President Trump's Tweets 2018

A Historical Archive of President Trump's Tweets

Anthony T. Michalisko

Anthony T. Michalisko

President Trumps Tweets 2018: A Historical Archive of President Trump's Tweets

Donald J. Trump ✓
@realDonaldTrump

The United States has foolishly given Pakistan more than 33 billion dollars in aid over the last 15 years, and they have given us nothing but lies & deceit, thinking of our leaders as fools. They give safe haven to the terrorists we hunt in Afghanistan, with little help. No more!
101,056 Retweets **304,676** Likes
4:12 AM - 1 Jan 2018

Donald J. Trump ✓
@realDonaldTrump

Iran is failing at every level despite the terrible deal made with them by the Obama Administration. The great Iranian people have been repressed for many years. They are hungry for food & for freedom. Along with human rights, the wealth of Iran is being looted. TIME FOR CHANGE!
29,046 Retweets **111,467** Likes
4:44 AM - 1 Jan 2018

Donald J. Trump ✓
@realDonaldTrump

Will be leaving Florida for Washington (D.C.) today at 4:00 P.M. Much work to be done, but it will be a great New Year!
16,884 Retweets **114,754** Likes
5:37 AM - 1 Jan 2018

Donald J. Trump ✓
@realDonaldTrump

The people of Iran are finally acting against the brutal and corrupt Iranian regime. All of the money that President Obama so foolishly gave them went into terrorism and into their "pockets." The people have little food, big inflation and no human rights. The U.S. is watching!
28,227 Retweets **105,965** Likes
4:09 AM - 2 Jan 2018

Donald J. Trump ✓
@realDonaldTrump

Crooked Hillary Clinton's top aid, Huma Abedin, has been accused of disregarding basic security protocols. She put Classified Passwords into the hands of foreign agents. Remember sailors pictures on submarine? Jail! Deep State Justice Dept must finally act? Also on Comey & others
37,561 Retweets **130,933** Likes
4:48 AM - 2 Jan 2018

Donald J. Trump ✓
@realDonaldTrump

Thank you to Brandon Judd of the National Border Patrol Council for your kind words on how well we are doing at the Border. We will be bringing in more & more of your great folks and will build the desperately needed WALL! @foxandfriends
14,478 Retweets **69,628** Likes
5:44 AM - 2 Jan 2018

Donald J. Trump ✓
@realDonaldTrump

Companies are giving big bonuses to their workers because of the Tax Cut Bill. Really great!
15,628 Retweets **87,020** Likes
5:49 AM - 2 Jan 2018

Donald J. Trump @realDonaldTrump

Sanctions and "other" pressures are beginning to have a big impact on North Korea. Soldiers are dangerously fleeing to South Korea. Rocket man now wants to talk to South Korea for first time. Perhaps that is good news, perhaps not - we will see!

17,379 Retweets **77,959** Likes
6:08 AM - 2 Jan 2018

Donald J. Trump @realDonaldTrump

Since taking office I have been very strict on Commercial Aviation. Good news - it was just reported that there were Zero deaths in 2017, the best and safest year on record!

16,249 Retweets **88,764** Likes
6:13 AM - 2 Jan 2018

Donald J. Trump @realDonaldTrump

The Failing New York Times has a new publisher, A.G. Sulzberger. Congratulations! Here is a last chance for the Times to fulfill the vision of its Founder, Adolph Ochs, "to give the news impartially, without fear or FAVOR, regardless of party, sect, or interests involved." Get...

18,011 Retweets **79,447** Likes
6:39 AM - 2 Jan 2018

Donald J. Trump @realDonaldTrump

....impartial journalists of a much higher standard, lose all of your phony and non-existent "sources," and treat the President of the United States FAIRLY, so that the next time I (and the people) win, you won't have to write an apology to your readers for a job poorly done! GL

16,565 Retweets **77,709** Likes
6:53 AM - 2 Jan 2018

Donald J. Trump @realDonaldTrump

Democrats are doing nothing for DACA - just interested in politics. DACA activists and Hispanics will go hard against Dems, will start "falling in love" with Republicans and their President! We are about RESULTS.

18,580 Retweets **87,703** Likes
7:16 AM - 2 Jan 2018

Donald J. Trump @realDonaldTrump

We will not rest until all of America's GREAT VETERANS can receive the care they so richly deserve. Tremendous progress has been made in a short period of time. Keep up the great work @SecShulkin @DeptVetAffairs!

16,301 Retweets **70,544** Likes
10:11 AM - 2 Jan 2018

Donald J. Trump @realDonaldTrump

Congratulations to Senator Orrin Hatch on an absolutely incredible career. He has been a tremendous supporter, and I will never forget the (beyond kind) statements he has made about me as President. He is my friend and he will be greatly missed in the U.S. Senate!

12,392 Retweets **63,280** Likes
2:23 PM - 2 Jan 2018

Donald J. Trump ✓
@realDonaldTrump

It's not only Pakistan that we pay billions of dollars to for nothing, but also many other countries, and others. As an example, we pay the Palestinians HUNDRED OF MILLIONS OF DOLLARS a year and get no appreciation or respect. They don't even want to negotiate a long overdue...
29,334 Retweets **118,505** Likes
2:37 PM - 2 Jan 2018

Donald J. Trump ✓
@realDonaldTrump

...peace treaty with Israel. We have taken Jerusalem, the toughest part of the negotiation, off the table, but Israel, for that, would have had to pay more. But with the Palestinians no longer willing to talk peace, why should we make any of these massive future payments to them?
20,000 Retweets **94,008** Likes
2:37 PM - 2 Jan 2018

Donald J. Trump ✓
@realDonaldTrump

North Korean Leader Kim Jong Un just stated that the "Nuclear Button is on his desk at all times." Will someone from his depleted and food starved regime please inform him that I too have a Nuclear Button, but it is a much bigger & more powerful one than his, and my Button works!
191,837 Retweets **499,183** Likes
4:49 PM - 2 Jan 2018

Donald J. Trump ✓
@realDonaldTrump

I will be announcing THE MOST DISHONEST & CORRUPT MEDIA AWARDS OF THE YEAR on Monday at 5:00 o'clock. Subjects will cover Dishonesty & Bad Reporting in various categories from the Fake News Media. Stay tuned!
51,056 Retweets **196,552** Likes
5:05 PM - 2 Jan 2018

Donald J. Trump ✓
@realDonaldTrump

"President Trump has something now he didn't have a year ago, that is a set of accomplishments that nobody can deny. The accomplishments are there, look at his record, he has had a very significant first year." @LouDobbs Show, David Asman & Ed Rollins
21,073 Retweets **98,208** Likes
8:03 PM - 2 Jan 2018

Donald J. Trump ✓
@realDonaldTrump

Such respect for the people of Iran as they try to take back their corrupt government. You will see great support from the United States at the appropriate time!
30,285 Retweets **147,921** Likes
5:37 AM - 3 Jan 2018

Donald J. Trump ✓
@realDonaldTrump

Melania and I are deeply saddened by the death of Thomas S. Monson, a beloved President of the Church of Jesus Christ of Latter-day Saints...
12,643 Retweets **59,848** Likes
5:06 PM - 3 Jan 2018

Donald J. Trump ✓
@realDonaldTrump

"Some 40 U.S. companies have responded to President Trump's tax cut and reform victory in Congress last year by handing out bonuses up to $2,000, increases in 401k matches and spending on charity, a much higher number than previously known."
16,718 Retweets **68,324** Likes
6:07 PM - 3 Jan 2018

Donald J. Trump ✓
@realDonaldTrump

Stock Market had another good day but, now that the Tax Cut Bill has passed, we have tremendous upward potential. Dow just short of 25,000, a number that few thought would be possible this soon into my administration. Also, unemployment went down to 4.1%. Only getting better!
19,850 Retweets **106,397** Likes
6:11 PM - 3 Jan 2018

Donald J. Trump ✓
@realDonaldTrump

MAKE AMERICA GREAT AGAIN!
37,992 Retweets **160,796** Likes
6:13 PM - 3 Jan 2018

Donald J. Trump ✓
@realDonaldTrump

Many mostly Democrat States refused to hand over data from the 2016 Election to the Commission On Voter Fraud. They fought hard that the Commission not see their records or methods because they know that many people are voting illegally. System is rigged, must go to Voter I.D.
30,929 Retweets **111,192** Likes
3:02 AM - 4 Jan 2018

Donald J. Trump ✓
@realDonaldTrump

As Americans, you need identification, sometimes in a very strong and accurate form, for almost everything you do.....except when it comes to the most important thing, VOTING for the people that run your country. Push hard for Voter Identification!
40,391 Retweets **155,369** Likes
3:11 AM - 4 Jan 2018

Donald J. Trump ✓
@realDonaldTrump

With all of the failed "experts" weighing in, does anybody really believe that talks and dialogue would be going on between North and South Korea right now if I wasn't firm, strong and willing to commit our total "might" against the North. Fools, but talks are a good thing!
19,831 Retweets **94,396** Likes
3:32 AM - 4 Jan 2018

Donald J. Trump ✓
@realDonaldTrump

So beautiful....Show this picture to the NFL players who still kneel!
32,849 Retweets **117,610** Likes
3:37 AM - 4 Jan 2018

Donald J. Trump ✓
@realDonaldTrump

Dow just crashes through 25,000. Congrats! Big cuts in unnecessary regulations continuing.
23,357 Retweets **118,129** Likes
7:48 AM - 4 Jan 2018

President Trumps Tweets 2018: A Historical Archive of President Trump's Tweets

Donald J. Trump ✓
@realDonaldTrump

Thank you to the great Republican Senators who showed up to our mtg on immigration reform. We must BUILD THE WALL, stop illegal immigration, end chain migration & cancel the visa lottery. The current system is unsafe & unfair to the great people of our country - time for change!
30,271 Retweets **137,534** Likes
3:53 PM - 4 Jan 2018

Donald J. Trump ✓
@realDonaldTrump

MAKING AMERICA GREAT AGAIN!
22,283 Retweets **93,496** Likes
4:11 PM - 4 Jan 2018

Donald J. Trump ✓
@realDonaldTrump

I authorized Zero access to White House (actually turned him down many times) for author of phony book! I never spoke to him for book. Full of lies, misrepresentations and sources that don't exist. Look at this guy's past and watch what happens to him and Sloppy Steve!
23,765 Retweets **101,209** Likes
7:52 PM - 4 Jan 2018

Donald J. Trump ✓
@realDonaldTrump

The Fake News Media barely mentions the fact that the Stock Market just hit another New Record and that business in the U.S. is booming...but the people know! Can you imagine if "O" was president and had these numbers - would be biggest story on earth! Dow now over 25,000.
28,059 Retweets **129,174** Likes
8:04 PM - 4 Jan 2018

Donald J. Trump ✓
@realDonaldTrump

Dow goes from 18,589 on November 9, 2016, to 25,075 today, for a new all-time Record. Jumped 1000 points in last 5 weeks, Record fastest 1000 point move in history. This is all about the Make America Great Again agenda! Jobs, Jobs, Jobs. Six trillion dollars in value created!
27,115 Retweets **123,316** Likes
3:35 AM - 5 Jan 2018

Donald J. Trump ✓
@realDonaldTrump

Well, now that collusion with Russia is proving to be a total hoax and the only collusion is with Hillary Clinton and the FBI/Russia, the Fake News Media (Mainstream) and this phony new book are hitting out at every new front imaginable. They should try winning an election. Sad!
33,002 Retweets **147,032** Likes
6:32 AM - 5 Jan 2018

Donald J. Trump ✓
@realDonaldTrump

The Mercer Family recently dumped the leaker known as Sloppy Steve Bannon. Smart!
15,927 Retweets **79,778** Likes
7:34 AM - 5 Jan 2018

Donald J. Trump ✓
@realDonaldTrump

Good idea Rand!
30,213 Retweets **121,202** Likes
8:19 PM - 5 Jan 2018

Donald J. Trump @
@realDonaldTrump

Michael Wolff is a total loser who made up stories in order to sell this really boring and untruthful book. He used Sloppy Steve Bannon, who cried when he got fired and begged for his job. Now Sloppy Steve has been dumped like a dog by almost everyone. Too bad!
23,915 Retweets **88,836** Likes
8:32 PM - 5 Jan 2018

Donald J. Trump @
@realDonaldTrump

The African American unemployment rate fell to 6.8%, the lowest rate in 45 years. I am so happy about this News! And, in the Washington Post (of all places), headline states, "Trumps first year jobs numbers were very, very good."
32,647 Retweets **144,628** Likes
3:49 AM - 6 Jan 2018

Donald J. Trump @
@realDonaldTrump

Brian Ross, the reporter who made a fraudulent live newscast about me that drove the Stock Market down 350 points (billions of dollars), was suspended for a month but is now back at ABC NEWS in a lower capacity. He is no longer allowed to report on Trump. Should have been fired!
23,403 Retweets **119,287** Likes
3:57 AM - 6 Jan 2018

Donald J. Trump @
@realDonaldTrump

Now that Russian collusion, after one year of intense study, has proven to be a total hoax on the American public, the Democrats and their lapdogs, the Fake News Mainstream Media, are taking out the old Ronald Reagan playbook and screaming mental stability and intelligence.....
35,083 Retweets **148,583** Likes
4:19 AM - 6 Jan 2018

Donald J. Trump @
@realDonaldTrump

....Actually, throughout my life, my two greatest assets have been mental stability and being, like, really smart. Crooked Hillary Clinton also played these cards very hard and, as everyone knows, went down in flames. I went from VERY successful businessman, to top T.V. Star.....
36,376 Retweets **134,915** Likes
4:27 AM - 6 Jan 2018

Donald J. Trump @
@realDonaldTrump

....to President of the United States (on my first try). I think that would qualify as not smart, but genius....and a very stable genius at that!
34,259 Retweets **142,407** Likes
4:30 AM - 6 Jan 2018

Donald J. Trump @
@realDonaldTrump

Leaving Camp David for the White House. Great meetings with the Cabinet and Military on many very important subjects including Border Security & the desperately needed Wall, the ever increasing Drug and Opioid Problem, Infrastructure, Military, Budget, Trade and DACA.
15,557 Retweets **81,553** Likes
6:33 AM - 7 Jan 2018

President Trumps Tweets 2018: A Historical Archive of President Trump's Tweets

Donald J. Trump ✓
@realDonaldTrump

I've had to put up with the Fake News from the first day I announced that I would be running for President. Now I have to put up with a Fake Book, written by a totally discredited author. Ronald Reagan had the same problem and handled it well. So will I!
31,447 Retweets **153,387** Likes
6:40 AM - 7 Jan 2018

Donald J. Trump ✓
@realDonaldTrump

Jake Tapper of Fake News CNN just got destroyed in his interview with Stephen Miller of the Trump Administration. Watch the hatred and unfairness of this CNN flunky!
29,604 Retweets **123,429** Likes
7:15 AM - 7 Jan 2018

Donald J. Trump ✓
@realDonaldTrump

The Fake News Awards, those going to the most corrupt & biased of the Mainstream Media, will be presented to the losers on Wednesday, January 17th, rather than this coming Monday. The interest in, and importance of, these awards is far greater than anyone could have anticipated!
37,762 Retweets **151,191** Likes
12:35 PM - 7 Jan 2018

Donald J. Trump ✓
@realDonaldTrump

The Stock Market has been creating tremendous benefits for our country in the form of not only Record Setting Stock Prices, but present and future Jobs, Jobs, Jobs. Seven TRILLION dollars of value created since our big election win!
20,322 Retweets **100,254** Likes
12:42 PM - 7 Jan 2018

Donald J. Trump ✓
@realDonaldTrump

"His is turning out to be an enormously consequential presidency. So much so that, despite my own frustration over his missteps, there has never been a day when I wished Hillary Clinton were president. Not one. Indeed, as Trump's accomplishments accumulate, the mere thought of...
16,880 Retweets **82,631** Likes
7:23 PM - 7 Jan 2018

Donald J. Trump ✓
@realDonaldTrump

...Clinton in the WH, doubling down on Barack Obama's failed policies, washes away any doubts that America made the right choice. This was truly a change election — and the changes Trump is bringing are far-reaching & necessary." Thank you Michael Goodwin!
18,904 Retweets **83,265** Likes
7:24 PM - 7 Jan 2018

Donald J. Trump ✓
@realDonaldTrump

African American unemployment is the lowest ever recorded in our country. The Hispanic unemployment rate dropped a full point in the last year and is close to the lowest in recorded history. Dems did nothing for you but get your vote! #NeverForget @foxandfriends
34,648 Retweets **132,122** Likes
6:20 AM - 8 Jan 2018

Donald J. Trump ✓
@realDonaldTrump

Can't wait to be back in the amazing state of Tennessee to address the 99th American @FarmBureau Federation's Annual Convention in Nashville! #AFBF18 On my way now - join me LIVE at 4:00pm
10,242 Retweets **54,355** Likes
11:06 AM - 8 Jan 2018

Donald J. Trump ✓
@realDonaldTrump

We have been working every day to DELIVER for America's Farmers just as they work every day to deliver FOR US. #AFBF18
11,561 Retweets **57,809** Likes
2:58 PM - 8 Jan 2018

Donald J. Trump ✓
@realDonaldTrump

In every decision we make, we are honoring America's PROUD FARMING LEGACY. Years of crushing taxes, crippling regs, & corrupt politics left our communities hurting, our economy stagnant, & millions of hardworking Americans COMPLETELY FORGOTTEN. But they are not forgotten ANYMORE!
17,769 Retweets **81,027** Likes
2:59 PM - 8 Jan 2018

Donald J. Trump ✓
@realDonaldTrump

We are fighting for our farmers, for our country, and for our GREAT AMERICAN FLAG. We want our flag respected - and we want our NATIONAL ANTHEM respected also!
22,044 Retweets **104,968** Likes
3:19 PM - 8 Jan 2018

Donald J. Trump ✓
@realDonaldTrump

Today, it was my great honor to sign a new Executive Order to ensure Veterans have the resources they need as they transition back to civilian life. We must ensure that our HEROES are given the care and support they so richly deserve!
19,481 Retweets **82,151** Likes
3:07 PM - 9 Jan 2018

Donald J. Trump ✓
@realDonaldTrump

As I made very clear today, our country needs the security of the Wall on the Southern Border, which must be part of any DACA approval.
24,552 Retweets **123,413** Likes
4:16 PM - 9 Jan 2018

Donald J. Trump ✓
@realDonaldTrump

Thank you @GOPLeader Kevin McCarthy! Couldn't agree w/you more. TOGETHER, we are #MAGA
11,893 Retweets **51,951** Likes
7:48 PM - 9 Jan 2018

President Trumps Tweets 2018: A Historical Archive of President Trump's Tweets

Donald J. Trump ✓
@realDonaldTrump

.@ICEgov HSI agents and ERO officers, on behalf of an entire Nation, THANK YOU for what you are doing 24/7/365 to keep fellow American's SAFE. Everyone is so grateful! #LawEnforcementAppreciationDay President @realDonaldTrump

13,822 Retweets **60,252** Likes
8:23 PM - 9 Jan 2018

Donald J. Trump ✓
@realDonaldTrump

It just shows everyone how broken and unfair our Court System is when the opposing side in a case (such as DACA) always runs to the 9th Circuit and almost always wins before being reversed by higher courts.

26,665 Retweets **108,152** Likes
6:11 AM - 10 Jan 2018

Donald J. Trump ✓
@realDonaldTrump

The fact that Sneaky Dianne Feinstein, who has on numerous occasions stated that collusion between Trump/Russia has not been found, would release testimony in such an underhanded and possibly illegal way, totally without authorization, is a disgrace. Must have tough Primary!

22,740 Retweets **92,227** Likes
7:00 AM - 10 Jan 2018

Donald J. Trump ✓
@realDonaldTrump

The single greatest Witch Hunt in American history continues. There was no collusion, everybody including the Dems knows there was no collusion, & yet on and on it goes. Russia & the world is laughing at the stupidity they are witnessing. Republicans should finally take control!

28,805 Retweets **119,548** Likes
7:14 AM - 10 Jan 2018

Donald J. Trump ✓
@realDonaldTrump

I want to thank my @Cabinet for working tirelessly on behalf of our country. 2017 was a year of monumental achievement and we look forward to the year ahead. Together, we are delivering results and MAKING AMERICA GREAT AGAIN!

11,875 Retweets **56,051** Likes
12:08 PM - 10 Jan 2018

Donald J. Trump ✓
@realDonaldTrump

Today, it was my great honor to welcome Prime Minister Erna Solberg of Norway to the @WhiteHouse - a great friend and ally of the United States! Joint press conference

9,570 Retweets **50,505** Likes
1:31 PM - 10 Jan 2018

Donald J. Trump ✓
@realDonaldTrump

The United States needs the security of the Wall on the Southern Border, which must be part of any DACA approval. The safety and security of our country is #1!

15,828 Retweets **69,057** Likes
3:07 PM - 10 Jan 2018

Anthony T. Michalisko

 **Donald J. Trump** ✓
@realDonaldTrump

Cutting taxes and simplifying regulations makes America the place to invest! Great news as Toyota and Mazda announce they are bringing 4,000 JOBS and investing $1.6 BILLION in Alabama, helping to further grow our economy!
23,085 Retweets **89,943** Likes
3:37 PM - 10 Jan 2018

 Donald J. Trump ✓
@realDonaldTrump

Good news: Toyota and Mazda announce giant new Huntsville, Alabama, plant which will produce over 300,000 cars and SUV's a year and employ 4000 people. Companies are coming back to the U.S. in a very big way. Congratulations Alabama!
36,627 Retweets **176,601** Likes
8:29 PM - 10 Jan 2018

 Donald J. Trump ✓
@realDonaldTrump

Disproven and paid for by Democrats "Dossier used to spy on Trump Campaign. Did FBI use Intel tool to influence the Election?" @foxandfriends Did Dems or Clinton also pay Russians? Where are hidden and smashed DNC servers? Where are Crooked Hillary Emails? What a mess!
22,798 Retweets **82,158** Likes
3:33 AM - 11 Jan 2018

 Donald J. Trump ✓
@realDonaldTrump

In new Quinnipiac Poll, 66% of people feel the economy is "Excellent or Good." That is the highest number ever recorded by this poll.
21,318 Retweets **96,789** Likes
3:43 AM - 11 Jan 2018

 Donald J. Trump ✓
@realDonaldTrump

"House votes on controversial FISA ACT today." This is the act that may have been used, with the help of the discredited and phony Dossier, to so badly surveil and abuse the Trump Campaign by the previous administration and others?
17,274 Retweets **72,410** Likes
4:33 AM - 11 Jan 2018

 Donald J. Trump ✓
@realDonaldTrump

"45 year low in illegal immigration this year." @foxandfriends
16,253 Retweets **84,555** Likes
5:11 AM - 11 Jan 2018

 Donald J. Trump ✓
@realDonaldTrump

With that being said, I have personally directed the fix to the unmasking process since taking office and today's vote is about foreign surveillance of foreign bad guys on foreign land. We need it! Get smart!
12,423 Retweets **60,560** Likes
6:14 AM - 11 Jan 2018

 Donald J. Trump ✓
@realDonaldTrump

Great news, as a result of our TAX CUTS & JOBS ACT!
15,213 Retweets **62,600** Likes
7:37 AM - 11 Jan 2018

President Trumps Tweets 2018: A Historical Archive of President Trump's Tweets

Donald J. Trump ✓
@realDonaldTrump

Yesterday, I signed the #INTERDICTAct (H.R. 2142) with bipartisan members of Congress to help end the flow of drugs into our country. Together, we are committed to doing everything we can to combat the deadly scourge of drug addiction and overdose in the United States!
13,781 Retweets **59,300** Likes
3:27 PM - 11 Jan 2018

Donald J. Trump ✓
@realDonaldTrump

Thank you Adam Levine, The Federalist, in interview on @foxandfriends "Donald Trump is the greatest President our Country has ever seen."
15,578 Retweets **76,146** Likes
6:43 PM - 11 Jan 2018

Donald J. Trump ✓
@realDonaldTrump

Small Business Poll has highest approval numbers in the polls history. All business is just at the beginning of something really special!
13,261 Retweets **68,224** Likes
6:47 PM - 11 Jan 2018

Donald J. Trump ✓
@realDonaldTrump

More great news as a result of historical Tax Cuts and Reform: Fiat Chrysler announces plan to invest more than $1 BILLION in Michigan plant, relocating their heavy-truck production from Mexico to Michigan, adding 2,500 new jobs and paying $2,000 bonus to U.S. employees!
19,199 Retweets **73,432** Likes
6:49 PM - 11 Jan 2018

Donald J. Trump ✓
@realDonaldTrump

Chrysler is moving a massive plant from Mexico to Michigan, reversing a years long opposite trend. Thank you Chrysler, a very wise decision. The voters in Michigan are very happy they voted for Trump/Pence. Plenty of more to follow!
26,034 Retweets **115,604** Likes
6:53 PM - 11 Jan 2018

Donald J. Trump ✓
@realDonaldTrump

Democrat Dianne Feinstein should never have released secret committee testimony to the public without authorization. Very disrespectful to committee members and possibly illegal. She blamed her poor decision on the fact she had a cold - a first!
23,043 Retweets **99,213** Likes
7:01 PM - 11 Jan 2018

Donald J. Trump ✓
@realDonaldTrump

The Democrats seem intent on having people and drugs pour into our country from the Southern Border, risking thousands of lives in the process. It is my duty to protect the lives and safety of all Americans. We must build a Great Wall, think Merit and end Lottery & Chain. USA!
29,526 Retweets **122,744** Likes
8:42 PM - 11 Jan 2018

Donald J. Trump ✓
@realDonaldTrump

Reason I canceled my trip to London is that I am not a big fan of the Obama Administration having sold perhaps the best located and finest embassy in London for "peanuts," only to build a new one in an off location for 1.2 billion dollars. Bad deal. Wanted me to cut ribbon-NO!

30,085 Retweets **125,213** Likes

8:57 PM - 11 Jan 2018

Donald J. Trump ✓
@realDonaldTrump

The so-called bipartisan DACA deal presented yesterday to myself and a group of Republican Senators and Congressmen was a big step backwards. Wall was not properly funded, Chain & Lottery were made worse and USA would be forced to take large numbers of people from high crime.....

21,748 Retweets **83,977** Likes

3:59 AM - 12 Jan 2018

Donald J. Trump ✓
@realDonaldTrump

....countries which are doing badly. I want a merit based system of immigration and people who will help take our country to the next level. I want safety and security for our people. I want to stop the massive inflow of drugs. I want to fund our military, not do a Dem defund....

24,462 Retweets **110,177** Likes

4:09 AM - 12 Jan 2018

Donald J. Trump ✓
@realDonaldTrump

....Because of the Democrats not being interested in life and safety, DACA has now taken a big step backwards. The Dems will threaten "shutdown," but what they are really doing is shutting down our military, at a time we need it most. Get smart, MAKE AMERICA GREAT AGAIN!

23,043 Retweets **92,162** Likes

4:20 AM - 12 Jan 2018

Donald J. Trump ✓
@realDonaldTrump

The language used by me at the DACA meeting was tough, but this was not the language used. What was really tough was the outlandish proposal made - a big setback for DACA!

24,795 Retweets **103,655** Likes

4:28 AM - 12 Jan 2018

Donald J. Trump ✓
@realDonaldTrump

Sadly, Democrats want to stop paying our troops and government workers in order to give a sweetheart deal, not a fair deal, for DACA. Take care of our Military, and our Country, FIRST!

32,123 Retweets **125,050** Likes

4:50 AM - 12 Jan 2018

Donald J. Trump ✓
@realDonaldTrump

Never said anything derogatory about Haitians other than Haiti is, obviously, a very poor and troubled country. Never said "take them out." Made up by Dems. I have a wonderful relationship with Haitians. Probably should record future meetings - unfortunately, no trust!

36,601 Retweets **138,855** Likes

5:48 AM - 12 Jan 2018

President Trumps Tweets 2018: A Historical Archive of President Trump's Tweets

Donald J. Trump ✓
@realDonaldTrump

Today, it was my great honor to proclaim January 15, 2018, as Martin Luther King Jr., Federal Holiday. I encourage all Americans to observe this day with appropriate civic, community, and service activities in honor of Dr. King's life and legacy.
26,544 Retweets **109,300** Likes
9:56 AM - 12 Jan 2018

Donald J. Trump ✓
@realDonaldTrump

Yesterday was a big day for the stock market. Jobs are coming back to America. Chrysler is coming back to the USA, from Mexico and many others will follow. Tax cut money to employees is pouring into our economy with many more companies announcing. American business is hot again!
24,624 Retweets **117,847** Likes
5:13 AM - 13 Jan 2018

Donald J. Trump ✓
@realDonaldTrump

The Democrats are all talk and no action. They are doing nothing to fix DACA. Great opportunity missed. Too bad!
21,951 Retweets **104,405** Likes
5:14 AM - 13 Jan 2018

Donald J. Trump ✓
@realDonaldTrump

AMERICA FIRST!
37,694 Retweets **152,962** Likes
5:14 AM - 13 Jan 2018

Donald J. Trump ✓
@realDonaldTrump

I don't believe the Democrats really want to see a deal on DACA. They are all talk and no action. This is the time but, day by day, they are blowing the one great opportunity they have. Too bad!
27,380 Retweets **124,729** Likes
6:20 AM - 13 Jan 2018

Donald J. Trump ✓
@realDonaldTrump

So much Fake News is being reported. They don't even try to get it right, or correct it when they are wrong. They promote the Fake Book of a mentally deranged author, who knowingly writes false information. The Mainstream Media is crazed that WE won the election!
34,708 Retweets **148,208** Likes
2:08 PM - 13 Jan 2018

Donald J. Trump ✓
@realDonaldTrump

The Wall Street Journal stated falsely that I said to them "I have a good relationship with Kim Jong Un" (of N. Korea). Obviously I didn't say that. I said "I'd have a good relationship with Kim Jong Un," a big difference. Fortunately we now record conversations with reporters...
22,639 Retweets **96,340** Likes
4:58 AM - 14 Jan 2018

Donald J. Trump ✓
@realDonaldTrump

...and they knew exactly what I said and meant. They just wanted a story. FAKE NEWS!
16,641 Retweets **83,609** Likes
5:01 AM - 14 Jan 2018

Donald J. Trump @realDonaldTrump

DACA is probably dead because the Democrats don't really want it, they just want to talk and take desperately needed money away from our Military.
27,910 Retweets **122,528** Likes
5:09 AM - 14 Jan 2018

 Donald J. Trump @realDonaldTrump

I, as President, want people coming into our Country who are going to help us become strong and great again, people coming in through a system based on MERIT. No more Lotteries! #AMERICA FIRST
39,822 Retweets **162,032** Likes
5:19 AM - 14 Jan 2018

 Donald J. Trump @realDonaldTrump

"President Trump is not getting the credit he deserves for the economy. Tax Cut bonuses to more than 2,000,000 workers. Most explosive Stock Market rally that we've seen in modern times. 18,000 to 26,000 from Election, and grounded in profitability and growth. All Trump, not O...
25,199 Retweets **112,365** Likes
5:50 AM - 14 Jan 2018

 Donald J. Trump @realDonaldTrump

...big unnecessary regulation cuts made it all possible" (among many other things). "President Trump reversed the policies of President Obama, and reversed our economic decline." Thank you Stuart Varney. @foxandfriends
19,249 Retweets **88,722** Likes
5:59 AM - 14 Jan 2018

 Donald J. Trump @realDonaldTrump

Statement by me last night in Florida: "Honestly, I don't think the Democrats want to make a deal. They talk about DACA, but they don't want to help..We are ready, willing and able to make a deal but they don't want to. They don't want security at the border, they don't want.....
22,262 Retweets **94,720** Likes
4:57 AM - 15 Jan 2018

 Donald J. Trump @realDonaldTrump

...to stop drugs, they want to take money away from our military which we cannot do." My standard is very simple, AMERICA FIRST & MAKE AMERICA GREAT AGAIN!
23,721 Retweets **113,504** Likes
5:02 AM - 15 Jan 2018

Donald J. Trump @realDonaldTrump

Senator Dicky Durbin totally misrepresented what was said at the DACA meeting. Deals can't get made when there is no trust! Durbin blew DACA and is hurting our Military.
30,428 Retweets **118,168** Likes
12:28 PM - 15 Jan 2018

President Trumps Tweets 2018: A Historical Archive of President Trump's Tweets

Donald J. Trump ✓
@realDonaldTrump

We must have Security at our VERY DANGEROUS SOUTHERN BORDER, and we must have a great WALL to help protect us, and to help stop the massive inflow of drugs pouring into our country!
25,132 Retweets **117,811** Likes
5:54 AM - 16 Jan 2018

Donald J. Trump ✓
@realDonaldTrump

The Democrats want to shut down the Government over Amnesty for all and Border Security. The biggest loser will be our rapidly rebuilding Military, at a time we need it more than ever. We need a merit based system of immigration, and we need it now! No more dangerous Lottery.
24,015 Retweets **100,620** Likes
6:07 AM - 16 Jan 2018

Donald J. Trump ✓
@realDonaldTrump

Do you notice the Fake News Mainstream Media never likes covering the great and record setting economic news, but rather talks about anything negative or that can be turned into the negative. The Russian Collusion Hoax is dead, except as it pertains to the Dems. Public gets it!
26,530 Retweets **111,945** Likes
6:19 AM - 16 Jan 2018

Donald J. Trump ✓
@realDonaldTrump

"90% of Trump 2017 news coverage was negative" -and much of it contrived!@foxandfriends
16,362 Retweets **73,687** Likes
6:24 AM - 16 Jan 2018

Donald J. Trump ✓
@realDonaldTrump

Unemployment for Black Americans is the lowest ever recorded. Trump approval ratings with Black Americans has doubled. Thank you, and it will get even (much) better! @FoxNews
28,302 Retweets **113,867** Likes
6:30 AM - 16 Jan 2018

Donald J. Trump ✓
@realDonaldTrump

"President Donald J. Trump Proclaims January 16, 2018, as Religious Freedom Day"
19,677 Retweets **74,030** Likes
11:43 AM - 16 Jan 2018

Donald J. Trump ✓
@realDonaldTrump

Today, it was my honor to welcome President Nursultan Nazarbayev of Kazakhstan to the @WhiteHouse!
10,012 Retweets **56,142** Likes
12:17 PM - 16 Jan 2018

Donald J. Trump ✓
@realDonaldTrump

New report from DOJ & DHS shows that nearly 3 in 4 individuals convicted of terrorism-related charges are foreign-born. We have submitted to Congress a list of resources and reforms....
26,005 Retweets **100,365** Likes
3:19 PM - 16 Jan 2018

Donald J. Trump ✓
@realDonaldTrump

....we need to keep America safe, including moving away from a random chain migration and lottery system, to one that is merit-based.
19,205 Retweets **81,945** Likes
3:20 PM - 16 Jan 2018

Donald J. Trump ✓
@realDonaldTrump

Eric Trump on @foxandfriends now!
6,775 Retweets **54,585** Likes
5:04 AM - 17 Jan 2018

Donald J. Trump ✓
@realDonaldTrump

Today, we witnessed an incredible moment in history – the presentation of Congress' highest civilian honor to our friend, and true AMERICAN HERO, Bob Dole. #CongressionalGoldMedal
15,592 Retweets **75,223** Likes
3:19 PM - 17 Jan 2018

Donald J. Trump ✓
@realDonaldTrump

I promised that my policies would allow companies like Apple to bring massive amounts of money back to the United States. Great to see Apple follow through as a result of TAX CUTS. Huge win for American workers and the USA!
24,533 Retweets **92,540** Likes
3:28 PM - 17 Jan 2018

Donald J. Trump ✓
@realDonaldTrump

During the campaign, I promised to MAKE AMERICA GREAT AGAIN by bringing businesses and jobs back to our country. I am very proud to see companies like Chrysler moving operations from Mexico to Michigan where there are so many great American workers!
24,791 Retweets **99,349** Likes
3:32 PM - 17 Jan 2018

Donald J. Trump ✓
@realDonaldTrump

Main Street is BACK! Strongest Holiday Sales bump since the Great Recession -- beating forecasts by BILLIONS OF DOLLARS.
15,704 Retweets **68,259** Likes
3:36 PM - 17 Jan 2018

Donald J. Trump ✓
@realDonaldTrump

And the FAKE NEWS winners are...
41,677 Retweets **112,931** Likes
5:00 PM - 17 Jan 2018

Donald J. Trump ✓
@realDonaldTrump

Despite some very corrupt and dishonest media coverage, there are many great reporters I respect and lots of GOOD NEWS for the American people to be proud of!
22,540 Retweets **112,497** Likes
5:05 PM - 17 Jan 2018

President Trumps Tweets 2018: A Historical Archive of President Trump's Tweets

Donald J. Trump ✓
@realDonaldTrump

ISIS is in retreat, our economy is booming, investments and jobs are pouring back into the country, and so much more! Together there is nothing we can't overcome--even a very biased media. We ARE Making America Great Again!
40,177 Retweets **179,374** Likes
5:11 PM - 17 Jan 2018

Donald J. Trump ✓
@realDonaldTrump

The Wall is the Wall, it has never changed or evolved from the first day I conceived of it. Parts will be, of necessity, see through and it was never intended to be built in areas where there is natural protection such as mountains, wastelands or tough rivers or water.....
21,731 Retweets **94,684** Likes
3:15 AM - 18 Jan 2018

Donald J. Trump ✓
@realDonaldTrump

....The Wall will be paid for, directly or indirectly, or through longer term reimbursement, by Mexico, which has a ridiculous $71 billion dollar trade surplus with the U.S. The $20 billion dollar Wall is "peanuts" compared to what Mexico makes from the U.S. NAFTA is a bad joke!
28,282 Retweets **112,438** Likes
3:25 AM - 18 Jan 2018

Donald J. Trump ✓
@realDonaldTrump

Will be going to Pennsylvania today in order to give my total support to RICK SACCONE, running for Congress in a Special Election (March 13). Rick is a great guy. We need more Republicans to continue our already successful agenda!
17,299 Retweets **85,634** Likes
4:53 AM - 18 Jan 2018

Donald J. Trump ✓
@realDonaldTrump

We need the Wall for the safety and security of our country. We need the Wall to help stop the massive inflow of drugs from Mexico, now rated the number one most dangerous country in the world. If there is no Wall, there is no Deal!
29,311 Retweets **124,070** Likes
5:16 AM - 18 Jan 2018

Donald J. Trump ✓
@realDonaldTrump

CHIP should be part of a long term solution, not a 30 Day, or short term, extension!
12,110 Retweets **62,752** Likes
5:37 AM - 18 Jan 2018

Donald J. Trump ✓
@realDonaldTrump

A government shutdown will be devastating to our military...something the Dems care very little about!
21,966 Retweets **90,978** Likes
5:49 AM - 18 Jan 2018

Donald J. Trump ✓
@realDonaldTrump

Departing Pittsburgh now, where it was my great honor to stand with our incredible workers, and to show the world that AMERICA is back - and we are coming back bigger and better and stronger than ever before!
15,312 Retweets **76,045** Likes
12:45 PM - 18 Jan 2018

 Donald J. Trump ✓
@realDonaldTrump

AMERICA will once again be a NATION that thinks big, dreams bigger, and always reaches for the stars. YOU are the ones who will shape America's destiny. YOU are the ones who will restore our prosperity. And YOU are the ones who are MAKING AMERICA GREAT AGAIN! #MAGA
26,240 Retweets **103,585** Likes
1:04 PM - 18 Jan 2018

 Donald J. Trump ✓
@realDonaldTrump

House of Representatives needs to pass Government Funding Bill tonight. So important for our country - our Military needs it!
20,416 Retweets **102,080** Likes
3:39 PM - 18 Jan 2018

 Donald J. Trump ✓
@realDonaldTrump

Government Funding Bill past last night in the House of Representatives. Now Democrats are needed if it is to pass in the Senate - but they want illegal immigration and weak borders. Shutdown coming? We need more Republican victories in 2018!
26,110 Retweets **110,987** Likes
4:04 AM - 19 Jan 2018

 **Donald J. Trump** ✓
@realDonaldTrump

.@WhiteHouse Briefing with Director Marc Short and Director Mick Mulvaney...
8,564 Retweets **44,108** Likes
8:14 AM - 19 Jan 2018

 Donald J. Trump ✓
@realDonaldTrump

"Shutting down the government is a very serious thing. People die, accidents happen. I don't know how I would vote right now on a CR, OK?" Sen. Dianne Feinstein (D-Calif)
15,651 Retweets **49,735** Likes
8:28 AM - 19 Jan 2018

 Donald J. Trump ✓
@realDonaldTrump

Today, I was honored and proud to address the 45th Annual @March_for_Life! You are living witnesses of this year's March for Life theme: #LoveSavesLives.
25,081 Retweets **96,877** Likes
10:39 AM - 19 Jan 2018

Donald J. Trump ✓
@realDonaldTrump

Just signed 702 Bill to reauthorize foreign intelligence collection. This is NOT the same FISA law that was so wrongly abused during the election. I will always do the right thing for our country and put the safety of the American people first!
28,082 Retweets **129,151** Likes
12:53 PM - 19 Jan 2018

Donald J. Trump ✓
@realDonaldTrump

Excellent preliminary meeting in Oval with @SenSchumer - working on solutions for Security and our great Military together with @SenateMajLdr McConnell and @SpeakerRyan. Making progress - four week extension would be best!

13,138 Retweets **65,007** Likes
2:17 PM - 19 Jan 2018

Donald J. Trump ✓
@realDonaldTrump

Not looking good for our great Military or Safety & Security on the very dangerous Southern Border. Dems want a Shutdown in order to help diminish the great success of the Tax Cuts, and what they are doing for our booming economy.

31,457 Retweets **117,670** Likes
6:28 PM - 19 Jan 2018

Donald J. Trump ✓
@realDonaldTrump

Democrats are far more concerned with Illegal Immigrants than they are with our great Military or Safety at our dangerous Southern Border. They could have easily made a deal but decided to play Shutdown politics instead. #WeNeedMoreRepublicansIn18 in order to power through mess!

42,612 Retweets **145,344** Likes
3:17 AM - 20 Jan 2018

Donald J. Trump ✓
@realDonaldTrump

This is the One Year Anniversary of my Presidency and the Democrats wanted to give me a nice present. #DemocratShutdown

30,695 Retweets **124,222** Likes
3:33 AM - 20 Jan 2018

Donald J. Trump ✓
@realDonaldTrump

For those asking, the Republicans only have 51 votes in the Senate, and they need 60. That is why we need to win more Republicans in 2018 Election! We can then be even tougher on Crime (and Border), and even better to our Military & Veterans!

40,265 Retweets **155,084** Likes
3:44 AM - 20 Jan 2018

Donald J. Trump ✓
@realDonaldTrump

#AMERICA FIRST!

31,872 Retweets **123,740** Likes
3:47 AM - 20 Jan 2018

Donald J. Trump ✓
@realDonaldTrump

Democrats are holding our Military hostage over their desire to have unchecked illegal immigration. Can't let that happen!

44,943 Retweets **168,968** Likes
6:27 AM - 20 Jan 2018

Donald J. Trump ✓
@realDonaldTrump

Beautiful weather all over our great country, a perfect day for all Women to March. Get out there now to celebrate the historic milestones and unprecedented economic success and wealth creation that has taken place over the last 12 months. Lowest female unemployment in 18 years!
53,725 Retweets **209,710** Likes
10:51 AM - 20 Jan 2018

Donald J. Trump ✓
@realDonaldTrump

Unprecedented success for our Country, in so many ways, since the Election. Record Stock Market, Strong on Military, Crime, Borders, & ISIS, Judicial Strength & Numbers, Lowest Unemployment for Women & ALL, Massive Tax Cuts, end of Individual Mandate - and so much more. Big 2018!
29,055 Retweets **130,892** Likes
2:31 PM - 20 Jan 2018

Donald J. Trump ✓
@realDonaldTrump

The Trump Administration has terminated more UNNECESSARY Regulation, in just twelve months, than any other Administration has terminated during their full term in office, no matter what the length. The good news is, THERE IS MUCH MORE TO COME!
31,921 Retweets **154,853** Likes
4:47 PM - 20 Jan 2018

Donald J. Trump ✓
@realDonaldTrump

Eric Trump on @JudgeJeanine on @FoxNews now!
6,389 Retweets **46,706** Likes
6:18 PM - 20 Jan 2018

Donald J. Trump ✓
@realDonaldTrump

Great to see how hard Republicans are fighting for our Military and Safety at the Border. The Dems just want illegal immigrants to pour into our nation unchecked. If stalemate continues, Republicans should go to 51% (Nuclear Option) and vote on real, long term budget, no C.R.'s!
47,818 Retweets **178,941** Likes
4:35 AM - 21 Jan 2018

Donald J. Trump ✓
@realDonaldTrump

Thank you to Brad Blakeman on @FoxNews for grading year one of my presidency with an "A"- and likewise to Doug Schoen for the very good grade and statements. Working hard!
23,749 Retweets **127,050** Likes
5:21 PM - 21 Jan 2018

Donald J. Trump ✓
@realDonaldTrump

The Democrats are turning down services and security for citizens in favor of services and security for non-citizens. Not good!
33,480 Retweets **132,396** Likes
5:07 AM - 22 Jan 2018

Donald J. Trump ✓
@realDonaldTrump

Democrats have shut down our government in the interests of their far left base. They don't want to do it but are powerless!
22,345 Retweets **109,898** Likes
5:15 AM - 22 Jan 2018

President Trumps Tweets 2018: A Historical Archive of President Trump's Tweets

Donald J. Trump ✓
@realDonaldTrump

End the Democrats Obstruction!
21,781 Retweets **93,311** Likes
7:13 AM - 22 Jan 2018

Donald J. Trump ✓
@realDonaldTrump

Big win for Republicans as Democrats cave on Shutdown. Now I want a big win for everyone, including Republicans, Democrats and DACA, but especially for our Great Military and Border Security. Should be able to get there. See you at the negotiating table!
28,224 Retweets **133,812** Likes
8:30 PM - 22 Jan 2018

Donald J. Trump ✓
@realDonaldTrump

Even Crazy Jim Acosta of Fake News CNN agrees: "Trump World and WH sources dancing in end zone: Trump wins again...Schumer and Dems caved...gambled and lost." Thank you for your honesty Jim!
27,462 Retweets **129,596** Likes
3:31 AM - 23 Jan 2018

Donald J. Trump ✓
@realDonaldTrump

In one of the biggest stories in a long time, the FBI now says it is now missing five months worth of lovers Strzok - Page texts, perhaps 50,000, all in prime time. Wow!
36,971 Retweets **134,949** Likes
3:55 AM - 23 Jan 2018

Donald J. Trump ✓
@realDonaldTrump

Nobody knows for sure that the Republicans & Democrats will be able to reach a deal on DACA by February 8, but everyone will be trying....with a big additional focus put on Military Strength and Border Security. The Dems have just learned that a Shutdown is not the answer!
24,229 Retweets **112,958** Likes
5:34 AM - 23 Jan 2018

Donald J. Trump ✓
@realDonaldTrump

Thank you to General John Kelly, who is doing a fantastic job, and all of the Staff and others in the White House, for a job well done. Long hours and Fake reporting makes your job more difficult, but it is always great to WIN, and few have won more than us!
21,698 Retweets **97,892** Likes
6:16 AM - 23 Jan 2018

Donald J. Trump ✓
@realDonaldTrump

Where are the 50,000 important text messages between FBI lovers Lisa Page and Peter Strzok? Blaming Samsung!
32,286 Retweets **127,998** Likes
7:54 PM - 23 Jan 2018

Donald J. Trump ✓
@realDonaldTrump

Cryin' Chuck Schumer fully understands, especially after his humiliating defeat, that if there is no Wall, there is no DACA. We must have safety and security, together with a strong Military, for our great people!
36,887 Retweets **155,261** Likes
8:07 PM - 23 Jan 2018

Donald J. Trump ✓
@realDonaldTrump

Tremendous investment by companies from all over the world being made in America. There has never been anything like it. Now Disney, J.P. Morgan Chase and many others. Massive Regulation Reduction and Tax Cuts are making us a powerhouse again. Long way to go! Jobs, Jobs, Jobs!
33,406 Retweets **147,591** Likes
3:58 AM - 24 Jan 2018

Donald J. Trump ✓
@realDonaldTrump

Earlier today, I spoke with @GovMattBevin of Kentucky regarding yesterday's shooting at Marshall County High School. My thoughts and prayers are with Bailey Holt, Preston Cope, their families, and all of the wounded victims who are in recovery. We are with you!
19,372 Retweets **98,925** Likes
12:26 PM - 24 Jan 2018

Donald J. Trump ✓
@realDonaldTrump

It was my great honor to welcome Mayor's from across America to the WH. My Administration will always support local government - and listen to the leaders who know their communities best. Together, we will usher in a bold new era of Peace and Prosperity!
16,891 Retweets **79,440** Likes
2:51 PM - 24 Jan 2018

Donald J. Trump ✓
@realDonaldTrump

Will soon be heading to Davos, Switzerland, to tell the world how great America is and is doing. Our economy is now booming and with all I am doing, will only get better...Our country is finally WINNING again!
28,521 Retweets **153,096** Likes
4:27 PM - 24 Jan 2018

Donald J. Trump ✓
@realDonaldTrump

Great bilateral meeting with Prime Minister Theresa May of the United Kingdom, affirming the special relationship and our commitment to work together on key national security challenges and economic opportunities. #WEF18
16,111 Retweets **76,560** Likes
9:25 AM - 25 Jan 2018

Donald J. Trump ✓
@realDonaldTrump

Very productive bilateral meeting with Prime Minister Benjamin @Netanyahu of Israel - in Davos, Switzerland! #WEF18
15,210 Retweets **73,018** Likes
10:03 AM - 25 Jan 2018

Donald J. Trump ✓
@realDonaldTrump

Today, Americans everywhere remember the brave men and women of @NASA who lost their lives in our Nation's eternal quest to expand the boundaries of human potential.
17,824 Retweets **84,228** Likes
2:38 PM - 25 Jan 2018

Donald J. Trump ✓
@realDonaldTrump

Will be interviewed on @SquawkCNBC by @JoeSquawk coming up at 6:00amE from Davos, Switzerland. Enjoy! #WEF18
6,604 Retweets **36,719** Likes
2:46 AM - 26 Jan 2018

Donald J. Trump ✓
@realDonaldTrump

It was an honor to meet with Republic of Rwanda President Paul Kagame this morning in Davos, Switzerland. Many great discussions! #WEF18
12,518 Retweets **63,689** Likes
2:46 AM - 26 Jan 2018

Donald J. Trump ✓
@realDonaldTrump

Great bilateral meeting with President @Alain_Berset of the Swiss Confederation - as we continue to strengthen our great friendship. Such an honor to be in Switzerland! #WEF18
10,795 Retweets **55,881** Likes
3:23 AM - 26 Jan 2018

Donald J. Trump ✓
@realDonaldTrump

Join me live at the 2018 World Economic Forum in Davos, Switzerland! #WEF18
10,132 Retweets **52,421** Likes
4:54 AM - 26 Jan 2018

Donald J. Trump ✓
@realDonaldTrump

Heading back from a very exciting two days in Davos, Switzerland. Speech on America's economic revival was well received. Many of the people I met will be investing in the U.S.A.! #MAGA
22,686 Retweets **112,306** Likes
9:12 AM - 26 Jan 2018

Donald J. Trump ✓
@realDonaldTrump

DACA has been made increasingly difficult by the fact that Cryin' Chuck Schumer took such a beating over the shutdown that he is unable to act on immigration!
26,389 Retweets **119,475** Likes
9:16 AM - 26 Jan 2018

Donald J. Trump ✓
@realDonaldTrump

Thank you for the wonderful welcome @WEF! #Davos2018
16,392 Retweets **72,341** Likes
3:27 PM - 26 Jan 2018

Donald J. Trump ✓
@realDonaldTrump

Thank you to Brandon Judd of the National Border Patrol Council for his strong statement on @foxandfriends that we very badly NEED THE WALL. Must also end loophole of "catch & release" and clean up the legal and other procedures at the border NOW for Safety & Security reasons.
29,292 Retweets **124,248** Likes
3:55 AM - 27 Jan 2018

Donald J. Trump ✓
@realDonaldTrump

On Holocaust Remembrance Day we mourn and grieve the murder of 6 million innocent Jewish men, women and children, and the millions of others who perished in the evil Nazi Genocide. We pledge with all of our might and resolve: Never Again!
25,987 Retweets **107,944** Likes
11:30 AM - 27 Jan 2018

Donald J. Trump ✓
@realDonaldTrump

Taliban targeted innocent Afghans, brave police in Kabul today. Our thoughts and prayers go to the victims, and first responders. We will not allow the Taliban to win!
22,155 Retweets **114,304** Likes
2:59 PM - 27 Jan 2018

Donald J. Trump ✓
@realDonaldTrump

I have offered DACA a wonderful deal, including a doubling in the number of recipients & a twelve year pathway to citizenship, for two reasons: (1) Because the Republicans want to fix a long time terrible problem. (2) To show that Democrats do not want to solve DACA, only use it!
47,047 Retweets **175,856** Likes
7:58 PM - 27 Jan 2018

Donald J. Trump ✓
@realDonaldTrump

Democrats are not interested in Border Safety & Security or in the funding and rebuilding of our Military. They are only interested in Obstruction!
35,964 Retweets **157,413** Likes
8:08 PM - 27 Jan 2018

Donald J. Trump ✓
@realDonaldTrump

Somebody please inform Jay-Z that because of my policies, Black Unemployment has just been reported to be at the LOWEST RATE EVER RECORDED!
64,122 Retweets **240,489** Likes
5:18 AM - 28 Jan 2018

Donald J. Trump ✓
@realDonaldTrump

Our economy is better than it has been in many decades. Businesses are coming back to America like never before. Chrysler, as an example, is leaving Mexico and coming back to the USA. Unemployment is nearing record lows. We are on the right track!
42,337 Retweets **199,787** Likes
5:18 AM - 28 Jan 2018

Donald J. Trump ✓
@realDonaldTrump

Congratulations to America's new Secretary of @HHSGov, Alex Azar!
16,431 Retweets **84,209** Likes
12:12 PM - 29 Jan 2018

Donald J. Trump ✓
@realDonaldTrump

Join me live for the #SOTU
22,023 Retweets **109,076** Likes
6:00 PM - 30 Jan 2018

Donald J. Trump ✓
@realDonaldTrump

Heading to beautiful West Virginia to be with great members of the Republican Party. Will be planning Infrastructure and discussing Immigration and DACA, not easy when we have no support from the Democrats. NOT ONE DEM VOTED FOR OUR TAX CUT BILL! Need more Republicans in '18.
28,485 Retweets **138,117** Likes
3:43 AM - 1 Feb 2018

Donald J. Trump ✓
@realDonaldTrump

March 5th is rapidly approaching and the Democrats are doing nothing about DACA. They Resist, Blame, Complain and Obstruct - and do nothing. Start pushing Nancy Pelosi and the Dems to work out a DACA fix, NOW!
29,920 Retweets **123,474** Likes
3:51 AM - 1 Feb 2018

Donald J. Trump ✓
@realDonaldTrump

Thank you for all of the nice compliments and reviews on the State of the Union speech. 45.6 million people watched, the highest number in history. @FoxNews beat every other Network, for the first time ever, with 11.7 million people tuning in. Delivered from the heart!
37,362 Retweets **184,812** Likes
4:02 AM - 1 Feb 2018

Donald J. Trump ✓
@realDonaldTrump

The Democrats just aren't calling about DACA. Nancy Pelosi and Chuck Schumer have to get moving fast, or they'll disappoint you again. We have a great chance to make a deal or, blame the Dems! March 5th is coming up fast.
28,843 Retweets **124,250** Likes
7:32 PM - 1 Feb 2018

Donald J. Trump ✓
@realDonaldTrump

The top Leadership and Investigators of the FBI and the Justice Department have politicized the sacred investigative process in favor of Democrats and against Republicans - something which would have been unthinkable just a short time ago. Rank & File are great people!
40,439 Retweets **139,322** Likes
3:33 AM - 2 Feb 2018

Donald J. Trump ✓
@realDonaldTrump

"You had Hillary Clinton and the Democratic Party try to hide the fact that they gave money to GPS Fusion to create a Dossier which was used by their allies in the Obama Administration to convince a Court misleadingly, by all accounts, to spy on the Trump Team." Tom Fitton, JW
52,193 Retweets **161,884** Likes
3:49 AM - 2 Feb 2018

Donald J. Trump @realDonaldTrump

With 3.5 million Americans receiving bonuses or other benefits from their employers as a result of TAX CUTS, 2018 is off to great start! Unemployment rate at 4.1%. Average earnings up 2.9% in the last year. 200,000 new American jobs. #MAGA
27,604 Retweets **108,146** Likes
10:05 AM - 2 Feb 2018

Donald J. Trump @realDonaldTrump

"Trump the orator outlines the greatness of America to Democrats' disgust"
17,672 Retweets **77,697** Likes
10:07 AM - 2 Feb 2018

Donald J. Trump @realDonaldTrump

Today, it was my honor to join the great men and women of @DHSgov, @CustomsBorder, @ICEgov and @USCIS at the U.S. Customs and Border Protection National Targeting Center in Sterling, Virginia. Fact sheet
14,643 Retweets **71,009** Likes
2:26 PM - 2 Feb 2018

Donald J. Trump @realDonaldTrump

Rasmussen just announced that my approval rating jumped to 49%, a far better number than I had in winning the Election, and higher than certain "sacred cows." Other Trump polls are way up also. So why does the media refuse to write this? Oh well, someday!
34,992 Retweets **156,630** Likes
6:40 AM - 3 Feb 2018

Donald J. Trump @realDonaldTrump

This memo totally vindicates "Trump" in probe. But the Russian Witch Hunt goes on and on. Their was no Collusion and there was no Obstruction (the word now used because, after one year of looking endlessly and finding NOTHING, collusion is dead). This is an American disgrace!
39,282 Retweets **141,909** Likes
6:40 AM - 3 Feb 2018

Donald J. Trump @realDonaldTrump

Great jobs numbers and finally, after many years, rising wages- and nobody even talks about them. Only Russia, Russia, Russia, despite the fact that, after a year of looking, there is No Collusion!
30,276 Retweets **136,102** Likes
4:26 PM - 3 Feb 2018

Donald J. Trump @realDonaldTrump

"The four page memo released Friday reports the disturbing fact about how the FBI and FISA appear to have been used to influence the 2016 election and its aftermath....The FBI failed to inform the FISA court that the Clinton campaign had funded the dossier....the FBI became....
37,037 Retweets **130,687** Likes
4:40 PM - 3 Feb 2018

President Trumps Tweets 2018: A Historical Archive of President Trump's Tweets

Donald J. Trump ✓
@realDonaldTrump

...a tool of anti-Trump political actors. This is unacceptable in a democracy and ought to alarm anyone who wants the FBI to be a nonpartisan enforcer of the law....The FBI wasn't straight with Congress, as it hid most of these facts from investigators." Wall Street Journal
35,940 Retweets **130,832** Likes
4:53 PM - 3 Feb 2018

Donald J. Trump ✓
@realDonaldTrump

My thoughts and prayers are with all of the victims involved in this mornings train collision in South Carolina. Thank you to our incredible First Responders for the work they've done!
22,937 Retweets **141,922** Likes
8:58 AM - 4 Feb 2018

Donald J. Trump ✓
@realDonaldTrump

Congratulations to the Philadelphia Eagles on a great Super Bowl victory!
36,253 Retweets **212,429** Likes
7:54 PM - 4 Feb 2018

Donald J. Trump ✓
@realDonaldTrump

The Democrats are pushing for Universal HealthCare while thousands of people are marching in the UK because their U system is going broke and not working. Dems want to greatly raise taxes for really bad and non-personal medical care. No thanks!
30,625 Retweets **120,989** Likes
4:11 AM - 5 Feb 2018

Donald J. Trump ✓
@realDonaldTrump

Thank you to @foxandfriends for exposing the truth. Perhaps that's why your ratings are soooo much better than your untruthful competition!
22,763 Retweets **107,638** Likes
4:17 AM - 5 Feb 2018

Donald J. Trump ✓
@realDonaldTrump

Little Adam Schiff, who is desperate to run for higher office, is one of the biggest liars and leakers in Washington, right up there with Comey, Warner, Brennan and Clapper! Adam leaves closed committee hearings to illegally leak confidential information. Must be stopped!
43,004 Retweets **142,317** Likes
4:39 AM - 5 Feb 2018

Donald J. Trump ✓
@realDonaldTrump

Any deal on DACA that does not include STRONG border security and the desperately needed WALL is a total waste of time. March 5th is rapidly approaching and the Dems seem not to care about DACA. Make a deal!
30,023 Retweets **123,371** Likes
6:36 AM - 5 Feb 2018

Donald J. Trump ✓
@realDonaldTrump

Representative Devin Nunes, a man of tremendous courage and grit, may someday be recognized as a Great American Hero for what he has exposed and what he has had to endure!
35,787 Retweets **133,744** Likes
7:08 AM - 5 Feb 2018

Donald J. Trump ✓
@realDonaldTrump

Thanks to the historic TAX CUTS that I signed into law, your paychecks are going way UP, your taxes are going way DOWN, and America is once again OPEN FOR BUSINESS!
22,886 Retweets **105,977** Likes
12:42 PM - 5 Feb 2018

Donald J. Trump ✓
@realDonaldTrump

So disgraceful that a person illegally in our country killed @Colts linebacker Edwin Jackson. This is just one of many such preventable tragedies. We must get the Dems to get tough on the Border, and with illegal immigration, FAST!
36,136 Retweets **142,978** Likes
5:32 AM - 6 Feb 2018

Donald J. Trump ✓
@realDonaldTrump

My prayers and best wishes are with the family of Edwin Jackson, a wonderful young man whose life was so senselessly taken. @Colts
20,956 Retweets **104,741** Likes
5:37 AM - 6 Feb 2018

Donald J. Trump ✓
@realDonaldTrump

Polling shows nearly 7 in 10 Americans support an immigration reform package that includes DACA, fully secures the border, ends chain migration & cancels the visa lottery. If D's oppose this deal, they aren't serious about DACA-they just want open borders.
23,645 Retweets **89,740** Likes
8:00 AM - 6 Feb 2018

Donald J. Trump ✓
@realDonaldTrump

We need a 21st century MERIT-BASED immigration system. Chain migration and the visa lottery are outdated programs that hurt our economic and national security.
25,680 Retweets **92,746** Likes
8:05 AM - 6 Feb 2018

Donald J. Trump ✓
@realDonaldTrump

Today, we heard the experiences of law enforcement professionals and community leaders working to combat the threat of MS-13, and the reforms we need from Congress to defeat it. Watch here
18,392 Retweets **76,121** Likes
2:45 PM - 6 Feb 2018

Donald J. Trump ✓
@realDonaldTrump

HAPPY BIRTHDAY to our 40th President of the United States of America, Ronald Reagan!
33,058 Retweets **181,719** Likes
4:48 PM - 6 Feb 2018

Donald J. Trump ✓
@realDonaldTrump

Congratulations @ElonMusk and @SpaceX on the successful #FalconHeavy launch. This achievement, along with @NASA's commercial and international partners, continues to show American ingenuity at its best!
31,726 Retweets **167,618** Likes
7:05 PM - 6 Feb 2018

President Trumps Tweets 2018: A Historical Archive of President Trump's Tweets

Donald J. Trump @realDonaldTrump

In the "old days," when good news was reported, the Stock Market would go up. Today, when good news is reported, the Stock Market goes down. Big mistake, and we have so much good (great) news about the economy!
22,005 Retweets **112,672** Likes
6:59 AM - 7 Feb 2018

Donald J. Trump @realDonaldTrump

NEW FBI TEXTS ARE BOMBSHELLS!
39,864 Retweets **138,202** Likes
8:10 AM - 7 Feb 2018

Donald J. Trump @realDonaldTrump

Best wishes to the Republic of Korea on hosting the @Olympics! What a wonderful opportunity to show everyone that you are a truly GREAT NATION!
12,803 Retweets **65,509** Likes
10:01 AM - 7 Feb 2018

Donald J. Trump @realDonaldTrump

Congratulations to the Republic of Korea on what will be a MAGNIFICENT Winter Olympics! What the South Korean people have built is truly an inspiration!
13349 Retweets **70576** Likes
2:13 PM - 7 Feb 2018

Donald J. Trump @realDonaldTrump

The Budget Agreement today is so important for our great Military. It ends the dangerous sequester and gives Secretary Mattis what he needs to keep America Great. Republicans and Democrats must support our troops and support this Bill!
23,230 Retweets **109,471** Likes
2:36 PM - 7 Feb 2018

Donald J. Trump @realDonaldTrump

Will be heading over shortly to make remarks at The National Prayer Breakfast in Washington. Great religious and political leaders, and many friends, including T.V. producer Mark Burnett of our wonderful 14 season Apprentice triumph, will be there. Looking forward to seeing all!
17,876 Retweets **106,381** Likes
3:08 AM - 8 Feb 2018

Donald J. Trump @realDonaldTrump

Our founders invoked our Creator four times in the Declaration of Independence. Our currency declares "IN GOD WE TRUST." And we place our hands on our hearts as we recite the Pledge of Allegiance and proclaim that we are "One Nation Under God." #NationalPrayerBreakfast
29,398 Retweets **107,158** Likes
9:13 AM - 8 Feb 2018

Donald J. Trump @realDonaldTrump

I will be meeting with Henry Kissinger at 1:45pm. Will be discussing North Korea, China and the Middle East.
13,629 Retweets **79,956** Likes
10:44 AM - 8 Feb 2018

Donald J. Trump ⊙
@realDonaldTrump

As long as we open our eyes to God's grace - and open our hearts to God's love - then America will forever be the land of the free, the home of the brave, and a light unto all nations. #NationalPrayerBreakfast
30,800 Retweets **110,326** Likes
12:10 PM - 8 Feb 2018

Donald J. Trump ⊙
@realDonaldTrump

Time to end the visa lottery. Congress must secure the immigration system and protect Americans.
24162 Retweets **97893** Likes
3:26 PM - 8 Feb 2018

Donald J. Trump ⊙
@realDonaldTrump

Wow! -Senator Mark Warner got caught having extensive contact with a lobbyist for a Russian oligarch. Warner did not want a "paper trail" on a "private" meeting (in London) he requested with Steele of fraudulent Dossier fame. All tied into Crooked Hillary.
39,958 Retweets **127,896** Likes
7:22 PM - 8 Feb 2018

Donald J. Trump ⊙
@realDonaldTrump

Just signed Bill. Our Military will now be stronger than ever before. We love and need our Military and gave them everything — and more. First time this has happened in a long time. Also means JOBS, JOBS, JOBS!
27,278 Retweets **130,615** Likes
5:39 AM - 9 Feb 2018

Donald J. Trump ⊙
@realDonaldTrump

Without more Republicans in Congress, we were forced to increase spending on things we do not like or want in order to finally, after many years of depletion, take care of our Military. Sadly, we needed some Dem votes for passage. Must elect more Republicans in 2018 Election!
28,187 Retweets **110,663** Likes
5:47 AM - 9 Feb 2018

Donald J. Trump ⊙
@realDonaldTrump

Costs on non-military lines will never come down if we do not elect more Republicans in the 2018 Election, and beyond. This Bill is a BIG VICTORY for our Military, but much waste in order to get Dem votes. Fortunately, DACA not included in this Bill, negotiations to start now!
21,465 Retweets **89,668** Likes
5:59 AM - 9 Feb 2018

Donald J. Trump ⊙
@realDonaldTrump

Jobless claims have dropped to a 45 year low!
13,834 Retweets **64,927** Likes
6:02 AM - 10 Feb 2018

Donald J. Trump @
@realDonaldTrump

The Democrats sent a very political and long response memo which they knew, because of sources and methods (and more), would have to be heavily redacted, whereupon they would blame the White House for lack of transparency. Told them to re-do and send back in proper form!
32,384 Retweets **117,713** Likes
6:20 AM - 10 Feb 2018

Donald J. Trump @
@realDonaldTrump

According to the @nytimes, a Russian sold phony secrets on "Trump" to the U.S. Asking price was $10 million, brought down to $1 million to be paid over time. I hope people are now seeing & understanding what is going on here. It is all now starting to come out - DRAIN THE SWAMP!
32,882 Retweets **105,760** Likes
7:20 AM - 10 Feb 2018

Donald J. Trump @
@realDonaldTrump

Peoples lives are being shattered and destroyed by a mere allegation. Some are true and some are false. Some are old and some are new. There is no recovery for someone falsely accused - life and career are gone. Is there no such thing any longer as Due Process?
37,304 Retweets **136,957** Likes
7:33 AM - 10 Feb 2018

Donald J. Trump @
@realDonaldTrump

"My view is that not only has Trump been vindicated in the last several weeks about the mishandling of the Dossier and the lies about the Clinton/DNC Dossier, it shows that he's been victimized. He's been victimized by the Obama Administration who were using all sorts of.......
25,875 Retweets **101,513** Likes
10:16 AM - 10 Feb 2018

Donald J. Trump @
@realDonaldTrump

....agencies, not just the FBI & DOJ, now the State Department to dig up dirt on him in the days leading up to the Election. Comey had conversations with Donald Trump, which I don't believe were accurate...he leaked information (corrupt)." Tom Fitton of Judicial Watch on @FoxNews
19,990 Retweets **75,810** Likes
10:34 AM - 10 Feb 2018

Donald J. Trump @
@realDonaldTrump

Republicans want to fix DACA far more than the Democrats do. The Dems had all three branches of government back in 2008-2011, and they decided not to do anything about DACA. They only want to use it as a campaign issue. Vote Republican!
30,571 Retweets **118,224** Likes
10:50 AM - 10 Feb 2018

Donald J. Trump @
@realDonaldTrump

My thoughts and prayers are with the two police officers, their families, and everybody at the @WestervillePD.
20,517 Retweets **85,046** Likes
1:18 PM - 10 Feb 2018

Donald J. Trump ✓
@realDonaldTrump

My Administration has identified three major priorities for creating a safe, modern and lawful immigration system: fully securing the border, ending chain migration, and canceling the visa lottery. Congress must secure the immigration system and protect Americans.
32,066 Retweets **119,333** Likes
3:34 PM - 10 Feb 2018

Donald J. Trump ✓
@realDonaldTrump

So many positive things going on for the U.S.A. and the Fake News Media just doesn't want to go there. Same negative stories over and over again! No wonder the People no longer trust the media, whose approval ratings are correctly at their lowest levels in history! #MAGA
31,128 Retweets **123,868** Likes
10:21 AM - 11 Feb 2018

Donald J. Trump ✓
@realDonaldTrump

4.2 million hard working Americans have already received a large Bonus and/or Pay Increase because of our recently Passed Tax Cut & Jobs Bill....and it will only get better! We are far ahead of schedule.
25,082 Retweets **125,039** Likes
11:15 AM - 11 Feb 2018

Donald J. Trump ✓
@realDonaldTrump

Rep. Lou Barletta, a Great Republican from Pennsylvania who was one of my very earliest supporters, will make a FANTASTIC Senator. He is strong & smart, loves Pennsylvania & loves our Country! Voted for Tax Cuts, unlike Bob Casey, who listened to Tax Hikers Pelosi and Schumer!
24,147 Retweets **97,505** Likes
12:26 PM - 11 Feb 2018

Donald J. Trump ✓
@realDonaldTrump

Just spoke to @JohnKasich to express condolences and prayers to all for the horrible shooting of two great police officers from @WestervillePD. This is a true tragedy!
14,954 Retweets **77,715** Likes
12:36 PM - 11 Feb 2018

Donald J. Trump ✓
@realDonaldTrump

Thank you to Sue Kruczek, who lost her wonderful and talented son Nick to the Opioid scourge, for your kind words while on @foxandfriends. We are fighting this terrible epidemic hard - Nick will not have died in vain!
16,854 Retweets **87,081** Likes
4:54 AM - 12 Feb 2018

Donald J. Trump ✓
@realDonaldTrump

The journey to #MAGA began @CPAC 2011 and the opportunity to reconnect with friends and supporters is something I look forward to every year. See you at #CPAC2018!
14,387 Retweets **67,800** Likes
12:48 PM - 12 Feb 2018

Donald J. Trump ✓
@realDonaldTrump

Our infrastructure plan has been put forward and has received great reviews by everyone except, of course, the Democrats. After many years we have taken care of our Military, now we have to fix our roads, bridges, tunnels, airports and more. Bipartisan, make deal Dems?

22,903 Retweets **105,996** Likes
2:43 AM - 13 Feb 2018

Donald J. Trump ✓
@realDonaldTrump

Negotiations on DACA have begun. Republicans want to make a deal and Democrats say they want to make a deal. Wouldn't it be great if we could finally, after so many years, solve the DACA puzzle. This will be our last chance, there will never be another opportunity! March 5th.

22,659 Retweets **107,190** Likes
2:52 AM - 13 Feb 2018

Donald J. Trump ✓
@realDonaldTrump

As we come together to celebrate the extraordinary contributions of African-Americans to our nation, our thoughts turn to the heroes of the civil rights movement whose courage and sacrifice have inspired us all. Proclamation

15,026 Retweets **65,423** Likes
10:15 AM - 14 Feb 2018

Donald J. Trump ✓
@realDonaldTrump

Today, I was honored to be joined by Republicans and Democrats from both the House and Senate, as well as members of my Cabinet - to discuss the urgent need to rebuild and restore America's depleted infrastructure.

11,359 Retweets **56,369** Likes
11:11 AM - 14 Feb 2018

Donald J. Trump ✓
@realDonaldTrump

My prayers and condolences to the families of the victims of the terrible Florida shooting. No child, teacher or anyone else should ever feel unsafe in an American school.

39,628 Retweets **174,183** Likes
12:50 PM - 14 Feb 2018

Donald J. Trump ✓
@realDonaldTrump

Just spoke to Governor Rick Scott. We are working closely with law enforcement on the terrible Florida school shooting.

19,524 Retweets **111,834** Likes
12:55 PM - 14 Feb 2018

Donald J. Trump ✓
@realDonaldTrump

So many signs that the Florida shooter was mentally disturbed, even expelled from school for bad and erratic behavior. Neighbors and classmates knew he was a big problem. Must always report such instances to authorities, again and again!

20,780 Retweets **89,071** Likes
4:12 AM - 15 Feb 2018

Donald J. Trump ✓
@realDonaldTrump

While the Republicans and Democrats in Congress are working hard to come up with a solution to DACA, they should be strongly considering a system of Merit Based Immigration so that we will have the people ready, willing and able to help all of those companies moving into the USA!
20,642 Retweets **100,976** Likes
6:57 AM - 15 Feb 2018

Donald J. Trump ✓
@realDonaldTrump

In times of tragedy, the bonds that sustain us are those of family, faith, community, and country. These bonds are stronger than the forces of hatred and evil - and these bonds grow even stronger in the hours of our greatest need.
19,695 Retweets **82,584** Likes
9:33 AM - 15 Feb 2018

Donald J. Trump ✓
@realDonaldTrump

The Schumer-Rounds-Collins immigration bill would be a total catastrophe. @DHSgov says it would be "the end of immigration enforcement in America." It creates a giant amnesty (including for dangerous criminals), doesn't build the wall, expands chain migration, keeps the visa...
20,026 Retweets **72,298** Likes
11:25 AM - 15 Feb 2018

Donald J. Trump ✓
@realDonaldTrump

...lottery, continues deadly catch-and-release, and bars enforcement even for FUTURE illegal immigrants. Voting for this amendment would be a vote AGAINST law enforcement, and a vote FOR open borders. If Dems are actually serious about DACA, they should support the Grassley bill!
15,254 Retweets **60,189** Likes
11:26 AM - 15 Feb 2018

Donald J. Trump ✓
@realDonaldTrump

Presidential Proclamation Honoring the Victims of the Tragedy in Parkland, Florida
13,591 Retweets **61,970** Likes
12:19 PM - 15 Feb 2018

Donald J. Trump ✓
@realDonaldTrump

I will be leaving for Florida today to meet with some of the bravest people on earth - but people whose lives have been totally shattered. Am also working with Congress on many fronts.
19,836 Retweets **120,054** Likes
6:37 AM - 16 Feb 2018

Donald J. Trump ✓
@realDonaldTrump

Cannot believe how BADLY DACA recipients have been treated by the Democrats...totally abandoned! Republicans are still working hard.
21,900 Retweets **97,235** Likes
6:49 AM - 16 Feb 2018

Donald J. Trump ✓
@realDonaldTrump

Russia started their anti-US campaign in 2014, long before I announced that I would run for President. The results of the election were not impacted. The Trump campaign did nothing wrong - no collusion!
37,049 Retweets **141,288** Likes
12:18 PM - 16 Feb 2018

Donald J. Trump ✓
@realDonaldTrump

Our entire Nation, w/one heavy heart, continues to pray for the victims & their families in Parkland, FL. To teachers, law enforcement, first responders & medical professionals who responded so bravely in the face of danger: We THANK YOU for your courage!
24,716 Retweets **118,119** Likes
8:53 PM - 16 Feb 2018

Donald J. Trump ✓
@realDonaldTrump

Melania and I met such incredible people last night in Broward County, Florida. Will never forget them, or the evening!
14,745 Retweets **97,126** Likes
11:04 AM - 17 Feb 2018

Donald J. Trump ✓
@realDonaldTrump

"Charges Deal Don A Big Win," written by Michael Goodwin of the @nypost, succinctly states that "the Russians had no impact on the election results." There was no Collusion with the Trump Campaign. "She lost the old-fashioned way, by being a terrible candidate. Case closed."
18,892 Retweets **71,274** Likes
11:26 AM - 17 Feb 2018

Donald J. Trump ✓
@realDonaldTrump

Deputy A.G. Rod Rosenstein stated at the News Conference: "There is no allegation in the indictment that any American was a knowing participant in this illegal activity. There is no allegation in the indictment that the charged conduct altered the outcome of the 2016 election.
21,867 Retweets **90,335** Likes
11:36 AM - 17 Feb 2018

Donald J. Trump ✓
@realDonaldTrump

Funny how the Fake News Media doesn't want to say that the Russian group was formed in 2014, long before my run for President. Maybe they knew I was going to run even though I didn't know!
25,523 Retweets **105,922** Likes
11:46 AM - 17 Feb 2018

Donald J. Trump ✓
@realDonaldTrump

The Fake News Media never fails. Hard to ignore this fact from the Vice President of Facebook Ads, Rob Goldman!
18,770 Retweets **60,818** Likes
12:11 PM - 17 Feb 2018

Donald J. Trump ✓
@realDonaldTrump

"I have seen all of the Russian ads and I can say very definitively that swaying the election was *NOT* the main goal." Rob Goldman Vice President of Facebook Ads
17,148 Retweets **58,403** Likes
12:16 PM - 17 Feb 2018

Donald J. Trump ✓
@realDonaldTrump

Just like they don't want to solve the DACA problem, why didn't the Democrats pass gun control legislation when they had both the House & Senate during the Obama Administration. Because they didn't want to, and now they just talk!
32,193 Retweets **122,987** Likes
3:45 PM - 17 Feb 2018

Donald J. Trump ✓
@realDonaldTrump

Very sad that the FBI missed all of the many signals sent out by the Florida school shooter. This is not acceptable. They are spending too much time trying to prove Russian collusion with the Trump campaign - there is no collusion. Get back to the basics and make us all proud!
37,025 Retweets **149,114** Likes
8:08 PM - 17 Feb 2018

Donald J. Trump ✓
@realDonaldTrump

General McMaster forgot to say that the results of the 2016 election were not impacted or changed by the Russians and that the only Collusion was between Russia and Crooked H, the DNC and the Dems. Remember the Dirty Dossier, Uranium, Speeches, Emails and the Podesta Company!
27,037 Retweets **96,734** Likes
8:22 PM - 17 Feb 2018

Donald J. Trump ✓
@realDonaldTrump

Never gotten over the fact that Obama was able to send $1.7 Billion Dollars in CASH to Iran and nobody in Congress, the FBI or Justice called for an investigation!
38,387 Retweets **124,701** Likes
4:02 AM - 18 Feb 2018

Donald J. Trump ✓
@realDonaldTrump

Finally, Liddle' Adam Schiff, the leakin' monster of no control, is now blaming the Obama Administration for Russian meddling in the 2016 Election. He is finally right about something. Obama was President, knew of the threat, and did nothing. Thank you Adam!
28,411 Retweets **108,688** Likes
4:22 AM - 18 Feb 2018

Donald J. Trump ✓
@realDonaldTrump

I never said Russia did not meddle in the election, I said "it may be Russia, or China or another country or group, or it may be a 400 pound genius sitting in bed and playing with his computer." The Russian "hoax" was that the Trump campaign colluded with Russia - it never did!
31,757 Retweets **127,176** Likes
4:33 AM - 18 Feb 2018

President Trumps Tweets 2018: A Historical Archive of President Trump's Tweets

Donald J. Trump ✓
@realDonaldTrump

Now that Adam Schiff is starting to blame President Obama for Russian meddling in the election, he is probably doing so as yet another excuse that the Democrats, lead by their fearless leader, Crooked Hillary Clinton, lost the 2016 election. But wasn't I a great candidate?
19,735 Retweets **90,179** Likes
4:43 AM - 18 Feb 2018

Donald J. Trump ✓
@realDonaldTrump

If it was the GOAL of Russia to create discord, disruption and chaos within the U.S. then, with all of the Committee Hearings, Investigations and Party hatred, they have succeeded beyond their wildest dreams. They are laughing their asses off in Moscow. Get smart America!
33,016 Retweets **118,306** Likes
5:11 AM - 18 Feb 2018

Donald J. Trump ✓
@realDonaldTrump

The Fake News of big ratings loser CNN.
19,637 Retweets **76,885** Likes
5:46 AM - 18 Feb 2018

Donald J. Trump ✓
@realDonaldTrump

Great Pollster John McLaughlin now has the GOP up in the Generic Congressional Ballot. Big gain over last 4 weeks. I guess people are loving the big Tax Cuts given them by the Republicans, the Cuts the Dems want to take away. We need more Republicans!
21,861 Retweets **97,209** Likes
5:55 AM - 18 Feb 2018

Donald J. Trump ✓
@realDonaldTrump

Thank you to KenStarr, former Independent Counsel, Whitewater, for your insight and powerful words on FISA abuse, Russian meddling etc. Really great interview with @MariaBartiromo
17,974 Retweets **77,496** Likes
9:10 AM - 18 Feb 2018

Donald J. Trump ✓
@realDonaldTrump

My great friends from NASCAR are having their big race today, The Daytona 500. Brian France and the France family are special people. Enjoy the race!
15,542 Retweets **102,112** Likes
11:13 AM - 18 Feb 2018

Donald J. Trump ✓
@realDonaldTrump

Just watched a very insecure Oprah Winfrey, who at one point I knew very well, interview a panel of people on 60 Minutes. The questions were biased and slanted, the facts incorrect. Hope Oprah runs so she can be exposed and defeated just like all of the others!
34,437 Retweets **153,608** Likes
8:28 PM - 18 Feb 2018

Donald J. Trump ✓
@realDonaldTrump

Have a great, but very reflective, President's Day!
23,877 Retweets **144,230** Likes
5:42 AM - 19 Feb 2018

Donald J. Trump ✓
@realDonaldTrump

Obama was President up to, and beyond, the 2016 Election. So why didn't he do something about Russian meddling?
22,285 Retweets **91,374** Likes
11:55 AM - 19 Feb 2018

Donald J. Trump ✓
@realDonaldTrump

.@MittRomney has announced he is running for the Senate from the wonderful State of Utah. He will make a great Senator and worthy successor to @OrrinHatch, and has my full support and endorsement!
9,387 Retweets **55,014** Likes
6:21 PM - 19 Feb 2018

Donald J. Trump ✓
@realDonaldTrump

The U.S. economy is looking very good, in my opinion, even better than anticipated. Companies are pouring back into our country, reversing the long term trend of leaving. The unemployment numbers are looking great, and Regulations & Taxes have been massively Cut! JOBS, JOBS, JOBS
25,306 Retweets **120,633** Likes
6:29 PM - 19 Feb 2018

Donald J. Trump ✓
@realDonaldTrump

"The Faith of Donald Trump," a book just out by David Brody and Scott Lamb, is a very interesting read. Enjoy!
13,259 Retweets **68,243** Likes
6:48 PM - 19 Feb 2018

Donald J. Trump ✓
@realDonaldTrump

Thank you to @foxandfriends for the great timeline on all of the failures the Obama Administration had against Russia, including Crimea, Syria and so much more. We are now starting to win again!
14,655 Retweets **66,368** Likes
4:24 AM - 20 Feb 2018

Donald J. Trump ✓
@realDonaldTrump

"There is no serious person out there who would suggest somehow that you could even rig America's elections, there's no evidence that that has happened in the past or that it will happen this time, and so I'd invite Mr. Trump to stop whining and make his case to get votes."
17,403 Retweets **67,815** Likes
4:37 AM - 20 Feb 2018

Donald J. Trump ✓
@realDonaldTrump

....The President Obama quote just before election. That's because he thought Crooked Hillary was going to win and he didn't want to "rock the boat." When I easily won the Electoral College, the whole game changed and the Russian excuse became the narrative of the Dems.
20,699 Retweets **85,341** Likes
4:46 AM - 20 Feb 2018

Donald J. Trump ✓
@realDonaldTrump

Republicans are now leading the Generic Poll, perhaps because of the popular Tax Cuts which the Dems want to take away. Actually, they want to raise you taxes, substantially. Also, they want to do nothing on DACA, R's want to fix!
17,161 Retweets **82,044** Likes
4:54 AM - 20 Feb 2018

Donald J. Trump ✓
@realDonaldTrump

Matt Schlapp and CPAC are getting ready for another exciting event. Big difference from those days when President Obama held the White House. You've come a long way Matt!
10,176 Retweets **51,701** Likes
5:03 AM - 20 Feb 2018

Donald J. Trump ✓
@realDonaldTrump

Hope Republicans in the Great State of Pennsylvania challenge the new "pushed" Congressional Map, all the way to the Supreme Court, if necessary. Your Original was correct! Don't let the Dems take elections away from you so that they can raise taxes & waste money!
20,211 Retweets **79,178** Likes
5:11 AM - 20 Feb 2018

Donald J. Trump ✓
@realDonaldTrump

I have been much tougher on Russia than Obama, just look at the facts. Total Fake News!
16,216 Retweets **77,951** Likes
5:38 AM - 20 Feb 2018

Donald J. Trump ✓
@realDonaldTrump

A woman I don't know and, to the best of my knowledge, never met, is on the FRONT PAGE of the Fake News Washington Post saying I kissed her (for two minutes yet) in the lobby of Trump Tower 12 years ago. Never happened! Who would do this in a public space with live security......
21,676 Retweets **96,352** Likes
7:16 AM - 20 Feb 2018

Donald J. Trump ✓
@realDonaldTrump

....cameras running. Another False Accusation. Why doesn't @washingtonpost report the story of the women taking money to make up stories about me? One had her home mortgage paid off. Only @FoxNews so reported...doesn't fit the Mainstream Media narrative.
19,693 Retweets **79,159** Likes
7:29 AM - 20 Feb 2018

Donald J. Trump ✓
@realDonaldTrump

Main Street is BOOMING thanks to our incredible TAX CUT and Reform law. "This shows small-business owners are more than just optimistic, they are ready to grow their businesses."
17,507 Retweets **74,716** Likes
9:49 AM - 20 Feb 2018

Donald J. Trump ✓
@realDonaldTrump

Bad ratings @CNN & @MSNBC got scammed when they covered the anti-Trump Russia rally wall-to-wall. They probably knew it was Fake News but, because it was a rally against me, they pushed it hard anyway. Two really dishonest newscasters, but the public is wise!
22,372 Retweets **95,052** Likes
5:08 PM - 20 Feb 2018

Donald J. Trump ✓
@realDonaldTrump

So true, thank you!
21,826 Retweets **97,813** Likes
5:14 PM - 20 Feb 2018

Donald J. Trump ✓
@realDonaldTrump

@CNN @MSNBC Whether we are Republican or Democrat, we must now focus on strengthening Background Checks!
16,129 Retweets **81,372** Likes
5:18 PM - 20 Feb 2018

Donald J. Trump ✓
@realDonaldTrump

The GREAT Billy Graham is dead. There was nobody like him! He will be missed by Christians and all religions. A very special man.
29,719 Retweets **150,289** Likes
6:22 AM - 21 Feb 2018

Donald J. Trump ✓
@realDonaldTrump

Question: If all of the Russian meddling took place during the Obama Administration, right up to January 20th, why aren't they the subject of the investigation? Why didn't Obama do something about the meddling? Why aren't Dem crimes under investigation? Ask Jeff Sessions!
32,325 Retweets **115,969** Likes
6:40 AM - 21 Feb 2018

Donald J. Trump ✓
@realDonaldTrump

Yesterday, it was my great honor to recognize extraordinary Law Enforcement Officers and First Responders, and to award them the the highest possible decoration for bravery by public safety officers, the Medal of Valor. #AmericanHeroes
15,075 Retweets **74,336** Likes
10:20 AM - 21 Feb 2018

Donald J. Trump ✓
@realDonaldTrump

.@FLOTUS Melania and I join millions of people around the world in mourning the passing of Billy Graham. Our prayers are with his children, grandchildren, great-grandchildren and all who worked closely with Reverend Graham in his lifelong ministry.
18,201 Retweets **83,667** Likes
1:12 PM - 21 Feb 2018

Donald J. Trump ✓
@realDonaldTrump

I will always remember the time I spent today with courageous students, teachers and families. So much love in the midst of so much pain. We must not let them down. We must keep our children safe!!
23,676 Retweets **105,342** Likes
5:40 PM - 21 Feb 2018

President Trumps Tweets 2018: A Historical Archive of President Trump's Tweets

Donald J. Trump ✓
@realDonaldTrump

I never said "give teachers guns" like was stated on Fake News @CNN & @NBC. What I said was to look at the possibility of giving "concealed guns to gun adept teachers with military or special training experience - only the best. 20% of teachers, a lot, would now be able to

22,391 Retweets **88,498** Likes
4:26 AM - 22 Feb 2018

Donald J. Trump ✓
@realDonaldTrump

....immediately fire back if a savage sicko came to a school with bad intentions. Highly trained teachers would also serve as a deterrent to the cowards that do this. Far more assets at much less cost than guards. A "gun free" school is a magnet for bad people. ATTACKS WOULD END!

22,428 Retweets **102,063** Likes
4:40 AM - 22 Feb 2018

Donald J. Trump ✓
@realDonaldTrump

....History shows that a school shooting lasts, on average, 3 minutes. It takes police & first responders approximately 5 to 8 minutes to get to site of crime. Highly trained, gun adept, teachers/coaches would solve the problem instantly, before police arrive. GREAT DETERRENT!

29,535 Retweets **125,135** Likes
4:54 AM - 22 Feb 2018

Donald J. Trump ✓
@realDonaldTrump

....If a potential "sicko shooter" knows that a school has a large number of very weapons talented teachers (and others) who will be instantly shooting, the sicko will NEVER attack that school. Cowards won't go there...problem solved. Must be offensive, defense alone won't work!

25,680 Retweets **106,687** Likes
5:05 AM - 22 Feb 2018

Donald J. Trump ✓
@realDonaldTrump

I will be strongly pushing Comprehensive Background Checks with an emphasis on Mental Health. Raise age to 21 and end sale of Bump Stocks! Congress is in a mood to finally do something on this issue - I hope!

36,750 Retweets **185,614** Likes
5:13 AM - 22 Feb 2018

Donald J. Trump ✓
@realDonaldTrump

What many people don't understand, or don't want to understand, is that Wayne, Chris and the folks who work so hard at the @NRA are Great People and Great American Patriots. They love our Country and will do the right thing. MAKE AMERICA GREAT AGAIN!

22,574 Retweets **92,246** Likes
6:31 AM - 22 Feb 2018

Donald J. Trump ✓
@realDonaldTrump

Will be meeting with Lawmakers today at 11:30 A.M. to discuss School Safety. Next week it will be with our Nation's Governors. It's been many years of all talk, no action. We'll get it done!

19,752 Retweets **106,094** Likes
6:53 AM - 22 Feb 2018

Donald J. Trump ⊘
@realDonaldTrump

On behalf of an entire Nation, CONGRATULATIONS to the U.S. Women's Hockey Team on winning the GOLD! #GoTeamUSA #Olympics
18,326 Retweets **103,358** Likes
8:29 AM - 22 Feb 2018

Donald J. Trump ⊘
@realDonaldTrump

Today, it was my great honor to host a School Safety Roundtable at the @WhiteHouse with State and local leaders, law enforcement officers, and education officials. There is nothing more important than protecting our children. They deserve to be safe, and we will deliver!
18,621 Retweets **83,274** Likes
12:07 PM - 22 Feb 2018

Donald J. Trump ⊘
@realDonaldTrump

"School shooting survivor says he quit @CNN Town Hall after refusing scripted question." @TuckerCarlson. Just like so much of CNN, Fake News. That's why their ratings are so bad! MSNBC may be worse.
32,011 Retweets **113,224** Likes
5:26 PM - 22 Feb 2018

Donald J. Trump ⊘
@realDonaldTrump

MS-13 gang members are being removed by our Great ICE and Border Patrol Agents by the thousands, but these killers come back in from El Salvador, and through Mexico, like water. El Salvador just takes our money, and Mexico must help MORE with this problem. We need The Wall!
28,423 Retweets **125,750** Likes
3:28 AM - 23 Feb 2018

Donald J. Trump ⊘
@realDonaldTrump

CPAC Today!
7,832 Retweets **47,061** Likes
5:01 AM - 23 Feb 2018

Donald J. Trump ⊘
@realDonaldTrump

My daughter, Ivanka, just arrived in South Korea. We cannot have a better, or smarter, person representing our country.
14,510 Retweets **98,737** Likes
5:07 AM - 23 Feb 2018

Donald J. Trump ⊘
@realDonaldTrump

For those of you who are still interested, the Democrats have totally forgotten about DACA. Not a lot of interest on this subject from them!
24,830 Retweets **98,027** Likes
5:09 AM - 23 Feb 2018

Donald J. Trump ⊘
@realDonaldTrump

After years of rebuilding OTHER nations, we are finally rebuilding OUR nation - and we are restoring our confidence and our pride! #CPAC2018
16,019 Retweets **69,607** Likes
9:06 AM - 23 Feb 2018

Donald J. Trump ✓
@realDonaldTrump

We salute our great American flag, we put our hands on our hearts for the pledge of Allegiance, and we all PROUDLY STAND for the National Anthem. #CPAC2018
18,212 Retweets **76,989** Likes
9:08 AM - 23 Feb 2018

Donald J. Trump ✓
@realDonaldTrump

Our nation's motto is IN GOD WE TRUST. This week, our nation lost an incredible leader who devoted his life to helping us understand what those words really mean. We will never forget the historic crowds, the voice, the energy, and the profound faith of Billy Graham! #CPAC2018
20,874 Retweets **85,902** Likes
9:12 AM - 23 Feb 2018

Donald J. Trump ✓
@realDonaldTrump

Today, @FLOTUS Melania and I were honored to welcome Prime Minister @TurnbullMalcolm and Mrs. Turnbull of Australia to the @WhiteHouse!
8,994 Retweets **47,602** Likes
1:19 PM - 23 Feb 2018

Donald J. Trump ✓
@realDonaldTrump

Thank you to the great men and women of the United States @SecretService for a job well done!
15,608 Retweets **87,142** Likes
2:46 PM - 23 Feb 2018

Donald J. Trump ✓
@realDonaldTrump

So true Wayne, and Lowest black unemployment in history!
20,535 Retweets **81,402** Likes
5:21 AM - 24 Feb 2018

Donald J. Trump ✓
@realDonaldTrump

Armed Educators (and trusted people who work within a school) love our students and will protect them. Very smart people. Must be firearms adept & have annual training. Should get yearly bonus. Shootings will not happen again - a big & very inexpensive deterrent. Up to States.
20,955 Retweets **86,414** Likes
10:54 AM - 24 Feb 2018

Donald J. Trump ✓
@realDonaldTrump

Democrat judges have totally redrawn election lines in the great State of Pennsylvania. @FoxNews. This is very unfair to Republicans and to our country as a whole. Must be appealed to the United States Supreme Court ASAP!
22,690 Retweets **80,461** Likes
12:16 PM - 24 Feb 2018

Donald J. Trump ✓
@realDonaldTrump

Unemployment claims are at the lowest level since 1973. Much of this has to do with the massive cutting of unnecessary and job killing Regulations!
16,109 Retweets **74,829** Likes
1:07 PM - 24 Feb 2018

Donald J. Trump ✓
@realDonaldTrump

Dems are no longer talking DACA! "Out of sight, out of mind," they say. DACA beneficiaries should not be happy. Nancy Pelosi truly doesn't care about them. Republicans stand ready to make a deal!
22,652 Retweets **94,448** Likes
1:18 PM - 24 Feb 2018

Donald J. Trump ✓
@realDonaldTrump

BIG CPAC STRAW POLL RESULTS: 93% APPROVE OF THE JOB PRESIDENT TRUMP IS DOING (Thank you!). 50% say President Trump should Tweet MORE or SAME (funny!). 79% say Republicans in Congress should do a better job of working with President Trump (starting to happen).
25,570 Retweets **99,968** Likes
2:26 PM - 24 Feb 2018

Donald J. Trump ✓
@realDonaldTrump

The Democrat memo response on government surveillance abuses is a total political and legal BUST. Just confirms all of the terrible things that were done. SO ILLEGAL!
20,911 Retweets **83,203** Likes
3:16 PM - 24 Feb 2018

Donald J. Trump ✓
@realDonaldTrump

Dem Memo: FBI did not disclose who the clients were - the Clinton Campaign and the DNC. Wow!
21,940 Retweets **80,551** Likes
3:20 PM - 24 Feb 2018

Donald J. Trump ✓
@realDonaldTrump

"Russians had no compromising information on Donald Trump" @FoxNews Of course not, because there is none, and never was. This whole Witch Hunt is an illegal disgrace...and Obama did nothing about Russia!
19,471 Retweets **74,190** Likes
3:44 PM - 24 Feb 2018

Donald J. Trump ✓
@realDonaldTrump

"Congressman Schiff omitted and distorted key facts" @FoxNews So, what else is new. He is a total phony!
19,619 Retweets **77,192** Likes
4:56 PM - 24 Feb 2018

Donald J. Trump ✓
@realDonaldTrump

I will be interviewed by @JudgeJeanine on @FoxNews at 9:00 P.M. Enjoy!
8,673 Retweets **50,149** Likes
5:00 PM - 24 Feb 2018

Donald J. Trump ✓
@realDonaldTrump

"He's got a very good point. Somebody in the Justice Department has a treasure trove of evidence of Mrs. Clinton's criminality at her own hands, or through others, that ought to be investigated. I fully agree with the President on that." @judgenapolitano on @marthamaccallum Show
19,756 Retweets **69,464** Likes
3:59 AM - 27 Feb 2018

Donald J. Trump ✓
@realDonaldTrump

"I've been skeptical about the collusion and obstruction claims for the last year. I just don't see the evidence....in terms of the collusion, it's all a bit implausible based on the evidence we have." Jonathan Turley on @FoxNews
14,848 Retweets **65,604** Likes
4:28 AM - 27 Feb 2018

Donald J. Trump ✓
@realDonaldTrump

"We've seen NO EVIDENCE OF COLLUSION....I have seen nothing, the firing of James Comey and all of the aftermath, that suggests that the President has obstructed justice because he's exercising his power as the President of the U.S. I just don't see it." Judge Ken Starr
23,576 Retweets **92,849** Likes
4:45 AM - 27 Feb 2018

Donald J. Trump ✓
@realDonaldTrump

WITCH HUNT!
24,267 Retweets **94,475** Likes
4:49 AM - 27 Feb 2018

Donald J. Trump ✓
@realDonaldTrump

I want to encourage all of my many Texas friends to vote in the primary for Governor Greg Abbott, Senator Ted Cruz, Lt. Gov. Dan Patrick, and Attorney General Ken Paxton. They are helping me to Make America Great Again! Vote early or on March 6th.
29,452 Retweets **106,481** Likes
10:11 AM - 27 Feb 2018

Donald J. Trump ✓
@realDonaldTrump

"American consumers are the most confident they've been since 2000....A strong job market is boosting confidence. The unemployment rate has stayed at a 17-year low."
13,566 Retweets **57,933** Likes
10:18 AM - 27 Feb 2018

Donald J. Trump ✓
@realDonaldTrump

Texas LC George P. Bush backed me when it wasn't the politically correct thing to do, and I back him now. Also, AC Sid Miller has been with me from the beginning, he is "Trump's Man in Texas." Also support Comptroller Glenn Hegar, and Railroad Commissioner Christi Craddick.
15,591 Retweets **65,317** Likes
2:55 PM - 27 Feb 2018

Donald J. Trump ✓
@realDonaldTrump

.@SenatorWicker of Mississippi has been a great supporter and incredible help in getting our massive Tax Cut Bill done and approved. Also big help on cutting regs. I am with him in his re-election all the way!
12,170 Retweets **50,474** Likes
2:58 PM - 27 Feb 2018

Donald J. Trump ✓
@realDonaldTrump

Such a beautiful map, thank you!
17,041 Retweets **71,290** Likes
8:20 PM - 27 Feb 2018

Donald J. Trump ✓
@realDonaldTrump

Big legal win today. U.S. judge sided with the Trump Administration and rejected the attempt to stop the government from building a great Border Wall on the Southern Border. Now this important project can go forward!
23,735 Retweets **100,927** Likes
8:28 PM - 27 Feb 2018

Donald J. Trump ✓
@realDonaldTrump

The Heritage Foundation has just stated that 64% of the Trump Agenda is already done, faster than even Ronald Reagan. "We're blown away," said Thomas Binion of Heritage, President Trump "is very active, very conservative and very effective. Huge volume & spectrum of issues."
23,665 Retweets **94,791** Likes
4:02 AM - 28 Feb 2018

Donald J. Trump ✓
@realDonaldTrump

I have decided that sections of the Wall that California wants built NOW will not be built until the whole Wall is approved. Big victory yesterday with ruling from the courts that allows us to proceed. OUR COUNTRY MUST HAVE BORDER SECURITY!
22,435 Retweets **101,499** Likes
4:29 AM - 28 Feb 2018

Donald J. Trump ✓
@realDonaldTrump

45 year low on illegal border crossings this year. Ice and Border Patrol Agents are doing a great job for our Country. MS-13 thugs being hit hard.
21,076 Retweets **112,466** Likes
6:08 AM - 28 Feb 2018

Donald J. Trump ✓
@realDonaldTrump

Why is A.G. Jeff Sessions asking the Inspector General to investigate potentially massive FISA abuse. Will take forever, has no prosecutorial power and already late with reports on Comey etc. Isn't the I.G. an Obama guy? Why not use Justice Department lawyers? DISGRACEFUL!
25,454 Retweets **90,393** Likes
6:34 AM - 28 Feb 2018

Donald J. Trump ✓
@realDonaldTrump

Today, in the center of this great Chamber lies Billy Graham – an Ambassador for Christ who reminded the world of the power of prayer and the gift of God's grace.
17,637 Retweets **75,066** Likes
9:10 AM - 28 Feb 2018

President Trumps Tweets 2018: A Historical Archive of President Trump's Tweets

Donald J. Trump ✓
@realDonaldTrump

Starting at a small Bible School in Florida, Billy Graham soon led a nationwide revival. From a large tent in Los Angeles, to one hundred thousand people in a single day at Yankee Stadium, to more than two million people at Madison Square Garden over sixteen weeks in 1957...
14,381 Retweets **66,631** Likes
10:36 AM - 28 Feb 2018

Donald J. Trump ✓
@realDonaldTrump

Today we honor Billy Graham as only three private citizens before him have been honored. We say a prayer for our country: that all across this land, the Lord will raise up men and women like Billy Graham to spread a message of love and hope to every precious child of God.
17,341 Retweets **73,093** Likes
11:01 AM - 28 Feb 2018

Donald J. Trump ✓
@realDonaldTrump

It was an honor to welcome bipartisan members of Congress for a discussion on SAFE schools and SAFE communities. As we continue to mourn the loss of so many precious young lives in Parkland, we are determined to turn our grief into action.
11,747 Retweets **53,608** Likes
1:34 PM - 28 Feb 2018

Donald J. Trump ✓
@realDonaldTrump

Many ideas, some good & some not so good, emerged from our bipartisan meeting on school safety yesterday at the White House. Background Checks a big part of conversation. Gun free zones are proven targets of killers. After many years, a Bill should emerge. Respect 2nd Amendment!
17,417 Retweets **79,666** Likes
3:53 AM - 1 Mar 2018

Donald J. Trump ✓
@realDonaldTrump

Our Steel and Aluminum industries (and many others) have been decimated by decades of unfair trade and bad policy with countries from around the world. We must not let our country, companies and workers be taken advantage of any longer. We want free, fair and SMART TRADE!
22,787 Retweets **103,843** Likes
4:12 AM - 1 Mar 2018

Donald J. Trump ✓
@realDonaldTrump

Unemployment filings are at their lowest level in over 48 years. Great news for workers and JOBS, JOBS, JOBS! #MAGA
15,070 Retweets **59,285** Likes
10:06 AM - 1 Mar 2018

Donald J. Trump ✓
@realDonaldTrump

"Manufacturing in U.S. Expands at Fastest Pace Since May 2004"
11,427 Retweets **48,759** Likes
10:26 AM - 1 Mar 2018

Donald J. Trump @realDonaldTrump

"Consumer Confidence in February Highest Since November 2000"
10,663 Retweets **47,092** Likes
12:40 PM - 1 Mar 2018

Donald J. Trump @realDonaldTrump

Together, we will face this challenge as a national family with conviction, with unity, and with a commitment to love and support our neighbors in times of dire need. Working together, we will defeat this #OpioidEpidemic.
11,798 Retweets **51,875** Likes
1:31 PM - 1 Mar 2018

Donald J. Trump @realDonaldTrump

Jobless claims at a 49 year low!
15,222 Retweets **76,116** Likes
4:51 PM - 1 Mar 2018

Donald J. Trump @realDonaldTrump

Manufacturing growing at the fastest pace in almost two decades!
14,796 Retweets **75,774** Likes
4:52 PM - 1 Mar 2018

Donald J. Trump @realDonaldTrump

Good (Great) meeting in the Oval Office tonight with the NRA!
17,475 Retweets **94,085** Likes
7:04 PM - 1 Mar 2018

Donald J. Trump @realDonaldTrump

When a country (USA) is losing many billions of dollars on trade with virtually every country it does business with, trade wars are good, and easy to win. Example, when we are down $100 billion with a certain country and they get cute, don't trade anymore-we win big. It's easy!
22,759 Retweets **100,825** Likes
2:50 AM - 2 Mar 2018

Donald J. Trump @realDonaldTrump

Alec Baldwin, whose dying mediocre career was saved by his terrible impersonation of me on SNL, now says playing me was agony. Alec, it was agony for those who were forced to watch. Bring back Darrell Hammond, funnier and a far greater talent!
28,791 Retweets **141,272** Likes
3:07 AM - 2 Mar 2018

Donald J. Trump @realDonaldTrump

Eric, we are all with you and your family! Look forward to seeing you back on T.V.
11,999 Retweets **54,647** Likes
3:18 AM - 2 Mar 2018

President Trumps Tweets 2018: A Historical Archive of President Trump's Tweets

Donald J. Trump ✓
@realDonaldTrump

We must protect our country and our workers. Our steel industry is in bad shape. IF YOU DON'T HAVE STEEL, YOU DON'T HAVE A COUNTRY!
22,024 Retweets **104,149** Likes
5:01 AM - 2 Mar 2018

Donald J. Trump ✓
@realDonaldTrump

When a country Taxes our products coming in at, say, 50%, and we Tax the same product coming into our country at ZERO, not fair or smart. We will soon be starting RECIPROCAL TAXES so that we will charge the same thing as they charge us. $800 Billion Trade Deficit-have no choice!
31,087 Retweets **124,145** Likes
5:57 AM - 2 Mar 2018

Donald J. Trump ✓
@realDonaldTrump

REST IN PEACE BILLY GRAHAM!
22,378 Retweets **112,277** Likes
11:48 AM - 2 Mar 2018

Donald J. Trump ✓
@realDonaldTrump

Happy National Anthem Day!
21,868 Retweets **94,540** Likes
6:15 AM - 3 Mar 2018

Donald J. Trump ✓
@realDonaldTrump

Mainstream Media in U.S. is being mocked all over the world. They've gone CRAZY!
20,619 Retweets **74,730** Likes
9:33 AM - 3 Mar 2018

Donald J. Trump ✓
@realDonaldTrump

The United States has an $800 Billion Dollar Yearly Trade Deficit because of our "very stupid" trade deals and policies. Our jobs and wealth are being given to other countries that have taken advantage of us for years. They laugh at what fools our leaders have been. No more!
31,042 Retweets **130,205** Likes
9:43 AM - 3 Mar 2018

Donald J. Trump ✓
@realDonaldTrump

If the E.U. wants to further increase their already massive tariffs and barriers on U.S. companies doing business there, we will simply apply a Tax on their Cars which freely pour into the U.S. They make it impossible for our cars (and more) to sell there. Big trade imbalance!
30,869 Retweets **124,849** Likes
9:53 AM - 3 Mar 2018

Donald J. Trump ✓
@realDonaldTrump

The Gridiron Dinner last night was great fun. I am accomplishing a lot in Washington and have never had a better time doing something, and especially since this is for the American People!
19,948 Retweets **102,246** Likes
9:42 AM - 4 Mar 2018

Donald J. Trump ✓
@realDonaldTrump

We are on the losing side of almost all trade deals. Our friends and enemies have taken advantage of the U.S. for many years. Our Steel and Aluminum industries are dead. Sorry, it's time for a change! MAKE AMERICA GREAT AGAIN!
26,614 Retweets **117,719** Likes
4:10 PM - 4 Mar 2018

Donald J. Trump ✓
@realDonaldTrump

We have large trade deficits with Mexico and Canada. NAFTA, which is under renegotiation right now, has been a bad deal for U.S.A. Massive relocation of companies & jobs. Tariffs on Steel and Aluminum will only come off if new & fair NAFTA agreement is signed. Also, Canada must..
19,316 Retweets **82,196** Likes
3:47 AM - 5 Mar 2018

Donald J. Trump ✓
@realDonaldTrump

...treat our farmers much better. Highly restrictive. Mexico must do much more on stopping drugs from pouring into the U.S. They have not done what needs to be done. Millions of people addicted and dying.
18,135 Retweets **86,041** Likes
3:53 AM - 5 Mar 2018

Donald J. Trump ✓
@realDonaldTrump

To protect our Country we must protect American Steel! #AMERICA FIRST
17,444 Retweets **83,955** Likes
4:57 AM - 5 Mar 2018

Donald J. Trump ✓
@realDonaldTrump

Why did the Obama Administration start an investigation into the Trump Campaign (with zero proof of wrongdoing) long before the Election in November? Wanted to discredit so Crooked H would win. Unprecedented. Bigger than Watergate! Plus, Obama did NOTHING about Russian meddling.
39,150 Retweets **131,365** Likes
5:22 AM - 5 Mar 2018

Donald J. Trump ✓
@realDonaldTrump

It's March 5th and the Democrats are nowhere to be found on DACA. Gave them 6 months, they just don't care. Where are they? We are ready to make a deal!
29,962 Retweets **114,127** Likes
12:37 PM - 5 Mar 2018

Donald J. Trump ✓
@realDonaldTrump

The new Fake News narrative is that there is CHAOS in the White House. Wrong! People will always come & go, and I want strong dialogue before making a final decision. I still have some people that I want to change (always seeking perfection). There is no Chaos, only great Energy!
22,761 Retweets **97,985** Likes
4:55 AM - 6 Mar 2018

Donald J. Trump ✓
@realDonaldTrump

Total inaction on DACA by Dems. Where are you? A deal can be made!
15,381 Retweets **72,464** Likes
5:00 AM - 6 Mar 2018

President Trumps Tweets 2018: A Historical Archive of President Trump's Tweets

Donald J. Trump ✓
@realDonaldTrump

We are getting it done - jobs and security!
13,033 Retweets **52,999** Likes
5:02 AM - 6 Mar 2018

Donald J. Trump ✓
@realDonaldTrump

We will see what happens!
9,932 Retweets **39,284** Likes
5:05 AM - 6 Mar 2018

Donald J. Trump ✓
@realDonaldTrump

Lowest rated Oscars in HISTORY. Problem is, we don't have Stars anymore - except your President (just kidding, of course)!
59,495 Retweets **213,557** Likes
5:25 AM - 6 Mar 2018

Donald J. Trump ✓
@realDonaldTrump

Federal Judge in Maryland has just ruled that "President Trump has the right to end DACA." President Obama had 8 years to fix this problem, and didn't. I am waiting for the Dems, they are running for the hills!
22,656 Retweets **85,659** Likes
5:46 AM - 6 Mar 2018

Donald J. Trump ✓
@realDonaldTrump

Possible progress being made in talks with North Korea. For the first time in many years, a serious effort is being made by all parties concerned. The World is watching and waiting! May be false hope, but the U.S. is ready to go hard in either direction!
27,861 Retweets **122,430** Likes
6:11 AM - 6 Mar 2018

Donald J. Trump ✓
@realDonaldTrump

Will be making a decision soon on the appointment of new Chief Economic Advisor. Many people wanting the job - will choose wisely!
16,558 Retweets **87,483** Likes
4:49 PM - 6 Mar 2018

Donald J. Trump ✓
@realDonaldTrump

Great couple, great book!
7,525 Retweets **38,204** Likes
2:44 AM - 7 Mar 2018

Donald J. Trump ✓
@realDonaldTrump

From Bush 1 to present, our Country has lost more than 55,000 factories, 6,000,000 manufacturing jobs and accumulated Trade Deficits of more than 12 Trillion Dollars. Last year we had a Trade Deficit of almost 800 Billion Dollars. Bad Policies & Leadership. Must WIN again! #MAGA
35,446 Retweets **128,219** Likes
3:40 AM - 7 Mar 2018

Donald J. Trump ✓
@realDonaldTrump

China has been asked to develop a plan for the year of a One Billion Dollar reduction in their massive Trade Deficit with the United States. Our relationship with China has been a very good one, and we look forward to seeing what ideas they come back with. We must act soon!
18,756 Retweets **86,274** Likes
7:10 AM - 7 Mar 2018

Donald J. Trump ✓
@realDonaldTrump

The U.S. is acting swiftly on Intellectual Property theft. We cannot allow this to happen as it has for many years!
19,409 Retweets **95,058** Likes
7:38 AM - 7 Mar 2018

Donald J. Trump ✓
@realDonaldTrump

Looking forward to 3:30 P.M. meeting today at the White House. We have to protect & build our Steel and Aluminum Industries while at the same time showing great flexibility and cooperation toward those that are real friends and treat us fairly on both trade and the military.
18,981 Retweets **92,589** Likes
4:38 AM - 8 Mar 2018

Donald J. Trump ✓
@realDonaldTrump

Happy #InternationalWomensDay "First Lady Melania Trump to Present the 2018 International Women of Courage Award"
11,823 Retweets **58,397** Likes
10:20 AM - 8 Mar 2018

Donald J. Trump ✓
@realDonaldTrump

Great meeting with @Cabinet at the @WhiteHouse today! #MAGA
9,207 Retweets **48,118** Likes
10:58 AM - 8 Mar 2018

Donald J. Trump ✓
@realDonaldTrump

"Presidential Proclamation on Adjusting Imports of Aluminum into the United States"
12,260 Retweets **52,868** Likes
2:17 PM - 8 Mar 2018

Donald J. Trump ✓
@realDonaldTrump

Kim Jong Un talked about denuclearization with the South Korean Representatives, not just a freeze. Also, no missile testing by North Korea during this period of time. Great progress being made but sanctions will remain until an agreement is reached. Meeting being planned!
45,093 Retweets **173,271** Likes
5:08 PM - 8 Mar 2018

Donald J. Trump ✓
@realDonaldTrump

JOBS, JOBS, JOBS! #MAGA
18,204 Retweets **71,253** Likes
8:47 AM - 9 Mar 2018

President Trumps Tweets 2018: A Historical Archive of President Trump's Tweets

Donald J. Trump ✓
@realDonaldTrump

Look forward to being in Pennsylvania tomorrow in support of Rick @Saccone4PA18. Big crowd expected in Moon Township. Vote Rick and see you there! #MAGA
12,364 Retweets **54,107** Likes
12:35 PM - 9 Mar 2018

Donald J. Trump ✓
@realDonaldTrump

That's right @RepBost! Thank you for your support in helping put America back to work. It's about JOBS, JOBS, JOBS for our incredible workers and putting AMERICA FIRST!
13,062 Retweets **54,704** Likes
12:40 PM - 9 Mar 2018

Donald J. Trump ✓
@realDonaldTrump

Spoke to PM @TurnbullMalcolm of Australia. He is committed to having a very fair and reciprocal military and trade relationship. Working very quickly on a security agreement so we don't have to impose steel or aluminum tariffs on our ally, the great nation of Australia!
17,200 Retweets **78,494** Likes
2:48 PM - 9 Mar 2018

Donald J. Trump ✓
@realDonaldTrump

The deal with North Korea is very much in the making and will be, if completed, a very good one for the World. Time and place to be determined.
26,834 Retweets **125,797** Likes
4:42 PM - 9 Mar 2018

Donald J. Trump ✓
@realDonaldTrump

We are deeply saddened by the tragic situation in Yountville and mourn the loss of three incredible women who cared for our Veterans.
13,996 Retweets **75,245** Likes
5:38 AM - 10 Mar 2018

Donald J. Trump ✓
@realDonaldTrump

Congratulations to Kristian Saucier, a man who has served proudly in the Navy, on your newly found Freedom. Now you can go out and have the life you deserve!
18,562 Retweets **85,934** Likes
7:52 AM - 10 Mar 2018

Donald J. Trump ✓
@realDonaldTrump

Chinese President XI JINPING and I spoke at length about the meeting with KIM JONG UN of North Korea. President XI told me he appreciates that the U.S. is working to solve the problem diplomatically rather than going with the ominous alternative. China continues to be helpful!
19,027 Retweets **91,296** Likes
8:15 AM - 10 Mar 2018

Donald J. Trump ✓
@realDonaldTrump

Spoke to Prime Minister Abe of Japan, who is very enthusiastic about talks with North Korea. Also discussing opening up Japan to much better trade with the U.S. Currently have a massive $100 Billion Trade Deficit. Not fair or sustainable. It will all work out!
16,736 Retweets **72,424** Likes
9:23 AM - 10 Mar 2018

Donald J. Trump ✓
@realDonaldTrump

Heading to Moon Township, Pennsylvania, to be with a really good person, State Representative Rick Saccone, who is running for Congress. Big & happy crowd (why not, some of the best economic numbers ever). Rick will help me a lot. Also, tough on crime & border. Loves 2nd A & VETS
13,733 Retweets **63,806** Likes
10:22 AM - 10 Mar 2018

Donald J. Trump ✓
@realDonaldTrump

North Korea has not conducted a Missile Test since November 28, 2017 and has promised not to do so through our meetings. I believe they will honor that commitment!
17,846 Retweets **90,360** Likes
10:38 AM - 10 Mar 2018

Donald J. Trump ✓
@realDonaldTrump

In the first hours after hearing that North Korea's leader wanted to meet with me to talk denuclearization and that missile launches will end, the press was startled & amazed. They couldn't believe it. But by the following morning the news became FAKE. They said so what, who cares!
21,453 Retweets **89,341** Likes
12:02 PM - 10 Mar 2018

Donald J. Trump ✓
@realDonaldTrump

The European Union, wonderful countries who treat the U.S. very badly on trade, are complaining about the tariffs on Steel & Aluminum. If they drop their horrific barriers & tariffs on U.S. products going in, we will likewise drop ours. Big Deficit. If not, we Tax Cars etc. FAIR!
23,972 Retweets **99,649** Likes
1:29 PM - 10 Mar 2018

Donald J. Trump ✓
@realDonaldTrump

Join me LIVE in Moon Township, Pennsylvania at 7:00pmE. Great crowd for a #MAGA rally!
7,642 Retweets **42,796** Likes
3:56 PM - 10 Mar 2018

Donald J. Trump ✓
@realDonaldTrump

Epic crowd in Moon Township, Pennsylvania tonight. Thank you! Get out on Tuesday and VOTE for Rick @Saccone4PA18. Together, we are MAKING AMERICA GREAT AGAIN!
18,986 Retweets **72,930** Likes
5:37 PM - 10 Mar 2018

Donald J. Trump ✓
@realDonaldTrump

The Failing New York Times purposely wrote a false story stating that I am unhappy with my legal team on the Russia case and am going to add another lawyer to help out. Wrong. I am VERY happy with my lawyers, John Dowd, Ty Cobb and Jay Sekulow. They are doing a great job and.....
20,912 Retweets **91,633** Likes
6:41 AM - 11 Mar 2018

Donald J. Trump ✓
@realDonaldTrump

...have shown conclusively that there was no Collusion with Russia..just excuse for losing. The only Collusion was that done by the DNC, the Democrats and Crooked Hillary. The writer of the story, Maggie Haberman, a Hillary flunky, knows nothing about me and is not given access.
19,824 Retweets **85,513** Likes
6:50 AM - 11 Mar 2018

Donald J. Trump ✓
@realDonaldTrump

The Republicans are 5-0 in recent Congressional races, a point which the Fake News Media continuously fails to mention. I backed and campaigned for all of the winners. They give me credit for one. Hopefully, Rick Saccone will be another big win on Tuesday.
18,305 Retweets **78,098** Likes
7:02 AM - 11 Mar 2018

Donald J. Trump ✓
@realDonaldTrump

The Democrats continue to Obstruct the confirmation of hundreds of good and talented people who are needed to run our government...A record in U.S. history. State Department, Ambassadors and many others are being slow walked. Senate must approve NOW!
24,923 Retweets **92,084** Likes
7:49 AM - 11 Mar 2018

Donald J. Trump ✓
@realDonaldTrump

Rasmussen and others have my approval ratings at around 50%, which is higher than Obama, and yet the political pundits love saying my approval ratings are "somewhat low." They know they are lying when they say it. Turn off the show - FAKE NEWS!
24,696 Retweets **106,270** Likes
8:16 AM - 11 Mar 2018

Donald J. Trump ✓
@realDonaldTrump

Secretary of Commerce Wilbur Ross will be speaking with representatives of the European Union about eliminating the large Tariffs and Barriers they use against the U.S.A. Not fair to our farmers and manufacturers.
15,345 Retweets **67,502** Likes
5:20 AM - 12 Mar 2018

Donald J. Trump ✓
@realDonaldTrump

Very strong improvement and strengthening of background checks will be fully backed by White House. Legislation moving forward. Bump Stocks will soon be out. Highly trained expert teachers will be allowed to conceal carry, subject to State Law. Armed guards OK, deterrent!.......
17,100 Retweets **81,658** Likes
6:15 AM - 12 Mar 2018

Donald J. Trump ✓
@realDonaldTrump

....On 18 to 21 Age Limits, watching court cases and rulings before acting. States are making this decision. Things are moving rapidly on this, but not much political support (to put it mildly).
11,016 Retweets **55,788** Likes
6:22 AM - 12 Mar 2018

Donald J. Trump ✓
@realDonaldTrump

If schools are mandated to be gun free zones, violence and danger are given an open invitation to enter. Almost all school shootings are in gun free zones. Cowards will only go where there is no deterrent!
18,503 Retweets **79,080** Likes
7:12 AM - 12 Mar 2018

Donald J. Trump ✓
@realDonaldTrump

The Pittsburgh Post Gazette just endorsed Rick Saccone for Congress. He will be much better for steel and business. Very strong on experience and what our Country needs. Lamb will always vote for Pelosi and Dems....Will raise taxes, weak on Crime and Border.
12,983 Retweets **50,956** Likes
7:43 AM - 12 Mar 2018

Donald J. Trump ✓
@realDonaldTrump

It was my great honor to welcome the 2017 World Series Champion Houston @Astros to the @WhiteHouse! #HoustonStrong
14,739 Retweets **75,712** Likes
2:13 PM - 12 Mar 2018

Donald J. Trump ✓
@realDonaldTrump

THE HOUSE INTELLIGENCE COMMITTEE HAS, AFTER A 14 MONTH LONG IN-DEPTH INVESTIGATION, FOUND NO EVIDENCE OF COLLUSION OR COORDINATION BETWEEN THE TRUMP CAMPAIGN AND RUSSIA TO INFLUENCE THE 2016 PRESIDENTIAL ELECTION.
44,798 Retweets **161,082** Likes
5:49 PM - 12 Mar 2018

Donald J. Trump ✓
@realDonaldTrump

The Economy is raging, at an all time high, and is set to get even better. Jobs and wages up. Vote for Rick Saccone and keep it going!
17,036 Retweets **75,793** Likes
5:28 AM - 13 Mar 2018

Donald J. Trump ✓
@realDonaldTrump

Mike Pompeo, Director of the CIA, will become our new Secretary of State. He will do a fantastic job! Thank you to Rex Tillerson for his service! Gina Haspel will become the new Director of the CIA, and the first woman so chosen. Congratulations to all!
40,910 Retweets **122,977** Likes
5:44 AM - 13 Mar 2018

Donald J. Trump ✓
@realDonaldTrump

Heading to see the BORDER WALL prototypes in California!
16,848 Retweets **86,859** Likes
7:37 AM - 13 Mar 2018

Donald J. Trump ✓
@realDonaldTrump

"According to the Center for Immigration Studies, the $18 billion wall will pay for itself by curbing the importation of crime, drugs and illegal immigrants who tend to go on the federal dole..."
20,236 Retweets **69,657** Likes
8:24 AM - 13 Mar 2018

President Trumps Tweets 2018: A Historical Archive of President Trump's Tweets

Donald J. Trump ✓
@realDonaldTrump

California's sanctuary policies are illegal and unconstitutional and put the safety and security of our entire nation at risk. Thousands of dangerous & violent criminal aliens are released as a result of sanctuary policies, set free to prey on innocent Americans. THIS MUST STOP!
32,824 Retweets **125,744** Likes
8:27 AM - 13 Mar 2018

Donald J. Trump ✓
@realDonaldTrump

If we don't have a wall system, we're not going to have a country. Congress must fund the BORDER WALL & prohibit grants to sanctuary jurisdictions that threaten the security of our country & the people of our country. We must enforce our laws & protect our people! #BuildTheWall
26,080 Retweets **95,236** Likes
3:23 PM - 13 Mar 2018

Donald J. Trump ✓
@realDonaldTrump

It was my great honor to deliver a message at the Marine Corps Air Station Miramar to our GREAT U.S. Military, straight from the heart of the American People: We support you, we thank you, we love you - and we will always have your back!
15,611 Retweets **72,714** Likes
5:25 PM - 13 Mar 2018

Donald J. Trump ✓
@realDonaldTrump

All across this nation, we pray for our country and we THANK GOD for our United States Marines! Thank you. God Bless You. And God Bless America!
19,110 Retweets **84,296** Likes
5:34 PM - 13 Mar 2018

Donald J. Trump ✓
@realDonaldTrump

Hundreds of good people, including very important Ambassadors and Judges, are being blocked and/or slow walked by the Democrats in the Senate. Many important positions in Government are unfilled because of this obstruction. Worst in U.S. history!
25,961 Retweets **90,583** Likes
6:02 AM - 14 Mar 2018

Donald J. Trump ✓
@realDonaldTrump

Perhaps at no time in history have the business fundamentals of U.S. companies been better than they are today!
13,681 Retweets **73,353** Likes
6:12 AM - 14 Mar 2018

Donald J. Trump ✓
@realDonaldTrump

Five of our incredible @Cabinet Secretaries are testifying on the Hill this morning on the need to rebuild our Nation's crumbling infrastructure. We need to build FAST & we need to build for our FUTURE. Thank you @SenateCommerce for hosting this hearing! #InfrastructureInAmerica
12,480 Retweets **56,101** Likes
6:54 AM - 14 Mar 2018

Anthony T. Michalisko

Donald J. Trump ✓
@realDonaldTrump

We cannot keep a blind eye to the rampant unfair trade practices against our Country!
16,142 Retweets **84,222** Likes
7:37 AM - 14 Mar 2018

Donald J. Trump ✓
@realDonaldTrump

Thank you for hosting! #MAGA
7,351 Retweets **38,552** Likes
2:20 PM - 14 Mar 2018

Donald J. Trump ✓
@realDonaldTrump

Today the House took major steps toward securing our schools by passing the STOP School Violence Act. We must put the safety of America's children FIRST by improving training and by giving schools and law enforcement better tools. A tragedy like Parkland can't happen ever again!
20,117 Retweets **93,275** Likes
2:25 PM - 14 Mar 2018

Donald J. Trump ✓
@realDonaldTrump

Together, we are MAKING AMERICA GREAT AGAIN!
13,978 Retweets **68,580** Likes
3:36 PM - 14 Mar 2018

Donald J. Trump ✓
@realDonaldTrump

It was wonderful to be back in Missouri where our push for historic TAX CUTS all began. Six months ago I promised that we would cut taxes to bring Main Street roaring back - and that is exactly what is happening!
14,588 Retweets **66,958** Likes
4:49 PM - 14 Mar 2018

Donald J. Trump ✓
@realDonaldTrump

Please join me with your thoughts and prayers for both aviators, their families and our incredible @USNavy.
15,035 Retweets **67,373** Likes
9:31 PM - 14 Mar 2018

Donald J. Trump ✓
@realDonaldTrump

Larry Kudlow will be my Chief Economic Advisor as Director of the National Economic Council. Our Country will have many years of Great Economic & Financial Success, with low taxes, unparalleled innovation, fair trade and an ever expanding labor force leading the way! #MAGA
17,466 Retweets **81,249** Likes
4:11 AM - 15 Mar 2018

Donald J. Trump ✓
@realDonaldTrump

We do have a Trade Deficit with Canada, as we do with almost all countries (some of them massive). P.M. Justin Trudeau of Canada, a very good guy, doesn't like saying that Canada has a Surplus vs. the U.S.(negotiating), but they do...they almost all do...and that's how I know!
16,996 Retweets **79,277** Likes
6:29 AM - 15 Mar 2018

President Trumps Tweets 2018: A Historical Archive of President Trump's Tweets

Donald J. Trump ✓
@realDonaldTrump

It was my honor to welcome Prime Minister Leo Varadkar of Ireland to the @WhiteHouse!
10,503 Retweets **61,410** Likes
10:47 AM - 15 Mar 2018

Donald J. Trump ✓
@realDonaldTrump

Continuing to monitor the heartbreaking bridge collapse at FIU - so tragic. Many brave First Responders rushed in to save lives. Thank you for your courage. Praying this evening for all who are affected.
19,337 Retweets **108,116** Likes
4:10 PM - 15 Mar 2018

Donald J. Trump ✓
@realDonaldTrump

"President Donald J. Trump Delivers Remarks at the Shamrock Bowl Presentation by Prime Minister Varadkar in the East Room of the White House"
12,311 Retweets **58,660** Likes
6:49 PM - 15 Mar 2018

Donald J. Trump ✓
@realDonaldTrump

Our thoughts and prayers go out to the families and loved ones of the brave troops lost in the helicopter crash on the Iraq-Syria border yesterday. Their sacrifice in service to our country will never be forgotten.
21,791 Retweets **114,201** Likes
7:40 AM - 16 Mar 2018

Donald J. Trump ✓
@realDonaldTrump

It would be great for the Republican Party of Nevada, and it's unity if good guy Danny Tarkanian would run for Congress and Dean Heller, who is doing a really good job, could run for Senate unopposed!
15,357 Retweets **71,927** Likes
9:27 AM - 16 Mar 2018

Donald J. Trump ✓
@realDonaldTrump

"U.S. Consumer Confidence Hits 14-Year High"
15,704 Retweets **66,344** Likes
10:42 AM - 16 Mar 2018

Donald J. Trump ✓
@realDonaldTrump

Andrew McCabe FIRED, a great day for the hard working men and women of the FBI - A great day for Democracy. Sanctimonious James Comey was his boss and made McCabe look like a choirboy. He knew all about the lies and corruption going on at the highest levels of the FBI!
47,996 Retweets **165,233** Likes
9:08 PM - 16 Mar 2018

Donald J. Trump ✓
@realDonaldTrump

Happy #StPatricksDay
17,249 Retweets **94,444** Likes
8:00 AM - 17 Mar 2018

Donald J. Trump ✓
@realDonaldTrump

As the House Intelligence Committee has concluded, there was no collusion between Russia and the Trump Campaign. As many are now finding out, however, there was tremendous leaking, lying and corruption at the highest levels of the FBI, Justice & State. #DrainTheSwamp
31,757 Retweets **115,876** Likes
10:11 AM - 17 Mar 2018

Donald J. Trump ✓
@realDonaldTrump

The Fake News is beside themselves that McCabe was caught, called out and fired. How many hundreds of thousands of dollars was given to wife's campaign by Crooked H friend, Terry M, who was also under investigation? How many lies? How many leaks? Comey knew it all, and much more!
39,341 Retweets **143,283** Likes
10:34 AM - 17 Mar 2018

Donald J. Trump ✓
@realDonaldTrump

The Mueller probe should never have been started in that there was no collusion and there was no crime. It was based on fraudulent activities and a Fake Dossier paid for by Crooked Hillary and the DNC, and improperly used in FISA COURT for surveillance of my campaign. WITCH HUNT!
29,521 Retweets **104,277** Likes
5:12 PM - 17 Mar 2018

Donald J. Trump ✓
@realDonaldTrump

Wow, watch Comey lie under oath to Senator G when asked "have you ever been an anonymous source...or known someone else to be an anonymous source...?" He said strongly "never, no." He lied as shown clearly on @foxandfriends.
27,440 Retweets **102,211** Likes
5:02 AM - 18 Mar 2018

Donald J. Trump ✓
@realDonaldTrump

Spent very little time with Andrew McCabe, but he never took notes when he was with me. I don't believe he made memos except to help his own agenda, probably at a later date. Same with lying James Comey. Can we call them Fake Memos?
31,695 Retweets **130,172** Likes
5:22 AM - 18 Mar 2018

Donald J. Trump ✓
@realDonaldTrump

Why does the Mueller team have 13 hardened Democrats, some big Crooked Hillary supporters, and Zero Republicans? Another Dem recently added...does anyone think this is fair? And yet, there is NO COLLUSION!
33,419 Retweets **126,139** Likes
5:35 AM - 18 Mar 2018

Donald J. Trump ✓
@realDonaldTrump

.@seanhannity on @foxandfriends now! Great! 8:18 A.M.
8,016 Retweets **50,101** Likes
5:16 AM - 19 Mar 2018

President Trumps Tweets 2018: A Historical Archive of President Trump's Tweets

Donald J. Trump ✓
@realDonaldTrump

A total WITCH HUNT with massive conflicts of interest!
24,770 Retweets **111,018** Likes
6:07 AM - 19 Mar 2018

Donald J. Trump ✓
@realDonaldTrump

The Democrats do not want to help DACA. Would be so easy to make a deal!
22,003 Retweets **99,230** Likes
5:28 PM - 19 Mar 2018

Donald J. Trump ✓
@realDonaldTrump

Our Nation was founded by farmers. Our independence was won by farmers. And our continent was tamed by farmers. Our farmers always lead the way -- we are PROUD of them, and we are DELIVERING for them! #NationalAgricultureDay
33,993 Retweets **140,902** Likes
8:36 AM - 20 Mar 2018

Donald J. Trump ✓
@realDonaldTrump

AUSTIN BOMBING SUSPECT IS DEAD. Great job by law enforcement and all concerned!
26,656 Retweets **137,016** Likes
3:28 AM - 21 Mar 2018

Donald J. Trump ✓
@realDonaldTrump

Department of Justice should have urged the Supreme Court to at least hear the Drivers License case on illegal immigrants in Arizona. I agree with @LouDobbs. Should have sought review.
14,868 Retweets **59,987** Likes
3:52 AM - 21 Mar 2018

Donald J. Trump ✓
@realDonaldTrump

...there was no probable cause for believing that there was any crime, collusion or otherwise, or obstruction of justice!" So stated by Harvard Law Professor Alan Dershowitz.
19,988 Retweets **83,557** Likes
4:11 AM - 21 Mar 2018

Donald J. Trump ✓
@realDonaldTrump

"Special Council is told to find crimes, whether a crime exists or not. I was opposed to the selection of Mueller to be Special Council. I am still opposed to it. I think President Trump was right when he said there never should have been a Special Council appointed because.....
18,721 Retweets **78,472** Likes
4:29 AM - 21 Mar 2018

Donald J. Trump ✓
@realDonaldTrump

I called President Putin of Russia to congratulate him on his election victory (in past, Obama called him also). The Fake News Media is crazed because they wanted me to excoriate him. They are wrong! Getting along with Russia (and others) is a good thing, not a bad thing.......
29,872 Retweets **131,185** Likes
11:56 AM - 21 Mar 2018

Donald J. Trump ✓
@realDonaldTrump

.....They can help solve problems with North Korea, Syria, Ukraine, ISIS, Iran and even the coming Arms Race. Bush tried to get along, but didn't have the "smarts." Obama and Clinton tried, but didn't have the energy or chemistry (remember RESET). PEACE THROUGH STRENGTH!
20,076 Retweets **85,386** Likes
12:05 PM - 21 Mar 2018

Donald J. Trump ✓
@realDonaldTrump

Got $1.6 Billion to start Wall on Southern Border, rest will be forthcoming. Most importantly, got $700 Billion to rebuild our Military, $716 Billion next year...most ever. Had to waste money on Dem giveaways in order to take care of military pay increase and new equipment.
24,772 Retweets **109,425** Likes
8:00 PM - 21 Mar 2018

Donald J. Trump ✓
@realDonaldTrump

Democrats refused to take care of DACA. Would have been so easy, but they just didn't care. I had to fight for Military and start of Wall.
18,336 Retweets **82,816** Likes
8:04 PM - 21 Mar 2018

Donald J. Trump ✓
@realDonaldTrump

Crazy Joe Biden is trying to act like a tough guy. Actually, he is weak, both mentally and physically, and yet he threatens me, for the second time, with physical assault. He doesn't know me, but he would go down fast and hard, crying all the way. Don't threaten people Joe!
75,713 Retweets **258,162** Likes
3:19 AM - 22 Mar 2018

Donald J. Trump ✓
@realDonaldTrump

Remember when they were saying, during the campaign, that Donald Trump is giving great speeches and drawing big crowds, but he is spending much less money and not using social media as well as Crooked Hillary's large and highly sophisticated staff. Well, not saying that anymore!
20,355 Retweets **94,790** Likes
3:40 AM - 22 Mar 2018

Donald J. Trump ✓
@realDonaldTrump

As a candidate, I pledged that if elected I would use every lawful tool to combat unfair trade, protect American workers, and defend our national security. Today, we took another critical step to fulfill that commitment.
15,736 Retweets **67,717** Likes
11:40 AM - 22 Mar 2018

Donald J. Trump ✓
@realDonaldTrump

My honor Charlie - thank you! #MAGA
10,877 Retweets **49,962** Likes
1:11 PM - 22 Mar 2018

Donald J. Trump ✓
@realDonaldTrump

I am pleased to announce that, effective 4/9/18, @AmbJohnBolton will be my new National Security Advisor. I am very thankful for the service of General H.R. McMaster who has done an outstanding job & will always remain my friend. There will be an official contact handover on 4/9.

24,242 Retweets **96,093** Likes
3:26 PM - 22 Mar 2018

Donald J. Trump ✓
@realDonaldTrump

House Intelligence Committee votes to release final report. FINDINGS: (1) No evidence provided of Collusion between Trump Campaign & Russia. (2) The Obama Administrations Post election response was insufficient. (3) Clapper provided inconsistent testimony on media contacts.

21,100 Retweets **77,515** Likes
3:07 AM - 23 Mar 2018

Donald J. Trump ✓
@realDonaldTrump

DACA was abandoned by the Democrats. Very unfair to them! Would have been tied to desperately needed Wall.

16,395 Retweets **73,007** Likes
5:26 AM - 23 Mar 2018

Donald J. Trump ✓
@realDonaldTrump

I am considering a VETO of the Omnibus Spending Bill based on the fact that the 800,000 plus DACA recipients have been totally abandoned by the Democrats (not even mentioned in Bill) and the BORDER WALL, which is desperately needed for our National Defense, is not fully funded.

37,288 Retweets **155,673** Likes
5:55 AM - 23 Mar 2018

Donald J. Trump ✓
@realDonaldTrump

News conference at the White House concerning the Omnibus Spending Bill. 1:00 P.M.

9,681 Retweets **47,571** Likes
9:32 AM - 23 Mar 2018

Donald J. Trump ✓
@realDonaldTrump

Obama Administration legalized bump stocks. BAD IDEA. As I promised, today the Department of Justice will issue the rule banning BUMP STOCKS with a mandated comment period. We will BAN all devices that turn legal weapons into illegal machine guns.

17,129 Retweets **81,865** Likes
1:50 PM - 23 Mar 2018

Donald J. Trump ✓
@realDonaldTrump

As a matter of National Security I've signed the Omnibus Spending Bill. I say to Congress: I will NEVER sign another bill like this again. To prevent this omnibus situation from ever happening again, I'm calling on Congress to give me a line-item veto for all govt spending bills!

19,345 Retweets **71,398** Likes
4:01 PM - 23 Mar 2018

Donald J. Trump ✓
@realDonaldTrump

Our thoughts and prayers are with the victims of the horrible attack in France yesterday, and we grieve the nation's loss. We also condemn the violent actions of the attacker and anyone who would provide him support. We are with you @EmmanuelMacron!
15,760 Retweets **83,062** Likes
9:40 AM - 24 Mar 2018

Donald J. Trump ✓
@realDonaldTrump

France honors a great hero. Officer died after bravely swapping places with hostage in ISIS related terror attack. So much bravery around the world constantly fighting radical Islamic terrorism. Even stronger measures needed, especially at borders!
19,653 Retweets **83,101** Likes
3:10 AM - 25 Mar 2018

Donald J. Trump ✓
@realDonaldTrump

Because of the $700 & $716 Billion Dollars gotten to rebuild our Military, many jobs are created and our Military is again rich. Building a great Border Wall, with drugs (poison) and enemy combatants pouring into our Country, is all about National Defense. Build WALL through M!
31,170 Retweets **117,696** Likes
3:33 AM - 25 Mar 2018

Donald J. Trump ✓
@realDonaldTrump

Much can be done with the $1.6 Billion given to building and fixing the border wall. It is just a down payment. Work will start immediately. The rest of the money will come - and remember DACA, the Democrats abandoned you (but we will not)!
19,683 Retweets **80,170** Likes
3:42 AM - 25 Mar 2018

Donald J. Trump ✓
@realDonaldTrump

Many lawyers and top law firms want to represent me in the Russia case...don't believe the Fake News narrative that it is hard to find a lawyer who wants to take this on. Fame & fortune will NEVER be turned down by a lawyer, though some are conflicted. Problem is that a new......
14,318 Retweets **66,686** Likes
4:40 AM - 25 Mar 2018

Donald J. Trump ✓
@realDonaldTrump

....lawyer or law firm will take months to get up to speed (if for no other reason than they can bill more), which is unfair to our great country - and I am very happy with my existing team. Besides, there was NO COLLUSION with Russia, except by Crooked Hillary and the Dems!
17,922 Retweets **82,458** Likes
4:49 AM - 25 Mar 2018

Donald J. Trump ✓
@realDonaldTrump

Happy National #MedalOfHonorDay to our HEROES. We love you!
15,023 Retweets **64,996** Likes
6:08 AM - 25 Mar 2018

President Trumps Tweets 2018: A Historical Archive of President Trump's Tweets

Donald J. Trump @
@realDonaldTrump

"President Donald J. Trump Proclaims March 25, 2018, as Greek Independence Day: A National Day of Celebration of Greek and American Democracy"
11,406 Retweets **51,735** Likes
6:45 AM - 25 Mar 2018

Donald J. Trump @
@realDonaldTrump

.@HowieCarrShow just wrote a book which everyone is talking about. He was a great help. He is a veteran journalist who had a great influence in NH and beyond. He calls it the most amazing political campaign of modern times. The book is called, "What Really Happened." Enjoy! #MAGA
20,641 Retweets **75,392** Likes
8:26 PM - 25 Mar 2018

Donald J. Trump @
@realDonaldTrump

The economy is looking really good. It has been many years that we have seen these kind of numbers. The underlying strength of companies has perhaps never been better.
19,715 Retweets **98,420** Likes
4:05 AM - 26 Mar 2018

Donald J. Trump @
@realDonaldTrump

So much Fake News. Never been more voluminous or more inaccurate. But through it all, our country is doing great!
27,436 Retweets **133,788** Likes
5:38 AM - 26 Mar 2018

Donald J. Trump @
@realDonaldTrump

Great news! #MAGA
15,786 Retweets **69,302** Likes
1:29 PM - 26 Mar 2018

Donald J. Trump @
@realDonaldTrump

Trade talks going on with numerous countries that, for many years, have not treated the United States fairly. In the end, all will be happy!
21,053 Retweets **104,664** Likes
5:44 PM - 26 Mar 2018

Donald J. Trump @
@realDonaldTrump

I am very pleased to welcome the opioid memorial to the President's Park in April. I encourage all to visit and remember those who we have lost to this deadly epidemic. We will keep fighting until we defeat the opioid crisis!
15,524 Retweets **68,129** Likes
11:35 AM - 27 Mar 2018

Donald J. Trump @
@realDonaldTrump

THE SECOND AMENDMENT WILL NEVER BE REPEALED! As much as Democrats would like to see this happen, and despite the words yesterday of former Supreme Court Justice Stevens, NO WAY. We need more Republicans in 2018 and must ALWAYS hold the Supreme Court!
59,143 Retweets **194,123** Likes
2:52 AM - 28 Mar 2018

Donald J. Trump ✓
@realDonaldTrump

For years and through many administrations, everyone said that peace and the denuclearization of the Korean Peninsula was not even a small possibility. Now there is a good chance that Kim Jong Un will do what is right for his people and for humanity. Look forward to our meeting!
26,517 Retweets **113,827** Likes
3:05 AM - 28 Mar 2018

 Donald J. Trump ✓
@realDonaldTrump

Received message last night from XI JINPING of China that his meeting with KIM JONG UN went very well and that KIM looks forward to his meeting with me. In the meantime, and unfortunately, maximum sanctions and pressure must be maintained at all cost!
24,254 Retweets **103,499** Likes
3:16 AM - 28 Mar 2018

 Donald J. Trump ✓
@realDonaldTrump

.@USTradeRep just announced an agreement in principle with South Korea on KORUS! A great deal for American and Korean workers. Let's now focus on our important security relationship.
12,228 Retweets **55,208** Likes
9:14 AM - 28 Mar 2018

 Donald J. Trump ✓
@realDonaldTrump

My Administration stands in solidarity with the brave citizens in Orange County defending their rights against California's illegal and unconstitutional Sanctuary policies. California's Sanctuary laws....
26,688 Retweets **111,399** Likes
9:18 AM - 28 Mar 2018

 Donald J. Trump ✓
@realDonaldTrump

....release known dangerous criminals into communities across the State. All citizens have the right to be protected by Federal law and strong borders.
15,087 Retweets **67,313** Likes
9:19 AM - 28 Mar 2018

 Donald J. Trump ✓
@realDonaldTrump

Great briefing this afternoon on the start of our Southern Border WALL!
32,111 Retweets **119,196** Likes
12:47 PM - 28 Mar 2018

 Donald J. Trump ✓
@realDonaldTrump

I am pleased to announce that I intend to nominate highly respected Admiral Ronny L. Jackson, MD, as the new Secretary of Veterans Affairs....
17,127 Retweets **78,712** Likes
2:31 PM - 28 Mar 2018

Donald J. Trump ✓
@realDonaldTrump

....In the interim, Hon. Robert Wilkie of DOD will serve as Acting Secretary. I am thankful for Dr. David Shulkin's service to our country and to our GREAT VETERANS!
9,891 Retweets **48,476** Likes
2:31 PM - 28 Mar 2018

Donald J. Trump
@realDonaldTrump

I have stated my concerns with Amazon long before the Election. Unlike others, they pay little or no taxes to state & local governments, use our Postal System as their Delivery Boy (causing tremendous loss to the U.S.), and are putting many thousands of retailers out of business!
33,388 Retweets **130,541** Likes
4:57 AM - 29 Mar 2018

Donald J. Trump
@realDonaldTrump

We are going to REBUILD our crumbling infrastructure, and there is no better place to begin this campaign than in the Great State of Ohio. A tremendous honor to be here today at a state-of-the-art training site, where the skills of the American Worker are forged and refined!
16,661 Retweets **74,693** Likes
12:44 PM - 29 Mar 2018

Donald J. Trump
@realDonaldTrump

Washington spent trillions building up foreign countries while allowing OUR OWN infrastructure to fall into a state of total disrepair. No more! It's time to REBUILD, and we will do it with American WORKERS, American GRIT, and American PRIDE!
26,959 Retweets **105,398** Likes
1:06 PM - 29 Mar 2018

Donald J. Trump
@realDonaldTrump

While we are on the subject, it is reported that the U.S. Post Office will lose $1.50 on average for each package it delivers for Amazon. That amounts to Billions of Dollars. The Failing N.Y. Times reports that "the size of the company's lobbying staff has ballooned," and that...
21,657 Retweets **82,372** Likes
5:45 AM - 31 Mar 2018

Donald J. Trump
@realDonaldTrump

...does not include the Fake Washington Post, which is used as a "lobbyist" and should so REGISTER. If the P.O. "increased its parcel rates, Amazon's shipping costs would rise by $2.6 Billion." This Post Office scam must stop. Amazon must pay real costs (and taxes) now!
22,610 Retweets **89,937** Likes
5:52 AM - 31 Mar 2018

Donald J. Trump
@realDonaldTrump

Governor Jerry "Moonbeam" Brown pardoned 5 criminal illegal aliens whose crimes include (1) Kidnapping and Robbery (2) Badly beating wife and threatening a crime with intent to terrorize (3) Dealing drugs. Is this really what the great people of California want? @FoxNews
32,577 Retweets **98,367** Likes
5:53 AM - 31 Mar 2018

Donald J. Trump
@realDonaldTrump

HAPPY EASTER!
41,508 Retweets **209,522** Likes
5:27 AM - 1 Apr 2018

Donald J. Trump ✓
@realDonaldTrump

Border Patrol Agents are not allowed to properly do their job at the Border because of ridiculous liberal (Democrat) laws like Catch & Release. Getting more dangerous. "Caravans" coming. Republicans must go to Nuclear Option to pass tough laws NOW. NO MORE DACA DEAL!
37,544 Retweets **132,851** Likes
6:56 AM - 1 Apr 2018

Donald J. Trump ✓
@realDonaldTrump

Mexico is doing very little, if not NOTHING, at stopping people from flowing into Mexico through their Southern Border, and then into the U.S. They laugh at our dumb immigration laws. They must stop the big drug and people flows, or I will stop their cash cow, NAFTA. NEED WALL!
33,429 Retweets **127,184** Likes
7:25 AM - 1 Apr 2018

Donald J. Trump ✓
@realDonaldTrump

These big flows of people are all trying to take advantage of DACA. They want in on the act!
19,875 Retweets **85,084** Likes
7:28 AM - 1 Apr 2018

Donald J. Trump ✓
@realDonaldTrump

Mexico has the absolute power not to let these large "Caravans" of people enter their country. They must stop them at their Northern Border, which they can do because their border laws work, not allow them to pass through into our country, which has no effective border laws.....
19,753 Retweets **76,422** Likes
4:02 AM - 2 Apr 2018

Donald J. Trump ✓
@realDonaldTrump

...Congress must immediately pass Border Legislation, use Nuclear Option if necessary, to stop the massive inflow of Drugs and People. Border Patrol Agents (and ICE) are GREAT, but the weak Dem laws don't allow them to do their job. Act now Congress, our country is being stolen!
23,709 Retweets **90,143** Likes
4:10 AM - 2 Apr 2018

Donald J. Trump ✓
@realDonaldTrump

DACA is dead because the Democrats didn't care or act, and now everyone wants to get onto the DACA bandwagon... No longer works. Must build Wall and secure our borders with proper Border legislation. Democrats want No Borders, hence drugs and crime!
23,176 Retweets **90,936** Likes
4:17 AM - 2 Apr 2018

Donald J. Trump ✓
@realDonaldTrump

Mexico is making a fortune on NAFTA...They have very strong border laws - ours are pathetic. With all of the money they make from the U.S., hopefully they will stop people from coming through their country and into ours, at least until Congress changes our immigration laws!
19,555 Retweets **77,338** Likes
6:08 AM - 2 Apr 2018

President Trumps Tweets 2018: A Historical Archive of President Trump's Tweets

Donald J. Trump ✓
@realDonaldTrump

So funny to watch Fake News Networks, among the most dishonest groups of people I have ever dealt with, criticize Sinclair Broadcasting for being biased. Sinclair is far superior to CNN and even more Fake NBC, which is a total joke.
19,085 Retweets **82,200** Likes
6:28 AM - 2 Apr 2018

Donald J. Trump ✓
@realDonaldTrump

Only fools, or worse, are saying that our money losing Post Office makes money with Amazon. THEY LOSE A FORTUNE, and this will be changed. Also, our fully tax paying retailers are closing stores all over the country...not a level playing field!
18,414 Retweets **77,519** Likes
6:35 AM - 2 Apr 2018

Donald J. Trump ✓
@realDonaldTrump

So sad that the Department of "Justice" and the FBI are slow walking, or even not giving, the unredacted documents requested by Congress. An embarrassment to our country!
21,137 Retweets **80,206** Likes
6:58 AM - 2 Apr 2018

Donald J. Trump ✓
@realDonaldTrump

An honor to host the Annual @WhiteHouse Easter Egg Roll!
9,611 Retweets **51,240** Likes
8:41 AM - 2 Apr 2018

Donald J. Trump ✓
@realDonaldTrump

"President Donald J. Trump Proclaims April 2, 2018, World Autism Awareness Day"
13,702 Retweets **56,478** Likes
9:38 AM - 2 Apr 2018

Donald J. Trump ✓
@realDonaldTrump

As ridiculous as it sounds, the laws of our country do not easily allow us to send those crossing our Southern Border back where they came from. A whole big wasted procedure must take place. Mexico & Canada have tough immigration laws, whereas ours are an Obama joke. ACT CONGRESS
24,596 Retweets **89,883** Likes
5:00 PM - 2 Apr 2018

Donald J. Trump ✓
@realDonaldTrump

Honduras, Mexico and many other countries that the U.S. is very generous to, sends many of their people to our country through our WEAK IMMIGRATION POLICIES. Caravans are heading here. Must pass tough laws and build the WALL. Democrats allow open borders, drugs and crime!
20,587 Retweets **79,542** Likes
5:12 PM - 2 Apr 2018

Donald J. Trump ✓
@realDonaldTrump

39% of my nominations, including Diplomats to foreign lands, have not been confirmed due to Democrat obstruction and delay. At this rate, it would take more than 7 years before I am allowed to have these great people start working. Never happened before. Disgraceful!
30,648 Retweets **103,239** Likes
5:24 PM - 2 Apr 2018

Donald J. Trump ✓
@realDonaldTrump

"President Trump's approval rate among likely U.S. voters hit 50 percent on Monday, which puts him higher than former President Barack Obama's score at the same point into his first term, according to a new poll." Via: @Anna_Giaritelli @DCExaminer
18,962 Retweets **74,243** Likes
5:34 PM - 2 Apr 2018

Donald J. Trump ✓
@realDonaldTrump

#AutismAwarenessDay #LightItUpBlue
18,328 Retweets **91,435** Likes
7:03 PM - 2 Apr 2018

Donald J. Trump ✓
@realDonaldTrump

The Fake News Networks, those that knowingly have a sick and biased AGENDA, are worried about the competition and quality of Sinclair Broadcast. The "Fakers" at CNN, NBC, ABC & CBS have done so much dishonest reporting that they should only be allowed to get awards for fiction!
21,418 Retweets **86,809** Likes
3:34 AM - 3 Apr 2018

Donald J. Trump ✓
@realDonaldTrump

The big Caravan of People from Honduras, now coming across Mexico and heading to our "Weak Laws" Border, had better be stopped before it gets there. Cash cow NAFTA is in play, as is foreign aid to Honduras and the countries that allow this to happen. Congress MUST ACT NOW!
25,533 Retweets **99,245** Likes
3:49 AM - 3 Apr 2018

Donald J. Trump ✓
@realDonaldTrump

Check out the fact that you can't get a job at ratings challenged @CNN unless you state that you are totally anti-Trump? Little Jeff Zuker, whose job is in jeopardy, is not having much fun lately. They should clean up and strengthen CNN and get back to honest reporting!
16,830 Retweets **70,804** Likes
3:58 AM - 3 Apr 2018

Donald J. Trump ✓
@realDonaldTrump

Thank you to Rasmussen for the honest polling. Just hit 50%, which is higher than Cheatin' Obama at the same time in his Administration.
22,540 Retweets **99,903** Likes
4:08 AM - 3 Apr 2018

Donald J. Trump ✓
@realDonaldTrump

I am right about Amazon costing the United States Post Office massive amounts of money for being their Delivery Boy. Amazon should pay these costs (plus) and not have them bourne by the American Taxpayer. Many billions of dollars. P.O. leaders don't have a clue (or do they?)!
20,292 Retweets **84,366** Likes
6:55 AM - 3 Apr 2018

Donald J. Trump ✓
@realDonaldTrump

Today, it was my honor to welcome Estonia President @KerstiKaljulaid, Lithuania President @Grybauskaite_LT, and Latvia President @Vejonis to the @WhiteHouse. Congratulations on your 100th anniversaries of independence! #BalticSummit
9,378 Retweets **45,429** Likes
12:15 PM - 3 Apr 2018

Donald J. Trump ✓
@realDonaldTrump

WE WILL PROTECT OUR SOUTHERN BORDER!
21,366 Retweets **84,819** Likes
12:59 PM - 3 Apr 2018

Donald J. Trump ✓
@realDonaldTrump

Was just briefed on the shooting at YouTube's HQ in San Bruno, California. Our thoughts and prayers are with everybody involved. Thank you to our phenomenal Law Enforcement Officers and First Responders that are currently on the scene.
19,983 Retweets **109,584** Likes
2:49 PM - 3 Apr 2018

Donald J. Trump ✓
@realDonaldTrump

Our Border Laws are very weak while those of Mexico & Canada are very strong. Congress must change these Obama era, and other, laws NOW! The Democrats stand in our way - they want people to pour into our country unchecked....CRIME! We will be taking strong action today.
24,527 Retweets **99,709** Likes
4:19 AM - 4 Apr 2018

Donald J. Trump ✓
@realDonaldTrump

We are not in a trade war with China, that war was lost many years ago by the foolish, or incompetent, people who represented the U.S. Now we have a Trade Deficit of $500 Billion a year, with Intellectual Property Theft of another $300 Billion. We cannot let this continue!
37,281 Retweets **144,378** Likes
4:22 AM - 4 Apr 2018

Donald J. Trump ✓
@realDonaldTrump

When you're already $500 Billion DOWN, you can't lose!
18,557 Retweets **88,304** Likes
6:20 AM - 4 Apr 2018

Anthony T. Michalisko

Donald J. Trump ✓
@realDonaldTrump

Our thoughts and prayers are with the four U.S. Marines from the 3rd Marine Aircraft Wing who lost their lives in yesterday's Southern California helicopter crash. We pray for their families, and our great @USMC.
18,139 Retweets **87,562** Likes
7:50 AM - 4 Apr 2018

Donald J. Trump ✓
@realDonaldTrump

Today we honor Dr. Martin Luther King, Jr. on the 50th anniversary of his assassination. Earlier this year I spoke about Dr. King's legacy of justice and peace, and his impact on uniting Americans. #MLK50
18,830 Retweets **74,530** Likes
8:05 AM - 4 Apr 2018

Donald J. Trump ✓
@realDonaldTrump

"Still Rising: Rasmussen Poll Shows Donald Trump Approval Ratings Now at 51 Percent"
23,985 Retweets **99,983** Likes
4:08 PM - 4 Apr 2018

Donald J. Trump ✓
@realDonaldTrump

The Caravan is largely broken up thanks to the strong immigration laws of Mexico and their willingness to use them so as not to cause a giant scene at our Border. Because of the Trump Administrations actions, Border crossings are at a still UNACCEPTABLE 46 year low. Stop drugs!
20,952 Retweets **93,713** Likes
4:40 AM - 5 Apr 2018

Donald J. Trump ✓
@realDonaldTrump

The Fake News Washington Post, Amazon's "chief lobbyist," has another (of many) phony headlines, "Trump Defiant As China Adds Trade Penalties." WRONG! Should read, "Trump Defiant as U.S. Adds Trade Penalties, Will End Barriers And Massive I.P. Theft." Typically bad reporting!
24,732 Retweets **93,542** Likes
6:10 AM - 5 Apr 2018

Donald J. Trump ✓
@realDonaldTrump

Thanks to our historic TAX CUTS, America is open for business, and millions of American workers are seeing more take-home pay through higher wages, salaries and bonuses!
15,547 Retweets **70,269** Likes
1:12 PM - 5 Apr 2018

Donald J. Trump ✓
@realDonaldTrump

Thank you @WVGovernor Jim Justice. It was my great honor to be with the amazing people of West Virginia today! #MAGA
10,557 Retweets **50,062** Likes
1:28 PM - 5 Apr 2018

Donald J. Trump ✓
@realDonaldTrump

Despite the Aluminum Tariffs, Aluminum prices are DOWN 4%. People are surprised, I'm not! Lots of money coming into U.S. coffers and Jobs, Jobs, Jobs!
18,995 Retweets **81,035** Likes
4:11 AM - 6 Apr 2018

Donald J. Trump ✓
@realDonaldTrump

China, which is a great economic power, is considered a Developing Nation within the World Trade Organization. They therefore get tremendous perks and advantages, especially over the U.S. Does anybody think this is fair. We were badly represented. The WTO is unfair to U.S.
24,512 Retweets **96,583** Likes
7:32 AM - 6 Apr 2018

Donald J. Trump ✓
@realDonaldTrump

Do you believe that the Fake News Media is pushing hard on a story that I am going to replace A.G. Jeff Sessions with EPA Chief Scott Pruitt, who is doing a great job but is TOTALLY under siege? Do people really believe this stuff? So much of the media is dishonest and corrupt!
22,927 Retweets **91,125** Likes
7:46 AM - 6 Apr 2018

Donald J. Trump ✓
@realDonaldTrump

AMERICA IS OPEN FOR BUSINESS!
16,538 Retweets **68,939** Likes
9:24 AM - 6 Apr 2018

Donald J. Trump ✓
@realDonaldTrump

"BET founder: Trump's economy is bringing black workers back into the labor force"
29,519 Retweets **97,151** Likes
1:23 PM - 6 Apr 2018

Donald J. Trump ✓
@realDonaldTrump

Congratulations to @bernieandsid on their new @77wabcradio morning radio show in New York City. It was an honor to join you two – good luck!
8,862 Retweets **40,931** Likes
1:26 PM - 6 Apr 2018

Donald J. Trump ✓
@realDonaldTrump

Just spoke to @JustinTrudeau to pay my highest respect and condolences to the families of the terrible Humboldt Team tragedy. May God be with them all!
18,070 Retweets **93,382** Likes
10:35 AM - 7 Apr 2018

Donald J. Trump ✓
@realDonaldTrump

The United States hasn't had a Trade Surplus with China in 40 years. They must end unfair trade, take down barriers and charge only Reciprocal Tariffs. The U.S. is losing $500 Billion a year, and has been losing Billions of Dollars for decades. Cannot continue!
22,193 Retweets **90,487** Likes
11:03 AM - 7 Apr 2018

Donald J. Trump ✓
@realDonaldTrump

We are sealing up our Southern Border. The people of our great country want Safety and Security. The Dems have been a disaster on this very important issue!
24,937 Retweets **107,845** Likes
11:11 AM - 7 Apr 2018

Donald J. Trump ✓
@realDonaldTrump

Lawmakers of the House Judiciary Committee are angrily accusing the Department of Justice of missing the Thursday Deadline for turning over UNREDACTED Documents relating to FISA abuse, FBI, Comey, Lynch, McCabe, Clinton Emails and much more. Slow walking - what is going on? BAD!
22,279 Retweets **79,442** Likes
1:52 PM - 7 Apr 2018

Donald J. Trump ✓
@realDonaldTrump

What does the Department of Justice and FBI have to hide? Why aren't they giving the strongly requested documents (unredacted) to the HOUSE JUDICIARY COMMITTEE? Stalling, but for what reason? Not looking good!
26,680 Retweets **94,298** Likes
2:00 PM - 7 Apr 2018

Donald J. Trump ✓
@realDonaldTrump

Fire at Trump Tower is out. Very confined (well built building). Firemen (and women) did a great job. THANK YOU!
24,434 Retweets **136,189** Likes
3:42 PM - 7 Apr 2018

Donald J. Trump ✓
@realDonaldTrump

While Security spending was somewhat more than his predecessor, Scott Pruitt has received death threats because of his bold actions at EPA. Record clean Air & Water while saving USA Billions of Dollars. Rent was about market rate, travel expenses OK. Scott is doing a great job!
18,413 Retweets **75,853** Likes
5:03 PM - 7 Apr 2018

Donald J. Trump ✓
@realDonaldTrump

"The FBI closed the case on Hillary, which was a rigged investigation. They exonerated her even before they ever interviewed her, they never even put her under oath....." and much more. So true Jesse! @WattersWorld
21,086 Retweets **78,671** Likes
4:27 AM - 8 Apr 2018

Donald J. Trump ✓
@realDonaldTrump

The Washington Post is far more fiction than fact. Story after story is made up garbage - more like a poorly written novel than good reporting. Always quoting sources (not names), many of which don't exist. Story on John Kelly isn't true, just another hit job!
20,487 Retweets **81,286** Likes
4:58 AM - 8 Apr 2018

Donald J. Trump ✓
@realDonaldTrump

President Xi and I will always be friends, no matter what happens with our dispute on trade. China will take down its Trade Barriers because it is the right thing to do. Taxes will become Reciprocal & a deal will be made on Intellectual Property. Great future for both countries!
23,906 Retweets **107,756** Likes
5:12 AM - 8 Apr 2018

President Trumps Tweets 2018: A Historical Archive of President Trump's Tweets

Donald J. Trump @
@realDonaldTrump

Many dead, including women and children, in mindless CHEMICAL attack in Syria. Area of atrocity is in lockdown and encircled by Syrian Army, making it completely inaccessible to outside world. President Putin, Russia and Iran are responsible for backing Animal Assad. Big price...
33,180 Retweets **101,864** Likes
6:00 AM - 8 Apr 2018

Donald J. Trump @
@realDonaldTrump

....to pay. Open area immediately for medical help and verification. Another humanitarian disaster for no reason whatsoever. SICK!
15,616 Retweets **67,780** Likes
6:04 AM - 8 Apr 2018

Donald J. Trump @
@realDonaldTrump

If President Obama had crossed his stated Red Line In The Sand, the Syrian disaster would have ended long ago! Animal Assad would have been history!
24,946 Retweets **91,711** Likes
6:12 AM - 8 Apr 2018

Donald J. Trump @
@realDonaldTrump

Congratulations to Patrick Reed on his great and courageous MASTERS win! When Patrick had his amazing win at Doral 5 years ago, people saw his great talent, and a bright future ahead. Now he is the Masters Champion!
12,862 Retweets **92,509** Likes
5:43 PM - 8 Apr 2018

Donald J. Trump @
@realDonaldTrump

When a car is sent to the United States from China, there is a Tariff to be paid of 2 1/2%. When a car is sent to China from the United States, there is a Tariff to be paid of 25%. Does that sound like free or fair trade. No, it sounds like STUPID TRADE - going on for years!
46,855 Retweets **176,652** Likes
3:03 AM - 9 Apr 2018

Donald J. Trump @
@realDonaldTrump

The Democrats are not doing what's right for our country. I will not rest until we have secured our borders and restored the rule of law!
27,106 Retweets **104,763** Likes
12:17 PM - 9 Apr 2018

Donald J. Trump @
@realDonaldTrump

Great @Cabinet meeting at the @WhiteHouse this morning!
10,494 Retweets **53,184** Likes
12:32 PM - 9 Apr 2018

Donald J. Trump @
@realDonaldTrump

Attorney–client privilege is dead!
27,107 Retweets **105,299** Likes
4:07 AM - 10 Apr 2018

Donald J. Trump ✓
@realDonaldTrump

A TOTAL WITCH HUNT!!!
31,061 Retweets **122,912** Likes
4:08 AM - 10 Apr 2018

Donald J. Trump ✓
@realDonaldTrump

Last night, it was my great honor to host America's senior defense and military leaders for dinner at the White House. America's military is the GREATEST fighting force in the history of the world. They all have my pledge of unwavering commitment to our men and women in uniform!
19,515 Retweets **87,735** Likes
6:30 AM - 10 Apr 2018

Donald J. Trump ✓
@realDonaldTrump

Very thankful for President Xi of China's kind words on tariffs and automobile barriers...also, his enlightenment on intellectual property and technology transfers. We will make great progress together!
22,531 Retweets **106,429** Likes
11:30 AM - 10 Apr 2018

Donald J. Trump ✓
@realDonaldTrump

Today, it was my great honor to welcome the 2017 NCAA Football National Champion, Alabama Crimson Tide - to the White House. Congratulations! #RollTide
16,582 Retweets **80,005** Likes
2:49 PM - 10 Apr 2018

Donald J. Trump ✓
@realDonaldTrump

The Failing New York Times wrote another phony story. It was political pundit Doug Schoen, not a Ukrainian businessman, who asked me to do a short speech by phone (Skype), hosted by Doug, in Ukraine. I was very positive about Ukraine-another negative to the Fake Russia C story!
17,026 Retweets **67,201** Likes
3:30 AM - 11 Apr 2018

Donald J. Trump ✓
@realDonaldTrump

So much Fake News about what is going on in the White House. Very calm and calculated with a big focus on open and fair trade with China, the coming North Korea meeting and, of course, the vicious gas attack in Syria. Feels great to have Bolton & Larry K on board. I (we) are
16,168 Retweets **69,376** Likes
3:38 AM - 11 Apr 2018

Donald J. Trump ✓
@realDonaldTrump

....doing things that nobody thought possible, despite the never ending and corrupt Russia Investigation, which takes tremendous time and focus. No Collusion or Obstruction (other than I fight back), so now they do the Unthinkable, and RAID a lawyers office for information! BAD!
17,886 Retweets **76,115** Likes
3:47 AM - 11 Apr 2018

Donald J. Trump ✓
@realDonaldTrump

Russia vows to shoot down any and all missiles fired at Syria. Get ready Russia, because they will be coming, nice and new and "smart!" You shouldn't be partners with a Gas Killing Animal who kills his people and enjoys it!
66,753 Retweets **173,428** Likes
3:57 AM - 11 Apr 2018

Donald J. Trump ✓
@realDonaldTrump

Our relationship with Russia is worse now than it has ever been, and that includes the Cold War. There is no reason for this. Russia needs us to help with their economy, something that would be very easy to do, and we need all nations to work together. Stop the arms race?
32,551 Retweets **125,691** Likes
4:37 AM - 11 Apr 2018

Donald J. Trump ✓
@realDonaldTrump

Much of the bad blood with Russia is caused by the Fake & Corrupt Russia Investigation, headed up by the all Democrat loyalists, or people that worked for Obama. Mueller is most conflicted of all (except Rosenstein who signed FISA & Comey letter). No Collusion, so they go crazy!
26,720 Retweets **97,922** Likes
6:00 AM - 11 Apr 2018

Donald J. Trump ✓
@realDonaldTrump

Speaker Paul Ryan is a truly good man, and while he will not be seeking re-election, he will leave a legacy of achievement that nobody can question. We are with you Paul!
9,909 Retweets **61,655** Likes
6:50 AM - 11 Apr 2018

Donald J. Trump ✓
@realDonaldTrump

The @WhiteHouse is partnering with @Interior and @NatlParkService to bring the @NSCsafety's "Prescribed to Death" Opioid Memorial to the Ellipse - beginning tomorrow, April 12th to April 18th.
8,589 Retweets **35,788** Likes
8:47 AM - 11 Apr 2018

Donald J. Trump ✓
@realDonaldTrump

"Trump just took a giant step towards actual welfare reform"
16,360 Retweets **69,453** Likes
12:47 PM - 11 Apr 2018

Donald J. Trump ✓
@realDonaldTrump

Honored to have Republican Congressional Leadership join me at the @WhiteHouse this evening. Lots to discuss as we continue MAKING AMERICA GREAT AGAIN!
11,140 Retweets **57,916** Likes
3:59 PM - 11 Apr 2018

Donald J. Trump ✓
@realDonaldTrump

Big show tonight on @seanhannity! 9:00 P.M. on @FoxNews
11,142 Retweets **55,637** Likes
5:48 PM - 11 Apr 2018

Donald J. Trump ✓
@realDonaldTrump

If I wanted to fire Robert Mueller in December, as reported by the Failing New York Times, I would have fired him. Just more Fake News from a biased newspaper!
19,214 Retweets **87,391** Likes
3:03 AM - 12 Apr 2018

Donald J. Trump ✓
@realDonaldTrump

California Governor Jerry Brown is doing the right thing and sending the National Guard to the Border. Thank you Jerry, good move for the safety of our Country!
14,804 Retweets **86,130** Likes
3:08 AM - 12 Apr 2018

Donald J. Trump ✓
@realDonaldTrump

Never said when an attack on Syria would take place. Could be very soon or not so soon at all! In any event, the United States, under my Administration, has done a great job of ridding the region of ISIS. Where is our "Thank you America?"
25,626 Retweets **113,966** Likes
3:15 AM - 12 Apr 2018

Donald J. Trump ✓
@realDonaldTrump

Good luck to Mike Pompeo during his Confirmation Hearing today. He will be a great Secretary of State!
12,413 Retweets **62,486** Likes
3:37 AM - 12 Apr 2018

Donald J. Trump ✓
@realDonaldTrump

On Yom HaShoah we remember the six million Jews slaughtered in the Holocaust. With each passing year, our duty to remember this atrocity increases as we pledge #NeverAgain. #HolocaustRemembranceDay
16,854 Retweets **65,767** Likes
9:42 AM - 12 Apr 2018

Donald J. Trump ✓
@realDonaldTrump

I have agreed with the historically cooperative, disciplined approach that we have engaged in with Robert Mueller (Unlike the Clintons!). I have full confidence in Ty Cobb, my Special Counsel, and have been fully advised throughout each phase of this process.
16,722 Retweets **82,895** Likes
9:46 AM - 12 Apr 2018

Donald J. Trump ✓
@realDonaldTrump

Thank you to all of the American workers who travelled here today! This event is dedicated to YOU: the hardworking Americans who make this nation run. You love your country, you provide for your family, you have PRIDE in your work and you cherish our GREAT AMERICAN FLAG! #TaxCuts
14,277 Retweets **65,421** Likes
11:32 AM - 12 Apr 2018

Donald J. Trump ✓
@realDonaldTrump

America's greatest treasure is our people – and my Administration HEARS YOUR VOICE and HAS YOUR BACK. We are fighting to give every American a future of dignity, purpose and pride. AMERICAN SPIRIT is back! #TaxCuts
19,953 Retweets **81,129** Likes
12:03 PM - 12 Apr 2018

Donald J. Trump ✓
@realDonaldTrump

Would only join TPP if the deal were substantially better than the deal offered to Pres. Obama. We already have BILATERAL deals with six of the eleven nations in TPP, and are working to make a deal with the biggest of those nations, Japan, who has hit us hard on trade for years!
16759 Retweets **78,686** Likes
8:15 PM - 12 Apr 2018

Donald J. Trump ✓
@realDonaldTrump

Tremendous pressure is building, like never before, for the Border Wall and an end to crime cradling Sanctuary Cities. Started the Wall in San Diego, where the people were pushing really hard to get it. They will soon be protected!
23,145 Retweets **108,689** Likes
4:44 AM - 13 Apr 2018

Donald J. Trump ✓
@realDonaldTrump

James Comey is a proven LEAKER & LIAR. Virtually everyone in Washington thought he should be fired for the terrible job he did-until he was, in fact, fired. He leaked CLASSIFIED information, for which he should be prosecuted. He lied to Congress under OATH. He is a weak and.....
33,432 Retweets **127,321** Likes
5:01 AM - 13 Apr 2018

Donald J. Trump ✓
@realDonaldTrump

....untruthful slime ball who was, as time has proven, a terrible Director of the FBI. His handling of the Crooked Hillary Clinton case, and the events surrounding it, will go down as one of the worst "botch jobs" of history. It was my great honor to fire James Comey!
35,266 Retweets **143,118** Likes
5:17 AM - 13 Apr 2018

Donald J. Trump ✓
@realDonaldTrump

We are bringing back our factories, we are bringing back our jobs, and we are bringing back those four beautiful words: MADE IN THE USA!
25,345 Retweets **111,025** Likes
9:21 AM - 13 Apr 2018

Donald J. Trump ✓
@realDonaldTrump

DOJ just issued the McCabe report - which is a total disaster. He LIED! LIED! LIED! McCabe was totally controlled by Comey - McCabe is Comey!! No collusion, all made up by this den of thieves and lowlifes!
36,632 Retweets **126,817** Likes
12:36 PM - 13 Apr 2018

Donald J. Trump ✓
@realDonaldTrump

A perfectly executed strike last night. Thank you to France and the United Kingdom for their wisdom and the power of their fine Military. Could not have had a better result. Mission Accomplished!
43,580 Retweets **200,070** Likes
5:21 AM - 14 Apr 2018

Donald J. Trump ✓
@realDonaldTrump

So proud of our great Military which will soon be, after the spending of billions of fully approved dollars, the finest that our Country has ever had. There won't be anything, or anyone, even close!
30,430 Retweets **160,818** Likes
5:29 AM - 14 Apr 2018

Donald J. Trump ✓
@realDonaldTrump

Unbelievably, James Comey states that Polls, where Crooked Hillary was leading, were a factor in the handling (stupidly) of the Clinton Email probe. In other words, he was making decisions based on the fact that he thought she was going to win, and he wanted a job. Slimeball!
27,603 Retweets **106,702** Likes
4:42 AM - 15 Apr 2018

Donald J. Trump ✓
@realDonaldTrump

The big questions in Comey's badly reviewed book aren't answered like, how come he gave up Classified Information (jail), why did he lie to Congress (jail), why did the DNC refuse to give Server to the FBI (why didn't they TAKE it), why the phony memos, McCabe's $700,000 & more?
27,729 Retweets **101,235** Likes
4:57 AM - 15 Apr 2018

Donald J. Trump ✓
@realDonaldTrump

Comey throws AG Lynch "under the bus!" Why can't we all find out what happened on the tarmac in the back of the plane with Wild Bill and Lynch? Was she promised a Supreme Court seat, or AG, in order to lay off Hillary. No golf and grandkids talk (give us all a break)!
26,569 Retweets **102,051** Likes
5:08 AM - 15 Apr 2018

Donald J. Trump ✓
@realDonaldTrump

The Syrian raid was so perfectly carried out, with such precision, that the only way the Fake News Media could demean was by my use of the term "Mission Accomplished." I knew they would seize on this but felt it is such a great Military term, it should be brought back. Use often!
24,048 Retweets **115,575** Likes
5:19 AM - 15 Apr 2018

Donald J. Trump ✓
@realDonaldTrump

I never asked Comey for Personal Loyalty. I hardly even knew this guy. Just another of his many lies. His "memos" are self serving and FAKE!
22,395 Retweets **102,330** Likes
5:32 AM - 15 Apr 2018

President Trumps Tweets 2018: A Historical Archive of President Trump's Tweets

Donald J. Trump ✓
@realDonaldTrump

Attorney Client privilege is now a thing of the past. I have many (too many!) lawyers and they are probably wondering when their offices, and even homes, are going to be raided with everything, including their phones and computers, taken. All lawyers are deflated and concerned!
24,019 Retweets **103,035** Likes
5:56 AM - 15 Apr 2018

Donald J. Trump ✓
@realDonaldTrump

Slippery James Comey, a man who always ends up badly and out of whack (he is not smart!), will go down as the WORST FBI Director in history, by far!
22,407 Retweets **99,162** Likes
6:07 AM - 15 Apr 2018

Donald J. Trump ✓
@realDonaldTrump

Just hit 50% in the Rasmussen Poll, much higher than President Obama at same point. With all of the phony stories and Fake News, it's hard to believe! Thank you America, we are doing Great Things.
29,754 Retweets **141,548** Likes
7:44 AM - 15 Apr 2018

Donald J. Trump ✓
@realDonaldTrump

Comey drafted the Crooked Hillary exoneration long before he talked to her (lied in Congress to Senator G), then based his decisions on her poll numbers. Disgruntled, he, McCabe, and the others, committed many crimes!
28,889 Retweets **112,636** Likes
5:25 AM - 16 Apr 2018

Donald J. Trump ✓
@realDonaldTrump

Russia and China are playing the Currency Devaluation game as the U.S. keeps raising interest rates. Not acceptable!
21,561 Retweets **97,741** Likes
5:31 AM - 16 Apr 2018

Donald J. Trump ✓
@realDonaldTrump

Employment is up, Taxes are DOWN. Enjoy!
24,896 Retweets **124,448** Likes
5:24 AM - 17 Apr 2018

Donald J. Trump ✓
@realDonaldTrump

I am in Florida and looking forward to my meeting with Prime Minister Abe of Japan. Working on Trade and Military Security.
11,779 Retweets **63,836** Likes
5:24 AM - 17 Apr 2018

Donald J. Trump ✓
@realDonaldTrump

Looks like Jerry Brown and California are not looking for safety and security along their very porous Border. He cannot come to terms for the National Guard to patrol and protect the Border. The high crime rate will only get higher. Much wanted Wall in San Diego already started!
15,332 Retweets **64,910** Likes
5:24 AM - 17 Apr 2018

Donald J. Trump ✓
@realDonaldTrump

So many people are seeing the benefits of the Tax Cut Bill. Everyone is talking, really nice to see!
15,379 Retweets **85,300** Likes
5:24 AM - 17 Apr 2018

Donald J. Trump ✓
@realDonaldTrump

Getting ready to meet Prime Minister Abe of Japan, a truly fine gentleman!
10,438 Retweets **67,802** Likes
10:51 AM - 17 Apr 2018

Donald J. Trump ✓
@realDonaldTrump

Rasmussen just came out at 51% Approval despite the Fake News Media. They were one of the three most accurate on Election Day. Just about the most inaccurate were CNN and ABC News/Washington Post, and they haven't changed (get new pollsters). Much of the media is a Scam!
18,409 Retweets **77,972** Likes
10:59 AM - 17 Apr 2018

Donald J. Trump ✓
@realDonaldTrump

Welcome Prime Minister Abe!
14,549 Retweets **58,345** Likes
1:45 PM - 17 Apr 2018

Donald J. Trump ✓
@realDonaldTrump

Today's Court decision means that Congress must close loopholes that block the removal of dangerous criminal aliens, including aggravated felons. This is a public safety crisis that can only be fixed by....
15,804 Retweets **66,855** Likes
2:34 PM - 17 Apr 2018

Donald J. Trump ✓
@realDonaldTrump

....Congress – House and Senate must quickly pass a legislative fix to ensure violent criminal aliens can be removed from our society. Keep America Safe!
13,120 Retweets **55,653** Likes
2:34 PM - 17 Apr 2018

Donald J. Trump ✓
@realDonaldTrump

States and Cities throughout our Country are being cheated and treated so badly by online retailers. Very unfair to traditional tax paying stores!
14,227 Retweets **70,002** Likes
3:59 PM - 17 Apr 2018

President Trumps Tweets 2018: A Historical Archive of President Trump's Tweets

Donald J. Trump ✓
@realDonaldTrump

.@FLOTUS Melania and I join the Nation in celebrating the life of Barbara Bush
10,206 Retweets **39,641** Likes
7:23 PM - 17 Apr 2018

Donald J. Trump ✓
@realDonaldTrump

It is my great honor to host @JPN_PMO @AbeShinzo!
9,760 Retweets **42,306** Likes
7:26 PM - 17 Apr 2018

Donald J. Trump ✓
@realDonaldTrump

Pastor Andrew Brunson, a fine gentleman and Christian leader in the United States, is on trial and being persecuted in Turkey for no reason. They call him a Spy, but I am more a Spy than he is. Hopefully he will be allowed to come home to his beautiful family where he belongs!
20,638 Retweets **84,836** Likes
7:32 PM - 17 Apr 2018

Donald J. Trump ✓
@realDonaldTrump

While Japan and South Korea would like us to go back into TPP, I don't like the deal for the United States. Too many contingencies and no way to get out if it doesn't work. Bilateral deals are far more efficient, profitable and better for OUR workers. Look how bad WTO is to U.S.
18,159 Retweets **78,191** Likes
7:49 PM - 17 Apr 2018

Donald J. Trump ✓
@realDonaldTrump

There is a Revolution going on in California. Soooo many Sanctuary areas want OUT of this ridiculous, crime infested & breeding concept. Jerry Brown is trying to back out of the National Guard at the Border, but the people of the State are not happy. Want Security & Safety NOW!
29,045 Retweets **115,384** Likes
2:59 AM - 18 Apr 2018

Donald J. Trump ✓
@realDonaldTrump

A sketch years later about a nonexistent man. A total con job, playing the Fake News Media for Fools (but they know it)!
17,869 Retweets **61,945** Likes
3:08 AM - 18 Apr 2018

Donald J. Trump ✓
@realDonaldTrump

Mike Pompeo met with Kim Jong Un in North Korea last week. Meeting went very smoothly and a good relationship was formed. Details of Summit are being worked out now. Denuclearization will be a great thing for World, but also for North Korea!
25,827 Retweets **101,034** Likes
3:42 AM - 18 Apr 2018

Donald J. Trump ✓
@realDonaldTrump

Slippery James Comey, the worst FBI Director in history, was not fired because of the phony Russia investigation where, by the way, there was NO COLLUSION (except by the Dems)!
22,580 Retweets **96,478** Likes
5:05 AM - 18 Apr 2018

Donald J. Trump ✓
@realDonaldTrump

Best wishes to Prime Minister @Netanyahu and all of the people of Israel on the 70th Anniversary of your Great Independence. We have no better friends anywhere. Looking forward to moving our Embassy to Jerusalem next month!
23,897 Retweets **102,082** Likes
9:30 AM - 18 Apr 2018

Donald J. Trump ✓
@realDonaldTrump

Prime Minister @AbeShinzo of Japan and myself this morning building an even deeper and better relationship while playing a quick round of golf at Trump International Golf Club.
15,309 Retweets **75,781** Likes
2:00 PM - 18 Apr 2018

Donald J. Trump ✓
@realDonaldTrump

Great working luncheon with U.S. and Japanese Delegations this afternoon!
12,621 Retweets **64,968** Likes
2:32 PM - 18 Apr 2018

Donald J. Trump ✓
@realDonaldTrump

It was my great honor to host my friend @JPN_PMO @AbeShinzo and his delegation at Mar-a-Lago for the past two days. Lots accomplished, thank you! #Success
14,662 Retweets **65,149** Likes
7:58 PM - 18 Apr 2018

Donald J. Trump ✓
@realDonaldTrump

Great meeting with Prime Minister Abe of Japan, who has just left Florida. Talked in depth about North Korea, Military and Trade. Good things will happen!
14,185 Retweets **71,412** Likes
7:45 AM - 19 Apr 2018

Donald J. Trump ✓
@realDonaldTrump

Thank you San Diego County for defending the rule of law and supporting our lawsuit against California's illegal and unconstitutional 'Sanctuary' policies. California's dangerous policies release violent criminals back into our communities, putting all Americans at risk.
20,044 Retweets **86,533** Likes
8:23 AM - 19 Apr 2018

Donald J. Trump ✓
@realDonaldTrump

Governor Jerry Brown announced he will deploy "up to 400 National Guard Troops" to do nothing. The crime rate in California is high enough, and the Federal Government will not be paying for Governor Brown's charade. We need border security and action, not words!
20,309 Retweets **84,456** Likes
8:48 AM - 19 Apr 2018

Donald J. Trump ✓
@realDonaldTrump

Just arrived @NASKeyWest! Heading to a briefing with the Joint Interagency Task Force South, NORTHCOM and SOUTHCOM.
9,194 Retweets **44,839** Likes
9:23 AM - 19 Apr 2018

President Trumps Tweets 2018: A Historical Archive of President Trump's Tweets

Donald J. Trump ◎
@realDonaldTrump

THANK YOU #JIATFSouth, @Norad_Northcom, @southcomwatch and @DHSgov. Keep up the GREAT work!
6,663 Retweets **31,574** Likes
11:33 AM - 19 Apr 2018

Donald J. Trump ◎
@realDonaldTrump

.@MarshaBlackburn is a wonderful woman who has always been there when we have needed her. Great on the Military, Border Security and Crime. Loves and works hard for the people of Tennessee. She has my full endorsement and I will be there to campaign with her!
15,076 Retweets **60,475** Likes
11:40 AM - 19 Apr 2018

Donald J. Trump ◎
@realDonaldTrump

Democrats are obstructing good (hopefully great) people wanting to give up a big portion of their life to work for our Government, hence, the American People. They are "slow walking" all of my nominations - hundreds of people. At this rate it would take 9 years for all approvals!
26,579 Retweets **96,971** Likes
1:21 PM - 19 Apr 2018

Donald J. Trump ◎
@realDonaldTrump

...Hopefully the Senate will not leave Washington until our Ambassadors, Judges and the people who make Washington work are approved. The Democrats are Obstructing the process and we need these people approved for the good of our Country!
19,050 Retweets **73,600** Likes
1:27 PM - 19 Apr 2018

Donald J. Trump ◎
@realDonaldTrump

Mike Pompeo is outstanding. First in his class at West Point. A top student at Harvard Law School. A success at whatever he has done. We need the Senate to approve Mike ASAP. He will be a great Secretary of State!
22,576 Retweets **91,256** Likes
1:31 PM - 19 Apr 2018

Donald J. Trump ◎
@realDonaldTrump

My thoughts, prayers and condolences are with the families, friends and colleagues of the two @GCSOFlorida deputies (HEROES) who lost their lives in the line of duty today.
14,458 Retweets **65,890** Likes
3:30 PM - 19 Apr 2018

Donald J. Trump ◎
@realDonaldTrump

Sanctuary Cities released at least 142 Gang Members across the United States, making it easy for them to commit all forms of violent crimes where none would have existed. We are doing a great job of law enforcement, but things such as this make safety in America difficult!
20,391 Retweets **74,265** Likes
3:30 PM - 19 Apr 2018

Donald J. Trump ✓
@realDonaldTrump

James Comey just threw Andrew McCabe "under the bus." Inspector General's Report on McCabe is a disaster for both of them! Getting a little (lot) of their own medicine?
21,804 Retweets **85,311** Likes
3:46 PM - 19 Apr 2018

Donald J. Trump ✓
@realDonaldTrump

James Comey Memos just out and show clearly that there was NO COLLUSION and NO OBSTRUCTION. Also, he leaked classified information. WOW! Will the Witch Hunt continue?
25,596 Retweets **102,289** Likes
8:37 PM - 19 Apr 2018

Donald J. Trump ✓
@realDonaldTrump

So General Michael Flynn's life can be totally destroyed while Shadey James Comey can Leak and Lie and make lots of money from a third rate book (that should never have been written). Is that really the way life in America is supposed to work? I don't think so!
30,399 Retweets **109,491** Likes
3:34 AM - 20 Apr 2018

Donald J. Trump ✓
@realDonaldTrump

So exciting! I have agreed to be the Commencement Speaker at our GREAT Naval Academy on May 25th in Annapolis, Maryland. Looking forward to being there.
19,924 Retweets **116,724** Likes
3:43 AM - 20 Apr 2018

Donald J. Trump ✓
@realDonaldTrump

Nancy Pelosi is going absolutely crazy about the big Tax Cuts given to the American People by the Republicans...got not one Democrat Vote! Here's a choice. They want to end them and raise your taxes substantially. Republicans are working on making them permanent and more cuts!
28,986 Retweets **110,478** Likes
3:50 AM - 20 Apr 2018

Donald J. Trump ✓
@realDonaldTrump

Looks like OPEC is at it again. With record amounts of Oil all over the place, including the fully loaded ships at sea, Oil prices are artificially Very High! No good and will not be accepted!
24,013 Retweets **98,516** Likes
3:57 AM - 20 Apr 2018

Donald J. Trump ✓
@realDonaldTrump

Can you believe that despite 93% bad stories from the Fake News Media (should be getting good stories), today we had just about our highest Poll Numbers, including those on Election Day? The American public is wise to the phony an dishonest press. Make America Great Again!
32,021 Retweets **131,814** Likes
1:25 PM - 20 Apr 2018

Donald J. Trump ✓
@realDonaldTrump

North Korea has agreed to suspend all Nuclear Tests and close up a major test site. This is very good news for North Korea and the World - big progress! Look forward to our Summit.
47,068 Retweets **186,635** Likes
3:50 PM - 20 Apr 2018

President Trumps Tweets 2018: A Historical Archive of President Trump's Tweets

Donald J. Trump @realDonaldTrump

Just heard the Campaign was sued by the Obstructionist Democrats. This can be good news in that we will now counter for the DNC Server that they refused to give to the FBI, the Debbie Wasserman Schultz Servers and Documents held by the Pakistani mystery man and Clinton Emails.

31,576 Retweets **111,546** Likes
4:19 PM - 20 Apr 2018

Donald J. Trump @realDonaldTrump

James Comey illegally leaked classified documents to the press in order to generate a Special Council? Therefore, the Special Council was established based on an illegal act? Really, does everybody know what that means?

28,786 Retweets **106,428** Likes
8:13 PM - 20 Apr 2018

Donald J. Trump @realDonaldTrump

A message from Kim Jong Un: "North Korea will stop nuclear tests and launches of intercontinental ballistic missiles." Also will "Shut down a nuclear test site in the country's Northern Side to prove the vow to suspend nuclear tests." Progress being made for all!

32,170 Retweets **142,849** Likes
8:22 PM - 20 Apr 2018

Donald J. Trump @realDonaldTrump

The New York Times and a third rate reporter named Maggie Haberman, known as a Crooked H flunkie who I don't speak to and have nothing to do with, are going out of their way to destroy Michael Cohen and his relationship with me in the hope that he will "flip." They use....

14,573 Retweets **59,973** Likes
6:10 AM - 21 Apr 2018

Donald J. Trump @realDonaldTrump

....non-existent "sources" and a drunk/drugged up loser who hates Michael, a fine person with a wonderful family. Michael is a businessman for his own account/lawyer who I have always liked & respected. Most people will flip if the Government lets them out of trouble, even if....

10,795 Retweets **49,503** Likes
6:10 AM - 21 Apr 2018

Donald J. Trump @realDonaldTrump

....it means lying or making up stories. Sorry, I don't see Michael doing that despite the horrible Witch Hunt and the dishonest media!

11,372 Retweets **53,280** Likes
6:10 AM - 21 Apr 2018

Donald J. Trump @realDonaldTrump

Join me in Washington, Michigan on Saturday, April 28, 2018 at 7:00pm! #MAGA

10,915 Retweets **41,148** Likes
6:18 AM - 21 Apr 2018

Donald J. Trump ✓
@realDonaldTrump

Fantastic crowd and great people yesterday in Key West, Florida. Thank you!
14,259 Retweets **68,675** Likes
8:44 AM - 21 Apr 2018

Donald J. Trump ✓
@realDonaldTrump

Today, my thoughts and prayers are with the entire Bush family. In memory of First Lady Barbara Bush, there is a remembrance display located at her portrait in the Center Hall of the @WhiteHouse.
13,088 Retweets **78,985** Likes
8:45 AM - 21 Apr 2018

Donald J. Trump ✓
@realDonaldTrump

Heading to the Southern White House to watch the Funeral Service of Barbara Bush. First Lady Melania has arrived in Houston to pay our respects. Will be a beautiful day!
12,051 Retweets **78,580** Likes
8:47 AM - 21 Apr 2018

Donald J. Trump ✓
@realDonaldTrump

So funny, the Democrats have sued the Republicans for Winning. Now he R's counter and force them to turn over a treasure trove of material, including Servers and Emails!
23,722 Retweets **96,367** Likes
11:52 AM - 21 Apr 2018

Donald J. Trump ✓
@realDonaldTrump

Sylvester Stallone called me with the story of heavyweight boxing champion Jack Johnson. His trials and tribulations were great, his life complex and controversial. Others have looked at this over the years, most thought it would be done, but yes, I am considering a Full Pardon!
20,946 Retweets **99,627** Likes
12:02 PM - 21 Apr 2018

Donald J. Trump ✓
@realDonaldTrump

James Comey's Memos are Classified, I did not Declassify them. They belong to our Government! Therefore, he broke the law! Additionally, he totally made up many of the things he said I said, and he is already a proven liar and leaker. Where are Memos on Clinton, Lynch & others?
20,807 Retweets **76,182** Likes
12:24 PM - 21 Apr 2018

Donald J. Trump ✓
@realDonaldTrump

The Washington Post said I refer to Jeff Sessions as "Mr. Magoo" and Rod Rosenstein as "Mr. Peepers." This is "according to people with whom the president has spoken." There are no such people and don't know these characters...just more Fake & Disgusting News to create ill will!
17,773 Retweets **68,920** Likes
1:13 PM - 21 Apr 2018

Donald J. Trump ✓
@realDonaldTrump

"At least two Memos Comey shared with a friend contained Classified Information." Wall Street Journal
22,217 Retweets **89,167** Likes
3:30 PM - 21 Apr 2018

Donald J. Trump ✓
@realDonaldTrump

"GOP Lawmakers asking Sessions to Investigate Comey and Hillary Clinton." @FoxNews Good luck with that request!
20,686 Retweets **88,624** Likes
5:22 AM - 22 Apr 2018

Donald J. Trump ✓
@realDonaldTrump

Sleepy Eyes Chuck Todd of Fake News NBC just stated that we have given up so much in our negotiations with North Korea, and they have given up nothing. Wow, we haven't given up anything & they have agreed to denuclearization (so great for World), site closure, & no more testing!
25,871 Retweets **102,315** Likes
5:50 AM - 22 Apr 2018

Donald J. Trump ✓
@realDonaldTrump

....We are a long way from conclusion on North Korea, maybe things will work out, and maybe they won't - only time will tell....But the work I am doing now should have been done a long time ago!
22,150 Retweets **106,161** Likes
6:02 AM - 22 Apr 2018

Donald J. Trump ✓
@realDonaldTrump

"I can die happy now with Trump Job performance," stated Mary Matalin. "A great overall President, stunning!" Thank you Mary.
16,995 Retweets **91,081** Likes
7:06 AM - 22 Apr 2018

Donald J. Trump ✓
@realDonaldTrump

A complete Witch Hunt!
20,160 Retweets **96,490** Likes
10:23 AM - 22 Apr 2018

Donald J. Trump ✓
@realDonaldTrump

Funny how all of the Pundits that couldn't come close to making a deal on North Korea are now all over the place telling me how to make a deal!
28474 Retweets **121404**Likes
11:43 AM - 22 Apr 2018

Donald J. Trump ✓
@realDonaldTrump

Kim Strassel of the WSJ just said, after reviewing the dumb Comey Memos, "you got to ask, what was the purpose of the Special Counsel? There's no there there." Dan Henninger of the WSJ said Memos would show that this would be one of the weakest obstruction cases ever brought!
24,359 Retweets **95,011** Likes
1:04 PM - 22 Apr 2018

Donald J. Trump ✓
@realDonaldTrump

Thank you to the incredible Law Enforcement Officers from the Palm Beach County Sheriff's Office. They keep us safe and are very cool about it!
17,457 Retweets **94,385** Likes
1:12 PM - 22 Apr 2018

Donald J. Trump ✓
@realDonaldTrump

Hard to believe Obstructionists May vote against Mike Pompeo for Secretary of State. The Dems will not approve hundreds of good people, including the Ambassador to Germany. They are maxing out the time on approval process for all, never happened before. Need more Republicans!
22,940 Retweets **89,895** Likes
6:15 AM - 23 Apr 2018

Donald J. Trump ✓
@realDonaldTrump

Despite the Democrat inspired laws on Sanctuary Cities and the Border being so bad and one sided, I have instructed the Secretary of Homeland Security not to let these large Caravans of people into our Country. It is a disgrace. We are the only Country in the World so naive! WALL
25,812 Retweets **103,828** Likes
6:44 AM - 23 Apr 2018

Donald J. Trump ✓
@realDonaldTrump

Mexico, whose laws on immigration are very tough, must stop people from going through Mexico and into the U.S. We may make this a condition of the new NAFTA Agreement. Our Country cannot accept what is happening! Also, we must get Wall funding fast.
25,412 Retweets **106,206** Likes
6:51 AM - 23 Apr 2018

Donald J. Trump ✓
@realDonaldTrump

Here's a great stat - since January 2017, the number of people forced to use food stamps is down 1.9 million. The American people are finally back to work!
32,487 Retweets **153,557** Likes
1:08 PM - 23 Apr 2018

Donald J. Trump ✓
@realDonaldTrump

Having great meetings and discussions with my friend, President @EmmanuelMacron of France. We are in the midst of meetings on Iran, Syria and Trade. We will be holding a joint press conference shortly, here at the @WhiteHouse.
10,395 Retweets **51,605** Likes
9:43 AM - 24 Apr 2018

Donald J. Trump ✓
@realDonaldTrump

Americans stand with you and all of Canada, Prime Minister @JustinTrudeau. Our thoughts and prayers are with you all. #TorontoStrong
7,037 Retweets **39,641** Likes
10:56 AM - 24 Apr 2018

Donald J. Trump ✓
@realDonaldTrump

Arizona, please get out today and vote @DebbieLesko for Congress in #AZ08. Strong on Border, Immigration and Crime. Great on the Military. Time is ticking down - get out and VOTE today. We need Debbie in Congress!
16,650 Retweets **60,869** Likes
11:02 AM - 24 Apr 2018

President Trumps Tweets 2018: A Historical Archive of President Trump's Tweets

Donald J. Trump ✓
@realDonaldTrump

"President Trump Calls the U.S.-France Relationship 'Unbreakable.' History Shows He's Right."
10,729 Retweets **54,984** Likes
11:41 AM - 24 Apr 2018

Donald J. Trump ✓
@realDonaldTrump

.@JimRenacci has worked so hard on Tax Reductions, Illegal Immigration, the Border and Crime. I need Jim very badly to help our agenda and to keep MAKING AMERICA GREAT AGAIN! He will be a fantastic Senator for the Great State of Ohio, and has my full endorsement!
14,847 Retweets **59,884** Likes
12:06 PM - 24 Apr 2018

Donald J. Trump ✓
@realDonaldTrump

Our two great republics are linked together by the timeless bonds of history, culture, and destiny. We are people who cherish our values, protect our civilization, and recognize the image of God in every human soul.
20,495 Retweets **94,091** Likes
1:18 PM - 24 Apr 2018

Donald J. Trump ✓
@realDonaldTrump

Congratulations to Republican Debbie Lesko on her big win in the Special Election for Arizona House seat. Debbie will do a Great Job! Press is so silent.
23,314 Retweets **112,562** Likes
4:53 AM - 25 Apr 2018

Donald J. Trump ✓
@realDonaldTrump

Busy day planned. Looking forward to watching President Macron of France address a Joint Session of Congress today. This is a great honor and seldom allowed to be done...he will be GREAT!
12,866 Retweets **74,295** Likes
6:29 AM - 25 Apr 2018

Donald J. Trump ✓
@realDonaldTrump

.@FLOTUS did a spectacular job hosting the President of France @EmmanuelMacron and his wife Brigitte. Every detail was done to perfection. The State Dining Room never looked more beautiful, and Washington is abuzz over what an incredible job Melania did.
17,345 Retweets **91,122** Likes
7:10 AM - 25 Apr 2018

Donald J. Trump ✓
@realDonaldTrump

Looking forward to my meeting with Tim Cook of Apple. We will be talking about many things, including how the U.S. has been treated unfairly for many years, by many countries, on trade.
15,984 Retweets **86,666** Likes
7:11 AM - 25 Apr 2018

Donald J. Trump ✓
@realDonaldTrump

Thank you Kanye, very cool!
108,482 Retweets **362,139** Likes
12:33 PM - 25 Apr 2018

Donald J. Trump
@realDonaldTrump

MAGA!
60,466 Retweets **233,819** Likes
2:18 PM - 25 Apr 2018

Donald J. Trump
@realDonaldTrump

Loved being on @foxandfriends this morning. Great show!
11,300 Retweets **82,395** Likes
3:17 PM - 26 Apr 2018

Donald J. Trump
@realDonaldTrump

The U.S. has put together a STRONG bid w/ Canada & Mexico for the 2026 World Cup. It would be a shame if countries that we always support were to lobby against the U.S. bid. Why should we be supporting these countries when they don't support us (including at the United Nations)?
22,891 Retweets **99,253** Likes
4:39 PM - 26 Apr 2018

Donald J. Trump
@realDonaldTrump

Is everybody believing what is going on. James Comey can't define what a leak is. He illegally leaked CLASSIFIED INFORMATION but doesn't understand what he did or how serious it is. He lied all over the place to cover it up. He's either very sick or very dumb. Remember sailor!
24,887 Retweets **107,727** Likes
3:26 AM - 27 Apr 2018

Donald J. Trump
@realDonaldTrump

After a furious year of missile launches and Nuclear testing, a historic meeting between North and South Korea is now taking place. Good things are happening, but only time will tell!
25,419 Retweets **120,404** Likes
3:41 AM - 27 Apr 2018

Donald J. Trump
@realDonaldTrump

KOREAN WAR TO END! The United States, and all of its GREAT people, should be very proud of what is now taking place in Korea!
39,343 Retweets **134,459** Likes
3:55 AM - 27 Apr 2018

Donald J. Trump
@realDonaldTrump

So great to have Staff Sgt. Dan Nevins and the incredible WOUNDED WARRIORS with me in the White House yesterday. These are truly brave and special people! @foxandfriends
11,991 Retweets **64,826** Likes
4:23 AM - 27 Apr 2018

Donald J. Trump
@realDonaldTrump

Please do not forget the great help that my good friend, President Xi of China, has given to the United States, particularly at the Border of North Korea. Without him it would have been a much longer, tougher, process!
24,960 Retweets **112,500** Likes
4:50 AM - 27 Apr 2018

Donald J. Trump ●
@realDonaldTrump

Kanye West has performed a great service to the Black Community - Big things are happening and eyes are being opened for the first time in Decades - Legacy Stuff! Thank you also to Chance and Dr. Darrell Scott, they really get it (lowest Black & Hispanic unemployment in history).
34,372 Retweets **146,080** Likes
6:11 AM - 27 Apr 2018

Donald J. Trump ●
@realDonaldTrump

Look forward to meeting with Chancellor Angela Merkel of Germany today. So much to discuss, so little time! It will be good for both of our great countries!
11,557 Retweets **73,114** Likes
6:28 AM - 27 Apr 2018

Donald J. Trump ●
@realDonaldTrump

Just Out: House Intelligence Committee Report released. "No evidence" that the Trump Campaign "colluded, coordinated or conspired with Russia." Clinton Campaign paid for Opposition Research obtained from Russia- Wow! A total Witch Hunt! MUST END NOW!
33,612 Retweets **120,517** Likes
7:14 AM - 27 Apr 2018

Donald J. Trump ●
@realDonaldTrump

I urge all Americans to participate in #takebackday tomorrow! Let's come together and BEAT last October's record of disposed prescription pills! Visit takebackday.dea.gov to learn more on how to participate Saturday and every day.
11,885 Retweets **49,952** Likes
12:23 PM - 27 Apr 2018

Donald J. Trump ●
@realDonaldTrump

House Intelligence Committee rules that there was NO COLLUSION between the Trump Campaign and Russia. As I have been saying all along, it is all a big Hoax by the Democrats based on payments and lies. There should never have been a Special Counsel appointed. Witch Hunt!
27,456 Retweets **114,185** Likes
7:04 PM - 27 Apr 2018

Donald J. Trump ●
@realDonaldTrump

Allegations made by Senator Jon Tester against Admiral/Doctor Ron Jackson are proving false. The Secret Service is unable to confirm (in fact they deny) any of the phony Democrat charges which have absolutely devastated the wonderful Jackson family. Tester should resign. The.....
25,854 Retweets **93,447** Likes
5:07 AM - 28 Apr 2018

Donald J. Trump ●
@realDonaldTrump

....great people of Montana will not stand for this kind of slander when talking of a great human being. Admiral Jackson is the kind of man that those in Montana would most respect and admire, and now, for no reason whatsoever, his reputation has been shattered. Not fair, Tester!
21,811 Retweets **94,360** Likes
5:15 AM - 28 Apr 2018

Donald J. Trump ✓
@realDonaldTrump

"Clapper lied about (fraudulent) Dossier leaks to CNN" @foxandfriends FoxNews He is a lying machine who now works for Fake News CNN.
21,053 Retweets **79,744** Likes
5:58 AM - 28 Apr 2018

Donald J. Trump ✓
@realDonaldTrump

Just had a long and very good talk with President Moon of South Korea. Things are going very well, time and location of meeting with North Korea is being set. Also spoke to Prime Minister Abe of Japan to inform him of the ongoing negotiations.
23,891 Retweets **101,227** Likes
6:45 AM - 28 Apr 2018

Donald J. Trump ✓
@realDonaldTrump

Look forward to being in the Great State of Michigan tonight. Major business expansion and jobs pouring into your State. Auto companies expanding at record pace. Big crowd tonight, will be live on T.V.
18,797 Retweets **97,399** Likes
6:54 AM - 28 Apr 2018

Donald J. Trump ✓
@realDonaldTrump

Secret Service has just informed me that Senator Jon Tester's statements on Admiral Jackson are not true. There were no such findings. A horrible thing that we in D.C. must live with, just like phony Russian Collusion. Tester should lose race in Montana. Very dishonest and sick!
38,924 Retweets **135,989** Likes
12:11 PM - 28 Apr 2018

Donald J. Trump ✓
@realDonaldTrump

Join me LIVE in Washington, Michigan at 7:00pmE on @FoxNews! #MAGA
8,610 Retweets **52,272** Likes
3:45 PM - 28 Apr 2018

Donald J. Trump ✓
@realDonaldTrump

Great evening last night in Washington, Michigan. The enthusiasm, knowledge and love in that room was unreal. To the many thousands of people who couldn't get in, I cherish you....and will be back!
21,203 Retweets **109,185** Likes
4:21 AM - 29 Apr 2018

Donald J. Trump ✓
@realDonaldTrump

While Washington, Michigan, was a big success, Washington, D.C., just didn't work. Everyone is talking about the fact that the White House Correspondents Dinner was a very big, boring bust...the so-called comedian really "bombed." @greggutfeld should host next year! @PeteHegseth
18,883 Retweets **85,594** Likes
4:45 AM - 29 Apr 2018

President Trumps Tweets 2018: A Historical Archive of President Trump's Tweets

Donald J. Trump ✓
@realDonaldTrump

Just got recent Poll - much higher than President O at same time....Well, much more has been accomplished!
26,971 Retweets **145,636** Likes
4:54 AM - 29 Apr 2018

Donald J. Trump ✓
@realDonaldTrump

"Trump's Triumphs are driving his critics Crazy!" Thank you Steve Hilton @NextRevFNC, just want to do what is right for our wonderful U.S.A.
15,024 Retweets **74,873** Likes
6:29 PM - 29 Apr 2018

Donald J. Trump ✓
@realDonaldTrump

The White House Correspondents' Dinner was a failure last year, but this year was an embarrassment to everyone associated with it. The filthy "comedian" totally bombed (couldn't even deliver her lines-much like the Seth Meyers weak performance). Put Dinner to rest, or start over!
22,982 Retweets **107,294** Likes
7:38 PM - 29 Apr 2018

Donald J. Trump ✓
@realDonaldTrump

Headline: "Kim Prepared to Cede Nuclear Weapons if U.S. Pledges Not to Invade" - from the Failing New York Times. Also, will shut down Nuclear Test Site in May.
19,825 Retweets **92,349** Likes
7:59 PM - 29 Apr 2018

Donald J. Trump ✓
@realDonaldTrump

The White House Correspondents' Dinner is DEAD as we know it. This was a total disaster and an embarrassment to our great Country and all that it stands for. FAKE NEWS is alive and well and beautifully represented on Saturday night!
23,530 Retweets **108,339** Likes
5:10 AM - 30 Apr 2018

Donald J. Trump ✓
@realDonaldTrump

Numerous countries are being considered for the MEETING, but would Peace House/Freedom House, on the Border of North & South Korea, be a more Representative, Important and Lasting site than a third party country? Just asking!
20,356 Retweets **93,838** Likes
5:19 AM - 30 Apr 2018

Donald J. Trump ✓
@realDonaldTrump

I recently had a terrific meeting with a bipartisan group of freshman lawmakers who feel very strongly in favor of Congressional term limits. I gave them my full support and endorsement for their efforts. #DrainTheSwamp
27,369 Retweets **115,496** Likes
11:54 AM - 30 Apr 2018

Donald J. Trump ✓
@realDonaldTrump

The migrant 'caravan' that is openly defying our border shows how weak & ineffective U.S. immigration laws are. Yet Democrats like Jon Tester continue to support the open borders agenda – Tester even voted to protect Sanctuary Cities. We need lawmakers who will put America First.
24,433 Retweets **98,179** Likes
3:38 PM - 30 Apr 2018

Donald J. Trump ✓
@realDonaldTrump

During Small Business Week, we celebrate the great, hard-working entrepreneurs across our country who have started and operate a small business!
16,431 Retweets **88,382** Likes
3:39 PM - 30 Apr 2018

Donald J. Trump ✓
@realDonaldTrump

The Fake News is going crazy making up false stories and using only unnamed sources (who don't exist). They are totally unhinged, and the great success of this Administration is making them do and say things that even they can't believe they are saying. Truly bad people!
26,345 Retweets **110,396** Likes
3:49 PM - 30 Apr 2018

Donald J. Trump ✓
@realDonaldTrump

The White House is running very smoothly despite phony Witch Hunts etc. There is great Energy and unending Stamina, both necessary to get things done. We are accomplishing the unthinkable and setting positive records while doing so! Fake News is going "bonkers!"
21,890 Retweets **96,062** Likes
4:02 PM - 30 Apr 2018

Donald J. Trump ✓
@realDonaldTrump

So disgraceful that the questions concerning the Russian Witch Hunt were "leaked" to the media. No questions on Collusion. Oh, I see...you have a made up, phony crime, Collusion, that never existed, and an investigation begun with illegally leaked classified information. Nice!
26,438 Retweets **110,536** Likes
3:47 AM - 1 May 2018

Donald J. Trump ✓
@realDonaldTrump

Delegation heading to China to begin talks on the Massive Trade Deficit that has been created with our Country. Very much like North Korea, this should have been fixed years ago, not now. Same with other countries and NAFTA...but it will all get done. Great Potential for USA!
18,400 Retweets **83,668** Likes
4:00 AM - 1 May 2018

Donald J. Trump ✓
@realDonaldTrump

It would seem very hard to obstruct justice for a crime that never happened! Witch Hunt!
27,034 Retweets **126,090** Likes
4:34 AM - 1 May 2018

Donald J. Trump ✓
@realDonaldTrump

Yesterday, it was my great honor to welcome President @MBuhari of the Federal Republic of Nigeria to the @WhiteHouse!
12,797 Retweets **56,212** Likes
8:23 AM - 1 May 2018

Donald J. Trump ✓
@realDonaldTrump

Today I had the great honor of awarding the Commander-in-Chief's Trophy, for the first time in 21 years, to the @ArmyWP_Football Black Knights at the @WhiteHouse. Congratulations!
13,271 Retweets **63,850** Likes
9:57 AM - 1 May 2018

Donald J. Trump ✓
@realDonaldTrump

Congratulations @ArmyWP_Football!
10,922 Retweets **55,178** Likes
11:14 AM - 1 May 2018

Donald J. Trump ✓
@realDonaldTrump

Today, it was my great honor to thank and welcome heroic crew members and passengers of Southwest Airlines Flight 1380 at the @WhiteHouse!
15,475 Retweets **85,015** Likes
12:42 PM - 1 May 2018

Donald J. Trump ✓
@realDonaldTrump

There was no Collusion (it is a Hoax) and there is no Obstruction of Justice (that is a setup & trap). What there is is Negotiations going on with North Korea over Nuclear War, Negotiations going on with China over Trade Deficits, Negotiations on NAFTA, and much more. Witch Hunt!
26,992 Retweets **108,877** Likes
4:45 AM - 2 May 2018

Donald J. Trump ✓
@realDonaldTrump

"The questions are an intrusion into the President's Article 2 powers under the Constitution to fire any Executive Branch Employee...what the President was thinking is an outrageous.....as to the President's unfettered power to fire anyone..." Joe Digenova, former US Attorney
17,399 Retweets **67,707** Likes
6:23 AM - 2 May 2018

Donald J. Trump ✓
@realDonaldTrump

NEW BOOK - A MUST READ! "The Russia Hoax - The Illicit Scheme to Clear Hillary Clinton and Frame Donald Trump" by the brilliant Fox News Legal Analyst Gregg Jarrett. A sad chapter for law enforcement. A rigged system!
24,919 Retweets **88,965** Likes
6:33 AM - 2 May 2018

Donald J. Trump ✓
@realDonaldTrump

A Rigged System - They don't want to turn over Documents to Congress. What are they afraid of? Why so much redacting? Why such unequal "justice?" At some point I will have no choice but to use the powers granted to the Presidency and get involved!
31,510 Retweets **115,465** Likes
7:45 AM - 2 May 2018

Donald J. Trump ✓
@realDonaldTrump

Congratulations @SecPompeo!
13,720 Retweets **63,536** Likes
11:16 AM - 2 May 2018

 Donald J. Trump ✓
@realDonaldTrump

I have been briefed on the U.S. C-130 "Hercules" cargo plane from the Puerto Rico National Guard that crashed near Savannah Hilton Head International Airport. Please join me in thoughts and prayers for the victims, their families and the great men and women of the National Guard.
19,945 Retweets **94,872** Likes
1:27 PM - 2 May 2018

 Donald J. Trump ✓
@realDonaldTrump

"This isn't some game. You are screwing with the work of the president of the United States." John Dowd, March 2018. With North Korea, China, the Middle East and so much more, there is not much time to be thinking about this, especially since there was no Russian "Collusion."
23,303 Retweets **92,123** Likes
3:40 PM - 2 May 2018

 Donald J. Trump ✓
@realDonaldTrump

As everybody is aware, the past Administration has long been asking for three hostages to be released from a North Korean Labor camp, but to no avail. Stay tuned!
23,236 Retweets **106,926** Likes
5:53 PM - 2 May 2018

 Donald J. Trump ✓
@realDonaldTrump

Ainsley Earnhardt, a truly great person, just wrote a wonderful book, "The Light Within Me," which is doing really well. She is very special and so is her new book...bring it to number one!
16,973 Retweets **85,852** Likes
8:37 PM - 2 May 2018

@realDonaldTrump

Our great financial team is in China trying to negotiate a level playing field on trade! I look forward to being with President Xi in the not too distant future. We will always have a good (great) relationship!
15,845 Retweets **78,483** Likes
8:45 PM - 2 May 2018

 Donald J. Trump ✓
@realDonaldTrump

Mr. Cohen, an attorney, received a monthly retainer, not from the campaign and having nothing to do with the campaign, from which he entered into, through reimbursement, a private contract between two parties, known as a non-disclosure agreement, or NDA. These agreements are.....
16,037 Retweets **71,577** Likes
3:46 AM - 3 May 2018

Donald J. Trump ✓
@realDonaldTrump

...very common among celebrities and people of wealth. In this case it is in full force and effect and will be used in Arbitration for damages against Ms. Clifford (Daniels). The agreement was used to stop the false and extortionist accusations made by her about an affair,......
16,677 Retweets **76,516** Likes
3:54 AM - 3 May 2018

Donald J. Trump ◎
@realDonaldTrump

...despite already having signed a detailed letter admitting that there was no affair. Prior to its violation by Ms. Clifford and her attorney, this was a private agreement. Money from the campaign, or campaign contributions, played no roll in this transaction.

17,510 Retweets **84,096** Likes
4:00 AM - 3 May 2018

Donald J. Trump ◎
@realDonaldTrump

Today, it was my great honor to celebrate the #NationalDayOfPrayer at the @WhiteHouse, in the Rose Garden!

13,486 Retweets **61,711** Likes
9:27 AM - 3 May 2018

Donald J. Trump ◎
@realDonaldTrump

This spring marks 4yrs since the Phoenix VA crisis. We won't forget what happened to our GREAT VETS. Choice is vital, but the program needs work & is running out of $. Congress must fix Choice Program by Memorial Day so VETS can get the care they deserve. I will sign immediately!

17,675 Retweets **76,734** Likes
9:49 AM - 3 May 2018

Donald J. Trump ◎
@realDonaldTrump

#NationalDayOfPrayer

15,879 Retweets **69,146** Likes
11:20 AM - 3 May 2018

Donald J. Trump ◎
@realDonaldTrump

Our Southern Border is under siege. Congress must act now to change our weak and ineffective immigration laws. Must build a Wall. Mexico, which has a massive crime problem, is doing little to help!

19,564 Retweets **81,112** Likes
3:22 AM - 4 May 2018

Donald J. Trump ◎
@realDonaldTrump

Because Jobs in the U.S. are doing so well, Americans receiving unemployment aid is the lowest since 1973. Great!

22,674 Retweets **111,048** Likes
3:28 AM - 4 May 2018

Donald J. Trump ◎
@realDonaldTrump

Andy McCarthy will be on @LouDobbs tonight. 7:00 P.M. , @FoxBusiness.

6,073 Retweets **32,879** Likes
3:37 AM - 4 May 2018

Donald J. Trump ◎
@realDonaldTrump

NBC NEWS is wrong again! They cite "sources" which are constantly wrong. Problem is, like so many others, the sources probably don't exist, they are fabricated, fiction! NBC, my former home with the Apprentice, is now as bad as Fake News CNN. Sad!

20,942 Retweets **87,371** Likes
3:45 AM - 4 May 2018

Donald J. Trump ✓
@realDonaldTrump

Going to Dallas (the GREAT State of Texas) today. Leaving soon!
12,482 Retweets **83,711** Likes
3:57 AM - 4 May 2018

Donald J. Trump ✓
@realDonaldTrump

JUST OUT: 3.9% Unemployment. 4% is Broken! In the meantime, WITCH HUNT!
30,969 Retweets **137,773** Likes
6:27 AM - 4 May 2018

Donald J. Trump ✓
@realDonaldTrump

All of us here today are united by the same timeless values. We believe that our liberty is a gift from our creator, and that no Government can ever take it away. We believe in the rule of law - and we support the men and women of law enforcement. We have pride in our history...
18,431 Retweets **72,832** Likes
1:37 PM - 4 May 2018

Donald J. Trump ✓
@realDonaldTrump

Democrats and liberals in Congress want to disarm law-abiding Americans at the same time they are releasing dangerous criminal aliens and savage gang members onto our streets. Politicians who put criminal aliens before American Citizens should be voted out of office!
36,132 Retweets **130,728** Likes
2:58 PM - 4 May 2018

Donald J. Trump ✓
@realDonaldTrump

We are going to demand Congress secure the border in the upcoming CR. Illegal immigration must end!
24,799 Retweets **115,794** Likes
2:59 PM - 4 May 2018

Donald J. Trump ✓
@realDonaldTrump

I want to thank all of our friends and patriots at the @NRA. We will never fail, and we will always protect your Second Amendment! God Bless you, and God Bless America!
18,287 Retweets **74,763** Likes
3:56 PM - 4 May 2018

Donald J. Trump ✓
@realDonaldTrump

Great book just out by very successful businessman @AndyPuzder. Always known as somebody who knows how to win, "Capitalist Comeback" will be a big hit!
9,758 Retweets **50,888** Likes
5:08 PM - 4 May 2018

Donald J. Trump ✓
@realDonaldTrump

Just returned home to the beautiful White House, from Dallas, where the Arena was packed to the rafters with the great fans and supporters of the @NRA. It was so wonderful to be there!
18,366 Retweets **97,524** Likes
5:17 PM - 4 May 2018

Donald J. Trump ✓
@realDonaldTrump

Our high level delegation is on the way back from China where they had long meetings with Chinese leaders and business representatives. We will be meeting tomorrow to determine the results, but it is hard for China in that they have become very spoiled with U.S. trade wins!
17,531 Retweets **81,030** Likes
5:31 PM - 4 May 2018

Donald J. Trump ✓
@realDonaldTrump

Thank you Cleveland, Ohio!
16,132 Retweets **77,424** Likes
2:35 PM - 5 May 2018

Donald J. Trump ✓
@realDonaldTrump

To the great people of West Virginia we have, together, a really great chance to keep making a big difference. Problem is, Don Blankenship, currently running for Senate, can't win the General Election in your State...No way! Remember Alabama. Vote Rep. Jenkins or A.G. Morrisey!
14,986 Retweets **59,710** Likes
3:53 AM - 7 May 2018

Donald J. Trump ✓
@realDonaldTrump

My highly respected nominee for CIA Director, Gina Haspel, has come under fire because she was too tough on Terrorists. Think of that, in these very dangerous times, we have the most qualified person, a woman, who Democrats want OUT because she is too tough on terror. Win Gina!
24,905 Retweets **92,738** Likes
4:04 AM - 7 May 2018

Donald J. Trump ✓
@realDonaldTrump

The Russia Witch Hunt is rapidly losing credibility. House Intelligence Committee found No Collusion, Coordination or anything else with Russia. So now the Probe says OK, what else is there? How about Obstruction for a made up, phony crime.There is no O, it's called Fighting Back
21,599 Retweets **90,295** Likes
4:27 AM - 7 May 2018

Donald J. Trump ✓
@realDonaldTrump

The 13 Angry Democrats in charge of the Russian Witch Hunt are starting to find out that there is a Court System in place that actually protects people from injustice...and just wait 'till the Courts get to see your unrevealed Conflicts of Interest!
29,963 Retweets **110,027** Likes
4:39 AM - 7 May 2018

Donald J. Trump ✓
@realDonaldTrump

"The Great Revolt" by Salena Zito and Brad Todd does much to tell the story of our great Election victory. The Forgotten Men & Women are forgotten no longer!
12,422 Retweets **58,674** Likes
6:00 AM - 7 May 2018

Donald J. Trump ✓
@realDonaldTrump

Good luck to Ric Grenell, our new Ambassador to Germany. A great and talented guy, he will represent our Country well!
11,874 Retweets **65,137** Likes
6:05 AM - 7 May 2018

Donald J. Trump ✓
@realDonaldTrump

Lisa Page, who may hold the record for the most Emails in the shortest period of time (to her Lover, Peter S), and attorney Baker, are out at the FBI as part of the Probers getting caught? Why is Peter S still there? What a total mess. Our Country has to get back to Business!
21,678 Retweets **87,664** Likes
6:29 AM - 7 May 2018

Donald J. Trump ✓
@realDonaldTrump

Is this Phony Witch Hunt going to go on even longer so it wrongfully impacts the Mid-Term Elections, which is what the Democrats always intended? Republicans better get tough and smart before it is too late!
23,371 Retweets **95,113** Likes
6:35 AM - 7 May 2018

Donald J. Trump ✓
@realDonaldTrump

The United States does not need John Kerry's possibly illegal Shadow Diplomacy on the very badly negotiated Iran Deal. He was the one that created this MESS in the first place!
33,028 Retweets **118,444** Likes
7:08 AM - 7 May 2018

Donald J. Trump ✓
@realDonaldTrump

National Prescription Drug #TakeBackDay numbers are in! Another record broken: nearly 1 MILLION pounds of Rx pills disposed! Let's keep fighting this opioid epidemic, America!
13,889 Retweets **67,219** Likes
10:20 AM - 7 May 2018

Donald J. Trump ✓
@realDonaldTrump

I will be announcing my decision on the Iran Deal tomorrow from the White House at 2:00pm.
27,350 Retweets **111,859** Likes
11:44 AM - 7 May 2018

Donald J. Trump ✓
@realDonaldTrump

Gina Haspel, my highly respected nominee to lead the CIA, is being praised for the fact that she has been, and alway will be, TOUGH ON TERROR! This is a woman who has been a leader wherever she has gone. The CIA wants her to lead them into America's bright and glorious future!
20,725 Retweets **91,660** Likes
4:09 AM - 8 May 2018

Donald J. Trump ✓
@realDonaldTrump

I will be speaking to my friend, President Xi of China, this morning at 8:30. The primary topics will be Trade, where good things will happen, and North Korea, where relationships and trust are building.
17,027 Retweets **86,673** Likes
4:22 AM - 8 May 2018

Donald J. Trump
@realDonaldTrump

John Kerry can't get over the fact that he had his chance and blew it! Stay away from negotiations John, you are hurting your country!

33,731 Retweets **138,154** Likes
4:30 AM - 8 May 2018

Donald J. Trump
@realDonaldTrump

Statement on the Iran Nuclear Deal

27,635 Retweets **90,458** Likes
11:52 AM - 8 May 2018

Donald J. Trump
@realDonaldTrump

The Iran Deal is defective at its core. If we do nothing, we know what will happen. In just a short time, the world's leading state sponsor of terror will be on the cusp of acquiring the world's most dangerous weapons....

24,488 Retweets **95,878** Likes
3:11 PM - 8 May 2018

Donald J. Trump
@realDonaldTrump

The Republican Party had a great night. Tremendous voter energy and excitement, and all candidates are those who have a great chance of winning in November. The Economy is sooo strong, and with Nancy Pelosi wanting to end the big Tax Cuts and Raise Taxes, why wouldn't we win?

19,227 Retweets **83,243** Likes
4:24 AM - 9 May 2018

Donald J. Trump
@realDonaldTrump

The Fake News is working overtime. Just reported that, despite the tremendous success we are having with the economy & all things else, 91% of the Network News about me is negative (Fake). Why do we work so hard in working with the media when it is corrupt? Take away credentials?

27,761 Retweets **120,207** Likes
4:38 AM - 9 May 2018

Donald J. Trump
@realDonaldTrump

Candace Owens of Turning Point USA is having a big impact on politics in our Country. She represents an ever expanding group of very smart "thinkers," and it is wonderful to watch and hear the dialogue going on...so good for our Country!

33,578 Retweets **137,792** Likes
4:48 AM - 9 May 2018

Donald J. Trump
@realDonaldTrump

Congratulations to Mike Dewine on his big win in the Great State of Ohio. He will be a great Governor with a heavy focus on HealthCare and Jobs. His Socialist opponent in November should not do well, a big failure in last job!

13,651 Retweets **66,703** Likes
5:00 AM - 9 May 2018

Donald J. Trump ✓
@realDonaldTrump

I am pleased to inform you that Secretary of State Mike Pompeo is in the air and on his way back from North Korea with the 3 wonderful gentlemen that everyone is looking so forward to meeting. They seem to be in good health. Also, good meeting with Kim Jong Un. Date & Place set.
45,129 Retweets **168,836** Likes
5:30 AM - 9 May 2018

Donald J. Trump ✓
@realDonaldTrump

Secretary Pompeo and his "guests" will be landing at Andrews Air Force Base at 2:00 A.M. in the morning. I will be there to greet them. Very exciting!
27,624 Retweets **121,081** Likes
5:35 AM - 9 May 2018

Donald J. Trump ✓
@realDonaldTrump

The Failing New York Times criticized Secretary of State Pompeo for being AWOL (missing), when in fact he was flying to North Korea. Fake News, so bad!
26,369 Retweets **106,024** Likes
3:38 PM - 9 May 2018

Donald J. Trump ✓
@realDonaldTrump

Looking forward to greeting the Hostages (no longer) at 2:00 A.M.
18,408 Retweets **109,817** Likes
3:41 PM - 9 May 2018

Donald J. Trump ✓
@realDonaldTrump

Gina Haspel did a spectacular job today. There is nobody even close to run the CIA!
19,144 Retweets **96,939** Likes
7:19 PM - 9 May 2018

Donald J. Trump ✓
@realDonaldTrump

On behalf of the American people, WELCOME HOME!
49,906 Retweets **190,559** Likes
3:01 AM - 10 May 2018

Donald J. Trump ✓
@realDonaldTrump

Senator Cryin' Chuck Schumer fought hard against the Bad Iran Deal, even going at it with President Obama, & then Voted AGAINST it! Now he says I should not have terminated the deal - but he doesn't really believe that! Same with Comey. Thought he was terrible until I fired him!
26,899 Retweets **107,059** Likes
7:30 AM - 10 May 2018

Donald J. Trump ✓
@realDonaldTrump

Five Most Wanted leaders of ISIS just captured!
68,865 Retweets **301,809** Likes
7:33 AM - 10 May 2018

President Trumps Tweets 2018: A Historical Archive of President Trump's Tweets

Donald J. Trump ✓
@realDonaldTrump

The highly anticipated meeting between Kim Jong Un and myself will take place in Singapore on June 12th. We will both try to make it a very special moment for World Peace!
62,922 Retweets **237,845** Likes
7:37 AM - 10 May 2018

Donald J. Trump ✓
@realDonaldTrump

Thank you Indiana! #MAGA
17,926 Retweets **83,089** Likes
5:49 PM - 10 May 2018

Donald J. Trump ✓
@realDonaldTrump

Today, my Administration is launching the most sweeping action in history to lower the price of prescription drugs for the American People. We will have tougher negotiation, more competition, and much lower prices at the pharmacy counter!
22,444 Retweets **92,740** Likes
12:30 PM - 11 May 2018

Donald J. Trump ✓
@realDonaldTrump

The American people deserve a healthcare system that takes care of them – not one that takes advantage of them. We will work every day to ensure all Americans have access to the quality, affordable medication they need and deserve. We will not rest until the job is done!
20,106 Retweets **87,242** Likes
1:56 PM - 11 May 2018

Donald J. Trump ✓
@realDonaldTrump

Big week next week when the American Embassy in Israel will be moved to Jerusalem. Congratulations to all!
31,130 Retweets **145,690** Likes
4:39 PM - 11 May 2018

Donald J. Trump ✓
@realDonaldTrump

Why doesn't the Fake News Media state that the Trump Administration's Anti-Trust Division has been, and is, opposed to the AT&T purchase of Time Warner in a currently ongoing Trial. Such a disgrace in reporting!
22,854 Retweets **94,539** Likes
4:49 PM - 11 May 2018

Donald J. Trump ✓
@realDonaldTrump

North Korea has announced that they will dismantle Nuclear Test Site this month, ahead of the big Summit Meeting on June 12th. Thank you, a very smart and gracious gesture!
34,489 Retweets **162,839** Likes
2:08 PM - 12 May 2018

Donald J. Trump ✓
@realDonaldTrump

Iran's Military Budget is up more than 40% since the Obama negotiated Nuclear Deal was reached...just another indicator that it was all a big lie. But not anymore!
28,057 Retweets **112,009** Likes
3:02 PM - 12 May 2018

Donald J. Trump ✓
@realDonaldTrump

The Senate should get funding done before the August break, or NOT GO HOME. Wall and Border Security should be included. Also waiting for approval of almost 300 nominations, worst in history. Democrats are doing everything possible to obstruct, all they know how to do. STAY!
31,475 Retweets **115,894** Likes
3:20 PM - 12 May 2018

Donald J. Trump ✓
@realDonaldTrump

Happy Mother's Day!!!
29,961 Retweets **132,005** Likes
5:29 AM - 13 May 2018

Donald J. Trump ✓
@realDonaldTrump

President Xi of China, and I, are working together to give massive Chinese phone company, ZTE, a way to get back into business, fast. Too many jobs in China lost. Commerce Department has been instructed to get it done!
17,379 Retweets **84,164** Likes
8:01 AM - 13 May 2018

Donald J. Trump ✓
@realDonaldTrump

China and the United States are working well together on trade, but past negotiations have been so one sided in favor of China, for so many years, that it is hard for them to make a deal that benefits both countries. But be cool, it will all work out!
19,916 Retweets **101,153** Likes
12:22 PM - 13 May 2018

Donald J. Trump ✓
@realDonaldTrump

Remember how badly Iran was behaving with the Iran Deal in place. They were trying to take over the Middle East by whatever means necessary. Now, that will not happen!
27,863 Retweets **125,028** Likes
1:11 PM - 13 May 2018

Donald J. Trump ✓
@realDonaldTrump

So sad to see the Terror Attack in Paris. At some point countries will have to open their eyes & see what is really going on. This kind of sickness & hatred is not compatible with a loving, peaceful, & successful country! Changes to our thought process on terror must be made.
31,816 Retweets **135,139** Likes
5:03 PM - 13 May 2018

Donald J. Trump ✓
@realDonaldTrump

U.S. Embassy opening in Jerusalem will be covered live on @FoxNews & @FoxBusiness. Lead up to 9:00 A.M. (eastern) event has already begun. A great day for Israel!
17,864 Retweets **85,368** Likes
3:54 AM - 14 May 2018

Donald J. Trump ✓
@realDonaldTrump

Big day for Israel. Congratulations!
31,824 Retweets **167,314** Likes
6:36 AM - 14 May 2018

President Trumps Tweets 2018: A Historical Archive of President Trump's Tweets

Donald J. Trump
@realDonaldTrump

#USEmbassyJerusalem
15,995 Retweets **64,468** Likes
8:16 AM - 14 May 2018

Donald J. Trump
@realDonaldTrump

ZTE, the large Chinese phone company, buys a big percentage of individual parts from U.S. companies. This is also reflective of the larger trade deal we are negotiating with China and my personal relationship with President Xi.
12,492 Retweets **63,013** Likes
1:06 PM - 14 May 2018

Donald J. Trump
@realDonaldTrump

The so-called leaks coming out of the White House are a massive over exaggeration put out by the Fake News Media in order to make us look as bad as possible. With that being said, leakers are traitors and cowards, and we will find out who they are!
26,539 Retweets **118,557** Likes
1:46 PM - 14 May 2018

Donald J. Trump
@realDonaldTrump

Heading over to Walter Reed Medical Center to see our great First Lady, Melania. Successful procedure, she is in good spirits. Thank you to all of the well-wishers!
22,743 Retweets **149,307** Likes
2:09 PM - 14 May 2018

Donald J. Trump
@realDonaldTrump

Our great First Lady is doing really well. Will be leaving hospital in 2 or 3 days. Thank you for so much love and support!
21,157 Retweets **159,303** Likes
5:26 AM - 15 May 2018

Donald J. Trump
@realDonaldTrump

Trade negotiations are continuing with China. They have been making hundreds of billions of dollars a year from the U.S., for many years. Stay tuned!
14,876 Retweets **78,011** Likes
5:35 AM - 15 May 2018

Donald J. Trump
@realDonaldTrump

Can you believe that with all of the made up, unsourced stories I get from the Fake News Media, together with the $10,000,000 Russian Witch Hunt (there is no Collusion), I now have my best Poll Numbers in a year. Much of the Media may be corrupt, but the People truly get it!
32,019 Retweets **140,443** Likes
7:08 AM - 15 May 2018

Donald J. Trump
@realDonaldTrump

Nebraska - make sure you get out to the polls and VOTE for Deb Fischer today!
12,007 Retweets **46,387** Likes
10:30 AM - 15 May 2018

Donald J. Trump ✓
@realDonaldTrump

Today is one of the most important and solemn occasions of the year – the day we pay tribute to the Law Enforcement Heroes who gave their lives in the line of duty. They made the ultimate sacrifice so that we could live in safety and peace. We stand with our police (HEROES) 100%!
18,688 Retweets **83,239** Likes
11:39 AM - 15 May 2018

Donald J. Trump ✓
@realDonaldTrump

#PeaceOfficersMemorialDay
11,165 Retweets **49,721** Likes
11:56 AM - 15 May 2018

Donald J. Trump ✓
@realDonaldTrump

Thank you to the Washington Examiner and @CortesSteve on the great article - on WINNING!
11,877 Retweets **48,828** Likes
1:29 PM - 15 May 2018

Donald J. Trump ✓
@realDonaldTrump

Congratulations to Lou Barletta of Pennsylvania. He will be a great Senator and will represent his people well - like they haven't been represented in many years. Lou is a friend of mine and a special guy, he will very much help MAKE AMERICA GREAT AGAIN!
17,390 Retweets **86,938** Likes
5:07 AM - 16 May 2018

Donald J. Trump ✓
@realDonaldTrump

Congratulations to Deb Fischer. The people of Nebraska have seen what a great job she is doing - and it showed up at the ballot box! #MAGA
12,282 Retweets **65,164** Likes
5:25 AM - 16 May 2018

Donald J. Trump ✓
@realDonaldTrump

The Washington Post and CNN have typically written false stories about our trade negotiations with China. Nothing has happened with ZTE except as it pertains to the larger trade deal. Our country has been losing hundreds of billions of dollars a year with China...
13,454 Retweets **58,814** Likes
6:09 AM - 16 May 2018

Donald J. Trump ✓
@realDonaldTrump

...We have not seen China's demands yet, which should be few in that previous U.S. Administrations have done so poorly in negotiating. China has seen our demands. There has been no folding as the media would love people to believe, the meetings...
8,977 Retweets **44,044** Likes
6:09 AM - 16 May 2018

Donald J. Trump ✓
@realDonaldTrump

...haven't even started yet! The U.S. has very little to give, because it has given so much over the years. China has much to give!
9,560 Retweets **47,640** Likes
6:09 AM - 16 May 2018

Donald J. Trump ✓
@realDonaldTrump

House votes today on Choice/MISSION Act. Who will stand with our Great Vets, caregivers, and Veterans Service Organizations? Must get Choice passed by Memorial Day!
15,110 Retweets **69,022** Likes
10:21 AM - 16 May 2018

Donald J. Trump ✓
@realDonaldTrump

Today, it was my great honor to welcome President Mirziyoyev of Uzbekistan to the @WhiteHouse!
8,504 Retweets **46,023** Likes
10:50 AM - 16 May 2018

Donald J. Trump ✓
@realDonaldTrump

Lou Barletta will be a great Senator for Pennsylvania but his opponent, Bob Casey, has been a do-nothing Senator who only shows up at election time. He votes along the Nancy Pelosi, Elizabeth Warren lines, loves sanctuary cities, bad and expensive healthcare...
14,350 Retweets **57,936** Likes
11:40 AM - 16 May 2018

Donald J. Trump ✓
@realDonaldTrump

...and voted against the massive Tax Cut Bill. He's also weak on borders and crime. Sadly, our great Military and Vets mean nothing to Bobby Jr. Lou Barletta will win! #MAGA
9,557 Retweets **44,552** Likes
11:40 AM - 16 May 2018

Donald J. Trump ✓
@realDonaldTrump

Gina Haspel is one step closer to leading our brave men and women at the CIA. She is exceptionally qualified and the Senate should confirm her immediately. We need her to keep our great country safe! #ConfirmGina
17,153 Retweets **82,321** Likes
3:57 PM - 16 May 2018

Donald J. Trump ✓
@realDonaldTrump

Congratulations America, we are now into the second year of the greatest Witch Hunt in American History...and there is still No Collusion and No Obstruction. The only Collusion was that done by Democrats who were unable to win an Election despite the spending of far more money!
30,199 Retweets **125,633** Likes
4:28 AM - 17 May 2018

Donald J. Trump ✓
@realDonaldTrump

Wow, word seems to be coming out that the Obama FBI "SPIED ON THE TRUMP CAMPAIGN WITH AN EMBEDDED INFORMANT." Andrew McCarthy says, "There's probably no doubt that they had at least one confidential informant in the campaign." If so, this is bigger than Watergate!
34,113 Retweets **115,217** Likes
5:45 AM - 17 May 2018

Donald J. Trump ✓
@realDonaldTrump

Despite the disgusting, illegal and unwarranted Witch Hunt, we have had the most successful first 17 month Administration in U.S. history - by far! Sorry to the Fake News Media and "Haters," but that's the way it is!
32,409 Retweets **137,132** Likes
6:52 AM - 17 May 2018

Donald J. Trump ✓
@realDonaldTrump

Congrats to the House for passing the VA MISSION Act yesterday. Without this funding our veterans will be forced to stand in never ending lines in order to receive care. Putting politics over our veterans care is UNACCEPTABLE – Senate must vote yes on this bill by Memorial Day!
19,148 Retweets **80,528** Likes
8:25 AM - 17 May 2018

Donald J. Trump ✓
@realDonaldTrump

Congratulations to our new CIA Director, Gina Haspel!
18,885 Retweets **83,891** Likes
2:00 PM - 17 May 2018

Donald J. Trump ✓
@realDonaldTrump

Talking trade with the Vice Premier of the People's Republic of China, Liu He.
8,042 Retweets **43,309** Likes
2:27 PM - 17 May 2018

Donald J. Trump ✓
@realDonaldTrump

Great talk with my friend President Mauricio Macri of Argentina this week. He is doing such a good job for Argentina. I support his vision for transforming his country's economy and unleashing its potential!
16,782 Retweets **82,601** Likes
2:53 PM - May 17 2018

Donald J. Trump ✓
@realDonaldTrump

Tomorrow, the House will vote on a strong Farm Bill, which includes work requirements. We must support our Nation's great farmers!
14,313 Retweets **73,335** Likes
3:14 PM - 17 May 2018

Donald J. Trump ✓
@realDonaldTrump

It was my great honor to visit with our HEROES last night at Walter Reed Medical Center. There is nobody like them!
13,429 Retweets **72,082** Likes
3:17 PM - 17 May 2018

Donald J. Trump ✓
@realDonaldTrump

"Apparently the DOJ put a Spy in the Trump Campaign. This has never been done before and by any means necessary, they are out to frame Donald Trump for crimes he didn't commit." David Asman @LouDobbs @GreggJarrett Really bad stuff!
21,466 Retweets **75,730** Likes
3:24 AM - 18 May 2018

President Trumps Tweets 2018: A Historical Archive of President Trump's Tweets

Donald J. Trump ✓
@realDonaldTrump

Fake News Media had me calling Immigrants, or Illegal Immigrants, "Animals." Wrong! They were begrudgingly forced to withdraw their stories. I referred to MS 13 Gang Members as "Animals," a big difference - and so true. Fake News got it purposely wrong, as usual!

43,408 Retweets **160,867** Likes
3:51 AM - 18 May 2018

Donald J. Trump ✓
@realDonaldTrump

Why isn't disgraced FBI official Andrew McCabe being investigated for the $700,000 Crooked Hillary Democrats in Virginia, led by Clinton best friend Terry M (under FBI investigation that they killed) gave to McCabe's wife in her run for office? Then dropped case on Clinton!

24,058 Retweets **88,886** Likes
6:38 AM - 18 May 2018

Donald J. Trump ✓
@realDonaldTrump

Reports are there was indeed at least one FBI representative implanted, for political purposes, into my campaign for president. It took place very early on, and long before the phony Russia Hoax became a "hot" Fake News story. If true - all time biggest political scandal!

27,122 Retweets **89,902** Likes
6:50 AM - 18 May 2018

Donald J. Trump ✓
@realDonaldTrump

School shooting in Texas. Early reports not looking good. God bless all!

17,610 Retweets **94,775** Likes
8:05 AM - 18 May 2018

Donald J. Trump ✓
@realDonaldTrump

We grieve for the terrible loss of life, and send our support and love to everyone affected by this horrible attack in Texas. To the students, families, teachers and personnel at Santa Fe High School – we are with you in this tragic hour, and we will be with you forever...

17,833 Retweets **81,252** Likes
9:34 AM - 18 May 2018

Donald J. Trump ✓
@realDonaldTrump

America is a Nation that believes in the power of redemption. America is a Nation that believes in second chances - and America is a Nation that believes that the best is always yet to come! #PrisonReform

14,474 Retweets **61,820** Likes
1:22 PM - 18 May 2018

Donald J. Trump ✓
@realDonaldTrump

Just met with UN Secretary-General António Guterres who is working hard to "Make the United Nations Great Again." When the UN does more to solve conflicts around the world, it means the U.S. has less to do and we save money. @NikkiHaley is doing a fantastic job!

10,937 Retweets **52,364** Likes
1:41 PM - 18 May 2018

Donald J. Trump ✓
@realDonaldTrump

California finally deserves a great Governor, one who understands borders, crime and lowering taxes. John Cox is the man - he'll be the best Governor you've ever had. I fully endorse John Cox for Governor and look forward to working with him to Make California Great Again!
25,000 Retweets **102,430** Likes
3:00 PM - 18 May 2018

Donald J. Trump ✓
@realDonaldTrump

America is blessed with extraordinary energy abundance, including more than 250 years worth of beautiful clean coal. We have ended the war on coal, and will continue to work to promote American energy dominance!
20,200 Retweets **99,464** Likes
3:57 PM - 18 May 2018

Donald J. Trump ✓
@realDonaldTrump

Happy #ArmedForcesDay to our GREAT military men and women for their selfless service to our Nation!
17,495 Retweets **76,249** Likes
11:00 AM - 19 May 2018

Donald J. Trump ✓
@realDonaldTrump

Great to have our incredible First Lady back home in the White House. Melania is feeling and doing really well. Thank you for all of your prayers and best wishes!
23,722 Retweets **159,552** Likes
11:37 AM - 19 May 2018

Donald J. Trump ✓
@realDonaldTrump

If the FBI or DOJ was infiltrating a campaign for the benefit of another campaign, that is a really big deal. Only the release or review of documents that the House Intelligence Committee (also, Senate Judiciary) is asking for can give the conclusive answers. Drain the Swamp!
36,127 Retweets **127,129** Likes
2:27 PM - 19 May 2018

Donald J. Trump ✓
@realDonaldTrump

Things are really getting ridiculous. The Failing and Crooked (but not as Crooked as Hillary Clinton) @nytimes has done a long & boring story indicating that the World's most expensive Witch Hunt has found nothing on Russia & me so now they are looking at the rest of the World!
22,894 Retweets **88,155** Likes
6:04 AM - 20 May 2018

Donald J. Trump ✓
@realDonaldTrump

....At what point does this soon to be $20,000,000 Witch Hunt, composed of 13 Angry and Heavily Conflicted Democrats and two people who have worked for Obama for 8 years, STOP! They have found no Collusion with Russia, No Obstruction, but they aren't looking at the corruption...
26,935 Retweets **100,528** Likes
6:11 AM - 20 May 2018

Donald J. Trump ✓
@realDonaldTrump

...in the Hillary Clinton Campaign where she deleted 33,000 Emails, got $145,000,000 while Secretary of State, paid McCabes wife $700,000 (and got off the FBI hook along with Terry M) and so much more. Republicans and real Americans should start getting tough on this Scam.
31,520 Retweets **115,544** Likes
6:19 AM - 20 May 2018

Donald J. Trump ✓
@realDonaldTrump

Now that the Witch Hunt has given up on Russia and is looking at the rest of the World, they should easily be able to take it into the Mid-Term Elections where they can put some hurt on the Republican Party. Don't worry about Dems FISA Abuse, missing Emails or Fraudulent Dossier!
23,569 Retweets **91,219** Likes
6:29 AM - 20 May 2018

Donald J. Trump ✓
@realDonaldTrump

What ever happened to the Server, at the center of so much Corruption, that the Democratic National Committee REFUSED to hand over to the hard charging (except in the case of Democrats) FBI? They broke into homes & offices early in the morning, but were afraid to take the Server?
32,045 Retweets **109,043** Likes
6:37 AM - 20 May 2018

Donald J. Trump ✓
@realDonaldTrump

....and why hasn't the Podesta brother been charged and arrested, like others, after being forced to close down his very large and successful firm? Is it because he is a VERY well connected Democrat working in the Swamp of Washington, D.C.?
30,789 Retweets **114,336** Likes
7:04 AM - 20 May 2018

Donald J. Trump ✓
@realDonaldTrump

The Witch Hunt finds no Collusion with Russia - so now they're looking at the rest of the World. Oh' great!
19,699 Retweets **90,327** Likes
10:13 AM - 20 May 2018

Donald J. Trump ✓
@realDonaldTrump

I hereby demand, and will do so officially tomorrow, that the Department of Justice look into whether or not the FBI/DOJ infiltrated or surveilled the Trump Campaign for Political Purposes - and if any such demands or requests were made by people within the Obama Administration!
53,994 Retweets **183,696** Likes
10:37 AM - 20 May 2018

Donald J. Trump ✓
@realDonaldTrump

I ask Senator Chuck Schumer, why didn't President Obama & the Democrats do something about Trade with China, including Theft of Intellectual Property etc.? They did NOTHING! With that being said, Chuck & I have long agreed on this issue! Fair Trade, plus, with China will happen!
17,442 Retweets **78,313** Likes
4:21 AM - 21 May 2018

Donald J. Trump @realDonaldTrump

China has agreed to buy massive amounts of ADDITIONAL Farm/Agricultural Products - would be one of the best things to happen to our farmers in many years!
17,347 Retweets **80,202** Likes
4:27 AM - 21 May 2018

Donald J. Trump @realDonaldTrump

On China, Barriers and Tariffs to come down for first time.
11,787 Retweets **57,657** Likes
4:31 AM - 21 May 2018

Donald J. Trump @realDonaldTrump

China must continue to be strong & tight on the Border of North Korea until a deal is made. The word is that recently the Border has become much more porous and more has been filtering in. I want this to happen, and North Korea to be VERY successful, but only after signing!
13,936 Retweets **64,527** Likes
4:40 AM - 21 May 2018

Donald J. Trump @realDonaldTrump

"John Brennan is panicking. He has disgraced himself, he has disgraced the Country, he has disgraced the entire Intelligence Community. He is the one man who is largely responsible for the destruction of American's faith in the Intelligence Community and in some people at the....
33,636 Retweets **113,672** Likes
4:53 AM - 21 May 2018

Donald J. Trump @realDonaldTrump

....top of the FBI. Brennan started this entire debacle about President Trump. We now know that Brennan had detailed knowledge of the (phony) Dossier...he knows about the Dossier, he denies knowledge of the Dossier, he briefs the Gang of 8 on the Hill about the Dossier, which....
21,045 Retweets **74,684** Likes
5:01 AM - 21 May 2018

Donald J. Trump @realDonaldTrump

...they then used to start an investigation about Trump. It is that simple. This guy is the genesis of this whole Debacle. This was a Political hit job, this was not an Intelligence Investigation. Brennan has disgraced himself, he's worried about staying out of Jail." Dan Bongino
22,897 Retweets **85,227** Likes
5:12 AM - 21 May 2018

Donald J. Trump @realDonaldTrump

The Wall Street Journal asks, "WHERE IN THE WORLD WAS BARACK OBAMA?" A very good question!
26,953 Retweets **114,177** Likes
5:51 AM - 21 May 2018

Donald J. Trump @realDonaldTrump

Under our potential deal with China, they will purchase from our Great American Farmers practically as much as our Farmers can produce.
20,464 Retweets **93,452** Likes
6:16 AM - 21 May 2018

Donald J. Trump
@realDonaldTrump

.@AsaHutchinson, the great Governor of Arkansas, is in a primary tomorrow. He has done an incredible job with a focus on lower taxes, border security, and crime prevention. Asa loves our military and our veterans. I fully endorse Asa for Governor!

18,313 Retweets **76,098** Likes
4:18 PM - 21 May 2018

Donald J. Trump
@realDonaldTrump

Today, it was my great honor to welcome President Moon Jae-in of the Republic of Korea to the @WhiteHouse!

13,963 Retweets **68,214** Likes
11:21 AM - 22 May 2018

Donald J. Trump
@realDonaldTrump

It was my honor to welcome @NASCAR Cup Series Champion @MartinTruex_Jr and his team to the @WhiteHouse yesterday!

10,776 Retweets **56,515** Likes
12:35 PM - 22 May 2018

Donald J. Trump
@realDonaldTrump

For the first time since Roe v. Wade, America has a Pro-Life President, a Pro-Life Vice President, a Pro-Life House of Representatives and 25 Pro-Life Republican State Capitals!

20,418 Retweets **83,467** Likes
5:40 PM - 22 May 2018

Donald J. Trump
@realDonaldTrump

If the person placed very early into my campaign wasn't a SPY put there by the previous Administration for political purposes, how come such a seemingly massive amount of money was paid for services rendered - many times higher than normal...

25,352 Retweets **92,898** Likes
6:13 PM - 22 May 2018

Donald J. Trump
@realDonaldTrump

...Follow the money! The spy was there early in the campaign and yet never reported Collusion with Russia, because there was no Collusion. He was only there to spy for political reasons and to help Crooked Hillary win - just like they did to Bernie Sanders, who got duped!

24,289 Retweets **85,532** Likes
6:13 PM - 22 May 2018

Donald J. Trump
@realDonaldTrump

@foxandfriends "New Bombshell in the Obama Spying Scandal. Did other Agencies SPY on Trump Campaign?" Even Clapper, worlds dumbest former Intelligence Head, who has the problem of lying a lot, used the word SPY when describing the illegal activities!

4,649 Retweets **11,397** Likes
3:45 AM - 23 May 2018

Donald J. Trump ✓
@realDonaldTrump

Look how things have turned around on the Criminal Deep State. They go after Phony Collusion with Russia, a made up Scam, and end up getting caught in a major SPY scandal the likes of which this country may never have seen before! What goes around, comes around!
34,137 Retweets **115,107** Likes
3:54 AM - 23 May 2018

Donald J. Trump ✓
@realDonaldTrump

"It's clear that they had eyes and ears all over the Trump Campaign" Judge Andrew Napolitano
15,403 Retweets **62,228** Likes
4:00 AM - 23 May 2018

Donald J. Trump ✓
@realDonaldTrump

SPYGATE could be one of the biggest political scandals in history!
24,518 Retweets **90,991** Likes
4:12 AM - 23 May 2018

Donald J. Trump ✓
@realDonaldTrump

Everybody is with Tomi Lahren, a truly outstanding and respected young woman! @foxandfriends
16,248 Retweets **88,285** Likes
4:22 AM - 23 May 2018

Donald J. Trump ✓
@realDonaldTrump

"Trump should be happy that the FBI was SPYING on his campaign" No, James Clapper, I am not happy. Spying on a campaign would be illegal, and a scandal to boot!
26,736 Retweets **94,546** Likes
4:33 AM - 23 May 2018

Donald J. Trump ✓
@realDonaldTrump

Our Trade Deal with China is moving along nicely, but in the end we will probably have to use a different structure in that this will be too hard to get done and to verify results after completion.
11,537 Retweets **57,699** Likes
4:55 AM - 23 May 2018

Donald J. Trump ✓
@realDonaldTrump

Big legislation will be signed by me shortly. After many years, RIGHT TO TRY and big changes to DODD FRANK.
13,988 Retweets **63,659** Likes
4:58 AM - 23 May 2018

Donald J. Trump ✓
@realDonaldTrump

There will be big news coming soon for our great American Autoworkers. After many decades of losing your jobs to other countries, you have waited long enough!
19,136 Retweets **87,991** Likes
6:18 AM - 23 May 2018

President Trumps Tweets 2018: A Historical Archive of President Trump's Tweets

Donald J. Trump ✓
@realDonaldTrump

WITCH HUNT!
23,707 Retweets **94,347** Likes
6:34 AM - 23 May 2018

Donald J. Trump ✓
@realDonaldTrump

Thank you @SBAList! #SBAGala
7,504 Retweets **34,365** Likes
9:19 AM - 23 May 2018

Donald J. Trump ✓
@realDonaldTrump

Today on Long Island, we were all moved to be joined by families who have suffered unthinkable heartbreak at the hands of MS-13. I was truly honored to be joined again by the courageous families who were my guests at the State of the Union...
13,822 Retweets **61,136** Likes
12:29 PM - 23 May 2018

Donald J. Trump ✓
@realDonaldTrump

Crippling loopholes in our laws have enabled MS-13 gang members and other criminals to infiltrate our communities - and Democrats in Congress REFUSE to close these loopholes, including the disgraceful practice known as Catch-and-Release. Democrats must abandon their resistance...
17,568 Retweets **63,373** Likes
12:35 PM - 23 May 2018

Donald J. Trump ✓
@realDonaldTrump

Thank you to all of the incredible law enforcement officers and firefighters in Bethpage, New York. Keep up the great work!
11,941 Retweets **58,450** Likes
4:41 PM - 23 May 2018

Donald J. Trump ✓
@realDonaldTrump

Great to be in New York for the day. Heading back to the @WhiteHouse now, lots of work to be done!
13,229 Retweets **69,464** Likes
5:08 PM - 23 May 2018

Donald J. Trump ✓
@realDonaldTrump

Will be interviewed on @foxandfriends tomorrow morning at 6:00 A.M. Enjoy!
12,512 Retweets **65,069** Likes
5:58 PM - 23 May 2018

Donald J. Trump ✓
@realDonaldTrump

Clapper has now admitted that there was Spying in my campaign. Large dollars were paid to the Spy, far beyond normal. Starting to look like one of the biggest political scandals in U.S. history. SPYGATE - a terrible thing!
31,366 Retweets **110,142** Likes
5:21 AM - 24 May 2018

Donald J. Trump ✓
@realDonaldTrump

Not surprisingly, the GREAT Men & Women of the FBI are starting to speak out against Comey, McCabe and all of the political corruption and poor leadership found within the top ranks of the FBI. Comey was a terrible and corrupt leader who inflicted great pain on the FBI! #SPYGATE
34535 Retweets **122597**Likes
5:34 AM - 24 May 2018

Donald J. Trump ✓
@realDonaldTrump

Sadly, I was forced to cancel the Summit Meeting in Singapore with Kim Jong Un.
16,919 Retweets **62,181** Likes
9:18 AM - 24 May 2018

Donald J. Trump ✓
@realDonaldTrump

It was my great honor to host a roundtable re: MS-13 yesterday in Bethpage, New York. Democrats must abandon their resistance to border security so that we can SUPPORT law enforcement and SAVE innocent lives!
12,964 Retweets **57,142** Likes
9:24 AM - 24 May 2018

Donald J. Trump ✓
@realDonaldTrump

I have decided to terminate the planned Summit in Singapore on June 12th. While many things can happen and a great opportunity lies ahead potentially, I believe that this is a tremendous setback for North Korea and indeed a setback for the world...
16,088 Retweets **62,717** Likes
9:57 AM - 24 May 2018

Donald J. Trump ✓
@realDonaldTrump

Today, it was my honor to sign #S2155, the "Economic Growth, Regulatory Relief, and Consumer Protection Act."
8,831 Retweets **39,293** Likes
10:54 AM - 24 May 2018

Donald J. Trump ✓
@realDonaldTrump

Today, it was my great honor to present the #MedalOfHonor to @USNavy (SEAL) Master Chief Special Warfare Operator Britt Slabinski in the East Room of the @WhiteHouse.
14,977 Retweets **70,215** Likes
2:18 PM - 24 May 2018

Donald J. Trump ✓
@realDonaldTrump

The Democrats are now alluding to the the concept that having an Informant placed in an opposing party's campaign is different than having a Spy, as illegal as that may be. But what about an "Informant" who is paid a fortune and who "sets up" way earlier than the Russian Hoax?
18,625 Retweets **68,649** Likes
5:04 AM - 25 May 2018

President Trumps Tweets 2018: A Historical Archive of President Trump's Tweets

Donald J. Trump ✓
@realDonaldTrump

Can anyone even imagine having Spies placed in a competing campaign, by the people and party in absolute power, for the sole purpose of political advantage and gain? And to think that the party in question, even with the expenditure of far more money, LOST!
23,521 Retweets **94,519** Likes
5:04 AM - 25 May 2018

Donald J. Trump ✓
@realDonaldTrump

"Everyone knows there was a Spy, and in fact the people who were involved in the Spying are admitting that there was a Spy...Widespread Spying involving multiple people." Mollie Hemingway, The Federalist Senior Editor But the corrupt Mainstream Media hates this monster story!
21,766 Retweets **78,598** Likes
5:04 AM - 25 May 2018

Donald J. Trump ✓
@realDonaldTrump

Democrats are so obviously rooting against us in our negotiations with North Korea. Just like they are coming to the defense of MS 13 thugs, saying that they are individuals & must be nurtured, or asking to end your big Tax Cuts & raise your taxes instead. Dems have lost touch!
26,952 Retweets **97,482** Likes
5:04 AM - 25 May 2018

Donald J. Trump ✓
@realDonaldTrump

Very good news to receive the warm and productive statement from North Korea. We will soon see where it will lead, hopefully to long and enduring prosperity and peace. Only time (and talent) will tell!
24,085 Retweets **101,539** Likes
5:14 AM - 25 May 2018

Donald J. Trump ✓
@realDonaldTrump

Today, it was my great honor to deliver the 2018 Commencement Address at the United States @NavalAcademy in Annapolis, Maryland. Congratulations! Good luck. Godspeed. And ANCHORS AWEIGH!
10,995 Retweets **54,433** Likes
10:12 AM - 25 May 2018

Donald J. Trump ✓
@realDonaldTrump

On behalf of the American People, CONGRATULATIONS! We love you!
18,660 Retweets **89,352** Likes
10:22 AM - 25 May 2018

Donald J. Trump ✓
@realDonaldTrump

To the @NavalAcademy Class of 2018, I say: We know you are up to the task. We know you will make us proud. We know that glory will be yours. Because you are WINNERS, you are WARRIORS, you are FIGHTERS, you are CHAMPIONS, and YOU will lead us to VICTORY! God Bless the U.S.A.!
17,499 Retweets **72,090** Likes
1:39 PM - 25 May 2018

Donald J. Trump ✓
@realDonaldTrump

Chicago Police have every right to legally protest against the mayor and an administration that just won't let them do their job. The killings are at a record pace and tough police work, which Chicago will not allow, would bring things back to order fast...the killings must stop!
25,737 Retweets **104,526** Likes
3:14 PM - 25 May 2018

Donald J. Trump ✓
@realDonaldTrump

Funny to watch the Democrats criticize Trade Deals being negotiated by me when they don't even know what the deals are and when for 8 years the Obama Administration did NOTHING on trade except let other countries rip off the United States. Lost almost $800 Billion/year under "O"
32,107 Retweets **118,321** Likes
3:45 PM - 25 May 2018

Donald J. Trump ✓
@realDonaldTrump

Senator Schumer and Obama Administration let phone company ZTE flourish with no security checks. I closed it down then let it reopen with high level security guarantees, change of management and board, must purchase U.S. parts and pay a $1.3 Billion fine. Dems do nothing....
24,835 Retweets **93,951** Likes
4:07 PM - 25 May 2018

Donald J. Trump ✓
@realDonaldTrump

...but complain and obstruct. They made only bad deals (Iran) and their so-called Trade Deals are the laughing stock of the world!
14,578 Retweets **65,667** Likes
4:13 PM - 25 May 2018

Donald J. Trump ✓
@realDonaldTrump

We are having very productive talks with North Korea about reinstating the Summit which, if it does happen, will likely remain in Singapore on the same date, June 12th., and, if necessary, will be extended beyond that date.
22,271 Retweets **90,098** Likes
5:37 PM - 25 May 2018

Donald J. Trump ✓
@realDonaldTrump

Good news about the release of the American hostage from Venezuela. Should be landing in D.C. this evening and be in the White House, with his family, at about 7:00 P.M. The great people of Utah will be very happy!
23,873 Retweets **96,129** Likes
6:22 AM - 26 May 2018

Donald J. Trump ✓
@realDonaldTrump

Put pressure on the Democrats to end the horrible law that separates children from there parents once they cross the Border into the U.S. Catch and Release, Lottery and Chain must also go with it and we MUST continue building the WALL! DEMOCRATS ARE PROTECTING MS-13 THUGS.
22,519 Retweets **90,018** Likes
6:59 AM - 26 May 2018

President Trumps Tweets 2018: A Historical Archive of President Trump's Tweets

Donald J. Trump @realDonaldTrump

Looking forward to seeing Joshua Holt this evening in the White House. The great people of Utah are Celebrating!
11,960 Retweets **59,892** Likes
7:38 AM - 26 May 2018

Donald J. Trump @realDonaldTrump

Thanks to very brave Teacher & Hero Jason Seaman of Noblesville, Indiana, for his heroic act in saving so many precious young lives. His quick and automatic action is being talked about all over the world!
22,282 Retweets **101,562** Likes
7:47 AM - 26 May 2018

Donald J. Trump @realDonaldTrump

Unlike what the Failing and Corrupt New York Times would like people to believe, there is ZERO disagreement within the Trump Administration as to how to deal with North Korea...and if there was, it wouldn't matter. The @nytimes has called me wrong right from the beginning!
15,224 Retweets **62,326** Likes
8:03 AM - 26 May 2018

Donald J. Trump @realDonaldTrump

The Failing @nytimes quotes "a senior White House official," who doesn't exist, as saying "even if the meeting were reinstated, holding it on June 12 would be impossible, given the lack of time and the amount of planning needed." WRONG AGAIN! Use real people, not phony sources.
22,560 Retweets **84,090** Likes
8:21 AM - 26 May 2018

Donald J. Trump @realDonaldTrump

With Spies, or "Informants" as the Democrats like to call them because it sounds less sinister (but it's not), all over my campaign, even from a very early date, why didn't the crooked highest levels of the FBI or "Justice" contact me to tell me of the phony Russia problem?
21,850 Retweets **82,408** Likes
12:28 PM - 26 May 2018

Donald J. Trump @realDonaldTrump

This whole Russia Probe is Rigged. Just an excuse as to why the Dems and Crooked Hillary lost the Election and States that haven't been lost in decades. 13 Angry Democrats, and all Dems if you include the people who worked for Obama for 8 years. #SPYGATE & CONFLICTS OF INTEREST!
21,733 Retweets **83,693** Likes
12:41 PM - 26 May 2018

Donald J. Trump @realDonaldTrump

When will the 13 Angry Democrats (& those who worked for President O), reveal their disqualifying Conflicts of Interest? It's been a long time now! Will they be indelibly written into the Report along with the fact that the only Collusion is with the Dems, Justice, FBI & Russia?
24,081 Retweets **90,904** Likes
12:56 PM - 26 May 2018

Donald J. Trump ⊙
@realDonaldTrump

WELCOME HOME JOSH!
23,012 Retweets **89,461** Likes
6:49 PM - 26 May 2018

Donald J. Trump ⊙
@realDonaldTrump

Who's going to give back the young and beautiful lives (and others) that have been devastated and destroyed by the phony Russia Collusion Witch Hunt? They journeyed down to Washington, D.C., with stars in their eyes and wanting to help our nation...They went back home in tatters!
21,683 Retweets **89,558** Likes
5:41 AM - 27 May 2018

Donald J. Trump ⊙
@realDonaldTrump

Fantastic to have 400,000 GREAT MEN & WOMEN of Rolling Thunder in D.C. showing their patriotism. They love our Country, they love our Flag, they stand for our National Anthem! Thanks to Executive Director Artie Muller.
26,645 Retweets **119,622** Likes
6:14 AM - 27 May 2018

Donald J. Trump ⊙
@realDonaldTrump

Why didn't the 13 Angry Democrats investigate the campaign of Crooked Hillary Clinton, many crimes, much Collusion with Russia? Why didn't the FBI take the Server from the DNC? Rigged Investigation!
27,160 Retweets **106,665** Likes
7:13 AM - 27 May 2018

Donald J. Trump ⊙
@realDonaldTrump

Our United States team has arrived in North Korea to make arrangements for the Summit between Kim Jong Un and myself. I truly believe North Korea has brilliant potential and will be a great economic and financial Nation one day. Kim Jong Un agrees with me on this. It will happen!
29,541 Retweets **119,545** Likes
1:09 PM - 27 May 2018

Donald J. Trump ⊙
@realDonaldTrump

Why didn't President Obama do something about the so-called Russian Meddling when he was told about it by the FBI before the Election? Because he thought Crooked Hillary was going to win, and he didn't want to upset the apple cart! He was in charge, not me, and did nothing.
34,148 Retweets **126,769** Likes
1:32 PM - 27 May 2018

Donald J. Trump ⊙
@realDonaldTrump

#MemorialDay
18,300 Retweets **71,269** Likes
4:01 AM - 28 May 2018

President Trumps Tweets 2018: A Historical Archive of President Trump's Tweets

Donald J. Trump ✓
@realDonaldTrump

Happy Memorial Day! Those who died for our great country would be very happy and proud at how well our country is doing today. Best economy in decades, lowest unemployment numbers for Blacks and Hispanics EVER (& women in 18years), rebuilding our Military and so much more. Nice!
27,460 Retweets **130,467** Likes
5:58 AM - 28 May 2018

Donald J. Trump ✓
@realDonaldTrump

"The President deserves some answers." @FoxNews in discussing "SPYGATE."
13,886 Retweets **62,886** Likes
6:55 AM - 28 May 2018

Donald J. Trump ✓
@realDonaldTrump

"Sally Yates is part of concerns people have raised about bias in the Justice Dept. I find her actions to be really quite unbelievable." Jonathan Turley
16,072 Retweets **66,471** Likes
7:08 AM - 28 May 2018

Donald J. Trump ✓
@realDonaldTrump

"We now find out that the Obama Administration put the opposing campaigns presidential candidate, or his campaign, under investigation. That raises legitimate questions. I just find this really odd...this goes to the heart of our electoral system." Jonathan Turley on @FoxNews
22,262 Retweets **80,702** Likes
7:32 AM - 28 May 2018

Donald J. Trump ✓
@realDonaldTrump

Thank you for joining us on this solemn day of remembrance. We are gathered here on the sacred soil of @ArlingtonNatl Cemetery to honor the lives and deeds of America's greatest heroes, the men and women who laid down their lives for our freedom. #MemorialDay
11,092 Retweets **52,534** Likes
10:13 AM - 28 May 2018

Donald J. Trump ✓
@realDonaldTrump

The heroes who rest in these hallowed fields, in cemeteries, battlefields, and burial grounds near and far are drawn the full tapestry of American life. They came from every generation from towering cities and wind swept prairies, from privilege and from poverty...
13,938 Retweets **65,498** Likes
10:14 AM - 28 May 2018

Donald J. Trump ✓
@realDonaldTrump

Our fallen heroes have not only written our history they have shaped our destiny. They saved the lives of the men and women with whom they served. They cared for their families more than anything in the world, they loved their families. They inspired their communities...
17,608 Retweets **80,464** Likes
10:19 AM - 28 May 2018

Donald J. Trump ✓
@realDonaldTrump

A Democratic lawmaker just introduced a bill to Repeal the GOP Tax Cuts (no chance). This is too good to be true for Republicans...Remember, the Nancy Pelosi Dems are also weak on Crime, the Border and want to be gentle and kind to MS-13 gang members...not good!
26,860 Retweets **95,744** Likes
2:22 PM - 28 May 2018

Donald J. Trump ✓
@realDonaldTrump

California has a rare opportunity to turn things around and solve its high crime, high tax, problems - along with so many others. On June 5th., vote for GOP Gubernatorial Candidate JOHN COX, a really good and highly competent man. He'll Make California Great Again!
24,860 Retweets **100,521** Likes
2:53 PM - 28 May 2018

Donald J. Trump ✓
@realDonaldTrump

Democrats mistakenly tweet 2014 pictures from Obama's term showing children from the Border in steel cages. They thought it was recent pictures in order to make us look bad, but backfires. Dems must agree to Wall and new Border Protection for good of country...Bipartisan Bill!
29,547 Retweets **104,188** Likes
3:07 AM - 29 May 2018

Donald J. Trump ✓
@realDonaldTrump

We have put a great team together for our talks with North Korea. Meetings are currently taking place concerning Summit, and more. Kim Young Chol, the Vice Chairman of North Korea, heading now to New York. Solid response to my letter, thank you!
17,016 Retweets **74,641** Likes
3:30 AM - 29 May 2018

Donald J. Trump ✓
@realDonaldTrump

"This investigation involved far more surveillance than we ever had any idea about. It wasn't just a wiretap against a campaign aide...it was secretly gathering information on the Trump Campaign...people call that Spying...this is unprecedented and scandalous." Mollie Hemingway
20,336 Retweets **75,856** Likes
3:49 AM - 29 May 2018

Donald J. Trump ✓
@realDonaldTrump

The 13 Angry Democrats (plus people who worked 8 years for Obama) working on the rigged Russia Witch Hunt, will be MEDDLING with the mid-term elections, especially now that Republicans (stay tough!) are taking the lead in Polls. There was no Collusion, except by the Democrats!
23,870 Retweets **97,966** Likes
4:00 AM - 29 May 2018

Donald J. Trump ✓
@realDonaldTrump

Why aren't the 13 Angry and heavily conflicted Democrats investigating the totally Crooked Campaign of totally Crooked Hillary Clinton. It's a Rigged Witch Hunt, that's why! Ask them if they enjoyed her after election celebration!
18,723 Retweets **79,525** Likes
4:09 AM - 29 May 2018

Donald J. Trump ✓
@realDonaldTrump

Sorry, I've got to start focusing my energy on North Korea Nuclear, bad Trade Deals, VA Choice, the Economy, rebuilding the Military, and so much more, and not on the Rigged Russia Witch Hunt that should be investigating Clinton/Russia/FBI/Justice/Obama/Comey/Lynch etc.

29,075 Retweets **121,391** Likes
4:27 AM - 29 May 2018

Donald J. Trump ✓
@realDonaldTrump

The Fake Mainstream Media has, from the time I announced I was running for President, run the most highly sophisticated & dishonest Disinformation Campaign in the history of politics. No matter how well WE do, they find fault. But the forgotten men & women WON, I'm President!

35,879 Retweets **139,197** Likes
6:30 AM - 29 May 2018

Donald J. Trump ✓
@realDonaldTrump

Rep.Trey Gowdy, "I don't think so, I think what the President is doing is expressing frustration that Attorney General Sessions should have shared these reasons for recusal before he took the job, not afterward. If I were the President and I picked someone to be the country's....

13,780 Retweets **58,646** Likes
5:46 AM - 30 May 2018

Donald J. Trump ✓
@realDonaldTrump

....chief law enforcement officer, and they told me later, 'oh by the way I'm not going to be able to participate in the most important case in the office, I would be frustrated too...and that's how I read that - Senator Sessions, why didn't you tell me before I picked you.....

15,677 Retweets **67,596** Likes
5:47 AM - 30 May 2018

Donald J. Trump ✓
@realDonaldTrump

....There are lots of really good lawyers in the country, he could have picked somebody else!" And I wish I did!

14,172 Retweets **71,673** Likes
5:47 AM - 30 May 2018

Donald J. Trump ✓
@realDonaldTrump

The Failing and Corrupt @nytimes estimated the crowd last night at "1000 people," when in fact it was many times that number - and the arena was rockin'. This is the way they demean and disparage. They are very dishonest people who don't "get" me, and never did!

19,627 Retweets **83,247** Likes
7:35 AM - 30 May 2018

Donald J. Trump ✓
@realDonaldTrump

Bob Iger of ABC called Valerie Jarrett to let her know that "ABC does not tolerate comments like those" made by Roseanne Barr. Gee, he never called President Donald J. Trump to apologize for the HORRIBLE statements made and said about me on ABC. Maybe I just didn't get the call?

45,555 Retweets **164,092** Likes
8:31 AM - 30 May 2018

Donald J. Trump ✓
@realDonaldTrump

Today I am proud to keep another promise to the American people as I sign the #RightToTry Legislation into law.
11,536 Retweets **58,157** Likes
10:09 AM - 30 May 2018

Donald J. Trump ✓
@realDonaldTrump

With the #RightToTry Law I signed today, patients with life threatening illnesses will finally have access to experimental treatments that could improve or even cure their conditions. These are experimental treatments and products that have shown great promise...
18,539 Retweets **78,198** Likes
10:11 AM - 30 May 2018

Donald J. Trump ✓
@realDonaldTrump

Moments ago, it was my great honor to sign #RightToTry into law!
12,871 Retweets **57,787** Likes
10:19 AM - 30 May 2018

Great meeting with @KimKardashian today, talked about prison reform and sentencing.
42,274 Retweets **158,925** Likes
3:59 PM - 30 May 2018

Donald J. Trump ✓
@realDonaldTrump

There is no one better to represent the people of N.Y. and Staten Island (a place I know very well) than @RepDanDonovan, who is strong on Borders & Crime, loves our Military & our Vets, voted for Tax Cuts and is helping me to Make America Great Again. Dan has my full endorsement!
12,558 Retweets **52,751** Likes
4:46 PM - 30 May 2018

Donald J. Trump ✓
@realDonaldTrump

Very importantly, @RepDanDonovan will win for the Republicans in November...and his opponent will not. Remember Alabama. We can't take any chances on losing to a Nancy Pelosi controlled Democrat!
13,554 Retweets **55,922** Likes
5:08 PM - 30 May 2018

Donald J. Trump ✓
@realDonaldTrump

The soon to be released book, "The Russia Hoax, The Illicit Scheme To Clear Hillary Clinton And Frame Donald Trump," written by Gregg Jarrett, looks like a real deal big hit. The Phony Witch Hunt will be opened up for the world to see! Out in 5 weeks.
21,900 Retweets **82,556** Likes
8:06 PM - 30 May 2018

Donald J. Trump ✓
@realDonaldTrump

"The recusal of Jeff Sessions was an unforced betrayal of the President of the United States." JOE DIGENOVA, former U.S. Attorney.
16,193 Retweets **64,846** Likes
8:21 PM - 30 May 2018

Donald J. Trump @realDonaldTrump

RUSH LIMBAUGH "If the FBI was so concerned, and if they weren't targeting Trump, they should have told Trump. If they were really concerned about the Russians infiltrating a campaign (hoax), then why not try to stop it? Why not tell Trump? Because they were pushing this scam."
24,331 Retweets **89,405** Likes
3:55 AM - 31 May 2018

Donald J. Trump @realDonaldTrump

Iger, where is my call of apology? You and ABC have offended millions of people, and they demand a response. How is Brian Ross doing? He tanked the market with an ABC lie, yet no apology. Double Standard!
24,735 Retweets **99,265** Likes
4:53 AM - 31 May 2018

Donald J. Trump @realDonaldTrump

The corrupt Mainstream Media is working overtime not to mention the infiltration of people, Spies (Informants), into my campaign! Surveillance much?
20,318 Retweets **86,977** Likes
5:05 AM - 31 May 2018

Donald J. Trump @realDonaldTrump

Not that it matters but I never fired James Comey because of Russia! The Corrupt Mainstream Media loves to keep pushing that narrative, but they know it is not true!
16,628 Retweets **74,634** Likes
5:11 AM - 31 May 2018

Donald J. Trump @realDonaldTrump

Very good meetings with North Korea.
20,506 Retweets **109,566** Likes
6:15 AM - 31 May 2018

Donald J. Trump @realDonaldTrump

Will be giving a Full Pardon to Dinesh D'Souza today. He was treated very unfairly by our government!
37,156 Retweets **153,677** Likes
6:18 AM - 31 May 2018

Donald J. Trump @realDonaldTrump

FAIR TRADE!
20,093 Retweets **98,108** Likes
2:19 PM - 31 May 2018

Donald J. Trump @realDonaldTrump

A.P. has just reported that the Russian Hoax Investigation has now cost our government over $17 million, and going up fast. No Collusion, except by the Democrats!
26,010 Retweets **97,681** Likes
4:05 AM - 1 Jun 2018

Donald J. Trump ✓
@realDonaldTrump

Why aren't they firing no talent Samantha Bee for the horrible language used on her low ratings show? A total double standard but that's O.K., we are Winning, and will be doing so for a long time to come!
32,370 Retweets **141,384** Likes
4:15 AM - 1 Jun 2018

Donald J. Trump ✓
@realDonaldTrump

Looking forward to seeing the employment numbers at 8:30 this morning.
11,588 Retweets **76,357** Likes
4:21 AM - 1 Jun 2018

Donald J. Trump ✓
@realDonaldTrump

Canada has treated our Agricultural business and Farmers very poorly for a very long period of time. Highly restrictive on Trade! They must open their markets and take down their trade barriers! They report a really high surplus on trade with us. Do Timber & Lumber in U.S.?
19,358 Retweets **81,997** Likes
6:18 AM - 1 Jun 2018

Donald J. Trump ✓
@realDonaldTrump

Today, it was my great honor to be with the brave men and women of the United States Coast Guard!
15,507 Retweets **83,616** Likes
2:40 PM - 1 Jun 2018

Donald J. Trump ✓
@realDonaldTrump

"We ran out of words to describe how good the jobs numbers are." Neil Irwin of the @nytimes.
16,426 Retweets **74,403** Likes
4:40 AM - 2 Jun 2018

Donald J. Trump ✓
@realDonaldTrump

"John Brennan, no single figure in American history has done more to discredit the intelligence community than this liar. Not only is he a liar, he's a liar about being a liar." Dan Bongino on @foxandfriends
23,815 Retweets **87,040** Likes
5:06 AM - 2 Jun 2018

Donald J. Trump ✓
@realDonaldTrump

...."$17 million spent, it's a scam Investigation. Americans are being worked. We now know there was Russian collusion, with Russians and the Democrats. The Mueller team is stacked with anti-Trumpers, who actually represented Clinton people (& gave $'s to Crooked H)." Dan Bongino
19,656 Retweets **74,759** Likes
5:40 AM - 2 Jun 2018

Donald J. Trump ✓
@realDonaldTrump

Now this is a record that will never be broken!
5,924 Retweets **35,149** Likes
9:13 AM - 2 Jun 2018

President Trumps Tweets 2018: A Historical Archive of President Trump's Tweets

Donald J. Trump ✓
@realDonaldTrump

Very surprised that China would be doing this?
7743 Retweets **33298**Likes
9:35 AM - 2 Jun 2018

Donald J. Trump ✓
@realDonaldTrump

Real @FoxNews is doing great, Fake News CNN is dead!
16,671 Retweets **69,999** Likes
9:46 AM - 2 Jun 2018

Donald J. Trump ✓
@realDonaldTrump

There was No Collusion with Russia (except by the Democrats). When will this very expensive Witch Hunt Hoax ever end? So bad for our Country. Is the Special Counsel/Justice Department leaking my lawyers letters to the Fake News Media? Should be looking at Dems corruption instead?
18,930 Retweets **76,465** Likes
10:43 AM - 2 Jun 2018

Donald J. Trump ✓
@realDonaldTrump

The United States must, at long last, be treated fairly on Trade. If we charge a country ZERO to sell their goods, and they charge us 25, 50 or even 100 percent to sell ours, it is UNFAIR and can no longer be tolerated. That is not Free or Fair Trade, it is Stupid Trade!
31,453 Retweets **127,689** Likes
10:51 AM - 2 Jun 2018

Donald J. Trump ✓
@realDonaldTrump

Why is it that the Wall Street Journal, though well meaning, never mentions the unfairness of the Tariffs routinely charged against the U.S. by other countries, or the many Billions of Dollars that the Tariffs we are now charging are, and will be, pouring into U.S. coffers?
19,150 Retweets **80,115** Likes
1:57 PM - 2 Jun 2018

Donald J. Trump ✓
@realDonaldTrump

When you're almost 800 Billion Dollars a year down on Trade, you can't lose a Trade War! The U.S. has been ripped off by other countries for years on Trade, time to get smart!
30.370 Retweets **129,712** Likes
2:23 PM - 2 Jun 2018

Donald J. Trump ✓
@realDonaldTrump

Jesse Watters "The only thing Trump obstructed was Hillary getting to the White House." So true!
30,019 Retweets **124,404** Likes
5:59 AM - 3 Jun 2018

Donald J. Trump ✓
@realDonaldTrump

As only one of two people left who could become President, why wouldn't the FBI or Department of "Justice" have told me that they were secretly investigating Paul Manafort (on charges that were 10 years old and had been previously dropped) during my campaign? Should have told me!
22,810 Retweets **95,387** Likes
6:25 AM - 3 Jun 2018

Donald J. Trump ✓
@realDonaldTrump

....Paul Manafort came into the campaign very late and was with us for a short period of time (he represented Ronald Reagan, Bob Dole & many others over the years), but we should have been told that Comey and the boys were doing a number on him, and he wouldn't have been hired!
20,706 Retweets **86,911** Likes
6:34 AM - 3 Jun 2018

Donald J. Trump ✓
@realDonaldTrump

Mark Penn "Why are there people from the Clinton Foundation on the Mueller Staff? Why is there an Independent Counsel? To go after people and their families for unrelated offenses...Constitution was set up to prevent this...Stormtrooper tactics almost." A disgrace!
31,190 Retweets **112,003** Likes
10:34 AM - 3 Jun 2018

Donald J. Trump ✓
@realDonaldTrump

This is my 500th. Day in Office and we have accomplished a lot - many believe more than any President in his first 500 days. Massive Tax & Regulation Cuts, Military & Vets, Lower Crime & Illegal Immigration, Stronger Borders, Judgeships, Best Economy & Jobs EVER, and much more...
28,077 Retweets **129,668** Likes
4:35 AM - 4 Jun 2018

Donald J. Trump ✓
@realDonaldTrump

....We had Repeal & Replace done (and the saving to our country of one trillion dollars) except for one person, but it is getting done anyway. Individual Mandate is gone and great, less expensive plans will be announced this month. Drug prices coming down & Right to Try!
15,561 Retweets **68,983** Likes
5:18 AM - 4 Jun 2018

Donald J. Trump ✓
@realDonaldTrump

"This is the best time EVER to look for a job." James Freeman of WSJ.
12,338 Retweets **60,703** Likes
5:20 AM - 4 Jun 2018

Donald J. Trump ✓
@realDonaldTrump

As has been stated by numerous legal scholars, I have the absolute right to PARDON myself, but why would I do that when I have done nothing wrong? In the meantime, the never ending Witch Hunt, led by 13 very Angry and Conflicted Democrats (& others) continues into the mid-terms!
21,695 Retweets **90,869** Likes
5:35 AM - 4 Jun 2018

President Trumps Tweets 2018: A Historical Archive of President Trump's Tweets

Donald J. Trump ✓
@realDonaldTrump

China already charges a tax of 16% on soybeans. Canada has all sorts of trade barriers on our Agricultural products. Not acceptable!
14,518 Retweets **64,831** Likes
5:41 AM - 4 Jun 2018

Donald J. Trump ✓
@realDonaldTrump

The U.S. has made such bad trade deals over so many years that we can only WIN!
12,293 Retweets **61,675** Likes
5:43 AM - 4 Jun 2018

Donald J. Trump ✓
@realDonaldTrump

Farmers have not been doing well for 15 years. Mexico, Canada, China and others have treated them unfairly. By the time I finish trade talks, that will change. Big trade barriers against U.S. farmers, and other businesses, will finally be broken. Massive trade deficits no longer!
19,743 Retweets **81,839** Likes
6:47 AM - 4 Jun 2018

Donald J. Trump ✓
@realDonaldTrump

The appointment of the Special Counsel is totally UNCONSTITUTIONAL! Despite that, we play the game because I, unlike the Democrats, have done nothing wrong!
18,822 Retweets **79,611** Likes
7:01 AM - 4 Jun 2018

Donald J. Trump ✓
@realDonaldTrump

#500Days of American Greatness
13,334 Retweets **52,990** Likes
12:05 PM - 4 Jun 2018

Donald J. Trump ✓
@realDonaldTrump

The Fake News Media is desperate to distract from the economy and record setting economic numbers and so they keep talking about the phony Russian Witch Hunt.
20,378 Retweets **89,591** Likes
1:41 PM - 4 Jun 2018

Donald J. Trump ✓
@realDonaldTrump

In many ways this is the greatest economy in the HISTORY of America and the best time EVER to look for a job!
17,811 Retweets **85,216** Likes
1:42 PM - 4 Jun 2018

Donald J. Trump ✓
@realDonaldTrump

Big Supreme Court ruling for Baker just out!
12,103 Retweets **69,556** Likes
6:10 PM - 4 Jun 2018

Donald J. Trump ✓
@realDonaldTrump

The Philadelphia Eagles Football Team was invited to the White House. Unfortunately, only a small number of players decided to come, and we canceled the event. Staying in the Locker Room for the playing of our National Anthem is as disrespectful to our country as kneeling. Sorry!
25,932 Retweets **118,218** Likes
7:55 PM - 4 Jun 2018

Donald J. Trump ✓
@realDonaldTrump

What is taking so long with the Inspector General's Report on Crooked Hillary and Slippery James Comey. Numerous delays. Hope Report is not being changed and made weaker! There are so many horrible things to tell, the public has the right to know. Transparency!
23,798 Retweets **84,346** Likes
3:38 AM - 5 Jun 2018

Donald J. Trump ✓
@realDonaldTrump

The U.S. has an increased economic value of more than 7 Trillion Dollars since the Election. May be the best economy in the history of our country. Record Jobs numbers. Nice!
16,331 Retweets **73,172** Likes
3:51 AM - 5 Jun 2018

Donald J. Trump ✓
@realDonaldTrump

We will proudly be playing the National Anthem and other wonderful music celebrating our Country today at 3 P.M., The White House, with the United States Marine Band and the United States Army Chorus. Honoring America! NFL, no escaping to Locker Rooms!
17,996 Retweets **81,223** Likes
4:08 AM - 5 Jun 2018

Donald J. Trump ✓
@realDonaldTrump

We have had many Championship teams recently at the White House including the Chicago Cubs, Houston Astros, Pittsburgh Penguins, New England Patriots, Alabama and Clemson National Champions, and many others. National Anthem & more great music today at 3:00 P.M.
11,117 Retweets **56,545** Likes
4:21 AM - 5 Jun 2018

Donald J. Trump ✓
@realDonaldTrump

The Russian Witch Hunt Hoax continues, all because Jeff Sessions didn't tell me he was going to recuse himself...I would have quickly picked someone else. So much time and money wasted, so many lives ruined...and Sessions knew better than most that there was No Collusion!
16,432 Retweets **65,499** Likes
4:31 AM - 5 Jun 2018

Donald J. Trump ✓
@realDonaldTrump

Meeting in Singapore with North Korea will hopefully be the start of something big...we will soon see!
15,708 Retweets **79,322** Likes
4:34 AM - 5 Jun 2018

Donald J. Trump ✓
@realDonaldTrump

....@NASCAR and Champion @MartinTruex_Jr were recently at the White House. It was a great day for a great sport!
7,649 Retweets **42,552** Likes
4:50 AM - 5 Jun 2018

Donald J. Trump ✓
@realDonaldTrump

Separating families at the Border is the fault of bad legislation passed by the Democrats. Border Security laws should be changed but the Dems can't get their act together! Started the Wall.
18,963 Retweets **82,234** Likes
4:58 AM - 5 Jun 2018

Donald J. Trump ✓
@realDonaldTrump

In High Tax, High Crime California, be sure to get out and vote for Republican John Cox for Governor. He will make a BIG difference!
14,391 Retweets **59,965** Likes
6:02 AM - 5 Jun 2018

Donald J. Trump ✓
@realDonaldTrump

Get the vote out in California today for Rep. Kevin McCarthy and all of the great GOP candidates for Congress. Keep our country out of the hands of High Tax, High Crime Nancy Pelosi.
18,339 Retweets **71,714** Likes
6:09 AM - 5 Jun 2018

Donald J. Trump ✓
@realDonaldTrump

Vote for Congressman Devin Nunes, a true American Patriot the likes of which we rarely see in our modern day world....he truly loves our country and deserves everyone's support!
21,535 Retweets **80,505** Likes
6:44 AM - 5 Jun 2018

Donald J. Trump ✓
@realDonaldTrump

Senator @RogerWicker of Mississippi has done everything necessary to Make America Great Again! Get out and vote for Roger, he has my total support!
99,73 Retweets **42,179** Likes
6:49 AM - 5 Jun 2018

Donald J. Trump ✓
@realDonaldTrump

Terrific new book out by the wonderful Harris Faulkner, "9 Rules of Engagement." Harris shares lessons from a military family. Enjoy!
10,749 Retweets **52,613** Likes
6:55 AM - 5 Jun 2018

Donald J. Trump ✓
@realDonaldTrump

The HISTORIC Rescissions Package we've proposed would cut $15,000,000,000 in Wasteful Spending! We are getting our government back on track.
18,726 Retweets **80,875** Likes
1:06 PM - 5 Jun 2018

Donald J. Trump ⊙
@realDonaldTrump

Imagine how much wasteful spending we'd save if we didn't have Chuck and Nancy standing in our way! For years, Democrats in Congress have depleted our military and busted our budgets on needless spending, and to what end? No more.
22,064 Retweets **89,733** Likes
1:07 PM - 5 Jun 2018

Donald J. Trump ⊙
@realDonaldTrump

Wow, Strzok-Page, the incompetent & corrupt FBI lovers, have texts referring to a counter-intelligence operation into the Trump Campaign dating way back to December, 2015. SPYGATE is in full force! Is the Mainstream Media interested yet? Big stuff!
28,483 Retweets **87,844** Likes
5:37 PM - 5 Jun 2018

Donald J. Trump ⊙
@realDonaldTrump

Great interview by @LouDobbs with Chris Farrell of Judicial Watch concerning the governments counter-intelligence operation into the Trump Campaign. SPYGATE at the highest level. Who would believe?
13,148 Retweets **53,343** Likes
6:02 PM - 5 Jun 2018

Donald J. Trump ⊙
@realDonaldTrump

Chris Farrell, Judicial Watch. "They were running an operation to undermine a candidate for President of the U.S. These are all violations of law. This is intelligence tradecraft to steer an election. There's nothing more grave when it comes to abuse of our intelligence system...
20,982 Retweets **75,260** Likes
6:23 PM - 5 Jun 2018

Donald J. Trump ⊙
@realDonaldTrump

...This is a level of criminality beyond the pale. This is such a grave abuse of power and authority, it's like nothing else we've seen in our history. This makes the Nixon Watergate burglary look like keystone cop stuff
22,374 Retweets **86,467** Likes
6:27 PM - 5 Jun 2018

Donald J. Trump ⊙
@realDonaldTrump

...The greatest Witch Hunt in political history!
16,752 Retweets **78,859** Likes
6:33 PM - 5 Jun 2018

Donald J. Trump ⊙
@realDonaldTrump

Mitch McConnell announced he will cancel the Senate's August Recess. Great, maybe the Democrats will finally get something done other than their acceptance of High Crime and High Taxes. We need Border Security!
19,895 Retweets **88,273** Likes
9:02 PM - 5 Jun 2018

Donald J. Trump ✓
@realDonaldTrump

Great night for Republicans! Congratulations to John Cox on a really big number in California. He can win. Even Fake News CNN said the Trump impact was really big, much bigger than they ever thought possible. So much for the big Blue Wave, it may be a big Red Wave. Working hard!
19,546 Retweets **85,754** Likes
6:16 AM - 6 Jun 2018

Donald J. Trump ✓
@realDonaldTrump

Gold Star father, Ceejay Metcalf, whose great son Michael was just honored at the White House, was fantastic this morning on @foxandfriends. He is a special man!
9,515 Retweets **53,228** Likes
6:37 AM - 6 Jun 2018

Donald J. Trump ✓
@realDonaldTrump

The Fake News Media has been so unfair, and vicious, to my wife and our great First Lady, Melania. During her recovery from surgery they reported everything from near death, to facelift, to left the W.H. (and me) for N.Y. or Virginia, to abuse. All Fake, she is doing really well!
26,463 Retweets **124,105** Likes
6:48 AM - 6 Jun 2018

Donald J. Trump ✓
@realDonaldTrump

...Four reporters spotted Melania in the White House last week walking merrily along to a meeting. They never reported the sighting because it would hurt the sick narrative that she was living in a different part of the world, was really ill, or whatever. Fake News is really bad!
22,197 Retweets **97,195** Likes
6:54 AM - 6 Jun 2018

Donald J. Trump ✓
@realDonaldTrump

Many more Republican voters showed up yesterday than the Fake News thought possible. The political pundits just don't get what is going on out there - or they do get it but refuse to report the facts! Remember, Dems are High Tax, High Crime, easy to beat!
20,181 Retweets **81,396** Likes
7:04 AM - 6 Jun 2018

Donald J. Trump ✓
@realDonaldTrump

Congratulations to Dana Rohrabacher on his big California win. We are proud of you Dana!
13,120 Retweets **71,784** Likes
7:43 AM - 6 Jun 2018

Donald J. Trump ✓
@realDonaldTrump

Today we mark another milestone: the 74th anniversary of #DDay, the Allied invasion of Normandy. On June 6, 1944, more than 70,000 brave young Americans charged out of landing craft, jumped out of airplanes, and stormed into hell...
14,462 Retweets **64,125** Likes
12:37 PM - 6 Jun 2018

Donald J. Trump ✓
@realDonaldTrump

We must always protect those who protect us. Today, it was my great honor to sign the #VAMissionAct and to make Veterans Choice the permanent law of the land!
15,681 Retweets **67,034** Likes
1:09 PM - 6 Jun 2018

Donald J. Trump ✓
@realDonaldTrump

Thank you to everyone at @FEMA HQ for today's briefing on preparations for the upcoming hurricane season. Disaster response and recovery is best achieved when it's federally supported, state managed, and locally executed – this is the successful model we will continue to build.
11,155 Retweets **52,301** Likes
2:41 PM - 6 Jun 2018

Donald J. Trump ✓
@realDonaldTrump

Isn't it Ironic? Getting ready to go to the G-7 in Canada to fight for our country on Trade (we have the worst trade deals ever made), then off to Singapore to meet with North Korea & the Nuclear Problem...But back home we still have the 13 Angry Democrats pushing the Witch Hunt!
20,828 Retweets **84,767** Likes
4:57 AM - 7 Jun 2018

Donald J. Trump ✓
@realDonaldTrump

Good luck to Alice Johnson. Have a wonderful life!
17,703 Retweets **92,030** Likes
5:07 AM - 7 Jun 2018

Donald J. Trump ✓
@realDonaldTrump

Alan Dershowitz, Harvard Law Professor: "It all proves that we never needed a Special Counsel....All of this could have been done by the Justice Dept. Don't need a multi-million dollar group of people with a target on someone's back. Not the way Justice should operate." So true!
18,188 Retweets **70,818** Likes
6:05 AM - 7 Jun 2018

Donald J. Trump ✓
@realDonaldTrump

When and where will all of the many conflicts of interest be listed by the 13 Angry Democrats (plus) working on the Witch Hunt Hoax. There has never been a group of people on a case so biased or conflicted. It is all a Democrat Excuse for LOSING the Election. Where is the server?
17,969 Retweets **72,540** Likes
6:07 AM - 7 Jun 2018

Donald J. Trump ✓
@realDonaldTrump

How could Jeff Flake, who is setting record low polling numbers in Arizona and was therefore humiliatingly forced out of his own Senate seat without even a fight (and who doesn't have a clue), think about running for office, even a lower one, again? Let's face it, he's a Flake!
17,501 Retweets **78,132** Likes
6:49 AM - 7 Jun 2018

Donald J. Trump ✓
@realDonaldTrump

Looking forward to seeing my friend Prime Minister @AbeShinzo of Japan at noon. Will be discussing North Korea and Trade.
9,997 Retweets **49,929** Likes
7:01 AM - 7 Jun 2018

President Trumps Tweets 2018: A Historical Archive of President Trump's Tweets

Donald J. Trump ✓
@realDonaldTrump

Our Justice Department must not let Awan & Debbie Wasserman Schultz off the hook. The Democrat I.T. scandal is a key to much of the corruption we see today. They want to make a "plea deal" to hide what is on their Server. Where is Server? Really bad!
33,335 Retweets **102,627** Likes
7:07 AM - 7 Jun 2018

Donald J. Trump ✓
@realDonaldTrump

When will people start saying, "thank you, Mr. President, for firing James Comey?"
16,231 Retweets **88,541** Likes
8:10 AM - 7 Jun 2018

Donald J. Trump ✓
@realDonaldTrump

The Obama Administration is now accused of trying to give Iran secret access to the financial system of the United States. This is totally illegal. Perhaps we could get the 13 Angry Democrats to divert some of their energy to this "matter" (as Comey would call it). Investigate!
31,685 Retweets **102,258** Likes
8:15 AM - 7 Jun 2018

Donald J. Trump ✓
@realDonaldTrump

MAKING AMERICA GREAT AGAIN!
36,273 Retweets **100,938** Likes
8:42 AM - 7 Jun 2018

Donald J. Trump ✓
@realDonaldTrump

"Total jobless claims running at lowest level in 44 years"
11,224 Retweets **46,716** Likes
8:49 AM - 7 Jun 2018

Donald J. Trump ✓
@realDonaldTrump

"$3 billion payoff: 101 utilities cut rates, credit GOP tax cuts"
10,792 Retweets **42,062** Likes
8:50 AM - 7 Jun 2018

Donald J. Trump ✓
@realDonaldTrump

It's my great honor to welcome Prime Minister @AbeShinzo back to the @WhiteHouse!
9,998 Retweets **50,463** Likes
10:20 AM - 7 Jun 2018

Donald J. Trump ✓
@realDonaldTrump

Today, I am greatly honored to welcome my good friend, PM Abe of Japan to the @WhiteHouse. Over the past 16 months the Prime Minister and I have worked closely together to address common challenges, of which there are many...
9,921 Retweets **49,804** Likes
12:51 PM - 7 Jun 2018

Donald J. Trump ✓
@realDonaldTrump

PM Abe and I are also working to improve the trading relationship between the U.S. and Japan, something we have to do. The U.S. seeks a bilateral deal with Japan that is based on the principle of fairness and reciprocity. We're working hard to reduce our trade imbalance...
10,312 Retweets **48,451** Likes
12:55 PM - 7 Jun 2018

Donald J. Trump ✓
@realDonaldTrump

Great day of meetings with Prime Minister @AbeShinzo of Japan!
11,599 Retweets **51,348** Likes
1:02 PM - 7 Jun 2018

Donald J. Trump ✓
@realDonaldTrump

Please tell Prime Minister Trudeau and President Macron that they are charging the U.S. massive tariffs and create non-monetary barriers. The EU trade surplus with the U.S. is $151 Billion, and Canada keeps our farmers and others out. Look forward to seeing them tomorrow.
23,855 Retweets **92,673** Likes
3:04 PM - 7 Jun 2018

Donald J. Trump ✓
@realDonaldTrump

Prime Minister Trudeau is being so indignant, bringing up the relationship that the U.S. and Canada had over the many years and all sorts of other things...but he doesn't bring up the fact that they charge us up to 300% on dairy — hurting our Farmers, killing our Agriculture!
30,132 Retweets **110,156** Likes
4:44 PM - 7 Jun 2018

Donald J. Trump ✓
@realDonaldTrump

Why isn't the European Union and Canada informing the public that for years they have used massive Trade Tariffs and non-monetary Trade Barriers against the U.S. Totally unfair to our farmers, workers & companies. Take down your tariffs & barriers or we will more than match you!
27,161 Retweets **98,572** Likes
7:15 PM - 7 Jun 2018

Donald J. Trump ✓
@realDonaldTrump

Obama, Schumer and Pelosi did NOTHING about North Korea, and now weak on Crime, High Tax Schumer is telling me what to do at the Summit the Dems could never set up. Schumer failed with North Korea and Iran, we don't need his advice!
29,695 Retweets **115,734** Likes
3:06 AM - 8 Jun 2018

Donald J. Trump ✓
@realDonaldTrump

Canada charges the U.S. a 270% tariff on Dairy Products! They didn't tell you that, did they? Not fair to our farmers!
26,419 Retweets **95,015** Likes
3:16 AM - 8 Jun 2018

President Trumps Tweets 2018: A Historical Archive of President Trump's Tweets

Donald J. Trump ✓
@realDonaldTrump

Looking forward to straightening out unfair Trade Deals with the G-7 countries. If it doesn't happen, we come out even better!
15,772 Retweets **77,480** Likes
3:25 AM - 8 Jun 2018

Donald J. Trump ✓
@realDonaldTrump

Congratulations to the Washington Capitals on their GREAT play and winning the Stanley Cup Championship. Alex Ovechkin, the team captain, was spectacular - a true Superstar! D.C. is popping, in many ways. What a time!
20,740 Retweets **119,538** Likes
4:12 AM - 8 Jun 2018

Donald J. Trump ✓
@realDonaldTrump

I am heading for Canada and the G-7 for talks that will mostly center on the long time unfair trade practiced against the United States. From there I go to Singapore and talks with North Korea on Denuclearization. Won't be talking about the Russian Witch Hunt Hoax for a while!
17,764 Retweets **83,159** Likes
4:22 AM - 8 Jun 2018

Donald J. Trump ✓
@realDonaldTrump

My thoughts and prayers are with the families of our serviceman who was killed and his fellow servicemen who were wounded in Somalia. They are truly all HEROES.
17,211 Retweets **97,009** Likes
9:22 PM - 8 Jun 2018

Donald J. Trump ✓
@realDonaldTrump

.@G7 Press Briefing in Charlevoix, Canada, prior to departing for Singapore!
11,251 Retweets **45,713** Likes
9:00 AM - 9 Jun 2018

Donald J. Trump ✓
@realDonaldTrump

Henry McMaster loves the people of South Carolina and was with me from the beginning. He is strong on Crime and Borders, great for our Military and our Vets. He is doing a fantastic job as your Governor, and has my full endorsement, a special guy. Vote on Tuesday!
17,215 Retweets **74,616** Likes
1:33 PM - 9 Jun 2018

Donald J. Trump ✓
@realDonaldTrump

Just met the new Prime Minister of Italy, @GiuseppeConteIT, a really great guy. He will be honored in Washington, at the @WhiteHouse, shortly. He will do a great job - the people of Italy got it right!
20,851 Retweets **86,798** Likes
1:43 PM - 9 Jun 2018

Donald J. Trump ✓
@realDonaldTrump

Just left the @G7 Summit in beautiful Canada. Great meetings and relationships with the six Country Leaders especially since they know I cannot allow them to apply large Tariffs and strong barriers to...
11,711 Retweets **60,203** Likes
1:56 PM - 9 Jun 2018

Donald J. Trump ✓
@realDonaldTrump

...U.S.A. Trade. They fully understand where I am coming from. After many decades, fair and reciprocal Trade will happen!
11,333 Retweets **56,433** Likes
1:56 PM - 9 Jun 2018

Donald J. Trump ✓
@realDonaldTrump

The United States will not allow other countries to impose massive Tariffs and Trade Barriers on its farmers, workers and companies. While sending their product into our country tax free. We have put up with Trade Abuse for many decades — and that is long enough.
30,027 Retweets **125,475** Likes
1:57 PM - 9 Jun 2018

Donald J. Trump ✓
@realDonaldTrump

I am on my way to Singapore where we have a chance to achieve a truly wonderful result for North Korea and the World. It will certainly be an exciting day and I know that Kim Jong-un will work very hard to do something that has rarely been done before...
23,325 Retweets **103,670** Likes
1:58 PM - 9 Jun 2018

Donald J. Trump ✓
@realDonaldTrump

...Create peace and great prosperity for his land. I look forward to meeting him and have a feeling that this one-time opportunity will not be wasted!
14,844 Retweets **71,110** Likes
1:58 PM - 9 Jun 2018

Donald J. Trump ✓
@realDonaldTrump

Based on Justin's false statements at his news conference, and the fact that Canada is charging massive Tariffs to our U.S. farmers, workers and companies, I have instructed our U.S. Reps not to endorse the Communique as we look at Tariffs on automobiles flooding the U.S. Market!
33,199 Retweets **131,937** Likes
4:03 PM - 9 Jun 2018

Donald J. Trump ✓
@realDonaldTrump

PM Justin Trudeau of Canada acted so meek and mild during our @G7 meetings only to give a news conference after I left saying that, "US Tariffs were kind of insulting" and he "will not be pushed around." Very dishonest & weak. Our Tariffs are in response to his of 270% on dairy!
35,318 Retweets **126,724** Likes
4:04 PM - 9 Jun 2018

President Trumps Tweets 2018: A Historical Archive of President Trump's Tweets

 Donald J. Trump ✓
@realDonaldTrump

Fair Trade is now to be called Fool Trade if it is not Reciprocal. According to a Canada release, they make almost 100 Billion Dollars in Trade with U.S. (guess they were bragging and got caught!). Minimum is 17B. Tax Dairy from us at 270%. Then Justin acts hurt when called out!
26,861 Retweets **105,242** Likes
6:05 PM - 10 Jun 2018

 Donald J. Trump ✓
@realDonaldTrump

Why should I, as President of the United States, allow countries to continue to make Massive Trade Surpluses, as they have for decades, while our Farmers, Workers & Taxpayers have such a big and unfair price to pay? Not fair to the PEOPLE of America! $800 Billion Trade Deficit...
33,611 Retweets **142,661** Likes
6:17 PM - 10 Jun 2018

 Donald J. Trump ✓
@realDonaldTrump

....And add to that the fact that the U.S. pays close to the entire cost of NATO-protecting many of these same countries that rip us off on Trade (they pay only a fraction of the cost-and laugh!). The European Union had a $151 Billion Surplus-should pay much more for Military!
25,234 Retweets **105,194** Likes
6:29 PM - 10 Jun 2018

 Donald J. Trump ✓
@realDonaldTrump

....Germany pays 1% (slowly) of GDP towards NATO, while we pay 4% of a MUCH larger GDP. Does anybody believe that makes sense? We protect Europe (which is good) at great financial loss, and then get unfairly clobbered on Trade. Change is coming!
33,307 Retweets **139,303** Likes
6:42 PM - 10 Jun 2018

 Donald J. Trump ✓
@realDonaldTrump

Great to be in Singapore, excitement in the air!
21,357 Retweets **113,137** Likes
6:45 PM - 10 Jun 2018

 Donald J. Trump ✓
@realDonaldTrump

Sorry, we cannot let our friends, or enemies, take advantage of us on Trade anymore. We must put the American worker first!
33,464 Retweets **154,319** Likes
7:41 PM - 10 Jun 2018

 Donald J. Trump ✓
@realDonaldTrump

Thank you Prime Minister Lee Hsien Loong!
19,109 Retweets **87,380** Likes
12:51 AM - 11 Jun 2018

 Donald J. Trump ✓
@realDonaldTrump

Meetings between staffs and representatives are going well and quickly....but in the end, that doesn't matter. We will all know soon whether or not a real deal, unlike those of the past, can happen!
21,180 Retweets **105,025** Likes
2:27 PM - 11 Jun 2018

Donald J. Trump ✓
@realDonaldTrump

Stock Market up almost 40% since the Election, with 7 Trillion Dollars of U.S. value built throughout the economy. Lowest unemployment rate in many decades, with Black & Hispanic unemployment lowest in History, and Female unemployment lowest in 21 years. Highest confidence ever!
32,153 Retweets **139,239** Likes
2:52 PM - 11 Jun 2018

Donald J. Trump ✓
@realDonaldTrump

The fact that I am having a meeting is a major loss for the U.S., say the haters & losers. We have our hostages, testing, research and all missle launches have stoped, and these pundits, who have called me wrong from the beginning, have nothing else they can say! We will be fine!
33,959 Retweets **150,303** Likes
3:04 PM - 11 Jun 2018

Donald J. Trump ✓
@realDonaldTrump

Just won big Supreme Court decision on Voting! Great News!
23,335 Retweets **117,708** Likes
5:03 PM - 11 Jun 2018

Donald J. Trump ✓
@realDonaldTrump

Our Great Larry Kudlow, who has been working so hard on trade and the economy, has just suffered a heart attack. He is now in Walter Reed Medical Center.
24,875 Retweets **100,792** Likes
5:35 PM - 11 Jun 2018

Donald J. Trump ✓
@realDonaldTrump

I strongly endorse Adam Laxalt for Governor of Nevada. Adam is smart, works hard, and knows how to win. He will be a great Governor. Also, will fight hard to lower your taxes and is tough on crime!
14,739 Retweets **64,500** Likes
12:30 PM - 12 Jun 2018

Donald J. Trump ✓
@realDonaldTrump

Mark Sanford has been very unhelpful to me in my campaign to MAGA. He is MIA and nothing but trouble. He is better off in Argentina. I fully endorse Katie Arrington for Congress in SC, a state I love. She is tough on crime and will continue our fight to lower taxes. VOTE Katie!
18,770 Retweets **79,157** Likes
1:12 PM - 12 Jun 2018

Donald J. Trump ✓
@realDonaldTrump

Heading back home from Singapore after a truly amazing visit. Great progress was made on the denuclearization of North Korea. Hostages are back home, will be getting the remains of our great heroes back to their families, no missiles shot, no research happening, sites closing...
19,402 Retweets **89,962** Likes
1:40 PM - 12 Jun 2018

Donald J. Trump ✓
@realDonaldTrump

...Got along great with Kim Jong-un who wants to see wonderful things for his country. As I said earlier today: Anyone can make war, but only the most courageous can make peace! #SingaporeSummit
18,324 Retweets **83,269** Likes
1:40 PM - 12 Jun 2018

Donald J. Trump ✓
@realDonaldTrump

Here is the video, "A Story of Opportunity" that I shared with Kim Jong-un at the #SingaporeSummit
15,673 Retweets **57,567** Likes
2:23 PM - 12 Jun 2018

Donald J. Trump ✓
@realDonaldTrump

It's time for another #MAGA rally. Join me in Duluth, Minnesota on Wednesday, June 20th at 6:30pm!
13,185 Retweets **52,719** Likes
4:37 PM - 12 Jun 2018

Donald J. Trump ✓
@realDonaldTrump

There is no limit to what NoKo can achieve when it gives up its nuclear weapons and embraces commerce & engagement w/ the world. Chairman Kim has before him the opportunity to be remembered as the leader who ushered in a glorious new era of security & prosperity for his citizens!
18,172 Retweets **83,487** Likes
5:02 PM - 12 Jun 2018

Donald J. Trump ✓
@realDonaldTrump

I want to thank Chairman Kim for taking the first bold step toward a bright new future for his people. Our unprecedented meeting – the first between an American President and a leader of North Korea – proves that real change is possible!
24,209 Retweets **111,870** Likes
5:11 PM - 12 Jun 2018

Donald J. Trump ✓
@realDonaldTrump

The World has taken a big step back from potential Nuclear catastrophe! No more rocket launches, nuclear testing or research! The hostages are back home with their families. Thank you to Chairman Kim, our day together was historic!
33,138 Retweets **153,658** Likes
5:27 PM - 12 Jun 2018

Donald J. Trump ✓
@realDonaldTrump

A year ago the pundits & talking heads, people that couldn't do the job before, were begging for conciliation and peace - "please meet, don't go to war." Now that we meet and have a great relationship with Kim Jong Un, the same haters shout out, "you shouldn't meet, do not meet!"
30,890 Retweets **127,515** Likes
6:14 PM - 12 Jun 2018

Donald J. Trump ✓
@realDonaldTrump

My political representatives didn't want me to get involved in the Mark Sanford primary thinking that Sanford would easily win - but with a few hours left I felt that Katie was such a good candidate, and Sanford was so bad, I had to give it a shot. Congrats to Katie Arrington!
12,221 Retweets **63,132** Likes
2:37 AM - 13 Jun 2018

Donald J. Trump ✓
@realDonaldTrump

Robert De Niro, a very Low IQ individual, has received too many shots to the head by real boxers in movies. I watched him last night and truly believe he may be "punch-drunk." I guess he doesn't...
20,145 Retweets **99,597** Likes
2:40 AM - 13 Jun 2018

Donald J. Trump ✓
@realDonaldTrump

...realize the economy is the best it's ever been with employment being at an all time high, and many companies pouring back into our country. Wake up Punchy!
13,662 Retweets **74,619** Likes
2:40 AM - 13 Jun 2018

Donald J. Trump ✓
@realDonaldTrump

Congratulations to Corey Stewart for his great victory for Senator from Virginia. Now he runs against a total stiff, Tim Kaine, who is weak on crime and borders, and wants to raise your taxes through the roof. Don't underestimate Corey, a major chance of winning!
16,367 Retweets **74,404** Likes
2:55 AM - 13 Jun 2018

Donald J. Trump ✓
@realDonaldTrump

Just landed - a long trip, but everybody can now feel much safer than the day I took office. There is no longer a Nuclear Threat from North Korea. Meeting with Kim Jong Un was an interesting and very positive experience. North Korea has great potential for the future!
21,715 Retweets **105,473** Likes
2:56 AM - 13 Jun 2018

Donald J. Trump ✓
@realDonaldTrump

Before taking office people were assuming that we were going to War with North Korea. President Obama said that North Korea was our biggest and most dangerous problem. No longer - sleep well tonight!
32,671 Retweets **146,005** Likes
3:01 AM - 13 Jun 2018

Donald J. Trump ✓
@realDonaldTrump

We save a fortune by not doing war games, as long as we are negotiating in good faith - which both sides are!
19,083 Retweets **102,890** Likes
4:10 AM - 13 Jun 2018

President Trumps Tweets 2018: A Historical Archive of President Trump's Tweets

Donald J. Trump ✓
@realDonaldTrump

The U.S., together with Mexico and Canada, just got the World Cup. Congratulations - a great deal of hard work!
20,013 Retweets **103,412** Likes
4:49 AM - 13 Jun 2018

Donald J. Trump ✓
@realDonaldTrump

Oil prices are too high, OPEC is at it again. Not good!
24,207 Retweets **112,519** Likes
4:52 AM - 13 Jun 2018

Donald J. Trump ✓
@realDonaldTrump

So funny to watch the Fake News, especially NBC and CNN. They are fighting hard to downplay the deal with North Korea. 500 days ago they would have "begged" for this deal-looked like war would break out. Our Country's biggest enemy is the Fake News so easily promulgated by fools!
42,887 Retweets **164,892** Likes
6:30 AM - 13 Jun 2018

Donald J. Trump ✓
@realDonaldTrump

Senator Claire McCaskill of the GREAT State of Missouri flew around in a luxurious private jet during her RV tour of the state. RV's are not for her. People are really upset, so phony! Josh Hawley should win big, and has my full endorsement.
24,270 Retweets **94,725** Likes
1:11 PM - 13 Jun 2018

Donald J. Trump ✓
@realDonaldTrump

Congratulations to Danny Tarkanian on his big GOP primary win in Nevada. Danny worked hard an got a great result. Looking good in November!
15,897 Retweets **82,619** Likes
1:17 PM - 13 Jun 2018

Donald J. Trump ✓
@realDonaldTrump

Congratulations to @KevinCramer on his huge win in North Dakota. We need Kevin in the Senate, and I strongly endorse him. Heidi voted NO on our Tax Cuts, and always will vote no when we need her. Kevin is strong on Crime & Borders, big on Cutting Taxes!
15,347 Retweets **71,212** Likes
1:50 PM - 13 Jun 2018

Donald J. Trump ✓
@realDonaldTrump

The Republican Party is starting to show very big numbers. People are starting to see what is being done. Results are speaking loudly. North Korea and our greatest ever economy are leading the way!
24,002 Retweets **114,918** Likes
5:34 AM - 14 Jun 2018

Donald J. Trump ✓
@realDonaldTrump

Now that I am back from Singapore, where we had a great result with respect to North Korea, the thought process must sadly go back to the Witch Hunt, always remembering that there was No Collusion and No Obstruction of the fabricated No Crime.
16,595 Retweets **78,334** Likes
8:08 AM - 14 Jun 2018

Donald J. Trump ✓
@realDonaldTrump

So, the Democrats make up a phony crime, Collusion with the Russians, pay a fortune to make the crime sound real, illegally leak (Comey) classified information so that a Special Councel will be appointed, and then Collude to make this pile of garbage take on life in Fake News!
31,670 Retweets **117,201** Likes
8:08 AM - 14 Jun 2018

Donald J. Trump ✓
@realDonaldTrump

The sleazy New York Democrats, and their now disgraced (and run out of town) A.G. Eric Schneiderman, are doing everything they can to sue me on a foundation that took in $18,800,000 and gave out to charity more money than it took in, $19,200,000. I won't settle this case!...
27,172 Retweets **111,718** Likes
8:09 AM - 14 Jun 2018

Donald J. Trump ✓
@realDonaldTrump

....Schneiderman, who ran the Clinton campaign in New York, never had the guts to bring this ridiculous case, which lingered in their office for almost 2 years. Now he resigned his office in disgrace, and his disciples brought it when we would not settle.
17,691 Retweets **76,042** Likes
8:09 AM - 14 Jun 2018

Donald J. Trump ✓
@realDonaldTrump

Happy 243rd Birthday to the @USArmy! Thank you for your bravery, sacrifices, and dedication to the U.S.A. We love you!
16,255 Retweets **78,373** Likes
9:33 AM - 14 Jun 2018

Donald J. Trump ✓
@realDonaldTrump

Happy #FlagDay
17,237 Retweets **84,620** Likes
10:34 AM - 14 Jun 2018

Donald J. Trump ✓
@realDonaldTrump

FBI Agent Peter Strzok, who headed the Clinton & Russia investigations, texted to his lover Lisa Page, in the IG Report, that "we'll stop" candidate Trump from becoming President. Doesn't get any lower than that!
23,712 Retweets **91,847** Likes
3:35 AM - 15 Jun 2018

President Trumps Tweets 2018: A Historical Archive of President Trump's Tweets

Donald J. Trump ✓
@realDonaldTrump

The IG Report is a total disaster for Comey, his minions and sadly, the FBI. Comey will now officially go down as the worst leader, by far, in the history of the FBI. I did a great service to the people in firing him. Good Instincts. Christopher Wray will bring it proudly back!
19,628 Retweets **85,926** Likes
3:55 AM - 15 Jun 2018

Donald J. Trump ✓
@realDonaldTrump

Thank you for all of the compliments on getting the World Cup to come to the U.S.A., Mexico and Canada. I worked hard on this, along with a Great Team of talented people. We never fail, and it will be a great World Cup! A special thanks to Bob Kraft for excellent advice.
13,446 Retweets **71,995** Likes
4:06 AM - 15 Jun 2018

Donald J. Trump ✓
@realDonaldTrump

U.S.A. Jobs numbers are the BEST in 44 years. If my opponent (the Democrats) had won the election, they would have raised taxes substantially and increased regulations - the economy, and jobs, would have been a disaster!
21,635 Retweets **98,957** Likes
4:45 AM - 15 Jun 2018

Donald J. Trump ✓
@realDonaldTrump

Wow, the highest rated (by far) morning show, @foxandfriends, is on the Front Lawn of the White House. Maybe I'll have to take an unannounced trip down to see them?
14,861 Retweets **88,138** Likes
4:50 AM - 15 Jun 2018

Donald J. Trump ✓
@realDonaldTrump

"Why in the world didn't Barack Obama fire this guy (Comey)?" asks Mark Levin!
13,677 Retweets **66,511** Likes
4:53 AM - 15 Jun 2018

Donald J. Trump ✓
@realDonaldTrump

"Donald Trump was 100% right to fire James Comey." Mark Levin
15,775 Retweets **77,657** Likes
5:03 AM - 15 Jun 2018

Donald J. Trump ✓
@realDonaldTrump

The Democrats are forcing the breakup of families at the Border with their horrible and cruel legislative agenda. Any Immigration Bill MUST HAVE full funding for the Wall, end Catch & Release, Visa Lottery and Chain, and go to Merit Based Immigration. Go for it! WIN!
28,609 Retweets **110,650** Likes
10:08 AM - 15 Jun 2018

Donald J. Trump ✓
@realDonaldTrump

Wow, what a tough sentence for Paul Manafort, who has represented Ronald Reagan, Bob Dole and many other top political people and campaigns. Didn't know Manafort was the head of the Mob. What about Comey and Crooked Hillary and all of the others? Very unfair!
25,324 Retweets **97,786** Likes
10:41 AM - 15 Jun 2018

Donald J. Trump ✓
@realDonaldTrump

I've had to beat 17 very talented people including the Bush Dynasty, then I had to beat the Clinton Dynasty, and now I have to beat a phony Witch Hunt and all of the dishonest people covered in the IG Report...and never forget the Fake News Media. It never ends!
37,551 Retweets **154,084** Likes
10:49 AM - 15 Jun 2018

Donald J. Trump ✓
@realDonaldTrump

I have a great relationship with Angela Merkel of Germany, but the Fake News Media only shows the bad photos (implying anger) of negotiating an agreement - where I am asking for things that no other American President would ask for!
21,846 Retweets **81,808** Likes
3:03 PM - 15 Jun 2018

Donald J. Trump ✓
@realDonaldTrump

The Fake News Media said that I did not get along with other Leaders at the #G7Summit in Canada. They are once again, WRONG!
17,801 Retweets **73,047** Likes
3:23 PM - 15 Jun 2018

Donald J. Trump ✓
@realDonaldTrump

Great discussions with European Union Commission President Jean-Claude Juncker and EU Council President Donald Tusk at the #G7Summit in Canada
9,088 Retweets **47,689** Likes
3:32 PM - 15 Jun 2018

Donald J. Trump ✓
@realDonaldTrump

Democrats can fix their forced family breakup at the Border by working with Republicans on new legislation, for a change! This is why we need more Republicans elected in November. Democrats are good at only three things, High Taxes, High Crime and Obstruction. Sad!
30,394 Retweets **119,553** Likes
6:03 AM - 16 Jun 2018

Donald J. Trump ✓
@realDonaldTrump

My supporters are the smartest, strongest, most hard working and most loyal that we have seen in our countries history. It is a beautiful thing to watch as we win elections and gather support from all over the country. As we get stronger, so does our country. Best numbers ever!
43,106 Retweets **183,643** Likes
6:12 AM - 16 Jun 2018

Donald J. Trump ✓
@realDonaldTrump

The IG Report totally destroys James Comey and all of his minions including the great lovers, Peter Strzok and Lisa Page, who started the disgraceful Witch Hunt against so many innocent people. It will go down as a dark and dangerous period in American History!
30,186 Retweets **119,661** Likes
7:01 AM - 16 Jun 2018

Donald J. Trump ✓
@realDonaldTrump

Chuck Schumer said "the Summit was what the Texans call all cattle and no hat." Thank you Chuck, but are you sure you got that right? No more nuclear testing or rockets flying all over the place, blew up launch sites. Hostages already back, hero remains coming home & much more!
19,640 Retweets **85,039** Likes
4:52 AM - 17 Jun 2018

Donald J. Trump ✓
@realDonaldTrump

Please clear up the Fake News!
12,335 Retweets **51,986** Likes
4:58 AM - 17 Jun 2018

Donald J. Trump ✓
@realDonaldTrump

Daniel Henninger of The Wall Street Journal: "This IG Report makes it clear, as did Rod Rosenstein's memo, that Trump was absolutely justified, unquestionably justified, in firing Jim Comey. So I think the Mueller Investigation is on pretty weak grounds right now." Witch Hunt!
17,300 Retweets **70,893** Likes
5:31 AM - 17 Jun 2018

Donald J. Trump ✓
@realDonaldTrump

Funny how the Fake News, in a coordinated effort with each other, likes to say I gave sooo much to North Korea because I "met." That's because that's all they have to disparage! We got so much for peace in the world, & more is being added in finals. Even got our hostages/remains!
17,152 Retweets **78,676** Likes
5:40 AM - 17 Jun 2018

Donald J. Trump ✓
@realDonaldTrump

Holding back the "war games" during the negotiations was my request because they are VERY EXPENSIVE and set a bad light during a good faith negotiation. Also, quite provocative. Can start up immediately if talks break down, which I hope will not happen!
15,119 Retweets **75,820** Likes
5:48 AM - 17 Jun 2018

Donald J. Trump ✓
@realDonaldTrump

The denuclearization deal with North Korea is being praised and celebrated all over Asia. They are so happy! Over here, in our country, some people would rather see this historic deal fail than give Trump a win, even if it does save potentially millions & millions of lives!
18,711 Retweets **79,452** Likes
6:01 AM - 17 Jun 2018

Donald J. Trump ✓
@realDonaldTrump

Our economy is perhaps BETTER than it has ever been. Companies doing really well, and moving back to America, and jobs numbers are the best in 44 years.
15,724 Retweets **82,528** Likes
6:08 AM - 17 Jun 2018

Donald J. Trump ✓
@realDonaldTrump

Washington Post employees want to go on strike because Bezos isn't paying them enough. I think a really long strike would be a great idea. Employees would get more money and we would get rid of Fake News for an extended period of time! Is @WaPo a registered lobbyist?
16,714 Retweets **70,925** Likes
6:26 AM - 17 Jun 2018

Donald J. Trump ✓
@realDonaldTrump

WITCH HUNT! There was no Russian Collusion. Oh, I see, there was no Russian Collusion, so now they look for obstruction on the no Russian Collusion. The phony Russian Collusion was a made up Hoax. Too bad they didn't look at Crooked Hillary like this. Double Standard!
30,555 Retweets **125,754** Likes
7:54 AM - 17 Jun 2018

Donald J. Trump ✓
@realDonaldTrump

Why was the FBI giving so much information to the Fake News Media. They are not supposed to be doing that, and knowing the enemy of the people Fake News, they put their own spin on it - truth doesn't matter to them!
24,521 Retweets **101,649** Likes
5:25 PM - 17 Jun 2018

Donald J. Trump ✓
@realDonaldTrump

Why was the FBI's sick loser, Peter Strzok, working on the totally discredited Mueller team of 13 Angry & Conflicted Democrats, when Strzok was giving Crooked Hillary a free pass yet telling his lover, lawyer Lisa Page, that "we'll stop" Trump from becoming President? Witch Hunt!
21,339 Retweets **84,263** Likes
5:42 PM - 17 Jun 2018

Donald J. Trump ✓
@realDonaldTrump

The Democrats should get together with their Republican counterparts and work something out on Border Security & Safety. Don't wait until after the election because you are going to lose!
20,034 Retweets **89,729** Likes
5:49 PM - 17 Jun 2018

Donald J. Trump ✓
@realDonaldTrump

"The highest level of bias I've ever witnessed in any law enforcement officer." Trey Gowdy on the FBI's own, Peter Strzok. Also remember that they all worked for Slippery James Comey and that Comey is best friends with Robert Mueller. A really sick deal, isn't it?
27,840 Retweets **106,014** Likes
6:03 PM - 17 Jun 2018

Donald J. Trump ✓
@realDonaldTrump

Why don't the Democrats give us the votes to fix the world's worst immigration laws? Where is the outcry for the killings and crime being caused by gangs and thugs, including MS-13, coming into our country illegally?
26,853 Retweets **109,438** Likes
5:46 AM - 18 Jun 2018

Donald J. Trump ✓
@realDonaldTrump

The people of Germany are turning against their leadership as migration is rocking the already tenuous Berlin coalition. Crime in Germany is way up. Big mistake made all over Europe in allowing millions of people in who have so strongly and violently changed their culture!
34,717 Retweets **117,299** Likes
6:02 AM - 18 Jun 2018

Donald J. Trump ✓
@realDonaldTrump

We don't want what is happening with immigration in Europe to happen with us!
32,692 Retweets **128,143** Likes
6:04 AM - 18 Jun 2018

Donald J. Trump ✓
@realDonaldTrump

Children are being used by some of the worst criminals on earth as a means to enter our country. Has anyone been looking at the Crime taking place south of the border. It is historic, with some countries the most dangerous places in the world. Not going to happen in the U.S.
30,031 Retweets **116,973** Likes
6:50 AM - 18 Jun 2018

Donald J. Trump ✓
@realDonaldTrump

CHANGE THE LAWS!
19,027 Retweets **85,385** Likes
6:50 AM - 18 Jun 2018

Donald J. Trump ✓
@realDonaldTrump

It is the Democrats fault for being weak and ineffective with Boarder Security and Crime. Tell them to start thinking about the people devastated by Crime coming from illegal immigration. Change the laws!
23,521 Retweets **100,445** Likes
6:53 AM - 18 Jun 2018

Donald J. Trump ✓
@realDonaldTrump

If President Obama (who got nowhere with North Korea and would have had to go to war with many millions of people being killed) had gotten along with North Korea and made the initial steps toward a deal that I have, the Fake News would have named him a national hero!
26,893 Retweets **120,464** Likes
7:57 AM - 18 Jun 2018

Donald J. Trump ✓
@realDonaldTrump

Comey gave Strozk his marching orders. Mueller is Comey's best friend. Witch Hunt!
21,407 Retweets **88,684** Likes
8:27 AM - 18 Jun 2018

Donald J. Trump ✓
@realDonaldTrump

I can't think of something more concerning than a law enforcement officer suggesting that their going to use their powers to affect an election!" Inspector General Horowitz on what was going on with numerous people regarding my election. A Rigged Witch Hunt!p
20,788 Retweets **85,067** Likes
6:52 AM - 19 Jun 2018

Donald J. Trump ✓
@realDonaldTrump

Crime in Germany is up 10% plus (officials do not want to report these crimes) since migrants were accepted. Others countries are even worse. Be smart America
19,736 Retweets **80,573** Likes
6:52 AM - 19 Jun 2018

Donald J. Trump ✓
@realDonaldTrump

If you don't have Borders, you don't have a Country!
42,024 Retweets **173,340** Likes
6:52 AM - 19 Jun 2018

Donald J. Trump ✓
@realDonaldTrump

Democrats are the problem. They don't care about crime and want illegal immigrants, no matter how bad they may be, to pour into and infest our Country, like MS-13. They can't win on their terrible policies, so they view them as potential voters!
28,272 Retweets **109,384** Likes
6:52 AM - 19 Jun 2018

Donald J. Trump ✓
@realDonaldTrump

We must always arrest people coming into our Country illegally. Of the 12,000 children, 10,000 are being sent by their parents on a very dangerous trip, and only 2000 are with their parents, many of whom have tried to enter our Country illegally on numerous occasions.
32,768 Retweets **122,189** Likes
7:07 AM - 19 Jun 2018

Donald J. Trump ✓
@realDonaldTrump

#CHANGETHELAWS Now is the best opportunity ever for Congress to change the ridiculous and obsolete laws on immigration. Get it done, always keeping in mind that we must have strong border security.
20,015 Retweets **80,534** Likes
7:11 AM - 19 Jun 2018

Donald J. Trump ✓
@realDonaldTrump

Join me tomorrow in Duluth, Minnesota for a #MAGA Rally!
10,619 Retweets **42,736** Likes
8:22 AM - 19 Jun 2018

Donald J. Trump ✓
@realDonaldTrump

THANK YOU @NFIB! #NFIB75
8,626 Retweets **38,632** Likes
10:35 AM - 19 Jun 2018

Donald J. Trump ✓
@realDonaldTrump

I want to take a moment to address the current illegal immigration crisis on the Southern Border...it has been going on for many, many decades...
22,068 Retweets **82,636** Likes
11:04 AM - 19 Jun 2018

President Trumps Tweets 2018: A Historical Archive of President Trump's Tweets

Donald J. Trump ✓
@realDonaldTrump

Homeland Security @SecNielsen did a fabulous job yesterday at the press conference explaining security at the border and for our country, while at the same time recommending changes to obsolete & nasty laws, which force family separation. We want "heart" and security in America!
22,451 Retweets **96,708** Likes
6:06 PM - 19 Jun 2018

Donald J. Trump ✓
@realDonaldTrump

Earlier today, @FLOTUS Melania and I were honored to welcome King Felipe VI and Queen Letizia of Spain to the @WhiteHouse!
13,128 Retweets **70,132** Likes
7:17 PM - 19 Jun 2018

Donald J. Trump ✓
@realDonaldTrump

THANK YOU @HouseGOP!
9,507 Retweets **48,199** Likes
7:36 PM - 19 Jun 2018

Donald J. Trump ✓
@realDonaldTrump

The Fake News is not mentioning the safety and security of our Country when talking about illegal immigration. Our immigration laws are the weakest and worst anywhere in the world, and the Dems will do anything not to change them & to obstruct-want open borders which means crime!
32,075 Retweets **126,623** Likes
5:25 AM - 20 Jun 2018

Donald J. Trump ✓
@realDonaldTrump

It's the Democrats fault, they won't give us the votes needed to pass good immigration legislation. They want open borders, which breeds horrible crime. Republicans want security. But I am working on something - it never ends!
23,501 Retweets **96,534** Likes
6:41 AM - 20 Jun 2018

Donald J. Trump ✓
@realDonaldTrump

"FBI texts have revealed anti-Trump Bias." @FoxNews Big News, but the Fake News doesn't want to cover. Total corruption - the Witch Hunt has turned out to be a scam! At some point soon the Mainstream Media will have to cover correctly, too big a story!
22,186 Retweets **83,338** Likes
7:00 AM - 20 Jun 2018

Donald J. Trump ✓
@realDonaldTrump

More records! #MAGA
10,841 Retweets **42,424** Likes
8:00 AM - 20 Jun 2018

Donald J. Trump ✓
@realDonaldTrump

Had a great meeting with the House GOP last night at the Capitol. They applauded and laughed loudly when I mentioned my experience with Mark Sanford. I have never been a fan of his!
10,029 Retweets **53,851** Likes
1:04 PM - 20 Jun 2018

Donald J. Trump @realDonaldTrump

Look what Fake ABC News put out. I guess they had it prepared from the 13 Angry Democrats leading the Witch Hunt! #StopTheBias
14,796 Retweets **51,871** Likes
1:34 PM - 20 Jun 2018

Donald J. Trump @realDonaldTrump

Don't worry, the Republicans, and your President, will fix it!
72,651 Retweets **188,618** Likes
1:39 PM - 20 Jun 2018

Donald J. Trump @realDonaldTrump

Just landed in Duluth, Minnesota. Two events planned - looking forward to them and being with @PeteStauber and his wonderful family!
9,771 Retweets **55,854** Likes
2:54 PM - 20 Jun 2018

Donald J. Trump @realDonaldTrump

So sorry, people wanting to get into the already packed arena - I LOVE YOU ALL!
21,779 Retweets **94,335** Likes
4:30 PM - 20 Jun 2018

Donald J. Trump @realDonaldTrump

Thank you Duluth, Minnesota. Together, we are MAKING AMERICA GREAT AGAIN!
16,437 Retweets **72,767** Likes
6:01 PM - 20 Jun 2018

Donald J. Trump @realDonaldTrump

Just returning from the Great State of Minnesota where we had an incredible rally with 9,000 people, and at least 10,000 who could not get in - I will return! Congratulations to @PeteStauber who is loved and respected in Minnesota!
16,971 Retweets **87,684** Likes
8:24 PM - 20 Jun 2018

Donald J. Trump @realDonaldTrump

ALL-TIME RECORD OPTIMISM!
18,665 Retweets **75,097** Likes
8:51 PM - 20 Jun 2018

Donald J. Trump @realDonaldTrump

We shouldn't be hiring judges by the thousands, as our ridiculous immigration laws demand, we should be changing our laws, building the Wall, hire Border Agents and Ice and not let people come into our country based on the legal phrase they are told to say as their password.
27,946 Retweets **105,311** Likes
5:12 AM - 21 Jun 2018

Donald J. Trump ✓
@realDonaldTrump

The Border has been a big mess and problem for many years. At some point Schumer and Pelosi, who are weak on Crime and Border security, will be forced to do a real deal, so easy, that solves this long time problem. Schumer used to want Border security - now he'll take Crime!
17,939 Retweets **72,348** Likes
5:29 AM - 21 Jun 2018

Donald J. Trump ✓
@realDonaldTrump

I will be going the Columbia, South Carolina, on Monday night to do a campaign speech for one of my very early supporters, a man who truly loves the people of South Carolina, Governor Henry McMaster. Henry worked so hard & was so loyal to me that I look forward to reciprocating!
17,163 Retweets **81,211** Likes
5:38 AM - 21 Jun 2018

Donald J. Trump ✓
@realDonaldTrump

Last night in Minnesota was incredible. What a crowd!
12,300 Retweets **76,157** Likes
5:50 AM - 21 Jun 2018

Donald J. Trump ✓
@realDonaldTrump

What is the purpose of the House doing good immigration bills when you need 9 votes by Democrats in the Senate, and the Dems are only looking to Obstruct (which they feel is good for them in the Mid-Terms). Republicans must get rid of the stupid Filibuster Rule-it is killing you!
20,623 Retweets **77,658** Likes
6:08 AM - 21 Jun 2018

Donald J. Trump ✓
@realDonaldTrump

Henry McMaster has done a great job as Governor of South Carolina. The state is BOOMING, with jobs and new industry setting records. He is tough on Crime and Strong on Borders, Healthcare, the Military and our great Vets. Henry has my full and complete Endrosement! #MAGA
9,527 Retweets **43,115** Likes
6:52 AM - 21 Jun 2018

Donald J. Trump ✓
@realDonaldTrump

Democrats want open Borders, where anyone can come into our Country, and stay. This is Nancy Pelosi's dream. It won't happen!
25,463 Retweets **104,682** Likes
7:38 AM - 21 Jun 2018

Donald J. Trump ✓
@realDonaldTrump

My Administration is acting swiftly to address the illegal immigration crisis on the Southern Border. Loopholes in our immigration laws all supported by extremist open border Democrats...and that's what they are - they're extremist open border Democrats....
19,376 Retweets **70,977** Likes
10:02 AM - 21 Jun 2018

Donald J. Trump ✓
@realDonaldTrump

"The real big story that affects everybody in America is the success of @POTUS's TAX CUT package and what it's done for our economy…" @Varneyco
11,608 Retweets **47,038** Likes
1:25 PM - 21 Jun 2018

Donald J. Trump ✓
@realDonaldTrump

I was thrilled to be back in Minnesota for a roundtable with hardworking American Patriots. Thank you!
10,215 Retweets **51,622** Likes
1:45 PM - 21 Jun 2018

Donald J. Trump ✓
@realDonaldTrump

Farm Bill just passed in the House. So happy to see work requirements included. Big win for the farmers!
15,866 Retweets **76,785** Likes
1:46 PM - 21 Jun 2018

Donald J. Trump ✓
@realDonaldTrump

Big Supreme Court win on internet sales tax - about time! Big victory for fairness and for our country. Great victory for consumers and retailers.
14,011 Retweets **67,027** Likes
1:46 PM - 21 Jun 2018

Donald J. Trump ✓
@realDonaldTrump

"I REALLY DON'T CARE, DO U?" written on the back of Melania's jacket, refers to the Fake News Media. Melania has learned how dishonest they are, and she truly no longer cares!
41,413 Retweets **159,572** Likes
2:51 PM - 21 Jun 2018

Donald J. Trump ✓
@realDonaldTrump

We have to maintain strong borders or we will no longer have a country that we can be proud of – and if we show any weakness, millions of people will journey into our country.
32,918 Retweets **144,945** Likes
3:40 PM - 21 Jun 2018

Donald J. Trump ✓
@realDonaldTrump

You cannot pass legislation on immigration whether it be for safety and security or any other reason including "heart," without getting Dem votes. Problem is, they don't care about security and R's do. Zero Dems voted to support the Goodlatte Bill. They won't vote for anything!
23,606 Retweets **84,563** Likes
4:07 PM - 21 Jun 2018

Donald J. Trump ✓
@realDonaldTrump

Our great Judge Jeanine Pirro is out with a new book, "Liars, Leakers and Liberals, the Case Against the Anti-Trump Conspiracy," which is fantastic. Go get it!
20,268 Retweets **88,791** Likes
3:41 AM - 22 Jun 2018

President Trumps Tweets 2018: A Historical Archive of President Trump's Tweets

Donald J. Trump ✓
@realDonaldTrump

Even if we get 100% Republican votes in the Senate, we need 10 Democrat votes to get a much needed Immigration Bill - & the Dems are Obstructionists who won't give votes for political reasons & because they don't care about Crime coming from Border! So we need to elect more R's!

20,462 Retweets **77,931** Likes
3:54 AM - 22 Jun 2018

Donald J. Trump ✓
@realDonaldTrump

Elect more Republicans in November and we will pass the finest, fairest and most comprehensive Immigration Bills anywhere in the world. Right now we have the dumbest and the worst. Dems are doing nothing but Obstructing. Remember their motto, RESIST! Ours is PRODUCE!

30,186 Retweets **106,188** Likes
4:00 AM - 22 Jun 2018

Donald J. Trump ✓
@realDonaldTrump

Republicans should stop wasting their time on Immigration until after we elect more Senators and Congressmen/women in November. Dems are just playing games, have no intention of doing anything to solves this decades old problem. We can pass great legislation after the Red Wave!

24,416 Retweets **90,620** Likes
4:06 AM - 22 Jun 2018

Donald J. Trump ✓
@realDonaldTrump

Governor Henry McMaster is a truly fine man who loves the People of South Carolina. He was one of my very early supporters and truly helped me to a Big South Carolina Victory. I will see you all in S.C on Monday and Vice President Pence will be there for Henry on Saturday!

13,123 Retweets **56,818** Likes
4:31 AM - 22 Jun 2018

Donald J. Trump ✓
@realDonaldTrump

Congresswoman Martha Roby of Alabama has been a consistent and reliable vote for our Make America Great Again Agenda. She is in a Republican Primary run-off against a recent Nancy Pelosi voting Democrat. I fully endorse Martha for Alabama 2nd Congressional District!

13,681 Retweets **54,609** Likes
4:46 AM - 22 Jun 2018

Donald J. Trump ✓
@realDonaldTrump

Congressman Ron DeSantis, a top student at Yale and Harvard Law School, is running for Governor of the Great State of Florida. Ron is strong on Borders, tough on Crime & big on Cutting Taxes - Loves our Military & our Vets. He will be a Great Governor & has my full Endorsement!

24,732 Retweets **100,231** Likes
4:58 AM - 22 Jun 2018

Donald J. Trump ✓
@realDonaldTrump

80% of Mexico's Exports come to the United States. They totally rely on us, which is fine with me. They do have, though, very strong Immigration Laws. The U.S. has pathetically weak and ineffective Immigration Laws that the Democrats refuse to help us fix. Will speak to Mexico!

22,846 Retweets **92,429** Likes
6:30 AM - 22 Jun 2018

Donald J. Trump ✓
@realDonaldTrump

We must maintain a Strong Southern Border. We cannot allow our Country to be overrun by illegal immigrants as the Democrats tell their phony stories of sadness and grief, hoping it will help them in the elections. Obama and others had the same pictures, and did nothing about it!
29,162 Retweets **109,245** Likes
6:43 AM - 22 Jun 2018

Donald J. Trump ✓
@realDonaldTrump

Hope OPEC will increase output substantially. Need to keep prices down!
13,239 Retweets **63,717** Likes
7:10 AM - 22 Jun 2018

Donald J. Trump ✓
@realDonaldTrump

We are gathered today to hear directly from the AMERICAN VICTIMS of ILLEGAL IMMIGRATION. These are the American Citizens permanently separated from their loved ones b/c they were killed by criminal illegal aliens. These are the families the media ignores...
28,839 Retweets **85,917** Likes
12:40 PM - 22 Jun 2018

Donald J. Trump ✓
@realDonaldTrump

Our first duty, and our highest loyalty, is to the citizens of the United States. We will not rest until our border is secure, our citizens are safe, and we finally end the immigration crisis once and for all.
23,743 Retweets **91,563** Likes
1:23 PM - 22 Jun 2018

Donald J. Trump ✓
@realDonaldTrump

Based on the Tariffs and Trade Barriers long placed on the U.S. & its great companies and workers by the European Union, if these Tariffs and Barriers are not soon broken down and removed, we will be placing a 20% Tariff on all of their cars coming into the U.S. Build them here!
18,720 Retweets **84,433** Likes
5:34 PM - 22 Jun 2018

Donald J. Trump ✓
@realDonaldTrump

Steel is coming back fast! U.S. Steel is adding great capacity also. So are others.
11,459 Retweets **49,862** Likes
4:15 AM - 23 Jun 2018

Donald J. Trump ✓
@realDonaldTrump

.@FoxNews Poll numbers plummet on the Democrat inspired and paid for Russian Witch Hunt. With all of the bias, lying and hate by the investigators, people want the investigators investigated. Much more will come out. A total scam and excuse for the Dems losing the Election!
20,804 Retweets **84,357** Likes
4:33 AM - 23 Jun 2018

Donald J. Trump ✓
@realDonaldTrump

The Russian Witch Hunt is Rigged!
17,107 Retweets **83,777** Likes
4:36 AM - 23 Jun 2018

President Trumps Tweets 2018: A Historical Archive of President Trump's Tweets

Donald J. Trump ✓
@realDonaldTrump

The National Association of Manufacturers just announced that 95.1% of Manufacturers "have a positive outlook for their companies." This is the best number in the Association's history!

18,264 Retweets **79,590** Likes
5:38 AM - 23 Jun 2018

Donald J. Trump ✓
@realDonaldTrump

"Disability applications plunge as economy strengthens" Failing New York Times

12,856 Retweets **61,990** Likes
5:42 AM - 23 Jun 2018

Donald J. Trump ✓
@realDonaldTrump

Drudge Report "OBAMA KEPT THEM IN CAGES, WRAPPED THEM IN FOIL" We do a much better job while at the same time maintaining a MUCH stronger Border! Mainstream Fake Media hates this story.

30,988 Retweets **111,361** Likes
5:52 AM - 23 Jun 2018

Donald J. Trump ✓
@realDonaldTrump

.@VP Pence is heading to Pittsburgh, Pennsylvania where we have both strongly endorsed one of the finest men around, Congressman Keith @RothfusForPA. He is running against #LambTheSham, who is telling...

9,750 Retweets **43,376** Likes
7:00 AM - 23 Jun 2018

Donald J. Trump ✓
@realDonaldTrump

...everyone how much he likes me, but he will only vote with Nancy Pelosi. Keith is strong on borders and tough on crime — and loves cutting taxes! #MAGA

7,774 Retweets **36,985** Likes
7:00 AM - 23 Jun 2018

Donald J. Trump ✓
@realDonaldTrump

My thoughts and prayers are with Representative Katie Arrington of South Carolina, including all of those involved in last nights car accident, and their families.

13,102 Retweets **58,091** Likes
7:53 AM - 23 Jun 2018

Donald J. Trump ✓
@realDonaldTrump

Heading to Nevada to talk trade and immigration with supporters. Country's economy is stronger than ever before with numbers that are getting better by the week. Tremendous potential, and trade deals are coming along well.

14,794 Retweets **77,984** Likes
9:57 AM - 23 Jun 2018

Donald J. Trump ✓
@realDonaldTrump

It's very sad that Nancy Pelosi and her sidekick, Cryin' Chuck Schumer, want to protect illegal immigrants far more than the citizens of our country. The United States cannot stand for this. We wants safety and security at our borders!

36,438 Retweets **150,085** Likes
10:05 AM - 23 Jun 2018

Donald J. Trump ✓
@realDonaldTrump

Happy Birthday to Supreme Court Justice Clarence Thomas, a friend and great man!
18,405 Retweets **91,154** Likes
10:12 AM - 23 Jun 2018

Donald J. Trump ✓
@realDonaldTrump

Thank you @NVGOP! #MAGA
9,161 Retweets **41,577** Likes
1:25 PM - 23 Jun 2018

Donald J. Trump ✓
@realDonaldTrump

AMERICA IS OPEN FOR BUSINESS!
16,171 Retweets **73,825** Likes
3:06 PM - 23 Jun 2018

Donald J. Trump ✓
@realDonaldTrump

Major Wall Street Journal opinion piece today talking about the Russian Witch Hunt and the disgrace that it is. So many people hurt, so bad for our country - a total sham!
24,327 Retweets **82,333** Likes
6:43 PM - 23 Jun 2018

Donald J. Trump ✓
@realDonaldTrump

Democrats, fix the laws. Don't RESIST. We are doing a far better job than Bush and Obama, but we need strength and security at the Border! Cannot accept all of the people trying to break into our Country. Strong Borders, No Crime!
30,122 Retweets **124,637** Likes
6:12 AM - 24 Jun 2018

Donald J. Trump ✓
@realDonaldTrump

We cannot allow all of these people to invade our Country. When somebody comes in, we must immediately, with no Judges or Court Cases, bring them back from where they came. Our system is a mockery to good immigration policy and Law and Order. Most children come without parents...
29,919 Retweets **118,256** Likes
8:02 AM - 24 Jun 2018

Donald J. Trump ✓
@realDonaldTrump

....Our Immigration policy, laughed at all over the world, is very unfair to all of those people who have gone through the system legally and are waiting on line for years! Immigration must be based on merit - we need people who will help to Make America Great Again!
30,321 Retweets **124,176** Likes
8:08 AM - 24 Jun 2018

Donald J. Trump ✓
@realDonaldTrump

The United States is insisting that all countries that have placed artificial Trade Barriers and Tariffs on goods going into their country, remove those Barriers & Tariffs or be met with more than Reciprocity by the U.S.A. Trade must be fair and no longer a one way street!
26,841 Retweets **110,562** Likes
1:12 PM - 24 Jun 2018

President Trumps Tweets 2018: A Historical Archive of President Trump's Tweets

Donald J. Trump ✓
@realDonaldTrump

.@jimmyfallon is now whimpering to all that he did the famous "hair show" with me (where he seriously messed up my hair), & that he would have now done it differently because it is said to have "humanized" me-he is taking heat. He called & said "monster ratings." Be a man Jimmy!
19,065 Retweets **92,867** Likes
5:01 PM - 24 Jun 2018

Donald J. Trump ✓
@realDonaldTrump

House Republicans could easily pass a Bill on Strong Border Security but remember, it still has to pass in the Senate, and for that we need 10 Democrat votes, and all they do is RESIST. They want Open Borders and don't care about Crime! Need more Republicans to WIN in November!
28,412 Retweets **109,425** Likes
5:08 PM - 24 Jun 2018

Donald J. Trump ✓
@realDonaldTrump

.@RepClayHiggins has been a great help to me on Cutting Taxes, creating great new healthcare programs at low cost, fighting for Border Security, our Military and are Vets. He is tough on Crime and has my full Endorsement. The Great State of Louisiana, we want Clay!
13,888 Retweets **60,764** Likes
6:08 PM - 24 Jun 2018

Donald J. Trump ✓
@realDonaldTrump

Former Attorney General Michael Mukasey said that President Trump is probably correct that there was surveillance on Trump Tower. Actually, far greater than would ever have been believed!
17,961 Retweets **72,144** Likes
4:28 AM - 25 Jun 2018

Donald J. Trump ✓
@realDonaldTrump

The Red Hen Restaurant should focus more on cleaning its filthy canopies, doors and windows (badly needs a paint job) rather than refusing to serve a fine person like Sarah Huckabee Sanders. I always had a rule, if a restaurant is dirty on the outside, it is dirty on the inside!
34,364 Retweets **136,352** Likes
4:41 AM - 25 Jun 2018

Donald J. Trump ✓
@realDonaldTrump

I have tried to stay uninvolved with the Department of Justice and FBI (although I do not legally have to), because of the now totally discredited and very expensive Witch Hunt currently going on. But you do have to ask why the DOJ & FBI aren't giving over requested documents?
29,187 Retweets **113,555** Likes
5:02 AM - 25 Jun 2018

Donald J. Trump ✓
@realDonaldTrump

Such a difference in the media coverage of the same immigration policies between the Obama Administration and ours. Actually, we have done a far better job in that our facilities are cleaner and better run than were the facilities under Obama. Fake News is working overtime!
25,797 Retweets **103,399** Likes
5:36 AM - 25 Jun 2018

Donald J. Trump ✓
@realDonaldTrump

Hiring manythousands of judges, and going through a long and complicated legal process, is not the way to go - will always be dysfunctional. People must simply be stopped at the Border and told they cannot come into the U.S. illegally. Children brought back to their country......
21,557 Retweets **90,886** Likes
5:43 AM - 25 Jun 2018

Donald J. Trump ✓
@realDonaldTrump

....If this is done, illegal immigration will be stopped in it's tracks - and at very little, by comparison, cost. This is the only real answer - and we must continue to BUILD THE WALL!
21,536 Retweets **93,131** Likes
5:54 AM - 25 Jun 2018

Donald J. Trump ✓
@realDonaldTrump

Will be heading to one of my favorite places, South Carolina, to fight for one of my original "fighters," Governor Henry McMaster. Speaking at 7:00 P.M.
14,456 Retweets **70,944** Likes
7:36 AM - 25 Jun 2018

Donald J. Trump ✓
@realDonaldTrump

Congresswoman Maxine Waters, an extraordinarily low IQ person, has become, together with Nancy Pelosi, the Face of the Democrat Party. She has just called for harm to supporters, of which there are many, of the Make America Great Again movement. Be careful what you wish for Max!
40,092 Retweets **141,932** Likes
10:11 AM - 25 Jun 2018

Donald J. Trump ✓
@realDonaldTrump

Surprised that Harley-Davidson, of all companies, would be the first to wave the White Flag. I fought hard for them and ultimately they will not pay tariffs selling into the E.U., which has hurt us badly on trade, down $151 Billion. Taxes just a Harley excuse - be patient! #MAGA
16,881 Retweets **73,870** Likes
2:28 PM - 25 Jun 2018

Donald J. Trump ✓
@realDonaldTrump

"Director David Lynch: Trump Could Go Down as One of the Greatest Presidents"
14,395 Retweets **60,683** Likes
4:06 PM - 25 Jun 2018

Donald J. Trump ✓
@realDonaldTrump

Why is Senator Mark Warner (D-VA), perhaps in a near drunken state, claiming he has information that only he and Bob Mueller, the leader of the 13 Angry Democrats on a Witch Hunt, knows? Isn't this highly illegal. Is it being investigated?
24,551 Retweets **90,067** Likes
4:22 PM - 25 Jun 2018

President Trumps Tweets 2018: A Historical Archive of President Trump's Tweets

Donald J. Trump ✓
@realDonaldTrump

The hearing of Peter Strzok and the other hating frauds at the FBI & DOJ should be shown to the public on live television, not a closed door hearing that nobody will see. We should expose these people for what they are - there should be total transparency!
37,554 Retweets **131,502** Likes
4:30 PM - 25 Jun 2018

Donald J. Trump ✓
@realDonaldTrump

Just landed in South Carolina - will be at the McMaster rally shortly! #MAGA
7,622 Retweets **51,750** Likes
4:44 PM - 25 Jun 2018

Donald J. Trump ✓
@realDonaldTrump

Thank you South Carolina. Now let's get out tomorrow and VOTE for @HenryMcMaster!
12,949 Retweets **55,392** Likes
6:35 PM - 25 Jun 2018

Donald J. Trump ✓
@realDonaldTrump

Early this year Harley-Davidson said they would move much of their plant operations in Kansas City to Thailand. That was long before Tariffs were announced. Hence, they were just using Tariffs/Trade War as an excuse. Shows how unbalanced & unfair trade is, but we will fix it.....
14,304 Retweets **64,499** Likes
4:16 AM - 26 Jun 2018

Donald J. Trump ✓
@realDonaldTrump

....We are getting other countries to reduce and eliminate tariffs and trade barriers that have been unfairly used for years against our farmers, workers and companies. We are opening up closed markets and expanding our footprint. They must play fair or they will pay tariffs!
13,946 Retweets **64,592** Likes
4:25 AM - 26 Jun 2018

Donald J. Trump ✓
@realDonaldTrump

....When I had Harley-Davidson officials over to the White House, I chided them about tariffs in other countries, like India, being too high. Companies are now coming back to America. Harley must know that they won't be able to sell back into U.S. without paying a big tax!
11,959 Retweets **56,864** Likes
4:37 AM - 26 Jun 2018

Donald J. Trump ✓
@realDonaldTrump

....We are finishing our study of Tariffs on cars from the E.U. in that they have long taken advantage of the U.S. in the form of Trade Barriers and Tariffs. In the end it will all even out - and it won't take very long!
12,041 Retweets **57,496** Likes
4:49 AM - 26 Jun 2018

Anthony T. Michalisko

Donald J. Trump ⊕
@realDonaldTrump

It was great being with Governor Henry McMaster last night in South Carolina. Henry is tough on Crime and Borders, loves our Military and our Vets and has created many jobs and a great economy. GO OUT AND VOTE FOR HENRY TODAY, HE WILL NEVER LET YOU DOWN!
15,055 Retweets **71,442** Likes
4:57 AM - 26 Jun 2018

Donald J. Trump ⊕
@realDonaldTrump

A Harley-Davidson should never be built in another country-never! Their employees and customers are already very angry at them. If they move, watch, it will be the beginning of the end - they surrendered, they quit! The Aura will be gone and they will be taxed like never before!
19,167 Retweets **87,652** Likes
5:17 AM - 26 Jun 2018

Donald J. Trump ⊕
@realDonaldTrump

The face of the Democrats is now Maxine Waters who, together with Nancy Pelosi, have established a fine leadership team. They should always stay together and lead the Democrats, who want Open Borders and Unlimited Crime, well into the future....and pick Crooked Hillary for Pres.
24,015 Retweets **96,900** Likes
5:36 AM - 26 Jun 2018

Donald J. Trump ⊕
@realDonaldTrump

"The most profound question of our era: Was there a conspiracy in the Obama Department of Justice and the FBI to prevent Donald Trump from becoming President of the U.S., and was Strzok at the core of the conspiracy?" Judge Andrew Napolitano
27,933 Retweets **105,727** Likes
6:30 AM - 26 Jun 2018

Donald J. Trump ⊕
@realDonaldTrump

SUPREME COURT UPHOLDS TRUMP TRAVEL BAN. Wow!
35,672 Retweets **167,232** Likes
7:40 AM - 26 Jun 2018

Donald J. Trump ⊕
@realDonaldTrump

Today, we tell the story of an incredible HERO who defended our nation in World War Two – First Lieutenant Garlin Murl Conner. Although he died 20 years ago, today he takes his rightful place in the Eternal Chronicle of American Valor...
14,919 Retweets **70,942** Likes
1:12 PM - 26 Jun 2018

Donald J. Trump ⊕
@realDonaldTrump

Congratulations to Governor Henry McMaster on your BIG election win! South Carolina loves you. We are all proud of you and Peggy! @henrymcmaster
12,853 Retweets **65,443** Likes
6:52 PM - 26 Jun 2018

Donald J. Trump ✓
@realDonaldTrump

Tremendous win for Congressman Dan Donovan. You showed great courage in a tough race! New York, and my many friends on Staten Island, have elected someone they have always been very proud of. Congratulations!
14,055 Retweets **73,868** Likes
7:05 PM - 26 Jun 2018

Donald J. Trump ✓
@realDonaldTrump

Wow! Big Trump Hater Congressman Joe Crowley, who many expected was going to take Nancy Pelosi's place, just LOST his primary election. In other words, he's out! That is a big one that nobody saw happening. Perhaps he should have been nicer, and more respectful, to his President!
23,672 Retweets **119,570** Likes
7:18 PM - 26 Jun 2018

Donald J. Trump ✓
@realDonaldTrump

The Democrats are in Turmoil! Open Borders and unchecked Crime a certain way to lose elections. Republicans are for Strong Borders, NO Crime! A BIG NIGHT!
17,929 Retweets **81,527** Likes
7:47 PM - 26 Jun 2018

Donald J. Trump ✓
@realDonaldTrump

A great First Lady!
15,173 Retweets **88,784** Likes
7:54 PM - 26 Jun 2018

Donald J. Trump ✓
@realDonaldTrump

The legendary Gary Player at Turnberry in Scotland!
4,882 Retweets **33,173** Likes
7:59 PM - 26 Jun 2018

Donald J. Trump ✓
@realDonaldTrump

Big and conclusive win by Mitt Romney. Congratulations! I look forward to working together - there is so much good to do. A great and loving family will be coming to D.C.
9,319 Retweets **62,080** Likes
8:52 PM - 26 Jun 2018

Donald J. Trump ✓
@realDonaldTrump

Congratulations to Maxine Waters, whose crazy rants have made her, together with Nancy Pelosi, the unhinged FACE of the Democrat Party. Together, they will Make America Weak Again! But have no fear, America is now stronger than ever before, and I'm not going anywhere!
36,724 Retweets **156,734** Likes
4:18 AM - 27 Jun 2018

Donald J. Trump ✓
@realDonaldTrump

HOUSE REPUBLICANS SHOULD PASS THE STRONG BUT FAIR IMMIGRATION BILL, KNOWN AS GOODLATTE II, IN THEIR AFTERNOON VOTE TODAY, EVEN THOUGH THE DEMS WON'T LET IT PASS IN THE SENATE. PASSAGE WILL SHOW THAT WE WANT STRONG BORDERS & SECURITY WHILE THE DEMS WANT OPEN BORDERS = CRIME. WIN!
21,991 Retweets **98,022** Likes
5:39 AM - 27 Jun 2018

Donald J. Trump ✓
@realDonaldTrump

Supreme Court rules in favor of non-union workers who are now, as an example, able to support a candidate of his or her choice without having those who control the Union deciding for them. Big loss for the coffers of the Democrats!
23,027 Retweets **102,751** Likes
7:11 AM - 27 Jun 2018

Donald J. Trump ✓
@realDonaldTrump

Harley-Davidson should stay 100% in America, with the people that got you your success. I've done so much for you, and then this. Other companies are coming back where they belong! We won't forget, and neither will your customers or your now very HAPPY competitors!
17,963 Retweets **83,318** Likes
8:26 AM - 27 Jun 2018

Donald J. Trump ✓
@realDonaldTrump

Today, I was thrilled to join student leaders from Colleges and Universities across the country...
11,016 Retweets **54,531** Likes
10:33 AM - 27 Jun 2018

Donald J. Trump ✓
@realDonaldTrump

Statement on Justice Anthony Kennedy. #SCOTUS
10,718 Retweets **46,708** Likes
12:13 PM - 27 Jun 2018

Donald J. Trump ✓
@realDonaldTrump

Heading to North Dakota to fully stand with and endorse Kevin Cramer for Senate. He is an extraordinary Congressman who will hopefully soon represent this great state as your Senator. He is tough on crime, strong on borders, loves our Military, and our Vets! #NDSen
12,826 Retweets **58,092** Likes
1:28 PM - 27 Jun 2018

Donald J. Trump ✓
@realDonaldTrump

Today, it was my great honor to welcome President Marcelo Rebelo de Sousa of Portugal to the @WhiteHouse!
10,277 Retweets **57,834** Likes
2:18 PM - 27 Jun 2018

Donald J. Trump ✓
@realDonaldTrump

Just landed in North Dakota with @SenJohnHoeven and @RepKevinCramer. We will see everyone at Scheels Arena shortly!
7,614 Retweets **43,979** Likes
4:14 PM - 27 Jun 2018

President Trumps Tweets 2018: A Historical Archive of President Trump's Tweets

Donald J. Trump ✓
@realDonaldTrump

Thank you North Dakota. Together, we are MAKING AMERICA SAFE AND GREAT AGAIN! #MAGA
15,372 Retweets **73,545** Likes
8:03 PM - 27 Jun 2018

Donald J. Trump ✓
@realDonaldTrump

In recent days we have heard shameless attacks on our courageous law enforcement officers. Extremist Democrat politicians have called for the complete elimination of ICE. Leftwing Activists are trying to block ICE officers from doing their jobs and publicly posting their...
20,988 Retweets **81,772** Likes
8:24 PM - 27 Jun 2018

Donald J. Trump ✓
@realDonaldTrump

...home addresses – putting these selfless public servants in harm's way. These radical protesters want ANARCHY – but the only response they will find from our government is LAW AND ORDER!
18,446 Retweets **79,650** Likes
8:24 PM - 27 Jun 2018

Donald J. Trump ✓
@realDonaldTrump

Lover FBI Agent Peter Strzok was given poor marks on yesterday's closed door testimony and, according to most reports, refused to answer many questions. There was no Collusion and the Witch Hunt, headed by 13 Angry Democrats and others who are totally conflicted, is Rigged!
18,418 Retweets **77,564** Likes
4:02 AM - 28 Jun 2018

Donald J. Trump ✓
@realDonaldTrump

Russia continues to say they had nothing to do with Meddling in our Election! Where is the DNC Server, and why didn't Shady James Comey and the now disgraced FBI agents take and closely examine it? Why isn't Hillary/Russia being looked at? So many questions, so much corruption!
22,480 Retweets **92,201** Likes
4:25 AM - 28 Jun 2018

Donald J. Trump ✓
@realDonaldTrump

Amy Kremer, Women for Trump, was so great on @foxandfriends. Brave and very smart, thank you Amy! @AmyKremer
9,205 Retweets **50,408** Likes
4:32 AM - 28 Jun 2018

Donald J. Trump ✓
@realDonaldTrump

Just watched @SharkGregNorman on @foxandfriends. Said "President is doing a great job. All over the world, people want to come back to the U.S." Thank you Greg, and you're looking and doing great!
11,637 Retweets **61,615** Likes
4:38 AM - 28 Jun 2018

Donald J. Trump ✓
@realDonaldTrump

Peter Strzok worked as the leader of the Rigged Witch Hunt for a long period of time - he got it started and was only fired because the gig was up. But remember, he took his orders from Comey and McCabe and they took their orders from you know who. Mueller/Comey best friends!
20,769 Retweets **80,110** Likes
5:30 AM - 28 Jun 2018

Donald J. Trump ✓
@realDonaldTrump

When is Bob Mueller going to list his Conflicts of Interest? Why has it taken so long? Will they be listed at the top of his $22,000,000 Report...And what about the 13 Angry Democrats, will they list their conflicts with Crooked H? How many people will be sent to jail and......
20,122 Retweets **78,853** Likes
5:43 AM - 28 Jun 2018

Donald J. Trump ✓
@realDonaldTrump

....persecuted on old and/or totally unrelated charges (there was no collusion and there was no obstruction of the no collusion)...And what is going on in the FBI & DOJ with Crooked Hillary, the DNC and all of the lies? A disgraceful situation!
16,715 Retweets **72,445** Likes
5:56 AM - 28 Jun 2018

Donald J. Trump ✓
@realDonaldTrump

I am in Milwaukee, Wisconsin, for meetings. Soon to leave for a big groundbreaking for Foxconn, which is building a great new electronics plant in Wisconsin. 15,000 Jobs, so great!
15,836 Retweets **87,968** Likes
6:06 AM - 28 Jun 2018

Donald J. Trump ✓
@realDonaldTrump

Today, we broke ground on a plant that will provide jobs for up to 15,000 Wisconsin Workers! As Foxconn has discovered, there is no better place to build, hire and grow than right here in the United States!
21,298 Retweets **94,785** Likes
11:57 AM - 28 Jun 2018

Donald J. Trump ✓
@realDonaldTrump

AMERICA IS OPEN FOR BUSINESS!
12,262 Retweets **55,013** Likes
12:09 PM - 28 Jun 2018

Donald J. Trump ✓
@realDonaldTrump

Prior to departing Wisconsin, I was briefed on the shooting at Capital Gazette in Annapolis, Maryland. My thoughts and prayers are with the victims and their families. Thank you to all of the First Responders who are currently on the scene.
17,553 Retweets **96,358** Likes
1:49 PM - 28 Jun 2018

President Trumps Tweets 2018: A Historical Archive of President Trump's Tweets

Donald J. Trump ✓
@realDonaldTrump

Before going any further today, I want to address the horrific shooting that took place yesterday at the Capital Gazette newsroom in Annapolis, Maryland. This attack shocked the conscience of our Nation, and filled our hearts with grief...
11,706 Retweets **58,414** Likes
10:59 AM - 29 Jun 2018

Donald J. Trump ✓
@realDonaldTrump

Six months after our TAX CUTS, more than 6 MILLION workers have received bonuses, pay raises, and retirement account contributions. #TaxCutsandJobsAct
18,894 Retweets **84,178** Likes
11:06 AM - 29 Jun 2018

Donald J. Trump ✓
@realDonaldTrump

The new plant being built by Foxconn in Wisconsin is incredible. Congratulations to the people of Wisconsin and to Governor Scott Walker @GovWalker and his talented representatives for having pulled it off. Great job!
14,978 Retweets **75,479** Likes
4:30 PM - 29 Jun 2018

Donald J. Trump ✓
@realDonaldTrump

The Democrats are making a strong push to abolish ICE, one of the smartest, toughest and most spirited law enforcement groups of men and women that I have ever seen. I have watched ICE liberate towns from the grasp of MS-13 & clean out the toughest of situations. They are great!
27,356 Retweets **113,034** Likes
4:07 AM - 30 Jun 2018

Donald J. Trump ✓
@realDonaldTrump

To the great and brave men and women of ICE, do not worry or lose your spirit. You are doing a fantastic job of keeping us safe by eradicating the worst criminal elements. So brave! The radical left Dems want you out. Next it will be all police. Zero chance, It will never happen!
38,646 Retweets **151,149** Likes
4:22 AM - 30 Jun 2018

Donald J. Trump ✓
@realDonaldTrump

Just spoke to King Salman of Saudi Arabia and explained to him that, because of the turmoil & disfunction in Iran and Venezuela, I am asking that Saudi Arabia increase oil production, maybe up to 2,000,000 barrels, to make up the difference...Prices to high! He has agreed!
41,617 Retweets **154,940** Likes
4:37 AM - 30 Jun 2018

Donald J. Trump ✓
@realDonaldTrump

I will be making my choice for Justice of the United States Supreme Court on the first Monday after the July 4th Holiday, July 9th!
21,404 Retweets **107,336** Likes
5:33 AM - 30 Jun 2018

Donald J. Trump ✓
@realDonaldTrump

A friend of mine and a man who has truly seen politics and life as few others ever will, Sean Spicer, has written a great new book, "The Briefing: Politics, the Press and the President." It is a story told with both heart and knowledge. Really good, go get it!
15,514 Retweets **78,272** Likes
12:05 PM - 30 Jun 2018

Donald J. Trump ✓
@realDonaldTrump

I never pushed the Republicans in the House to vote for the Immigration Bill, either GOODLATTE 1 or 2, because it could never have gotten enough Democrats as long as there is the 60 vote threshold. I released many prior to the vote knowing we need more Republicans to win in Nov.
15,407 Retweets **69,000** Likes
12:17 PM - 30 Jun 2018

Donald J. Trump ✓
@realDonaldTrump

Either we need to elect more Republicans in November or Republicans must end the ridiculous 60 vote, or Filibuster, rule - or better yet, do both. Cryin' Chuck would do it on day one, but we'll never give him the chance. Some great legislation awaits - be smart!
23,594 Retweets **95,837** Likes
12:26 PM - 30 Jun 2018

Donald J. Trump ✓
@realDonaldTrump

I will be interviewed by @MariaBartiromo on Sunday on @FoxNews at 10:00 A. M. Enjoy!
9,864 Retweets **50,760** Likes
12:31 PM - 30 Jun 2018

Donald J. Trump ✓
@realDonaldTrump

When people come into our Country illegally, we must IMMEDIATELY escort them back out without going through years of legal maneuvering. Our laws are the dumbest anywhere in the world. Republicans want Strong Borders and no Crime. Dems want Open Borders and are weak on Crime!
38,990 Retweets **155,402** Likes
12:44 PM - 30 Jun 2018

Donald J. Trump ✓
@realDonaldTrump

I will be interviewed by @MariaBartiromo at 10:00 A.M. on @FoxNews
8,301 Retweets **50,863** Likes
5:00 AM - 1 Jul 2018

Donald J. Trump ✓
@realDonaldTrump

The Liberal Left, also known as the Democrats, want to get rid of ICE, who do a fantastic job, and want Open Borders. Crime would be rampant and uncontrollable! Make America Great Again
30,653 Retweets **133,568** Likes
5:11 AM - 1 Jul 2018

Donald J. Trump ✓
@realDonaldTrump

A big week, especially with our numerous victories in the Supreme Court. Heading back to the White House now. Focus will be on the selection of a new Supreme Court Justice. Exciting times for our country. Economy may be stronger than it has ever been!
26,419 Retweets **126,018** Likes
12:39 PM - 1 Jul 2018

President Trumps Tweets 2018: A Historical Archive of President Trump's Tweets

Donald J. Trump ✓
@realDonaldTrump

Congratulations to Andres Manuel Lopez Obrador on becoming the next President of Mexico. I look very much forward to working with him. There is much to be done that will benefit both the United States and Mexico!

67,944 Retweets **211,701** Likes
8:01 PM - 1 Jul 2018

Donald J. Trump ✓
@realDonaldTrump

Today, it was my great honor to welcome Prime Minister Mark Rutte of the Netherlands, to the @WhiteHouse!

12,257 Retweets **68,349** Likes
2:48 PM - 2 Jul 2018

Donald J. Trump ✓
@realDonaldTrump

Many Democrats are deeply concerned about the fact that their "leadership" wants to denounce and abandon the great men and women of ICE, thereby declaring war on Law & Order. These people will be voting for Republicans in November and, in many cases, joining the Republican Party!

26,608 Retweets **112,425** Likes
7:43 PM - 2 Jul 2018

Donald J. Trump ✓
@realDonaldTrump

Crazy Maxine Waters, said by some to be one of the most corrupt people in politics, is rapidly becoming, together with Nancy Pelosi, the FACE of the Democrat Party. Her ranting and raving, even referring to herself as a wounded animal, will make people flee the Democrats!

19,571 Retweets **86,022** Likes
3:16 AM - 3 Jul 2018

Donald J. Trump ✓
@realDonaldTrump

I interviewed 4 very impressive people yesterday. On Monday I will be announcing my decision for Justice of the United States Supreme Court!

14,187 Retweets **75,430** Likes
3:25 AM - 3 Jul 2018

Donald J. Trump ✓
@realDonaldTrump

The economy is doing perhaps better than ever before, and that's prior to fixing some of the worst and most unfair Trade Deals ever made by any country. In any event, they are coming along very well. Most countries agree that they must be changed, but nobody ever asked!

14,724 Retweets **67,668** Likes
3:33 AM - 3 Jul 2018

Donald J. Trump ✓
@realDonaldTrump

When we have an "infestation" of MS-13 GANGS in certain parts of our country, who do we send to get them out? ICE! They are tougher and smarter than these rough criminal elelments that bad immigration laws allow into our country. Dems do not appreciate the great job they do! Nov.

22,371 Retweets **96,354** Likes
3:49 AM - 3 Jul 2018

Donald J. Trump ✓
@realDonaldTrump

How can the Democrats, who are weak on the Border and weak on Crime, do well in November. The people of our Country want and demand Safety and Security, while the Democrats are more interested in ripping apart and demeaning (and not properly funding) our great Law Enforcement!
20,771 Retweets **88,158** Likes
3:57 AM - 3 Jul 2018

Donald J. Trump ✓
@realDonaldTrump

Many good conversations with North Korea-it is going well! In the meantime, no Rocket Launches or Nuclear Testing in 8 months. All of Asia is thrilled. Only the Opposition Party, which includes the Fake News, is complaining. If not for me, we would now be at War with North Korea!
19,276 Retweets **83,420** Likes
4:16 AM - 3 Jul 2018

Donald J. Trump ✓
@realDonaldTrump

Just out that the Obama Administration granted citizenship, during the terrible Iran Deal negotiation, to 2,500 Iranians - including to government officials. How big (and bad) is that?
29,751 Retweets **94,900** Likes
5:03 AM - 3 Jul 2018

Donald J. Trump ✓
@realDonaldTrump

Now that Harley-Davidson is moving part of its operation out of the U.S., my Administration is working with other Motor Cycle companies who want to move into the U.S. Harley customers are not happy with their move - sales are down 7% in 2017. The U.S. is where the Action is!
18,312 Retweets **87,917** Likes
7:00 AM - 3 Jul 2018

Donald J. Trump ✓
@realDonaldTrump

Wow! The NSA has deleted 685 million phone calls and text messages. Privacy violations? They blame technical irregularities. Such a disgrace. The Witch Hunt continues!
28,453 Retweets **109,026** Likes
7:18 AM - 3 Jul 2018

Donald J. Trump ✓
@realDonaldTrump

Heading to West Virginia to be with my friend, @WVGovernor Jim Justice, at his beautiful Greenbrier Resort. He works hard, does a great job, and raises lots of money for charities!
9,292 Retweets **52,633** Likes
2:26 PM - 3 Jul 2018

Donald J. Trump ✓
@realDonaldTrump

The Washington Post is constantly quoting "anonymous sources" that do not exist. Rarely do they use the name of anyone because there is no one to give them the kind of negative quote that they are looking for. They are a disgrace to journalism but then again, so are many others!
23,407 Retweets **98,967** Likes
2:35 PM - 3 Jul 2018

President Trumps Tweets 2018: A Historical Archive of President Trump's Tweets

Donald J. Trump ✓
@realDonaldTrump

After having written many best selling books, and somewhat priding myself on my ability to write, it should be noted that the Fake News constantly likes to pore over my tweets looking for a mistake. I capitalize certain words only for emphasis, not b/c they should be capitalized!
15,333 Retweets **88,278** Likes
4:13 PM - 3 Jul 2018

Donald J. Trump ✓
@realDonaldTrump

Thank you, @WVGovernor Jim Justice, for that warm introduction. Tonight, it was my great honor to attend the "Greenbrier Classic – Salute to Service Dinner" in West Virginia! God Bless our Veterans. God Bless America - and HAPPY INDEPENDENCE DAY TO ALL!
10,256 Retweets **49,400** Likes
4:19 PM - 3 Jul 2018

Donald J. Trump ✓
@realDonaldTrump

Tonight we gathered to celebrate the courageous men and women who make freedom possible: our brave service members, and our wonderful Veterans. For 242 years, American Independence...
18,613 Retweets **92,312** Likes
4:52 PM - 3 Jul 2018

Donald J. Trump ✓
@realDonaldTrump

...has endured because of the sweat, blood and sacrifice of the American Armed Forces – the greatest force for peace and justice in the history of the world!
12,972 Retweets **67,073** Likes
4:52 PM - 3 Jul 2018

Donald J. Trump ✓
@realDonaldTrump

Tomorrow, families across our Nation will gather to celebrate the Fourth of July. As we do, we will think of the men & women serving overseas at this very moment, far away from their families, protecting America - & we will thank GOD for blessing us with these incredible HEROES!
20,776 Retweets **90,767** Likes
5:36 PM - 3 Jul 2018

Donald J. Trump ✓
@realDonaldTrump

Happy Fourth of July....Our Country is doing GREAT!
46,295 Retweets **227,562** Likes
7:42 AM - 4 Jul 2018

Donald J. Trump ✓
@realDonaldTrump

The OPEC Monopoly must remember that gas prices are up & they are doing little to help. If anything, they are driving prices higher as the United States defends many of their members for very little $'s. This must be a two way street. REDUCE PRICING NOW!
26,956 Retweets **114,781** Likes
1:46 PM - 4 Jul 2018

Donald J. Trump ✓
@realDonaldTrump

Happy Birthday, America!
33,677 Retweets **185,695** Likes
7:47 PM - 4 Jul 2018

Donald J. Trump ✓
@realDonaldTrump

Congress must pass smart, fast and reasonable Immigration Laws now. Law Enforcement at the Border is doing a great job, but the laws they are forced to work with are insane. When people, with or without children, enter our Country, they must be told to leave without our........
19,830 Retweets **84,022** Likes
7:08 AM - 5 Jul 2018

Donald J. Trump ✓
@realDonaldTrump

......Country being forced to endure a long and costly trial. Tell the people "OUT," and they must leave, just as they would if they were standing on your front lawn. Hiring thousands of "judges" does not work and is not acceptable - only Country in the World that does this!
20,471 Retweets **86,500** Likes
7:16 AM - 5 Jul 2018

Donald J. Trump ✓
@realDonaldTrump

Congress - FIX OUR INSANE IMMIGRATION LAWS NOW!
26,448 Retweets **114,948** Likes
7:17 AM - 5 Jul 2018

Donald J. Trump ✓
@realDonaldTrump

I have accepted the resignation of Scott Pruitt as the Administrator of the Environmental Protection Agency. Within the Agency Scott has done an outstanding job, and I will always be thankful to him for this. The Senate confirmed Deputy at EPA, Andrew Wheeler, will...
15,218 Retweets **65,928** Likes
12:37 PM - 5 Jul 2018

Donald J. Trump ✓
@realDonaldTrump

...on Monday assume duties as the acting Administrator of the EPA. I have no doubt that Andy will continue on with our great and lasting EPA agenda. We have made tremendous progress and the future of the EPA is very bright!
9,579 Retweets **46,816** Likes
12:37 PM - 5 Jul 2018

Donald J. Trump ✓
@realDonaldTrump

It was my great honor to join proud, hardworking American Patriots in Montana tonight. I love you - thank you! #MAGA
14,036 Retweets **66,063** Likes
5:11 PM - 5 Jul 2018

Donald J. Trump ✓
@realDonaldTrump

A vote for Democrats in November is a vote to let MS-13 run wild in our communities, to let drugs pour into our cities, and to take jobs and benefits away from hardworking Americans. Democrats want anarchy, amnesty and chaos - Republicans want LAW, ORDER and JUSTICE!
33,537 Retweets **131,672** Likes
5:44 PM - 5 Jul 2018

President Trumps Tweets 2018: A Historical Archive of President Trump's Tweets

Donald J. Trump ✓
@realDonaldTrump

Every day, the brave men and women of ICE are liberating communities from savage gangs like MS-13. We will NOT stand for these vile Democrat smears in law enforcement. We will always stand proudly with the BRAVE HEROES of ICE and BORDER PATROL!
26,234 Retweets **117,336** Likes
5:58 PM - 5 Jul 2018

Donald J. Trump ✓
@realDonaldTrump

Thanks to REPUBLICAN LEADERSHIP, America is WINNING AGAIN - and America is being RESPECTED again all over the world. Because we are finally putting AMERICA FIRST!
23,755 Retweets **119,877** Likes
6:06 PM - 5 Jul 2018

Donald J. Trump ✓
@realDonaldTrump

JOBS, JOBS, JOBS!
21,912 Retweets **91,503** Likes
9:12 AM - 6 Jul 2018

Donald J. Trump ✓
@realDonaldTrump

Just won lawsuit filed by the DNC and a bunch of Democrat crazies trying to claim the Trump Campaign (and others), colluded with Russia. They haven't figured out that this was an excuse for them losing the election!
35,227 Retweets **151,126** Likes
9:57 AM - 6 Jul 2018

Donald J. Trump ✓
@realDonaldTrump

Twitter is getting rid of fake accounts at a record pace. Will that include the Failing New York Times and propaganda machine for Amazon, the Washington Post, who constantly quote anonymous sources that, in my opinion, don't exist - They will both be out of business in 7 years!
30,058 Retweets **126,598** Likes
6:21 AM - 7 Jul 2018

Donald J. Trump ✓
@realDonaldTrump

Big decision will soon be made on our next Justice of the Supreme Court!
17,775 Retweets **103,820** Likes
6:24 AM - 7 Jul 2018

Donald J. Trump ✓
@realDonaldTrump

Public opinion has turned strongly against the Rigged Witch Hunt and the "Special" Counsel because the public understands that there was no Collusion with Russia (so ridiculous), that the two FBI lovers were a fraud against our Nation & that the only Collusion was with the Dems!
28,190 Retweets **116,645** Likes
1:42 PM - 7 Jul 2018

Donald J. Trump ✓
@realDonaldTrump

The Rigged Witch Hunt, originally headed by FBI lover boy Peter S (for one year) & now, 13 Angry Democrats, should look into the missing DNC Server, Crooked Hillary's illegally deleted Emails, the Pakistani Fraudster, Uranium One, Podesta & so much more. It's a Democrat Con Job!
35,792 Retweets **130,602** Likes
3:24 PM - 7 Jul 2018

Donald J. Trump ✓
@realDonaldTrump

The U.S. is working very closely with the Government of Thailand to help get all of the children out of the cave and to safety. Very brave and talented people!
36,186 Retweets **141,762** Likes
6:14 AM - 8 Jul 2018

Donald J. Trump ✓
@realDonaldTrump

Iranian Harassment of U.S. Warships: 2015: 22 2016: 36 2017: 14 2018: 0 Source: @USNavy
38,628 Retweets **156,777** Likes
1:29 PM - 8 Jul 2018

Donald J. Trump ✓
@realDonaldTrump

Looking forward to announcing my final decision on the United States Supreme Court Justice at 9:00pmE tomorrow night at the @WhiteHouse. An exceptional person will be chosen!
20,934 Retweets **107,798** Likes
2:27 PM - 8 Jul 2018

Donald J. Trump ✓
@realDonaldTrump

They just didn't get it, but they do now!
108,798 Retweets **317,534** Likes
2:58 PM - 8 Jul 2018

Donald J. Trump ✓
@realDonaldTrump

The United States is spending far more on NATO than any other Country. This is not fair, nor is it acceptable. While these countries have been increasing their contributions since I took office, they must do much more. Germany is at 1%, the U.S. is at 4%, and NATO benefits......
17,558 Retweets **73,300** Likes
4:55 AM - 9 Jul 2018

Donald J. Trump ✓
@realDonaldTrump

...Europe far more than it does the U.S. By some accounts, the U.S. is paying for 90% of NATO, with many countries nowhere close to their 2% commitment. On top of this the European Union has a Trade Surplus of $151 Million with the U.S., with big Trade Barriers on U.S. goods. NO!
16,185 Retweets **71,693** Likes
5:04 AM - 9 Jul 2018

Donald J. Trump ✓
@realDonaldTrump

I have long heard that the most important decision a U.S. President can make is the selection of a Supreme Court Justice - Will be announced tonight at 9:00 P.M.
21,476 Retweets **116,459** Likes
5:14 AM - 9 Jul 2018

Donald J. Trump ✓
@realDonaldTrump

I have confidence that Kim Jong Un will honor the contract we signed &, even more importantly, our handshake. We agreed to the denuclearization of North Korea. China, on the other hand, may be exerting negative pressure on a deal because of our posture on Chinese Trade-Hope Not!

20,173 Retweets **92,956** Likes
7:25 AM - 9 Jul 2018

Donald J. Trump ✓
@realDonaldTrump

The failing NY Times Fake News story today about breast feeding must be called out. The U.S. strongly supports breast feeding but we don't believe women should be denied access to formula. Many women need this option because of malnutrition and poverty.

22,998 Retweets **99,823** Likes
10:04 AM - 9 Jul 2018

Donald J. Trump ✓
@realDonaldTrump

Pfizer & others should be ashamed that they have raised drug prices for no reason. They are merely taking advantage of the poor & others unable to defend themselves, while at the same time giving bargain basement prices to other countries in Europe & elsewhere. We will respond!

28,852 Retweets **112,761** Likes
10:08 AM - 9 Jul 2018

Donald J. Trump ✓
@realDonaldTrump

HAPPY 100TH BIRTHDAY to our amazing current and former Army Warrant Officers. Thank you for your century of service, as the indispensable guardians of our great @USArmy's technology! #CenturyOfService

14,118 Retweets **65,605** Likes
3:22 PM - 9 Jul 2018

Donald J. Trump ✓
@realDonaldTrump

Tonight, it was my honor and privilege to nominate Judge Brett Kavanaugh to the United States Supreme Court. #SCOTUS

16,162 Retweets **80,919** Likes
7:54 PM - 9 Jul 2018

Donald J. Trump ✓
@realDonaldTrump

Getting ready to leave for Europe. First meeting - NATO. The U.S. is spending many times more than any other country in order to protect them. Not fair to the U.S. taxpayer. On top of that we lose $151 Billion on Trade with the European Union. Charge us big Tariffs (& Barriers)!

15,620 Retweets **71,535** Likes
2:35 AM - 10 Jul 2018

Donald J. Trump ✓
@realDonaldTrump

NATO countries must pay MORE, the United States must pay LESS. Very Unfair!

14,005 Retweets **68,991** Likes
3:42 AM - 10 Jul 2018

Donald J. Trump ✓
@realDonaldTrump

Thank you to all of my great supporters, really big progress being made. Other countries wanting to fix crazy trade deals. Economy is ROARING. Supreme Court pick getting GREAT REVIEWS. New Poll says Trump, at over 90%, is the most popular Republican in history of the Party. Wow!
25,810 Retweets **124,606** Likes
3:59 AM - 10 Jul 2018

Donald J. Trump ✓
@realDonaldTrump

On behalf of the United States, congratulations to the Thai Navy SEALs and all on the successful rescue of the 12 boys and their coach from the treacherous cave in Thailand. Such a beautiful moment - all freed, great job!
40,357 Retweets **185,811** Likes
5:39 AM - 10 Jul 2018

Donald J. Trump ✓
@realDonaldTrump

I am on Air Force One flying to NATO and hear reports that the FBI lovers, Peter Strzok and Lisa Page are getting cold feet on testifying about the Rigged Witch Hunt headed by 13 Angry Democrats and people that worked for Obama for 8 years. Total disgrace!
25,348 Retweets **107,691** Likes
7:40 AM - 10 Jul 2018

Donald J. Trump ✓
@realDonaldTrump

Informing the Republican Senators of my nomination of Judge Brett Kavanaugh. #SCOTUS
9,526 Retweets **50,793** Likes
7:49 AM - 10 Jul 2018

Donald J. Trump ✓
@realDonaldTrump

Many countries in NATO, which we are expected to defend, are not only short of their current commitment of 2% (which is low), but are also delinquent for many years in payments that have not been made. Will they reimburse the U.S.?
18,483 Retweets **77,497** Likes
10:01 AM - 10 Jul 2018

Donald J. Trump ✓
@realDonaldTrump

A recent Emerson College ePoll said that most Americans, especially Hispanics, feel that they are better off under President Trump than they were under President Obama.
21,716 Retweets **106,543** Likes
11:42 AM - 10 Jul 2018

Donald J. Trump ✓
@realDonaldTrump

The European Union makes it impossible for our farmers and workers and companies to do business in Europe (U.S. has a $151 Billion trade deficit), and then they want us to happily defend them through NATO, and nicely pay for it. Just doesn't work!
24,458 Retweets **99,823** Likes
11:52 AM - 10 Jul 2018

President Trumps Tweets 2018: A Historical Archive of President Trump's Tweets

Donald J. Trump ✓
@realDonaldTrump

Just talked with Pfizer CEO and @SecAzar on our drug pricing blueprint. Pfizer is rolling back price hikes, so American patients don't pay more. We applaud Pfizer for this decision and hope other companies do the same. Great news for the American people!
25,601 Retweets **108,068** Likes
3:37 PM - 10 Jul 2018

Donald J. Trump ✓
@realDonaldTrump

Bilateral Breakfast with NATO Secretary General in Brussels, Belgium...
19,380 Retweets **77,139** Likes
1:04 AM - 11 Jul 2018

Donald J. Trump ✓
@realDonaldTrump

I am in Brussels, but always thinking about our farmers. Soy beans fell 50% from 2012 to my election. Farmers have done poorly for 15 years. Other countries' trade barriers and tariffs have been destroying their businesses. I will open...
17,371 Retweets **81,131** Likes
5:40 AM - 11 Jul 2018

Donald J. Trump ✓
@realDonaldTrump

...things up, better than ever before, but it can't go too quickly. I am fighting for a level playing field for our farmers, and will win!
13,687 Retweets **70,612** Likes
5:40 AM - 11 Jul 2018

Donald J. Trump ✓
@realDonaldTrump

Democrats in Congress must no longer Obstruct - vote to fix our terrible Immigration Laws now. I am watching what is going on from Europe - it would be soooo simple to fix. Judges run the system and illegals and traffickers know how it works. They are just using children!
22,389 Retweets **91,255** Likes
9:41 AM - 11 Jul 2018

Donald J. Trump ✓
@realDonaldTrump

What good is NATO if Germany is paying Russia billions of dollars for gas and energy? Why are there only 5 out of 29 countries that have met their commitment? The U.S. is paying for Europe's protection, then loses billions on Trade. Must pay 2% of GDP IMMEDIATELY, not by 2025.
29,470 Retweets **119,730** Likes
10:07 AM - 11 Jul 2018

Donald J. Trump ✓
@realDonaldTrump

If the Democrats want to win Supreme Court and other Court picks, don't Obstruct and Resist, but rather do it the good ol' fashioned way, WIN ELECTIONS!
18,454 Retweets **84,532** Likes
2:09 PM - 11 Jul 2018

Donald J. Trump ✓
@realDonaldTrump

Ex-FBI LAYER Lisa Page today defied a House of Representatives issued Subpoena to testify before Congress! Wow, but is anybody really surprised! Together with her lover, FBI Agent Peter Strzok, she worked on the Rigged Witch Hunt, perhaps the most tainted and corrupt case EVER!
24,084 Retweets **94,749** Likes
2:53 PM - 11 Jul 2018

Donald J. Trump ✓
@realDonaldTrump

How can the Rigged Witch Hunt proceed when it was started, influenced and worked on, for an extended period of time, by former FBI Agent/Lover Peter Strzok? Read his hate filled and totally biased Emails and the answer is clear!
21,619 Retweets **87,721** Likes
3:47 PM - 11 Jul 2018

Donald J. Trump ✓
@realDonaldTrump

Billions of additional dollars are being spent by NATO countries since my visit last year, at my request, but it isn't nearly enough. U.S. spends too much. Europe's borders are BAD! Pipeline dollars to Russia are not acceptable!
19,094 Retweets **82,413** Likes
4:33 PM - 11 Jul 2018

Donald J. Trump ✓
@realDonaldTrump

As I head out to a very important NATO meeting, I see that FBI Lover/Agent Lisa Page is dodging a Subpoena & is refusing to show up and testify. What can she possibly say about her statements and lies. So much corruption on the other side. Where is the Attorney General? @FoxNews
18,572 Retweets **81,600** Likes
10:55 PM - 11 Jul 2018

Donald J. Trump ✓
@realDonaldTrump

Presidents have been trying unsuccessfully for years to get Germany and other rich NATO Nations to pay more toward their protection from Russia. They pay only a fraction of their cost. The U.S. pays tens of Billions of Dollars too much to subsidize Europe, and loses Big on Trade!
17,565 Retweets **77,174** Likes
11:03 PM - 11 Jul 2018

Donald J. Trump ✓
@realDonaldTrump

....On top of it all, Germany just started paying Russia, the country they want protection from, Billions of Dollars for their Energy needs coming out of a new pipeline from Russia. Not acceptable! All NATO Nations must meet their 2% commitment, and that must ultimately go to 4%!
20,410 Retweets **88,176** Likes
11:12 PM - 11 Jul 2018

Donald J. Trump ✓
@realDonaldTrump

#NATOSummit2018 Press Conference in Brussels, Belgium
10,489 Retweets **42,675** Likes
3:57 AM - 12 Jul 2018

President Trumps Tweets 2018: A Historical Archive of President Trump's Tweets

Donald J. Trump ✓
@realDonaldTrump

Thank you #NATO2018!
12,900 Retweets **64,034** Likes
7:12 AM - 12 Jul 2018

Donald J. Trump ✓
@realDonaldTrump

"Trump has been the most consequential president in history when it comes to minority employment. In June, for instance, the unemployment rate for Hispanics and Latinos 16 years and older fell to 4.6%, its lowest level ever, from 4.9% in May."
18,420 Retweets **68,641** Likes
8:10 AM - 12 Jul 2018

Donald J. Trump ✓
@realDonaldTrump

A very nice note from Chairman Kim of North Korea. Great progress being made!
25,416 Retweets **93,288** Likes
9:32 AM - 12 Jul 2018

Donald J. Trump ✓
@realDonaldTrump

Great success today at NATO! Billions of additional dollars paid by members since my election. Great spirit!
21,067 Retweets **108,325** Likes
10:52 AM - 12 Jul 2018

Donald J. Trump ✓
@realDonaldTrump

Congressman Matt Gaetz of Florida is one of the finest and most talented people in Congress. Strong on Crime, the Border, Illegal Immigration, the 2nd Amendment, our great Military & Vets, Matt worked tirelessly on helping to get our Massive Tax Cuts. He has my Full Endorsement!
21,827 Retweets **91,728** Likes
11:02 PM - 12 Jul 2018

Donald J. Trump ✓
@realDonaldTrump

Joint Press Conference with Prime Minister Theresa May...
11,101 Retweets **51,789** Likes
7:07 AM - 13 Jul 2018

Donald J. Trump ✓
@realDonaldTrump

This is now changing - for the first time!
12,395 Retweets **58,116** Likes
2:18 AM - 14 Jul 2018

Donald J. Trump ✓
@realDonaldTrump

I have arrived in Scotland and will be at Trump Turnberry for two days of meetings, calls and hopefully, some golf - my primary form of exercise! The weather is beautiful, and this place is incredible! Tomorrow I go to Helsinki for a Monday meeting with Vladimir Putin.
15,190 Retweets **85,783** Likes
2:43 AM - 14 Jul 2018

Donald J. Trump ✓
@realDonaldTrump

The Stock Market hit 25,000 yesterday. Jobs are at an all time record - and that is before we fix some of the worst trade deals and conditions ever seen by any government. It is all happening!
23,753 Retweets **111,378** Likes
2:46 AM - 14 Jul 2018

Donald J. Trump ✓
@realDonaldTrump

....Where is the DNC Server, and why didn't the FBI take possession of it? Deep State?
28,753 Retweets **103,384** Likes
2:57 AM - 14 Jul 2018

Donald J. Trump ✓
@realDonaldTrump

The stories you heard about the 12 Russians yesterday took place during the Obama Administration, not the Trump Administration. Why didn't they do something about it, especially when it was reported that President Obama was informed by the FBI in September, before the Election?
38,526 Retweets **127,895** Likes
3:08 AM - 14 Jul 2018

Donald J. Trump ✓
@realDonaldTrump

So funny! I just checked out Fake News CNN, for the first time in a long time (they are dying in the ratings), to see if they covered my takedown yesterday of Jim Acosta (actually a nice guy). They didn't! But they did say I already lost in my meeting with Putin. Fake News......
21,629 Retweets **95,859** Likes
4:24 AM - 14 Jul 2018

Donald J. Trump ✓
@realDonaldTrump

....Remember, it was Little Jeff Z and his people, who are told exactly what to say, who said I could not win the election in that "there was no way to 270" (over & over again) in the Electoral College. I got 306! They were sooooo wrong in their election coverage. Still hurting!
17,809 Retweets **87,888** Likes
4:34 AM - 14 Jul 2018

Donald J. Trump ✓
@realDonaldTrump

Our prayers are with those affected by the flooding in Japan. We commend the rescue efforts and offer condolences to all who were injured or lost loved ones.
17,301 Retweets **71,718** Likes
5:44 AM - 14 Jul 2018

Donald J. Trump ✓
@realDonaldTrump

These Russian individuals did their work during the Obama years. Why didn't Obama do something about it? Because he thought Crooked Hillary Clinton would win, that's why. Had nothing to do with the Trump Administration, but Fake News doesn't want to report the truth, as usual!
40,945 Retweets **147,696** Likes
11:17 AM - 14 Jul 2018

Donald J. Trump ✓
@realDonaldTrump

There hasn't been a missile or rocket fired in 9 months in North Korea, there have been no nuclear tests and we got back our hostages. Who knows how it will all turn out in the end, but why isn't the Fake News talking about these wonderful facts? Because it is FAKE NEWS!
30,467 Retweets **127,281** Likes
9:11 AM - 15 Jul 2018

Donald J. Trump ✓
@realDonaldTrump

Heading to Helsinki, Finland – looking forward to meeting with President Putin tomorrow. Unfortunately, no matter how well I do at the Summit, if I was given the great city of Moscow as retribution for all of the sins and evils committed by Russia...
15,751 Retweets **78,971** Likes
9:18 AM - 15 Jul 2018

Donald J. Trump ✓
@realDonaldTrump

...over the years, I would return to criticism that it wasn't good enough – that I should have gotten Saint Petersburg in addition! Much of our news media is indeed the enemy of the people and all the Dems...
12,989 Retweets **67,761** Likes
9:18 AM - 15 Jul 2018

Donald J. Trump ✓
@realDonaldTrump

...know how to do is resist and obstruct! This is why there is such hatred and dissension in our country – but at some point, it will heal!
14,131 Retweets **75,002** Likes
9:18 AM - 15 Jul 2018

Donald J. Trump ✓
@realDonaldTrump

Congratulations to France, who played extraordinary soccer, on winning the 2018 World Cup. Additionally, congratulations to President Putin and Russia for putting on a truly great World Cup Tournament -- one of the best ever!
35,575 Retweets **153,006** Likes
10:03 AM - 15 Jul 2018

Donald J. Trump ✓
@realDonaldTrump

Received many calls from leaders of NATO countries thanking me for helping to bring them together and to get them focused on financial obligations, both present & future. We had a truly great Summit that was inaccurately covered by much of the media. NATO is now strong & rich!
21,687 Retweets **102,254** Likes
10:23 PM - 15 Jul 2018

Donald J. Trump ✓
@realDonaldTrump

President Obama thought that Crooked Hillary was going to win the election, so when he was informed by the FBI about Russian Meddling, he said it couldn't happen, was no big deal, & did NOTHING about it. When I won it became a big deal and the Rigged Witch Hunt headed by Strzok!
35,163 Retweets **134,117** Likes
10:37 PM - 15 Jul 2018

Donald J. Trump ✓
@realDonaldTrump

Our relationship with Russia has NEVER been worse thanks to many years of U.S. foolishness and stupidity and now, the Rigged Witch Hunt!
23,288 Retweets **104,347** Likes
11:05 PM - 15 Jul 2018

Donald J. Trump ✓
@realDonaldTrump

It was an honor to join you this morning. Thank you!
10,747 Retweets **58,516** Likes
1:56 AM - 16 Jul 2018

Donald J. Trump ✓
@realDonaldTrump

Joint Press Conference from Helsinki, Finland
13,330 Retweets **53,115** Likes
9:11 AM - 16 Jul 2018

Donald J. Trump ✓
@realDonaldTrump

Thank you Helsinki, Finland!
17,148 Retweets **90,958** Likes
9:51 AM - 16 Jul 2018

Donald J. Trump ✓
@realDonaldTrump

As I said today and many times before, "I have GREAT confidence in MY intelligence people." However, I also recognize that in order to build a brighter future, we cannot exclusively focus on the past – as the world's two largest nuclear powers, we must get along! #HELSINKI2018
30,096 Retweets **127,784** Likes
12:40 PM - 16 Jul 2018

Donald J. Trump ✓
@realDonaldTrump

I would rather take a political risk in pursuit of peace, than to risk peace in pursuit of politics. #HELSINKI2018
35,487 Retweets **125,110** Likes
1:29 PM - 16 Jul 2018

Donald J. Trump ✓
@realDonaldTrump

A productive dialogue is not only good for the United States and good for Russia, but it is good for the world. #HELSINKI2018
21,539 Retweets **82,643** Likes
1:34 PM - 16 Jul 2018

Donald J. Trump ✓
@realDonaldTrump

Will be interviewed on @seanhannity tonight at 9pmE and @TuckerCarlson tomorrow night at 8pmE. Enjoy!
14,926 Retweets **73,281** Likes
3:53 PM - 16 Jul 2018

President Trumps Tweets 2018: A Historical Archive of President Trump's Tweets

Donald J. Trump ✓
@realDonaldTrump

I had a great meeting with NATO. They have paid $33 Billion more and will pay hundreds of Billions of Dollars more in the future, only because of me. NATO was weak, but now it is strong again (bad for Russia). The media only says I was rude to leaders, never mentions the money!
22,466 Retweets **100,990** Likes
6:53 AM - 17 Jul 2018

Donald J. Trump ✓
@realDonaldTrump

While I had a great meeting with NATO, raising vast amounts of money, I had an even better meeting with Vladimir Putin of Russia. Sadly, it is not being reported that way - the Fake News is going Crazy!
23,733 Retweets **98,305** Likes
7:22 AM - 17 Jul 2018

Donald J. Trump ✓
@realDonaldTrump

Thank you @RandPaul. "The President has gone through a year and a half of totally partisan investigations - what's he supposed to think?"
21,193 Retweets **94,505** Likes
7:33 AM - 17 Jul 2018

Donald J. Trump ✓
@realDonaldTrump

The economy of the United States is stronger than ever before!
24,077 Retweets **124,376** Likes
7:39 AM - 17 Jul 2018

Donald J. Trump ✓
@realDonaldTrump

The meeting between President Putin and myself was a great success, except in the Fake News Media!
22,981 Retweets **106,481** Likes
5:21 PM - 17 Jul 2018

Donald J. Trump ✓
@realDonaldTrump

The Democrats want to abolish ICE, which will mean more crime in our country. I want to give ICE a big cheer! Vote Republican in November.
30,279 Retweets **125,995** Likes
5:27 PM - 17 Jul 2018

Donald J. Trump ✓
@realDonaldTrump

"Prosperity is returning. Donald Trump is doing exactly what he said he would do as a candidate, now as the most effective president, the most successful president, in modern American history." Thank you to the great Lou Dobbs!
22,539 Retweets **101,546** Likes
9:10 PM - 17 Jul 2018

Donald J. Trump ✓
@realDonaldTrump

So many people at the higher ends of intelligence loved my press conference performance in Helsinki. Putin and I discussed many important subjects at our earlier meeting. We got along well which truly bothered many haters who wanted to see a boxing match. Big results will come!
20,814 Retweets **90,828** Likes
2:53 AM - 18 Jul 2018

Donald J. Trump ✓
@realDonaldTrump

While the NATO meeting in Brussels was an acknowledged triumph, with billions of dollars more being put up by member countries at a faster pace, the meeting with Russia may prove to be, in the long run, an even greater success. Many positive things will come out of that meeting..
16,639 Retweets **74,814** Likes
3:08 AM - 18 Jul 2018

Donald J. Trump ✓
@realDonaldTrump

....Russia has agreed to help with North Korea, where relationships with us are very good and the process is moving along. There is no rush, the sanctions remain! Big benefits and exciting future for North Korea at end of process!
16,321 Retweets **69,365** Likes
3:16 AM - 18 Jul 2018

Donald J. Trump ✓
@realDonaldTrump

Congratulations to Martha Roby of The Great State of Alabama on her big GOP Primary win for Congress. My endorsement came appropriately late, but when it came the "flood gates" opened and you had the kind of landslide victory that you deserve. Enjoy!
12,748 Retweets **64,622** Likes
3:44 AM - 18 Jul 2018

Donald J. Trump ✓
@realDonaldTrump

"A lot of Democrats wished they voted for the Tax Cuts because the economy is booming - we could have 4% growth now and the Fed said yesterday that unemployment could drop again." @foxandfriends @kilmeade
16,120 Retweets **71,039** Likes
4:03 AM - 18 Jul 2018

Donald J. Trump ✓
@realDonaldTrump

Some people HATE the fact that I got along well with President Putin of Russia. They would rather go to war than see this. It's called Trump Derangement Syndrome!
33,325 Retweets **130,187** Likes
4:27 AM - 18 Jul 2018

Donald J. Trump ✓
@realDonaldTrump

3.4 million jobs created since our great Election Victory - far greater than ever anticipated, and only getting better as new and greatly improved Trade Deals start coming to fruition!
22,779 Retweets **102,872** Likes
4:33 AM - 18 Jul 2018

Donald J. Trump ✓
@realDonaldTrump

Brian Kemp is running for Governor of the great state of Georgia. The Primary is on Tuesday. Brian is tough on crime, strong on the border and illegal immigration. He loves our Military and our Vets and protects our Second Amendment. I give him my full and total endorsement.
25,507 Retweets **101,027** Likes
12:25 PM - 18 Jul 2018

Donald J. Trump ✓
@realDonaldTrump

Thank you to Congressman Kevin Yoder! He secured $5 BILLION for Border Security. Now we need Congress to support. Kevin has been strong on Crime, the Border, the 2nd Amendment, and he loves our Military and Vets. @RepKevinYoder has my full and total endorsement!
17,213 Retweets **70,380** Likes
2:29 PM - 18 Jul 2018

Donald J. Trump ✓
@realDonaldTrump

The two biggest opponents of ICE in America today are the Democratic Party and MS-13!
29,239 Retweets **106,500** Likes
2:30 PM - 18 Jul 2018

Donald J. Trump ✓
@realDonaldTrump

A total disgrace that Turkey will not release a respected U.S. Pastor, Andrew Brunson, from prison. He has been held hostage far too long. @RT_Erdogan should do something to free this wonderful Christian husband & father. He has done nothing wrong, and his family needs him!
31,676 Retweets **112,456** Likes
6:35 PM - 18 Jul 2018

Donald J. Trump ✓
@realDonaldTrump

Thank you to Novartis for not increasing your prices on prescription drugs. Likewise to Pfizer. We are making a big push to actually reduce the prices, maybe substantially, on prescription drugs.
15,847 Retweets **76,642** Likes
3:23 AM - 19 Jul 2018

Donald J. Trump ✓
@realDonaldTrump

The Democrats have a death wish, in more ways than one - they actually want to abolish ICE. This should cost them heavily in the Midterms. Yesterday, the Republicans overwhelmingly passed a bill supporting ICE!
18,853 Retweets **78,801** Likes
3:29 AM - 19 Jul 2018

Donald J. Trump ✓
@realDonaldTrump

The Fake News Media is going Crazy! They make up stories without any backup, sources or proof. Many of the stories written about me, and the good people surrounding me, are total fiction. Problem is, when you complain you just give them more publicity. But I'll complain anyway!
26,071 Retweets **114,313** Likes
3:37 AM - 19 Jul 2018

Donald J. Trump ✓
@realDonaldTrump

The Fake News Media wants so badly to see a major confrontation with Russia, even a confrontation that could lead to war. They are pushing so recklessly hard and hate the fact that I'll probably have a good relationship with Putin. We are doing MUCH better than any other country!
22,658 Retweets **91,171** Likes
3:59 AM - 19 Jul 2018

Donald J. Trump ✓
@realDonaldTrump

"Trump recognized Russian Meddling MANY TIMES." Thank you to @foxandfriends and @FoxNews for actually showing the clips. The Fake News wants no part of that narrative! Too bad they don't want to focus on all of the ECONOMIC and JOBS records being set.
17,120 Retweets **69,609** Likes
4:13 AM - 19 Jul 2018

Donald J. Trump ✓
@realDonaldTrump

Really big jobs meeting today at the White House! 3 P.M.
11,311 Retweets **62,129** Likes
4:37 AM - 19 Jul 2018

Donald J. Trump ✓
@realDonaldTrump

I told you so! The European Union just slapped a Five Billion Dollar fine on one of our great companies, Google. They truly have taken advantage of the U.S., but not for long!
24,778 Retweets **98,835** Likes
6:11 AM - 19 Jul 2018

Donald J. Trump ✓
@realDonaldTrump

The Summit with Russia was a great success, except with the real enemy of the people, the Fake News Media. I look forward to our second meeting so that we can start implementing some of the many things discussed, including stopping terrorism, security for Israel, nuclear........
23,783 Retweets **101,069** Likes
6:24 AM - 19 Jul 2018

Donald J. Trump ✓
@realDonaldTrump

....proliferation, cyber attacks, trade, Ukraine, Middle East peace, North Korea and more. There are many answers, some easy and some hard, to these problems...but they can ALL be solved!
16,336 Retweets **72,109** Likes
6:30 AM - 19 Jul 2018

Donald J. Trump ✓
@realDonaldTrump

"Trump recognized Russian Meddling MANY TIMES"
15,033 Retweets **53,909** Likes
6:35 AM - 19 Jul 2018

Donald J. Trump ✓
@realDonaldTrump

Will the Dems and Fake News ever learn? This is classic!
42,344 Retweets **114,026** Likes
11:14 AM - 19 Jul 2018

Donald J. Trump ✓
@realDonaldTrump

My deepest sympathies to the families and friends of those involved in the terrible boat accident which just took place in Missouri. Such a tragedy, such a great loss. May God be with you all!
17,054 Retweets **86,807** Likes
5:31 AM - 20 Jul 2018

Donald J. Trump ✓
@realDonaldTrump

China, the European Union and others have been manipulating their currencies and interest rates lower, while the U.S. is raising rates while the dollars gets stronger and stronger with each passing day - taking away our big competitive edge. As usual, not a level playing field...
17,104 Retweets **70,562** Likes
5:43 AM - 20 Jul 2018

Donald J. Trump ✓
@realDonaldTrump

....The United States should not be penalized because we are doing so well. Tightening now hurts all that we have done. The U.S. should be allowed to recapture what was lost due to illegal currency manipulation and BAD Trade Deals. Debt coming due & we are raising rates - Really?
20,108 Retweets **87,449** Likes
5:51 AM - 20 Jul 2018

Donald J. Trump ✓
@realDonaldTrump

Farmers have been on a downward trend for 15 years. The price of soybeans has fallen 50% since 5 years before the Election. A big reason is bad (terrible) Trade Deals with other countries. They put on massive Tariffs and Barriers. Canada charges 275% on Dairy. Farmers will WIN!
18,755 Retweets **75,987** Likes
6:04 AM - 20 Jul 2018

Donald J. Trump ✓
@realDonaldTrump

So important. Should have been done years ago!
12,881 Retweets **56,868** Likes
7:35 AM - 20 Jul 2018

Donald J. Trump ✓
@realDonaldTrump

I got severely criticized by the Fake News Media for being too nice to President Putin. In the Old Days they would call it Diplomacy. If I was loud & vicious, I would have been criticized for being too tough. Remember when they said I was too tough with Chairman Kim? Hypocrites!
37,244 Retweets **153,003** Likes
2:50 PM - 20 Jul 2018

Donald J. Trump ✓
@realDonaldTrump

The NFL National Anthem Debate is alive and well again - can't believe it! Isn't it in contract that players must stand at attention, hand on heart? The $40,000,000 Commissioner must now make a stand. First time kneeling, out for game. Second time kneeling, out for season/no pay!
30,295 Retweets **127,161** Likes
3:17 PM - 20 Jul 2018

Donald J. Trump ✓
@realDonaldTrump

Inconceivable that the government would break into a lawyer's office (early in the morning) - almost unheard of. Even more inconceivable that a lawyer would tape a client - totally unheard of & perhaps illegal. The good news is that your favorite President did nothing wrong!
40,787 Retweets **179,931** Likes
5:10 AM - 21 Jul 2018

Donald J. Trump ✓
@realDonaldTrump

The Rigged Witch Hunt, headed by the 13 Angry Democrats (and now 4 more have been added, one who worked directly for Obama W.H.), seems intent on damaging the Republican Party's chances in the November Election. This Democrat excuse for losing the '16 Election never ends!
23,415 Retweets **91,436** Likes
3:40 PM - 21 Jul 2018

Donald J. Trump ✓
@realDonaldTrump

No Collusion, No Obstruction - but that doesn't matter because the 13 Angry Democrats, who are only after Republicans and totally protecting Democrats, want this Witch Hunt to drag out to the November Election. Republicans better get smart fast and expose what they are doing!
28,590 Retweets **101,514** Likes
3:50 PM - 21 Jul 2018

Donald J. Trump ✓
@realDonaldTrump

Brian Kemp, who is running for Governor of Georgia and has my full endorsement, is campaigning tonight with VP @mike_pence. Brian is very strong on Crime and Borders, LOVES our Military, Vets and the 2nd Amendment. He will be a GREAT Governor!
16,345 Retweets **66,429** Likes
4:10 PM - 21 Jul 2018

Donald J. Trump ✓
@realDonaldTrump

Troy Balderson of Ohio is running for Congress against a Nancy Pelosi Liberal who is WEAK on Crime & Borders. Troy is the total opposite, and loves our Military, Vets & 2nd Amendment. EARLY VOTING just started with Election Day on August 7th. Troy has my Full & Total Endorsement!
25,924 Retweets **97,108** Likes
4:23 PM - 21 Jul 2018

Donald J. Trump ✓
@realDonaldTrump

Congratulations to @JudicialWatch and @TomFitton on being successful in getting the Carter Page FISA documents. As usual they are ridiculously heavily redacted but confirm with little doubt that the Department of "Justice" and FBI misled the courts. Witch Hunt Rigged, a Scam!
26,923 Retweets **90,752** Likes
3:28 AM - 22 Jul 2018

Donald J. Trump ✓
@realDonaldTrump

Looking more & more like the Trump Campaign for President was illegally being spied upon (surveillance) for the political gain of Crooked Hillary Clinton and the DNC. Ask her how that worked out - she did better with Crazy Bernie. Republicans must get tough now. An illegal Scam!
33,001 Retweets **120,227** Likes
3:49 AM - 22 Jul 2018

Donald J. Trump ✓
@realDonaldTrump

Andrew McCarthy - "I said this could never happen. This is so bad that they should be looking at the judges who signed off on this stuff, not just the people who gave it. It is so bad it screams out at you." On the whole FISA scam which led to the rigged Mueller Witch Hunt!
34,649 Retweets **120,280** Likes
5:22 AM - 22 Jul 2018

President Trumps Tweets 2018: A Historical Archive of President Trump's Tweets

Donald J. Trump ✓
@realDonaldTrump

.@PeteHegseth on @FoxNews "Source #1 was the (Fake) Dossier. Yes, the Dirty Dossier, paid for by Democrats as a hit piece against Trump, and looking for information that could discredit Candidate #1 Trump. Carter Page was just the foot to surveil the Trump campaign..." ILLEGAL!
21,089 Retweets **76,806** Likes
5:56 AM - 22 Jul 2018

Donald J. Trump ✓
@realDonaldTrump

I had a GREAT meeting with Putin and the Fake News used every bit of their energy to try and disparage it. So bad for our country!
22,520 Retweets **107,819** Likes
6:15 AM - 22 Jul 2018

Donald J. Trump ✓
@realDonaldTrump

Happy Birthday @SenatorDole!
8,874 Retweets **54,407** Likes
1:58 PM - 22 Jul 2018

Donald J. Trump ✓
@realDonaldTrump

So President Obama knew about Russia before the Election. Why didn't he do something about it? Why didn't he tell our campaign? Because it is all a big hoax, that's why, and he thought Crooked Hillary was going to win!!!
41,545 Retweets **156,311** Likes
3:23 PM - 22 Jul 2018

Donald J. Trump ✓
@realDonaldTrump

To Iranian President Rouhani: NEVER, EVER THREATEN THE UNITED STATES AGAIN OR YOU WILL SUFFER CONSEQUENCES THE LIKES OF WHICH FEW THROUGHOUT HISTORY HAVE EVER SUFFERED BEFORE. WE ARE NO LONGER A COUNTRY THAT WILL STAND FOR YOUR DEMENTED WORDS OF VIOLENCE & DEATH. BE CAUTIOUS!
107,757 Retweets **332,225** Likes
8:24 PM - 22 Jul 2018

Donald J. Trump ✓
@realDonaldTrump

Tom Fitton on @foxandfriends at 6:15 A.M. NOW! Judicial Watch.
7,435 Retweets **43,616** Likes
3:13 AM - 23 Jul 2018

Donald J. Trump ✓
@realDonaldTrump

So we now find out that it was indeed the unverified and Fake Dirty Dossier, that was paid for by Crooked Hillary Clinton and the DNC, that was knowingly & falsely submitted to FISA and which was responsible for starting the totally conflicted and discredited Mueller Witch Hunt!
28,700 Retweets **106,276** Likes
3:30 AM - 23 Jul 2018

Donald J. Trump ✓
@realDonaldTrump

"It was classified to cover up misconduct by the FBI and the Justice Department in misleading the Court by using this Dossier in a dishonest way to gain a warrant to target the Trump Team. This is a Clinton Campaign document. It was a fraud and a hoax designed to target Trump....
25,063 Retweets **94,003** Likes
3:52 AM - 23 Jul 2018

Donald J. Trump ✓
@realDonaldTrump

....and the DOJ, FBI and Obama Gang need to be held to account. Source #1 was the major source. Avoided talking about it being the Clinton campaign behind it. Misled the Court to provide a pretext to SPY on the Trump Team. Not about Carter Page..was all about getting Trump.....
22,058 Retweets **80,632** Likes
4:01 AM - 23 Jul 2018

Donald J. Trump ✓
@realDonaldTrump

....."Carter Page wasn't a spy, wasn't an agent of the Russians - he would have cooperated with the FBI. It was a fraud and a hoax designed to target Trump." Tom Fitton @JudicialWatch A disgrace to America. They should drop the discredited Mueller Witch Hunt now!
19,773 Retweets **75,433** Likes
4:09 AM - 23 Jul 2018

Donald J. Trump ✓
@realDonaldTrump

When you hear the Fake News talking negatively about my meeting with President Putin, and all that I gave up, remember, I gave up NOTHING, we merely talked about future benefits for both countries. Also, we got along very well, which is a good thing, except for the Corrupt Media!
24,541 Retweets **104,142** Likes
5:25 AM - 23 Jul 2018

Donald J. Trump ✓
@realDonaldTrump

A Rocket has not been launched by North Korea in 9 months. Likewise, no Nuclear Tests. Japan is happy, all of Asia is happy. But the Fake News is saying, without ever asking me (always anonymous sources), that I am angry because it is not going fast enough. Wrong, very happy!
30,489 Retweets **126,860** Likes
6:06 AM - 23 Jul 2018

Donald J. Trump ✓
@realDonaldTrump

The Amazon Washington Post has gone crazy against me ever since they lost the Internet Tax Case in the U.S. Supreme Court two months ago. Next up is the U.S. Post Office which they use, at a fraction of real cost, as their "delivery boy" for a BIG percentage of their packages....
20,498 Retweets **85,390** Likes
6:21 AM - 23 Jul 2018

Donald J. Trump ✓
@realDonaldTrump

....In my opinion the Washington Post is nothing more than an expensive (the paper loses a fortune) lobbyist for Amazon. Is it used as protection against antitrust claims which many feel should be brought?
18,549 Retweets **82,618** Likes
6:35 AM - 23 Jul 2018

President Trumps Tweets 2018: A Historical Archive of President Trump's Tweets

Donald J. Trump ✓
@realDonaldTrump

Robert will do a great job for our Vets. We also recently won Choice!
10,996 Retweets **54,527** Likes
6:35 PM - 23 Jul 2018

Donald J. Trump ✓
@realDonaldTrump

Lou Barletta was one of my first supporters. He is tough on Crime and Borders. Will be a great Senator from Pennsylvania. His opponent is WEAK on Crime, ICE and Borders. We need Lou!
16,049 Retweets **61,053** Likes
6:44 PM - 23 Jul 2018

Donald J. Trump ✓
@realDonaldTrump

#MadeInAmerica Showcase!
18,251 Retweets **72,214** Likes
7:07 PM - 23 Jul 2018

Donald J. Trump ✓
@realDonaldTrump

Countries that have treated us unfairly on trade for years are all coming to Washington to negotiate. This should have taken place many years ago but, as the saying goes, better late than never!
21,414 Retweets **100,190** Likes
4:09 AM - 24 Jul 2018

Donald J. Trump ✓
@realDonaldTrump

Tariffs are the greatest! Either a country which has treated the United States unfairly on Trade negotiates a fair deal, or it gets hit with Tariffs. It's as simple as that - and everybody's talking! Remember, we are the "piggy bank" that's being robbed. All will be Great!
21,582 Retweets **94,195** Likes
4:29 AM - 24 Jul 2018

Donald J. Trump ✓
@realDonaldTrump

Today is the day to vote for Brian Kemp. Will be great for Georgia, full Endorsement!
12,037 Retweets **49,254** Likes
6:39 AM - 24 Jul 2018

Donald J. Trump ✓
@realDonaldTrump

Our Country is doing GREAT. Best financial numbers on the Planet. Great to have USA WINNING AGAIN!
21,333 Retweets **102,150** Likes
6:46 AM - 24 Jul 2018

Donald J. Trump ✓
@realDonaldTrump

Heading to Missouri to be with many of my great friends. VFW here we come!
10,760 Retweets **65,012** Likes
6:52 AM - 24 Jul 2018

Donald J. Trump ✓
@realDonaldTrump

MAKE AMERICA GREAT AGAIN!
32,860 Retweets **134,635**Likes
6:54 AM - 24 Jul 2018

Donald J. Trump ✓
@realDonaldTrump

I'm very concerned that Russia will be fighting very hard to have an impact on the upcoming Election. Based on the fact that no President has been tougher on Russia than me, they will be pushing very hard for the Democrats. They definitely don't want Trump!
24,460 Retweets **104,844** Likes
8:50 AM - 24 Jul 2018

Donald J. Trump ✓
@realDonaldTrump

#VFWConvention @VFWHQ
8,322 Retweets **37,744** Likes
10:51 AM - 24 Jul 2018

Donald J. Trump ✓
@realDonaldTrump

I want to thank the @VFWHQ for your devotion to our fallen heroes, unknown soldiers, Prisoners of War, those Missing in Action, and their families. #VFWConvention
11,046 Retweets **51,332** Likes
12:15 PM - 24 Jul 2018

Donald J. Trump ✓
@realDonaldTrump

On the heels of the VERY successful launch of the @WhiteHouse National Council for the American Worker, Congress should reauthorize #PerkinsCTE and ensure the American workforce remains stronger than EVER! #Jobs #Workforce
11,093 Retweets **52,021** Likes
3:25 PM - 24 Jul 2018

Donald J. Trump ✓
@realDonaldTrump

Today, it was my great honor to be in Kansas City, Missouri to pay tribute to the men and women who make FREEDOM possible! Thank you @VFWHQ! #VFWConvention
12,193 Retweets **56,779** Likes
3:33 PM - 24 Jul 2018

Donald J. Trump ✓
@realDonaldTrump

The European Union is coming to Washington tomorrow to negotiate a deal on Trade. I have an idea for them. Both the U.S. and the E.U. drop all Tariffs, Barriers and Subsidies! That would finally be called Free Market and Fair Trade! Hope they do it, we are ready - but they won't!
31,469 Retweets **121,472** Likes
5:08 PM - 24 Jul 2018

Donald J. Trump ✓
@realDonaldTrump

So sad and unfair that the FCC wouldn't approve the Sinclair Broadcast merger with Tribune. This would have been a great and much needed Conservative voice for and of the People. Liberal Fake News NBC and Comcast gets approved, much bigger, but not Sinclair. Disgraceful!
22,482 Retweets **87,260** Likes
5:39 PM - 24 Jul 2018

Donald J. Trump
@realDonaldTrump

"The Russia Hoax, The Illicit Scheme To Clear Hillary Clinton & Frame Donald Trump" is a Hot Seller, already Number One! More importantly, it is a great book that everyone is talking about. It covers the Rigged Witch Hunt brilliantly. Congratulations to Gregg Jarrett!

23,880 Retweets **86,911** Likes
6:05 PM - 24 Jul 2018

Donald J. Trump
@realDonaldTrump

Every time I see a weak politician asking to stop Trade talks or the use of Tariffs to counter unfair Tariffs, I wonder, what can they be thinking? Are we just going to continue and let our farmers and country get ripped off? Lost $817 Billion on Trade last year. No weakness!

21,625 Retweets **88,799** Likes
4:01 AM - 25 Jul 2018

Donald J. Trump
@realDonaldTrump

When you have people snipping at your heels during a negotiation, it will only take longer to make a deal, and the deal will never be as good as it could have been with unity. Negotiations are going really well, be cool. The end result will be worth it!

22,458 Retweets **102,370** Likes
4:08 AM - 25 Jul 2018

Donald J. Trump
@realDonaldTrump

China is targeting our farmers, who they know I love & respect, as a way of getting me to continue allowing them to take advantage of the U.S. They are being vicious in what will be their failed attempt. We were being nice - until now! China made $517 Billion on us last year.

21,332 Retweets **82,825** Likes
4:20 AM - 25 Jul 2018

Donald J. Trump
@realDonaldTrump

What kind of a lawyer would tape a client? So sad! Is this a first, never heard of it before? Why was the tape so abruptly terminated (cut) while I was presumably saying positive things? I hear there are other clients and many reporters that are taped - can this be so? Too bad!

23,932 Retweets **109,155** Likes
5:34 AM - 25 Jul 2018

Donald J. Trump
@realDonaldTrump

Congratulations to Brian Kemp on your very big win in Georgia last night. Wow, 69-30, those are big numbers. Now go win against the open border, crime loving opponent that the Democrats have given you. She is weak on Vets, the Military and the 2nd Amendment. Win!

18,831 Retweets **84,814** Likes
5:41 AM - 25 Jul 2018

Donald J. Trump
@realDonaldTrump

The United States and the European Union have a $1 TRILLION bilateral trade relationship – the largest economic relationship in the world. We want to further strengthen this trade relationship to the benefit of all American and European citizens...

18,450 Retweets **71,266** Likes
1:57 PM - 25 Jul 2018

Donald J. Trump ✓
@realDonaldTrump

This week, my Administration is hosting the first-ever #IRFMinisterial. The U.S. will continue to promote #ReligiousFreedom around the world. Nations that support religious freedom are far more free, prosperous & peaceful. Great job, @VP, @SecPompeo, @IRF_Ambassador & @StateDept!
12,572 Retweets **52,366** Likes
3:33 PM - 25 Jul 2018

 Donald J. Trump ✓
@realDonaldTrump

Sergio Marchionne, who passed away today, was one of the most brilliant & successful car executives since the days of the legendary Henry Ford. It was a great honor for me to get to know Sergio as POTUS, he loved the car industry, and fought hard for it. He will be truly missed!
11,896 Retweets **62,125** Likes
3:45 PM - 25 Jul 2018

 Donald J. Trump ✓
@realDonaldTrump

Thank you very much, working hard!
23,130 Retweets **102,339** Likes
3:59 PM - 25 Jul 2018

 Donald J. Trump ✓
@realDonaldTrump

Great meeting on Trade today with @JunckerEU and representatives of the European Union. We have come to a very strong understanding and are all believers in no tariffs, no barriers and no subsidies. Work on documents has already started and the process is moving...
13,051 Retweets **60,165** Likes
4:42 PM - 25 Jul 2018

 Donald J. Trump ✓
@realDonaldTrump

...along quickly. European Union Nations will be open to the United States and at the same time benefiting by everything we are doing for them. There was great warmth and feeling in the room - a breakthrough has been quickly made that nobody thought possible!
10,787 Retweets **50,035** Likes
4:42 PM - 25 Jul 2018

 Donald J. Trump ✓
@realDonaldTrump

Obviously the European Union, as represented by @JunckerEU and the United States, as represented by yours truly, love each other!
11,952 Retweets **52,406** Likes
4:49 PM - 25 Jul 2018

Donald J. Trump ✓
@realDonaldTrump

Thank you Georgia! They say that my endorsement last week of Brian Kemp, in the Republican Primary for Governor against a very worthy opponent, lifted him from 5 points down to a 70% to 30% victory! Two very good and talented men in a great race, but congratulations to Brian!
13,593 Retweets **69,301** Likes
5:16 PM - 25 Jul 2018

Donald J. Trump ✓
@realDonaldTrump

Great to be back on track with the European Union. This was a big day for free and fair trade!
21,560 Retweets **105,281** Likes
6:01 PM - 25 Jul 2018

President Trumps Tweets 2018: A Historical Archive of President Trump's Tweets

Donald J. Trump ✓
@realDonaldTrump

European Union representatives told me that they would start buying soybeans from our great farmers immediately. Also, they will be buying vast amounts of LNG!
20,220 Retweets **91,623** Likes
6:07 PM - 25 Jul 2018

Donald J. Trump ✓
@realDonaldTrump

Twitter "SHADOW BANNING" prominent Republicans. Not good. We will look into this discriminatory and illegal practice at once! Many complaints.
50,130 Retweets **159,804** Likes
4:46 AM - 26 Jul 2018

Donald J. Trump ✓
@realDonaldTrump

Heading to Dubuque, Iowa and then Granite City, Illinois. Looking forward to being with many great friends!
11,856 Retweets **67,926** Likes
7:11 AM - 26 Jul 2018

Donald J. Trump ✓
@realDonaldTrump

This is great - on my way, see you soon @IAGovernor Kim Reynolds!
8,736 Retweets **41,256** Likes
7:52 AM - 26 Jul 2018

Donald J. Trump ✓
@realDonaldTrump

The United States will impose large sanctions on Turkey for their long time detainment of Pastor Andrew Brunson, a great Christian, family man and wonderful human being. He is suffering greatly. This innocent man of faith should be released immediately!
33,097 Retweets **122,313** Likes
8:22 AM - 26 Jul 2018

Donald J. Trump ✓
@realDonaldTrump

Thank you @U_S_Steel and Granite City, Illinois!
10,629 Retweets **47,188** Likes
2:12 PM - 26 Jul 2018

Donald J. Trump ✓
@realDonaldTrump

PROMISES KEPT!
17,790 Retweets **75,571** Likes
2:43 PM - 26 Jul 2018

Donald J. Trump ✓
@realDonaldTrump

.@AlanDersh, a brilliant lawyer, who although a Liberal Democrat who probably didn't vote for me, has discussed the Witch Hunt with great clarity and in a very positive way. He has written a new and very important book...
16,652 Retweets **72,787** Likes
3:48 PM - 26 Jul 2018

Donald J. Trump ✓
@realDonaldTrump

...called "The Case Against Impeaching Trump," which I would encourage all people with Trump Derangement Syndrome to read!
14,528 Retweets **66,953** Likes
3:48 PM - 26 Jul 2018

Donald J. Trump ✓
@realDonaldTrump

America is OPEN FOR BUSINESS and U.S. Steel is back!
21,865 Retweets **90,662** Likes
7:37 PM - 26 Jul 2018

Donald J. Trump ✓
@realDonaldTrump

The Remains of American Servicemen will soon be leaving North Korea and heading to the United States! After so many years, this will be a great moment for so many families. Thank you to Kim Jong Un.
22,907 Retweets **104,925** Likes
8:50 PM - 26 Jul 2018

Donald J. Trump ✓
@realDonaldTrump

Way to go Jerry. This is what the league should do!
12,486 Retweets **59,398** Likes
3:56 AM - 27 Jul 2018

Donald J. Trump ✓
@realDonaldTrump

Arrived back in Washington last night from a very emotional reopening of a major U.S. Steel plant in Granite City, Illinois, only to be greeted with the ridiculous news that the highly conflicted Robert Mueller and his gang of 13 Angry Democrats obviously cannot find Collusion...
18,912 Retweets **82,459** Likes
4:26 AM - 27 Jul 2018

Donald J. Trump ✓
@realDonaldTrump

.....,the only Collusion with Russia was with the Democrats, so now they are looking at my Tweets (along with 53 million other people) - the rigged Witch Hunt continues! How stupid and unfair to our Country....And so the Fake News doesn't waste my time with dumb questions, NO,....
22,957 Retweets **98,240** Likes
4:38 AM - 27 Jul 2018

Donald J. Trump ✓
@realDonaldTrump

.....I did NOT know of the meeting with my son, Don jr. Sounds to me like someone is trying to make up stories in order to get himself out of an unrelated jam (Taxi cabs maybe?). He even retained Bill and Crooked Hillary's lawyer. Gee, I wonder if they helped him make the choice!
20,471 Retweets **86,807** Likes
4:56 AM - 27 Jul 2018

Donald J. Trump ✓
@realDonaldTrump

GREAT GDP numbers just released. Will be having a news conference soon!
14,798 Retweets **79,239** Likes
6:17 AM - 27 Jul 2018

Donald J. Trump ✓
@realDonaldTrump

.@JohnJamesMI, who is running in the Republican Primary in the great state of Michigan, is SPECTACULAR! Vote on August 7th. Rarely have I seen a candidate with such great potential. West Point graduate, successful businessman and a African American leader...
19,280 Retweets **70,735** Likes
8:53 AM - 27 Jul 2018

Donald J. Trump ✓
@realDonaldTrump

...John is strong on crime and borders, loves our Military, our Vets and our Second Amendment. He will be a star. He has my full and total Endorsement!
12,493 Retweets **53,484** Likes
8:53 AM - 27 Jul 2018

Donald J. Trump ✓
@realDonaldTrump

.@Troy_Balderson of Ohio is running for Congress - so important to the Republican Party. Cast you early vote or vote on August 7th. Troy is strong on crime and borders, loves our Military, our Vets and our Second Amendment. He has my full and total Endorsement!
12,197 Retweets **47,293** Likes
8:58 AM - 27 Jul 2018

Donald J. Trump ✓
@realDonaldTrump

I am thrilled to announce that in the second quarter of this year, the U.S. Economy grew at the amazing rate of 4.1%!
22,075 Retweets **90,779** Likes
9:12 AM - 27 Jul 2018

Donald J. Trump ✓
@realDonaldTrump

We have accomplished an economic turnaround of HISTORIC proportions!
17,193 Retweets **67,318** Likes
9:20 AM - 27 Jul 2018

Donald J. Trump ✓
@realDonaldTrump

The @USNavy's first female Admiral, Alene Duerk once said: "It was a nice distinction to have, and to be recognized as the first, but I wanted to make certain that I used that notoriety to do as much positive as I could." Alene did just that, and America is forever grateful!
12,594 Retweets **54,602** Likes
11:16 AM - 27 Jul 2018

Donald J. Trump ✓
@realDonaldTrump

Private business investment has surged from 1.8 percent the year BEFORE I came into office to 9.4 percent this year -- that means JOBS, JOBS, JOBS!
16,058 Retweets **59,904** Likes
12:23 PM - 27 Jul 2018

Donald J. Trump ✓
@realDonaldTrump

Congressman David Kustoff has been a champion for the Trump Agenda - I greatly appreciate his support. David is strong on crime and borders, loves our Military, Vets and Second Amendment. Get out and vote for David on Thursday, August 2nd. He has my full and total Endorsement!
17,754 Retweets **72,793** Likes
1:08 PM - 27 Jul 2018

Donald J. Trump ✓
@realDonaldTrump

Democrats, who want Open Borders and care little about Crime, are incompetent, but they have the Fake News Media almost totally on their side!
29,051 Retweets **118,933** Likes
3:45 PM - 27 Jul 2018

Donald J. Trump ✓
@realDonaldTrump

The only things the Democrats do well is "Resist," which is their campaign slogan, and "Obstruct." Cryin' Chuck Schumer has almost 400 great American people that are waiting "forever" to serve our Country! A total disgrace. Mitch M should not let them go home until all approved!
30,440 Retweets **118,530** Likes
5:47 PM - 27 Jul 2018

@realDonaldTrump

Join me in Tampa, Florida next Tuesday, July 31st at 7:00pmE for a #MAGA Rally!
15,188 Retweets **55,585** Likes
6:53 PM - 27 Jul 2018

Donald J. Trump ✓
@realDonaldTrump

Tom Homan, fmr ICE Director: "There is nobody that has done more for border security & public safety than President Trump. I've worked for six presidents, and I respect them all, but nobody has done more than this Administration & President Trump, that's just a stone cold fact!"
22,644 Retweets **87,009** Likes
4:31 AM - 29 Jul 2018

Donald J. Trump ✓
@realDonaldTrump

Wow, highest Poll Numbers in the history of the Republican Party. That includes Honest Abe Lincoln and Ronald Reagan. There must be something wrong, please recheck that poll!
22,102 Retweets **102,444** Likes
4:44 AM - 29 Jul 2018

Donald J. Trump ✓
@realDonaldTrump

Do you think the Fake News Media will ever report on this tweet from Michael?
14,368 Retweets **50,407** Likes
4:52 AM - 29 Jul 2018

Donald J. Trump ✓
@realDonaldTrump

Please understand, there are consequences when people cross our Border illegally, whether they have children or not - and many are just using children for their own sinister purposes. Congress must act on fixing the DUMBEST & WORST immigration laws anywhere in the world! Vote "R"
33,183 Retweets **127,626** Likes
4:58 AM - 29 Jul 2018

Donald J. Trump ✓
@realDonaldTrump

Had a very good and interesting meeting at the White House with A.G. Sulzberger, Publisher of the New York Times. Spent much time talking about the vast amounts of Fake News being put out by the media & how that Fake News has morphed into phrase, "Enemy of the People." Sad!
18,359 Retweets **75,592** Likes
5:30 AM - 29 Jul 2018

Donald J. Trump ✓
@realDonaldTrump

The biggest and best results coming out of the good GDP report was that the quarterly Trade Deficit has been reduced by $52 Billion and, of course, the historically low unemployment numbers, especially for African Americans, Hispanics, Asians and Women.
21,443 Retweets **88,751** Likes
5:42 AM - 29 Jul 2018

Donald J. Trump ✓
@realDonaldTrump

I would be willing to "shut down" government if the Democrats do not give us the votes for Border Security, which includes the Wall! Must get rid of Lottery, Catch & Release etc. and finally go to system of Immigration based on MERIT! We need great people coming into our Country!
34,842 Retweets **135,850** Likes
6:13 AM - 29 Jul 2018

Donald J. Trump ✓
@realDonaldTrump

When the media - driven insane by their Trump Derangement Syndrome - reveals internal deliberations of our government, it truly puts the lives of many, not just journalists, at risk! Very unpatriotic! Freedom of the press also comes with a responsibility to report the news...
22,434 Retweets **91,737** Likes
12:09 PM - 29 Jul 2018

Donald J. Trump ✓
@realDonaldTrump

...accurately. 90% of media coverage of my Administration is negative, despite the tremendously positive results we are achieving, it's no surprise that confidence in the media is at an all time low! I will not allow our great country to be sold out by anti-Trump haters in the...
13,322 Retweets **44,052** Likes
12:09 PM - 29 Jul 2018

Donald J. Trump ✓
@realDonaldTrump

...dying newspaper industry. No matter how much they try to distract and cover it up, our country is making great progress under my leadership and I will never stop fighting for the American people! As an example, the failing New York Times...
15,209 Retweets **68,586** Likes
12:09 PM - 29 Jul 2018

Donald J. Trump ✓
@realDonaldTrump

...and the Amazon Washington Post do nothing but write bad stories even on very positive achievements - and they will never change!
14,594 Retweets **66,480** Likes
12:09 PM - 29 Jul 2018

Donald J. Trump @realDonaldTrump

There is No Collusion! The Robert Mueller Rigged Witch Hunt, headed now by 17 (increased from 13, including an Obama White House lawyer) Angry Democrats, was started by a fraudulent Dossier, paid for by Crooked Hillary and the DNC. Therefore, the Witch Hunt is an illegal Scam!
31,048 Retweets **115,212** Likes
12:35 PM - 29 Jul 2018

Donald J. Trump @realDonaldTrump

Is Robert Mueller ever going to release his conflicts of interest with respect to President Trump, including the fact that we had a very nasty & contentious business relationship, I turned him down to head the FBI (one day before appointment as S.C.) & Comey is his close friend...
24,839 Retweets **87,857** Likes
1:12 PM - 29 Jul 2018

Donald J. Trump @realDonaldTrump

....Also, why is Mueller only appointing Angry Dems, some of whom have worked for Crooked Hillary, others, including himself, have worked for Obama....And why isn't Mueller looking at all of the criminal activity & real Russian Collusion on the Democrats side-Podesta, Dossier?
25,755 Retweets **96,234** Likes
1:20 PM - 29 Jul 2018

Donald J. Trump @realDonaldTrump

We must have Border Security, get rid of Chain, Lottery, Catch & Release Sanctuary Cities - go to Merit based Immigration. Protect ICE and Law Enforcement and, of course, keep building, but much faster, THE WALL!
29,494 Retweets **116,486** Likes
4:57 AM - 30 Jul 2018

Donald J. Trump @realDonaldTrump

It is my great honor to welcome Prime Minister @GiuseppeConteIT of Italy to the @WhiteHouse! Join us at 2:00pmE for our joint press conference
10,545 Retweets **49,097** Likes
10:22 AM - 30 Jul 2018

Donald J. Trump @realDonaldTrump

Congratulations to General John Kelly. Today we celebrate his first full year as @WhiteHouse Chief of Staff!
12,906 Retweets **67,743** Likes
2:20 PM - 30 Jul 2018

Donald J. Trump @realDonaldTrump

.@Troy_Balderson of Ohio is running for Congress - so important to the Republican Party. Troy is strong on crime and Borders, loves our Military, our Vets and our Second Amendment. Troy will strongly protect...
8,773 Retweets **38,263** Likes
3:28 PM - 30 Jul 2018

President Trumps Tweets 2018: A Historical Archive of President Trump's Tweets

Donald J. Trump ✓
@realDonaldTrump

...your Social Security and Medicare! Cast your early vote, or vote on August 7th, Election Day. He has my full and total Endorsement!
5,871 Retweets **29,448** Likes
3:28 PM - 30 Jul 2018

Donald J. Trump ✓
@realDonaldTrump

Congratulations to Judge Jeanine on the tremendous success of her new #1 best-selling book, "Liars, Leakers, and Liberals – The Case Against the Anti-Trump Conspiracy!"
18,383 Retweets **90,837** Likes
3:31 PM - 30 Jul 2018

Donald J. Trump ✓
@realDonaldTrump

Illegal immigration is a top National Security problem. After decades of playing games, with the whole World laughing at the stupidity of our immigration laws, and with Democrats thinking...
19,050 Retweets **80,965** Likes
3:34 PM - 30 Jul 2018

Donald J. Trump ✓
@realDonaldTrump

...that Open Borders, large scale Crime, and abolishing ICE is good for them, we must get smart and finally do what must be done for the Safety and Security of our Country!
13,975 Retweets **62,004** Likes
3:34 PM - 30 Jul 2018

Donald J. Trump ✓
@realDonaldTrump

Thank you to @RandPaul for your YES on a future great Justice of the Supreme Court, Brett Kavanaugh. Your vote means a lot to me, and to everyone who loves our Country!
16,807 Retweets **79,854** Likes
3:36 PM - 30 Jul 2018

Donald J. Trump ✓
@realDonaldTrump

Congratulations to our new @DeptVetAffairs Secretary, Robert Wilkie!
8,963 Retweets **42,660** Likes
3:44 PM - 30 Jul 2018

Donald J. Trump ✓
@realDonaldTrump

A highly respected Federal judge today stated that the "Trump Administration gets great credit" for reuniting illegal families. Thank you, and please look at the previous administrations record - not good!
21,905 Retweets **88,708** Likes
5:56 PM - 30 Jul 2018

Donald J. Trump ✓
@realDonaldTrump

MAKING AMERICA GREAT AGAIN!
36,406 Retweets **110,155** Likes
7:01 PM - 30 Jul 2018

Donald J. Trump ✓
@realDonaldTrump

The globalist Koch Brothers, who have become a total joke in real Republican circles, are against Strong Borders and Powerful Trade. I never sought their support because I don't need their money or bad ideas. They love my Tax & Regulation Cuts, Judicial picks & more. I made.....
22,095 Retweets **88,242** Likes
3:14 AM - 31 Jul 2018

Donald J. Trump ✓
@realDonaldTrump

....them richer. Their network is highly overrated, I have beaten them at every turn. They want to protect their companies outside the U.S. from being taxed, I'm for America First & the American Worker - a puppet for no one. Two nice guys with bad ideas. Make America Great Again!
16,864 Retweets **74,917** Likes
3:23 AM - 31 Jul 2018

Donald J. Trump ✓
@realDonaldTrump

Rush Limbaugh is a great guy who truly gets it!
15,348 Retweets **74,560** Likes
3:50 AM - 31 Jul 2018

Donald J. Trump ✓
@realDonaldTrump

One of the reasons we need Great Border Security is that Mexico's murder rate in 2017 increased by 27% to 31,174 people killed, a record! The Democrats want Open Borders. I want Maximum Border Security and respect for ICE and our great Law Enforcement Professionals! @FoxNews
24,687 Retweets **91,904** Likes
4:00 AM - 31 Jul 2018

Donald J. Trump ✓
@realDonaldTrump

Collusion is not a crime, but that doesn't matter because there was No Collusion (except by Crooked Hillary and the Democrats)!
19,514 Retweets **86,389** Likes
4:58 AM - 31 Jul 2018

Donald J. Trump ✓
@realDonaldTrump

I am looking into 3-D Plastic Guns being sold to the public. Already spoke to NRA, doesn't seem to make much sense!
10,376 Retweets **52,390** Likes
5:03 AM - 31 Jul 2018

Donald J. Trump ✓
@realDonaldTrump

Will be in Tampa tonight. A big year for @RepDeSantis, who will be a great governor for Florida. Strong on Crime, Borders and our 2nd Amendment. Big help on Tax & Regulation Cuts. Loves our Military & our Vets. Has my Full & Total Endorsement!
13,410 Retweets **56,186** Likes
5:21 AM - 31 Jul 2018

President Trumps Tweets 2018: A Historical Archive of President Trump's Tweets

Donald J. Trump ✓
@realDonaldTrump

The Fake News Media is going CRAZY! They are totally unhinged and in many ways, after witnessing first hand the damage they do to so many innocent and decent people, I enjoy watching. In 7 years, when I am no longer in office, their ratings will dry up and they will be gone!

24,610 Retweets **102,238** Likes
6:34 AM - 31 Jul 2018

Donald J. Trump ✓
@realDonaldTrump

Congressman David Kustoff has been a champion for the Trump Agenda - I greatly appreciate his support. David is strong on crime and borders, loves our Military, Vets and Second Amendment. Get out and vote for David on Thursday, August 2nd. He has my Full and Total Endorsement!

13,301 Retweets **56,547** Likes
10:09 AM - 31 Jul 2018

Donald J. Trump ✓
@realDonaldTrump

.@SenJohnBarrasso has a Primary on August 21st. He doesn't need any help because he is absolutely outstanding in every way, but I hope the great people of Wyoming will go out and show their support anyway. John is absolutely top of the line & has my Complete & Total Endorsement!

11,264 Retweets **46,723** Likes
10:13 AM - 31 Jul 2018

Donald J. Trump ✓
@realDonaldTrump

I don't care what the political ramifications are, our immigration laws and border security have been a complete and total disaster for decades, and there is no way that the Democrats will allow it to be fixed without a Government Shutdown...

26,354 Retweets **107,985** Likes
10:33 AM - 31 Jul 2018

Donald J. Trump ✓
@realDonaldTrump

...Border Security is National Security, and National Security is the long-term viability of our Country. A Government Shutdown is a very small price to pay for a safe and Prosperous America!

17,024 Retweets **74,147** Likes
10:33 AM - 31 Jul 2018

Donald J. Trump ✓
@realDonaldTrump

"Worker pay rate hits highest level since 2008"

18,921 Retweets **74,178** Likes
1:39 PM - 31 Jul 2018

Donald J. Trump ✓
@realDonaldTrump

On my way to Tampa, Florida. Look forward to seeing everyone soon!

8,441 Retweets **50,791** Likes
1:49 PM - 31 Jul 2018

Donald J. Trump ✓
@realDonaldTrump

Thank you Florida. I love you!
17,690 Retweets **75,106** Likes
5:24 PM - 31 Jul 2018

Donald J. Trump ✓
@realDonaldTrump

"FBI Agent Peter Strzok (on the Mueller team) should have recused himself on day one. He was out to STOP THE ELECTION OF DONALD TRUMP. He needed an insurance policy. Those are illegal, improper goals, trying to influence the Election. He should never, ever been allowed to........
20,828 Retweets **82,452** Likes
6:03 AM - 1 Aug 2018

Donald J. Trump ✓
@realDonaldTrump

......remain in the FBI while he himself was being investigated. This is a real issue. It won't go into a Mueller Report because Mueller is going to protect these guys. Mueller has an interest in creating the illusion of objectivity around his investigation." ALAN DERSHOWITZ....
16,547 Retweets **64,593** Likes
6:15 AM - 1 Aug 2018

Donald J. Trump ✓
@realDonaldTrump

..This is a terrible situation and Attorney General Jeff Sessions should stop this Rigged Witch Hunt right now, before it continues to stain our country any further. Bob Mueller is totally conflicted, and his 17 Angry Democrats that are doing his dirty work are a disgrace to USA!
25,318 Retweets **96,678** Likes
6:24 AM - 1 Aug 2018

Donald J. Trump ✓
@realDonaldTrump

Paul Manafort worked for Ronald Reagan, Bob Dole and many other highly prominent and respected political leaders. He worked for me for a very short time. Why didn't government tell me that he was under investigation. These old charges have nothing to do with Collusion - a Hoax!
23,314 Retweets **89,238** Likes
6:34 AM - 1 Aug 2018

Donald J. Trump ✓
@realDonaldTrump

Russian Collusion with the Trump Campaign, one of the most successful in history, is a TOTAL HOAX. The Democrats paid for the phony and discredited Dossier which was, along with Comey, McCabe, Strzok and his lover, the lovely Lisa Page, used to begin the Witch Hunt. Disgraceful!
22,187 Retweets **84,988** Likes
7:01 AM - 1 Aug 2018

Donald J. Trump ✓
@realDonaldTrump

Looking back on history, who was treated worse, Alfonse Capone, legendary mob boss, killer and "Public Enemy Number One," or Paul Manafort, political operative & Reagan/Dole darling, now serving solitary confinement - although convicted of nothing? Where is the Russian Collusion?
18,537 Retweets **71,912** Likes
8:35 AM - 1 Aug 2018

President Trumps Tweets 2018: A Historical Archive of President Trump's Tweets

Donald J. Trump ✓
@realDonaldTrump

"We already have a smoking gun about a campaign getting dirt on their opponent, it was Hillary Clinton. How is it OK for Hillary Clinton to proactively seek dirt from the Russians but the Trump campaign met at the Russians request and that is bad?" Marc Thiessen, Washington Post
21,566 Retweets **79,041** Likes
8:56 AM - 1 Aug 2018

Donald J. Trump ✓
@realDonaldTrump

It was my great honor to be joined by leading pastors and faith leaders from across our Nation today at the @WhiteHouse!
15,638 Retweets **65,957** Likes
11:55 AM - 1 Aug 2018

Donald J. Trump ✓
@realDonaldTrump

#PledgeToAmericasWorkers
11,876 Retweets **50,277** Likes
12:22 PM - 1 Aug 2018

Donald J. Trump ✓
@realDonaldTrump

Join me tomorrow night at 7pmE in Wilkes-Barre Township, Pennsylvania for a MAKE AMERICA GREAT AGAIN RALLY!
11,284 Retweets **45,573** Likes
2:04 PM - 1 Aug 2018

Donald J. Trump ✓
@realDonaldTrump

"Private payrolls boom in July, increasing by 219,000 vs 185,000 estimate: ADP"
14,477 Retweets **59,365** Likes
2:16 PM - 1 Aug 2018

Donald J. Trump ✓
@realDonaldTrump

Incredibly beautiful ceremony as U.S. Korean War remains are returned to American soil. Thank you to Honolulu and all of our great Military participants on a job well done. A special thanks to Vice President Mike Pence on delivering a truly magnificent tribute!
17,350 Retweets **86,814** Likes
8:32 PM - 1 Aug 2018

Donald J. Trump ✓
@realDonaldTrump

Congratulations to @GreggJarrett on The TREMENDOUS success of his just out book, "The Russia Hoax, The Illicit Scheme To Clear Hillary Clinton & Frame Donald Trump." Already number one on Amazon. Hard work from a brilliant guy. It's the Real Story of the Rigged Witch Hunt!
17,180 Retweets **70,597** Likes
9:38 PM - 1 Aug 2018

Donald J. Trump ✓
@realDonaldTrump

Thank you to Chairman Kim Jong Un for keeping your word & starting the process of sending home the remains of our great and beloved missing fallen! I am not at all surprised that you took this kind action. Also, thank you for your nice letter - I look forward to seeing you soon!
26,299 Retweets **130,250** Likes
9:47 PM - 1 Aug 2018

Donald J. Trump ✓
@realDonaldTrump

Charles Koch of Koch Brothers, who claims to be giving away millions of dollars to politicians even though I know very few who have seen this (?), now makes the ridiculous statement that what President Trump is doing is unfair to "foreign workers." He is correct, AMERICA FIRST!
25,836 Retweets **102,889** Likes
3:38 AM - 2 Aug 2018

 Donald J. Trump ✓
@realDonaldTrump

Wow, @foxandfriends is blowing away the competition in the morning ratings. Morning Joe is a dead show with very few people watching and sadly, Fake News CNN is also doing poorly. Too much hate and inaccurately reported stories - too predictable!
21,829 Retweets **97,812** Likes
4:04 AM - 2 Aug 2018

 Donald J. Trump ✓
@realDonaldTrump

Working hard, thank you!
21,721 Retweets **92,481** Likes
10:23 AM - 2 Aug 2018

 Donald J. Trump ✓
@realDonaldTrump

Looking forward to being in the Great State of Pennsylvania where we had a tremendous victory in the Election. Will be campaigning hard for an original supporter, Lou Barletta, to replace a weak an ineffective Senator, Bob Casey. Lou is tough and smart, loves PA and our Country!
13,812 Retweets **64,860** Likes
11:53 AM - 2 Aug 2018

 Donald J. Trump ✓
@realDonaldTrump

Pennsylvania has to love Trump because unlike all of the others before me, I am bringing STEEL BACK in a VERY BIG way. Plants opening up in Pennsylvania, and all over the Country, and Congressman Lou Barletta, who is running for the Senate in Pennsylvania, is really helping!
17,076 Retweets **80,304** Likes
11:55 AM - 2 Aug 2018

 Donald J. Trump ✓
@realDonaldTrump

When the House and Senate meet on the very important Farm Bill – we love our farmers - hopefully they will be able to leave the WORK REQUIREMENTS FOR FOOD STAMPS PROVISION that the House approved. Senate should go to 51 votes!
13,769 Retweets **63,019** Likes
11:57 AM - 2 Aug 2018

Donald J. Trump ✓
@realDonaldTrump

Looking forward to being in the Great State of Ohio on Saturday night where I will be campaigning hard for a truly talented future Congressman, @Troy_Balderson. See you all then!
9,501 Retweets **40,419** Likes
12:08 PM - 2 Aug 2018

Donald J. Trump ✓
@realDonaldTrump

They asked my daughter Ivanka whether or not the media is the enemy of the people. She correctly said no. It is the FAKE NEWS, which is a large percentage of the media, that is the enemy of the people!

34,404 Retweets **145,812** Likes
1:24 PM - 2 Aug 2018

Donald J. Trump ✓
@realDonaldTrump

Thank you Pennsylvania. I love you!

18,236 Retweets **80,610** Likes
5:30 PM - 2 Aug 2018

Donald J. Trump ✓
@realDonaldTrump

Congratulations to Bill Lee of Tennessee on his big primary win for Governor last night. He ran a great campaign and now will finish off the job in November. Bill has my total and enthusiastic Endorsement!

16,043 Retweets **77,708** Likes
7:21 AM - 3 Aug 2018

Donald J. Trump ✓
@realDonaldTrump

Congratulations Marsha!

8,647 Retweets **41,383** Likes
10:39 AM - 3 Aug 2018

Donald J. Trump ✓
@realDonaldTrump

"Pastor praises Trump as 'pro-black' at prison reform event"

15,398 Retweets **60,075** Likes
1:31 PM - 3 Aug 2018

Donald J. Trump ✓
@realDonaldTrump

Marsha Blackburn had a BIG win last night in the Tennessee primary for U.S. Senate. She is an outstanding person & great supporter of mine. Congratulations Marsha, we need you very badly in the Senate to vote for our agenda. Your next opponent will vote against all we are doing!

15,808 Retweets **70,395** Likes
3:00 PM - 3 Aug 2018

Donald J. Trump ✓
@realDonaldTrump

July is just the ninth month since 1970 that unemployment has fallen below 4%. Our economy has added 3.7 million jobs since I won the Election. 4.1 GDP. More than 4 million people have received a pay raise due to tax reform. $400 Billion brought back from "overseas." @FoxNews

18,443 Retweets **77,998** Likes
3:10 PM - 3 Aug 2018

Donald J. Trump ✓
@realDonaldTrump

NASA, which is making a BIG comeback under the Trump Administration, has just named 9 astronauts for Boeing and Spacex space flights. We have the greatest facilities in the world and we are now letting the private sector pay to use them. Exciting things happening. Space Force!

17,608 Retweets **81,570** Likes
3:43 PM - 3 Aug 2018

Donald J. Trump ✓
@realDonaldTrump

"The media are good news fire extinguishers!" @greggutfeld @TheFive
10,310 Retweets **46,532** Likes
3:55 PM - 3 Aug 2018

Donald J. Trump ✓
@realDonaldTrump

Almost 500,000 Manufacturing Jobs created since I won the Election. Remember when my opponents were saying that we couldn't create this type of job anymore. Wrong, in fact these are among our best and most important jobs!
22,625 Retweets **98,844** Likes
3:59 PM - 3 Aug 2018

Donald J. Trump ✓
@realDonaldTrump

Great photo from Ocean City, Maryland. Thank you. MAKE AMERICA GREAT AGAIN!
21,640 Retweets **86,511** Likes
6:06 PM - 3 Aug 2018

Donald J. Trump ✓
@realDonaldTrump

Congratulations to Gregg Jarrett on his book, "THE RUSSIA HOAX, THE ILLICIT SCHEME TO CLEAR HILLARY CLINTON AND FRAME DONALD TRUMP," going to #1 on @nytimes and Amazon. It is indeed a HOAX and WITCH HUNT, illegally started by people who have already been disgraced. Great book!
13,932 Retweets **60,344** Likes
8:01 PM - 3 Aug 2018

Donald J. Trump ✓
@realDonaldTrump

...Dianne is the person leading our Nation on "Collusion" with Russia (only done by Dems). Will she now investigate herself?
18,732 Retweets **57,212** Likes
8:28 PM - 3 Aug 2018

Donald J. Trump ✓
@realDonaldTrump

Lebron James was just interviewed by the dumbest man on television, Don Lemon. He made Lebron look smart, which isn't easy to do. I like Mike!
49,313 Retweets **180,381** Likes
8:37 PM - 3 Aug 2018

Donald J. Trump ✓
@realDonaldTrump

Will be going to Ohio tonight to campaign for Troy Balderson for the big Congressional Special Election on Tuesday. Early voting is on. Troy is strong on Crime, the Border & loves our Military, Vets & 2nd Amendment. His opponent is a puppet of Nancy Pelosi/high taxes.
15,637 Retweets **70,696** Likes
5:49 AM - 4 Aug 2018

Donald J. Trump ✓
@realDonaldTrump

Troy Balderson, running for Congress from Ohio, is in a big Election fight with a candidate who just got caught lying about his relationship with Nancy Pelosi, who is weak on Crime, Borders & your 2nd Amendment-and wants to raise your Taxes (by a lot). Vote for Troy on Tuesday!
19,899 Retweets **76,470** Likes
6:02 AM - 4 Aug 2018

President Trumps Tweets 2018: A Historical Archive of President Trump's Tweets

Donald J. Trump ✓
@realDonaldTrump

HAPPY BIRTHDAY @USCG!
12,303 Retweets **60,706** Likes
8:18 AM - 4 Aug 2018

Donald J. Trump ✓
@realDonaldTrump

Tariffs are working far better than anyone ever anticipated. China market has dropped 27% in last 4months, and they are talking to us. Our market is stronger than ever, and will go up dramatically when these horrible Trade Deals are successfully renegotiated. America First.......
20,071 Retweets **86,527** Likes
12:47 PM - 4 Aug 2018

Donald J. Trump ✓
@realDonaldTrump

....Tariffs have had a tremendous positive impact on our Steel Industry. Plants are opening all over the U.S., Steelworkers are working again, and big dollars are flowing into our Treasury. Other countries use Tariffs against, but when we use them, foolish people scream!
13,722 Retweets **61,221** Likes
12:53 PM - 4 Aug 2018

Donald J. Trump ✓
@realDonaldTrump

....Tariffs will make our country much richer than it is today. Only fools would disagree. We are using them to negotiate fair trade deals and, if countries are still unwilling to negotiate, they will pay us vast sums of money in the form of Tariffs. We win either way......
17,819 Retweets **81,002** Likes
12:58 PM - 4 Aug 2018

Donald J. Trump ✓
@realDonaldTrump

....China, which is for the first time doing poorly against us, is spending a fortune on ads and P.R. trying to convince and scare our politicians to fight me on Tariffs- because they are really hurting their economy. Likewise other countries. We are Winning, but must be strong!
16,553 Retweets **69,589** Likes
1:03 PM - 4 Aug 2018

Donald J. Trump ✓
@realDonaldTrump

Heading to Ohio!
9,075 Retweets **64,584** Likes
1:28 PM - 4 Aug 2018

Donald J. Trump ✓
@realDonaldTrump

Iran, and it's economy, is going very bad, and fast! I will meet, or not meet, it doesn't matter - it is up to them!
18,571 Retweets **87,241** Likes
1:53 PM - 4 Aug 2018

Donald J. Trump ✓
@realDonaldTrump

Thank you Ohio. I love you!
13,891 Retweets **61,483** Likes
5:28 PM - 4 Aug 2018

Donald J. Trump ✓
@realDonaldTrump

A great night in Ohio's 12th Congressional District with Troy Balderson! Troy loves Ohio, and he loves the people of Ohio. He will be fighting for you all the way...
16,505 Retweets **78,784** Likes
6:43 PM - 4 Aug 2018

 Donald J. Trump ✓
@realDonaldTrump

...Danny O'Connor is a total puppet for Nancy Pelosi and Maxine Waters – Danny wants to raise your taxes, open your borders, and take away your 2nd Amendment. Vote for Troy on Tuesday!
15,195 Retweets **63,195** Likes
6:43 PM - 4 Aug 2018

 Donald J. Trump ✓
@realDonaldTrump

The Fake News hates me saying that they are the Enemy of the People only because they know it's TRUE. I am providing a great service by explaining this to the American People. They purposely cause great division & distrust. They can also cause War! They are very dangerous & sick!
33,755 Retweets **124,918** Likes
4:38 AM - 5 Aug 2018

 Donald J. Trump ✓
@realDonaldTrump

Tariffs are working big time. Every country on earth wants to take wealth out of the U.S., always to our detriment. I say, as they come, Tax them. If they don't want to be taxed, let them make or build the product in the U.S. In either event, it means jobs and great wealth.....
16,604 Retweets **75,150** Likes
4:59 AM - 5 Aug 2018

 Donald J. Trump ✓
@realDonaldTrump

..Because of Tariffs we will be able to start paying down large amounts of the $21 Trillion in debt that has been accumulated, much by the Obama Administration, while at the same time reducing taxes for our people. At minimum, we will make much better Trade Deals for our country!
19,789 Retweets **81,856** Likes
5:06 AM - 5 Aug 2018

 Donald J. Trump ✓
@realDonaldTrump

Fake News reporting, a complete fabrication, that I am concerned about the meeting my wonderful son, Donald, had in Trump Tower. This was a meeting to get information on an opponent, totally legal and done all the time in politics - and it went nowhere. I did not know about it!
20,549 Retweets **83,174** Likes
5:35 AM - 5 Aug 2018

Donald J. Trump ✓
@realDonaldTrump

...Why aren't Mueller and the 17 Angry Democrats looking at the meetings concerning the Fake Dossier and all of the lying that went on in the FBI and DOJ? This is the most one sided Witch Hunt in the history of our country. Fortunately, the facts are all coming out, and fast!
26,382 Retweets **104,190** Likes
5:45 AM - 5 Aug 2018

President Trumps Tweets 2018: A Historical Archive of President Trump's Tweets

Donald J. Trump
@realDonaldTrump

Too bad a large portion of the Media refuses to report the lies and corruption having to do with the Rigged Witch Hunt - but that is why we call them FAKE NEWS!
22,057 Retweets **93,211** Likes
5:49 AM - 5 Aug 2018

Donald J. Trump
@realDonaldTrump

Presidential Approval numbers are very good - strong economy, military and just about everything else. Better numbers than Obama at this point, by far. We are winning on just about every front and for that reason there will not be a Blue Wave, but there might be a Red Wave!
29,214 Retweets **135,598** Likes
1:01 PM - 5 Aug 2018

Donald J. Trump
@realDonaldTrump

"Collusion with Russia was very real. Hillary Clinton and her team 100% colluded with the Russians, and so did Adam Schiff who is on tape trying to collude with what he thought was Russians to obtain compromising material on DJT. We also know that Hillary Clinton paid through....
25,103 Retweets **86,757** Likes
7:13 AM - 6 Aug 2018

Donald J. Trump
@realDonaldTrump

....a law firm, eventually Kremlin connected sources, to gather info on Donald Trump. Collusion is very real with Russia, but only with Hillary and the Democrats, and we should demand a full investigation." Dan Bongino on @foxandfriends Looking forward to the new IG Report!
18,269 Retweets **70,555** Likes
7:25 AM - 6 Aug 2018

Donald J. Trump
@realDonaldTrump

Great financial numbers being announced on an almost daily basis. Economy has never been better, jobs at best point in history. Fixing our terrible Trade Deals is a priority-and going very well. Immigration on Merit Based System to take care of the companies coming back to U.S.A.
17,792 Retweets **74,883** Likes
7:52 AM - 6 Aug 2018

Donald J. Trump
@realDonaldTrump

Kris Kobach, a strong and early supporter of mine, is running for Governor of the Great State of Kansas. He is a fantastic guy who loves his State and our Country - he will be a GREAT Governor and has my full & total Endorsement! Strong on Crime, Border & Military. VOTE TUESDAY!
18,391 Retweets **76,717** Likes
8:48 AM - 6 Aug 2018

Donald J. Trump
@realDonaldTrump

Governor Jerry Brown must allow the Free Flow of the vast amounts of water coming from the North and foolishly being diverted into the Pacific Ocean. Can be used for fires, farming and everything else. Think of California with plenty of Water - Nice! Fast Federal govt. approvals.
19,515 Retweets **75,138** Likes
10:43 AM - 6 Aug 2018

Donald J. Trump ✓
@realDonaldTrump

John James is a potential Republican Star who has a Senate primary election tomorrow in Michigan. If he becomes the Republican candidate, he will beat the Open Borders, weak on Crime, Democrat, Debbie Stabenow. Vote for John James and Make America Great Again!
20,720 Retweets **75,321** Likes
12:13 PM - 6 Aug 2018

Donald J. Trump ✓
@realDonaldTrump

Democrats want Open Borders and they want to abolish ICE, the brave men and women that are protecting our Country from some of the most vicious and dangerous people on earth! Sorry, we can't let that happen! Also, change the rules in the Senate and approve STRONG Border Security!
24,719 Retweets **95,140** Likes
2:46 PM - 6 Aug 2018

Donald J. Trump ✓
@realDonaldTrump

California wildfires are being magnified & made so much worse by the bad environmental laws which aren't allowing massive amounts of readily available water to be properly utilized. It is being diverted into the Pacific Ocean. Must also tree clear to stop fire from spreading!
18,211 Retweets **77,997** Likes
2:53 PM - 6 Aug 2018

Donald J. Trump ✓
@realDonaldTrump

The Iran sanctions have officially been cast. These are the most biting sanctions ever imposed, and in November they ratchet up to yet another level. Anyone doing business with Iran will NOT be doing business with the United States. I am asking for WORLD PEACE, nothing less!
37,124 Retweets **137,023** Likes
2:31 AM - 7 Aug 2018

Donald J. Trump ✓
@realDonaldTrump

Ohio, vote today for Troy Balderson for Congress. His opponent, controlled by Nancy Pelosi, is weak on Crime, the Border, Military, Vets, your 2nd Amendment - and will end your Tax Cuts. Troy will be a great Congressman. #MAGA
22,308 Retweets **84,622** Likes
3:46 AM - 7 Aug 2018

Donald J. Trump ✓
@realDonaldTrump

Today, on the 236th anniversary of the Purple Heart, we honor the members of our Armed Forces for serving as the vanguard of American democracy and freedom around the world. #PurpleHeartDay
16,917 Retweets **74,931** Likes
11:25 AM - 7 Aug 2018

Donald J. Trump ✓
@realDonaldTrump

When I decided to go to Ohio for Troy Balderson, he was down in early voting 64 to 36. That was not good. After my speech on Saturday night, there was a big turn for the better. Now Troy wins a great victory during a very tough time of the year for voting. He will win BIG in Nov.
20,677 Retweets **100,341** Likes
7:59 PM - 7 Aug 2018

President Trumps Tweets 2018: A Historical Archive of President Trump's Tweets

Donald J. Trump ✓
@realDonaldTrump

.....Congratulations to Troy Balderson on a great win in Ohio. A very special and important race!
16,811 Retweets **83,437** Likes
8:18 PM - 7 Aug 2018

Donald J. Trump ✓
@realDonaldTrump

Congratulations to a future STAR of the Republican Party, future Senator John James. A big and bold victory tonight in the Great State of Michigan - the first of many. November can't come fast enough!
23,723 Retweets **107,531** Likes
8:23 PM - 7 Aug 2018

Donald J. Trump ✓
@realDonaldTrump

Congratulations to Bill Schuette. You will have a Big win in November and be a tremendous Governor for the Great State of Michigan. Lots of car and other companies moving back!
16,434 Retweets **80,623** Likes
8:52 PM - 7 Aug 2018

Donald J. Trump ✓
@realDonaldTrump

Congratulations to Josh Hawley on your big Senate Primary win in Missouri. I look forward to working with you toward a big win in November. We need you in Washington!
16,129 Retweets **76,981** Likes
9:28 PM - 7 Aug 2018

Donald J. Trump ✓
@realDonaldTrump

5 for 5!
19,664 Retweets **95,136** Likes
7:31 AM - 8 Aug 2018

Donald J. Trump ✓
@realDonaldTrump

The Republicans have now won 8 out of 9 House Seats, yet if you listen to the Fake News Media you would think we are being clobbered. Why can't they play it straight, so unfair to the Republican Party and in particular, your favorite President!
36,082 Retweets **152,820** Likes
8:14 AM - 8 Aug 2018

Donald J. Trump ✓
@realDonaldTrump

As long as I campaign and/or support Senate and House candidates (within reason), they will win! I LOVE the people, & they certainly seem to like the job I'm doing. If I find the time, in between China, Iran, the Economy and much more, which I must, we will have a giant Red Wave!
21,445 Retweets **95,310** Likes
8:25 AM - 8 Aug 2018

Donald J. Trump ✓
@realDonaldTrump

Congratulations to @LenaEpstein of Michigan on a job well done. Also, thanks for your great support!
11,358 Retweets **61,473** Likes
11:07 AM - 8 Aug 2018

Donald J. Trump @realDonaldTrump

RED WAVE!
32,189 Retweets **135,418** Likes
11:51 AM - 8 Aug 2018

Donald J. Trump @realDonaldTrump

"There has been no evidence whatsoever that Donald Trump or the campaign was involved in any kind of collusion to fix the 2016 election. In fact the evidence is the opposite, that Hillary Clinton & the Democrats colluded with the Russians to fix the 2016 election." @GrahamLedger
26,362 Retweets **100,528** Likes
6:22 AM - 9 Aug 2018

Donald J. Trump @realDonaldTrump

This is an illegally brought Rigged Witch Hunt run by people who are totally corrupt and/or conflicted. It was started and paid for by Crooked Hillary and the Democrats. Phony Dossier, FISA disgrace and so many lying and dishonest people already fired. 17 Angry Dems? Stay tuned!
26,447 Retweets **101,540** Likes
9:02 AM - 9 Aug 2018

Space Force all the way!
38,036 Retweets **144,861** Likes
9:03 AM - 9 Aug 2018

Donald J. Trump @realDonaldTrump

Congressman Ted Yoho of Florida is doing a fantastic job and has my complete and total Endorsement! Tough on Crime and Borders, Ted was really helpful on Tax Cuts. Vote all the way for Ted in the upcoming Primary - he will never let you down!
18,215 Retweets **77,731** Likes
10:00 AM - 9 Aug 2018

Donald J. Trump @realDonaldTrump

@LindseyGrahamSC "Why didn't the FBI tell President Trump that they had concerns about Carter Page? Is there a double standard here?" They told Senator Diane Feinstein that she had a spy - but not Trump. Is that entrapment or did they just want to use Page as an excuse to SPY?
6,715 Retweets **13,653** Likes
12:43 PM - 9 Aug 2018

Donald J. Trump @realDonaldTrump

Jenna Ellis "FBI thought they wouldn't get caught because they thought that Hillary was going to win. There is overt bias and that depends on whether you are Democrat or Republican - a double standard that needs to stop."
29,464 Retweets **112,260** Likes
3:50 PM - 9 Aug 2018

Donald J. Trump @realDonaldTrump

.@MariaBartiromo "No evidence to launch even an investigation into potential collusion between Donald Trump and the Russians - and here we are, a year and a half later."
18,410 Retweets **75,989** Likes
4:49 AM - 10 Aug 2018

President Trumps Tweets 2018: A Historical Archive of President Trump's Tweets

Donald J. Trump ✓
@realDonaldTrump

The NFL players are at it again - taking a knee when they should be standing proudly for the National Anthem. Numerous players, from different teams, wanted to show their "outrage" at something that most of them are unable to define. They make a fortune doing what they love......
25,476 Retweets **111,461** Likes
5:18 AM - 10 Aug 2018

Donald J. Trump ✓
@realDonaldTrump

.....Be happy, be cool! A football game, that fans are paying soooo much money to watch and enjoy, is no place to protest. Most of that money goes to the players anyway. Find another way to protest. Stand proudly for your National Anthem or be Suspended Without Pay!
34,559 Retweets **170,619** Likes
5:32 AM - 10 Aug 2018

Donald J. Trump ✓
@realDonaldTrump

I have just authorized a doubling of Tariffs on Steel and Aluminum with respect to Turkey as their currency, the Turkish Lira, slides rapidly downward against our very strong Dollar! Aluminum will now be 20% and Steel 50%. Our relations with Turkey are not good at this time!
37,812 Retweets **122,264** Likes
5:47 AM - 10 Aug 2018

Donald J. Trump ✓
@realDonaldTrump

Democrats, please do not distance yourselves from Nancy Pelosi. She is a wonderful person whose ideas & policies may be bad, but who should definitely be given a 4th chance. She is trying very hard & has every right to take down the Democrat Party if she has veered too far left!
32,663 Retweets **141,243** Likes
2:30 PM - 10 Aug 2018

Donald J. Trump ✓
@realDonaldTrump

Had a very good phone call with @EmmanuelMacron, President of France. Discussed various subjects, in particular Security and Trade. Many other calls and conversations today. Looking forward to dinner tonight with Tim Cook of Apple. He is investing big dollars in U.S.A.
16,408 Retweets **79,785** Likes
3:47 PM - 10 Aug 2018

Donald J. Trump ✓
@realDonaldTrump

Thank you to Kanye West and the fact that he is willing to tell the TRUTH. One new and great FACT - African American unemployment is the lowest ever recorded in the history of our Country. So honored by this. Thank you Kanye for your support. It is making a big difference!
35,927 Retweets **148,131** Likes
3:58 PM - 10 Aug 2018

Donald J. Trump ✓
@realDonaldTrump

Deal with Mexico is coming along nicely. Autoworkers and farmers must be taken care of or there will be no deal. New President of Mexico has been an absolute gentleman. Canada must wait. Their Tariffs and Trade Barriers are far too high. Will tax cars if we can't make a deal!
24,781 Retweets **101,159** Likes
4:12 PM - 10 Aug 2018

Donald J. Trump ⊗
@realDonaldTrump

Why isn't the FBI giving Andrew McCabe text messages to Judicial Watch or appropriate governmental authorities. FBI said they won't give up even one (I may have to get involved, DO NOT DESTROY). What are they hiding? McCabe wife took big campaign dollars from Hillary people.....
22,359 Retweets **80,765** Likes
6:17 AM - 11 Aug 2018

Donald J. Trump ⊗
@realDonaldTrump

.....Will the FBI ever recover it's once stellar reputation, so badly damaged by Comey, McCabe, Peter S and his lover, the lovely Lisa Page, and other top officials now dismissed or fired? So many of the great men and women of the FBI have been hurt by these clowns and losers!
25,591 Retweets **104,931** Likes
6:18 AM - 11 Aug 2018

Donald J. Trump ⊗
@realDonaldTrump

The riots in Charlottesville a year ago resulted in senseless death and division. We must come together as a nation. I condemn all types of racism and acts of violence. Peace to ALL Americans!
33,037 Retweets **136,300** Likes
6:26 AM - 11 Aug 2018

@realDonaldTrump

I am proud to have fought for and secured the LOWEST African American and Hispanic unemployment rates in history. Now I'm pushing for prison reform to give people who have paid their debt to society a second chance. I will never stop fighting for ALL Americans!
36,242 Retweets **152,272** Likes
6:41 AM - 11 Aug 2018

Donald J. Trump ⊗
@realDonaldTrump

The big story that the Fake News Media refuses to report is lowlife Christopher Steele's many meetings with Deputy A.G. Bruce Ohr and his beautiful wife, Nelly. It was Fusion GPS that hired Steele to write the phony & discredited Dossier, paid for by Crooked Hillary & the DNC....
25,284 Retweets **88,682** Likes
11:28 AM - 11 Aug 2018

Donald J. Trump ⊗
@realDonaldTrump

....Do you believe Nelly worked for Fusion and her husband STILL WORKS FOR THE DEPARTMENT OF "JUSTICE." I have never seen anything so Rigged in my life. Our A.G. is scared stiff and Missing in Action. It is all starting to be revealed - not pretty. IG Report soon? Witch Hunt!
30,395 Retweets **106,463** Likes
11:54 AM - 11 Aug 2018

Donald J. Trump ⊗
@realDonaldTrump

Hundreds of Bikers for Trump just joined me at Bedminster. Quite a scene - great people who truly love our Country!
26,336 Retweets **134,095** Likes
11:59 AM - 11 Aug 2018

President Trumps Tweets 2018: A Historical Archive of President Trump's Tweets

Donald J. Trump ✓
@realDonaldTrump

Bikers for Trump at Bedminster earlier today. Thank you!
22,659 Retweets **99,752** Likes
6:51 PM - 11 Aug 2018

Donald J. Trump ✓
@realDonaldTrump

.@JudgeJeanine "Bob Mueller, isn't your whole investigation premised on a Fake Dossier, paid for by Hillary, created by a man who hates Donald Trump, & used to con a FISA Court Judge. Bob, I really think it's time for you to give up your phony investigation." No Collusion!
24,267 Retweets **91,756** Likes
5:24 AM - 12 Aug 2018

Donald J. Trump ✓
@realDonaldTrump

.@GovMikeHuckabee "Your paycheck is bigger, your pension is stronger." @foxandfriends Unemployment numbers are better than they have been in 50 years, & perhaps ever. Our country is booming like never before - and it will get even better! Many companies moving back to the U.S.A.
22,278 Retweets **95,322** Likes
5:34 AM - 12 Aug 2018

Donald J. Trump ✓
@realDonaldTrump

Many @harleydavidson owners plan to boycott the company if manufacturing moves overseas. Great! Most other companies are coming in our direction, including Harley competitors. A really bad move! U.S. will soon have a level playing field, or better.
18,412 Retweets **84,447** Likes
5:57 AM - 12 Aug 2018

Donald J. Trump ✓
@realDonaldTrump

"Seems like the Department of Justice (and FBI) had a program to keep Donald Trump from becoming President". @DarrellIssa @foxandfriends If this had happened to the other side, everybody involved would be in jail. This is a Media coverup of the biggest story of our time.
33,759 Retweets **106,933** Likes
6:25 AM - 12 Aug 2018

Donald J. Trump ✓
@realDonaldTrump

Wacky Omarosa, who got fired 3 times on the Apprentice, now got fired for the last time. She never made it, never will. She begged me for a job, tears in her eyes, I said Ok. People in the White House hated her. She was vicious, but not smart. I would rarely see her but heard....
20,450 Retweets **87,627** Likes
6:27 AM - 13 Aug 2018

Donald J. Trump ✓
@realDonaldTrump

...really bad things. Nasty to people & would constantly miss meetings & work. When Gen. Kelly came on board he told me she was a loser & nothing but problems. I told him to try working it out, if possible, because she only said GREAT things about me - until she got fired!
18,386 Retweets **80,892** Likes
6:50 AM - 13 Aug 2018

Donald J. Trump ✓
@realDonaldTrump

While I know it's "not presidential" to take on a lowlife like Omarosa, and while I would rather not be doing so, this is a modern day form of communication and I know the Fake News Media will be working overtime to make even Wacky Omarosa look legitimate as possible. Sorry!
23,204 Retweets **107,572** Likes
7:21 AM - 13 Aug 2018

Donald J. Trump ✓
@realDonaldTrump

The very unpopular Governor of Ohio (and failed presidential candidate) @JohnKasich hurt Troy Balderson's recent win by tamping down enthusiasm for an otherwise great candidate. Even Kasich's Lt. Governor lost Gov. race because of his unpopularity. Credit to Troy on the BIG WIN!
14,897 Retweets **64,632** Likes
8:12 AM - 13 Aug 2018

Donald J. Trump ✓
@realDonaldTrump

Agent Peter Strzok was just fired from the FBI - finally. The list of bad players in the FBI & DOJ gets longer & longer. Based on the fact that Strzok was in charge of the Witch Hunt, will it be dropped? It is a total Hoax. No Collusion, No Obstruction - I just fight back!
24,182 Retweets **94,990** Likes
9:04 AM - 13 Aug 2018

Donald J. Trump ✓
@realDonaldTrump

Just fired Agent Strzok, formerly of the FBI, was in charge of the Crooked Hillary Clinton sham investigation. It was a total fraud on the American public and should be properly redone!
29,004 Retweets **114,825** Likes
9:09 AM - 13 Aug 2018

Donald J. Trump ✓
@realDonaldTrump

Wacky Omarosa already has a fully signed Non-Disclosure Agreement!
14,794 Retweets **66,845** Likes
9:13 AM - 13 Aug 2018

Donald J. Trump ✓
@realDonaldTrump

Brooks Koepka just won his third Golf Major, and he did it not only with his powerful game, but with his powerful mind. He has been a man of steel on the Tour and will have many Victories, including Majors, ahead of him. Congrats to Brooks and his great team on a job well done!
10,375 Retweets **70,143** Likes
10:11 AM - 13 Aug 2018

Donald J. Trump ✓
@realDonaldTrump

Just landed at Fort Drum, New York. Looking forward to making a speech about our GREAT HEROES!
10,942 Retweets **63,774** Likes
11:19 AM - 13 Aug 2018

Donald J. Trump ✓
@realDonaldTrump

Great to be in Fort Drum, New York with our HEROES!
10,974 Retweets **49,883** Likes
12:37 PM - 13 Aug 2018

President Trumps Tweets 2018: A Historical Archive of President Trump's Tweets

Donald J. Trump ✓
@realDonaldTrump

Pete Stauber is running for Congress in Minnesota. He will make for a great Congressman. Pete is strong on crime and borders, loves our Military, Vets and Second Amendment. Vote for Pete tomorrow. He has my full and total Endorsement!
16,611 Retweets **63,277** Likes
1:42 PM - 13 Aug 2018

Donald J. Trump ✓
@realDonaldTrump

It was my great honor to sign our new Defense Bill into law and to pay tribute to the greatest soldiers in the history of the world: THE U.S. ARMY. The National Defense Authorization Act is the most significant investment in our Military and our warfighters in modern history!
15,163 Retweets **66,167** Likes
3:36 PM - 13 Aug 2018

Donald J. Trump ✓
@realDonaldTrump

"Trump's foreign policy is actually boosting America's standing"
15,199 Retweets **62,537** Likes
5:11 PM - 13 Aug 2018

Donald J. Trump ✓
@realDonaldTrump

Scott Walker of Wisconsin is a tremendous Governor who has done incredible things for that Great State. He has my complete & total Endorsement! He brought the amazing Foxconn to Wisconsin with its 15,000 Jobs-and so much more. Vote for Scott on Tuesday in the Republican Primary!
18,492 Retweets **76,016** Likes
6:37 PM - 13 Aug 2018

Donald J. Trump ✓
@realDonaldTrump

.@MarkBurnettTV called to say that there are NO TAPES of the Apprentice where I used such a terrible and disgusting word as attributed by Wacky and Deranged Omarosa. I don't have that word in my vocabulary, and never have. She made it up. Look at her MANY recent quotes saying....
16,393 Retweets **66,658** Likes
6:50 PM - 13 Aug 2018

Donald J. Trump ✓
@realDonaldTrump

....such wonderful and powerful things about me - a true Champion of Civil Rights - until she got fired. Omarosa had Zero credibility with the Media (they didn't want interviews) when she worked in the White House. Now that she says bad about me, they will talk to her. Fake News!
16,968 Retweets **74,771** Likes
6:57 PM - 13 Aug 2018

Donald J. Trump ✓
@realDonaldTrump

Tom Fitton of Judicial Watch: "The Strzok firing is as much about the Mueller operation as anything else. There would be no Mueller Special Councel to investigate so called collusion but for the machinations of Strzok & his colleagues at the top levels of the FBI. We know this...
18,871 Retweets **75,498** Likes
3:59 AM - 14 Aug 2018

Donald J. Trump ✓
@realDonaldTrump

....guy was corrupt and had anti-Trump animus. Strzok and others at the FBI should be criminally investigated for the way the conducted this investigation. Instead, Mueller is pretending nothing went wrong. He used Strzok, he used the Clinton DNC Dossier...the whole thing....
14,104 Retweets **57,675** Likes
4:07 AM - 14 Aug 2018

Donald J. Trump ✓
@realDonaldTrump

....should be shut down. The Strzok firing shows that the fundamental underpinnings of the investigation were corrupt. It should be shut down by the courts or by honest prosecutors." Thank you Judicial Watch, I couldn't have said it better myself!
15,683 Retweets **66,489** Likes
4:13 AM - 14 Aug 2018

Donald J. Trump ✓
@realDonaldTrump

When you give a crazed, crying lowlife a break, and give her a job at the White House, I guess it just didn't work out. Good work by General Kelly for quickly firing that dog!
21,625 Retweets **92,317** Likes
4:31 AM - 14 Aug 2018

Donald J. Trump ✓
@realDonaldTrump

Another terrorist attack in London...These animals are crazy and must be dealt with through toughness and strength!
30,906 Retweets **131,440** Likes
4:42 AM - 14 Aug 2018

Donald J. Trump ✓
@realDonaldTrump

Bruce Ohr of the "Justice" Department (can you believe he is still there) is accused of helping disgraced Christopher Steele "find dirt on Trump." Ohr's wife, Nelly, was in on the act big time - worked for Fusion GPS on Fake Dossier. @foxandfriends
17,242 Retweets **66,054** Likes
4:55 AM - 14 Aug 2018

Donald J. Trump ✓
@realDonaldTrump

"They were all in on it, clear Hillary Clinton and FRAME Donald Trump for things he didn't do." Gregg Jarrett on @foxandfriends If we had a real Attorney General, this Witch Hunt would never have been started! Looking at the wrong people.
19,742 Retweets **73,779** Likes
5:06 AM - 14 Aug 2018

Donald J. Trump ✓
@realDonaldTrump

Fired FBI Agent Peter Strzok is a fraud, as is the rigged investigation he started. There was no Collusion or Obstruction with Russia, and everybody, including the Democrats, know it. The only Collusion and Obstruction was by Crooked Hillary, the Democrats and the DNC!
24,154 Retweets **97,054** Likes
6:01 AM - 14 Aug 2018

Donald J. Trump ✓
@realDonaldTrump

Strzok started the illegal Rigged Witch Hunt - why isn't this so-called "probe" ended immediately? Why aren't these angry and conflicted Democrats instead looking at Crooked Hillary?
22,093 Retweets **91,079** Likes
6:10 AM - 14 Aug 2018

Donald J. Trump ✓
@realDonaldTrump

Lou Dobbs: "This cannot go forward...this Special Counsel with all of his conflicts, with his 17 Angry Democrats, without any evidence of collusion by the Trump Campaign and Russia. The Dems are the ones who should be investigated." Thank you Lou, so true!
21,009 Retweets **82,356** Likes
6:15 AM - 14 Aug 2018

Donald J. Trump ✓
@realDonaldTrump

"Hope and Change in an Alabama Coal Mine"
12,774 Retweets **54,284** Likes
11:21 AM - 14 Aug 2018

Donald J. Trump ✓
@realDonaldTrump

Great Republican election results last night. So far we have the team we want. 8 for 9 in Special Elections. Red Wave!
19,473 Retweets **91,690** Likes
5:30 AM - 15 Aug 2018

Donald J. Trump ✓
@realDonaldTrump

Congratulations to Leah Vukmir of Wisconsin on your great win last night. You beat a very tough and good competitor and will make a fantastic Senator after winning in November against someone who has done very little. You have my complete and total Endorsement!
10,460 Retweets **49,196** Likes
5:54 AM - 15 Aug 2018

Donald J. Trump ✓
@realDonaldTrump

Scott Walker is very special and will have another great win in November. He has done a fantastic job as Governor of Wisconsin and will always have my full support and Endorsement!
10,758 Retweets **49,953** Likes
6:07 AM - 15 Aug 2018

Donald J. Trump ✓
@realDonaldTrump

Jeff Johnson of Minnesota had a big night in winning the Republican nomination for Governor against a very strong and well known opponent! Thanks for all of the support you showed me. You have my complete and total Endorsement. You will win in November!
10,438 Retweets **48,658** Likes
6:12 AM - 15 Aug 2018

Donald J. Trump ✓
@realDonaldTrump

Congratulations to Bryan Steil on a wonderful win last night. You will be replacing a great guy in Paul Ryan, and your win in November will make the entire State of Wisconsin very proud. You have my complete and total Endorsement!
10,000 Retweets **46,806** Likes
6:14 AM - 15 Aug 2018

Donald J. Trump ✓
@realDonaldTrump

"People who enter the United States without our permission are illegal aliens and illegal aliens should not be treated the same as people who entered the U.S. legally." Chuck Schumer in 2009, before he went left and haywire! @foxandfriends
24,294 Retweets **86,233** Likes
6:18 AM - 15 Aug 2018

Donald J. Trump ✓
@realDonaldTrump

.@PeteStauber won big last night in Minnesota. A big star in Hockey, he will be an even bigger star in politics. It all begins with a win in November. Pete has my complete and total Endorsement!
10,061 Retweets **47,074** Likes
6:31 AM - 15 Aug 2018

Donald J. Trump ✓
@realDonaldTrump

It is about time that Connecticut had a real and talented Governor. Bob Stefanowski is the person needed to do the job. Tough on crime, Bob is also a big cutter of Taxes. He will win in November and make a Great Governor, a major difference maker. Bob has my total Endorsement!
14,425 Retweets **62,799** Likes
6:39 AM - 15 Aug 2018

Donald J. Trump ✓
@realDonaldTrump

My friend and very early supporter Kris Kobach won the Republican Nomination for Governor of Kansas last night in a tough race against a very fine opponent. Kris will win in November and be a great Governor. He has my complete and total Endorsement!
11,765 Retweets **55,895** Likes
6:51 AM - 15 Aug 2018

Donald J. Trump ✓
@realDonaldTrump

The Rigged Russian Witch Hunt goes on and on as the "originators and founders" of this scam continue to be fired and demoted for their corrupt and illegal activity. All credibility is gone from this terrible Hoax, and much more will be lost as it proceeds. No Collusion!
19,234 Retweets **78,501** Likes
7:08 AM - 15 Aug 2018

Donald J. Trump ✓
@realDonaldTrump

"The action (the Strzok firing) was a decisive step in the right direction in correcting the wrongs committed by what has been described as Comey's skinny inner circle." Chris Swecker, former FBI Assistant Director.
16,687 Retweets **69,798** Likes
7:15 AM - 15 Aug 2018

President Trumps Tweets 2018: A Historical Archive of President Trump's Tweets

Donald J. Trump
@realDonaldTrump

Happy Birthday to the leader of the Democrat Party, Maxine Waters!
18,708 Retweets **93,574** Likes
7:57 AM - 15 Aug 2018

Donald J. Trump
@realDonaldTrump

Our Country was built on Tariffs, and Tariffs are now leading us to great new Trade Deals - as opposed to the horrible and unfair Trade Deals that I inherited as your President. Other Countries should not be allowed to come in and steal the wealth of our great U.S.A. No longer!
20,036 Retweets **82,415** Likes
8:04 AM - 15 Aug 2018

Donald J. Trump
@realDonaldTrump

Chuck Schumer, I agree!
30,854 Retweets **87,311** Likes
11:34 AM - 15 Aug 2018

Donald J. Trump
@realDonaldTrump

"John Brennan is a stain on the Country, we deserve better than this." Former Secret Service Agent and author of new book, "Spygate, the Attempted Sabotage of Donald J. Trump," Dan Bongino. Thank you Dan, and good luck with the book!
24,821 Retweets **93,900** Likes
6:00 PM - 15 Aug 2018

Donald J. Trump
@realDonaldTrump

"Hillary Clinton clearly got a pass by the FBI. We have the unfortunate situation where they then decided they were going to frame Donald Trump" concerning the Rigged Witch Hunt. JOE DIGENOVA, former U.S. Attorney.
24,361 Retweets **93,179** Likes
6:14 PM - 15 Aug 2018

Donald J. Trump
@realDonaldTrump

"WE'RE NOT GOING TO MAKE AMERICA GREAT AGAIN, IT WAS NEVER THAT GREAT." Can you believe this is the Governor of the Highest Taxed State in the U.S., Andrew Cuomo, having a total meltdown!
34,935 Retweets **127,810** Likes
7:02 PM - 15 Aug 2018

Donald J. Trump
@realDonaldTrump

Mark Levin "When they had power they didn't stop the Russians, the Chinese, the North Koreans, they funded the Iranians & are responsible for the greatest scandal in American history by interfering with our election & trying to undermine the Trump Campaign and Trump Presidency."
30,896 Retweets **102,505** Likes
7:31 PM - 15 Aug 2018

Donald J. Trump ✓
@realDonaldTrump

"I'd strip the whole bunch of them. They're all corrupt. They've all abused their power. They've all betrayed the American people with a political agenda. They tried to steal and influence an election in the United States." @seanhannity
29,422 Retweets **109,905** Likes
7:40 PM - 15 Aug 2018

Donald J. Trump ✓
@realDonaldTrump

Our Economy is doing better than ever. Money is pouring into our cherished DOLLAR like rarely before, companies earnings are higher than ever, inflation is low & business optimism is higher than it has ever been. For the first time in many decades, we are protecting our workers!
22,013 Retweets **91,682** Likes
5:43 AM - 16 Aug 2018

Donald J. Trump ✓
@realDonaldTrump

THE FAKE NEWS MEDIA IS THE OPPOSITION PARTY. It is very bad for our Great Country....BUT WE ARE WINNING!
25,316 Retweets **105,165** Likes
5:50 AM - 16 Aug 2018

Donald J. Trump ✓
@realDonaldTrump

The Boston Globe, which was sold to the the Failing New York Times for 1.3 BILLION DOLLARS (plus 800 million dollars in losses & investment), or 2.1 BILLION DOLLARS, was then sold by the Times for 1 DOLLAR. Now the Globe is in COLLUSION with other papers on free press. PROVE IT!
16,770 Retweets **66,579** Likes
7:00 AM - 16 Aug 2018

Donald J. Trump ✓
@realDonaldTrump

There is nothing that I would want more for our Country than true FREEDOM OF THE PRESS. The fact is that the Press is FREE to write and say anything it wants, but much of what it says is FAKE NEWS, pushing a political agenda or just plain trying to hurt people. HONESTY WINS!
36,491 Retweets **135,175** Likes
7:10 AM - 16 Aug 2018

Donald J. Trump ✓
@realDonaldTrump

The Queen of Soul, Aretha Franklin, is dead. She was a great woman, with a wonderful gift from God, her voice. She will be missed!
27,700 Retweets **147,536** Likes
8:36 AM - 16 Aug 2018

Donald J. Trump ✓
@realDonaldTrump

Great @Cabinet meeting today at the @WhiteHouse!
10,760 Retweets **53,002** Likes
11:43 AM - 16 Aug 2018

Donald J. Trump ✓
@realDonaldTrump

Thank you for the kind words Omarosa!
25,400 Retweets **86,352** Likes
11:55 AM - 16 Aug 2018

President Trumps Tweets 2018: A Historical Archive of President Trump's Tweets

Donald J. Trump ✓
@realDonaldTrump

Turkey has taken advantage of the United States for many years. They are now holding our wonderful Christian Pastor, who I must now ask to represent our Country as a great patriot hostage. We will pay nothing for the release of an innocent man, but we are cutting back on Turkey!
23,080 Retweets **87,039** Likes
4:30 PM - 16 Aug 2018

Donald J. Trump ✓
@realDonaldTrump

"The FBI received documents from Bruce Ohr (of the Justice Department & whose wife Nelly worked for Fusion GPS)." Disgraced and fired FBI Agent Peter Strzok. This is too crazy to be believed! The Rigged Witch Hunt has zero credibility.
21,100 Retweets **79,565** Likes
4:37 PM - 16 Aug 2018

Donald J. Trump ✓
@realDonaldTrump

"While Steele shopped the document to multiple media outlets, he also asked for help with a RUSSIAN Oligarch." Catherine Herridge of @FoxNews @LouDobbs In other words, they were colluding with Russia!
17,833 Retweets **62,892** Likes
4:45 PM - 16 Aug 2018

Donald J. Trump ✓
@realDonaldTrump

"Very concerned about Comey's firing, afraid they will be exposed," said Bruce Ohr. DOJ's Emails & Notes show Bruce Ohr's connection to (phony & discredited) Trump Dossier. A creep thinking he would get caught in a dishonest act. Rigged Witch Hunt!
21,651 Retweets **76,957** Likes
4:53 PM - 16 Aug 2018

Donald J. Trump ✓
@realDonaldTrump

.@TuckerCarlson speaking of John Brennan: "How did somebody so obviously limited intellectually get to be CIA Director in the first place?" Now that is a really good question! Then followed by "Richard Blumenthal of Connecticut is a FAKE War Hero..." So true, a total Fake!
19,048 Retweets **72,942** Likes
5:45 PM - 16 Aug 2018

Donald J. Trump ✓
@realDonaldTrump

How can "Senator" Richard Blumenthal, who went around for twenty years as a Connecticut politician bragging that he was a great Marine war hero in Vietnam (then got caught and sobbingly admitted he was neither a Marine nor ever in Vietnam), pass judgement on anyone? Loser!
30,040 Retweets **110,496** Likes
5:56 PM - 16 Aug 2018

Donald J. Trump ✓
@realDonaldTrump

"....An incredibly corrupt FBI & DOJ trying to steer the outcome of a Presidential Election. Brennan has gone off the deep end, he's disgraced and discredited himself. His conduct has been outrageous." Chris Farrell, Judicial Watch.
21,646 Retweets **83,290** Likes
6:49 PM - 16 Aug 2018

Donald J. Trump ✓
@realDonaldTrump

"Director Brennan's recent statements purport to know as fact that the Trump campaign colluded with a foreign power. If Director Brennan's statement is based on intelligence he received while leading the CIA, why didn't he include it in the Intelligence Community Assessment......
18,995 Retweets **71,461** Likes
6:54 PM - 16 Aug 2018

Donald J. Trump ✓
@realDonaldTrump

.....released in 2017. If his statement is based on intelligence he has seen since leaving office, it constitutes an intelligence breach......" Richard Burr (R-NC) Senate Intel Cmte Chair @LouDobbs
13,705 Retweets **53,783** Likes
7:04 PM - 16 Aug 2018

Donald J. Trump ✓
@realDonaldTrump

In speaking with some of the world's top business leaders I asked what it is that would make business (jobs) even better in the U.S. "Stop quarterly reporting & go to a six month system," said one. That would allow greater flexibility & save money. I have asked the SEC to study!
16,741 Retweets **75,930** Likes
4:30 AM - 17 Aug 2018

Donald J. Trump ✓
@realDonaldTrump

How does a politician, Cuomo, known for pushing people and businesses out of his state, not to mention having the highest taxes in the U.S., survive making the statement, WE'RE NOT GOING TO MAKE AMERICA GREAT AGAIN, IT WAS NEVER THAT GREAT? Which section of the sentence is worse?
20,620 Retweets **78,103** Likes
4:44 AM - 17 Aug 2018

Donald J. Trump ✓
@realDonaldTrump

The local politicians who run Washington, D.C. (poorly) know a windfall when they see it. When asked to give us a price for holding a great celebratory military parade, they wanted a number so ridiculously high that I cancelled it. Never let someone hold you up! I will instead...
18,468 Retweets **83,128** Likes
4:57 AM - 17 Aug 2018

Donald J. Trump ✓
@realDonaldTrump

....attend the big parade already scheduled at Andrews Air Force Base on a different date, & go to the Paris parade, celebrating the end of the War, on November 11th. Maybe we will do something next year in D.C. when the cost comes WAY DOWN. Now we can buy some more jet fighters!
15,472 Retweets **70,688** Likes
5:10 AM - 17 Aug 2018

Donald J. Trump ✓
@realDonaldTrump

Just announced, youth unemployment is at a 50 year low! @foxandfriends
19,523 Retweets **88,731** Likes
5:29 AM - 17 Aug 2018

President Trumps Tweets 2018: A Historical Archive of President Trump's Tweets

Donald J. Trump ✓
@realDonaldTrump

The U.S. has more than double the growth rate than it had 18 months ago.
19,545 Retweets **87,496** Likes
5:38 AM - 17 Aug 2018

Donald J. Trump ✓
@realDonaldTrump

Wow! Big pushback on Governor Andrew Cuomo of New York for his really dumb statement about America's lack of greatness. I have already MADE America Great Again, just look at the markets, jobs, military- setting records, and we will do even better. Andrew "choked" badly, mistake!
21,178 Retweets **90,668** Likes
7:10 AM - 17 Aug 2018

Donald J. Trump ✓
@realDonaldTrump

When a politician admits that "We're not going to make America great again," there doesn't seem to be much reason to ever vote for him. This could be a career threatening statement by Andrew Cuomo, with many wanting him to resign-he will get higher ratings than his brother Chris!
21,888 Retweets **88,873** Likes
7:17 AM - 17 Aug 2018

Donald J. Trump ✓
@realDonaldTrump

Which is worse, Hightax Andrew Cuomo's statement, "WE'RE NOT GOING TO MAKE AMERICA GREAT AGAIN, IT WAS NEVER THAT GREAT" or Hillary Clinton's "DEPLORABLES" statement...
18,617 Retweets **76,418** Likes
12:25 PM - 17 Aug 2018

Donald J. Trump ✓
@realDonaldTrump

...I say Andrew's was a bigger and more incompetent blunder. He should easily win his race against a Super Liberal Actress, but his political career is over!
12,377 Retweets **56,971** Likes
12:25 PM - 17 Aug 2018

Donald J. Trump ✓
@realDonaldTrump

"Fox News has learned that Bruce Ohr wrote Christopher Steele following the firing of James Comey saying that he was afraid the anti-Trump Russia probe will be exposed." Charles Payne @FoxBusiness How much more does Mueller have to see? They have blinders on - RIGGED!
28,033 Retweets **94,085** Likes
3:29 PM - 17 Aug 2018

Donald J. Trump ✓
@realDonaldTrump

"Bruce Ohr of DOJ is in legal jeopardy, it's astonishing that he's still employed. Bruce & Nelly Ohr's bank account is getting fatter & fatter because of the Dossier that they are both peddling. He doesn't disclose it under Fed Regs. Using your Federal office for personal.......
21534 Retweets **77,845** Likes
6:46 PM - 17 Aug 2018

Donald J. Trump ✓
@realDonaldTrump

....financial gain is a Federal Gratuity Statute Violation, Bribery Statute Violation, Honest Services Violation....all Major Crimes....because the DOJ is run by BLANK Jeff Sessions......" Gregg Jarrett. So when does Mueller do what must be done? Probably never! @FoxNews
17,813 Retweets **70,389** Likes
6:47 PM - 17 Aug 2018

Donald J. Trump ✓
@realDonaldTrump

Social Media is totally discriminating against Republican/Conservative voices. Speaking loudly and clearly for the Trump Administration, we won't let that happen. They are closing down the opinions of many people on the RIGHT, while at the same time doing nothing to others.......
36,914 Retweets **114,344** Likes
4:23 AM - 18 Aug 2018

Donald J. Trump ✓
@realDonaldTrump

.....Censorship is a very dangerous thing & absolutely impossible to police. If you are weeding out Fake News, there is nothing so Fake as CNN & MSNBC, & yet I do not ask that their sick behavior be removed. I get used to it and watch with a grain of salt, or don't watch at all..
33,662 Retweets **125,370** Likes
4:32 AM - 18 Aug 2018

Donald J. Trump ✓
@realDonaldTrump

....Too many voices are being destroyed, some good & some bad, and that cannot be allowed to happen. Who is making the choices, because I can already tell you that too many mistakes are being made. Let everybody participate, good & bad, and we will all just have to figure it out!
27,825 Retweets **106,836** Likes
4:40 AM - 18 Aug 2018

Donald J. Trump ✓
@realDonaldTrump

All of the fools that are so focused on looking only at Russia should start also looking in another direction, China. But in the end, if we are smart, tough and well prepared, we will get along with everyone!
20,696 Retweets **87,374** Likes
4:46 AM - 18 Aug 2018

Donald J. Trump ✓
@realDonaldTrump

Has anyone looked at the mistakes that John Brennan made while serving as CIA Director? He will go down as easily the WORST in history & since getting out, he has become nothing less than a loudmouth, partisan, political hack who cannot be trusted with the secrets to our country!
29,516 Retweets **116,017** Likes
6:12 AM - 18 Aug 2018

Donald J. Trump ✓
@realDonaldTrump

Great Job Rachel Campos-Duffy on @foxandfriends.
8,571 Retweets **48,439** Likes
6:34 AM - 18 Aug 2018

Donald J. Trump
@realDonaldTrump

The Economy is stronger and better than ever before. Importantly, there remains tremendous potential - it will only get better with time!

22,640 Retweets **108,880** Likes
6:39 AM - 18 Aug 2018

Donald J. Trump
@realDonaldTrump

The United States has ended the ridiculous 230 Million Dollar yearly development payment to Syria. Saudi Arabia and other rich countries in the Middle East will start making payments instead of the U.S. I want to develop the U.S., our military and countries that help us!

39,806 Retweets **158,426** Likes
2:51 PM - 18 Aug 2018

Donald J. Trump
@realDonaldTrump

I allowed White House Counsel Don McGahn, and all other requested members of the White House Staff, to fully cooperate with the Special Counsel. In addition we readily gave over one million pages of documents. Most transparent in history. No Collusion, No Obstruction. Witch Hunt!

24,090 Retweets **95,534** Likes
3:12 PM - 18 Aug 2018

Donald J. Trump
@realDonaldTrump

The failing @nytimes wrote a Fake piece today implying that because White House Councel Don McGahn was giving hours of testimony to the Special Councel, he must be a John Dean type "RAT." But I allowed him and all others to testify - I didn't have to. I have nothing to hide......

17,727 Retweets **71,686** Likes
4:01 AM - 19 Aug 2018

Donald J. Trump
@realDonaldTrump

....and have demanded transparency so that this Rigged and Disgusting Witch Hunt can come to a close. So many lives have been ruined over nothing - McCarthyism at its WORST! Yet Mueller & his gang of Dems refuse to look at the real crimes on the other side - Media is even worse!

19,915 Retweets **80,789** Likes
4:15 AM - 19 Aug 2018

Donald J. Trump
@realDonaldTrump

No Collusion and No Obstruction, except by Crooked Hillary and the Democrats. All of the resignations and corruption, yet heavily conflicted Bob Mueller refuses to even look in that direction. What about the Brennan, Comey, McCabe, Strzok lies to Congress, or Crooked's Emails!

29,848 Retweets **116,507** Likes
4:30 AM - 19 Aug 2018

Donald J. Trump
@realDonaldTrump

The Failing New York Times wrote a story that made it seem like the White House Councel had TURNED on the President, when in fact it is just the opposite - & the two Fake reporters knew this. This is why the Fake News Media has become the Enemy of the People. So bad for America!

26,504 Retweets **99,816** Likes
5:06 AM - 19 Aug 2018

Anthony T. Michalisko

Donald J. Trump ✓
@realDonaldTrump

Some members of the media are very Angry at the Fake Story in the New York Times. They actually called to complain and apologize - a big step forward. From the day I announced, the Times has been Fake News, and with their disgusting new Board Member, it will only get worse!
22,600 Retweets **88,499** Likes
5:14 AM - 19 Aug 2018

Donald J. Trump ✓
@realDonaldTrump

Study the late Joseph McCarthy, because we are now in period with Mueller and his gang that make Joseph McCarthy look like a baby! Rigged Witch Hunt!
24,681 Retweets **96,746** Likes
5:24 AM - 19 Aug 2018

Donald J. Trump ✓
@realDonaldTrump

Disgraced and discredited Bob Mueller and his whole group of Angry Democrat Thugs spent over 30 hours with the White House Councel, only with my approval, for purposes of transparency. Anybody needing that much time when they know there is no Russian Collusion is just someone....
18,757 Retweets **75,766** Likes
4:28 AM - 20 Aug 2018

Donald J. Trump ✓
@realDonaldTrump

....looking for trouble. They are enjoying ruining people's lives and REFUSE to look at the real corruption on the Democrat side - the lies, the firings, the deleted Emails and soooo much more! Mueller's Angry Dems are looking to impact the election. They are a National Disgrace!
21,586 Retweets **82,923** Likes
4:38 AM - 20 Aug 2018

Donald J. Trump ✓
@realDonaldTrump

Where's the Collusion? They made up a phony crime called Collusion, and when there was no Collusion they say there was Obstruction (of a phony crime that never existed). If you FIGHT BACK or say anything bad about the Rigged Witch Hunt, they scream Obstruction!
24,175 Retweets **94,672** Likes
4:48 AM - 20 Aug 2018

Donald J. Trump ✓
@realDonaldTrump

I hope John Brennan, the worst CIA Director in our country's history, brings a lawsuit. It will then be very easy to get all of his records, texts, emails and documents to show not only the poor job he did, but how he was involved with the Mueller Rigged Witch Hunt. He won't sue!
30,909 Retweets **113,982** Likes
7:13 AM - 20 Aug 2018

Donald J. Trump ✓
@realDonaldTrump

Everybody wants to keep their Security Clearance, it's worth great prestige and big dollars, even board seats, and that is why certain people are coming forward to protect Brennan. It certainly isn't because of the good job he did! He is a political "hack."
27,143 Retweets **104,676** Likes
7:23 AM - 20 Aug 2018

Donald J. Trump ✓
@realDonaldTrump

Will Bruce Ohr, whose family received big money for helping to create the phony, dirty and discredited Dossier, ever be fired from the Jeff Sessions "Justice" Department? A total joke!
21,378 Retweets **80,910** Likes
7:36 AM - 20 Aug 2018

Donald J. Trump ✓
@realDonaldTrump

"Bruce Ohr is at the center of FALSE ALLEGATIONS which led to a multi-million dollar investigation into what apparently didn't happen." Darrell Issa, House Oversight. We can take out the word "apparently." @FoxNews
17,795 Retweets **67,332** Likes
7:46 AM - 20 Aug 2018

Donald J. Trump ✓
@realDonaldTrump

It is outrageous that Poisonous Synthetic Heroin Fentanyl comes pouring into the U.S. Postal System from China. We can, and must, END THIS NOW! The Senate should pass the STOP ACT – and firmly STOP this poison from killing our children and destroying our country. No more delay!
28,452 Retweets **104,181** Likes
10:14 AM - 20 Aug 2018

Donald J. Trump ✓
@realDonaldTrump

.@DianeHarkey is an extraordinary woman of great accomplishment & potential. She is running as a very popular Republican for the Congressional seat of my friend Darrell Issa-with his complete support. Diane is strong on crime, loves our Military & Vets-has my total Endorsement!
13,679 Retweets **55,059** Likes
6:46 PM - 20 Aug 2018

Donald J. Trump ✓
@realDonaldTrump

Just watched former Intelligence Official Phillip Mudd become totally unglued and weird while debating wonderful @PARISDENNARD over Brennan's Security Clearance. Dennard destroyed him but Mudd is in no mental condition to have such a Clearance. Should be REVOKED? @seanhannity
21,652 Retweets **82,480** Likes
7:06 PM - 20 Aug 2018

Donald J. Trump ✓
@realDonaldTrump

Will be going to the Great State of West Virginia on Tuesday Night to campaign & do a Rally Speech for a hard working and spectacular person, A.G. Patrick Morrisey, who is running for the U.S. Senate. Patrick has great Energy & Stamina-I need his VOTE to MAGA. Total Endorsement!
15,119 Retweets **63,699** Likes
8:40 PM - 20 Aug 2018

Donald J. Trump ✓
@realDonaldTrump

I am hearing so many great things about the Republican Party's California Gubernatorial Candidate, John Cox. He is a very successful businessman who is tired of high Taxes & Crime. He will Make California Great Again & make you proud of your Great State again. Total Endorsement!
21,378 Retweets **84,894** Likes
8:53 PM - 20 Aug 2018

Donald J. Trump ✓
@realDonaldTrump

A Blue Wave means Crime and Open Borders. A Red Wave means Safety and Strength!
28,715 Retweets **101,895** Likes
3:38 AM - 21 Aug 2018

Donald J. Trump ✓
@realDonaldTrump

Even James Clapper has admonished John Brennan for having gone totally off the rails. Maybe Clapper is being nice to me so he doesn't lose his Security Clearance for lying to Congress!
18,089 Retweets **78,190** Likes
3:55 AM - 21 Aug 2018

Donald J. Trump ✓
@realDonaldTrump

Fake News, of which there is soooo much (this time the very tired New Yorker) falsely reported that I was going to take the extraordinary step of denying Intelligence Briefings to President Obama. Never discussed or thought of!
16,463 Retweets **71,694** Likes
4:10 AM - 21 Aug 2018

Donald J. Trump ✓
@realDonaldTrump

I am sorry to have to reiterate that there are serious and unpleasant consequences to crossing the Border into the United States ILLEGALLY! If there were no serious consequences, our country would be overrun with people trying to get in, and our system could not handle it!
26,633 Retweets **110,535** Likes
4:41 AM - 21 Aug 2018

Donald J. Trump ✓
@realDonaldTrump

Big Rally tonight in West Virginia. Patrick Morrisey is running a GREAT race for U.S. Senate. I have done so much for West Virginia, against all odds, and having Patrick, a real fighter, by my side, would make things so much easier. See you later. CLEAN COAL!!!!
17,484 Retweets **75,164** Likes
4:57 AM - 21 Aug 2018

Donald J. Trump ✓
@realDonaldTrump

Bill DeBlasio, the high taxing Mayor of NYC, just stole my campaign slogan: PROMISES MADE PROMISES KEPT! That's not at all nice. No imagination! @foxandfriends
19,394 Retweets **79,926** Likes
7:15 AM - 21 Aug 2018

Donald J. Trump ✓
@realDonaldTrump

To the incredible people of the Great State of Wyoming: Go VOTE TODAY for Foster Friess - He will be a fantastic Governor! Strong on Crime, Borders & 2nd Amendment. Loves our Military & our Vets. He has my complete and total Endorsement!
18,562 Retweets **77,686** Likes
7:56 AM - 21 Aug 2018

Donald J. Trump ✓
@realDonaldTrump

Join me tonight at the Charleston Civic Center in West Virginia at 7:00pmE!
10,669 Retweets **46,402** Likes
8:22 AM - 21 Aug 2018

President Trumps Tweets 2018: A Historical Archive of President Trump's Tweets

Donald J. Trump ✓
@realDonaldTrump

Just landed in West Virginia. Big crowd, looking forward to seeing everyone soon! #MAGA
13,866 Retweets **78,123** Likes
2:32 PM - 21 Aug 2018

Donald J. Trump ✓
@realDonaldTrump

MAKING AMERICA GREAT AGAIN!
17,538 Retweets **70,961** Likes
5:38 PM - 21 Aug 2018

Donald J. Trump ✓
@realDonaldTrump

Thank you West Virginia. I love you!
17,281 Retweets **80,950** Likes
5:45 PM - 21 Aug 2018

Donald J. Trump ✓
@realDonaldTrump

If anyone is looking for a good lawyer, I would strongly suggest that you don't retain the services of Michael Cohen!
36,940 Retweets **151,479** Likes
5:44 AM - 22 Aug 2018

Donald J. Trump ✓
@realDonaldTrump

I feel very badly for Paul Manafort and his wonderful family. "Justice" took a 12 year old tax case, among other things, applied tremendous pressure on him and, unlike Michael Cohen, he refused to "break" - make up stories in order to get a "deal." Such respect for a brave man!
22,662 Retweets **96,678** Likes
6:21 AM - 22 Aug 2018

Donald J. Trump ✓
@realDonaldTrump

A large number of counts, ten, could not even be decided in the Paul Manafort case. Witch Hunt!
13,619 Retweets **63,687** Likes
6:34 AM - 22 Aug 2018

Donald J. Trump ✓
@realDonaldTrump

Michael Cohen plead guilty to two counts of campaign finance violations that are not a crime. President Obama had a big campaign finance violation and it was easily settled!
26,791 Retweets **99,653** Likes
6:37 AM - 22 Aug 2018

Donald J. Trump ✓
@realDonaldTrump

Thank you to Democrat Assemblyman Dov Hikind of New York for your very gracious remarks on @foxandfriends for our deporting a longtime resident Nazi back to Germany! Others worked on this for decades.
14,052 Retweets **66,160** Likes
6:52 AM - 22 Aug 2018

Donald J. Trump ✓
@realDonaldTrump

Everyone in the path of #HurricaneLane please prepare yourselves, heed the advice of State and local officials, and follow @NWSHonolulu for updates. Be safe!
11,352 Retweets **45,879** Likes
8:05 AM - 22 Aug 2018

Donald J. Trump ✓
@realDonaldTrump

Longest bull run in the history of the stock market, congratulations America!
24,042 Retweets **106,347** Likes
1:07 PM - 22 Aug 2018

Donald J. Trump ✓
@realDonaldTrump

I will be interviewed on @foxandfriends by @ainsleyearhardt tomorrow from 6:00 A.M. to 9:00 A.M. Enjoy!
10,909 Retweets **53,048** Likes
5:51 PM - 22 Aug 2018

Donald J. Trump ✓
@realDonaldTrump

The only thing that I have done wrong is to win an election that was expected to be won by Crooked Hillary Clinton and the Democrats. The problem is, they forgot to campaign in numerous states!
37,868 Retweets **154,809** Likes
5:56 PM - 22 Aug 2018

Donald J. Trump ✓
@realDonaldTrump

I have asked Secretary of State @SecPompeo to closely study the South Africa land and farm seizures and expropriations and the large scale killing of farmers. "South African Government is now seizing land from white farmers." @TuckerCarlson @FoxNews
46,100 Retweets **135,647** Likes
7:28 PM - 22 Aug 2018

Donald J. Trump ✓
@realDonaldTrump

NO COLLUSION - RIGGED WITCH HUNT!
26,791 Retweets **119,003** Likes
10:10 PM - 22 Aug 2018

Donald J. Trump ✓
@realDonaldTrump

It was my great honor to host the Foreign Investment Risk Review Modernization Act Roundtable today at the @WhiteHouse!
11,050 Retweets **52,112** Likes
11:08 AM - 23 Aug 2018

Donald J. Trump ✓
@realDonaldTrump

I have authorized an emergency disaster declaration to provide Hawaii the necessary support ahead of #HurricaneLane. Our teams are closely coordinating with the state and local authorities. You are in our thoughts!
14,326 Retweets **63,582** Likes
12:21 PM - 23 Aug 2018

President Trumps Tweets 2018: A Historical Archive of President Trump's Tweets

Donald J. Trump ●
@realDonaldTrump

.@cindyhydesmith has helped me put America First! She's strong on the Wall, is helping me create Jobs, loves our Vets and fights for our conservative judges...
14,777 Retweets **64,826** Likes
2:10 PM - 23 Aug 2018

Donald J. Trump ●
@realDonaldTrump

...Cindy has voted for our Agenda in the Senate 100% of the time and has my complete and total Endorsement. We need Cindy to win in Mississippi!
12,965 Retweets **55,165** Likes
2:10 PM - 23 Aug 2018

Donald J. Trump ●
@realDonaldTrump

...And according to Polls, would do even better today!
16,610 Retweets **71,503** Likes
9:21 PM - 23 Aug 2018

Donald J. Trump ●
@realDonaldTrump

Target CEO raves about the Economy. "This is the best consumer environment I've seen in my career." A big statement from a top executive. But virtually everybody is saying this, & when our Trade Deals are made, & cost cutting done, you haven't seen anything yet! @DRUDGE_REPORT
17,389 Retweets **69,975** Likes
2:57 AM - 24 Aug 2018

Donald J. Trump ●
@realDonaldTrump

Our Economy is setting records on virtually every front - Probably the best our country has ever done. Tremendous value created since the Election. The World is respecting us again! Companies are moving back to the U.S.A.
20,612 Retweets **84,624** Likes
3:04 AM - 24 Aug 2018

Donald J. Trump ●
@realDonaldTrump

"Department of Justice will not be improperly influenced by political considerations." Jeff, this is GREAT, what everyone wants, so look into all of the corruption on the "other side" including deleted Emails, Comey lies & leaks, Mueller conflicts, McCabe, Strzok, Page, Ohr......
32,815 Retweets **110,890** Likes
3:17 AM - 24 Aug 2018

Donald J. Trump ●
@realDonaldTrump

....FISA abuse, Christopher Steele & his phony and corrupt Dossier, the Clinton Foundation, illegal surveillance of Trump Campaign, Russian collusion by Dems - and so much more. Open up the papers & documents without redaction? Come on Jeff, you can do it, the country is waiting!
29,769 Retweets **104,378** Likes
3:28 AM - 24 Aug 2018

Donald J. Trump ✓
@realDonaldTrump

Ex-NSA contractor to spend 63 months in jail over "classified" information. Gee, this is "small potatoes" compared to what Hillary Clinton did! So unfair Jeff, Double Standard.
30,150 Retweets **106,311** Likes
4:10 AM - 24 Aug 2018

Donald J. Trump ✓
@realDonaldTrump

Social Media Giants are silencing millions of people. Can't do this even if it means we must continue to hear Fake News like CNN, whose ratings have suffered gravely. People have to figure out what is real, and what is not, without censorship!
53,254 Retweets **184,573** Likes
4:34 AM - 24 Aug 2018

Donald J. Trump ✓
@realDonaldTrump

I have asked Secretary of State Mike Pompeo not to go to North Korea, at this time, because I feel we are not making sufficient progress with respect to the denuclearization of the Korean Peninsula...
18,026 Retweets **79,161** Likes
10:36 AM - 24 Aug 2018

Donald J. Trump ✓
@realDonaldTrump

...Additionally, because of our much tougher Trading stance with China, I do not believe they are helping with the process of denuclearization as they once were (despite the UN Sanctions which are in place)...
11,571 Retweets **53,963** Likes
10:36 AM - 24 Aug 2018

Donald J. Trump ✓
@realDonaldTrump

...Secretary Pompeo looks forward to going to North Korea in the near future, most likely after our Trading relationship with China is resolved. In the meantime I would like to send my warmest regards and respect to Chairman Kim. I look forward to seeing him soon!
12,928 Retweets **58,199** Likes
10:36 AM - 24 Aug 2018

Donald J. Trump ✓
@realDonaldTrump

Thank you. I love you Ohio!
13,405 Retweets **61,041** Likes
4:26 PM - 24 Aug 2018

Donald J. Trump ✓
@realDonaldTrump

I spoke with Governor David Ige of Hawaii today to express our full support for the people of Hawaii as the State is impacted by #HurricaneLane. The Federal Government is fully committed to helping the people of Hawaii.
10,454 Retweets **52,504** Likes
5:20 PM - 24 Aug 2018

Donald J. Trump ✓
@realDonaldTrump

Congratulations to new Australian Prime Minister Scott Morrison. There are no greater friends than the United States and Australia!
14,696 Retweets **79,200** Likes
5:27 PM - 24 Aug 2018

President Trumps Tweets 2018: A Historical Archive of President Trump's Tweets

Donald J. Trump @realDonaldTrump

Great to see the Senate working on solutions to end the secrecy around ridiculously high drug prices, something I called for in my drug pricing Blueprint. Will now work with the House to help American patients! #AmericanPatientsFirst
17,772 Retweets **71,614** Likes
5:40 PM - 24 Aug 2018

Donald J. Trump @realDonaldTrump

Great #StateDinner2018 in Ohio tonight! Together, we are MAKING AMERICA GREAT AGAIN!
12,723 Retweets **52,713** Likes
7:13 PM - 24 Aug 2018

Donald J. Trump @realDonaldTrump

Happy birthday Vince, you are truly one of the greats!
13,216 Retweets **66,586** Likes
8:35 PM - 24 Aug 2018

Donald J. Trump @realDonaldTrump

Michaels Cohen's attorney clarified the record, saying his client does not know if President Trump knew about the Trump Tower meeting (out of which came nothing!). The answer is that I did NOT know about the meeting. Just another phony story by the Fake News Media!
21,849 Retweets **81,294** Likes
5:16 AM - 25 Aug 2018

Donald J. Trump @realDonaldTrump

Jeff Sessions said he wouldn't allow politics to influence him only because he doesn't understand what is happening underneath his command position. Highly conflicted Bob Mueller and his gang of 17 Angry Dems are having a field day as real corruption goes untouched. No Collusion!
24,600 Retweets **94,556** Likes
5:36 AM - 25 Aug 2018

Donald J. Trump @realDonaldTrump

.@LindseyGrahamSC "Every President deserves an Attorney General they have confidence in. I believe every President has a right to their Cabinet, these are not lifetime appointments. You serve at the pleasure of the President."
18,493 Retweets **76,758** Likes
5:46 AM - 25 Aug 2018

Donald J. Trump @realDonaldTrump

Big story out that the FBI ignored tens of thousands of Crooked Hillary Emails, many of which are REALLY BAD. Also gave false election info. I feel sure that we will soon be getting to the bottom of all of this corruption. At some point I may have to get involved!
42,247 Retweets **153,410** Likes
6:05 AM - 25 Aug 2018

Donald J. Trump ✓
@realDonaldTrump

"The FBI only looked at 3000 of 675,000 Crooked Hillary Clinton Emails." They purposely didn't look at the disasters. This news is just out. @FoxNews
34,133 Retweets **109,806** Likes
6:11 AM - 25 Aug 2018

Donald J. Trump ✓
@realDonaldTrump

"The FBI looked at less than 1%" of Crooked's Emails!
29,187 Retweets **102,682** Likes
6:14 AM - 25 Aug 2018

Donald J. Trump ✓
@realDonaldTrump

Our relationship with Mexico is getting closer by the hour. Some really good people within both the new and old government, and all working closely together....A big Trade Agreement with Mexico could be happening soon!
21,779 Retweets **99,077** Likes
6:22 AM - 25 Aug 2018

Donald J. Trump ✓
@realDonaldTrump

Stock Market hit all time high on Friday. Congratulations U.S.A.!
27,466 Retweets **136,617** Likes
4:45 PM - 25 Aug 2018

Donald J. Trump ✓
@realDonaldTrump

My deepest sympathies and respect go out to the family of Senator John McCain. Our hearts and prayers are with you!
39,308 Retweets **219,967** Likes
5:44 PM - 25 Aug 2018

Donald J. Trump ✓
@realDonaldTrump

...And it will get, as I have always said, much better from even here!
17,887 Retweets **77,434** Likes
7:27 AM - 26 Aug 2018

Donald J. Trump ✓
@realDonaldTrump

Fantastic numbers on consumer spending released on Friday. Stock Market hits all time high!
22,426 Retweets **106,913** Likes
7:31 AM - 26 Aug 2018

Donald J. Trump ✓
@realDonaldTrump

"Mainstream Media tries to rewrite history to credit Obama for Trump accomplishments. Since President Trump took office, the economy is booming. The stronger the economy gets, the more desperate his critics are. O had weakest recovery since Great Depression." @WashTimes
30,202 Retweets **113,445** Likes
3:01 PM - 26 Aug 2018

Donald J. Trump ✓
@realDonaldTrump

Over 90% approval rating for your all time favorite (I hope) President within the Republican Party and 52% overall. This despite all of the made up stories by the Fake News Media trying endlessly to make me look as bad and evil as possible. Look at the real villains please!
43,510 Retweets **181,471** Likes
5:39 PM - 26 Aug 2018

Donald J. Trump ✓
@realDonaldTrump

Thank you to the great @JimBrownNFL32, perhaps the greatest running back of all time, for your wonderful words and support. Since our meeting in New York, African-American UNEMPLOYMENT has reached the LOWEST LEVEL IN HISTORY. You get it!
21,239 Retweets **86,854** Likes
5:57 AM - 27 Aug 2018

Donald J. Trump ✓
@realDonaldTrump

The Fake News Media worked hard to get Tiger Woods to say something that he didn't want to say. Tiger wouldn't play the game - he is very smart. More importantly, he is playing great golf again!
30,710 Retweets **154,072** Likes
6:37 AM - 27 Aug 2018

Donald J. Trump ✓
@realDonaldTrump

A big deal looking good with Mexico!
22,070 Retweets **113,780** Likes
6:39 AM - 27 Aug 2018

Donald J. Trump ✓
@realDonaldTrump

Rick Scott of Florida is doing a fantastic job as Governor. Jobs are pouring into the State and its economic health is better than ever before. He is strong on Crime, Borders, and loves our Military and Vets. Vote for Rick on Tuesday!
18,084 Retweets **72,053** Likes
10:19 AM - 27 Aug 2018

Donald J. Trump ✓
@realDonaldTrump

Congressman Ron DeSantis is a special person who has done an incredible job. He is running in Tuesdays Primary for Governor of Florida....Strong on Crime, Borders and wants Low Taxes. He will be a great Governor and has my full and total Endorsement!
18,995 Retweets **69,605** Likes
10:20 AM - 27 Aug 2018

Donald J. Trump ✓
@realDonaldTrump

Governor Doug Ducey of Arizona is doing a great job. It would be really nice to show your support tomorrow by voting for him in Tuesdays Primary. Doug is strong on Crime, the Border, and our Second Amendment. Loves our Military & our Vets. He has my full and complete Endorsement.
18,686 Retweets **73,165** Likes
10:22 AM - 27 Aug 2018

Donald J. Trump ✓
@realDonaldTrump

United States-Mexico Trade Agreement
15,849 Retweets **59,962** Likes
11:11 AM - 27 Aug 2018

Donald J. Trump ✓
@realDonaldTrump

.@FLOTUS Melania and I were honored to welcome the President of the Republic of Kenya, @UKenyatta and Mrs. Margaret Kenyatta to the @WhiteHouse today!
16,707 Retweets **71,595** Likes
3:07 PM - 27 Aug 2018

Donald J. Trump ✓
@realDonaldTrump

VOTE FOR RON!
19,382 Retweets **69,901** Likes
6:18 PM - 27 Aug 2018

Donald J. Trump ✓
@realDonaldTrump

"President Trump has done more for minority groups in this country than any president in decades." @LouDobbs
19,524 Retweets **80,170** Likes
2:54 AM - 28 Aug 2018

Donald J. Trump ✓
@realDonaldTrump

NASDAQ has just gone above 8000 for the first time in history!
28,408 Retweets **121,129** Likes
2:57 AM - 28 Aug 2018

Donald J. Trump ✓
@realDonaldTrump

I smile at Senators and others talking about how good free trade is for the U.S. What they don't say is that we lose Jobs and over 800 Billion Dollars a year on really dumb Trade Deals....and these same countries Tariff us to death. These lawmakers are just fine with this!
24,056 Retweets **89,711** Likes
7:21 AM - 28 Aug 2018

Donald J. Trump ✓
@realDonaldTrump

Google search results for "Trump News" shows only the viewing/reporting of Fake News Media. In other words, they have it RIGGED, for me & others, so that almost all stories & news is BAD. Fake CNN is prominent. Republican/Conservative & Fair Media is shut out. Illegal? 96% of....
27,090 Retweets **94,669** Likes
8:02 AM - 28 Aug 2018

Donald J. Trump ✓
@realDonaldTrump

....results on "Trump News" are from National Left-Wing Media, very dangerous. Google & others are suppressing voices of Conservatives and hiding information and news that is good. They are controlling what we can & cannot see. This is a very serious situation-will be addressed!
20,381 Retweets **73,497** Likes
8:02 AM - 28 Aug 2018

President Trumps Tweets 2018: A Historical Archive of President Trump's Tweets

Donald J. Trump
@realDonaldTrump

"Consumer confidence pops in August to highest level since October 2000"
16,662 Retweets **64,362** Likes
10:28 AM - 28 Aug 2018

Donald J. Trump
@realDonaldTrump

Such a fantastic win for Ron DeSantis and the people of the Great State of Florida. Ron will be a fantastic Governor. On to November!
18,618 Retweets **81,597** Likes
5:32 PM - 28 Aug 2018

Donald J. Trump
@realDonaldTrump

Congratulations to Governor Rick Scott of Florida on his conclusive Republican Primary Win. He will be a great Senator!
15,648 Retweets **71,782** Likes
5:48 PM - 28 Aug 2018

Donald J. Trump
@realDonaldTrump

Report just out: "China hacked Hillary Clinton's private Email Server." Are they sure it wasn't Russia (just kidding!)? What are the odds that the FBI and DOJ are right on top of this? Actually, a very big story. Much classified information!
37,264 Retweets **124,354** Likes
6:16 PM - 28 Aug 2018

Donald J. Trump
@realDonaldTrump

Add the 2026 World Cup to our long list of accomplishments!
18,077 Retweets **96,193** Likes
6:21 PM - 28 Aug 2018

Donald J. Trump
@realDonaldTrump

Our new Trade Deal with Mexico focuses on FARMERS, GROWTH for our country, tearing down TRADE BARRIERS, JOBS and having companies continue to POUR BACK INTO OUR COUNTRY. It will be a big hit!
18,883 Retweets **79,471** Likes
7:19 PM - 28 Aug 2018

Donald J. Trump
@realDonaldTrump

New Poll - A majority of Americans think that John Brennan and James Comey should have their Security Clearances Revoked. Not surprised! @FoxNews
24,060 Retweets **102,214** Likes
7:26 PM - 28 Aug 2018

Donald J. Trump
@realDonaldTrump

Hillary Clinton's Emails, many of which are Classified Information, got hacked by China. Next move better be by the FBI & DOJ or, after all of their other missteps (Comey, McCabe, Strzok, Page, Ohr, FISA, Dirty Dossier etc.), their credibility will be forever gone!
31,073 Retweets **99,120** Likes
9:11 PM - 28 Aug 2018

Donald J. Trump ✓
@realDonaldTrump

Martha McSally, running in the Arizona Primary for U.S. Senate, was endorsed by rejected Senator Jeff Flake....and turned it down - a first! Now Martha, a great U.S. Military fighter jet pilot and highly respected member of Congress, WINS BIG. Congratulations, and on to November!
15,090 Retweets **69,322** Likes
9:44 PM - 28 Aug 2018

Donald J. Trump ✓
@realDonaldTrump

Not only did Congressman Ron DeSantis easily win the Republican Primary, but his opponent in November is his biggest dream....a failed Socialist Mayor named Andrew Gillum who has allowed crime & many other problems to flourish in his city. This is not what Florida wants or needs!
18,822 Retweets **72,449** Likes
5:00 AM - 29 Aug 2018

Donald J. Trump ✓
@realDonaldTrump

"The Obama people did something that's never been done...They spied on a rival presidential campaign. Would it be OK if Trump did it next? I am losing faith that our system is on the level. I'm beginning to think it is rotten & corrupt. Scary stuff Obama did." @TuckerCarlson DOJ
26,031 Retweets **84,671** Likes
5:12 AM - 29 Aug 2018

Donald J. Trump ✓
@realDonaldTrump

"Hillary Clinton and the DNC paid for information from the Russian government to use against her government - there's no doubt about that!" @TuckerCarlson
20,222 Retweets **71,361** Likes
5:18 AM - 29 Aug 2018

Donald J. Trump ✓
@realDonaldTrump

Big Election Wins last night! The Republican Party will MAKE AMERICA GREAT AGAIN! Actually, it is happening faster than anybody thought possible! It is morphing into KEEP AMERICA GREAT!
17,989 Retweets **74,917** Likes
5:23 AM - 29 Aug 2018

Donald J. Trump ✓
@realDonaldTrump

"Anonymous Sources are really starting to BURN the media." @FoxNews The fact is that many anonymous sources don't even exist. They are fiction made up by the Fake News reporters. Look at the lie that Fake CNN is now in. They got caught red handed! Enemy of the People!
29,373 Retweets **104,187** Likes
5:40 AM - 29 Aug 2018

Donald J. Trump ✓
@realDonaldTrump

When you see "anonymous source," stop reading the story, it is fiction!
38,294 Retweets **148,974** Likes
5:41 AM - 29 Aug 2018

Donald J. Trump ✓
@realDonaldTrump

Martha McSally is an extraordinary woman. She was a very talented fighter jet pilot and is now a highly respected member of Congress. She is Strong on Crime, the Border and our under siege 2nd Amendment. Loves our Military and our Vets. Has my total and complete Endorsement!
14,051 Retweets **61,585** Likes
5:52 AM - 29 Aug 2018

Donald J. Trump ✓
@realDonaldTrump

White House Counsel Don McGahn will be leaving his position in the fall, shortly after the confirmation (hopefully) of Judge Brett Kavanaugh to the United States Supreme Court. I have worked with Don for a long time and truly appreciate his service!
12,778 Retweets **61,538** Likes
7:30 AM - 29 Aug 2018

Donald J. Trump ✓
@realDonaldTrump

Consumer Confidence Index, just out, is the HIGHEST IN 18 YEARS! Also, GDP revised upward to 4.2 from 4.1. Our country is doing great!
20,813 Retweets **80,697** Likes
7:56 AM - 29 Aug 2018

Donald J. Trump ✓
@realDonaldTrump

How the hell is Bruce Ohr still employed at the Justice Department? Disgraceful! Witch Hunt!
26,276 Retweets **101,929** Likes
8:12 AM - 29 Aug 2018

Donald J. Trump ✓
@realDonaldTrump

#StopTheBias
40,174 Retweets **108,279** Likes
1:55 PM - 29 Aug 2018

Donald J. Trump ✓
@realDonaldTrump

STATEMENT FROM THE WHITE HOUSE President Donald J. Trump feels strongly that North Korea is under tremendous pressure from China because of our major trade disputes with the Chinese Government. At the same time, we also know that China is providing North Korea with...
15,918 Retweets **61,394** Likes
2:23 PM - 29 Aug 2018

Donald J. Trump ✓
@realDonaldTrump

...considerable aid, including money, fuel, fertilizer and various other commodities. This is not helpful! Nonetheless, the President believes that his relationship with Kim Jong Un is a very good and warm one, and there is no reason at this time to be spending large amounts...
9,065 Retweets **32,908** Likes
2:23 PM - 29 Aug 2018

Donald J. Trump ✓
@realDonaldTrump

...of money on joint U.S.-South Korea war games. Besides, the President can instantly start the joint exercises again with South Korea, and Japan, if he so chooses. If he does, they will be far bigger than ever before. As for the U.S.–China trade disputes, and other...
10,310 Retweets **45,102** Likes
2:23 PM - 29 Aug 2018

Donald J. Trump @
@realDonaldTrump

...differences, they will be resolved in time by President Trump and China's great President Xi Jinping. Their relationship and bond remain very strong.
10,749 Retweets **47,994** Likes
2:23 PM - 29 Aug 2018

Donald J. Trump @
@realDonaldTrump

CNN is being torn apart from within based on their being caught in a major lie and refusing to admit the mistake. Sloppy @carlbernstein, a man who lives in the past and thinks like a degenerate fool, making up story after story, is being laughed at all over the country! Fake News
30,856 Retweets **116,583** Likes
3:43 PM - 29 Aug 2018

Donald J. Trump @
@realDonaldTrump

"Lanny Davis admits being anonymous source in CNN Report." @BretBaier Oh well, so much for CNN saying it wasn't Lanny. No wonder their ratings are so low, it's FAKE NEWS!
22,285 Retweets **84,341** Likes
5:44 PM - 29 Aug 2018

Donald J. Trump @
@realDonaldTrump

"Ohr told the FBI it (the Fake Dossier) wasn't true, it was a lie and the FBI was determined to use it anyway to damage Trump and to perpetrate a fraud on the court to spy on the Trump campaign. This is a fraud on the court. The Chief Justice of the U.S. Supreme Court is in......
21,628 Retweets **73,508** Likes
6:43 PM - 29 Aug 2018

Donald J. Trump @
@realDonaldTrump

...charge of the FISA court. He should direct the Presiding Judge, Rosemary Collier, to hold a hearing, haul all of these people from the DOJ & FBI in there, & if she finds there were crimes committed, and there were, there should be a criminal referral by her...." @GreggJarrett
20,389 Retweets **70,883** Likes
6:51 PM - 29 Aug 2018

Donald J. Trump @
@realDonaldTrump

Watch: Kanye West Says Trump Wants to Be the 'Greatest President' for Black Americans
20,945 Retweets **72,658** Likes
7:27 PM - 29 Aug 2018

Donald J. Trump @
@realDonaldTrump

The hatred and extreme bias of me by @CNN has clouded their thinking and made them unable to function. But actually, as I have always said, this has been going on for a long time. Little Jeff Z has done a terrible job, his ratings suck, & AT&T should fire him to save credibility!
23,904 Retweets **100,345** Likes
3:50 AM - 30 Aug 2018

President Trumps Tweets 2018: A Historical Archive of President Trump's Tweets

Donald J. Trump ✓
@realDonaldTrump

What's going on at @CNN is happening, to different degrees, at other networks - with @NBCNews being the worst. The good news is that Andy Lack(y) is about to be fired(?) for incompetence, and much worse. When Lester Holt got caught fudging my tape on Russia, they were hurt badly!
18,808 Retweets **71,978** Likes
4:02 AM - 30 Aug 2018

Donald J. Trump ✓
@realDonaldTrump

I just cannot state strongly enough how totally dishonest much of the Media is. Truth doesn't matter to them, they only have their hatred & agenda. This includes fake books, which come out about me all the time, always anonymous sources, and are pure fiction. Enemy of the People!
31,482 Retweets **127,265** Likes
4:11 AM - 30 Aug 2018

Donald J. Trump ✓
@realDonaldTrump

The news from the Financial Markets is even better than anticipated. For all of you that have made a fortune in the markets, or seen your 401k's rise beyond your wildest expectations, more good news is coming!
18,690 Retweets **80,998** Likes
4:20 AM - 30 Aug 2018

Donald J. Trump ✓
@realDonaldTrump

Ivanka Trump & Jared Kushner had NOTHING to do with the so called "pushing out" of Don McGahn.The Fake News Media has it, purposely,so wrong! They love to portray chaos in the White House when they know that chaos doesn't exist-just a "smooth running machine" with changing parts!
18,616 Retweets **77,237** Likes
4:44 AM - 30 Aug 2018

Donald J. Trump ✓
@realDonaldTrump

The only thing James Comey ever got right was when he said that President Trump was not under investigation!
16,911 Retweets **71,462** Likes
4:56 AM - 30 Aug 2018

Donald J. Trump ✓
@realDonaldTrump

Wow, Nellie Ohr, Bruce Ohr's wife, is a Russia expert who is fluent in Russian. She worked for Fusion GPS where she was paid a lot. Collusion! Bruce was a boss at the Department of Justice and is, unbelievably, still there!
26,670 Retweets **88,416** Likes
5:54 AM - 30 Aug 2018

Donald J. Trump ✓
@realDonaldTrump

The Rigged Russia Witch Hunt did not come into play, even a little bit, with respect to my decision on Don McGahn!
12,878 Retweets **59,766** Likes
6:17 AM - 30 Aug 2018

Donald J. Trump ✓
@realDonaldTrump

I am very excited about the person who will be taking the place of Don McGahn as White House Counsel! I liked Don, but he was NOT responsible for me not firing Bob Mueller or Jeff Sessions. So much Fake Reporting and Fake News!
14,294 Retweets **62,295** Likes
6:39 AM - 30 Aug 2018

Donald J. Trump ✓
@realDonaldTrump

Will be going to Evansville, Indiana, tonight for a big crowd rally with Mike Braun, a very successful businessman who is campaigning to be Indiana's next U.S. Senator. He is strong on Crime & Borders, the 2nd Amendment, and loves our Military & Vets. Will be a big night!
18,983 Retweets **79,319** Likes
6:49 AM - 30 Aug 2018

Donald J. Trump ✓
@realDonaldTrump

CNN is working frantically to find their "source." Look hard because it doesn't exist. Whatever was left of CNN's credibility is now gone!
33,097 Retweets **129,670** Likes
9:54 AM - 30 Aug 2018

Donald J. Trump ✓
@realDonaldTrump

Kevin Stitt ran a great winning campaign against a very tough opponent in Oklahoma. Kevin is a very successful businessman who will be a fantastic Governor. He is strong on Crime & Borders, the 2nd Amendment, & loves our Military & Vets. He has my complete and total Endorsement!
17,071 Retweets **72,612** Likes
11:30 AM - 30 Aug 2018

Donald J. Trump ✓
@realDonaldTrump

Throwback Thursday! #MAGA
27,530 Retweets **98,311** Likes
12:59 PM - 30 Aug 2018

Donald J. Trump ✓
@realDonaldTrump

Thank you Indiana, I love you!
20,352 Retweets **85,353** Likes
6:50 PM - 30 Aug 2018

Donald J. Trump ✓
@realDonaldTrump

I will be doing a major rally for Senator Ted Cruz in October. I'm picking the biggest stadium in Texas we can find. As you know, Ted has my complete and total Endorsement. His opponent is a disaster for Texas - weak on Second Amendment, Crime, Borders, Military, and Vets!
32,605 Retweets **122,409** Likes
10:09 AM - 31 Aug 2018

Donald J. Trump ✓
@realDonaldTrump

Wow, I made OFF THE RECORD COMMENTS to Bloomberg concerning Canada, and this powerful understanding was BLATANTLY VIOLATED. Oh well, just more dishonest reporting. I am used to it. At least Canada knows where I stand!
27,281 Retweets **120,070** Likes
11:37 AM - 31 Aug 2018

President Trumps Tweets 2018: A Historical Archive of President Trump's Tweets

Donald J. Trump ✓
@realDonaldTrump

"President Donald J. Trump is Strengthening Retirement Security for American Workers"
14,371 Retweets **57,390** Likes
3:07 PM - 31 Aug 2018

Donald J. Trump ✓
@realDonaldTrump

.@Rasmussen_Poll just came out at 48% approval rate despite the constant and intense Fake News. Higher than Election Day and higher than President Obama. Rasmussen was one of the most accurate Election Day polls!
20,400 Retweets **84,744** Likes
7:25 PM - 31 Aug 2018

Donald J. Trump ✓
@realDonaldTrump

The ABC/Washington Post Poll was by far the least accurate one 2 weeks out from the 2016 Election. I call it a suppression poll - but by Election Day they brought us, out of shame, to about even. They will never learn!
14,825 Retweets **66,829** Likes
7:35 PM - 31 Aug 2018

Donald J. Trump ✓
@realDonaldTrump

Great day in North Carolina where Republicans will do very well!
11,749 Retweets **63,505** Likes
7:36 PM - 31 Aug 2018

Donald J. Trump ✓
@realDonaldTrump

Still can't believe that Bloomberg violated a firm OFF THE RECORD statement. Will they put out an apology?
16,811 Retweets **76,391** Likes
7:40 PM - 31 Aug 2018

Donald J. Trump ✓
@realDonaldTrump

"I think today what has happened is that news reporting has become part of the adversary system." Alan Dershowitz It has become tainted and corrupt! DJT
17,483 Retweets **70,926** Likes
4:19 AM - 1 Sep 2018

Donald J. Trump ✓
@realDonaldTrump

I love Canada, but they've taken advantage of our Country for many years!
17,383 Retweets **85,115** Likes
4:21 AM - 1 Sep 2018

Donald J. Trump ✓
@realDonaldTrump

Report: There were no FISA hearings held over Spy documents."It is astonishing that the FISA courts couldn't hold hearings on Spy Warrants targeting Donald Trump. It isn't about Carter Page, it's about the Trump Campaign. You've got corruption at the DOJ & FBI. The leadership....
19,901 Retweets **72,506** Likes
5:26 AM - 1 Sep 2018

 Donald J. Trump ✓
@realDonaldTrump

....of the DOJ & FBI are completely out to lunch in terms of exposing and holding those accountable who are responsible for that corruption." @TomFitton @JudicialWatch
15,523 Retweets **59,435** Likes
5:32 AM - 1 Sep 2018

 Donald J. Trump ✓
@realDonaldTrump

"You have a Fake Dossier, gathered by Steele, paid by the Clinton team to get information on Trump. The Dossier is Fake, nothing in it has been verified. It then filters into our American court system in order to spy on Barrack Obama and Hillary Clinton's political opponent......
22,652 Retweets **82,755** Likes
6:19 AM - 1 Sep 2018

 Donald J. Trump ✓
@realDonaldTrump

....Donald Trump, and now we find out that there wasn't even a hearing - that Donald Trump's 4th Amendment right to privacy was signed away...and someone in there is swearing that this stuff is true, when it wasn't? This is the scandal here - a police state." Dan Bongino
23,781 Retweets **85,148** Likes
6:27 AM - 1 Sep 2018

 Donald J. Trump ✓
@realDonaldTrump

There is no political necessity to keep Canada in the new NAFTA deal. If we don't make a fair deal for the U.S. after decades of abuse, Canada will be out. Congress should not interfere w/ these negotiations or I will simply terminate NAFTA entirely & we will be far better off...
25,981 Retweets **105,815** Likes
8:03 AM - 1 Sep 2018

 Donald J. Trump ✓
@realDonaldTrump

....Remember, NAFTA was one of the WORST Trade Deals ever made. The U.S. lost thousands of businesses and millions of jobs. We were far better off before NAFTA - should never have been signed. Even the Vat Tax was not accounted for. We make new deal or go back to pre-NAFTA!
19,907 Retweets **81,782** Likes
8:12 AM - 1 Sep 2018

 Donald J. Trump ✓
@realDonaldTrump

No Deal! Trade Talks with Canada Conclude for the Week with No Agreement | Breitbart
11,956 Retweets **48,934** Likes
3:51 PM - 1 Sep 2018

 **Donald J. Trump** ✓
@realDonaldTrump

MAKE AMERICA GREAT AGAIN!
44,735 Retweets **178,928** Likes
3:53 PM - 1 Sep 2018

Donald J. Trump ✓
@realDonaldTrump

We shouldn't have to buy our friends with bad Trade Deals and Free Military Protection!
25,467 Retweets **108,482** Likes
3:55 PM - 1 Sep 2018

President Trumps Tweets 2018: A Historical Archive of President Trump's Tweets

Donald J. Trump ✓
@realDonaldTrump

"There's no fairness here, if you're a Democrat or a friend of Hillary you get immunity or off scott free. If you're connected to Donald Trump, you get people like Robert Mueller & Andrew Weissman, and his team of partisans, coming after you with a vengeance and abusing their....
25,213 Retweets **94,871** Likes
5:46 PM - 1 Sep 2018

Donald J. Trump ✓
@realDonaldTrump

....positions of power. That's part of the story of the Russia Hoax. Christopher Steele is on the payroll of Hillary Clinton & the FBI, & when they fired him for lying, they continued to use him. Violation of FBI regulations. Kept trying to verify the unverifiable." @GreggJarrett
16,746 Retweets **64,001** Likes
5:53 PM - 1 Sep 2018

Donald J. Trump ✓
@realDonaldTrump

"No information was ever given by the Trump Team to Russia, yet the Hillary Clinton campaign paid for information from Kremlin sources and just washed it through an intermediary, Christopher Steele." Jesse Waters
21,798 Retweets **82,234** Likes
6:01 PM - 1 Sep 2018

Donald J. Trump ✓
@realDonaldTrump

"There is no possible way the Trump Tower meeting between Don Trump jr and a couple of Russians, who have very deep connections to both the Clintons & Fusion GPS, & where no information on the Clintons was exchanged, is a crime. Dems are blinded by their hatred of Trump." Bongino
23,148 Retweets **95,685** Likes
6:21 PM - 1 Sep 2018

Donald J. Trump ✓
@realDonaldTrump

Tiger Woods showed great class in the way he answered the question about the Office of the Presidency and me. Now they say the so-called "left" is angry at him. So sad, but the "center & right" loves Tiger, Kanye, George Foreman, Jim Brown & so many other greats, even more.......
26,403 Retweets **125,168** Likes
6:28 AM - 2 Sep 2018

Donald J. Trump ✓
@realDonaldTrump

....The fact is that African/American unemployment is now the lowest in the history of our country. Same with Asian, Hispanic and almost every other group. The Democrats have been all talk and no action. My Administration has already produced like no other, and everyone sees it!
32,533 Retweets **137,610** Likes
6:37 AM - 2 Sep 2018

Donald J. Trump ✓
@realDonaldTrump

Happy Labor Day! Our country is doing better than ever before with unemployment setting record lows. The U.S. has tremendous upside potential as we go about fixing some of the worst Trade Deals ever made by any country in the world. Big progress being made!
27,895 Retweets **124,606** Likes
4:28 AM - 3 Sep 2018

Anthony T. Michalisko

Donald J. Trump ✓
@realDonaldTrump

The Worker in America is doing better than ever before. Celebrate Labor Day!
19,755 Retweets **93,634** Likes
5:23 AM - 3 Sep 2018

Donald J. Trump ✓
@realDonaldTrump

Richard Trumka, the head of the AFL-CIO, represented his union poorly on television this weekend. Some of the things he said were so against the working men and women of our country, and the success of the U.S. itself, that it is easy to see why unions are doing so poorly. A Dem!
15,429 Retweets **63,480** Likes
8:28 AM - 3 Sep 2018

Donald J. Trump ✓
@realDonaldTrump

The U.S. is respected again!
15,054 Retweets **67,735** Likes
10:50 AM - 3 Sep 2018

Donald J. Trump ✓
@realDonaldTrump

Two long running, Obama era, investigations of two very popular Republican Congressmen were brought to a well publicized charge, just ahead of the Mid-Terms, by the Jeff Sessions Justice Department. Two easy wins now in doubt because there is not enough time. Good job Jeff......
20,064 Retweets **79,126** Likes
11:25 AM - 3 Sep 2018

Donald J. Trump ✓
@realDonaldTrump

....The Democrats, none of whom voted for Jeff Sessions, must love him now. Same thing with Lyin' James Comey. The Dems all hated him, wanted him out, thought he was disgusting - UNTIL I FIRED HIM! Immediately he became a wonderful man, a saint like figure in fact. Really sick!
23,819 Retweets **100,016** Likes
11:39 AM - 3 Sep 2018

Donald J. Trump ✓
@realDonaldTrump

I see that John Kerry, the father of the now terminated Iran deal, is thinking of running for President. I should only be so lucky - although the field that is currently assembling looks really good - FOR ME!
25,251 Retweets **111,098** Likes
11:55 AM - 3 Sep 2018

Donald J. Trump ✓
@realDonaldTrump

According to the Failing New York Times, the FBI started a major effort to flip Putin loyalists in 2014-2016. "It wasn't about Trump, he wasn't even close to a candidate yet." Rigged Witch Hunt!
18,704 Retweets **72,600** Likes
12:21 PM - 3 Sep 2018

Donald J. Trump ✓
@realDonaldTrump

President Bashar al-Assad of Syria must not recklessly attack Idlib Province. The Russians and Iranians would be making a grave humanitarian mistake to take part in this potential human tragedy. Hundreds of thousands of people could be killed. Don't let that happen!
22,823 Retweets **88,416** Likes
3:20 PM - 3 Sep 2018

Donald J. Trump ✓
@realDonaldTrump

NBC FAKE NEWS, which is under intense scrutiny over their killing the Harvey Weinstein story, is now fumbling around making excuses for their probably highly unethical conduct. I have long criticized NBC and their journalistic standards-worse than even CNN. Look at their license?
25,962 Retweets **104,415** Likes
7:58 AM - 4 Sep 2018

Donald J. Trump ✓
@realDonaldTrump

Everyone in the path of #Gordon please heed the advice of State and local officials and follow @NHC_Atlantic for updates. The Federal Government stands ready to assist. Be safe!
11,461 Retweets **46,430** Likes
11:24 AM - 4 Sep 2018

Donald J. Trump ✓
@realDonaldTrump

Jon Kyl will be an extraordinary Senator representing an extraordinary state, Arizona. I look forward to working with him!
12,602 Retweets **58,461** Likes
1:40 PM - 4 Sep 2018

Donald J. Trump ✓
@realDonaldTrump

The Brett Kavanaugh hearings for the future Justice of the Supreme Court are truly a display of how mean, angry, and despicable the other side is. They will say anything, and are only....
21,966 Retweets **90,541** Likes
1:41 PM - 4 Sep 2018

Donald J. Trump ✓
@realDonaldTrump

....looking to inflict pain and embarrassment to one of the most highly renowned jurists to ever appear before Congress. So sad to see!
15,490 Retweets **66,613** Likes
1:41 PM - 4 Sep 2018

Donald J. Trump ✓
@realDonaldTrump

"Pledge to America's Workers"
10,319 Retweets **43,016** Likes
1:44 PM - 4 Sep 2018

Donald J. Trump ✓
@realDonaldTrump

Paul Cook is a decorated Marine Corps Veteran who loves and supports our Military and Vets. He is Strong on Crime, the Border, and supported Tax Cuts for the people of California. Paul has my total and complete Endorsement!
16,062 Retweets **64,539** Likes
1:55 PM - 4 Sep 2018

Donald J. Trump ✓
@realDonaldTrump

"Judge Brett Kavanaugh is an Exceptionally Qualified and Deserving Nominee for the Supreme Court"
15,184 Retweets **58,914** Likes
2:03 PM - 4 Sep 2018

Donald J. Trump ✓
@realDonaldTrump

Statement from Secretary of Defense, James Mattis
21,557 Retweets **67,922** Likes
3:37 PM - 4 Sep 2018

Donald J. Trump ✓
@realDonaldTrump

Statement from White House Chief of Staff, General John Kelly
20,314 Retweets **66,605** Likes
3:38 PM - 4 Sep 2018

Donald J. Trump ✓
@realDonaldTrump

Statement from White House @PressSec, Sarah Sanders
15,810 Retweets **56,201** Likes
3:49 PM - 4 Sep 2018

Donald J. Trump ✓
@realDonaldTrump

The Woodward book has already been refuted and discredited by General (Secretary of Defense) James Mattis and General (Chief of Staff) John Kelly. Their quotes were made up frauds, a con on the public. Likewise other stories and quotes. Woodward is a Dem operative? Notice timing?
23,494 Retweets **83,890** Likes
4:18 PM - 4 Sep 2018

Donald J. Trump ✓
@realDonaldTrump

Sleepy Eyes Chuck Todd of Fake NBC News said it's time for the Press to stop complaining and to start fighting back. Actually Chuck, they've been doing that from the day I announced for President. They've gone all out, and I WON, and now they're going CRAZY!
26,168 Retweets **107,623** Likes
7:50 PM - 4 Sep 2018

Donald J. Trump ✓
@realDonaldTrump

The already discredited Woodward book, so many lies and phony sources, has me calling Jeff Sessions "mentally retarded" and "a dumb southerner." I said NEITHER, never used those terms on anyone, including Jeff, and being a southerner is a GREAT thing. He made this up to divide!
22,078 Retweets **87,246** Likes
8:01 PM - 4 Sep 2018

Donald J. Trump ✓
@realDonaldTrump

Jim Mattis Calls Woodward Book 'Fiction': 'Product of Someone's Rich Imagination'
12,273 Retweets **46,774** Likes
8:32 PM - 4 Sep 2018

Donald J. Trump ✓
@realDonaldTrump

"Secretary Mattis Nukes Woodward Allegations"
14,595 Retweets **53,122** Likes
8:35 PM - 4 Sep 2018

President Trumps Tweets 2018: A Historical Archive of President Trump's Tweets

Donald J. Trump ✓
@realDonaldTrump

Isn't it a shame that someone can write an article or book, totally make up stories and form a picture of a person that is literally the exact opposite of the fact, and get away with it without retribution or cost. Don't know why Washington politicians don't change libel laws?
25,541 Retweets **114,928** Likes
4:33 AM - 5 Sep 2018

Donald J. Trump ✓
@realDonaldTrump

Almost everyone agrees that my Administration has done more in less than two years than any other Administration in the history of our Country. I'm tough as hell on people & if I weren't, nothing would get done. Also, I question everybody & everything-which is why I got elected!
28,860 Retweets **118,462** Likes
6:20 AM - 5 Sep 2018

Donald J. Trump ✓
@realDonaldTrump

The Trump Economy is booming with help of House and Senate GOP. #FarmBill with SNAP work requirements will bolster farmers and get America back to work. Pass the Farm Bill with SNAP work requirements!
13,994 Retweets **60,250** Likes
6:21 AM - 5 Sep 2018

Donald J. Trump ✓
@realDonaldTrump

Just like the NFL, whose ratings have gone WAY DOWN, Nike is getting absolutely killed with anger and boycotts. I wonder if they had any idea that it would be this way? As far as the NFL is concerned, I just find it hard to watch, and always will, until they stand for the FLAG!
27,547 Retweets **121,039** Likes
6:39 AM - 5 Sep 2018

Donald J. Trump ✓
@realDonaldTrump

Thank you General Kelly, book is total fiction!
14,809 Retweets **58,827** Likes
6:51 AM - 5 Sep 2018

Donald J. Trump ✓
@realDonaldTrump

Thank you General Mattis, book is boring & untrue!
15,430 Retweets **62,276** Likes
6:54 AM - 5 Sep 2018

Donald J. Trump ✓
@realDonaldTrump

Join me tomorrow night at 7:00pm MDT in Billings, Montana for a MAKE AMERICA GREAT AGAIN RALLY!
14,923 Retweets **55,583** Likes
12:09 PM - 5 Sep 2018

Donald J. Trump ✓
@realDonaldTrump

Today, it was my honor to welcome the Amir of Kuwait to the @WhiteHouse!
12,204 Retweets **49,881** Likes
2:10 PM - 5 Sep 2018

Donald J. Trump ✓
@realDonaldTrump

The Failing New York Times!
25,528 Retweets **88,162** Likes
2:45 PM - 5 Sep 2018

Donald J. Trump ✓
@realDonaldTrump

TREASON?
34,012 Retweets **121,342** Likes
3:15 PM - 5 Sep 2018

Donald J. Trump ✓
@realDonaldTrump

Does the so-called "Senior Administration Official" really exist, or is it just the Failing New York Times with another phony source? If the GUTLESS anonymous person does indeed exist, the Times must, for National Security purposes, turn him/her over to government at once!
31,916 Retweets **120,458** Likes
4:40 PM - 5 Sep 2018

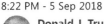

Donald J. Trump ✓
@realDonaldTrump

I'm draining the Swamp, and the Swamp is trying to fight back. Don't worry, we will win!
53,170 Retweets **203,256** Likes
8:22 PM - 5 Sep 2018

Donald J. Trump ✓
@realDonaldTrump

Kim Jong Un of North Korea proclaims "unwavering faith in President Trump." Thank you to Chairman Kim. We will get it done together!
26,147 Retweets **110,587** Likes
3:58 AM - 6 Sep 2018

Donald J. Trump ✓
@realDonaldTrump

The Deep State and the Left, and their vehicle, the Fake News Media, are going Crazy - & they don't know what to do. The Economy is booming like never before, Jobs are at Historic Highs, soon TWO Supreme Court Justices & maybe Declassification to find Additional Corruption. Wow!
36,407 Retweets **129,230** Likes
4:19 AM - 6 Sep 2018

Donald J. Trump ✓
@realDonaldTrump

Cosumer confidence highest in 18 years, Atlanta Fed forecasts 4.7 GDP, manufacturing jobs highest in many years. "It's the story of the Trump Administration, the Economic Success, that's unnerving his detractors." @MariaBartiromo
19,110 Retweets **76,621** Likes
4:31 AM - 6 Sep 2018

Donald J. Trump ✓
@realDonaldTrump

"The record is quite remarkable. The President has faithfully followed the agenda he campaigned on in 2016. People should focus on the results, and they're extraordinary!" James Freeman - Wall Street Journal
25,245 Retweets **97,379** Likes
7:09 AM - 6 Sep 2018

President Trumps Tweets 2018: A Historical Archive of President Trump's Tweets

Donald J. Trump ✓
@realDonaldTrump

Look forward to seeing everyone in Montana tonight! #MAGA
13,209 Retweets **56,324** Likes
10:16 AM - 6 Sep 2018

Donald J. Trump ✓
@realDonaldTrump

Are the investigative "journalists" of the New York Times going to investigate themselves - who is the anonymous letter writer?
18,804 Retweets **86,141** Likes
4:12 PM - 6 Sep 2018

Donald J. Trump ✓
@realDonaldTrump

Landing in Montana now to support Matt Rosendale for U.S. Senate! #MAGA
11,046 Retweets **52,569** Likes
4:15 PM - 6 Sep 2018

Donald J. Trump ✓
@realDonaldTrump

Getting ready to go on stage for Matt Rosendale, who will be a great Senator. Jon Tester has let the people of Montana down & does not deserve another six years. Matt is strong on Crime, the Borders, & will save your Second Amendment from the onslaught. Loves our Military & Vets!
16,358 Retweets **75,391** Likes
6:06 PM - 6 Sep 2018

Donald J. Trump ✓
@realDonaldTrump

MAKE AMERICA GREAT AGAIN!
17,418 Retweets **67,872** Likes
7:38 PM - 6 Sep 2018

Donald J. Trump ✓
@realDonaldTrump

Thank you Montana, I love you!
16,071 Retweets **76,228** Likes
7:48 PM - 6 Sep 2018

Donald J. Trump ✓
@realDonaldTrump

What was Nike thinking?
30,036 Retweets **151,673** Likes
3:56 AM - 7 Sep 2018

Donald J. Trump ✓
@realDonaldTrump

Matt Rosendale will be a Great Senator from a Great State, Montana! He is a fighter who will be tough on Crime and the Border, fight hard for our 2nd Amendment and loves our Military and our Vets. He has my full and complete Endorsement!
15,928 Retweets **68,260** Likes
4:11 AM - 7 Sep 2018

Anthony T. Michalisko

Donald J. Trump ✓
@realDonaldTrump

The Woodward book is a scam. I don't talk the way I am quoted. If I did I would not have been elected President. These quotes were made up. The author uses every trick in the book to demean and belittle. I wish the people could see the real facts - and our country is doing GREAT!
29,430 Retweets **127,236** Likes
4:32 AM - 7 Sep 2018

Donald J. Trump ✓
@realDonaldTrump

Under our horrible immigration laws, the Government is frequently blocked from deporting criminal aliens with violent felony convictions. House GOP just passed a bill to increase our ability to deport violent felons (Crazy Dems opposed). Need to get this bill to my desk fast!
30,246 Retweets **112,398** Likes
9:35 AM - 7 Sep 2018

Donald J. Trump ✓
@realDonaldTrump

"Unprecedented Jobs Growth Streak Continues as Wages Rise"
14,739 Retweets **56,501** Likes
1:16 PM - 7 Sep 2018

Donald J. Trump ✓
@realDonaldTrump

14 days for $28 MILLION - $2 MILLION a day, No Collusion. A great day for America!
21,096 Retweets **87,063** Likes
2:39 PM - 7 Sep 2018

Donald J. Trump ✓
@realDonaldTrump

Dave Hughes is running for Congress in the Great State of Minnesota. He will help us accomplish our America First policies, is strong on Crime, the Border, our 2nd Amendmen, Trade, Military and Vets. Running against Pelosi Liberal Puppet Petterson. Dave has my Total Endorsement!
16,085 Retweets **63,385** Likes
7:44 AM - 8 Sep 2018

Donald J. Trump ✓
@realDonaldTrump

"To this point, President Trump's achievements are unprecedented." @LouDobbs
15,434 Retweets **68,415** Likes
7:47 AM - 8 Sep 2018

Donald J. Trump ✓
@realDonaldTrump

We are breaking all Jobs and Economic Records but, importantly, our Country has TREMENDOUS FUTURE POTENTIAL. We have just begun!
24,477 Retweets **103,159** Likes
7:51 AM - 8 Sep 2018

Donald J. Trump ✓
@realDonaldTrump

Apple prices may increase because of the massive Tariffs we may be imposing on China - but there is an easy solution where there would be ZERO tax, and indeed a tax incentive. Make your products in the United States instead of China. Start building new plants now. Exciting! #MAGA
28,281 Retweets **112,546** Likes
8:45 AM - 8 Sep 2018

President Trumps Tweets 2018: A Historical Archive of President Trump's Tweets

Donald J. Trump ✓
@realDonaldTrump

So true! "Mr. Trump remains the single most popular figure in the Republican Party, whose fealty has helped buoy candidates in competitive Republican primaries and remains a hot commodity among general election candidates." Nicholas Fandos, @nytimes
16,272 Retweets **73,477** Likes
2:08 PM - 8 Sep 2018

Donald J. Trump ✓
@realDonaldTrump

Our Social Media (and beyond) Stars, @DiamondandSilk, are terrific people who are doing really well. We are all very proud of them, and their great success!
19,391 Retweets **87,579** Likes
5:07 PM - 8 Sep 2018

Donald J. Trump ✓
@realDonaldTrump

Republicans are doing really well with the Senate Midterms. Races that we were not even thinking about winning are now very close, or even leading. Election night will be very interesting indeed!
21,355 Retweets **93,794** Likes
6:38 PM - 8 Sep 2018

Donald J. Trump ✓
@realDonaldTrump

The Dems have tried every trick in the playbook-call me everything under the sun. But if I'm all of those terrible things, how come I beat them so badly, 306-223? Maybe they're just not very good! The fact is they are going CRAZY only because they know they can't beat me in 2020!
29,744 Retweets **125,431** Likes
6:47 PM - 8 Sep 2018

Donald J. Trump ✓
@realDonaldTrump

So nice, thank you both!
19,817 Retweets **85,874** Likes
6:51 PM - 8 Sep 2018

Donald J. Trump ✓
@realDonaldTrump

Happy Anniversary! #ProudDeplorable
27,742 Retweets **87,873** Likes
6:01 AM - 9 Sep 2018

Donald J. Trump ✓
@realDonaldTrump

"Barack Obama talked a lot about hope, but Donald Trump delivered the American Dream. All the economic indicators, what's happening overseas, Donald Trump has proven to be far more successful than Barack Obama. President Trump is delivering the American Dream." Jason Chaffetz
25,068 Retweets **95,006** Likes
6:32 AM - 9 Sep 2018

Donald J. Trump ✓
@realDonaldTrump

"Ford has abruptly killed a plan to sell a Chinese-made small vehicle in the U.S. because of the prospect of higher U.S. Tariffs." CNBC. This is just the beginning. This car can now be BUILT IN THE U.S.A. and Ford will pay no tariffs!
20,383 Retweets **84,225** Likes
6:49 AM - 9 Sep 2018

Donald J. Trump ✓
@realDonaldTrump

If the U.S. sells a car into China, there is a tax of 25%. If China sells a car into the U.S., there is a tax of 2%. Does anybody think that is FAIR? The days of the U.S. being ripped-off by other nations is OVER!
32,757 Retweets **133,067** Likes
7:01 AM - 9 Sep 2018

Donald J. Trump ✓
@realDonaldTrump

"Trump has set Economic Growth on fire. During his time in office, the economy has achieved feats most experts thought impossible. GDP is growing at a 3 percent-plus rate. The unemployment rate is near a 50 year low." CNBC...Also, the Stock Market is up almost 50% since Election!
19,063 Retweets **77,923** Likes
7:12 AM - 9 Sep 2018

Donald J. Trump ✓
@realDonaldTrump

Wow, NFL first game ratings are way down over an already really bad last year comparison. Viewership declined 13%, the lowest in over a decade. If the players stood proudly for our Flag and Anthem, and it is all shown on broadcast, maybe ratings could come back? Otherwise worse!
22,782 Retweets **106,928** Likes
7:42 AM - 9 Sep 2018

Donald J. Trump ✓
@realDonaldTrump

North Korea has just staged their parade, celebrating 70th anniversary of founding, without the customary display of nuclear missiles. Theme was peace and economic development. "Experts believe that North Korea cut out the nuclear missiles to show President Trump......
21,120 Retweets **83,328** Likes
8:21 AM - 9 Sep 2018

Donald J. Trump ✓
@realDonaldTrump

...its commitment to denuclearize." @FoxNews This is a big and very positive statement from North Korea. Thank you To Chairman Kim. We will both prove everyone wrong! There is nothing like good dialogue from two people that like each other! Much better than before I took office.
17,417 Retweets **70,482** Likes
8:31 AM - 9 Sep 2018

Donald J. Trump ✓
@realDonaldTrump

Melania and I wish all Jewish people Shana Tova and send our warmest greetings to those celebrating Rosh Hashanah and the start of the High Holy Days...
15,880 Retweets **66,752** Likes
10:28 AM - 9 Sep 2018

Donald J. Trump ✓
@realDonaldTrump

The GDP Rate (4.2%) is higher than the Unemployment Rate (3.9%) for the first time in over 100 years!

25,215 Retweets **90,857** Likes
4:03 AM - 10 Sep 2018

Donald J. Trump ✓
@realDonaldTrump

If the Democrats had won the Election in 2016, GDP, which was about 1% and going down, would have been minus 4% instead of up 4.2%. I opened up our beautiful economic engine with Regulation and Tax Cuts. Our system was choking and would have been made worse. Still plenty to do!

15,995 Retweets **65,807** Likes
4:10 AM - 10 Sep 2018

Donald J. Trump ✓
@realDonaldTrump

The Woodward book is a Joke - just another assault against me, in a barrage of assaults, using now disproven unnamed and anonymous sources. Many have already come forward to say the quotes by them, like the book, are fiction. Dems can't stand losing. I'll write the real book!

17,211 Retweets **76,167** Likes
4:22 AM - 10 Sep 2018

Donald J. Trump ✓
@realDonaldTrump

The White House is a "smooth running machine." We are making some of the biggest and most important deals in our country's history - with many more to come! The Dems are going crazy!

16,439 Retweets **71,651** Likes
4:35 AM - 10 Sep 2018

Donald J. Trump ✓
@realDonaldTrump

"I'm taking this book with a grain of salt & everyone should do the same. Multiple sources, but almost every one of them has come out and discredited the claims made by Woodward. You cannot take this book too seriously." Katelyn Caralle, Washington Examiner

12,282 Retweets **53,974** Likes
4:46 AM - 10 Sep 2018

Donald J. Trump ✓
@realDonaldTrump

"It is mostly anonymous sources in here, why should anyone trust you? General Mattis, General Kelly said it's not true." @SavannahGuthrie @TODAYshow Bob Woodward is a liar who is like a Dem operative prior to the Midterms. He was caught cold, even by NBC.

14,920 Retweets **57,772** Likes
5:36 AM - 10 Sep 2018

Donald J. Trump ✓
@realDonaldTrump

The Economy is soooo good, perhaps the best in our country's history (remember, it's the economy stupid!), that the Democrats are flailing & lying like CRAZY! Phony books, articles and T.V. "hits" like no other pol has had to endure-and they are losing big. Very dishonest people!

22,256 Retweets **90,056** Likes
6:57 AM - 10 Sep 2018

 **Donald J. Trump** @realDonaldTrump

"President Trump would need a magic wand to get to 4% GDP," stated President Obama. I guess I have a magic wand, 4.2%, and we will do MUCH better than this! We have just begun.
42,135 Retweets **152,901** Likes
7:42 AM - 10 Sep 2018

 Donald J. Trump @realDonaldTrump

The Storms in the Atlantic are very dangerous. We encourage anyone in the path of these storms to prepare themselves and to heed the warnings of State and Local officials. The Federal Government is closely monitoring and ready to assist. We are with you!
18,132 Retweets **80,243** Likes
12:35 PM - 10 Sep 2018

 Donald J. Trump @realDonaldTrump

To the incredible citizens of North Carolina, South Carolina and the entire East Coast - the storm looks very bad! Please take all necessary precautions. We have already began mobilizing our assets to respond accordingly, and we are here for you!
27,869 Retweets **114,933** Likes
12:41 PM - 10 Sep 2018

 Donald J. Trump @realDonaldTrump

Chuck Schumer is holding up 320 appointments (Ambassadors, Executives, etc.) of great people who have left jobs and given up so much in order to come into Government. Schumer and the Democrats continue to OBSTRUCT!
29,429 Retweets **90,214** Likes
2:18 PM - 10 Sep 2018

 Donald J. Trump @realDonaldTrump

Was just briefed via phone by @DHSgov @SecNielsen and @FEMA @FEMA_Brock, along with @VP Mike Pence and Chief of Staff, John Kelly on incoming storm which is very dangerous. Heed the directions of your State and Local Officials - and know that WE are here for you. Be SAFE!
12,357 Retweets **49,951** Likes
2:52 PM - 10 Sep 2018

 Donald J. Trump @realDonaldTrump

My people just informed me that this is one of the worst storms to hit the East Coast in many years. Also, looking like a direct hit on North Carolina, South Carolina and Virginia. Please be prepared, be careful and be SAFE!
22,422 Retweets **95,600** Likes
4:17 PM - 10 Sep 2018

 Donald J. Trump @realDonaldTrump

Just had calls with South Carolina Governor Henry McMaster, North Carolina Governor Roy Cooper, and Virginia Governor Ralph Northam regarding the incoming storm. Federal Government stands by, ready to assist 24/7.
15,191 Retweets **69,310** Likes
4:21 PM - 10 Sep 2018

President Trumps Tweets 2018: A Historical Archive of President Trump's Tweets

Donald J. Trump ✓
@realDonaldTrump

"We have found nothing to show collusion between President Trump & Russia, absolutely zero, but every day we get more documentation showing collusion between the FBI & DOJ, the Hillary campaign, foreign spies & Russians, incredible." @SaraCarterDC @LouDobbs
22,624 Retweets **78,569** Likes
4:08 AM - 11 Sep 2018

Donald J. Trump ✓
@realDonaldTrump

#NeverForget #September11th
16,328 Retweets **60,786** Likes
4:12 AM - 11 Sep 2018

Donald J. Trump ✓
@realDonaldTrump

New Strzok-Page texts reveal "Media Leak Strategy." @FoxNews So terrible, and NOTHING is being done at DOJ or FBI - but the world is watching, and they get it completely.
22,610 Retweets **82,847** Likes
4:19 AM - 11 Sep 2018

Donald J. Trump ✓
@realDonaldTrump

"ERIC Holder could be running the Justice Department right now and it would be behaving no differently than it is." @LouDobbs
13,753 Retweets **57,659** Likes
4:41 AM - 11 Sep 2018

Donald J. Trump ✓
@realDonaldTrump

Rudy Giuliani did a GREAT job as Mayor of NYC during the period of September 11th. His leadership, bravery and skill must never be forgotten. Rudy is a TRUE WARRIOR!
24,404 Retweets **116,879** Likes
4:59 AM - 11 Sep 2018

Donald J. Trump ✓
@realDonaldTrump

Departing Washington, D.C. to attend a Flight 93 September 11th Memorial Service in Shanksville, Pennsylvania with Melania. #NeverForget
14,912 Retweets **66,010** Likes
5:24 AM - 11 Sep 2018

Donald J. Trump ✓
@realDonaldTrump

17 years since September 11th!
22,422 Retweets **99,109** Likes
5:58 AM - 11 Sep 2018

Donald J. Trump ✓
@realDonaldTrump

#NeverForget #September11th
12,941 Retweets **49,546** Likes
8:32 AM - 11 Sep 2018

Donald J. Trump ✓
@realDonaldTrump

Small Business Optimism Soars to Highest Level Ever | Breitbart
13,347 Retweets **50,928** Likes
9:48 AM - 11 Sep 2018

Donald J. Trump ✓
@realDonaldTrump

The safety of American people is my absolute highest priority. Heed the directions of your State and Local Officials. Please be prepared, be careful and be SAFE!
15,666 Retweets **62,924** Likes
1:16 PM - 11 Sep 2018

Donald J. Trump ✓
@realDonaldTrump

#NeverForget #September11th
14,843 Retweets **60,006** Likes
5:19 PM - 11 Sep 2018

Donald J. Trump ✓
@realDonaldTrump

"You know who's at fault for this more than anyone else, Comey, because he leaked information and laundered it through a professor at Columbia Law School. Shame on that professor, and shame on Comey. He snuck the information to a law professor who collaborated with him in........
21,065 Retweets **82,077** Likes
6:16 PM - 11 Sep 2018

Donald J. Trump ✓
@realDonaldTrump

....giving the information, and causing the appointment of a Special C without having the courage of his own convictions....." Alan Dershowitz @TuckerCarlson In other words, the whole thing was illegally and very unfairly set up?
15,904 Retweets **61,918** Likes
6:28 PM - 11 Sep 2018

Donald J. Trump ✓
@realDonaldTrump

Crazy Maxine Waters: "After we impeach Trump, we'll go after Mike Pence. We'll get him." @FoxNews Where are the Democrats coming from? The best Economy in the history of our country would totally collapse if they ever took control!
28,470 Retweets **109,586** Likes
6:55 PM - 11 Sep 2018

Donald J. Trump ✓
@realDonaldTrump

"The President has absolutely demonstrated no wrongdoing whatsoever & that the Special Counsel has no evidence of any wrongdoing. In other words, it's time to end this Witch Hunt." @LouDobbs Russian "collusion" was just an excuse by the Democrats for having lost the Election!
17,704 Retweets **70,293** Likes
3:30 AM - 12 Sep 2018

Donald J. Trump ✓
@realDonaldTrump

We got A Pluses for our recent hurricane work in Texas and Florida (and did an unappreciated great job in Puerto Rico, even though an inaccessible island with very poor electricity and a totally incompetent Mayor of San Juan). We are ready for the big one that is coming!
16,495 Retweets **77,537** Likes
3:51 AM - 12 Sep 2018

President Trumps Tweets 2018: A Historical Archive of President Trump's Tweets

Donald J. Trump ✓
@realDonaldTrump

Hurricane Florence is looking even bigger than anticipated. It will be arriving soon. FEMA, First Responders and Law Enforcement are supplied and ready. Be safe!
14,575 Retweets **69,288** Likes
3:58 AM - 12 Sep 2018

Donald J. Trump ✓
@realDonaldTrump

Hurricane Florence may now be dipping a bit south and hitting a portion of the Great State of Georgia. Be ready, be prepared!
14,106 Retweets **63,590** Likes
6:58 AM - 12 Sep 2018

Donald J. Trump ✓
@realDonaldTrump

"I can say, as it relates to the Senate Intelligence Committee Investigation, that we have NO hard evidence of Collusion." Richard Burr (R-NC) Senate Intelligence Committee, Chairman
17,728 Retweets **71,348** Likes
7:06 AM - 12 Sep 2018

Donald J. Trump ✓
@realDonaldTrump

It is imperative that everyone follow local evacuation orders. This storm is extremely dangerous. Be SAFE! #HurricaneFlorence
18,044 Retweets **65,031** Likes
9:37 AM - 12 Sep 2018

Donald J. Trump ✓
@realDonaldTrump

#HurricaneFlorence
7,965 Retweets **33,188** Likes
4:16 PM - 12 Sep 2018

Donald J. Trump ✓
@realDonaldTrump

Tonight, it was my great honor to host a Congressional Medal of Honor Society Reception at the @WhiteHouse!
12,206 Retweets **53,539** Likes
4:21 PM - 12 Sep 2018

Donald J. Trump ✓
@realDonaldTrump

The problem with banker Jamie Dimon running for President is that he doesn't have the aptitude or "smarts" & is a poor public speaker & nervous mess - otherwise he is wonderful. I've made a lot of bankers, and others, look much smarter than they are with my great economic policy!
11,842 Retweets **59,886** Likes
4:22 AM - 13 Sep 2018

Donald J. Trump ✓
@realDonaldTrump

We are completely ready for hurricane Florence, as the storm gets even larger and more powerful. Be careful!
8,507 Retweets **46,984** Likes
4:39 AM - 13 Sep 2018

Donald J. Trump ✓
@realDonaldTrump

More text messages between former FBI employees Peter Strzok and Lisa Page are a disaster and embarrassment to the FBI & DOJ. This should never have happened but we are learning more and more by the hour. "Others were leaking like mad" in order to get the President!....
16,690 Retweets **59,307** Likes
5:06 AM - 13 Sep 2018

Donald J. Trump ✓
@realDonaldTrump

....."It is a cesspool of corruption, and the people who did this need to be brought to justice." @GreggJarrett
10,772 Retweets **43,508** Likes
5:10 AM - 13 Sep 2018

Donald J. Trump ✓
@realDonaldTrump

"Middle-Class Income Hits All-Time High!" @foxandfriends And will continue to rise (unless the Dems get in and destroy what we have built).
16,820 Retweets **65,135** Likes
5:25 AM - 13 Sep 2018

Donald J. Trump ✓
@realDonaldTrump

3000 people did not die in the two hurricanes that hit Puerto Rico. When I left the Island, AFTER the storm had hit, they had anywhere from 6 to 18 deaths. As time went by it did not go up by much. Then, a long time later, they started to report really large numbers, like 3000...
20,699 Retweets **77,663** Likes
5:37 AM - 13 Sep 2018

Donald J. Trump ✓
@realDonaldTrump

.....This was done by the Democrats in order to make me look as bad as possible when I was successfully raising Billions of Dollars to help rebuild Puerto Rico. If a person died for any reason, like old age, just add them onto the list. Bad politics. I love Puerto Rico!
21,598 Retweets **90,523** Likes
5:49 AM - 13 Sep 2018

Donald J. Trump ✓
@realDonaldTrump

The Wall Street Journal has it wrong, we are under no pressure to make a deal with China, they are under pressure to make a deal with us. Our markets are surging, theirs are collapsing. We will soon be taking in Billions in Tariffs & making products at home. If we meet, we meet?
23,038 Retweets **87,737** Likes
7:15 AM - 13 Sep 2018

Donald J. Trump ✓
@realDonaldTrump

Thank you @USCG!
10,539 Retweets **46,440** Likes
8:14 AM - 13 Sep 2018

Donald J. Trump ✓
@realDonaldTrump

I was just briefed on Hurricane Florence. FEMA, First Responders and Law Enforcement are supplied and ready. We are with you!
12,401 Retweets **54,406** Likes
10:26 AM - 13 Sep 2018

President Trumps Tweets 2018: A Historical Archive of President Trump's Tweets

Donald J. Trump ✓
@realDonaldTrump

Thank you @USNationalGuard! #HurricaneFlorence
7,931 Retweets **34,794** Likes
10:41 AM - 13 Sep 2018

Donald J. Trump ✓
@realDonaldTrump

Senator Debbie Stabenow and the Democrats are totally against approving the Farm Bill. They are fighting tooth and nail to not allow our Great Farmers to get what they so richly deserve. Work requirements are imperative and the Dems are a NO. Not good!
21,003 Retweets **69,694** Likes
10:56 AM - 13 Sep 2018

Donald J. Trump ✓
@realDonaldTrump

John Kerry had illegal meetings with the very hostile Iranian Regime, which can only serve to undercut our great work to the detriment of the American people. He told them to wait out the Trump Administration! Was he registered under the Foreign Agents Registration Act? BAD!
39,118 Retweets **124,575** Likes
6:10 PM - 13 Sep 2018

Donald J. Trump ✓
@realDonaldTrump

Gina is Great!
9,089 Retweets **41,619** Likes
7:37 PM - 13 Sep 2018

Donald J. Trump ✓
@realDonaldTrump

Incredible job being done by FEMA, First Responders, Law Enforcement and all. Thank you!
18,686 Retweets **95,258** Likes
5:19 AM - 14 Sep 2018

Donald J. Trump ✓
@realDonaldTrump

We love the #CajunNavy - THANK YOU! #FlorenceHurricane2018
16,837 Retweets **66,442** Likes
2:40 PM - 14 Sep 2018

Donald J. Trump ✓
@realDonaldTrump

Keep up the great work - THANK YOU!
10,438 Retweets **47,070** Likes
2:43 PM - 14 Sep 2018

Donald J. Trump ✓
@realDonaldTrump

"They say all these people died in the storm in Puerto Rico, yet 70% of the power was out before the storm. So when did people start dying? At what point do you recognize that what they are doing is a political agenda couched in the nice language of journalism?" @GeraldoRivera
20,783 Retweets **80,616** Likes
3:35 PM - 14 Sep 2018

Donald J. Trump ✓
@realDonaldTrump

"The story of Puerto Rico is the rebuilding that has occurred. The President has done an extraordinary job of cleanup, rebuilding electrical stuff and everything else." @EdRollins "The people of Puerto Rico have one of the most corrupt governments in our country." @LouDobbs
14,297 Retweets **54,931** Likes
5:31 PM - 14 Sep 2018

Donald J. Trump ✓
@realDonaldTrump

My thoughts and prayers are with Evelyn Rodriguez this evening, along with her family and friends. #RIPEvelyn
17,364 Retweets **57,813** Likes
5:43 PM - 14 Sep 2018

Donald J. Trump ✓
@realDonaldTrump

Great job FEMA, First Responders and Law Enforcement - not easy, very dangerous, tremendous talent. America is proud of you. Keep it all going - finish strong!
15,667 Retweets **73,233** Likes
6:54 PM - 14 Sep 2018

Donald J. Trump ✓
@realDonaldTrump

"When Trump visited the island territory last October, OFFICIALS told him in a briefing 16 PEOPLE had died from Maria." The Washington Post. This was long AFTER the hurricane took place. Over many months it went to 64 PEOPLE. Then, like magic, "3000 PEOPLE KILLED." They hired....
16,171 Retweets **62,263** Likes
7:05 PM - 14 Sep 2018

Donald J. Trump ✓
@realDonaldTrump

....GWU Research to tell them how many people had died in Puerto Rico (how would they not know this?). This method was never done with previous hurricanes because other jurisdictions know how many people were killed. FIFTY TIMES LAST ORIGINAL NUMBER - NO WAY!
15,143 Retweets **65,392** Likes
7:23 PM - 14 Sep 2018

Donald J. Trump ✓
@realDonaldTrump

When President Obama said that he has been to "57 States," very little mention in Fake News Media. Can you imagine if I said that...story of the year! @IngrahamAngle
25,734 Retweets **104,570** Likes
8:08 PM - 14 Sep 2018

Donald J. Trump ✓
@realDonaldTrump

Thank you @nycemergencymgt!
7,460 Retweets **34,785** Likes
1:26 PM - 15 Sep 2018

Donald J. Trump ✓
@realDonaldTrump

Thank you Brock – it is my honor! "We (@FEMA) have never had the support that we have had from this President." Administrator @FEMA_Brock
14,728 Retweets **54,838** Likes
1:41 PM - 15 Sep 2018

President Trumps Tweets 2018: A Historical Archive of President Trump's Tweets

Donald J. Trump ✓
@realDonaldTrump

Congressman Pete Sessions of Texas is doing a great job. He is a fighter who will be tough on Crime and the Border, fight hard for our Second Amendment and loves our Military and our Vets. He has my full and complete Endorsement!
13,474 Retweets **53,017** Likes
1:43 PM - 15 Sep 2018

Donald J. Trump ✓
@realDonaldTrump

Congressman Keith Rothfus continues to do a great job for the people of Pennsylvania. Keith is strong on Crime, the Border, and our Second Amendment. Loves our Military and our Vets. He has my total Endorsement!
12,891 Retweets **51,990** Likes
1:54 PM - 15 Sep 2018

Donald J. Trump ✓
@realDonaldTrump

.@DannyTarkanian of Nevada is a great friend who supports the Trump Agenda. He is Strong on Crime, the Border and our under siege 2nd Amendment. Danny Loves our Military and our Vets. He has my total and complete Endorsement!
11,552 Retweets **45,292** Likes
1:57 PM - 15 Sep 2018

Donald J. Trump ✓
@realDonaldTrump

While my (our) poll numbers are good, with the Economy being the best ever, if it weren't for the Rigged Russian Witch Hunt, they would be 25 points higher! Highly conflicted Bob Mueller & the 17 Angry Democrats are using this Phony issue to hurt us in the Midterms. No Collusion!
21,389 Retweets **83,819** Likes
3:08 PM - 15 Sep 2018

Donald J. Trump ✓
@realDonaldTrump

When will Republican leadership learn that they are being played like a fiddle by the Democrats on Border Security and Building the Wall? Without Borders, we don't have a country. With Open Borders, which the Democrats want, we have nothing but crime! Finish the Wall!
31,415 Retweets **116,402** Likes
3:38 PM - 15 Sep 2018

Donald J. Trump ✓
@realDonaldTrump

Five deaths have been recorded thus far with regard to hurricane Florence! Deepest sympathies and warmth go out to the families and friends of the victims. May God be with them!
15,176 Retweets **77,738** Likes
3:42 PM - 15 Sep 2018

Donald J. Trump ✓
@realDonaldTrump

Exclusive -- Donald Trump Jr. to Obama: My Dad Fixed the Economy You Could Not
19,503 Retweets **67,705** Likes
7:27 PM - 15 Sep 2018

Donald J. Trump ✓
@realDonaldTrump

The illegal Mueller Witch Hunt continues in search of a crime. There was never Collusion with Russia, except by the Clinton campaign, so the 17 Angry Democrats are looking at anything they can find. Very unfair and BAD for the country. ALSO, not allowed under the LAW!
25,751 Retweets **98,778** Likes
7:20 AM - 16 Sep 2018

Donald J. Trump ✓
@realDonaldTrump

FEMA, First Responders and Law Enforcement are working really hard on hurricane Florence. As the storm begins to finally recede, they will kick into an even higher gear. Very Professional!
12,674 Retweets **62,983** Likes
9:09 AM - 16 Sep 2018

Donald J. Trump ✓
@realDonaldTrump

Congratulations to all of our Mexican friends on National Independence Day. We will be doing great things together!
16,166 Retweets **86,362** Likes
2:28 PM - 16 Sep 2018

Donald J. Trump ✓
@realDonaldTrump

Watch @MariaBartiromo at 6:00 P.M. on @FoxBusiness. Russian Hoax the big topic! Mainstream Media, often referred to as the Fake News Media, hates to discuss the real facts!
10,224 Retweets **44,001** Likes
2:40 PM - 16 Sep 2018

Donald J. Trump ✓
@realDonaldTrump

Best economic numbers in decades. If the Democrats take control, kiss your newfound wealth goodbye!
25,856 Retweets **102,204** Likes
3:18 PM - 16 Sep 2018

Donald J. Trump ✓
@realDonaldTrump

Consumer Sentiment hit its highest level in 17 years this year. Sentiment fell 11% in 2015, an Obama year, and rose 16% since the Election, #TrumpTime!
14,904 Retweets **63,198** Likes
6:06 PM - 16 Sep 2018

Donald J. Trump ✓
@realDonaldTrump

"A lot of small & medium size enterprises are registering very good profit, sometimes record profits-there stocks are doing very well, low income workers are getting big raises. There are an awful lot of good things going on that weren't during Pres. Obama's Watch." Peter Morici
14,721 Retweets **61,799** Likes
3:01 AM - 17 Sep 2018

Donald J. Trump ✓
@realDonaldTrump

Tariffs have put the U.S. in a very strong bargaining position, with Billions of Dollars, and Jobs, flowing into our Country - and yet cost increases have thus far been almost unnoticeable. If countries will not make fair deals with us, they will be "Tariffed!"
18,011 Retweets **78,851** Likes
3:11 AM - 17 Sep 2018

President Trumps Tweets 2018: A Historical Archive of President Trump's Tweets

Donald J. Trump ✓
@realDonaldTrump

Our Steel Industry is the talk of the World. It has been given new life, and is thriving. Billions of Dollars is being spent on new plants all around the country!
18,088 Retweets **75,366** Likes
3:15 AM - 17 Sep 2018

Donald J. Trump ✓
@realDonaldTrump

"Lisa Page Testimony- NO EVIDENCE OF COLLUSION BEFORE MUELLER APPOINTMENT." @FoxNews by Catherine Herridge. Therefore, the case should never have been allowed to be brought. It is a totally illegal Witch Hunt!
22,975 Retweets **80,400** Likes
7:23 AM - 17 Sep 2018

Donald J. Trump ✓
@realDonaldTrump

Immediately after Comey's firing Peter Strzok texted to his lover, Lisa Page "We need to Open the case we've been waiting on now while Andy (McCabe, also fired) is acting. Page answered, "We need to lock in (redacted). In a formal chargeable way. Soon." Wow, a conspiracy caught?
31,318 Retweets **102,371** Likes
7:36 AM - 17 Sep 2018

Donald J. Trump ✓
@realDonaldTrump

Americans deserve to know the lowest drug price at their pharmacy, but "gag clauses" prevent your pharmacist from telling you! I support legislation that will remove gag clauses and urge the Senate to act. #AmericanPatientsFirst
23,716 Retweets **87,932** Likes
11:10 AM - 17 Sep 2018

Donald J. Trump ✓
@realDonaldTrump

Join me in Las Vegas, Nevada at 7:00pm for a MAKE AMERICA GREAT AGAIN RALLY!
12,348 Retweets **45,738** Likes
11:22 AM - 17 Sep 2018

Donald J. Trump ✓
@realDonaldTrump

Happy Constitution Day!
14,986 Retweets **60,547** Likes
12:27 PM - 17 Sep 2018

Donald J. Trump ✓
@realDonaldTrump

It was my great honor to host today's Inaugural Meeting of the "President's National Council for the American Worker" in the Roosevelt Room!
9,684 Retweets **44,773** Likes
2:53 PM - 17 Sep 2018

Donald J. Trump ✓
@realDonaldTrump

Just met John James of Michigan. He has every single quality to be your next Great Senator from Michigan. When the people of Michigan get to know John, they will say he is a true star. Also, distinguished Military and a Combat Vet!
21,938 Retweets **80,236** Likes
3:07 PM - 17 Sep 2018

Donald J. Trump ✓
@realDonaldTrump

Today, as we celebrate Hispanic Heritage Month, we share our gratitude for all the ways Hispanic-Americans make our country flourish and prosper. Today, and every day, we honor, cherish, and celebrate Hispanic-American Workers, Families, Students, Businesses, and Leaders...
19,363 Retweets **76,890** Likes
5:21 PM - 17 Sep 2018

Donald J. Trump ✓
@realDonaldTrump

"What will be disclosed is that there was no basis for these FISA Warrants, that the important information was kept from the court, there's going to be a disproportionate influence of the (Fake) Dossier. Basically you have a counter terrorism tool used to spy on a presidential...
22,835 Retweets **77,212** Likes
5:42 AM - 18 Sep 2018

Donald J. Trump ✓
@realDonaldTrump

....campaign, which is unprecedented in our history." Congressman Peter King Really bad things were happening, but they are now being exposed. Big stuff!
14,974 Retweets **59,393** Likes
5:45 AM - 18 Sep 2018

Donald J. Trump ✓
@realDonaldTrump

China has openly stated that they are actively trying to impact and change our election by attacking our farmers, ranchers and industrial workers because of their loyalty to me. What China does not understand is that these people are great patriots and fully understand that.....
20,397 Retweets **86,435** Likes
5:50 AM - 18 Sep 2018

Donald J. Trump ✓
@realDonaldTrump

.....China has been taking advantage of the United States on Trade for many years. They also know that I am the one that knows how to stop it. There will be great and fast economic retaliation against China if our farmers, ranchers and/or industrial workers are targeted!
16,569 Retweets **67,518** Likes
5:55 AM - 18 Sep 2018

Donald J. Trump ✓
@realDonaldTrump

Happy 71st Birthday to our GREAT United States Air Force!
16,784 Retweets **75,599** Likes
6:26 AM - 18 Sep 2018

Donald J. Trump ✓
@realDonaldTrump

Right now, everybody is saying what a great job we are doing with Hurricane Florence – and they are 100% correct. But don't be fooled, at some point in the near future the Democrats will start ranting...
15,505 Retweets **71,470** Likes
8:50 AM - 18 Sep 2018

Donald J. Trump ✓
@realDonaldTrump

...that FEMA, our Military, and our First Responders, who are all unbelievable, are a disaster and not doing a good job. This will be a total lie, but that's what they do, and everybody knows it!
10,930 Retweets **51,785** Likes
8:50 AM - 18 Sep 2018

President Trumps Tweets 2018: A Historical Archive of President Trump's Tweets

Donald J. Trump @realDonaldTrump

Thank you to our great Coast Guard for doing such a tremendous job - thousands of lives being saved!
13,183 Retweets **62,420** Likes
8:59 AM - 18 Sep 2018

Donald J. Trump @realDonaldTrump

Today, I took action to strengthen our Nation's defenses against biological threats. For the first time in history, the Federal Government has a National Biodefense Strategy to address the FULL RANGE of biological threats!
18,033 Retweets **73,217** Likes
11:21 AM - 18 Sep 2018

Donald J. Trump @realDonaldTrump

Today, it was my great honor to welcome @prezydentpl Andrzej Duda of Poland to the @WhiteHouse!
9,979 Retweets **47,057** Likes
2:20 PM - 18 Sep 2018

Donald J. Trump @realDonaldTrump

The Supreme Court is one of the main reasons I got elected President. I hope Republican Voters, and others, are watching, and studying, the Democrats Playbook.
32,155 Retweets **118,509** Likes
8:45 PM - 18 Sep 2018

Donald J. Trump @realDonaldTrump

Kim Jong Un has agreed to allow Nuclear inspections, subject to final negotiations, and to permanently dismantle a test site and launch pad in the presence of international experts. In the meantime there will be no Rocket or Nuclear testing. Hero remains to continue being........
26,173 Retweets **102,073** Likes
9:04 PM - 18 Sep 2018

Donald J. Trump @realDonaldTrump

....returned home to the United States. Also, North and South Korea will file a joint bid to host the 2032 Olympics. Very exciting!
17,236 Retweets **77,048** Likes
9:11 PM - 18 Sep 2018

Donald J. Trump @realDonaldTrump

"The recovery got started on Election Day 2016. It took Trump's Tax Cuts and Regulation Cuts to get the economy booming. Before that it was the worst and slowest economic recovery since the Great Depression. It took just 6 months for Trump to get to 3%, even though they said.....
19,078 Retweets **78,493** Likes
4:34 AM - 19 Sep 2018

Donald J. Trump ✓
@realDonaldTrump

....it was impossible - and then already it's over 4%, and I expect it's going to grow faster and faster. We're just getting started here." Peter Ferrara, former advisor to President Reagan. @foxandfriends
14,930 Retweets **65,748** Likes
4:40 AM - 19 Sep 2018

Donald J. Trump ✓
@realDonaldTrump

"North Korea recommits to denuclearization - we've come a long way." @FoxNews
21,671 Retweets **100,372** Likes
4:43 AM - 19 Sep 2018

Donald J. Trump ✓
@realDonaldTrump

"President Donald J. Trump's Administration is Providing Support to Those Impacted by Hurricane Florence"
10,953 Retweets **48,799** Likes
10:49 AM - 19 Sep 2018

Donald J. Trump ✓
@realDonaldTrump

Just returned to the White House from the Great States of North Carolina and South Carolina where incredible work is being done on the ongoing fight against hurricane Florence. Tremendous talent and spirit!
15,963 Retweets **82,617** Likes
4:37 PM - 19 Sep 2018

Donald J. Trump ✓
@realDonaldTrump

Great new book by Jason Chaffetz appropriately called "The Deep State." Very interesting indeed!
19,179 Retweets **81,041** Likes
4:57 PM - 19 Sep 2018

Donald J. Trump ✓
@realDonaldTrump

Financial and jobs numbers are fantastic. There are plenty of new, high paying jobs available in our great and very vibrant economy. If you are not happy where you are, start looking - but also remember, our economy is only getting better. Vote in Midterms!
17,464 Retweets **70,699** Likes
4:05 AM - 20 Sep 2018

Donald J. Trump ✓
@realDonaldTrump

We protect the countries of the Middle East, they would not be safe for very long without us, and yet they continue to push for higher and higher oil prices! We will remember. The OPEC monopoly must get prices down now!
19,731 Retweets **81,211** Likes
4:13 AM - 20 Sep 2018

President Trumps Tweets 2018: A Historical Archive of President Trump's Tweets

Donald J. Trump
@realDonaldTrump

"We can't secure the Border because of the Democrats historic level of Obstruction. The Presidents fed up with this. His agenda is working. The economy is growing at twice the rate it did under Obama. We've nominated and confirmed 68 Federal Judges, 26 Court of Appeals Judges....
15,347 Retweets **60,642** Likes
4:32 AM - 20 Sep 2018

Donald J. Trump
@realDonaldTrump

....The thing that's lacking is we can't properly secure the Border because of the Democrats historic level of Obstruction." Senator David Perdue of Georgia.
13,003 Retweets **53,916** Likes
4:37 AM - 20 Sep 2018

Donald J. Trump
@realDonaldTrump

I want to know, where is the money for Border Security and the WALL in this ridiculous Spending Bill, and where will it come from after the Midterms? Dems are obstructing Law Enforcement and Border Security. REPUBLICANS MUST FINALLY GET TOUGH!
30,030 Retweets **114,699** Likes
4:43 AM - 20 Sep 2018

Donald J. Trump
@realDonaldTrump

S&P 500 HITS ALL-TIME HIGH Congratulations USA!
20,109 Retweets **89,709** Likes
6:34 AM - 20 Sep 2018

Donald J. Trump
@realDonaldTrump

.@JayWebberNJ is running for Congress in the 11th District of New Jersey. He is outstanding in every way. Strong on Borders, loves our Military and our Vets. Big Crime fighter. Jay has my Full and Total Endorsement!
11,353 Retweets **42,864** Likes
10:30 AM - 20 Sep 2018

Donald J. Trump
@realDonaldTrump

Congratulations to my good friend Prime Minister @AbeShinzo on his HUGE election victory in Japan. I'm looking forward to many more years of working together. See you in New York next week!
15,475 Retweets **69,312** Likes
10:39 AM - 20 Sep 2018

Donald J. Trump
@realDonaldTrump

Army Master Sgt. Charles H. McDaniel, 32, of Vernon, Indiana, and Army Pfc. William H. Jones, 19, of Nash County, North Carolina, are the first American remains from...
12,774 Retweets **54,911** Likes
11:10 AM - 20 Sep 2018

Anthony T. Michalisko

Donald J. Trump ✓
@realDonaldTrump

...North Korea to be identified as a result of my Summit with Chairman Kim. These HEROES are home, they may Rest In Peace, and hopefully their families can have closure.
11,191 Retweets **50,928** Likes
11:10 AM - 20 Sep 2018

Donald J. Trump ✓
@realDonaldTrump

On my way to Las Vegas, Nevada. Look forward to seeing everyone tonight! #MAGA
12,209 Retweets **55,746** Likes
2:54 PM - 20 Sep 2018

Donald J. Trump ✓
@realDonaldTrump

Landing in Las Vegas now for a Make America Great Again Rally supporting @DeanHeller and @DannyTarkanian. Also doing interview there with @seanhannity live on @FoxNews. Big crowd, long lines. Will be great! #MAGA
10,566 Retweets **52,840** Likes
6:27 PM - 20 Sep 2018

Donald J. Trump ✓
@realDonaldTrump

MAKE AMERICA GREAT AGAIN!
13,707 Retweets **53,188** Likes
8:29 PM - 20 Sep 2018

Donald J. Trump ✓
@realDonaldTrump

Thank you Las Vegas, Nevada - I love you! #MAGA
10,741 Retweets **48,792** Likes
8:33 PM - 20 Sep 2018

Donald J. Trump ✓
@realDonaldTrump

AMERICA IS WINNING AGAIN!
19,135 Retweets **79,047** Likes
9:05 PM - 20 Sep 2018

Donald J. Trump ✓
@realDonaldTrump

Judge Brett Kavanaugh is a fine man, with an impeccable reputation, who is under assault by radical left wing politicians who don't want to know the answers, they just want to destroy and delay. Facts don't matter. I go through this with them every single day in D.C.
29,293 Retweets **113,450** Likes
5:56 AM - 21 Sep 2018

Donald J. Trump ✓
@realDonaldTrump

I have no doubt that, if the attack on Dr. Ford was as bad as she says, charges would have been immediately filed with local Law Enforcement Authorities by either her or her loving parents. I ask that she bring those filings forward so that we can learn date, time, and place!
26,233 Retweets **110,748** Likes
6:14 AM - 21 Sep 2018

President Trumps Tweets 2018: A Historical Archive of President Trump's Tweets

Donald J. Trump ✓
@realDonaldTrump

I will Chair the United Nations Security Council meeting on Iran next week!
15,323 Retweets **68,800** Likes
6:23 AM - 21 Sep 2018

Donald J. Trump ✓
@realDonaldTrump

The radical left lawyers want the FBI to get involved NOW. Why didn't someone call the FBI 36 years ago?
16,855 Retweets **80,907** Likes
6:29 AM - 21 Sep 2018

Donald J. Trump ✓
@realDonaldTrump

I met with the DOJ concerning the declassification of various UNREDACTED documents. They agreed to release them but stated that so doing may have a perceived negative impact on the Russia probe. Also, key Allies' called to ask not to release. Therefore, the Inspector General.....
15,322 Retweets **56,908** Likes
7:35 AM - 21 Sep 2018

Donald J. Trump ✓
@realDonaldTrump

....has been asked to review these documents on an expedited basis. I believe he will move quickly on this (and hopefully other things which he is looking at). In the end I can always declassify if it proves necessary. Speed is very important to me - and everyone!
16,672 Retweets **67,483** Likes
7:41 AM - 21 Sep 2018

Donald J. Trump ✓
@realDonaldTrump

Senator Feinstein and the Democrats held the letter for months, only to release it with a bang after the hearings were OVER - done very purposefully to Obstruct & Resist & Delay. Let her testify, or not, and TAKE THE VOTE!
26,673 Retweets **92,136** Likes
8:29 AM - 21 Sep 2018

Donald J. Trump ✓
@realDonaldTrump

Throughout American history, the men and women of our Armed Forces have selflessly served our Country, making tremendous sacrifices to defend our liberty. On National POW/MIA Recognition Day, we honor all American Prisoners of War
10,889 Retweets **43,762** Likes
10:22 AM - 21 Sep 2018

Donald J. Trump ✓
@realDonaldTrump

Promises Kept for our GREAT Veterans!
11,049 Retweets **45,782** Likes
1:11 PM - 21 Sep 2018

Donald J. Trump ✓
@realDonaldTrump

Remarks by President Trump at the Signing of H.R. 5895
7,746 Retweets **34,706** Likes
2:44 PM - 21 Sep 2018

Anthony T. Michalisko

Donald J. Trump ✓
@realDonaldTrump

Thank you Missouri - I love you!
14,393 Retweets **59,518** Likes
6:05 PM - 21 Sep 2018

Donald J. Trump ✓
@realDonaldTrump

Thank you Missouri - Together, we are MAKING AMERICA GREAT AGAIN!
12,672 Retweets **56,090** Likes
6:31 PM - 21 Sep 2018

Donald J. Trump ✓
@realDonaldTrump

GOD BLESS THE U.S.A.!
24,515 Retweets **100,914** Likes
8:20 PM - 21 Sep 2018

Donald J. Trump ✓
@realDonaldTrump

New Economic Records being set on a daily basis - and it is not by accident!
21,836 Retweets **102,801** Likes
7:01 AM - 22 Sep 2018

Donald J. Trump ✓
@realDonaldTrump

Tiger is playing great. Looks like a big win could happen. Very exciting! @TigerWoods
16,111 Retweets **104,389** Likes
1:43 PM - 23 Sep 2018

Donald J. Trump ✓
@realDonaldTrump

Going to New York. Will be with Prime Minister Abe of Japan tonight, talking Military and Trade. We have done much to help Japan, would like to see more of a reciprocal relationship. It will all work out!
18,173 Retweets **90,886** Likes
1:52 PM - 23 Sep 2018

Donald J. Trump ✓
@realDonaldTrump

Prime Minster @AbeShinzo is coming up to Trump Tower for dinner but, most importantly, he just had a great landslide victory in Japan. I will congratulate him on behalf of the American people!
18,058 Retweets **89,591** Likes
3:48 PM - 23 Sep 2018

Donald J. Trump ✓
@realDonaldTrump

"Remarks by President Trump at 'Global Call to Action on the World Drug Problem' Event" #UNGA
8,216 Retweets **36,554** Likes
7:17 AM - 24 Sep 2018

Donald J. Trump ✓
@realDonaldTrump

Today, we commit to fighting the drug epidemic together! #UNGA
12,692 Retweets **57,775** Likes
9:55 AM - 24 Sep 2018

President Trumps Tweets 2018: A Historical Archive of President Trump's Tweets

Donald J. Trump ✓
@realDonaldTrump

It was my great honor to welcome and meet with President @moonriver365 Jae-in of South Korea today, in New York City!
8,886 Retweets **36,804** Likes
1:42 PM - 24 Sep 2018

Donald J. Trump ✓
@realDonaldTrump

US-Korea Free Trade Agreement Signing Ceremony!
13,808 Retweets **54,088** Likes
1:44 PM - 24 Sep 2018

Donald J. Trump ✓
@realDonaldTrump

Brett Kavanaugh and his wife, Ashley, will be interviewed tonight at 7pmE on @marthamaccallum @FoxNews. This is an outstanding family who must be treated fairly!
19,121 Retweets **87,097** Likes
2:33 PM - 24 Sep 2018

Donald J. Trump ✓
@realDonaldTrump

Joint Statement on the United States-Korea Free Trade Agreement
8,696 Retweets **37,843** Likes
2:46 PM - 24 Sep 2018

Donald J. Trump ✓
@realDonaldTrump

It was my great honor to welcome President @AlsisiOfficial of Egypt to the United States this afternoon, in New York City. Great meetings! #UNGA
7,857 Retweets **36,903** Likes
3:33 PM - 24 Sep 2018

Donald J. Trump ✓
@realDonaldTrump

It was my great honor to welcome President @EmmanuelMacron of France to the United States, here in New York City, this evening! #UNGA
7,707 Retweets **39,362** Likes
4:41 PM - 24 Sep 2018

Donald J. Trump ✓
@realDonaldTrump

REMEMBER THE MIDTERMS!
30,149 Retweets **109,226** Likes
7:38 PM - 24 Sep 2018

Donald J. Trump ✓
@realDonaldTrump

The Democrats are working hard to destroy a wonderful man, and a man who has the potential to be one of our greatest Supreme Court Justices ever, with an array of False Accusations the likes of which have never been seen before!
30,357 Retweets **115,208** Likes
7:50 PM - 24 Sep 2018

 Donald J. Trump ✓
@realDonaldTrump

Republican Party Favorability is the highest it has been in 7 years - 3 points higher than Democrats! Gallup
16,947 Retweets **77,478** Likes
3:41 AM - 25 Sep 2018

 Donald J. Trump ✓
@realDonaldTrump

Despite requests, I have no plans to meet Iranian President Hassan Rouhani. Maybe someday in the future. I am sure he is an absolutely lovely man!
15,473 Retweets **80,931** Likes
3:53 AM - 25 Sep 2018

  ✓
@realDonaldTrump

Will be speaking at the United Nations this morning. Our country is much stronger and much richer than it was when I took office less than two years ago. We are also MUCH safer!
16,066 Retweets **85,962** Likes
6:14 AM - 25 Sep 2018

 Donald J. Trump ✓
@realDonaldTrump

Thank you Mark!
15,597 Retweets **71,995** Likes
9:36 AM - 25 Sep 2018

 Donald J. Trump ✓
@realDonaldTrump

Thank you Dr. Jeffress!
14,219 Retweets **58,273** Likes
9:37 AM - 25 Sep 2018

 Donald J. Trump ✓
@realDonaldTrump

Rush Limbaugh to Republicans: "You can kiss the MIDTERMS goodbye if you don't get highly qualified Kavanaugh approved."
27,013 Retweets **96,699** Likes
9:45 AM - 25 Sep 2018

 Donald J. Trump ✓
@realDonaldTrump

"Remarks by President Trump to the 73rd Session of the United Nations General Assembly"
9,625 Retweets **41,125** Likes
10:19 AM - 25 Sep 2018

Donald J. Trump ✓
@realDonaldTrump

"Remarks by President Trump at a Luncheon Hosted by the Secretary-General of the United Nations"
9,802 Retweets **41,744** Likes
12:28 PM - 25 Sep 2018

Donald J. Trump ✓
@realDonaldTrump

"Consumer confidence rose in September, notching its highest level in about 18 years. The Consumer Board's index rose to 138.4 this month from 134.7 in August..."
13,445 Retweets **55,504** Likes
1:27 PM - 25 Sep 2018

President Trumps Tweets 2018: A Historical Archive of President Trump's Tweets

Donald J. Trump ✓
@realDonaldTrump

73rd Session of the United Nations General Assembly #UNGA
12,380 Retweets **53,232** Likes
3:06 PM - 25 Sep 2018

Donald J. Trump ✓
@realDonaldTrump

"These law enforcement people took the law into their own hands when it came to President Trump." @LindseyGrahamSC
13,461 Retweets **57,179** Likes
7:38 PM - 25 Sep 2018

Donald J. Trump ✓
@realDonaldTrump

The Democrats are playing a high level CON GAME in their vicious effort to destroy a fine person. It is called the politics of destruction. Behind the scene the Dems are laughing. Pray for Brett Kavanaugh and his family!
34,761 Retweets **127,414** Likes
7:55 PM - 25 Sep 2018

Donald J. Trump ✓
@realDonaldTrump

Consumer confidence hits an 18 year high, close to breaking the all-time record. A big jump from last 8 years. People are excited about the USA again! We are getting Bigger and Richer and Stronger. WAY MORE TO GO!
20,532 Retweets **92,071** Likes
3:54 AM - 26 Sep 2018

Donald J. Trump ✓
@realDonaldTrump

Jobless Claims fell to their lowest level in 49 years!
20,615 Retweets **96,037** Likes
3:57 AM - 26 Sep 2018

Donald J. Trump ✓
@realDonaldTrump

Avenatti is a third rate lawyer who is good at making false accusations, like he did on me and like he is now doing on Judge Brett Kavanaugh. He is just looking for attention and doesn't want people to look at his past record and relationships - a total low-life!
34,814 Retweets **138,700** Likes
9:47 AM - 26 Sep 2018

Donald J. Trump ✓
@realDonaldTrump

China is actually placing propaganda ads in the Des Moines Register and other papers, made to look like news. That's because we are beating them on Trade, opening markets, and the farmers will make a fortune when this is over!
19,303 Retweets **59,948** Likes
10:26 AM - 26 Sep 2018

Donald J. Trump ✓
@realDonaldTrump

Congressman Lee Zeldin is doing a fantastic job in D.C. Tough and smart, he loves our Country and will always be there to do the right thing. He has my Complete and Total Endorsement!
15,009 Retweets **66,506** Likes
10:34 AM - 26 Sep 2018

Donald J. Trump ✓
@realDonaldTrump

Join me this Saturday in Wheeling, West Virginia at 7pmE!
14,398 Retweets **54,364** Likes
1:48 PM - 26 Sep 2018

Donald J. Trump ✓
@realDonaldTrump

Judge Kavanaugh showed America exactly why I nominated him. His testimony was powerful, honest, and riveting. Democrats' search and destroy strategy is disgraceful and this process has been a total sham and effort to delay, obstruct, and resist. The Senate must vote!
84,180 Retweets **320,104** Likes
3:46 PM - 27 Sep 2018

Donald J. Trump ✓
@realDonaldTrump

Just started, tonight, our 7th FBI investigation of Judge Brett Kavanaugh. He will someday be recognized as a truly great Justice of The United States Supreme Court!
40,636 Retweets **177,927** Likes
5:27 PM - 28 Sep 2018

Donald J. Trump ✓
@realDonaldTrump

Senator Richard Blumenthal must talk about his fraudulent service in Vietnam, where for 12 years he told the people of Connecticut, as their Attorney General, that he was a great Marine War Hero. Talked about his many battles of near death, but was never in Vietnam. Total Phony!
46,252 Retweets **142,169** Likes
1:33 PM - 29 Sep 2018

Donald J. Trump ✓
@realDonaldTrump

Heading to West Virginia now. Big Rally. Will be live on @FoxNews tonight. Long lines, but will be great!
13,470 Retweets **74,598** Likes
1:36 PM - 29 Sep 2018

Donald J. Trump ✓
@realDonaldTrump

Thank you West Virginia - I love you!
17,544 Retweets **83,974** Likes
5:52 PM - 29 Sep 2018

Donald J. Trump ✓
@realDonaldTrump

NBC News incorrectly reported (as usual) that I was limiting the FBI investigation of Judge Kavanaugh, and witnesses, only to certain people. Actually, I want them to interview whoever they deem appropriate, at their discretion. Please correct your reporting!
45,075 Retweets **159,356** Likes
7:49 PM - 29 Sep 2018

Donald J. Trump ✓
@realDonaldTrump

Like many, I don't watch Saturday Night Live (even though I past hosted it) - no longer funny, no talent or charm. It is just a political ad for the Dems. Word is that Kanye West, who put on a MAGA hat after the show (despite being told "no"), was great. He's leading the charge!
46,040 Retweets **221,791** Likes
9:57 AM - 30 Sep 2018

President Trumps Tweets 2018: A Historical Archive of President Trump's Tweets

Donald J. Trump ✓
@realDonaldTrump

So if African-American unemployment is now at the lowest number in history, median income the highest, and you then add all of the other things I have done, how do Democrats, who have done NOTHING for African-Americans but TALK, win the Black Vote? And it will only get better!
34,181 Retweets **136,934** Likes
10:47 AM - 30 Sep 2018

Donald J. Trump ✓
@realDonaldTrump

Wow! Just starting to hear the Democrats, who are only thinking Obstruct and Delay, are starting to put out the word that the "time" and "scope" of FBI looking into Judge Kavanaugh and witnesses is not enough. Hello! For them, it will never be enough - stay tuned and watch!
37,794 Retweets **141,208** Likes
11:56 AM - 30 Sep 2018

Donald J. Trump ✓
@realDonaldTrump

Late last night, our deadline, we reached a wonderful new Trade Deal with Canada, to be added into the deal already reached with Mexico. The new name will be The United States Mexico Canada Agreement, or USMCA. It is a great deal for all three countries, solves the many......
28,659 Retweets **128,871** Likes
3:30 AM - 1 Oct 2018

Donald J. Trump ✓
@realDonaldTrump

....deficiencies and mistakes in NAFTA, greatly opens markets to our Farmers and Manufacturers, reduces Trade Barriers to the U.S. and will bring all three Great Nations together in competition with the rest of the world. The USMCA is a historic transaction!
18,158 Retweets **79,307** Likes
3:53 AM - 1 Oct 2018

Donald J. Trump ✓
@realDonaldTrump

Congratulations to Mexico and Canada!
19,069 Retweets **103,661** Likes
3:56 AM - 1 Oct 2018

Donald J. Trump ✓
@realDonaldTrump

News conference on the USMCA this morning at 11:00 - Rose Garden of White House.
12,285 Retweets **64,636** Likes
5:08 AM - 1 Oct 2018

Donald J. Trump ✓
@realDonaldTrump

Thank you Tennessee - I love you!
15,901 Retweets **73,602** Likes
5:37 PM - 1 Oct 2018

Donald J. Trump ✓
@realDonaldTrump

WOW - THANK YOU TENNESSEE!
27,116 Retweets **115,528** Likes
5:50 PM - 1 Oct 2018

Donald J. Trump ✓
@realDonaldTrump

Happy 7th birthday to Tristan, a very special member of the Trump family!
11,979 Retweets **85,333** Likes
7:52 AM - 2 Oct 2018

Donald J. Trump ✓
@realDonaldTrump

Great reviews on the new USMCA. Thank you! Mexico and Canada will be wonderful partners in Trade (and more) long into the future.
15,267 Retweets **74,222** Likes
8:02 AM - 2 Oct 2018

Donald J. Trump ✓
@realDonaldTrump

THE ONLY REASON TO VOTE FOR A DEMOCRAT IS IF YOU'RE TIRED OF WINNING!
45,533 Retweets **169,591** Likes
9:08 AM - 2 Oct 2018

Donald J. Trump ✓
@realDonaldTrump

Yesterday, it was my great honor to present the Medal of Honor to Ronald J. Shurer II, for his actions on April 6, 2008, when he braved enemy fire to treat multiple injured Soldiers. Read more
12,195 Retweets **56,312** Likes
9:18 AM - 2 Oct 2018

Donald J. Trump ✓
@realDonaldTrump

Proud of our great First Lady - and she loves doing this!
18,653 Retweets **90,565** Likes
10:22 AM - 2 Oct 2018

Donald J. Trump ✓
@realDonaldTrump

"USMCA Wins Praise as a Victory for American Industries and Workers"
9,715 Retweets **43,190** Likes
11:18 AM - 2 Oct 2018

Donald J. Trump ✓
@realDonaldTrump

This is really an incredible time for our Nation - WE are RESPECTED AGAIN!
15,582 Retweets **69,554** Likes
2:20 PM - 2 Oct 2018

Donald J. Trump ✓
@realDonaldTrump

Thank you Mississippi - I love you!
11,406 Retweets **51,334** Likes
6:18 PM - 2 Oct 2018

Donald J. Trump ✓
@realDonaldTrump

GOD BLESS THE U.S.A.! #MAGA
21,274 Retweets **84,510** Likes
6:25 PM - 2 Oct 2018

President Trumps Tweets 2018: A Historical Archive of President Trump's Tweets

 Donald J. Trump ✓
@realDonaldTrump

"National wage growth is at the highest it's been in nearly 17 months -- and, according to a new study released by Glassdoor, it's not expected to slow down anytime soon...."
12,636 Retweets **52,131** Likes
7:15 PM - 2 Oct 2018

 Donald J. Trump ✓
@realDonaldTrump

Today, my Administration provided HISTORIC levels of funding to improve school safety through STOP School Violence grants – a top priority for @sandyhook. I am committed to keeping our children SAFE in their schools!
17,730 Retweets **76,326** Likes
7:18 PM - 2 Oct 2018

 Donald J. Trump ✓
@realDonaldTrump

Thank you Mississippi - Together, we are MAKING AMERICA GREAT AGAIN!
11,026 Retweets **51,047** Likes
7:58 PM - 2 Oct 2018

 Donald J. Trump ✓
@realDonaldTrump

Congressman @PeteSessions of Texas is a true fighter and patriot. Highly respected in D.C. by all, he always gets what his district, and our country, wants and needs. Strong on Crime, Border, Military, Vets and 2nd Amendment. Pete has my Full and Total Endorsement. A great guy!
12,374 Retweets **53,036** Likes
5:35 AM - 3 Oct 2018

 Donald J. Trump ✓
@realDonaldTrump

The Failing New York Times did something I have never seen done before. They used the concept of "time value of money" in doing a very old, boring and often told hit piece on me. Added up, this means that 97% of their stories on me are bad. Never recovered from bad election call!
18,236 Retweets **81,741** Likes
5:53 AM - 3 Oct 2018

 Donald J. Trump ✓
@realDonaldTrump

The Stock Market just reached an All-Time High during my Administration for the 102nd Time, a presidential record, by far, for less than two years. So much potential as Trade and Military Deals are completed.
20,538 Retweets **91,906** Likes
6:04 AM - 3 Oct 2018

 **Donald J. Trump** ✓
@realDonaldTrump

Thank you Governor Phil Bryant - it was my great honor to be there! #MAGA
9,832 Retweets **47,201** Likes
6:23 AM - 3 Oct 2018

Donald J. Trump ✓
@realDonaldTrump

Thank you to Congressman Tom Reed of New York for your wonderful comments on our great new Trade Deal with Mexico and Canada, the USMCA. I have long ago given you my Full Endorsement, and for good reason. Keep up the Great Work! @Varneyco
9,885 Retweets **47,553** Likes
7:02 AM - 3 Oct 2018

Donald J. Trump ✓
@realDonaldTrump

Blowout numbers on New Jobs and, separately, Services. Market up!
13,208 Retweets **62,615** Likes
7:05 AM - 3 Oct 2018

Donald J. Trump ✓
@realDonaldTrump

Mexico, Canada and the United States are a great partnership and will be a very formidable trading force. We will now, because of the USMCA, work very well together. Great Spirit!
14,469 Retweets **69,609** Likes
7:13 AM - 3 Oct 2018

Donald J. Trump ✓
@realDonaldTrump

I see it each time I go out to Rallies in order to help some of our great Republican candidates. VOTERS ARE REALLY ANGRY AT THE VICIOUS AND DESPICABLE WAY DEMOCRATS ARE TREATING BRETT KAVANAUGH! He and his wonderful family deserve much better.
26,592 Retweets **103,846** Likes
7:29 AM - 3 Oct 2018

Donald J. Trump ✓
@realDonaldTrump

Just spoke to President-Elect Andres Manuel Lopez Obrador of Mexico. Great call, we will work well together!
14,191 Retweets **70,909** Likes
7:35 AM - 3 Oct 2018

Donald J. Trump ✓
@realDonaldTrump

My thoughts and prayers are with the Florence County Sheriff's Office and the Florence Police Department tonight, in South Carolina. We are forever grateful for what our Law Enforcement Officers do 24/7/365.
20,749 Retweets **85,256** Likes
5:01 PM - 3 Oct 2018

Donald J. Trump ✓
@realDonaldTrump

Wow, such enthusiasm and energy for Judge Brett Kavanaugh. Look at the Energy, look at the Polls. Something very big is happening. He is a fine man and great intellect. The country is with him all the way!
37,889 Retweets **157,867** Likes
7:23 PM - 3 Oct 2018

Donald J. Trump ✓
@realDonaldTrump

The harsh and unfair treatment of Judge Brett Kavanaugh is having an incredible upward impact on voters. The PEOPLE get it far better than the politicians. Most importantly, this great life cannot be ruined by mean & despicable Democrats and totally uncorroborated allegations!
34,356 Retweets **139,389** Likes
5:16 AM - 4 Oct 2018

President Trumps Tweets 2018: A Historical Archive of President Trump's Tweets

Donald J. Trump ✓
@realDonaldTrump

Our country's great First Lady, Melania, is doing really well in Africa. The people love her, and she loves them! It is a beautiful thing to see.
23,172 Retweets **134,529** Likes
6:34 AM - 4 Oct 2018

Donald J. Trump ✓
@realDonaldTrump

This is a very important time in our country. Due Process, Fairness and Common Sense are now on trial!
28,178 Retweets **115,007** Likes
6:54 AM - 4 Oct 2018

Donald J. Trump ✓
@realDonaldTrump

This is now the 7th. time the FBI has investigated Judge Kavanaugh. If we made it 100, it would still not be good enough for the Obstructionist Democrats.
30,705 Retweets **122,924** Likes
7:17 AM - 4 Oct 2018

Donald J. Trump ✓
@realDonaldTrump

Working hard, thank you!
21,889 Retweets **95,626** Likes
10:38 AM - 4 Oct 2018

Donald J. Trump ✓
@realDonaldTrump

Statement on National Strategy for Counterterrorism
10,910 Retweets **40,060** Likes
12:17 PM - 4 Oct 2018

Donald J. Trump ✓
@realDonaldTrump

"U.S. Stocks Widen Global Lead"
12,858 Retweets **52,687** Likes
12:29 PM - 4 Oct 2018

Donald J. Trump ✓
@realDonaldTrump

Congressman Bishop is doing a GREAT job! He helped pass tax reform which lowered taxes for EVERYONE! Nancy Pelosi is spending hundreds of thousands of dollars on his opponent because they both support a liberal agenda of higher taxes and wasteful spending!
17,129 Retweets **70,888** Likes
3:17 PM - 4 Oct 2018

Donald J. Trump ✓
@realDonaldTrump

Just made my second stop in Minnesota for a MAKE AMERICA GREAT AGAIN rally. We need to elect @KarinHousley to the U.S. Senate, and we need the strong leadership of @TomEmmer, @Jason2CD, @JimHagedornMN and @PeteStauber in the U.S. House!
14,343 Retweets **60,313** Likes
3:58 PM - 4 Oct 2018

Donald J. Trump ✓
@realDonaldTrump

Thank you Minnesota - I love you!
17,899 Retweets **82,812** Likes
5:52 PM - 4 Oct 2018

Donald J. Trump ✓
@realDonaldTrump

Beautiful evening in Rochester, Minnesota. VOTE, VOTE, VOTE!
15,500 Retweets **70,217** Likes
6:03 PM - 4 Oct 2018

Donald J. Trump ✓
@realDonaldTrump

The very rude elevator screamers are paid professionals only looking to make Senators look bad. Don't fall for it! Also, look at all of the professionally made identical signs. Paid for by Soros and others. These are not signs made in the basement from love! #Troublemakers
53,468 Retweets **179,025** Likes
6:03 AM - 5 Oct 2018

Donald J. Trump ✓
@realDonaldTrump

Just out: 3.7% Unemployment is the lowest number since 1969!
37,512 Retweets **159,724** Likes
6:06 AM - 5 Oct 2018

Donald J. Trump ✓
@realDonaldTrump

Very proud of the U.S. Senate for voting "YES" to advance the nomination of Judge Brett Kavanaugh!
40,450 Retweets **199,902** Likes
7:59 AM - 5 Oct 2018

Donald J. Trump ✓
@realDonaldTrump

Women for Kavanaugh, and many others who support this very good man, are gathering all over Capitol Hill in preparation for a 3-5 P.M. VOTE. It is a beautiful thing to see - and they are not paid professional protesters who are handed expensive signs. Big day for America!
29,482 Retweets **132,372** Likes
9:08 AM - 6 Oct 2018

Donald J. Trump ✓
@realDonaldTrump

I have asked Steve Daines, our great Republican Senator from Montana, to attend his daughter Annie's wedding rather than coming to today's vote. Steve was ready to do whatever he had to, but we had the necessary number. To the Daines Family, congratulations-have a wonderful day!
28,008 Retweets **156,497** Likes
1:06 PM - 6 Oct 2018

Donald J. Trump ✓
@realDonaldTrump

I applaud and congratulate the U.S. Senate for confirming our GREAT NOMINEE, Judge Brett Kavanaugh, to the United States Supreme Court. Later today, I will sign his Commission of Appointment, and he will be officially sworn in. Very exciting!
62,475 Retweets **262,765** Likes
1:15 PM - 6 Oct 2018

President Trumps Tweets 2018: A Historical Archive of President Trump's Tweets

Donald J. Trump ✓
@realDonaldTrump

The crowd in front of the U.S. Supreme Court is tiny, looks like about 200 people (& most are onlookers) - that wouldn't even fill the first couple of rows of our Kansas Rally, or any of our Rallies for that matter! The Fake News Media tries to make it look sooo big, & it's not!
37,880 Retweets **162,935** Likes
2:57 PM - 6 Oct 2018

Donald J. Trump ✓
@realDonaldTrump

Thank you Kansas - I love you!
15,474 Retweets **73,059** Likes
5:49 PM - 6 Oct 2018

Donald J. Trump ✓
@realDonaldTrump

Beautiful evening in Topeka, Kansas. VOTE, VOTE, VOTE! #MAGA
15,263 Retweets **69,247** Likes
6:15 PM - 6 Oct 2018

Donald J. Trump ✓
@realDonaldTrump

You don't hand matches to an arsonist, and you don't give power to an angry left-wing mob. Democrats have become too EXTREME and TOO DANGEROUS to govern. Republicans believe in the rule of law - not the rule of the mob. VOTE REPUBLICAN!
67746 Retweets **228025** Likes
6:21 PM - 6 Oct 2018

Donald J. Trump ✓
@realDonaldTrump

.@SecPompeo had a good meeting with Chairman Kim today in Pyongyang. Progress made on Singapore Summit Agreements! I look forward to seeing Chairman Kim again, in the near future.
19,807 Retweets **87,311** Likes
7:42 AM - 7 Oct 2018

Donald J. Trump ✓
@realDonaldTrump

Christopher Columbus's spirit of determination & adventure has provided inspiration to generations of Americans. On #ColumbusDay, we honor his remarkable accomplishments as a navigator, & celebrate his voyage into the unknown expanse of the Atlantic Ocean.
19,213 Retweets **76,200** Likes
6:36 AM - 8 Oct 2018

Donald J. Trump ✓
@realDonaldTrump

Departing Washington, D.C. for the International Association of Chiefs of Police Annual Convention in Orlando, Florida. Look forward to seeing everyone soon! #IACP2018
8,270 Retweets **43,063** Likes
8:31 AM - 8 Oct 2018

Donald J. Trump ✓
@realDonaldTrump

It was my great honor to address the International Association of Chiefs of Police Annual Convention in Orlando, Florida. Thank you! #IACP2018 #LESM
9,518 Retweets **44,503** Likes
11:32 AM - 8 Oct 2018

Donald J. Trump ✓
@realDonaldTrump

America's police officers have earned the everlasting gratitude of our Nation. In moments of danger & despair you are the reason we never lose hope – because there are men & women in uniform who face down evil & stand for all that is GOOD and JUST and DECENT and RIGHT! #IACP2018
16,053 Retweets **70,979** Likes
11:57 AM - 8 Oct 2018

Donald J. Trump ✓
@realDonaldTrump

We thank you. We salute you. We honor you. And we promise you: we will ALWAYS have your BACK – now and FOREVER! #IACP2018
15,246 Retweets **66,208** Likes
12:27 PM - 8 Oct 2018

Donald J. Trump ✓
@realDonaldTrump

Every day, our police officers race into darkened allies, deserted streets, & onto the doorsteps of the most hardened criminals. They see the worst of humanity & they respond with the best of the American Spirit. America's LEOs have earned the everlasting gratitude of our Nation!
15,026 Retweets **61,252** Likes
12:37 PM - 8 Oct 2018

Donald J. Trump ✓
@realDonaldTrump

Great to see @AGPamBondi launch a cutting-edge statewide school safety APP in Florida today - named by Parkland Survivors. BIG PRIORITY and Florida is getting it done! #FortifyFL
11,014 Retweets **48,534** Likes
12:44 PM - 8 Oct 2018

Donald J. Trump ✓
@realDonaldTrump

The paid D.C. protesters are now ready to REALLY protest because they haven't gotten their checks - in other words, they weren't paid! Screamers in Congress, and outside, were far too obvious - less professional than anticipated by those paying (or not paying) the bills!
25,502 Retweets **94,224** Likes
5:32 AM - 9 Oct 2018

Donald J. Trump ✓
@realDonaldTrump

Great evening last night at the White House honoring Justice Kavanaugh and family. Our country is very proud of them!
15,959 Retweets **89,845** Likes
5:37 AM - 9 Oct 2018

Donald J. Trump ✓
@realDonaldTrump

Will be going to Iowa tonight for Rally, and more! The Farmers (and all) are very happy with USMCA!
11,636 Retweets **55,642** Likes
6:10 AM - 9 Oct 2018

Donald J. Trump ✓
@realDonaldTrump

Big announcement with my friend Ambassador Nikki Haley in the Oval Office at 10:30am.
13,417 Retweets **66,424** Likes
7:18 AM - 9 Oct 2018

President Trumps Tweets 2018: A Historical Archive of President Trump's Tweets

Donald J. Trump ●
@realDonaldTrump

Hurricane on its way to the Florida Pan Handle with major elements arriving tomorrow. Could also hit, in later stage, parts of Georgia, and unfortunately North Carolina, and South Carolina, again...
8,742 Retweets **37,931** Likes
9:00 AM - 9 Oct 2018

Donald J. Trump ●
@realDonaldTrump

...Looks to be a Cat. 3 which is even more intense than Florence. Good news is, the folks in the Pan Handle can take care of anything. @FEMA and First Responders are ready - be prepared! #HurricaneMichael
5,960 Retweets **28,349** Likes
9:00 AM - 9 Oct 2018

Donald J. Trump ●
@realDonaldTrump

FLORIDA - It is imperative that you heed the directions of your State and Local Officials. Please be prepared, be careful and be SAFE! #HurricaneMichael
11,483 Retweets **45,318** Likes
9:07 AM - 9 Oct 2018

Donald J. Trump ●
@realDonaldTrump

REGISTER TO VOTE!
17,992 Retweets **48,430** Likes
9:36 AM - 9 Oct 2018

Donald J. Trump ●
@realDonaldTrump

"President Donald J. Trump Approves Florida Emergency Declaration"
7,724 Retweets **34,804** Likes
12:08 PM - 9 Oct 2018

Donald J. Trump ●
@realDonaldTrump

.@FLGovScott has been relentless in securing the funding to fix the algae problem from Lake Okeechobee - we will solve this! Congress must follow through on the Government's plan on the Everglades Reservoir. Bill Nelson has been no help!
14,657 Retweets **57,361** Likes
2:39 PM - 9 Oct 2018

Donald J. Trump ●
@realDonaldTrump

Beautiful evening in Iowa. GOD BLESS THE U.S.A.! #MAGA
18,514 Retweets **78,472** Likes
6:09 PM - 9 Oct 2018

Donald J. Trump ●
@realDonaldTrump

THANK YOU IOWA & NEBRASKA! VOTE, VOTE, VOTE!
13,172 Retweets **54,312** Likes
6:23 PM - 9 Oct 2018

Anthony T. Michalisko

Donald J. Trump ✓
@realDonaldTrump

Walker Stapleton is running as the highly respected Republican Candidate for Governor of the Great State of Colorado. His credentials and talents are impeccable. He has my complete and total Endorsement!
14,545 Retweets **57,022** Likes
5:47 AM - 10 Oct 2018

Donald J. Trump ✓
@realDonaldTrump

Despite so many positive events and victories, Media Reseach Center reports that 92% of stories on Donald Trump are negative on ABC, CBS and ABC. It is FAKE NEWS! Don't worry, the Failing New York Times didn't even put the Brett Kavanaugh victory on the Front Page yesterday-A17!
25,499 Retweets **93,308** Likes
6:01 AM - 10 Oct 2018

Donald J. Trump ✓
@realDonaldTrump

We are with you Florida!
12,172 Retweets **53,793** Likes
9:05 AM - 10 Oct 2018

Donald J. Trump ✓
@realDonaldTrump

Departing the @WhiteHouse for Erie, Pennsylvania. I cannot disappoint the thousands of people that are there - and the thousands that are going. I look forward to seeing everyone this evening.
14,890 Retweets **80,036** Likes
12:52 PM - 10 Oct 2018

Donald J. Trump ✓
@realDonaldTrump

Couldn't let these great people down. They have been lined up since last night - see you soon Pennsylvania!
11,788 Retweets **53,981** Likes
2:01 PM - 10 Oct 2018

Donald J. Trump ✓
@realDonaldTrump

Thank you Erie, Pennsylvania! Remember to get out and VOTE! #MAGA
11,285 Retweets **46,233** Likes
5:52 PM - 10 Oct 2018

Donald J. Trump ✓
@realDonaldTrump

Massive overflow crowd tonight in Erie, Pennsylvania. THANK YOU to everyone who came out and joined us. Together, we are MAKING AMERICA GREAT AGAIN!
23,802 Retweets **92,539** Likes
6:00 PM - 10 Oct 2018

Donald J. Trump ✓
@realDonaldTrump

Thank you Jacksonville Sheriff's Office! #HurricaneMichael
10,402 Retweets **47,413** Likes
6:33 PM - 10 Oct 2018

President Trumps Tweets 2018: A Historical Archive of President Trump's Tweets

Donald J. Trump ✓
@realDonaldTrump

Thank you to @FEMA and all First Responders! #HurricaneMichael
9,842 Retweets **48,376** Likes
6:35 PM - 10 Oct 2018

Donald J. Trump ✓
@realDonaldTrump

Florida Highway Patrol Troopers are all en route to the Panhandle, from all across the state of Florida - to help those affected by #HurricaneMichael. If you see them, be sure to shake their hands and say THANK YOU! #LESM
18,518 Retweets **83,413** Likes
8:44 PM - 10 Oct 2018

Donald J. Trump ✓
@realDonaldTrump

Working very hard on Pastor Brunson!
12,514 Retweets **68,058** Likes
6:42 AM - 12 Oct 2018

Donald J. Trump ✓
@realDonaldTrump

So nice, everyone wants Ivanka Trump to be the new United Nations Ambassador. She would be incredible, but I can already hear the chants of Nepotism! We have great people that want the job.
14,131 Retweets **76,446** Likes
6:54 AM - 12 Oct 2018

Donald J. Trump ✓
@realDonaldTrump

My thoughts and prayers are with Pastor Brunson, and we hope to have him safely back home soon!
13,840 Retweets **77,930** Likes
6:59 AM - 12 Oct 2018

Donald J. Trump ✓
@realDonaldTrump

PASTOR BRUNSON JUST RELEASED. WILL BE HOME SOON!
27,625 Retweets **125,672** Likes
7:26 AM - 12 Oct 2018

Donald J. Trump ✓
@realDonaldTrump

REGISTER TO VOTE!
13,815 Retweets **43,308** Likes
8:57 AM - 12 Oct 2018

Donald J. Trump ✓
@realDonaldTrump

PROMISES MADE, PROMISES KEPT!
18,566 Retweets **60,597** Likes
9:43 AM - 12 Oct 2018

Donald J. Trump ✓
@realDonaldTrump

People have no idea how hard Hurricane Michael has hit the great state of Georgia. I will be visiting both Florida and Georgia early next week. We are working very hard on every area and every state that was hit - we are with you!
16,976 Retweets **82,790** Likes
11:09 AM - 12 Oct 2018

Donald J. Trump ✓
@realDonaldTrump

Don't miss our GREAT @FLOTUS, Melania, on @ABC @ABC2020 tonight at 10pmE. Enjoy!
11,251 Retweets **57,063** Likes
12:10 PM - 12 Oct 2018

Donald J. Trump ✓
@realDonaldTrump

Happy #NationalFarmersDay! With the recent #USMCA our GREAT FARMERS will do better than ever before!!
8,398 Retweets **38,336** Likes
12:37 PM - 12 Oct 2018

Donald J. Trump ✓
@realDonaldTrump

The GREAT football (and lacrosse) player, Jim Brown outside the West Wing of the @WhiteHouse. He is also a tremendous man and mentor to many young people!
21,564 Retweets **87,883** Likes
3:14 PM - 12 Oct 2018

Donald J. Trump ✓
@realDonaldTrump

Beautiful MAKE AMERICA GREAT AGAIN rally in Lebanon, Ohio. Thank you! #ICYMI
10,638 Retweets **48,028** Likes
5:30 PM - 12 Oct 2018

Donald J. Trump ✓
@realDonaldTrump

Happy 243rd Birthday to our GREAT @USNavy! #243NavyBday
12,713 Retweets **57,185** Likes
6:31 AM - 13 Oct 2018

Donald J. Trump ✓
@realDonaldTrump

Pastor Andrew Brunson, released by Turkey, will be with me in the Oval Office at 2:30 P.M. (this afternoon). It will be wonderful to see and meet him. He is a great Christian who has been through such a tough experience. I would like to thank President @RT_Erdogan for his help!
16,916 Retweets **75,130** Likes
7:06 AM - 13 Oct 2018

Donald J. Trump ✓
@realDonaldTrump

There was NO DEAL made with Turkey for the release and return of Pastor Andrew Brunson. I don't make deals for hostages. There was, however, great appreciation on behalf of the United States, which will lead to good, perhaps great, relations between the United States & Turkey!
24,261 Retweets **101,249** Likes
7:17 AM - 13 Oct 2018

President Trumps Tweets 2018: A Historical Archive of President Trump's Tweets

Donald J. Trump ✓
@realDonaldTrump

"From a Turkish prison to the White House in 24 hours." Kristin Fisher of @FoxNews Very cool!
14,849 Retweets **73,661** Likes
10:03 AM - 13 Oct 2018

Donald J. Trump ✓
@realDonaldTrump

Highly respected Congressman Keith Rothfus (R) of Pennsylvania is in the fight of his life because the Dems changed the District Map. He must win. Strong on crime, borders, big tax & reg cuts, Military & Vets. Opponent Lamb a Pelosi puppet-weak on crime. BIG ENDORSEMENT FOR KEITH
26,519 Retweets **91,501** Likes
10:43 AM - 13 Oct 2018

Donald J. Trump ✓
@realDonaldTrump

Heading to the Great State of Kentucky - Big Rally for Congressman Andy Barr - Fantastic guy, need his vote for MAGA! Strong on Crime, Tax Cuts, Military, Vets & 2nd A. His opponent will NEVER vote for us, only for Pelosi. Andy has my Strongest Endorsement!!! See you in Kentucky.
15,940 Retweets **72,264** Likes
10:52 AM - 13 Oct 2018

Donald J. Trump ✓
@realDonaldTrump

WELCOME HOME PASTOR ANDREW BRUNSON!
19,823 Retweets **86,481** Likes
1:48 PM - 13 Oct 2018

Donald J. Trump ✓
@realDonaldTrump

On my way to Richmond, Kentucky for a MAKE AMERICA GREAT AGAIN rally at 7:00pmE. The crowds are once again, massive. See everyone in a couple of hours! #MAGA
9,896 Retweets **46,627** Likes
2:06 PM - 13 Oct 2018

Donald J. Trump ✓
@realDonaldTrump

Thank you Kentucky! #MAGA
12,754 Retweets **55,710** Likes
6:16 PM - 13 Oct 2018

Donald J. Trump ✓
@realDonaldTrump

Big day! Pastor Andrew Brunson, who could have spent 35 years in a Turkish prison, was returned safely home to his family today. Met in Oval Office, great people! Then off to Kentucky for a Rally for Congressman Andy Barr. Tremendous crowd & spirit! Just returned to White House.
16,885 Retweets **87,639** Likes
8:42 PM - 13 Oct 2018

Donald J. Trump ✓
@realDonaldTrump

Congratulations to Tucker Carlson on the great success of his book, "Ship of Fools." It just went to NUMBER ONE!
20,295 Retweets **100,420** Likes
8:53 PM - 13 Oct 2018

Donald J. Trump ✓
@realDonaldTrump

NBC News has totally and purposely changed the point and meaning of my story about General Robert E Lee and General Ulysses Grant. Was actually a shoutout to warrior Grant and the great state in which he was born. As usual, dishonest reporting. Even mainstream media embarrassed!
30,920 Retweets **117,653** Likes
6:56 AM - 14 Oct 2018

Donald J. Trump ✓
@realDonaldTrump

Princess Eugenie of York was a truly beautiful bride yesterday. She has been through so much, and has come out a total winner!
10,345 Retweets **70,726** Likes
7:02 AM - 14 Oct 2018

Donald J. Trump ✓
@realDonaldTrump

I will be interviewed on "60 Minutes" tonight at 7:00 P.M., after NFL game. Enjoy!
12,126 Retweets **71,664** Likes
12:39 PM - 14 Oct 2018

Donald J. Trump ✓
@realDonaldTrump

Thank you!
15,753 Retweets **74,452** Likes
12:45 PM - 14 Oct 2018

Donald J. Trump ✓
@realDonaldTrump

Thank you to NBC for the correction!
18,641 Retweets **77,749** Likes
12:54 PM - 14 Oct 2018

Donald J. Trump ✓
@realDonaldTrump

"The only way to shut down the Democrats new Mob Rule strategy is to stop them cold at the Ballot Box. The fight for America's future is never over!" Ben Shapiro
26,942 Retweets **100,364** Likes
4:46 AM - 15 Oct 2018

Donald J. Trump ✓
@realDonaldTrump

The crowds at my Rallies are far bigger than they have ever been before, including the 2016 election. Never an empty seat in these large venues, many thousands of people watching screens outside. Enthusiasm & Spirit is through the roof. SOMETHING BIG IS HAPPENING - WATCH!
28,046 Retweets **117,484** Likes
5:11 AM - 15 Oct 2018

Donald J. Trump ✓
@realDonaldTrump

Will be leaving for Florida and Georgia with the First Lady to tour the hurricane damage and visit with FEMA, First Responders and Law Enforcement. Maximum effort is taking place, everyone is working very hard. Worst hit in 50 years!
11,710 Retweets **62,217** Likes
5:25 AM - 15 Oct 2018

President Trumps Tweets 2018: A Historical Archive of President Trump's Tweets

Donald J. Trump ✓
@realDonaldTrump

Just spoke to the King of Saudi Arabia who denies any knowledge of whatever may have happened "to our Saudi Arabian citizen." He said that they are working closely with Turkey to find answer. I am immediately sending our Secretary of State to meet with King!
21,273 Retweets **83,290** Likes
5:37 AM - 15 Oct 2018

Donald J. Trump ✓
@realDonaldTrump

On our way to Florida and Georgia!
9,396 Retweets **64,737** Likes
6:48 AM - 15 Oct 2018

Donald J. Trump ✓
@realDonaldTrump

Just arrived in Florida. Also thinking about our GREAT Alabama farmers and our many friends in North and South Carolina today. We are with you!
12,979 Retweets **71,582** Likes
8:45 AM - 15 Oct 2018

Donald J. Trump ✓
@realDonaldTrump

Open enrollment starts today on lower-priced Medicare Advantage plans so loved by our great seniors. Crazy Bernie and his band of Congressional Dems will outlaw these plans. Disaster!
20,232 Retweets **76,165** Likes
4:51 PM - 15 Oct 2018

Donald J. Trump ✓
@realDonaldTrump

TOGETHER, WE WILL PREVAIL!
18,861 Retweets **85,114** Likes
5:26 PM - 15 Oct 2018

Donald J. Trump ✓
@realDonaldTrump

Pocahontas (the bad version), sometimes referred to as Elizabeth Warren, is getting slammed. She took a bogus DNA test and it showed that she may be 1/1024, far less than the average American. Now Cherokee Nation denies her, "DNA test is useless." Even they don't want her. Phony!
28,140 Retweets **121,754** Likes
5:06 AM - 16 Oct 2018

Donald J. Trump ✓
@realDonaldTrump

Now that her claims of being of Indian heritage have turned out to be a scam and a lie, Elizabeth Warren should apologize for perpetrating this fraud against the American Public. Harvard called her "a person of color" (amazing con), and would not have taken her otherwise!
22,831 Retweets **91,857** Likes
5:16 AM - 16 Oct 2018

Donald J. Trump ✓
@realDonaldTrump

Thank you to the Cherokee Nation for revealing that Elizabeth Warren, sometimes referred to as Pocahontas, is a complete and total Fraud!
29,846 Retweets **122,783** Likes
5:24 AM - 16 Oct 2018

Donald J. Trump ✓
@realDonaldTrump

"Op-Ed praises Trump Administrations efforts at the Border." @FoxNews The Washington Examiner States, "Finally, the government has taken steps to stop releasing unaccompanied minors to criminals and traffickers." This was done by the Obama Administration!
13410 Retweets **52,994** Likes
5:55 AM - 16 Oct 2018

Donald J. Trump ✓
@realDonaldTrump

The United States has strongly informed the President of Honduras that if the large Caravan of people heading to the U.S. is not stopped and brought back to Honduras, no more money or aid will be given to Honduras, effective immediately!
42,070 Retweets **143,613** Likes
6:05 AM - 16 Oct 2018

Donald J. Trump ✓
@realDonaldTrump

"8X more new manufacturing jobs now than with Obama." @FoxNews @cvpayne
15,776 Retweets **68,976** Likes
6:08 AM - 16 Oct 2018

Donald J. Trump ✓
@realDonaldTrump

For the record, I have no financial interests in Saudi Arabia (or Russia, for that matter). Any suggestion that I have is just more FAKE NEWS (of which there is plenty)!
20,394 Retweets **77,598** Likes
6:15 AM - 16 Oct 2018

Donald J. Trump ✓
@realDonaldTrump

Incredible number just out, 7,036,000 job openings. Astonishing - it's all working! Stock Market up big on tremendous potential of USA. Also, Strong Profits. We are Number One in World, by far!
22,836 Retweets **89,441** Likes
7:12 AM - 16 Oct 2018

Donald J. Trump ✓
@realDonaldTrump

"Federal Judge throws out Stormy Danials lawsuit versus Trump. Trump is entitled to full legal fees." @FoxNews Great, now I can go after Horseface and her 3rd rate lawyer in the Great State of Texas. She will confirm the letter she signed! She knows nothing about me, a total con!
28,414 Retweets **122,638** Likes
8:04 AM - 16 Oct 2018

Donald J. Trump ✓
@realDonaldTrump

"Conflict between Glen Simpson's testimony to another House Panel about his contact with Justice Department official Bruce Ohr. Ohr was used by Simpson and Steele as a Back Channel to get (FAKE) Dossier to FBI. Simpson pleading Fifth." Catherine Herridge. Where is Jeff Sessions?
12,973 Retweets **46,688** Likes
8:18 AM - 16 Oct 2018

President Trumps Tweets 2018: A Historical Archive of President Trump's Tweets

Donald J. Trump ✓
@realDonaldTrump

Is it really possible that Bruce Ohr, whose wife Nellie was paid by Simpson and GPS Fusion for work done on the Fake Dossier, and who was used as a Pawn in this whole SCAM (WITCH HUNT), is still working for the Department of Justice????? Can this really be so?????
24,807 Retweets **82,900** Likes
8:26 AM - 16 Oct 2018

Donald J. Trump ✓
@realDonaldTrump

REGISTER TO Vote.GOP! #MAGA
12,848 Retweets **43,910** Likes
9:22 AM - 16 Oct 2018

Donald J. Trump ✓
@realDonaldTrump

Just spoke with the Crown Prince of Saudi Arabia who totally denied any knowledge of what took place in their Turkish Consulate. He was with Secretary of State Mike Pompeo...
13,828 Retweets **52,922** Likes
11:40 AM - 16 Oct 2018

Donald J. Trump ✓
@realDonaldTrump

...during the call, and told me that he has already started, and will rapidly expand, a full and complete investigation into this matter. Answers will be forthcoming shortly.
10,273 Retweets **44,451** Likes
11:40 AM - 16 Oct 2018

Donald J. Trump ✓
@realDonaldTrump

WOW, John James is making headway in Michigan. We are bringing jobs back to the State, and the People of Michigan appreciate it. Debbie Stabenow has been no help, if anything, a major hindrance. John James is a star, I hope the voters see it. Polls are tightening!
27,033 Retweets **97,159** Likes
11:50 AM - 16 Oct 2018

Donald J. Trump ✓
@realDonaldTrump

I will be interviewed tonight by Trish Regan on @FoxBusiness at 8:00 P.M., right after the great Lou Dobbs!
8,215 Retweets **44,908** Likes
4:43 PM - 16 Oct 2018

Donald J. Trump ✓
@realDonaldTrump

We have today informed the countries of Honduras, Guatemala and El Salvador that if they allow their citizens, or others, to journey through their borders and up to the United States, with the intention of entering our country illegally, all payments made to them will STOP (END)!
36,164 Retweets **134,998** Likes
6:19 PM - 16 Oct 2018

Donald J. Trump ✓
@realDonaldTrump

Anybody entering the United States illegally will be arrested and detained, prior to being sent back to their country!
42,553 Retweets **170,768** Likes
6:24 PM - 16 Oct 2018

Donald J. Trump ✓
@realDonaldTrump

Elizabeth Warren is being hammered, even by the Left. Her false claim of Indian heritage is only selling to VERY LOW I.Q. individuals!
20,544 Retweets **91,859** Likes
7:36 PM - 16 Oct 2018

Donald J. Trump ✓
@realDonaldTrump

Stock Market up 548 points today. Also, GREAT jobs numbers!
13,600 Retweets **70,215** Likes
7:39 PM - 16 Oct 2018

Donald J. Trump ✓
@realDonaldTrump

"Trump could be the most honest president in modern history. When you look at the real barometer of presidential truthfulness, which is promise keeping, he is probably the most honest president in American history. He's done exactly what he said he would do." Marc Thiessen, WPost
22,603 Retweets **87,996** Likes
4:30 AM - 17 Oct 2018

Donald J. Trump ✓
@realDonaldTrump

Watched the debate last night & Beto O'Rourke, who wants higher taxes and far more regulations, is not in the same league with Ted Cruz & what the great people of Texas stand for & want. Ted is strong on Crime, Border & 2nd A, loves our Military, Vets, Low Taxes. Beto is a Flake!
20,321 Retweets **78,161** Likes
4:52 AM - 17 Oct 2018

Donald J. Trump ✓
@realDonaldTrump

Ted Cruz has done so much for Texas, including massive cuts in taxes and regulations - which has brought Texas to the best jobs numbers in the history of the state. He watches carefully over your 2nd Amendment. O'Rourke would blow it all! Ted has long had my Strong Endorsement!
20,115 Retweets **80,076** Likes
5:00 AM - 17 Oct 2018

Donald J. Trump ✓
@realDonaldTrump

AP headline was very different from my quote and meaning in the story. They just can't help themselves. FAKE NEWS!
13,921 Retweets **59,262** Likes
5:09 AM - 17 Oct 2018

Donald J. Trump ✓
@realDonaldTrump

August job openings hit a record 7.14 million. Congratulations USA!
16,936 Retweets **75,826** Likes
5:31 AM - 17 Oct 2018

Donald J. Trump ✓
@realDonaldTrump

"Network News gave Zero coverage to the Big Day the Stock Market had yesterday." @foxandfriends
14,039 Retweets **58,839** Likes
5:40 AM - 17 Oct 2018

Donald J. Trump ✓
@realDonaldTrump

Hard to believe that with thousands of people from South of the Border, walking unimpeded toward our country in the form of large Caravans, that the Democrats won't approve legislation that will allow laws for the protection of our country. Great Midterm issue for Republicans!

25,401 Retweets **85,614** Likes

6:45 AM - 17 Oct 2018

Donald J. Trump ✓
@realDonaldTrump

Republicans must make the horrendous, weak and outdated immigration laws, and the Border, a part of the Midterms!

17,319 Retweets **66,398** Likes

6:48 AM - 17 Oct 2018

Donald J. Trump ✓
@realDonaldTrump

"President Donald J. Trump is Following Through on His Promise to Cut Burdensome Red Tape and Unleash the American Economy"

8,878 Retweets **35,943** Likes

10:18 AM - 17 Oct 2018

Donald J. Trump ✓
@realDonaldTrump

College educated women want safety, security and healthcare protections – very much along with financial and economic health for themselves and our Country. I supply all of this far better than any Democrat (for decades, actually). That's why they will be voting for me!

22,981 Retweets **101,102** Likes

12:24 PM - 17 Oct 2018

Donald J. Trump ✓
@realDonaldTrump

Congressman Neal Dunn (@DunnCampaign) of Florida has done an outstanding job at everything having to do with #MAGA. Now working hard on hurricane relief and rebuild. Strong on Crime, strong on Borders, loves our Military and our Vets. Neal has my highest Endorsement!

12,253 Retweets **47,578** Likes

12:36 PM - 17 Oct 2018

Donald J. Trump ✓
@realDonaldTrump

This afternoon, it was my great honor to present @USMC Sergeant Major John Canley the Medal of Honor in the East Room of the @WhiteHouse!

11,683 Retweets **56,327** Likes

3:03 PM - 17 Oct 2018

Donald J. Trump ✓
@realDonaldTrump

Ever since his vicious and totally false statements about Admiral Ron Jackson, the highly respected White House Doctor for Obama, Bush & me, Senator John Tester looks to be in big trouble in the Great State of Montana! He behaved worse than the Democrat Mob did with Justice K!

23,979 Retweets **89,908** Likes

7:03 PM - 17 Oct 2018

Anthony T. Michalisko

Donald J. Trump ✓
@realDonaldTrump

I am watching the Democrat Party led (because they want Open Borders and existing weak laws) assault on our country by Guatemala, Honduras and El Salvador, whose leaders are doing little to stop this large flow of people, INCLUDING MANY CRIMINALS, from entering Mexico to U.S.....
23,266 Retweets **85,238** Likes
4:25 AM - 18 Oct 2018

Donald J. Trump ✓
@realDonaldTrump

....In addition to stopping all payments to these countries, which seem to have almost no control over their population, I must, in the strongest of terms, ask Mexico to stop this onslaught - and if unable to do so I will call up the U.S. Military and CLOSE OUR SOUTHERN BORDER!..
39,817 Retweets **150,942** Likes
4:35 AM - 18 Oct 2018

Donald J. Trump ✓
@realDonaldTrump

....The assault on our country at our Southern Border, including the Criminal elements and DRUGS pouring in, is far more important to me, as President, than Trade or the USMCA. Hopefully Mexico will stop this onslaught at their Northern Border. All Democrats fault for weak laws!
24,107 Retweets **90,065** Likes
4:45 AM - 18 Oct 2018

Donald J. Trump ✓
@realDonaldTrump

Congressman @DaveBratVA7th is one of the hardest working, and smartest, people in Washington. He is strong on the Border, Crime, the Military, our Vets and the 2nd Amendment. He is a powerful vote for MAGA and loves the Great State of Virginia. Dave has my Total Endorsement!
13,909 Retweets **54,007** Likes
6:28 AM - 18 Oct 2018

Donald J. Trump ✓
@realDonaldTrump

Secretary of State Mike Pompeo returned last night from Saudi Arabia and Turkey. I met with him this morning wherein the Saudi situation was discussed in great detail, including his meeting with...
9,078 Retweets **44,145** Likes
8:40 AM - 18 Oct 2018

Donald J. Trump ✓
@realDonaldTrump

...the Crown Prince. He is waiting for the results of the investigations being done by the Saudis and Turkey, and just gave a news conference to that effect.
7,626 Retweets **37,354** Likes
8:40 AM - 18 Oct 2018

Donald J. Trump ✓
@realDonaldTrump

.@StateDept @SecPompeo outside of the West Wing after our meeting this morning in the Oval Office...
8,768 Retweets **36,030** Likes
8:53 AM - 18 Oct 2018

President Trumps Tweets 2018: A Historical Archive of President Trump's Tweets

Donald J. Trump @
@realDonaldTrump

See you tonight Missoula, Montana! #MAGARally
9,772 Retweets **41,583** Likes
9:46 AM - 18 Oct 2018

Donald J. Trump @
@realDonaldTrump

All Republicans support people with pre-existing conditions, and if they don't, they will after I speak to them. I am in total support. Also, Democrats will destroy your Medicare, and I will keep it healthy and well!
28,187 Retweets **100,413** Likes
12:43 PM - 18 Oct 2018

Donald J. Trump @
@realDonaldTrump

Can you believe this, and what Democrats are allowing to be done to our Country?
26,523 Retweets **68,403** Likes
1:04 PM - 18 Oct 2018

Donald J. Trump @
@realDonaldTrump

Look forward to being there. Something's happening! #MAGA
13,930 Retweets **53,314** Likes
2:22 PM - 18 Oct 2018

Donald J. Trump @
@realDonaldTrump

Thank you Mexico, we look forward to working with you!
22,170 Retweets **79,234** Likes
3:51 PM - 18 Oct 2018

Donald J. Trump @
@realDonaldTrump

Prime Minister @AbeShinzo of Japan has been working with me to help balance out the one-sided Trade with Japan. These are some of the investments they are making in our Country - just the beginning!
14,243 Retweets **49,094** Likes
4:49 PM - 18 Oct 2018

Donald J. Trump @
@realDonaldTrump

Will be landing soon. Looking forward to seeing our next Senator from Montana, Matt Rosendale. He will represent our Country well, far better than Jon Tester who will vote with Cryin' Chuck Schumer and Nancy Pelosi - never with us!
13,560 Retweets **62,640** Likes
5:04 PM - 18 Oct 2018

Donald J. Trump @
@realDonaldTrump

The only thing keeping Tester alive is he has millions and millions of dollars from outside liberals and leftists, who couldn't care less about our Country!
17,698 Retweets **70,271** Likes
5:11 PM - 18 Oct 2018

Anthony T. Michalisko

Donald J. Trump ✓
@realDonaldTrump

Thank you Missoula, Montana. Get out and VOTE for @MattForMontana and @GregForMontana!! #MAGA
11,691 Retweets **46,496** Likes
6:54 PM - 18 Oct 2018

Donald J. Trump ✓
@realDonaldTrump

Jon Tester says one thing to voters and does the EXACT OPPOSITE in Washington. Tester takes his orders form Pelosi & Schumer. Tester wants to raise your taxes, take away your 2A, open your borders, and deliver MOB RULE. Retire Tester & Elect America-First Patriot Matt Rosendale!
22,422 Retweets **77,524** Likes
8:11 PM - 18 Oct 2018

Donald J. Trump ✓
@realDonaldTrump

#JobsNotMobs!
29,518 Retweets **99,009** Likes
8:23 PM - 18 Oct 2018

Donald J. Trump ✓
@realDonaldTrump

Congressman Andy Biggs is doing a great job for Arizona and our Country!
11308 Retweets **46774**Likes
7:02 AM - 19 Oct 2018

Donald J. Trump ✓
@realDonaldTrump

When referring to the USA, I will always capitalize the word Country!
19,967 Retweets **108,497** Likes
7:04 AM - 19 Oct 2018

Donald J. Trump ✓
@realDonaldTrump

Secretary of State Mike Pompeo was never given or shown a Transcript or Video of the Saudi Consulate event. FAKE NEWS!
32,297 Retweets **80,294** Likes
10:26 AM - 19 Oct 2018

Donald J. Trump ✓
@realDonaldTrump

Beto O'Rourke is a total lightweight compared to Ted Cruz, and he comes nowhere near representing the values and desires of the people of the Great State of Texas. He will never be allowed to turn Texas into Venezuela!
27,178 Retweets **99,454** Likes
10:34 AM - 19 Oct 2018

Donald J. Trump ✓
@realDonaldTrump

#JobsNotMobs!
21,237 Retweets **73,712** Likes
11:41 AM - 19 Oct 2018

Donald J. Trump ✓
@realDonaldTrump

This is what it is all about for the Republican Party! #JobsNotMobs
23,141 Retweets **84,582** Likes
4:47 PM - 19 Oct 2018

President Trumps Tweets 2018: A Historical Archive of President Trump's Tweets

Donald J. Trump ✓
@realDonaldTrump

WOW - Mesa, Arizona! Look forward to joining everyone soon. Something's happening!! #MAGA
16,335 Retweets **67,517** Likes
5:51 PM - 19 Oct 2018

Donald J. Trump ✓
@realDonaldTrump

On my way - see you all shortly! Vote.GOP
11,615 Retweets **54,655** Likes
6:23 PM - 19 Oct 2018

Donald J. Trump ✓
@realDonaldTrump

This was outside of the massive totally full hangar tonight in Mesa, Arizona! Vote.GOP #MAGA
24,115 Retweets **91,331** Likes
8:13 PM - 19 Oct 2018

Donald J. Trump ✓
@realDonaldTrump

Beautiful evening in Mesa, Arizona with GREAT PATRIOTS - thank you! Vote.GOP #MAGARally
11,754 Retweets **50,064** Likes
8:17 PM - 19 Oct 2018

Donald J. Trump ✓
@realDonaldTrump

If the Democrats would stop being obstructionists and come together, we could write up and agree to new immigration laws in less than one hour. Look at the needless pain and suffering that they are causing. Look at the horrors taking place on the Border. Chuck & Nancy, call me!
32,030 Retweets **110,699** Likes
7:35 AM - 20 Oct 2018

Donald J. Trump ✓
@realDonaldTrump

Georgia Secretary of State Brian Kemp will be a great governor. He has been successful at whatever he has done, and has prepared for this very difficult and complex job for many years. He has my Strong Endorsement. His opponent is totally unqualified. Would destroy a great state!
17,070 Retweets **66,334** Likes
7:43 AM - 20 Oct 2018

Donald J. Trump ✓
@realDonaldTrump

Get out and Early Vote for Brian Kemp. He will be a GREAT GOVERNOR for the State of Georgia!
16,221 Retweets **61,981** Likes
7:46 AM - 20 Oct 2018

Donald J. Trump ✓
@realDonaldTrump

Ron @RonDeSantisFL DeSantis is working hard. A great Congressman and top student at Harvard & Yale, Ron will be a record setting governor for Florida. Rick Scott gave him tremendous foundations to further build on. His opponent runs one of the worst & most corrupt cities in USA!
18,604 Retweets **64,395** Likes
7:56 AM - 20 Oct 2018

Donald J. Trump ✓
@realDonaldTrump

Rick Scott is known as easily one of the best Governors in the USA. Florida is setting records in almost every category of success. Amazing achievement-the envy of the World. Ron DeSantis will build on this success. His incompetent opponent will destroy Florida - next Venezuela!
18,722 Retweets **67,448** Likes
8:03 AM - 20 Oct 2018

Donald J. Trump ✓
@realDonaldTrump

Leaving Arizona after a fantastic Rally last night, in Mesa, honoring, and for, Martha @RepMcSally McSally. She is an inspiration & will be a GREAT SENATOR for the people of Arizona. Her opponent is a Nancy Pelosi puppet, really bad for State. Early Voting NOW! Will be back soon.
15,167 Retweets **65,821** Likes
9:19 AM - 20 Oct 2018

Donald J. Trump ✓
@realDonaldTrump

Heading to Nevada to help a man who has become a good friend, Senator Dean Heller. He is all about #MAGA and I need his Help and Talent in Washington. Also, Adam Laxalt will be a GREAT GOVERNOR, and has my complete and total Endorsement. Winners Both!
14,669 Retweets **61,412** Likes
9:30 AM - 20 Oct 2018

Donald J. Trump ✓
@realDonaldTrump

Beautiful afternoon in Elko, Nevada. Thank you! Get out and VOTE TODAY!! #MAGA #JobsNotMobs Vote.GOP
11,561 Retweets **49,297** Likes
1:12 PM - 20 Oct 2018

Donald J. Trump ✓
@realDonaldTrump

All levels of government and Law Enforcement are watching carefully for VOTER FRAUD, including during EARLY VOTING. Cheat at your own peril. Violators will be subject to maximum penalties, both civil and criminal!
45,084 Retweets **141,329** Likes
5:36 PM - 20 Oct 2018

Donald J. Trump ✓
@realDonaldTrump

Watched North Dakota's Rep. Kevin Cramer easily win debate with Senator Heidi Heitkamp. Great job Kevin, you will be a great Senator!
20,807 Retweets **93,931** Likes
7:45 PM - 20 Oct 2018

Donald J. Trump ✓
@realDonaldTrump

Full efforts are being made to stop the onslaught of illegal aliens from crossing our Souther Border. People have to apply for asylum in Mexico first, and if they fail to do that, the U.S. will turn them away. The courts are asking the U.S. to do things that are not doable!
28,591 Retweets **111,021** Likes
12:11 PM - 21 Oct 2018

President Trumps Tweets 2018: A Historical Archive of President Trump's Tweets

Donald J. Trump ✓
@realDonaldTrump

The Caravans are a disgrace to the Democrat Party. Change the immigration laws NOW!
26,281 Retweets **104,872** Likes
12:14 PM - 21 Oct 2018

Donald J. Trump ✓
@realDonaldTrump

Best Jobs Numbers in the history of our great Country! Many other things likewise. So why wouldn't we win the Midterms? Dems can never do even nearly as well! Think of what will happen to your now beautiful 401-k's!
24,007 Retweets **99,191** Likes
12:26 PM - 21 Oct 2018

Donald J. Trump ✓
@realDonaldTrump

Facebook has just stated that they are setting up a system to "purge" themselves of Fake News. Does that mean CNN will finally be put out of business?
46,785 Retweets **185,630** Likes
3:48 PM - 21 Oct 2018

Donald J. Trump ✓
@realDonaldTrump

Ron @RonDeSantisFL DeSantis had a great debate victory tonight against Andrew Gillum, a mayor who presides over one of the worst run, and most corrupt, cities in Florida. Ron will build on the great job done by Governor Rick Scott. Gillum will make Florida the next Venezuela!
23,251 Retweets **79,393** Likes
6:49 PM - 21 Oct 2018

Donald J. Trump ✓
@realDonaldTrump

Congressman Tom Reed of New York's 23rd District has done a great job. He has my complete and total Endorsement!
11,577 Retweets **49,415** Likes
5:26 AM - 22 Oct 2018

Donald J. Trump ✓
@realDonaldTrump

Sadly, it looks like Mexico's Police and Military are unable to stop the Caravan heading to the Southern Border of the United States. Criminals and unknown Middle Easterners are mixed in. I have alerted Border Patrol and Military that this is a National Emergy. Must change laws!
38,048 Retweets **142,983** Likes
5:37 AM - 22 Oct 2018

Donald J. Trump ✓
@realDonaldTrump

Every time you see a Caravan, or people illegally coming, or attempting to come, into our Country illegally, think of and blame the Democrats for not giving us the votes to change our pathetic Immigration Laws! Remember the Midterms! So unfair to those who come in legally.
39,052 Retweets **137,935** Likes
5:49 AM - 22 Oct 2018

Anthony T. Michalisko

Donald J. Trump ✓
@realDonaldTrump

Guatemala, Honduras and El Salvador were not able to do the job of stopping people from leaving their country and coming illegally to the U.S. We will now begin cutting off, or substantially reducing, the massive foreign aid routinely given to them.
37,865 Retweets **142,330** Likes
5:57 AM - 22 Oct 2018

Donald J. Trump ✓
@realDonaldTrump

Big Night In Texas!!!!
14,373 Retweets **70,859** Likes
5:58 AM - 22 Oct 2018

Donald J. Trump ✓
@realDonaldTrump

"Shock report: US paying more for illegal immigrant births than Trump's wall"
27,762 Retweets **63,697** Likes
10:52 AM - 22 Oct 2018

Donald J. Trump ✓
@realDonaldTrump

"America: the Cleanest Air in the World - BY FAR!"
16,802 Retweets **56,922** Likes
11:00 AM - 22 Oct 2018

Donald J. Trump ✓
@realDonaldTrump

The Fake News Media has been talking about recent approval ratings of me by countries around the world, including the European Union, as being very low....
13,323 Retweets **62,309** Likes
12:18 PM - 22 Oct 2018

Donald J. Trump ✓
@realDonaldTrump

....I say of course they're low - because for the first time in 50 years I am making them pay a big price for doing business with America. Why should they like me? — But I still like them!
14,032 Retweets **72,813** Likes
12:18 PM - 22 Oct 2018

Donald J. Trump ✓
@realDonaldTrump

WOW - thank you Houston, Texas! I am departing @Andrews_JBA now. See you in a few hours!! #MAGA
14,457 Retweets **56,953** Likes
12:27 PM - 22 Oct 2018

Donald J. Trump ✓
@realDonaldTrump

Last day to register to VOTE in Alabama, California, South Dakota and Wyoming! #JobsNotMobs Vote.GOP
9,723 Retweets **33,903** Likes
12:54 PM - 22 Oct 2018

Donald J. Trump ✓
@realDonaldTrump

Let's go FLORIDA! Vote.GOP
11,902 Retweets **40,792** Likes
12:55 PM - 22 Oct 2018

President Trumps Tweets 2018: A Historical Archive of President Trump's Tweets

Donald J. Trump ✓
@realDonaldTrump

Massive crowds inside and outside of the @ToyotaCenter in Houston, Texas. Landing shortly - see everyone soon! #MAGA
17,085 Retweets **66,915** Likes
2:35 PM - 22 Oct 2018

Donald J. Trump ✓
@realDonaldTrump

THANK YOU HOUSTON, TEXAS. Get out and Vote.GOP! #JobsNotMobs
17,103 Retweets **61,896** Likes
6:30 PM - 22 Oct 2018

Donald J. Trump ✓
@realDonaldTrump

Congressman Erik Paulsen of the Great State of Minnesota has done a fantastic job in cutting Taxes and Job Killing Regulations. Hard working and very smart. Keep Erik in Congress. He has my Strong Endorsement!
15,216 Retweets **62,267** Likes
9:22 PM - 22 Oct 2018

Donald J. Trump ✓
@realDonaldTrump

Jay Webber of New Jersey, running for Congress, is doing a great job against a person who is looking to raise Taxes substantially. Jay wants big Tax Cuts and Changes. A Harvard graduate and father of seven, Jay will be great for New Jersey and get the job done-and I will help!
15,183 Retweets **60,145** Likes
6:53 AM - 23 Oct 2018

Donald J. Trump ✓
@realDonaldTrump

The people of Puerto Rico are wonderful but the inept politicians are trying to use the massive and ridiculously high amounts of hurricane/disaster funding to pay off other obligations. The U.S. will NOT bail out long outstanding & unpaid obligations with hurricane relief money!
24,465 Retweets **94,401** Likes
8:24 AM - 23 Oct 2018

Donald J. Trump ✓
@realDonaldTrump

Congressman John Faso of New York has worked hard and smart. Strong on Crime, Borders and our 2nd Amendment, John is respected by all. Vote for John. He has my complete and total Endorsement!
13,620 Retweets **52,884** Likes
8:41 AM - 23 Oct 2018

Donald J. Trump ✓
@realDonaldTrump

#JobsNotMobs Vote.GOP
12,287 Retweets **45,539** Likes
9:29 AM - 23 Oct 2018

Donald J. Trump ✓
@realDonaldTrump

Billions of dollars are, and will be, coming into United States coffers because of Tariffs. Great also for negotiations - if a country won't give us a fair Trade Deal, we will institute Tariffs on them. Used or not, jobs and businesses will be created. U.S. respected again!
23,601 Retweets **103,218** Likes
9:43 AM - 23 Oct 2018

Donald J. Trump ✓
@realDonaldTrump

I agree with President Obama 100%!
82,875 Retweets **229,574** Likes
4:18 PM - 23 Oct 2018

Donald J. Trump ✓
@realDonaldTrump

For those who want and advocate for illegal immigration, just take a good look at what has happened to Europe over the last 5 years. A total mess! They only wish they had that decision to make over again.
36,608 Retweets **128,399** Likes
4:52 AM - 24 Oct 2018

Donald J. Trump ✓
@realDonaldTrump

We are a great Sovereign Nation. We have Strong Borders and will never accept people coming into our Country illegally!
30,272 Retweets **126,841** Likes
4:56 AM - 24 Oct 2018

Donald J. Trump ✓
@realDonaldTrump

Brian Kemp will be a GREAT Governor of Georgia. Stacey Abrams will destroy the State. Sooooo important, get out and VOTE for Brian!
17,809 Retweets **65,542** Likes
5:35 AM - 24 Oct 2018

Donald J. Trump ✓
@realDonaldTrump

Republicans will totally protect people with Pre-Existing Conditions, Democrats will not! Vote Republican.
25,586 Retweets **97,861** Likes
5:45 AM - 24 Oct 2018

Donald J. Trump ✓
@realDonaldTrump

I agree wholeheartedly!
22,430 Retweets **101,124** Likes
9:04 AM - 24 Oct 2018

Donald J. Trump ✓
@realDonaldTrump

The safety of the American People is my highest priority. I have just concluded a briefing with the FBI, Department of Justice, Department of Homeland Security, and the U.S. Secret Service...
21,909 Retweets **83,918** Likes
11:55 AM - 24 Oct 2018

Donald J. Trump ✓
@realDonaldTrump

Just arrived in Wisconsin to help two great people, @ScottWalker and @LeahVukmir!
15,477 Retweets **67,603** Likes
4:54 PM - 24 Oct 2018

President Trumps Tweets 2018: A Historical Archive of President Trump's Tweets

Donald J. Trump ✓
@realDonaldTrump

Just leaving Wisconsin. @ScottWalker and @LeahVukmir are fantastic people, badly needed for our Country! #MAGA
12,969 Retweets **54,424** Likes
6:43 PM - 24 Oct 2018

Donald J. Trump ✓
@realDonaldTrump

The so-called experts on Trump over at the New York Times wrote a long and boring article on my cellphone usage that is so incorrect I do not have time here to correct it. I only use Government Phones, and have only one seldom used government cell phone. Story is soooo wrong!
20,274 Retweets **78,067** Likes
3:54 AM - 25 Oct 2018

Donald J. Trump ✓
@realDonaldTrump

Brandon Judd of the National Border Patrol Council is right when he says on @foxandfriends that the Democrat inspired laws make it tough for us to stop people at the Border. MUST BE CHANDED, but I am bringing out the military for this National Emergency. They will be stopped!
22,133 Retweets **86,861** Likes
4:05 AM - 25 Oct 2018

Donald J. Trump ✓
@realDonaldTrump

A very big part of the Anger we see today in our society is caused by the purposely false and inaccurate reporting of the Mainstream Media that I refer to as Fake News. It has gotten so bad and hateful that it is beyond description. Mainstream Media must clean up its act, FAST!
50,880 Retweets **180,911** Likes
4:18 AM - 25 Oct 2018

Donald J. Trump ✓
@realDonaldTrump

The New York Times has a new Fake Story that now the Russians and Chinese (glad they finally added China) are listening to all of my calls on cellphones. Except that I rarely use a cellphone, & when I do it's government authorized. I like Hard Lines. Just more made up Fake News!
28,834 Retweets **101,687** Likes
6:57 AM - 25 Oct 2018

Donald J. Trump ✓
@realDonaldTrump

"Remarks by President Trump on a Year of Historic Progress and Action to Combat the Opioid Crisis"
9,861 Retweets **40,777** Likes
9:21 AM - 25 Oct 2018

Donald J. Trump ✓
@realDonaldTrump

To those in the Caravan, turnaround, we are not letting people into the United States illegally. Go back to your Country and if you want, apply for citizenship like millions of others are doing!
44,901 Retweets **156,071** Likes
11:31 AM - 25 Oct 2018

Anthony T. Michalisko

Donald J. Trump ✓
@realDonaldTrump

Spoke with French President @EmmanuelMacron this morning. Discussed many topics including the very exciting upcoming visit to Paris where @FLOTUS Melania and I will attend the Armistice Day Centennial Commemoration!
8,789 Retweets **43,354** Likes
11:42 AM - 25 Oct 2018

Donald J. Trump ✓
@realDonaldTrump

Just spoke with Prime Minister @GiuseppeConteIT of Italy concerning many subjects, including the fact that Italy is now taking a very hard line on illegal immigration...
14,276 Retweets **61,329** Likes
11:47 AM - 25 Oct 2018

Donald J. Trump ✓
@realDonaldTrump

...I agree with their stance 100%, and the United States is likewise taking a very hard line on illegal immigration. The Prime Minister is working very hard on the economy of Italy - he will be successful!
12,232 Retweets **52,543** Likes
11:47 AM - 25 Oct 2018

Donald J. Trump ✓
@realDonaldTrump

.@JohnChrin of Pennsylvania is fantastic. He is strong on the Border, Crime, the Military, our Vets and the 2nd Amendment. He is a powerful vote for #MAGA and loves the Great State of Pennsylvania. Please get out and vote for John, he has my Total and very Strong Endorsement!
9,702 Retweets **37,505** Likes
12:55 PM - 25 Oct 2018

Donald J. Trump ✓
@realDonaldTrump

.@Troy_Balderson of Ohio is doing a great job as your Congressman, already very respected in Washington. Get out and VOTE for Troy - we need him – great guy – has my Total Endorsement!
10,519 Retweets **41,251** Likes
12:56 PM - 25 Oct 2018

Donald J. Trump ✓
@realDonaldTrump

.@LloydSmuckerPA is doing a great job for the people of Pennsylvania. He is strong on the Border, Crime, the Military, our Vets and the 2nd Amendment. Lloyd has my Total Endorsement!
10,229 Retweets **39,838** Likes
1:22 PM - 25 Oct 2018

Donald J. Trump ✓
@realDonaldTrump

.@MikeDunleavyGov will make a fantastic Governor of Alaska. Mike is for Energy and Jobs, is tough on Crime, loves our Vets and our Great Second Amendment. Mike has my Complete and Total Endorsement!
10,618 Retweets **42,245** Likes
1:24 PM - 25 Oct 2018

President Trumps Tweets 2018: A Historical Archive of President Trump's Tweets

Donald J. Trump ✓
@realDonaldTrump

.@BrucePoliquin from Maine is a great Congressman. He is in a tough fight against a very liberal Nancy Pelosi Democrat. Bruce has helped bring JOBS back to his State and totally protects your Great Second Amendment. We need to keep Bruce in Washington. He has my Full Endorsement!
13,669 Retweets **51,611** Likes
1:39 PM - 25 Oct 2018

Donald J. Trump ✓
@realDonaldTrump

We are gathered together on this solemn occasion to fulfill our most reverent and sacred duty. 35 years ago, 241 American service members were murdered in the terrorist attack on our Marine Barracks in Beirut, Lebanon. Today, we honor our fallen heroes...
16,032 Retweets **65,423** Likes
4:13 PM - 25 Oct 2018

Donald J. Trump ✓
@realDonaldTrump

In 1983, roughly 1,800 Marines were in Beirut to keep the peace in a Nation torn apart by Civil War. Terrorists had bombed the U.S. Embassy earlier that year, killing 63 people, including 17 Americans...
11,534 Retweets **47,163** Likes
4:19 PM - 25 Oct 2018

Donald J. Trump ✓
@realDonaldTrump

The Service Members who died that day included brave young Marines just out of high school, accomplished officers in the middle of their military careers, and enlisted men who had served in theaters all over the world...
13,171 Retweets **56,245** Likes
4:21 PM - 25 Oct 2018

Donald J. Trump ✓
@realDonaldTrump

Funny how lowly rated CNN, and others, can criticize me at will, even blaming me for the current spate of Bombs and ridiculously comparing this to September 11th and the Oklahoma City bombing, yet when I criticize them they go wild and scream, "it's just not Presidential!"
37,097 Retweets **148,166** Likes
12:14 AM - 26 Oct 2018

Donald J. Trump ✓
@realDonaldTrump

The United States has been spending Billions of Dollars a year on Illegal Immigration. This will not continue. Democrats must give us the votes to pass strong (but fair) laws. If not, we will be forced to play a much tougher hand.
24,615 Retweets **90,279** Likes
6:55 AM - 26 Oct 2018

Donald J. Trump ✓
@realDonaldTrump

Twitter has removed many people from my account and, more importantly, they have seemingly done something that makes it much harder to join - they have stifled growth to a point where it is obvious to all. A few weeks ago it was a Rocket Ship, now it is a Blimp! Total Bias?
41,805 Retweets **141,176** Likes
7:05 AM - 26 Oct 2018

Donald J. Trump ✓
@realDonaldTrump

Republicans are doing so well in early voting, and at the polls, and now this "Bomb" stuff happens and the momentum greatly slows - news not talking politics. Very unfortunate, what is going on. Republicans, go out and vote!
30,034 Retweets **109,223** Likes
7:19 AM - 26 Oct 2018

Donald J. Trump ✓
@realDonaldTrump

I will be speaking at the Young Black Leadership Summit in 15 minutes where I will address the investigation into the bomb packages.
16,255 Retweets **82,089** Likes
8:41 AM - 26 Oct 2018

Donald J. Trump ✓
@realDonaldTrump

I would like to begin today's remarks by providing an update on the packages and devices that have been mailed to high-profile figures throughout our Country, and a media org. I am pleased to inform you that law enforcement has apprehended the suspect and taken him into custody.
13,483 Retweets **56,697** Likes
10:23 AM - 26 Oct 2018

Donald J. Trump ✓
@realDonaldTrump

I want to applaud the FBI, Secret Service, Department of Justice, the U.S. Attorneys' Office for the Southern District of New York, the NYPD, and all Law Enforcement partners across the Country for their incredible work, skill and determination!
18,319 Retweets **87,979** Likes
10:59 AM - 26 Oct 2018

Donald J. Trump ✓
@realDonaldTrump

It is my great honor to be with so many brilliant, courageous, patriotic, and PROUD AMERICANS. Seeing all of you here today fills me with extraordinary confidence in America's future. Each of you is taking part in the Young Black Leadership Summit because you are true leaders...
16,446 Retweets **61,716** Likes
11:22 AM - 26 Oct 2018

Donald J. Trump ✓
@realDonaldTrump

Whether you are African-American, Hispanic-American or ANY AMERICAN at all – you have the right to live in a Country that puts YOUR NEEDS FIRST!
24,697 Retweets **86,054** Likes
11:48 AM - 26 Oct 2018

Donald J. Trump ✓
@realDonaldTrump

It was my great honor, thank you!
19,648 Retweets **76,984** Likes
2:22 PM - 26 Oct 2018

Donald J. Trump ✓
@realDonaldTrump

If you meet every day with optimism – if you confront every obstacle with determination – if you refuse to give up, if you never quit, if you face every challenge with confidence and pride – then there is no goal you cannot achieve, and no dream beyond your reach! #YBLS2018
28,360 Retweets **84,560** Likes
2:47 PM - 26 Oct 2018

President Trumps Tweets 2018: A Historical Archive of President Trump's Tweets

Donald J. Trump ✓
@realDonaldTrump

Fantastic evening in Charlotte, North Carolina with great PATRIOTS. Get out and VOTE for @buddforcongress and @MarkHarrisNC9! Vote.GOP #MAGARally
12,521 Retweets **48,420** Likes
5:58 PM - 26 Oct 2018

Donald J. Trump ✓
@realDonaldTrump

Trump Thunders at Media for Smearing His Supporters after Bomb Scares
10,580 Retweets **39,581** Likes
6:28 AM - 27 Oct 2018

Donald J. Trump ✓
@realDonaldTrump

A big change is coming - don't want the Dems anymore!
20,844 Retweets **72,477** Likes
6:38 AM - 27 Oct 2018

Donald J. Trump ✓
@realDonaldTrump

Good luck Mary!
9,178 Retweets **38,295** Likes
6:41 AM - 27 Oct 2018

Donald J. Trump ✓
@realDonaldTrump

Martha McSally is a great warrior, her opponent a Nancy Pelosi Wacko!
18,292 Retweets **62,466** Likes
6:51 AM - 27 Oct 2018

Donald J. Trump ✓
@realDonaldTrump

Budd and Mark, two great patriots for Congress!
8,598 Retweets **35,725** Likes
6:54 AM - 27 Oct 2018

Donald J. Trump ✓
@realDonaldTrump

#Walkaway Walkaway from the Democrat Party movement marches today in D.C. Congratulations to Brandon Straka for starting something very special. @foxandfriends
28,168 Retweets **90,055** Likes
7:02 AM - 27 Oct 2018

Donald J. Trump ✓
@realDonaldTrump

Watching the events unfolding in Pittsburgh, Pennsylvania. Law enforcement on the scene. People in Squirrel Hill area should remain sheltered. Looks like multiple fatalities. Beware of active shooter. God Bless All!
19,725 Retweets **84,944** Likes
8:08 AM - 27 Oct 2018

Anthony T. Michalisko

Donald J. Trump ✓
@realDonaldTrump

Events in Pittsburgh are far more devastating than originally thought. Spoke with Mayor and Governor to inform them that the Federal Government has been, and will be, with them all the way. I will speak to the media shortly and make further statement at Future Farmers of America.
19,942 Retweets **88,602** Likes
9:26 AM - 27 Oct 2018

Donald J. Trump ✓
@realDonaldTrump

As you know, earlier today there was a horrific shooting targeting and killing Jewish Americans at the Tree of Life Synagogue in Pittsburgh, Pennsylvania. The shooter is in custody, and federal authorities have been dispatched to support state and local police...
14,824 Retweets **59,427** Likes
12:43 PM - 27 Oct 2018

Donald J. Trump ✓
@realDonaldTrump

All of America is in mourning over the mass murder of Jewish Americans at the Tree of Life Synagogue in Pittsburgh. We pray for those who perished and their loved ones, and our hearts go out to the brave police officers who sustained serious injuries...
24,084 Retweets **103,982** Likes
2:41 PM - 27 Oct 2018

Donald J. Trump ✓
@realDonaldTrump

...This evil Anti-Semitic attack is an assault on humanity. It will take all of us working together to extract the poison of Anti-Semitism from our world. We must unite to conquer hate.
21,100 Retweets **86,741** Likes
2:41 PM - 27 Oct 2018

Donald J. Trump ✓
@realDonaldTrump

Watching the Dodgers/Red Sox final innings. It is amazing how a manager takes out a pitcher who is loose & dominating through almost 7 innings, Rich Hill of Dodgers, and brings in nervous reliever(s) who get shellacked. 4 run lead gone. Managers do it all the time, big mistake!
33,927 Retweets **152,189** Likes
8:46 PM - 27 Oct 2018

Donald J. Trump ✓
@realDonaldTrump

Very interesting!
27,286 Retweets **84,162** Likes
8:57 PM - 27 Oct 2018

Donald J. Trump ✓
@realDonaldTrump

Thank you to Steve Rogers, FBI Joint Terror Task Force (Ret), for his very kind and generous remarks about me and my relationship to Law Enforcement. @JudgeJeanine
16,534 Retweets **74,509** Likes
9:53 AM - 28 Oct 2018

President Trumps Tweets 2018: A Historical Archive of President Trump's Tweets

Donald J. Trump ✓
@realDonaldTrump

Just watched Wacky Tom Steyer, who I have not seen in action before, be interviewed by @jaketapper. He comes off as a crazed & stumbling lunatic who should be running out of money pretty soon. As bad as their field is, if he is running for President, the Dems will eat him alive!

20,056 Retweets **84,712** Likes
10:03 AM - 28 Oct 2018

Donald J. Trump ✓
@realDonaldTrump

The Fake News is doing everything in their power to blame Republicans, Conservatives and me for the division and hatred that has been going on for so long in our Country. Actually, it is their Fake & Dishonest reporting which is causing problems far greater than they understand!

50,126 Retweets **186,262** Likes
5:12 PM - 28 Oct 2018

Donald J. Trump ✓
@realDonaldTrump

There is great anger in our Country caused in part by inaccurate, and even fraudulent, reporting of the news. The Fake News Media, the true Enemy of the People, must stop the open & obvious hostility & report the news accurately & fairly. That will do much to put out the flame...

36,723 Retweets **134,425** Likes
5:03 AM - 29 Oct 2018

Donald J. Trump ✓

....of Anger and Outrage and we will then be able to bring all sides together in Peace and Harmony. Fake News Must End!

19,630 Retweets **80,430** Likes
5:07 AM - 29 Oct 2018

Donald J. Trump ✓
@realDonaldTrump

Had a very good conversation with the newly elected President of Brazil, Jair Bolsonaro, who won his race by a substantial margin. We agreed that Brazil and the United States will work closely together on Trade, Military and everything else! Excellent call, wished him congrats!

92,699 Retweets **341,189** Likes
5:28 AM - 29 Oct 2018

Donald J. Trump ✓
@realDonaldTrump

Many Gang Members and some very bad people are mixed into the Caravan heading to our Southern Border. Please go back, you will not be admitted into the United States unless you go through the legal process. This is an invasion of our Country and our Military is waiting for you!

40,646 Retweets **142,735** Likes
7:41 AM - 29 Oct 2018

Donald J. Trump ✓
@realDonaldTrump

In Florida there is a choice between a Harvard/Yale educated man named @RonDeSantisFL who has been a great Congressman and will be a great Governor - and a Dem who is a thief and who is Mayor of poorly run Tallahassee, said to be one of the most corrupt cities in the Country!

29,404 Retweets **91,680** Likes
7:54 AM - 29 Oct 2018

Anthony T. Michalisko

Donald J. Trump ✓
@realDonaldTrump

Great job being done by Congressman Keith Rothfus of Pennsylvania. Thank you Keith!
11,757 Retweets **55,178** Likes
7:57 AM - 29 Oct 2018

Donald J. Trump ✓
@realDonaldTrump

CNN and others in the Fake News Business keep purposely and inaccurately reporting that I said the "Media is the Enemy of the People." Wrong! I said that the "Fake News (Media) is the Enemy of the People," a very big difference. When you give out false information - not good!
34,185 Retweets **122,099** Likes
5:00 PM - 29 Oct 2018

Donald J. Trump ✓
@realDonaldTrump

Check out tweets from last two days. I refer to Fake News Media when mentioning Enemy of the People - but dishonest reporters use only the word "Media." The people of our Great Country are angry and disillusioned at receiving so much Fake News. They get it, and fully understand!
25,535 Retweets **93,493** Likes
5:14 PM - 29 Oct 2018

Donald J. Trump ✓
@realDonaldTrump

I will be interviewed by Laura Ingraham tonight at 10:00 P.M. on @FoxNews
10,203 Retweets **52,668** Likes
5:31 PM - 29 Oct 2018

Donald J. Trump ✓
@realDonaldTrump

So Revealing!
49,911 Retweets **93,429** Likes
5:39 PM - 29 Oct 2018

Donald J. Trump ✓
@realDonaldTrump

.@Troy_Balderson is doing a great job as Congressman from Ohio. We need him in D.C. Vote for Troy - He has my total Endorsement!
13,344 Retweets **49,699** Likes
7:11 PM - 29 Oct 2018

Donald J. Trump ✓
@realDonaldTrump

.@Denver4VA of the 5th District in Virginia is a popular guy who really knows how to get the job done! Really big help with Tax Cuts, the Military and our great Vets. He has my Total Endorsement!
9,917 Retweets **39,632** Likes
8:05 PM - 29 Oct 2018

Donald J. Trump ✓
@realDonaldTrump

Congressman @RodBlum of Iowa got a desperately needed Flood Wall for Cedar Rapids that was almost impossible to get. He makes a BIG difference for Iowa! Border, Military, Vets etc. We need Rod in D.C. He has my Strong Endorsement!
13,485 Retweets **48,531** Likes
8:07 PM - 29 Oct 2018

President Trumps Tweets 2018: A Historical Archive of President Trump's Tweets

Donald J. Trump ✓
@realDonaldTrump

Congresswoman @cathymcmorris of Washington State is an incredible leader who is respected by everyone in Congress. We need her badly in D.C. to keep building on #MAGA. She has my Strong Endorsement!
10,527 Retweets **39,455** Likes
8:13 PM - 29 Oct 2018

Donald J. Trump ✓
@realDonaldTrump

Congressman @DaveBratVA7th is a fighter who is doing a great job for Virginia and for our Country. Border, Military, Vets, 2nd Amendment and all else. We need Dave in D.C. He has my Strong Endorsement!
12,765 Retweets **46,669** Likes
8:19 PM - 29 Oct 2018

Donald J. Trump ✓
@realDonaldTrump

.@Erik_Paulsen, @Jason2CD, @JimHagedornMN and @PeteStauber love our Country and the Great State of Minnesota. They are winners and always get the job done. We need them all in Congress for #MAGA. Border, Military, Vets, 2nd A. Go Vote Minnesota. They have my Strong Endorsement!
11,798 Retweets **43,760** Likes
8:21 PM - 29 Oct 2018

Donald J. Trump ✓
@realDonaldTrump

Congressman Andy Barr of Kentucky, who just had a great debate with his Nancy Pelosi run opponent, has been a winner for his State. Strong on Crime, the Border, Tax Cuts, Military, Vets and 2nd Amendment, we need Andy in D.C. He has my Strong Endorsement!
14,645 Retweets **56,169** Likes
5:12 AM - 30 Oct 2018

Donald J. Trump ✓
@realDonaldTrump

Congressman Kevin Brady of Texas is so popular in his District, and far beyond, that he doesn't need any help - but I am giving it to him anyway. He is a great guy and the absolute "King" of Cutting Taxes. Highly respected by all, he loves his State & Country. Strong Endorsement!
14,199 Retweets **57,038** Likes
5:25 AM - 30 Oct 2018

Donald J. Trump ✓
@realDonaldTrump

The Stock Market is up massively since the Election, but is now taking a little pause - people want to see what happens with the Midterms. If you want your Stocks to go down, I strongly suggest voting Democrat. They like the Venezuela financial model, High Taxes & Open Borders!
30,245 Retweets **112,456** Likes
5:33 AM - 30 Oct 2018

Donald J. Trump ✓
@realDonaldTrump

"If the Fed backs off and starts talking a little more Dovish, I think we're going to be right back to our 2,800 to 2,900 target range that we've had for the S&P 500." Scott Wren, Wells Fargo.
14,921 Retweets **61,386** Likes
5:53 AM - 30 Oct 2018

Donald J. Trump ✓
@realDonaldTrump

Just out: Consumer Confidence hits highest level since 2000.
22,529 Retweets **96,404** Likes
8:10 AM - 30 Oct 2018

Donald J. Trump ✓
@realDonaldTrump

.@MikeDeWine will be a great Governor for the People of Ohio. He is an outstanding man who loves his State – and always produces big....
12,473 Retweets **48,091** Likes
10:37 AM - 30 Oct 2018

Donald J. Trump ✓
@realDonaldTrump

....Richard Cordray will let you down, just like he did when he destroyed the government agency that he ran. Clone of Pocahontas, that's not for Ohio. Mike has my Total Endorsement!
11,012 Retweets **42,059** Likes
10:37 AM - 30 Oct 2018

Donald J. Trump ✓
@realDonaldTrump

Congressman @KevinYoder has fought hard for the People of Kansas. Highly respected, strong on Crime, the Border, Military, Vets and Second Amendment. Kevin has my Total Endorsement!
14,190 Retweets **54,129** Likes
10:38 AM - 30 Oct 2018

Donald J. Trump ✓
@realDonaldTrump

The Caravans are made up of some very tough fighters and people. Fought back hard and viciously against Mexico at Northern Border before breaking through. Mexican soldiers hurt, were unable, or unwilling to stop Caravan. Should stop them before they reach our Border, but won't!
19,498 Retweets **71,923** Likes
5:38 AM - 31 Oct 2018

Donald J. Trump ✓
@realDonaldTrump

Our military is being mobilized at the Southern Border. Many more troops coming. We will NOT let these Caravans, which are also made up of some very bad thugs and gang members, into the U.S. Our Border is sacred, must come in legally. TURN AROUND!
33,112 Retweets **127,361** Likes
5:45 AM - 31 Oct 2018

Donald J. Trump ✓
@realDonaldTrump

Stock Market up more than 400 points yesterday. Today looks to be another good one. Companies earnings are great!
12,641 Retweets **60,741** Likes
6:04 AM - 31 Oct 2018

Donald J. Trump ✓
@realDonaldTrump

Melania and I were treated very nicely yesterday in Pittsburgh. The Office of the President was shown great respect on a very sad & solemn day. We were treated so warmly. Small protest was not seen by us, staged far away. The Fake News stories were just the opposite-Disgraceful!
18,018 Retweets **71,496** Likes
6:09 AM - 31 Oct 2018

President Trumps Tweets 2018: A Historical Archive of President Trump's Tweets

Donald J. Trump ✓
@realDonaldTrump

So-called Birthright Citizenship, which costs our Country billions of dollars and is very unfair to our citizens, will be ended one way or the other. It is not covered by the 14th Amendment because of the words "subject to the jurisdiction thereof." Many legal scholars agree.....
27,788 Retweets **103,636** Likes
6:25 AM - 31 Oct 2018

Donald J. Trump ✓
@realDonaldTrump

....Harry Reid was right in 1993, before he and the Democrats went insane and started with the Open Borders (which brings massive Crime) "stuff." Don't forget the nasty term Anchor Babies. I will keep our Country safe. This case will be settled by the United States Supreme Court!
18,947 Retweets **66,971** Likes
7:17 AM - 31 Oct 2018

Donald J. Trump ✓
@realDonaldTrump

The World is using our laws to our detriment. They laugh at the Stupidity they see!
18,255 Retweets **74,445** Likes
7:19 AM - 31 Oct 2018

Donald J. Trump ✓
@realDonaldTrump

"Donald Trump has made good on his promises, and it drives Democrats Crazy!" Brad Blakeman @FoxNews
14,624 Retweets **62,029** Likes
8:25 AM - 31 Oct 2018

Donald J. Trump ✓
@realDonaldTrump

Republicans will protect people with pre-existing conditions far better than the Dems!
19,880 Retweets **78,062** Likes
8:28 AM - 31 Oct 2018

Donald J. Trump ✓
@realDonaldTrump

Paul Ryan should be focusing on holding the Majority rather than giving his opinions on Birthright Citizenship, something he knows nothing about! Our new Republican Majority will work on this, Closing the Immigration Loopholes and Securing our Border!
32,418 Retweets **122,475** Likes
9:43 AM - 31 Oct 2018

Donald J. Trump ✓
@realDonaldTrump

Harry Reid, when he was sane, agreed with us on Birthright Citizenship!
25,405 Retweets **76,687** Likes
10:19 AM - 31 Oct 2018

Donald J. Trump ✓
@realDonaldTrump

Yesterday in Pittsburgh I was really impressed with Congressman Keith Rothfus (far more so than any other local political figure). His sincere level of compassion, grief and sorrow for the events that took place was, in its own way, very inspiring. Vote for Keith!
14,461 Retweets **61,563** Likes
12:24 PM - 31 Oct 2018

Donald J. Trump ✓
@realDonaldTrump

#JOBSNOTMOBS! VOTE REPUBLICAN NOW!!
28,670 Retweets **76,880** Likes
12:25 PM - 31 Oct 2018

Donald J. Trump ✓
@realDonaldTrump

It is outrageous what the Democrats are doing to our Country. Vote Republican now! Vote.GOP
41,895 Retweets **97,576** Likes
1:18 PM - 31 Oct 2018

Donald J. Trump ✓
@realDonaldTrump

THANK YOU FLORIDA! Get out and VOTE Republican! #MAGA
16,488 Retweets **58,652** Likes
5:53 PM - 31 Oct 2018

Donald J. Trump ✓
@realDonaldTrump

Fantastic evening in Florida with great PATRIOTS at a beautiful #MAGARally. Get out and Vote.GOP so we can continue MAKING AMERICA SAFE & GREAT AGAIN!
12,775 Retweets **48,260** Likes
6:43 PM - 31 Oct 2018

Donald J. Trump ✓
@realDonaldTrump

That's because they treat me fairly! "@FoxNews tops @CNN and @MSNBC combined in October cable news ratings"
19,417 Retweets **75,779** Likes
8:33 PM - 31 Oct 2018

Donald J. Trump ✓
@realDonaldTrump

Just had a long and very good conversation with President Xi Jinping of China. We talked about many subjects, with a heavy emphasis on Trade. Those discussions are moving along nicely with meetings being scheduled at the G-20 in Argentina. Also had good discussion on North Korea!
21,436 Retweets **93,732** Likes
7:09 AM - 1 Nov 2018

Donald J. Trump ✓
@realDonaldTrump

Thank you to Rick Breckenridge and congratulations to Matt Rosendale (@MattForMontana). This is very big - see you in Montana on Saturday!
8,806 Retweets **35,391** Likes
11:33 AM - 1 Nov 2018

Donald J. Trump ✓
@realDonaldTrump

.@WalkerStapleton will be an extraordinary Governor for the State of Colorado. He is strong, smart, and has been successful at everything he has ever done....
11,718 Retweets **47,891** Likes
11:37 AM - 1 Nov 2018

President Trumps Tweets 2018: A Historical Archive of President Trump's Tweets

Donald J. Trump ✓
@realDonaldTrump

....His opponent, Jared Polis, is weak on crime and weak on borders – could never do the job. Get out and VOTE – Walker has my Complete and Total Endorsement!
8,474 Retweets **35,011** Likes
11:37 AM - 1 Nov 2018

Donald J. Trump ✓
@realDonaldTrump

Illegal immigration affects the lives of all Americans. Illegal Immigration hurts American workers, burdens American taxpayers, undermines public safety, and places enormous strain on local schools, hospitals and communities...
29,041 Retweets **94,089** Likes
1:54 PM - 1 Nov 2018

Donald J. Trump ✓
@realDonaldTrump

On my way to Columbia, Missouri for a #MAGARally. Look forward to seeing everyone soon!
8,685 Retweets **42,056** Likes
3:11 PM - 1 Nov 2018

Donald J. Trump ✓
@realDonaldTrump

Together, we are Making America Safe and Great Again!
23,848 Retweets **83,554** Likes
3:46 PM - 1 Nov 2018

Donald J. Trump ✓
@realDonaldTrump

Beautiful evening at a #MAGARally with great American Patriots. Loyal citizens like you helped build this Country and together, we are taking back this Country – returning power to YOU, the AMERICAN PEOPLE. Get out and Vote.GOP!
17,539 Retweets **63,662** Likes
7:23 PM - 1 Nov 2018

Donald J. Trump ✓
@realDonaldTrump

I love you Missouri! Under Republican leadership, America is BOOMING, America is THRIVING, and America is WINNING - because we are finally putting AMERICA FIRST. Get out and VOTE Josh @HawleyMO for the United States Senate! #MAGA
14,995 Retweets **57,362** Likes
7:43 PM - 1 Nov 2018

Donald J. Trump ✓
@realDonaldTrump

Wow! The U.S. added 250,000 Jobs in October - and this was despite the hurricanes. Unemployment at 3.7%. Wages UP! These are incredible numbers. Keep it going, Vote Republican!
29,517 Retweets **117,224** Likes
6:46 AM - 2 Nov 2018

Donald J. Trump ✓
@realDonaldTrump

Will be going to West Virginia and Indiana today, TWO RALLIES! Don't tell anyone (big secret), but I will be bringing Coach Bobby Knight to Indiana. He's been a supporter right from the beginning of the Greatest Political Movement in American History!
20,225 Retweets **86,249** Likes
6:54 AM - 2 Nov 2018

Donald J. Trump ✓
@realDonaldTrump

Fantastic #MAGARally in West Virginia, thank you. Everyone get out and VOTE for Patrick @MorriseyWV and @CarolMillerWV!
12,274 Retweets **47,536** Likes
2:54 PM - 2 Nov 2018

Donald J. Trump ✓
@realDonaldTrump

JOBS, JOBS, JOBS! #MAGA
15,797 Retweets **58,823** Likes
3:14 PM - 2 Nov 2018

Donald J. Trump ✓
@realDonaldTrump

THANK YOU WEST VIRGINIA! Vote.GOV
10,051 Retweets **47,603** Likes
3:45 PM - 2 Nov 2018

Donald J. Trump ✓
@realDonaldTrump

Just landed - will see everyone in Southport, Indiana shortly! #MAGARally
8,441 Retweets **40,555** Likes
3:51 PM - 2 Nov 2018

Donald J. Trump ✓
@realDonaldTrump

I need the people of West Virginia to send a message to Chuck Schumer, Maxine Waters, Nancy Pelosi and the Radical Democrats by voting for Carol Miller and Patrick Morrisey!
14,917 Retweets **51,095** Likes
4:18 PM - 2 Nov 2018

Donald J. Trump ✓
@realDonaldTrump

In just 4 days, the people of Indiana are going to send Mike @braun4indiana to the United States Senate, so we can keep MAKING AMERICA GREAT AGAIN! Get out and VOTE!!
11,607 Retweets **43,363** Likes
5:40 PM - 2 Nov 2018

Donald J. Trump ✓
@realDonaldTrump

Republicans believe our Country should be a Sanctuary for law-abiding Americans – not criminal aliens. And Republicans will ALWAYS stand with the HEROES of @ICEgov, @CBP, and Law Enforcement!
13,484 Retweets **51,124** Likes
5:49 PM - 2 Nov 2018

Donald J. Trump ✓
@realDonaldTrump

Massive #MAGARally tonight in Indiana, thank you. Everyone get out and Vote.GOP!
12,492 Retweets **47,833** Likes
6:27 PM - 2 Nov 2018

Donald J. Trump ✓
@realDonaldTrump

Scott Perry of Pennsylvania is fantastic. He is strong on the Border, Crime, the Military, our Vets and the Second Amendment. Scott has my Total Endorsement!
15,228 Retweets **63,617** Likes
7:56 PM - 2 Nov 2018

President Trumps Tweets 2018: A Historical Archive of President Trump's Tweets

Donald J. Trump ✓
@realDonaldTrump

Congresswoman Maxine Waters was called the most Corrupt Member of Congress! @FoxNews If Dems win, she would be put in charge of our Country's finances. The beginning of the end!
26,152 Retweets **86,027** Likes
3:54 AM - 3 Nov 2018

Donald J. Trump ✓
@realDonaldTrump

Indiana Rally, and Coach Bobby Knight, were incredible last night. Packed House in Honor of Mike Braun for Senate. Mike will be a GREAT Senator. Don't forget to VOTE!
13,250 Retweets **59,601** Likes
4:49 AM - 3 Nov 2018

Donald J. Trump ✓
@realDonaldTrump

Heading to Montana and Florida today! Everyone is excited about the Jobs Numbers - 250,000 new jobs in October. Also, wages rising. Wow!
14,020 Retweets **60,026** Likes
5:04 AM - 3 Nov 2018

Donald J. Trump ✓
@realDonaldTrump

Thank you to @PeteHegseth and @KatiePavlich for your nice, and very wise, statements on the Economy. You both really get it! @foxandfriends
10,023 Retweets **44,849** Likes
6:24 AM - 3 Nov 2018

Donald J. Trump ✓
@realDonaldTrump

A vicious accuser of Justice Kavanaugh has just admitted that she was lying, her story was totally made up, or FAKE! Can you imagine if he didn't become a Justice of the Supreme Court because of her disgusting False Statements. What about the others? Where are the Dems on this?
47,334 Retweets **151,598** Likes
6:38 AM - 3 Nov 2018

Donald J. Trump ✓
@realDonaldTrump

Get out and VOTE for @DeanHeller!
11,060 Retweets **43,020** Likes
9:32 AM - 3 Nov 2018

Donald J. Trump ✓
@realDonaldTrump

New York, get out and VOTE for @JohnFasoNy, a great and hardworking Congressman. We need John's voice in D.C. His opponent just moved to the area - is Pro-Iran and Anti-Israel. Vote for John. Has my Strong Endorsement!
15,006 Retweets **54,742** Likes
9:48 AM - 3 Nov 2018

Donald J. Trump ✓
@realDonaldTrump

Landing in Montana now - at least everybody admits that my lines and crowds are far bigger than Barack Obama's...
17,927 Retweets **74,116** Likes
11:03 AM - 3 Nov 2018

Donald J. Trump ✓
@realDonaldTrump

If Chuck Schumer and Nancy Pelosi gain the majority, they will try to raise your taxes, restore job-killing regulations, shut down your coal mines and timber mills, take away your healthcare, impose socialism, and ERASE your borders. VOTE for @MattForMontana and @GregForMontana!
18,479 Retweets **58,442** Likes
1:38 PM - 3 Nov 2018

Donald J. Trump ✓
@realDonaldTrump

Arizona is such a Great State but it needs Border Security which @MarthaMcSally will provide, and Krysten Sinema doesn't even think about. If it were up to Sinema - drugs, crime and illegal traffic will be flowing into Arizona at an ever increasing pace. Vote for Martha!
16,531 Retweets **58,727** Likes
1:57 PM - 3 Nov 2018

Donald J. Trump ✓
@realDonaldTrump

Rumor has it that Senator Joe Donnelly of Indiana is paying for Facebook ads for his so-called opponent on the libertarian ticket. Donnelly is trying to steal the election? Isn't that what Russia did!?
27,385 Retweets **97,596** Likes
2:05 PM - 3 Nov 2018

Donald J. Trump ✓
@realDonaldTrump

In all the time I've been President, almost two years, never once did Senator Bill Nelson call me to ask for help for the Great State of Florida. I never see him until election time....
16,644 Retweets **62,489** Likes
2:12 PM - 3 Nov 2018

Donald J. Trump ✓
@realDonaldTrump

....Lake Okeechobee and all of the hurricane money were a passion for Rick Scott, who called endlessly on behalf of the People of Florida. Vote @ScottforFlorida!
12,456 Retweets **47,306** Likes
2:12 PM - 3 Nov 2018

Donald J. Trump ✓
@realDonaldTrump

Governor @DougDucey of Arizona is doing a great job. Doug is strong on Crime, the Border, and our Second Amendment. Loves our Military & our Vets. Vote for Doug, he has my full and Complete Endorsement!
10,480 Retweets **40,376** Likes
4:00 PM - 3 Nov 2018

Donald J. Trump ✓
@realDonaldTrump

Heading to Pensacola, Florida - will be there soon. Amazing lines of people wanting to get in - what a crowd! Is this a sign of Republican Strength on Tuesday?
9,522 Retweets **42,709** Likes
4:05 PM - 3 Nov 2018

President Trumps Tweets 2018: A Historical Archive of President Trump's Tweets

Donald J. Trump ✓
@realDonaldTrump

Another fantastic #MAGARally tonight in the Great State of Florida. In just 3 days, the People of Florida are going to elect @ScottforFlorida and @RonDeSantisFL to protect your jobs, defend your BORDERS, and CONTINUE MAKING AMERICA GREAT AGAIN!
14,042 Retweets **49,722** Likes
6:29 PM - 3 Nov 2018

Donald J. Trump ✓
@realDonaldTrump

.@DannyTarkanian is a great guy and a team player. He will represent his District, State and Country at the highest level. Danny is strong on Military, our Vets, Second Amendment and all of the things that we so strongly stand for. Vote for Danny - he has my Strong Endorsement!
14,135 Retweets **54,560** Likes
6:39 PM - 3 Nov 2018

Donald J. Trump ✓
@realDonaldTrump

If you want to protect criminal aliens – VOTE DEMOCRAT. If you want to protect Law-Abiding Americans – VOTE REPUBLICAN!
16,078 Retweets **55,520** Likes
6:46 PM - 3 Nov 2018

Donald J. Trump ✓
@realDonaldTrump

Unbelievable crowd in Florida tonight. Get out and VOTE! #MAGA
20,607 Retweets **78,506** Likes
7:47 PM - 3 Nov 2018

Donald J. Trump ✓
@realDonaldTrump

New Fox Poll shows a "40% Approval Rating by African Americans for President Trump, a record for Republicans." Thank you, a great honor!
27,339 Retweets **111,774** Likes
7:15 AM - 4 Nov 2018

Donald J. Trump ✓
@realDonaldTrump

WOW - Departing the White House shortly. See you soon Georgia! #MAGA
15,409 Retweets **59,415** Likes
10:35 AM - 4 Nov 2018

Donald J. Trump ✓
@realDonaldTrump

On my way to Macon, Georgia where the crowds are massive, for a 4pmE #MAGARally. Will be in Chattanooga, Tennessee tonight, seen below, for a 7pmE rally. Something's happening! Everyone needs to get out and VOTE!
13,499 Retweets **52,064** Likes
12:02 PM - 4 Nov 2018

Donald J. Trump ✓
@realDonaldTrump

Thank you Macon, Georgia! Get out on Tuesday, November 6th and VOTE for @BrianKempGA as your next Governor to protect your jobs, defend your borders, fight for your values, and continue MAKING AMERICA GREAT AGAIN!
13,410 Retweets **52,339** Likes
3:05 PM - 4 Nov 2018

Anthony T. Michalisko

Donald J. Trump ✓
@realDonaldTrump

Great to be back in Tennessee. On our way to the McKenzie Arena in Chattanooga for a huge #MAGARally - see everyone soon!
12,494 Retweets **53,361** Likes
3:47 PM - 4 Nov 2018

Donald J. Trump ✓
@realDonaldTrump

Thank you for joining us tonight in Tennessee, @TheLeeGreenwood. GOD BLESS THE U.S.A.!
23,545 Retweets **85,935** Likes
5:36 PM - 4 Nov 2018

Donald J. Trump ✓
@realDonaldTrump

In just 2 days, the people of Tennessee are going to elect @VoteMarsha Blackburn to the United States Senate to protect your jobs, defend your borders, and CONTINUE MAKING AMERICA GREAT AGAIN! Get out on Tuesday and VOTE for Marsha!
13,730 Retweets **49,281** Likes
6:00 PM - 4 Nov 2018

Donald J. Trump ✓
@realDonaldTrump

John James, running as a Republican for the Senate from Michigan, is a spectacular young star of the future. We should make him a star of the present. A distinguished West Point Grad and Vet, people should Vote Out Schumer Puppet Debbie Stabenow, who does nothing for Michigan!
23,662 Retweets **81,174** Likes
9:04 PM - 4 Nov 2018

Donald J. Trump ✓
@realDonaldTrump

Dana Rohrabacher has been a great Congressman for his District and for the people of Cal. He works hard and is respected by all - he produces! Dems are desperate to replace Dana by spending vast sums to elect a super liberal who is weak on Crime and bad for our Military & Vets!
15,285 Retweets **55,489** Likes
9:32 PM - 4 Nov 2018

Donald J. Trump ✓
@realDonaldTrump

.@DebbieStabenow voted against Tax Cuts, great Healthcare, Supreme Court Justices and all of the many things the people of Michigan wanted and need. She is an automatic far left vote, controlled by her bosses. John James can be a truly great Senator!
14,973 Retweets **50,467** Likes
5:13 AM - 5 Nov 2018

Donald J. Trump ✓
@realDonaldTrump

If @AndrewGillum did the same job with Florida that he has done in Tallahassee as Mayor, the State will be a crime ridden, overtaxed mess. @RonDeSantisFL will be a great Governor. VOTE!!!!!!
18,592 Retweets **60,703** Likes
5:21 AM - 5 Nov 2018

President Trumps Tweets 2018: A Historical Archive of President Trump's Tweets

Donald J. Trump ✓
@realDonaldTrump

No matter what she says, Senator Claire McCaskill will always vote against us and the Great State of Missouri! Vote for Josh Hawley - he will be a great Senator!
20,920 Retweets **78,128** Likes
5:36 AM - 5 Nov 2018

Donald J. Trump ✓
@realDonaldTrump

I need @claudiatenney of #NY22 to be re-elected in order to get our big plans moving. Her opponent would be a disaster. Nobody works harder than Claudia, and she is a producer. I look forward to working together with her - she has my Strongest Endorsement! Vote Claudia!
13,337 Retweets **48,122** Likes
7:01 AM - 5 Nov 2018

Donald J. Trump ✓
@realDonaldTrump

So funny to see the CNN Fake Suppression Polls and false rhetoric. Watch for real results Tuesday. We are lucky CNN's ratings are so low. Don't fall for the Suppression Game. Go out & VOTE. Remember, we now have perhaps the greatest Economy (JOBS) in the history of our Country!
31,464 Retweets **105,477** Likes
7:18 AM - 5 Nov 2018

Donald J. Trump ✓
@realDonaldTrump

REMEMBER FLORIDA: I have been President of the United States for almost two years. During that time Senator Bill Nelson didn't call me once. Rick Scott called constantly requesting dollars plus for Florida. Did a GREAT job on hurricanes. VOTE SCOTT!
21,963 Retweets **78,359** Likes
7:35 AM - 5 Nov 2018

Donald J. Trump ✓
@realDonaldTrump

Law Enforcement has been strongly notified to watch closely for any ILLEGAL VOTING which may take place in Tuesday's Election (or Early Voting). Anyone caught will be subject to the Maximum Criminal Penalties allowed by law. Thank you!
36,667 Retweets **129,974** Likes
7:41 AM - 5 Nov 2018

Donald J. Trump ✓
@realDonaldTrump

"Bill Nelson is kind of an empty figure in Washington. You never hear his name, he's never in debates on key issues - he is just under the radar." Chris Wallace on @FoxNews In other words, Nelson is a "stiff."
16,198 Retweets **61,156** Likes
9:59 AM - 5 Nov 2018

Donald J. Trump ✓
@realDonaldTrump

Something's happening America! Get out tomorrow and Vote.GOP so together, we can KEEP MAKING AMERICA GREAT AGAIN!!
18,080 Retweets **57,446** Likes
12:59 PM - 5 Nov 2018

Donald J. Trump ✓
@realDonaldTrump

Thank you Ohio! When you enter the voting booth tomorrow you will be making a simple choice. A vote for Republicans is a vote to continue our extraordinary prosperity. A vote for Dems is a vote to bring this Economic Boom crashing to a sudden, screeching halt. Vote @MikeDeWine!
11,197 Retweets **41,329** Likes
1:26 PM - 5 Nov 2018

Donald J. Trump ✓
@realDonaldTrump

Republicans have created the best economy in the HISTORY of our Country – and the hottest jobs market on planet earth. The Democrat Agenda is a Socialist Nightmare. The Republican Agenda is the AMERICAN DREAM!
13,206 Retweets **44,652** Likes
1:40 PM - 5 Nov 2018

Donald J. Trump ✓
@realDonaldTrump

Just landed in Fort Wayne, Indiana for a #MAGARally at the Allen County War Memorial Coliseum. See everyone soon!
8,995 Retweets **38,970** Likes
2:28 PM - 5 Nov 2018

Donald J. Trump ✓
@realDonaldTrump

Thank you Indiana! A vote for Mike @Braun4Indiana is a vote to keep your jobs going up, your wages going up, and your healthcare costs coming down. It's a vote to keep your families safe & to keep criminals, traffickers & drug dealers OUT of our Country! Get out and for for Mike!
9,551 Retweets **36,802** Likes
5:02 PM - 5 Nov 2018

Donald J. Trump ✓
@realDonaldTrump

There is only one way to stop this Democrat-Led assault on our sovereignty – you have to VOTE Republican TOMORROW! Polling locations: Vote.GOP
12,752 Retweets **42,901** Likes
5:05 PM - 5 Nov 2018

Donald J. Trump ✓
@realDonaldTrump

Massive crowd inside and outside the Allen County War Memorial Coliseum in Fort Wayne, Indiana! Thank you for joining us tonight - and make sure you get out and Vote.GOP tomorrow!
15,711 Retweets **59,267** Likes
5:26 PM - 5 Nov 2018

Donald J. Trump ✓
@realDonaldTrump

On my way, see you soon Cape Girardeau, Missouri! #MAGARally
10,652 Retweets **46,501** Likes
5:47 PM - 5 Nov 2018

Donald J. Trump ✓
@realDonaldTrump

You have been loyal and faithful to your Country, and now you have a President that is loyal and faithful to you. Get out tomorrow, and Vote.GOP!
18,633 Retweets **60,906** Likes
6:14 PM - 5 Nov 2018

President Trumps Tweets 2018: A Historical Archive of President Trump's Tweets

Donald J. Trump ✓
@realDonaldTrump

A vote for Claire McCaskill is a vote for Schumer, Pelosi, Waters, and their socialist agenda. Claire voted IN FAVOR of deadly Sanctuary Cities - she would rather protect criminal aliens than American citizens, which is why she needs to be voted out of office. Vote @HawleyMO!
12,569 Retweets **44,016** Likes
9:12 PM - 5 Nov 2018

Donald J. Trump ✓
@realDonaldTrump

A fantastic evening in Cape Girardeau, Missouri. Josh @HawleyMO will be a tireless champion for YOU. He is great on jobs, great on tax cuts, and tough on crime. He shares your values, and he will always support our Military, Vets and Police! Get out tomorrow and VOTE for Josh!!
11,798 Retweets **46,028** Likes
10:36 PM - 5 Nov 2018

Donald J. Trump ✓
@realDonaldTrump

There is a rumor, put out by the Democrats, that Josh Hawley of Missouri left the Arena last night early. It is Fake News. He met me at the plane when I arrived, spoke at the great Rally, & stayed to the very end. In fact, I said goodbye to him and left before he did. Deception!
25,541 Retweets **93,103** Likes
7:20 AM - 6 Nov 2018

Donald J. Trump ✓
@realDonaldTrump

Congressman Peter King of New York is a hardworking gem. Loves his Country and his State. Get out and VOTE for Peter!
9,650 Retweets **40,612** Likes
7:44 AM - 6 Nov 2018

Donald J. Trump ✓
@realDonaldTrump

POLLING LOCATIONS: Vote.GOP
9,917 Retweets **36,979** Likes
9:58 AM - 6 Nov 2018

Donald J. Trump ✓
@realDonaldTrump

Bob Hugin, successful all of his life, would be a Great Senator from New Jersey. He has my complete and total Endorsement! Get out and Vote for Bob.
15,338 Retweets **64,500** Likes
10:08 AM - 6 Nov 2018

Donald J. Trump ✓
@realDonaldTrump

Epstein all the way in Michigan House 11. She is a wonderful person and, at the same time, a real fighter. Has my Strong Endorsement!
12,101 Retweets **54,295** Likes
10:48 AM - 6 Nov 2018

Donald J. Trump ✓
@realDonaldTrump

Florida, very important - get out and vote for Florida Congressional Candidate Michael Waltz (R). He has my Strong Endorsement!
16,385 Retweets **75,166** Likes
11:52 AM - 6 Nov 2018

Donald J. Trump ✓
@realDonaldTrump

Congressman Randy Hultgren (R) of Illinois is doing a great job. Get out and Vote for Randy - Total Endorsement!
13,843 Retweets **65,785** Likes
11:56 AM - 6 Nov 2018

Donald J. Trump ✓
@realDonaldTrump

Tremendous success tonight. Thank you to all!
49,931 Retweets **252,480** Likes
8:14 PM - 6 Nov 2018

Donald J. Trump ✓
@realDonaldTrump

"There's only been 5 times in the last 105 years that an incumbent President has won seats in the Senate in the off year election. Mr. Trump has magic about him. This guy has magic coming out of his ears. He is an astonishing vote getter & campaigner. The Republicans are.........
23,025 Retweets **100,087** Likes
10:27 PM - 6 Nov 2018

Donald J. Trump ✓
@realDonaldTrump

....unbelievably lucky to have him and I'm just awed at how well they've done. It's all the Trump magic - Trump is the magic man. Incredible, he's got the entire media against him, attacking him every day, and he pulls out these enormous wins." Ben Stein, "The Capitalist Code"
18,906 Retweets **88,457** Likes
10:37 PM - 6 Nov 2018

Donald J. Trump ✓
@realDonaldTrump

.@DavidAsmanfox "How do the Democrats respond to this? Think of how his position with Republicans improves-all the candidates who won tonight. They realize how important he is because of what he did in campaigning for them. They owe him their political career." Thanks, I agree!
12,614 Retweets **62,877** Likes
10:49 PM - 6 Nov 2018

Donald J. Trump ✓
@realDonaldTrump

Received so many Congratulations from so many on our Big Victory last night, including from foreign nations (friends) that were waiting me out, and hoping, on Trade Deals. Now we can all get back to work and get things done!
22,296 Retweets **110,248** Likes
3:21 AM - 7 Nov 2018

Donald J. Trump ✓
@realDonaldTrump

Ron DeSantis showed great courage in his hard fought campaign to become the Governor of Florida. Congratulations to Ron and family!
16,381 Retweets **87,315** Likes
3:55 AM - 7 Nov 2018

Donald J. Trump
@realDonaldTrump

Those that worked with me in this incredible Midterm Election, embracing certain policies and principles, did very well. Those that did not, say goodbye! Yesterday was such a very Big Win, and all under the pressure of a Nasty and Hostile Media!
24,165 Retweets **109,847** Likes
4:07 AM - 7 Nov 2018

Donald J. Trump
@realDonaldTrump

I will be doing a news conference at The White House - 11:30 A.M. Will be discussing our success in the Midterms!
13,464 Retweets **68,992** Likes
4:36 AM - 7 Nov 2018

Donald J. Trump
@realDonaldTrump

To any of the pundits or talking heads that do not give us proper credit for this great Midterm Election, just remember two words - FAKE NEWS!
29,074 Retweets **138,690** Likes
4:52 AM - 7 Nov 2018

Donald J. Trump
@realDonaldTrump

If the Democrats think they are going to waste Taxpayer Money investigating us at the House level, then we will likewise be forced to consider investigating them for all of the leaks of Classified Information, and much else, at the Senate level. Two can play that game!
45,878 Retweets **177,925** Likes
5:04 AM - 7 Nov 2018

Donald J. Trump
@realDonaldTrump

In all fairness, Nancy Pelosi deserves to be chosen Speaker of the House by the Democrats. If they give her a hard time, perhaps we will add some Republican votes. She has earned this great honor!
18,157 Retweets **88,740** Likes
5:31 AM - 7 Nov 2018

Donald J. Trump
@realDonaldTrump

According to NBC News, Voters Nationwide Disapprove of the so-called Mueller Investigation (46%) more than they Approve (41%). You mean they are finally beginning to understand what a disgusting Witch Hunt, led by 17 Angry Democrats, is all about!
28,199 Retweets **122,357** Likes
7:39 AM - 7 Nov 2018

Donald J. Trump
@realDonaldTrump

We are pleased to announce that Matthew G. Whitaker, Chief of Staff to Attorney General Jeff Sessions at the Department of Justice, will become our new Acting Attorney General of the United States. He will serve our Country well....
29,616 Retweets **121,133** Likes
11:44 AM - 7 Nov 2018

Anthony T. Michalisko

Donald J. Trump ✓
@realDonaldTrump

....We thank Attorney General Jeff Sessions for his service, and wish him well! A permanent replacement will be nominated at a later date.
19,873 Retweets **89,159** Likes
11:44 AM - 7 Nov 2018

Donald J. Trump ✓
@realDonaldTrump

I have been fully briefed on the terrible shooting in California. Law Enforcement and First Responders, together with the FBI, are on scene. 13 people, at this time, have been reported dead. Likewise, the shooter is dead, along with the first police officer to enter the bar....
19,965 Retweets **94,326** Likes
4:38 AM - 8 Nov 2018

Donald J. Trump ✓
@realDonaldTrump

....Great bravery shown by police. California Highway Patrol was on scene within 3 minutes, with first officer to enter shot numerous times. That Sheriff's Sergeant died in the hospital. God bless all of the victims and families of the victims. Thank you to Law Enforcement.
24,628 Retweets **127,120** Likes
4:51 AM - 8 Nov 2018

Donald J. Trump ✓
@realDonaldTrump

Law Enforcement is looking into another big corruption scandal having to do with Election Fraud in #Broward and Palm Beach. Florida voted for Rick Scott!
41,257 Retweets **134,859** Likes
6:38 PM - 8 Nov 2018

Donald J. Trump ✓
@realDonaldTrump

"Presidential Proclamation Addressing Mass Migration Through the Southern Border of the United States"
17,272 Retweets **56,063** Likes
6:54 AM - 9 Nov 2018

Donald J. Trump ✓
@realDonaldTrump

.@BrianKempGA ran a great race in Georgia – he won. It is time to move on!
20,315 Retweets **85,215** Likes
7:55 AM - 9 Nov 2018

Donald J. Trump ✓
@realDonaldTrump

You mean they are just now finding votes in Florida and Georgia – but the Election was on Tuesday? Let's blame the Russians and demand an immediate apology from President Putin!
41,893 Retweets **151,370** Likes
7:58 AM - 9 Nov 2018

Donald J. Trump ✓
@realDonaldTrump

As soon as Democrats sent their best Election stealing lawyer, Marc Elias, to Broward County they miraculously started finding Democrat votes. Don't worry, Florida - I am sending much better lawyers to expose the FRAUD!
43,706 Retweets **135,525** Likes
8:52 AM - 9 Nov 2018

Donald J. Trump ✓
@realDonaldTrump

Jeff Flake(y) doesn't want to protect the Non-Senate confirmed Special Counsel, he wants to protect his future after being unelectable in Arizona for the "crime" of doing a terrible job! A weak and ineffective guy!
20,672 Retweets **84,552** Likes
9:10 AM - 9 Nov 2018

Donald J. Trump ✓
@realDonaldTrump

Rick Scott was up by 50,000+ votes on Election Day, now they "found" many votes and he is only up 15,000 votes. "The Broward Effect." How come they never find Republican votes?
33,793 Retweets **113,555** Likes
9:36 AM - 9 Nov 2018

Donald J. Trump ✓
@realDonaldTrump

Mayor Gillum conceded on Election Day and now Broward County has put him "back into play." Bill Nelson conceded Election - now he's back in play!? This is an embarrassment to our Country and to Democracy!
35,860 Retweets **128,691** Likes
10:14 AM - 9 Nov 2018

Donald J. Trump ✓
@realDonaldTrump

In the 2016 Election I was winning by so much in Florida that Broward County, which was very late with vote tabulation and probably getting ready to do a "number," couldn't do it because not enough people live in Broward for them to falsify a victory!
23,262 Retweets **86,386** Likes
10:20 AM - 9 Nov 2018

Donald J. Trump ✓
@realDonaldTrump

Thank you @marcorubio for helping to expose the potential corruption going on with respect to Election Theft in Broward and Palm Beach Counties. The WORLD is now watching closely!
29,769 Retweets **106,522** Likes
10:39 AM - 9 Nov 2018

Donald J. Trump ✓
@realDonaldTrump

Just out — in Arizona, SIGNATURES DON'T MATCH. Electoral corruption - Call for a new Election? We must protect our Democracy!
51,468 Retweets **165,943** Likes
12:33 PM - 9 Nov 2018

Donald J. Trump ✓
@realDonaldTrump

President Macron of France has just suggested that Europe build its own military in order to protect itself from the U.S., China and Russia. Very insulting, but perhaps Europe should first pay its fair share of NATO, which the U.S. subsidizes greatly!
39,996 Retweets **148,502** Likes
1:10 PM - 9 Nov 2018

Donald J. Trump ✓
@realDonaldTrump

Matthew G. Whitaker is a highly respected former U.S. Attorney from Iowa. He was chosen by Jeff Sessions to be his Chief of Staff. I did not know Mr. Whitaker. Likewise, as Chief, I did not know Mr. Whitaker except primarily as he traveled with A.G. Sessions. No social contact...
18,273 Retweets **76,252** Likes
7:52 PM - 9 Nov 2018

Donald J. Trump ✓
@realDonaldTrump

....Mr. Whitaker is very highly thought of by @SenJoniErnst, Senator @ChuckGrassley, Ambassador @TerryBranstad, Leonard Leo of Federalist Society, and many more. I feel certain he will make an outstanding Acting Attorney General!
14,498 Retweets **60,765** Likes
8:04 PM - 9 Nov 2018

Donald J. Trump ✓
@realDonaldTrump

There is no reason for these massive, deadly and costly forest fires in California except that forest management is so poor. Billions of dollars are given each year, with so many lives lost, all because of gross mismanagement of the forests. Remedy now, or no more Fed payments!
28,877 Retweets **126,161** Likes
12:08 AM - 10 Nov 2018

Donald J. Trump ✓
@realDonaldTrump

I am in Paris getting ready to celebrate the end of World War One. Is there anything better to celebrate than the end of a war, in particular that one, which was one of the bloodiest and worst of all time?
24,776 Retweets **140,736** Likes
12:17 AM - 10 Nov 2018

Donald J. Trump ✓
@realDonaldTrump

Happy 243rd Birthday to our GREAT U.S. Marine Corps
23,582 Retweets **102,693** Likes
6:09 AM - 10 Nov 2018

Donald J. Trump ✓
@realDonaldTrump

Had very productive meetings and calls for our Country today. Meeting tonight with World Leaders!
16,098 Retweets **87,953** Likes
11:06 AM - 10 Nov 2018

Donald J. Trump ✓
@realDonaldTrump

Trying to STEAL two big elections in Florida! We are watching closely!
31,297 Retweets **120,239** Likes
11:09 AM - 10 Nov 2018

Donald J. Trump ✓
@realDonaldTrump

More than 4,000 are fighting the Camp and Woolsey Fires in California that have burned over 170,000 acres. Our hearts are with those fighting the fires, the 52,000 who have evacuated, and the families of the 11 who have died. The destruction is catastrophic. God Bless them all.
24,688 Retweets **119,407** Likes
2:19 PM - 10 Nov 2018

President Trumps Tweets 2018: A Historical Archive of President Trump's Tweets

Donald J. Trump ✓
@realDonaldTrump

These California fires are expanding very, very quickly (in some cases 80-100 acres a minute). If people don't evacuate quickly, they risk being overtaken by the fire. Please listen to evacuation orders from State and local officials!
20,764 Retweets **88,081** Likes
2:20 PM - 10 Nov 2018

Donald J. Trump ✓
@realDonaldTrump

With proper Forest Management, we can stop the devastation constantly going on in California. Get Smart!
22,411 Retweets **108,365** Likes
1:40 AM - 11 Nov 2018

Donald J. Trump ✓
@realDonaldTrump

On this Veterans Day — the 100th Anniversary of the end of WWI, we honor the brave HEROES who fought for America in the Great War, and every Veteran who has worn the uniform and kept our Nation Safe, Strong and FREE!
20,362 Retweets **77,635** Likes
6:16 AM - 11 Nov 2018

Donald J. Trump ✓
@realDonaldTrump

Beautiful ceremony today in Paris commemorating the end of World War One. Many World leaders in attendance. Thank you to @EmmanuelMacron, President of France! Now off to Suresnes American Cemetery to make speech in honor of our great heroes! Then back to the U.S.A.
18,771 Retweets **95,502** Likes
6:52 AM - 11 Nov 2018

Donald J. Trump ✓
@realDonaldTrump

Poland, a great country - Congratulations on the 100th Anniversary of your Independence. I will never forget my time there!
24,156 Retweets **109,220** Likes
8:03 AM - 11 Nov 2018

Donald J. Trump ✓
@realDonaldTrump

Exactly 100 years ago today, on November 11th, 1918, World War I came to an end. We are gathered together, at this hallowed resting place, to pay tribute to the brave Americans who gave their last breath in that mighty struggle....
20,988 Retweets **93,273** Likes
8:38 PM - 11 Nov 2018

Donald J. Trump ✓
@realDonaldTrump

Just returned from France where much was accomplished in my meetings with World Leaders. Never easy bringing up the fact that the U.S. must be treated fairly, which it hasn't, on both Military and Trade. We pay for LARGE portions of other countries military protection,........
24,416 Retweets **107,533** Likes
4:03 AM - 12 Nov 2018

Donald J. Trump ✓
@realDonaldTrump

.....hundreds of billions of dollars, for the great privilege of losing hundreds of billions of dollars with these same countries on trade. I told them that this situation cannot continue - It is, and always has been, ridiculously unfair to the United States. Massive amounts.....
18,266 Retweets **79,950** Likes
4:10 AM - 12 Nov 2018

Donald J. Trump ✓
@realDonaldTrump

.....of money spent on protecting other countries, and we get nothing but Trade Deficits and Losses. It is time that these very rich countries either pay the United States for its great military protection, or protect themselves...and Trade must be made FREE and FAIR!
22,058 Retweets **94,338** Likes
4:21 AM - 12 Nov 2018

Donald J. Trump ✓
@realDonaldTrump

The Florida Election should be called in favor of Rick Scott and Ron DeSantis in that large numbers of new ballots showed up out of nowhere, and many ballots are missing or forged. An honest vote count is no longer possible-ballots massively infected. Must go with Election Night!
34,108 Retweets **120,216** Likes
4:44 AM - 12 Nov 2018

Donald J. Trump ✓
@realDonaldTrump

The prospect of Presidential Harassment by the Dems is causing the Stock Market big headaches!
20,268 Retweets **82,850** Likes
7:34 AM - 12 Nov 2018

Donald J. Trump ✓
@realDonaldTrump

The California Fire Fighters, FEMA and First Responders are amazing and very brave. Thank you and God Bless you all!
22,229 Retweets **123,755** Likes
8:31 AM - 12 Nov 2018

Donald J. Trump ✓
@realDonaldTrump

American Cable Association has big problems with Comcast. They say that Comcast routinely violates Antitrust Laws. "These guys are acting much worse, and have much more potential for damage to consumers, than anything AT&T-Time Warner would do." Charlie Gasparino
17,735 Retweets **68,240** Likes
10:13 AM - 12 Nov 2018

Donald J. Trump ✓
@realDonaldTrump

Hopefully, Saudi Arabia and OPEC will not be cutting oil production. Oil prices should be much lower based on supply!
17,856 Retweets **75,667** Likes
10:21 AM - 12 Nov 2018

President Trumps Tweets 2018: A Historical Archive of President Trump's Tweets

Donald J. Trump ✓
@realDonaldTrump

I just approved an expedited request for a Major Disaster Declaration for the State of California. Wanted to respond quickly in order to alleviate some of the incredible suffering going on. I am with you all the way. God Bless all of the victims and families affected.
27,766 Retweets **136,850** Likes
5:19 PM - 12 Nov 2018

Donald J. Trump ✓
@realDonaldTrump

Emmanuel Macron suggests building its own army to protect Europe against the U.S., China and Russia. But it was Germany in World Wars One & Two - How did that work out for France? They were starting to learn German in Paris before the U.S. came along. Pay for NATO or not!
36,442 Retweets **124,632** Likes
3:50 AM - 13 Nov 2018

Donald J. Trump ✓
@realDonaldTrump

On Trade, France makes excellent wine, but so does the U.S. The problem is that France makes it very hard for the U.S. to sell its wines into France, and charges big Tariffs, whereas the U.S. makes it easy for French wines, and charges very small Tariffs. Not fair, must change!
28,695 Retweets **119,923** Likes
5:07 AM - 13 Nov 2018

Donald J. Trump ✓
@realDonaldTrump

The problem is that Emmanuel suffers from a very low Approval Rating in France, 26%, and an unemployment rate of almost 10%. He was just trying to get onto another subject. By the way, there is no country more Nationalist than France, very proud people-and rightfully so!........
28,655 Retweets **108,932** Likes
5:17 AM - 13 Nov 2018

Donald J. Trump ✓
@realDonaldTrump

......MAKE FRANCE GREAT AGAIN!
41,695 Retweets **155,839** Likes
5:18 AM - 13 Nov 2018

Donald J. Trump ✓
@realDonaldTrump

By the way, when the helicopter couldn't fly to the first cemetery in France because of almost zero visibility, I suggested driving. Secret Service said NO, too far from airport & big Paris shutdown. Speech next day at American Cemetery in pouring rain! Little reported-Fake News!
30,563 Retweets **120,946** Likes
7:49 AM - 13 Nov 2018

Donald J. Trump ✓
@realDonaldTrump

When will Bill Nelson concede in Florida? The characters running Broward and Palm Beach voting will not be able to "find" enough votes, too much spotlight on them now!
25,943 Retweets **101,627** Likes
8:32 AM - 13 Nov 2018

Anthony T. Michalisko

Donald J. Trump ✓
@realDonaldTrump

The story in the New York Times concerning North Korea developing missile bases is inaccurate. We fully know about the sites being discussed, nothing new - and nothing happening out of the normal. Just more Fake News. I will be the first to let you know if things go bad!
33,684 Retweets **124,735** Likes
9:07 AM - 13 Nov 2018

Donald J. Trump ✓
@realDonaldTrump

We mourn for the lives lost and we pray for the victims of the California Wildfires. I want to thank the Firefighters and First Responders for their incredible courage in the face of grave danger....
15,574 Retweets **68,741** Likes
11:38 AM - 13 Nov 2018

Donald J. Trump ✓
@realDonaldTrump

Today, we gathered for Diwali, a holiday observed by Buddhists, Sikhs, and Jains throughout the United States & around the world. Hundreds of millions of people have gathered with family & friends to light the Diya and to mark the beginning of a New Year.
11,281 Retweets **50,592** Likes
1:03 PM - 13 Nov 2018

Donald J. Trump ✓
@realDonaldTrump

It was my great honor to host a celebration of Diwali, the Hindu Festival of Lights, in the Roosevelt Room at the @WhiteHouse this afternoon. Very, very special people!
17,827 Retweets **77,288** Likes
1:20 PM - 13 Nov 2018

Donald J. Trump ✓
@realDonaldTrump

"Boom: Record high business optimism, need for employees at 45-year high"
22,613 Retweets **82,549** Likes
1:35 PM - 13 Nov 2018

Donald J. Trump ✓
@realDonaldTrump

Not seen in many years, America's steelworkers get a hard-earned raise because of my Administration's policies to help bring back the U.S. steel industry, which is critical to our National Security. I will always protect America and its workers!
22,541 Retweets **100,528** Likes
11:28 AM - 14 Nov 2018

Donald J. Trump ✓
@realDonaldTrump

Was just briefed by @FEMA_Brock and @SecretaryZinke, who are in California. Thank you to the great Firefighters, First Responders and @FEMA for the incredible job they are doing w/ the California Wildfires. Our Nation appreciates your heroism, courage & genius. God Bless you all!
12,652 Retweets **60,166** Likes
11:35 AM - 14 Nov 2018

Donald J. Trump ✓
@realDonaldTrump

Just spoke to Governor Jerry Brown to let him know that we are with him, and the people of California, all the way!
16,962 Retweets **100,277** Likes
11:58 AM - 14 Nov 2018

President Trumps Tweets 2018: A Historical Archive of President Trump's Tweets

Donald J. Trump ✓
@realDonaldTrump

I am grateful to be here today w/ Members of the House & Senate who have poured their time, heart and energy into the crucial issue of Prison Reform. Working together w/ my Admin over the last two years, these members have reached a bipartisan agreement...

17,880 Retweets **71,778** Likes
2:10 PM - 14 Nov 2018

Donald J. Trump ✓
@realDonaldTrump

Our pledge to hire American includes those leaving prison and looking for a very fresh start — new job, and new life. The legislation I am supporting today contains many significant reforms.

16,830 Retweets **67,035** Likes
3:26 PM - 14 Nov 2018

Donald J. Trump ✓
@realDonaldTrump

The White House is running very smoothly and the results for our Nation are obviously very good. We are the envy of the world. But anytime I even think about making changes, the FAKE NEWS MEDIA goes crazy, always seeking to make us look as bad as possible! Very dishonest!

25,420 Retweets **107,851** Likes
3:59 AM - 15 Nov 2018

Donald J. Trump ✓
@realDonaldTrump

The inner workings of the Mueller investigation are a total mess. They have found no collusion and have gone absolutely nuts. They are screaming and shouting at people, horribly threatening them to come up with the answers they want. They are a disgrace to our Nation and don't...

29,032 Retweets **110,132** Likes
4:14 AM - 15 Nov 2018

Donald J. Trump ✓
@realDonaldTrump

....care how many lives the ruin. These are Angry People, including the highly conflicted Bob Mueller, who worked for Obama for 8 years. They won't even look at all of the bad acts and crimes on the other side. A TOTAL WITCH HUNT LIKE NO OTHER IN AMERICAN HISTORY!

28,815 Retweets **114,556** Likes
4:32 AM - 15 Nov 2018

Donald J. Trump ✓
@realDonaldTrump

Universities will someday study what highly conflicted (and NOT Senate approved) Bob Mueller and his gang of Democrat thugs have done to destroy people. Why is he protecting Crooked Hillary, Comey, McCabe, Lisa Page & her lover, Peter S, and all of his friends on the other side?

30,608 Retweets **113,603** Likes
6:49 AM - 15 Nov 2018

Donald J. Trump ✓
@realDonaldTrump

The only "Collusion" is that of the Democrats with Russia and many others. Why didn't the FBI take the Server from the DNC? They still don't have it. Check out how biased Facebook, Google and Twitter are in favor of the Democrats. That's the real Collusion!

31,772 Retweets **111,120** Likes
6:59 AM - 15 Nov 2018

Donald J. Trump ✓
@realDonaldTrump

.@FLOTUS Melania and I were honored to visit with our GREAT U.S. MARINES at the Marine Barracks here in Washington, D.C. We love you @USMC @MBWDC!
14,804 Retweets **63,340** Likes
12:08 PM - 15 Nov 2018

Donald J. Trump ✓
@realDonaldTrump

It was my great honor to host a @WhiteHouse Conference on Supporting Veterans & Military Families... To everyone here today who has served our Country in uniform, & to every Veteran & Military family across our land, I want to express the eternal gratitude of our entire Nation!
13,583 Retweets **58,707** Likes
12:34 PM - 15 Nov 2018

Donald J. Trump ✓
@realDonaldTrump

Last year, I signed the landmark VA Accountability Act to ensure those who mistreat our Veterans can be held fully accountable. Since my inauguration, we have removed more than 3,600 government employees who were not giving our Vets the care they deserve....
19,203 Retweets **77,938** Likes
12:39 PM - 15 Nov 2018

Donald J. Trump ✓
@realDonaldTrump

It is our sacred duty to support America's Service Members every single day they wear the uniform – and every day after when they return home as Veterans. Together we will HONOR those who defend us, we will CHERISH those who protect us, and we will celebrate the amazing heroes...
17,764 Retweets **74,203** Likes
12:43 PM - 15 Nov 2018

Donald J. Trump ✓
@realDonaldTrump

Today in the East Room of the @WhiteHouse, it was my true privilege to award seven extraordinary Americans with the Presidential Medal of Freedom...
12,103 Retweets **51,684** Likes
11:35 AM - 16 Nov 2018

Donald J. Trump ✓
@realDonaldTrump

People are not being told that the Republican Party is on track to pick up two seats in the U.S. Senate, and epic victory: 53 to 47. The Fake News Media only wants to speak of the House, where the Midterm results were better than other sitting Presidents.
26,477 Retweets **103,743** Likes
11:41 AM - 16 Nov 2018

Donald J. Trump ✓
@realDonaldTrump

PRESIDENTIAL MEDAL OF FREEDOM
12,112 Retweets **57,004** Likes
1:47 PM - 16 Nov 2018

President Trumps Tweets 2018: A Historical Archive of President Trump's Tweets

Donald J. Trump ✓
@realDonaldTrump

Congratulations to Ron DeSantis on becoming the new Governor of Florida. Against all odds, he fought & fought & fought, the result being a historic victory. He never gave up and never will. He will be a great Governor!
22,249 Retweets **102,392** Likes
4:36 PM - 16 Nov 2018

Donald J. Trump ✓
@realDonaldTrump

Congratulations to Brian Kemp on becoming the new Governor of Georgia. Stacey Abrams fought brilliantly and hard - she will have a terrific political future! Brian was unrelenting and will become a great Governor for the truly Wonderful People of Georgia!
20,251 Retweets **104,526** Likes
4:37 PM - 16 Nov 2018

Donald J. Trump ✓
@realDonaldTrump

Isn't it ironic that large Caravans of people are marching to our border wanting U.S.A. asylum because they are fearful of being in their country - yet they are proudly waving....
30,494 Retweets **120,807** Likes
4:43 PM - 16 Nov 2018

Donald J. Trump ✓
@realDonaldTrump

....their country's flag. Can this be possible? Yes, because it is all a BIG CON, and the American taxpayer is paying for it!
26,273 Retweets **111,566** Likes
4:43 PM - 16 Nov 2018

Donald J. Trump ✓
@realDonaldTrump

Thank you @JerryBrownGov. Look forward to joining you and @GavinNewsom tomorrow in California. We are with you!
10,646 Retweets **49,420** Likes
7:14 PM - 16 Nov 2018

Donald J. Trump ✓
@realDonaldTrump

I can get Nancy Pelosi as many votes as she wants in order for her to be Speaker of the House. She deserves this victory, she has earned it - but there are those in her party who are trying to take it away. She will win! @TomReedCongress
13,937 Retweets **66,336** Likes
3:37 AM - 17 Nov 2018

Donald J. Trump ✓
@realDonaldTrump

Congratulations to Andrew Gillum on having run a really tough and competitive race for Governor of the Great State of Florida. He will be a strong Democrat warrior long into the future - a force to reckon with!
10,869 Retweets **68,690** Likes
8:39 AM - 17 Nov 2018

Donald J. Trump ✓
@realDonaldTrump

The New York Times did a phony story, as usual, about my relationship with @VP Mike Pence. They made up sources and refused to ask me, the only one that would know, for a quote....
18,296 Retweets **78,340** Likes
8:42 AM - 17 Nov 2018

Donald J. Trump ✓
@realDonaldTrump

....I can't imagine any President having a better or closer relationship with their Vice President then the two of us. Just more FAKE NEWS, the Enemy of the People!
19,875 Retweets **84,668** Likes
8:42 AM - 17 Nov 2018

Donald J. Trump ✓
@realDonaldTrump

Heading to California with @GOPLeader Kevin McCarthy, @RepLaMalfa, and @KenCalvert. Look forward to being with our brave Firefighters, First Responders and @FEMA, along with the many brave People of California. We are with you all the way – God Bless you all!
11,062 Retweets **59,048** Likes
8:47 AM - 17 Nov 2018

Donald J. Trump ✓
@realDonaldTrump

Incredible to be with our GREAT HEROES today in California. We will always be with you!
22,883 Retweets **105,635** Likes
6:48 PM - 17 Nov 2018

Donald J. Trump ✓
@realDonaldTrump

I will be interviewed by Chris Wallace on @FoxNews at 2:00 P.M. and 7:00 P.M. Enjoy!
9,591 Retweets **58,122** Likes
9:30 AM - 18 Nov 2018

Donald J. Trump ✓
@realDonaldTrump

So funny to see little Adam Schitt (D-CA) talking about the fact that Acting Attorney General Matt Whitaker was not approved by the Senate, but not mentioning the fact that Bob Mueller (who is highly conflicted) was not approved by the Senate!
36,809 Retweets **133,250** Likes
10:01 AM - 18 Nov 2018

Donald J. Trump ✓
@realDonaldTrump

The Mayor of Tijuana, Mexico, just stated that "the City is ill-prepared to handle this many migrants, the backlog could last 6 months." Likewise, the U.S. is ill-prepared for this invasion, and will not stand for it. They are causing crime and big problems in Mexico. Go home!
31,813 Retweets **113,279** Likes
10:42 AM - 18 Nov 2018

Donald J. Trump ✓
@realDonaldTrump

Catch and Release is an obsolete term. It is now Catch and Detain. Illegal Immigrants trying to come into the U.S.A., often proudly flying the flag of their nation as they ask for U.S. Asylum, will be detained or turned away. Dems must approve Border Security & Wall NOW!
38,765 Retweets **149,684** Likes
11:55 AM - 18 Nov 2018

President Trumps Tweets 2018: A Historical Archive of President Trump's Tweets

Donald J. Trump ✓
@realDonaldTrump

From day one Rick Scott never wavered. He was a great Governor and will be even a greater Senator in representing the People of Florida. Congratulations to Rick on having waged such a courageous and successful campaign!
18,192 Retweets **85,160** Likes
11:59 AM - 18 Nov 2018

Donald J. Trump ✓
@realDonaldTrump

.@cindyhydesmith loves Mississippi and our Great U.S.A.
10,099 Retweets **42,436** Likes
6:30 AM - 19 Nov 2018

Donald J. Trump ✓
@realDonaldTrump

Of course we should have captured Osama Bin Laden long before we did. I pointed him out in my book just BEFORE the attack on the World Trade Center. President Clinton famously missed his shot. We paid Pakistan Billions of Dollars & they never told us he was living there. Fools!..
37,999 Retweets **148,642** Likes
7:26 AM - 19 Nov 2018

Donald J. Trump ✓
@realDonaldTrump

....We no longer pay Pakistan the $Billions because they would take our money and do nothing for us, Bin Laden being a prime example, Afghanistan being another. They were just one of many countries that take from the United States without giving anything in return. That's ENDING!
42,439 Retweets **173,471** Likes
7:41 AM - 19 Nov 2018

Donald J. Trump ✓
@realDonaldTrump

The Fake News is showing old footage of people climbing over our Ocean Area Fence. This is what it really looks like - no climbers anymore under our Administration!
51,765 Retweets **174,421** Likes
11:10 AM - 19 Nov 2018

Donald J. Trump ✓
@realDonaldTrump

I hope the discovery and eventual recovery of the Argentine submarine San Juan brings needed closure to the wonderful families of those brave missing sailors. I look forward to hearing more from my friend President @MauricioMacri in Argentina later this month.
18,288 Retweets **91,128** Likes
8:19 PM - 19 Nov 2018

Donald J. Trump ✓
@realDonaldTrump

So-called comedian Michelle Wolf bombed so badly last year at the White House Correspondents' Dinner that this year, for the first time in decades, they will have an author instead of a comedian. Good first step in comeback of a dying evening and tradition! Maybe I will go?
22,461 Retweets **123,576** Likes
7:43 PM - 20 Nov 2018

Donald J. Trump ✓
@realDonaldTrump

AMERICA FIRST!
43,074 Retweets **183,664** Likes
8:40 PM - 20 Nov 2018

Donald J. Trump ✓
@realDonaldTrump

Oil prices getting lower. Great! Like a big Tax Cut for America and the World. Enjoy! $54, was just $82. Thank you to Saudi Arabia, but let's go lower!
30,478 Retweets **115,893** Likes
4:49 AM - 21 Nov 2018

Donald J. Trump ✓
@realDonaldTrump

MAKE AMERICA GREAT AGAIN!
42,711 Retweets **195,294** Likes
4:50 AM - 21 Nov 2018

Donald J. Trump ✓
@realDonaldTrump

"'Trump Imitation Syndrome' is afflicting the president's liberal enemies" Thank you @MGoodwin_NYPost!
11,275 Retweets **42,332** Likes
6:16 AM - 21 Nov 2018

Donald J. Trump ✓
@realDonaldTrump

Great new book out, "Mad Politics: Keeping Your Sanity in a World Gone Crazy" by @RealDrGina Loudon. Go out and get your copy today — a great read!
12,836 Retweets **55,311** Likes
7:13 AM - 21 Nov 2018

Donald J. Trump ✓
@realDonaldTrump

Sorry Chief Justice John Roberts, but you do indeed have "Obama judges," and they have a much different point of view than the people who are charged with the safety of our country. It would be great if the 9th Circuit was indeed an "independent judiciary," but if it is why......
23,967 Retweets **88,727** Likes
12:51 PM - 21 Nov 2018

Donald J. Trump ✓
@realDonaldTrump

.....are so many opposing view (on Border and Safety) cases filed there, and why are a vast number of those cases overturned. Please study the numbers, they are shocking. We need protection and security - these rulings are making our country unsafe! Very dangerous and unwise!
22,417 Retweets **89,238** Likes
1:09 PM - 21 Nov 2018

Donald J. Trump ✓
@realDonaldTrump

"Thank you to President Trump on the Border. No American President has ever done this before." Hector Garza, National Border Patrol Council
18,323 Retweets **78,881** Likes
1:31 PM - 21 Nov 2018

President Trumps Tweets 2018: A Historical Archive of President Trump's Tweets

Donald J. Trump ✓
@realDonaldTrump

There are a lot of CRIMINALS in the Caravan. We will stop them. Catch and Detain! Judicial Activism, by people who know nothing about security and the safety of our citizens, is putting our country in great danger. Not good!
25,090 Retweets **100,552** Likes
1:42 PM - 21 Nov 2018

Donald J. Trump ✓
@realDonaldTrump

"79% of these decisions have been overturned in the 9th Circuit." @FoxNews A terrible, costly and dangerous disgrace. It has become a dumping ground for certain lawyers looking for easy wins and delays. Much talk over dividing up the 9th Circuit into 2 or 3 Circuits. Too big!
20,603 Retweets **77,622** Likes
2:17 PM - 21 Nov 2018

Donald J. Trump ✓
@realDonaldTrump

Brutal and Extended Cold Blast could shatter ALL RECORDS - Whatever happened to Global Warming?
28,427 Retweets **114,148** Likes
4:23 PM - 21 Nov 2018

Donald J. Trump ✓
@realDonaldTrump

You just can't win with the Fake News Media. A big story today is that because I have pushed so hard and gotten Gasoline Prices so low, more people are driving and I have caused traffic jams throughout our Great Nation. Sorry everyone!
38,571 Retweets **169,831** Likes
4:36 PM - 21 Nov 2018

Donald J. Trump ✓
@realDonaldTrump

"It's a mean & nasty world out there, the Middle East in particular. This is a long and historic commitment, & one that is absolutely vital to America's national security." @SecPompeo I agree 100%. In addition, many Billions of Dollars of purchases made in U.S., big Jobs & Oil!
12,844 Retweets **57,554** Likes
3:58 AM - 22 Nov 2018

Donald J. Trump ✓
@realDonaldTrump

HAPPY THANKSGIVING TO ALL!
33,877 Retweets **202,283** Likes
4:01 AM - 22 Nov 2018

Donald J. Trump ✓
@realDonaldTrump

Justice Roberts can say what he wants, but the 9th Circuit is a complete & total disaster. It is out of control, has a horrible reputation, is overturned more than any Circuit in the Country, 79%, & is used to get an almost guaranteed result. Judges must not Legislate Security...
27,034 Retweets **106,655** Likes
4:21 AM - 22 Nov 2018

Donald J. Trump ✓
@realDonaldTrump

....and Safety at the Border, or anywhere else. They know nothing about it and are making our Country unsafe. Our great Law Enforcement professionals MUST BE ALLOWED TO DO THEIR JOB! If not there will be only bedlam, chaos, injury and death. We want the Constitution as written!
23,501 Retweets **97,395** Likes
4:30 AM - 22 Nov 2018

Donald J. Trump ✓
@realDonaldTrump

Will be speaking with our great military in different parts of the world, through teleconference, at 9:00 A.M. Eastern. Then it will be off to see our Coast Guard patriots & to thank them for the great job they have been doing, especially with the hurricanes. Happy Thanksgiving!
16,717 Retweets **84,492** Likes
5:42 AM - 22 Nov 2018

Donald J. Trump ✓
@realDonaldTrump

This is the coldest weather in the history of the Thanksgiving Day Parade in NYC, and one of the coldest Thanksgivings on record!
15,873 Retweets **90,827** Likes
1:26 PM - 22 Nov 2018

Donald J. Trump ✓
@realDonaldTrump

Our highly trained security professionals are not allowed to do their job on the Border because of the Judicial Activism and Interference by the 9th Circuit. Nevertheless, they are working hard to make America a safer place, though hard to do when anybody filing a lawsuit wins!
28,093 Retweets **116,801** Likes
3:07 PM - 22 Nov 2018

Donald J. Trump ✓
@realDonaldTrump

Republicans and Democrats MUST come together, finally, with a major Border Security package, which will include funding for the Wall. After 40 years of talk, it is finally time for action. Fix the Border, for once and for all, NOW!
38,114 Retweets **163,397** Likes
4:41 AM - 23 Nov 2018

Donald J. Trump ✓
@realDonaldTrump

Really good Criminal Justice Reform has a true shot at major bipartisan support. @senatemajldr Mitch McConnell and @SenSchumer have a real chance to do something so badly needed in our country. Already passed, with big vote, in House. Would be a major victory for ALL!
17,301 Retweets **74,443** Likes
9:14 AM - 23 Nov 2018

Donald J. Trump ✓
@realDonaldTrump

I am extremely happy and proud of the job being done by @USTreasury Secretary @StevenMnuchin1. The FAKE NEWS likes to write stories to the contrary, quoting phony sources or jealous people, but they aren't true. They never like to ask me for a quote b/c it would kill their story.
20,326 Retweets **90,763** Likes
3:48 PM - 23 Nov 2018

President Trumps Tweets 2018: A Historical Archive of President Trump's Tweets

Donald J. Trump ✓
@realDonaldTrump

Migrants at the Southern Border will not be allowed into the United States until their claims are individually approved in court. We only will allow those who come into our Country legally. Other than that our very strong policy is Catch and Detain. No "Releasing" into the U.S...
38,100 Retweets **166,298** Likes
3:49 PM - 24 Nov 2018

Donald J. Trump ✓
@realDonaldTrump

....All will stay in Mexico. If for any reason it becomes necessary, we will CLOSE our Southern Border. There is no way that the United States will, after decades of abuse, put up with this costly and dangerous situation anymore!
34,401 Retweets **145,270** Likes
3:56 PM - 24 Nov 2018

Donald J. Trump ✓
@realDonaldTrump

Victor Davis Hanson was a very good and interesting guest of Mark Levin on @FoxNews. He wrote a highly touted book called "The Second World Wars" and a new book will soon be coming out called "The Case For Trump." Recommend both. @marklevinshow
14,504 Retweets **61,137** Likes
4:12 AM - 25 Nov 2018

Donald J. Trump ✓
@realDonaldTrump

I will be in Gulfport and Tupelo, Mississippi, on Monday night doing two Rallies for Senator Hyde-Smith, who has a very important Election on Tuesday. She is an outstanding person who is strong on the Border, Crime, Military, our great Vets, Healthcare & the 2nd A. Needed in D.C.
18,759 Retweets **75,882** Likes
4:30 AM - 25 Nov 2018

Donald J. Trump ✓
@realDonaldTrump

The large and violent French protests don't take into account how badly the United States has been treated on Trade by the European Union or on fair and reasonable payments for our GREAT military protection. Both of these topics must be remedied soon.
17,939 Retweets **76,443** Likes
5:16 AM - 25 Nov 2018

Donald J. Trump ✓
@realDonaldTrump

Would be very SMART if Mexico would stop the Caravans long before they get to our Southern Border, or if originating countries would not let them form (it is a way they get certain people out of their country and dump in U.S. No longer). Dems created this problem. No crossings!
30,904 Retweets **128,893** Likes
5:28 AM - 25 Nov 2018

Donald J. Trump ✓
@realDonaldTrump

So great that oil prices are falling (thank you President T). Add that, which is like a big Tax Cut, to our other good Economic news. Inflation down (are you listening Fed)!
23,248 Retweets **111,647** Likes
5:46 AM - 25 Nov 2018

Donald J. Trump ✓
@realDonaldTrump

Mississippi, Vote for @cindyhydesmith on Tuesday. Respected by all. We need her in Washington!. Thanks!
14,803 Retweets **57,850** Likes
12:13 PM - 25 Nov 2018

Donald J. Trump ✓
@realDonaldTrump

General Anthony Tata: "President Trump is a man of his word & he said he was going to be tough on the Border, and he is tough on the Border. He has rightfully strengthened the Border in the face of an unprecedented threat. It's the right move by President Trump." Thanks General!
21,474 Retweets **84,645** Likes
12:20 PM - 25 Nov 2018

Donald J. Trump ✓
@realDonaldTrump

Europe has to pay their fair share for Military Protection. The European Union, for many years, has taken advantage of us on Trade, and then they don't live up to their Military commitment through NATO. Things must change fast!
21,522 Retweets **88,108** Likes
12:27 PM - 25 Nov 2018

Donald J. Trump ✓
@realDonaldTrump

Clinton Foundation donations drop 42% - which shows that they illegally played the power game. They monetized their political influence through the Foundation. "During her tenure the State Department was put in the service of the Clinton Foundation." Andrew McCarthy
36,864 Retweets **121,797** Likes
12:39 PM - 25 Nov 2018

Donald J. Trump ✓
@realDonaldTrump

.@60Minutes did a phony story about child separation when they know we had the exact same policy as the Obama Administration. In fact a picture of children in jails was used by other Fake Media to show how bad (cruel) we are, but it was in 2014 during O years. Obama separated....
29,830 Retweets **103,732** Likes
5:59 PM - 25 Nov 2018

Donald J. Trump ✓
@realDonaldTrump

....children from parents, as did Bush etc., because that is the policy and law. I tried to keep them together but the problem is, when you do that, vast numbers of additional people storm the Border. So with Obama seperation is fine, but with Trump it's not. Fake 60 Minutes!
28,221 Retweets **114,356** Likes
6:07 PM - 25 Nov 2018

Donald J. Trump ✓
@realDonaldTrump

When Mueller does his final report, will he be covering all of his conflicts of interest in a preamble, will he be recommending action on all of the crimes of many kinds from those "on the other side"(whatever happened to Podesta?), and will he be putting in statements from.....
26,651 Retweets **100,397** Likes
6:33 AM - 26 Nov 2018

 Donald J. Trump ✓
@realDonaldTrump

....hundreds of people closely involved with my campaign who never met, saw or spoke to a Russian during this period? So many campaign workers, people inside from the beginning, ask me why they have not been called (they want to be). There was NO Collusion & Mueller knows it!

22,863 Retweets **93,887** Likes
6:44 AM - 26 Nov 2018

 Donald J. Trump ✓
@realDonaldTrump

On the ten-year anniversary of the Mumbai terror attack, the U.S. stands with the people of India in their quest for justice. The attack killed 166 innocents, including six Americans. We will never let terrorists win, or even come close to winning!

25,128 Retweets **104,730** Likes
11:45 AM - 26 Nov 2018

 Donald J. Trump ✓
@realDonaldTrump

While CNN doesn't do great in the United States based on ratings, outside of the U.S. they have very little competition. Throughout the world, CNN has a powerful voice portraying the United States in an unfair....

21,997 Retweets **82,928** Likes
11:47 AM - 26 Nov 2018

 Donald J. Trump ✓
@realDonaldTrump

....and false way. Something has to be done, including the possibility of the United States starting our own Worldwide Network to show the World the way we really are, GREAT!

19,972 Retweets **82,507** Likes
11:47 AM - 26 Nov 2018

 Donald J. Trump ✓
@realDonaldTrump

Brad Raffensperger will be a fantastic Secretary of State for Georgia - will work closely with @BrianKempGA. It is really important that you get out and vote for Brad - early voting....

12,276 Retweets **49,799** Likes
12:20 PM - 26 Nov 2018

 Donald J. Trump ✓
@realDonaldTrump

....starts today, election is on December 4th. @VoteBradRaff is tough on Crime and Borders, Loves our Military and Vets. He will be great for jobs!

9,886 Retweets **40,162** Likes
12:20 PM - 26 Nov 2018

Donald J. Trump ✓
@realDonaldTrump

The Phony Witch Hunt continues, but Mueller and his gang of Angry Dems are only looking at one side, not the other. Wait until it comes out how horribly & viciously they are treating people, ruining lives for them refusing to lie. Mueller is a conflicted prosecutor gone rogue....

25,750 Retweets **93,537** Likes
4:30 AM - 27 Nov 2018

Donald J. Trump ✓
@realDonaldTrump

....The Fake News Media builds Bob Mueller up as a Saint, when in actuality he is the exact opposite. He is doing TREMENDOUS damage to our Criminal Justice System, where he is only looking at one side and not the other. Heroes will come of this, and it won't be Mueller and his...
24,939 Retweets **94,209** Likes
4:42 AM - 27 Nov 2018

Donald J. Trump ✓
@realDonaldTrump

....terrible Gang of Angry Democrats. Look at their past, and look where they come from. The now $30,000,000 Witch Hunt continues and they've got nothing but ruined lives. Where is the Server? Let these terrible people go back to the Clinton Foundation and "Justice" Department!
28,872 Retweets **105,226** Likes
5:07 AM - 27 Nov 2018

Donald J. Trump ✓
@realDonaldTrump

Polls are open in Mississippi. We need Cindy Hyde-Smith in Washington. GO OUT AND VOTE. Thanks!
17,248 Retweets **69,573** Likes
5:32 AM - 27 Nov 2018

Donald J. Trump ✓
@realDonaldTrump

Very disappointed with General Motors and their CEO, Mary Barra, for closing plants in Ohio, Michigan and Maryland. Nothing being closed in Mexico & China. The U.S. saved General Motors, and this is the THANKS we get! We are now looking at cutting all @GM subsidies, including....
31,187 Retweets **124,746** Likes
11:05 AM - 27 Nov 2018

Donald J. Trump ✓
@realDonaldTrump

....for electric cars. General Motors made a big China bet years ago when they built plants there (and in Mexico) - don't think that bet is going to pay off. I am here to protect America's Workers!
24,945 Retweets **109,307** Likes
11:05 AM - 27 Nov 2018

Donald J. Trump ✓
@realDonaldTrump

The Mueller Witch Hunt is a total disgrace. They are looking at supposedly stolen Crooked Hillary Clinton Emails (even though they don't want to look at the DNC Server), but have no interest in the Emails that Hillary DELETED & acid washed AFTER getting a Congressional Subpoena!
30,843 Retweets **110,777** Likes
4:31 PM - 27 Nov 2018

Donald J. Trump ✓
@realDonaldTrump

Brenda Snipes, in charge of voting in Broward County, Florida, was just spotted wearing a beautiful dress with 300 I VOTED signs on it. Just kidding, she is a fine, very honorable and highly respected voting tactician!
19,577 Retweets **93,850** Likes
7:38 PM - 27 Nov 2018

President Trumps Tweets 2018: A Historical Archive of President Trump's Tweets

Donald J. Trump ✓
@realDonaldTrump

Congratulations to Senator Cindy Hyde-Smith on your big WIN in the Great State of Mississippi. We are all very proud of you!
21,557 Retweets **107,408** Likes
7:42 PM - 27 Nov 2018

Donald J. Trump ✓
@realDonaldTrump

While the disgusting Fake News is doing everything within their power not to report it that way, at least 3 major players are intimating that the Angry Mueller Gang of Dems is viciously telling witnesses to lie about facts & they will get relief. This is our Joseph McCarthy Era!
27,912 Retweets **95,339** Likes
5:39 AM - 28 Nov 2018

Donald J. Trump ✓
@realDonaldTrump

The reason that the small truck business in the U.S. is such a go to favorite is that, for many years, Tariffs of 25% have been put on small trucks coming into our country. It is called the "chicken tax." If we did that with cars coming in, many more cars would be built here.....
17,319 Retweets **71,225** Likes
6:43 AM - 28 Nov 2018

Donald J. Trump ✓
@realDonaldTrump

.....and G.M. would not be closing their plants in Ohio, Michigan & Maryland. Get smart Congress. Also, the countries that send us cars have taken advantage of the U.S. for decades. The President has great power on this issue - Because of the G.M. event, it is being studied now!
17,602 Retweets **73,674** Likes
6:49 AM - 28 Nov 2018

Donald J. Trump ✓
@realDonaldTrump

Steel Dynamics announced that it will build a brand new 3 million ton steel mill in the Southwest that will create 600 good-paying U.S. JOBS. Steel JOBS are coming back to America, just like I predicted. Congratulations to Steel Dynamics!
27,325 Retweets **114,488** Likes
8:09 AM - 28 Nov 2018

Donald J. Trump ✓
@realDonaldTrump

On behalf of @FLOTUS Melania and the entire Trump family, I want to wish you all a very MERRY CHRISTMAS! May this Christmas Season bring peace to your hearts, warmth to your homes, cheer to your spirits and JOY TO THE WORLD! #NCTL2018
29,737 Retweets **125,182** Likes
3:32 PM - 28 Nov 2018

Donald J. Trump ✓
@realDonaldTrump

Sebastian Gorka, a very talented man who I got to know well while he was working at the White House, has just written an excellent book, "Why We Fight." Much will be learned from this very good read!
16,902 Retweets **78,717** Likes
8:36 PM - 28 Nov 2018

Donald J. Trump ✓
@realDonaldTrump

So much happening with the now discredited Witch Hunt. This total Hoax will be studied for years!
19,805 Retweets **86,250** Likes
8:39 PM - 28 Nov 2018

Donald J. Trump ✓
@realDonaldTrump

General Motors is very counter to what other auto, and other, companies are doing. Big Steel is opening and renovating plants all over the country. Auto companies are pouring into the U.S., including BMW, which just announced a major new plant. The U.S.A. is booming!
18,834 Retweets **83,713** Likes
3:37 AM - 29 Nov 2018

Donald J. Trump ✓
@realDonaldTrump

Did you ever see an investigation more in search of a crime? At the same time Mueller and the Angry Democrats aren't even looking at the atrocious, and perhaps subversive, crimes that were committed by Crooked Hillary Clinton and the Democrats. A total disgrace!
26,413 Retweets **99,632** Likes
3:54 AM - 29 Nov 2018

Donald J. Trump ✓
@realDonaldTrump

When will this illegal Joseph McCarthy style Witch Hunt, one that has shattered so many innocent lives, ever end-or will it just go on forever? After wasting more than $40,000,000 (is that possible?), it has proven only one thing-there was NO Collusion with Russia. So Ridiculous!
23,745 Retweets **88,691** Likes
4:16 AM - 29 Nov 2018

Donald J. Trump ✓
@realDonaldTrump

Billions of Dollars are pouring into the coffers of the U.S.A. because of the Tariffs being charged to China, and there is a long way to go. If companies don't want to pay Tariffs, build in the U.S.A. Otherwise, lets just make our Country richer than ever before!
21,663 Retweets **94,046** Likes
4:32 AM - 29 Nov 2018

Donald J. Trump ✓
@realDonaldTrump

Based on the fact that the ships and sailors have not been returned to Ukraine from Russia, I have decided it would be best for all parties concerned to cancel my previously scheduled meeting....
19,346 Retweets **82,126** Likes
8:34 AM - 29 Nov 2018

Donald J. Trump ✓
@realDonaldTrump

....in Argentina with President Vladimir Putin. I look forward to a meaningful Summit again as soon as this situation is resolved!
13,108 Retweets **60,098** Likes
8:34 AM - 29 Nov 2018

Donald J. Trump ✓
@realDonaldTrump

.@SteveScalise has written an absolutely fascinating book (BACK IN THE GAME) on the world of D.C. politics, and more. He has experienced so much, in a short period of time. Few people have had his bravery or courage, and he has come all the way back. A big power and great person!
12,618 Retweets **53,689** Likes
2:03 PM - 29 Nov 2018

President Trumps Tweets 2018: A Historical Archive of President Trump's Tweets

Donald J. Trump ✓
@realDonaldTrump

.@StephenMoore and Arthur Laffer, two very talented men, have just completed an incredible book on my Economic Policies or, as they call it, #TRUMPONOMICS....
9,967 Retweets **44,479** Likes
2:14 PM - 29 Nov 2018

Donald J. Trump ✓
@realDonaldTrump

....They have really done a great job in capturing my long-held views and ideas. This book is on sale now - a terrific read of a really interesting subject!
8,385 Retweets **39,316** Likes
2:14 PM - 29 Nov 2018

Donald J. Trump ✓
@realDonaldTrump

.@DBongino's new book, "Spygate: The Attempted Sabotage of Donald J. Trump," is terrific. He's tough, he's smart, and he really gets it. His book is on sale now, I highly recommend!
17,218 Retweets **66,019** Likes
2:34 PM - 29 Nov 2018

Donald J. Trump ✓
@realDonaldTrump

With all of the new books coming out you can't forget two of the great originals written by @GreggJarrett and @JudgeJeanine Pirro. Their books both went to #1. Go get them now, the phony Witch Hunt is well explained!
12,797 Retweets **52,172** Likes
2:43 PM - 29 Nov 2018

Donald J. Trump ✓
@realDonaldTrump

We have been working hard on this - and it's only going to get better!
11,936 Retweets **45,905** Likes
2:47 PM - 29 Nov 2018

Donald J. Trump ✓
@realDonaldTrump

As RNC Chair Ronna McDaniel oversaw history defying gains in the Senate and unprecedented fundraising strength. I have asked her to serve another term for my 2020 re-elect, because there is no one better for the job!
15,071 Retweets **70,007** Likes
4:04 PM - 29 Nov 2018

Donald J. Trump ✓
@realDonaldTrump

Just landed in Argentina with @FLOTUS Melania! #G20Summit
9,065 Retweets **47,793** Likes
5:41 PM - 29 Nov 2018

Donald J. Trump ✓
@realDonaldTrump

"This demonstrates the Robert Mueller and his partisans have no evidence, not a whiff of collusion, between Trump and the Russians. Russian project legal. Trump Tower meeting (son Don), perfectly legal. He wasn't involved with hacking." Gregg Jarrett. A total Witch Hunt!
19,109 Retweets **73,215** Likes
6:50 PM - 29 Nov 2018

Donald J. Trump ✓
@realDonaldTrump

Alan Dershowitz: "These are not crimes. He (Mueller) has no authority to be a roving Commissioner. I don't see any evidence of crimes." This is an illegal Hoax that should be ended immediately. Mueller refuses to look at the real crimes on the other side. Where is the IG REPORT?
27,963 Retweets **96,393** Likes
7:04 PM - 29 Nov 2018

Donald J. Trump ✓
@realDonaldTrump

Arrived in Argentina with a very busy two days planned. Important meetings scheduled throughout. Our great Country is extremely well represented. Will be very productive!
15,862 Retweets **84,672** Likes
7:31 PM - 29 Nov 2018

Donald J. Trump ✓
@realDonaldTrump

Oh, I get it! I am a very good developer, happily living my life, when I see our Country going in the wrong direction (to put it mildly). Against all odds, I decide to run for President & continue to run my business-very legal & very cool, talked about it on the campaign trail...
31,895 Retweets **156,832** Likes
1:52 AM - 30 Nov 2018

Donald J. Trump ✓
@realDonaldTrump

....Lightly looked at doing a building somewhere in Russia. Put up zero money, zero guarantees and didn't do the project. Witch Hunt!
19,094 Retweets **86,967** Likes
1:59 AM - 30 Nov 2018

@realDonaldTrump

#USMCA
12,170 Retweets **48,997** Likes
5:08 AM - 30 Nov 2018

Donald J. Trump ✓
@realDonaldTrump

Just signed one of the most important, and largest, Trade Deals in U.S. and World History. The United States, Mexico and Canada worked so well together in crafting this great document. The terrible NAFTA will soon be gone. The USMCA will be fantastic for all!
27,974 Retweets **125,660** Likes
6:45 AM - 30 Nov 2018

Donald J. Trump ✓
@realDonaldTrump

To the Great people of Alaska. You have been hit hard by a "big one." Please follow the directions of the highly trained professionals who are there to help you. Your Federal Government will spare no expense. God Bless you ALL!
21,401 Retweets **105,545** Likes
12:19 PM - 30 Nov 2018

Donald J. Trump ✓
@realDonaldTrump

Great reviews on the USMCA - sooo much better than NAFTA!
13,169 Retweets **64,861** Likes
12:23 PM - 30 Nov 2018

President Trumps Tweets 2018: A Historical Archive of President Trump's Tweets

Donald J. Trump ●
@realDonaldTrump

Great day at the #G20Summit in Buenos Aires, Argentina. Thank you!
18,514 Retweets **82,263** Likes
4:23 PM - 30 Nov 2018

Donald J. Trump ●
@realDonaldTrump

Watch @seanhannity on @FoxNews NOW. Enjoy!
10,233 Retweets **56,790** Likes
6:03 PM - 30 Nov 2018

Donald J. Trump ●
@realDonaldTrump

Statement from President Donald J. Trump and First Lady Melania Trump on the Passing of Former President George H.W. Bush
27,387 Retweets **105,955** Likes
9:49 PM - 30 Nov 2018

Donald J. Trump ●
@realDonaldTrump

President George H.W. Bush led a long, successful and beautiful life. Whenever I was with him I saw his absolute joy for life and true pride in his family. His accomplishments were great from beginning to end. He was a truly wonderful man and will be missed by all!
32,754 Retweets **216,587** Likes
3:16 AM - 1 Dec 2018

Donald J. Trump ●
@realDonaldTrump

I was very much looking forward to having a press conference just prior to leaving Argentina because we have had such great success in our dealing with various countries and their leaders at the G20....
16,032 Retweets **86,430** Likes
7:21 AM - 1 Dec 2018

Donald J. Trump ●
@realDonaldTrump

....However, out of respect for the Bush Family and former President George H.W. Bush we will wait until after the funeral to have a press conference.
15,409 Retweets **88,644** Likes
7:21 AM - 1 Dec 2018

Donald J. Trump ●
@realDonaldTrump

This week, Jews around the world will celebrate the miracles of Hanukkah. @FLOTUS Melania and I send our very best wishes for a blessed and Happy Hanukkah!
17,277 Retweets **75,249** Likes
12:15 PM - 2 Dec 2018

Donald J. Trump ●
@realDonaldTrump

China has agreed to reduce and remove tariffs on cars coming into China from the U.S. Currently the tariff is 40%.
31,945 Retweets **141,328** Likes
8:00 PM - 2 Dec 2018

Donald J. Trump ✓
@realDonaldTrump

My meeting in Argentina with President Xi of China was an extraordinary one. Relations with China have taken a BIG leap forward! Very good things will happen. We are dealing from great strength, but China likewise has much to gain if and when a deal is completed. Level the field!
16,456 Retweets **73,335** Likes
4:54 AM - 3 Dec 2018

Donald J. Trump ✓
@realDonaldTrump

Farmers will be a a very BIG and FAST beneficiary of our deal with China. They intend to start purchasing agricultural product immediately. We make the finest and cleanest product in the World, and that is what China wants. Farmers, I LOVE YOU!
26,165 Retweets **116,728** Likes
5:01 AM - 3 Dec 2018

Donald J. Trump ✓
@realDonaldTrump

President Xi and I have a very strong and personal relationship. He and I are the only two people that can bring about massive and very positive change, on trade and far beyond, between our two great Nations. A solution for North Korea is a great thing for China and ALL!
14,471 Retweets **65,427** Likes
5:18 AM - 3 Dec 2018

Donald J. Trump ✓
@realDonaldTrump

I am certain that, at some time in the future, President Xi and I, together with President Putin of Russia, will start talking about a meaningful halt to what has become a major and uncontrollable Arms Race. The U.S. spent 716 Billion Dollars this year. Crazy!
21,346 Retweets **91,956** Likes
5:30 AM - 3 Dec 2018

Donald J. Trump ✓
@realDonaldTrump

We would save Billions of Dollars if the Democrats would give us the votes to build the Wall. Either way, people will NOT be allowed into our Country illegally! We will close the entire Southern Border if necessary. Also, STOP THE DRUGS!
26,903 Retweets **105,758** Likes
5:45 AM - 3 Dec 2018

Donald J. Trump ✓
@realDonaldTrump

"Michael Cohen asks judge for no Prison Time." You mean he can do all of the TERRIBLE, unrelated to Trump, things having to do with fraud, big loans, Taxis, etc., and not serve a long prison term? He makes up stories to get a GREAT & ALREADY reduced deal for himself, and get.....
18,288 Retweets **74,551** Likes
7:24 AM - 3 Dec 2018

Donald J. Trump ✓
@realDonaldTrump

....his wife and father-in-law (who has the money?) off Scott Free. He lied for this outcome and should, in my opinion, serve a full and complete sentence.
14,527 Retweets **67,271** Likes
7:29 AM - 3 Dec 2018

Donald J. Trump ✓
@realDonaldTrump

"I will never testify against Trump." This statement was recently made by Roger Stone, essentially stating that he will not be forced by a rogue and out of control prosecutor to make up lies and stories about "President Trump." Nice to know that some people still have "guts!"
23,763 Retweets **99,508** Likes
7:48 AM - 3 Dec 2018

Donald J. Trump ✓
@realDonaldTrump

Bob Mueller (who is a much different man than people think) and his out of control band of Angry Democrats, don't want the truth, they only want lies. The truth is very bad for their mission!
26,098 Retweets **100,413** Likes
7:56 AM - 3 Dec 2018

Donald J. Trump ✓
@realDonaldTrump

Looking forward to being with the Bush Family to pay my respects to President George H.W. Bush.
13,015 Retweets **89,014** Likes
8:37 AM - 3 Dec 2018

Donald J. Trump ✓
@realDonaldTrump

Congratulations to newly inaugurated Mexican President @lopezobrador_. He had a tremendous political victory with the great support of the Mexican People. We will work well together for many years to come!
18,455 Retweets **86,417** Likes
11:42 AM - 3 Dec 2018

Donald J. Trump ✓
@realDonaldTrump

#Remembering41
22,031 Retweets **114,936** Likes
6:21 PM - 3 Dec 2018

Donald J. Trump ✓
@realDonaldTrump

Looking forward to being with the wonderful Bush family at Blair House today. The former First Lady will be coming over to the White House this morning to be given a tour of the Christmas decorations by Melania. The elegance & precision of the last two days have been remarkable!
12,945 Retweets **70,814** Likes
6:22 AM - 4 Dec 2018

Donald J. Trump ✓
@realDonaldTrump

The negotiations with China have already started. Unless extended, they will end 90 days from the date of our wonderful and very warm dinner with President Xi in Argentina. Bob Lighthizer will be working closely with Steve Mnuchin, Larry Kudlow, Wilbur Ross and Peter Navarro.....
14,067 Retweets **64,692** Likes
6:30 AM - 4 Dec 2018

Donald J. Trump ✓
@realDonaldTrump

......on seeing whether or not a REAL deal with China is actually possible. If it is, we will get it done. China is supposed to start buying Agricultural product and more immediately. President Xi and I want this deal to happen, and it probably will. But if not remember,......
11,715 Retweets **54,617** Likes
6:55 AM - 4 Dec 2018

Donald J. Trump ✓
@realDonaldTrump

....I am a Tariff Man. When people or countries come in to raid the great wealth of our Nation, I want them to pay for the privilege of doing so. It will always be the best way to max out our economic power. We are right now taking in $billions in Tariffs. MAKE AMERICA RICH AGAIN
25,270 Retweets **122,159** Likes
7:03 AM - 4 Dec 2018

Donald J. Trump ✓
@realDonaldTrump

.....But if a fair deal is able to be made with China, one that does all of the many things we know must be finally done, I will happily sign. Let the negotiations begin. MAKE AMERICA GREAT AGAIN!
13,058 Retweets **59,933** Likes
7:10 AM - 4 Dec 2018

Donald J. Trump ✓
@realDonaldTrump

Could somebody please explain to the Democrats (we need their votes) that our Country losses 250 Billion Dollars a year on illegal immigration, not including the terrible drug flow. Top Border Security, including a Wall, is $25 Billion. Pays for itself in two months. Get it done!
36,409 Retweets **121,752** Likes
8:22 AM - 4 Dec 2018

Donald J. Trump ✓
@realDonaldTrump

I am glad that my friend @EmmanuelMacron and the protestors in Paris have agreed with the conclusion I reached two years ago. The Paris Agreement is fatally flawed because it raises the price of energy for responsible countries while whitewashing some of the worst polluters....
29,321 Retweets **113,272** Likes
2:56 PM - 4 Dec 2018

Donald J. Trump ✓
@realDonaldTrump

....in the world. I want clean air and clean water and have been making great strides in improving America's environment. But American taxpayers – and American workers – shouldn't pay to clean up others countries' pollution.
23,877 Retweets **99,706** Likes
2:56 PM - 4 Dec 2018

Donald J. Trump ✓
@realDonaldTrump

We are either going to have a REAL DEAL with China, or no deal at all - at which point we will be charging major Tariffs against Chinese product being shipped into the United States. Ultimately, I believe, we will be making a deal - either now or into the future....
18,156 Retweets **83,739** Likes
4:20 PM - 4 Dec 2018

President Trumps Tweets 2018: A Historical Archive of President Trump's Tweets

Donald J. Trump ●
@realDonaldTrump

.....China does not want Tariffs!
13,486 Retweets **71,200** Likes
4:21 PM - 4 Dec 2018

Donald J. Trump ●
@realDonaldTrump

"China officially echoed President Donald Trump's optimism over bilateral trade talks. Chinese officials have begun preparing to restart imports of U.S. Soybeans & Liquified Natural Gas, the first sign confirming the claims of President Donald Trump and the White House that......
14,786 Retweets **65,166** Likes
4:46 AM - 5 Dec 2018

Donald J. Trump ●
@realDonaldTrump

.....China had agreed to start "immediately" buying U.S. products." @business
13,117 Retweets **62,984** Likes
4:49 AM - 5 Dec 2018

Donald J. Trump ●
@realDonaldTrump

Very strong signals being sent by China once they returned home from their long trip, including stops, from Argentina. Not to sound naive or anything, but I believe President Xi meant every word of what he said at our long and hopefully historic meeting. ALL subjects discussed!
17,072 Retweets **86,340** Likes
5:19 AM - 5 Dec 2018

Donald J. Trump ●
@realDonaldTrump

One of the very exciting things to come out of my meeting with President Xi of China is his promise to me to criminalize the sale of deadly Fentanyl coming into the United States. It will now be considered a "controlled substance." This could be a game changer on what is.......
14,540 Retweets **66,465** Likes
5:44 AM - 5 Dec 2018

Donald J. Trump ●
@realDonaldTrump

.....considered to be the worst and most dangerous, addictive and deadly substance of them all. Last year over 77,000 people died from Fentanyl. If China cracks down on this "horror drug," using the Death Penalty for distributors and pushers, the results will be incredible!
17,607 Retweets **79,452** Likes
5:51 AM - 5 Dec 2018

Donald J. Trump ●
@realDonaldTrump

Looking forward to being with the Bush family. This is not a funeral, this is a day of celebration for a great man who has led a long and distinguished life. He will be missed!
18,431 Retweets **126,149** Likes
5:56 AM - 5 Dec 2018

Donald J. Trump ●
@realDonaldTrump

Hopefully OPEC will be keeping oil flows as is, not restricted. The World does not want to see, or need, higher oil prices!
17,329 Retweets **85,502** Likes
6:44 AM - 5 Dec 2018

Donald J. Trump ✓
@realDonaldTrump

Doug Wead, a truly great presidential historian, had a wonderful take on a very beautiful moment in history, the funeral service today of President Bush. Doug was able to brilliantly cover some very important and interesting periods of time! @LouDobbs
13,197 Retweets **73,312** Likes
6:24 PM - 5 Dec 2018

Donald J. Trump ✓
@realDonaldTrump

Working hard, thank you!
29,437 Retweets **142,221** Likes
7:32 PM - 5 Dec 2018

Donald J. Trump ✓
@realDonaldTrump

Without the phony Russia Witch Hunt, and with all that we have accomplished in the last almost two years (Tax & Regulation Cuts, Judge's, Military, Vets, etc.) my approval rating would be at 75% rather than the 50% just reported by Rasmussen. It's called Presidential Harassment!
27,486 Retweets **119,107** Likes
7:17 AM - 6 Dec 2018

Donald J. Trump ✓
@realDonaldTrump

My thoughts and prayers are with the @USMC crew members who were involved in a mid-air collision off the coast of Japan. Thank you to @USForcesJapan for their immediate response and rescue efforts. Whatever you need, we are here for you. @IIIMEF
15,926 Retweets **77,617** Likes
9:07 AM - 6 Dec 2018

Donald J. Trump ✓
@realDonaldTrump

Does the Fake News Media ever mention the fact that Republicans, with the very important help of my campaign Rallies, WON THE UNITED STATES SENATE, 53 to 47? All I hear is that the Open Border Dems won the House. Senate alone approves judges & others. Big Republican Win!
25,194 Retweets **110,890** Likes
4:27 PM - 6 Dec 2018

Donald J. Trump ✓
@realDonaldTrump

Statement from China: "The teams of both sides are now having smooth communications and good cooperation with each other. We are full of confidence that an agreement can be reached within the next 90 days." I agree!
17,722 Retweets **78,942** Likes
4:56 PM - 6 Dec 2018

Donald J. Trump ✓
@realDonaldTrump

Jerome Corsi: "This is not justice, this is not America. This is a political prosecution. The Special Prosecutor (Counsel), to get this plea deal, demanded I lie and violate the law. They're the criminals." He is not alone. 17 Angry Dems. People forced to lie. Sad! @Trish_Regan
17,132 Retweets **60,597** Likes
6:58 PM - 6 Dec 2018

President Trumps Tweets 2018: A Historical Archive of President Trump's Tweets

Donald J. Trump ✓
@realDonaldTrump

Trish_Regan: "Did the FBI follow protocol to obtain the FISA warrant? I don't think so. The Dossier was opposition research funded by opponents. Don't use Government resources to take down political foes. Weaponizing Government for gain." Is this really America? Witch Hunt!
18,582 Retweets **67,811** Likes
7:07 PM - 6 Dec 2018

Donald J. Trump ✓
@realDonaldTrump

FAKE NEWS - THE ENEMY OF THE PEOPLE!
39,522 Retweets **145,583** Likes
7:08 PM - 6 Dec 2018

Donald J. Trump ✓
@realDonaldTrump

Arizona, together with our Military and Border Patrol, is bracing for a massive surge at a NON-WALLED area. WE WILL NOT LET THEM THROUGH. Big danger. Nancy and Chuck must approve Boarder Security and the Wall!
25,886 Retweets **102,204** Likes
7:15 PM - 6 Dec 2018

Donald J. Trump ✓
@realDonaldTrump

Robert Mueller and Leakin' Lyin' James Comey are Best Friends, just one of many Mueller Conflicts of Interest. And bye the way, wasn't the woman in charge of prosecuting Jerome Corsi (who I do not know) in charge of "legal" at the corrupt Clinton Foundation? A total Witch Hunt...
22,732 Retweets **86,498** Likes
3:18 AM - 7 Dec 2018

Donald J. Trump ✓
@realDonaldTrump

....Will Robert Mueller's big time conflicts of interest be listed at the top of his Republicans only Report. Will Andrew Weissman's horrible and vicious prosecutorial past be listed in the Report. He wrongly destroyed people's lives, took down great companies, only to be........
16,962 Retweets **64,369** Likes
3:28 AM - 7 Dec 2018

Donald J. Trump ✓
@realDonaldTrump

.....overturned, 9-0, in the United States Supreme Court. Doing same thing to people now. Will all of the substantial & many contributions made by the 17 Angry Democrats to the Campaign of Crooked Hillary be listed in top of Report. Will the people that worked for the Clinton....
15,173 Retweets **58,913** Likes
3:40 AM - 7 Dec 2018

Donald J. Trump ✓
@realDonaldTrump

....Foundation be listed at the top of the Report? Will the scathing document written about Lyin' James Comey, by the man in charge of the case, Rod Rosenstein (who also signed the FISA Warrant), be a big part of the Report? Isn't Rod therefore totally conflicted? Will all of....
17,047 Retweets **68,705** Likes
3:53 AM - 7 Dec 2018

Donald J. Trump ✓
@realDonaldTrump

...the lying and leaking by the people doing the Report, & also Bruce Ohr (and his lovely wife Molly), Comey, Brennan, Clapper, & all of the many fired people of the FBI, be listed in the Report? Will the corruption within the DNC & Clinton Campaign be exposed?..And so much more!
21,570 Retweets **86,083** Likes
4:15 AM - 7 Dec 2018

Donald J. Trump ✓
@realDonaldTrump

China talks are going very well!
14,753 Retweets **89,620** Likes
5:13 AM - 7 Dec 2018

Donald J. Trump ✓
@realDonaldTrump

It has been incorrectly reported that Rudy Giuliani and others will not be doing a counter to the Mueller Report. That is Fake News. Already 87 pages done, but obviously cannot complete until we see the final Witch Hunt Report.
20,914 Retweets **81,905** Likes
5:39 AM - 7 Dec 2018

Donald J. Trump ✓
@realDonaldTrump

Today, we honor those who perished 77 years ago at Pearl Harbor, and we salute every veteran who served in World War II over the 4 years that followed that horrific attack. God Bless America!
16,884 Retweets **66,709** Likes
6:46 AM - 7 Dec 2018

Donald J. Trump ✓
@realDonaldTrump

We will be doing a major Counter Report to the Mueller Report. This should never again be allowed to happen to a future President of the United States!
23,149 Retweets **86,395** Likes
6:56 AM - 7 Dec 2018

Donald J. Trump ✓
@realDonaldTrump

I am pleased to announce that Heather Nauert, Spokeswoman for the United States Department of State, will be nominated to serve as United Nations Ambassador. I want to congratulate Heather, and thank Ambassador Nikki Haley for her great service to our Country!
15,855 Retweets **76,719** Likes
8:16 AM - 7 Dec 2018

Donald J. Trump ✓
@realDonaldTrump

I am pleased to announce that I will be nominating The Honorable William P. Barr for the position of Attorney General of the United States. As the former AG for George H.W. Bush....
13,779 Retweets **65,313** Likes
8:18 AM - 7 Dec 2018

Donald J. Trump ✓
@realDonaldTrump

....and one of the most highly respected lawyers and legal minds in the Country, he will be a great addition to our team. I look forward to having him join our very successful Administration!
11,110 Retweets **54,308** Likes
8:18 AM - 7 Dec 2018

President Trumps Tweets 2018: A Historical Archive of President Trump's Tweets

Donald J. Trump ✓
@realDonaldTrump

Mike Pompeo is doing a great job, I am very proud of him. His predecessor, Rex Tillerson, didn't have the mental capacity needed. He was dumb as a rock and I couldn't get rid of him fast enough. He was lazy as hell. Now it is a whole new ballgame, great spirit at State!
28,822 Retweets **111,720** Likes
12:02 PM - 7 Dec 2018

Donald J. Trump ✓
@realDonaldTrump

Hopefully Mitch McConnell will ask for a VOTE on Criminal Justice Reform. It is extremely popular and has strong bipartisan support. It will also help a lot of people, save taxpayer dollars, and keep our communities safe. Go for it Mitch!
17,851 Retweets **81,241** Likes
12:56 PM - 7 Dec 2018

Donald J. Trump ✓
@realDonaldTrump

It is being reported that Leakin' James Comey was told by Department of Justice attorneys not to answer the most important questions. Total bias and corruption at the highest levels of previous Administration. Force him to answer the questions under oath!
28,696 Retweets **105,887** Likes
1:49 PM - 7 Dec 2018

Donald J. Trump ✓
@realDonaldTrump

Totally clears the President. Thank you!
23,438 Retweets **113,867** Likes
3:00 PM - 7 Dec 2018

Donald J. Trump ✓
@realDonaldTrump

The Paris Agreement isn't working out so well for Paris. Protests and riots all over France. People do not want to pay large sums of money, much to third world countries (that are questionably run), in order to maybe protect the environment. Chanting "We Want Trump!" Love France.
36,801 Retweets **137,558** Likes
4:34 AM - 8 Dec 2018

Donald J. Trump ✓
@realDonaldTrump

The idea of a European Military didn't work out too well in W.W. I or 2. But the U.S. was there for you, and always will be. All we ask is that you pay your fair share of NATO. Germany is paying 1% while the U.S. pays 4.3% of a much larger GDP - to protect Europe. Fairness!
24,304 Retweets **97,365** Likes
4:52 AM - 8 Dec 2018

Donald J. Trump ✓
@realDonaldTrump

AFTER TWO YEARS AND MILLIONS OF PAGES OF DOCUMENTS (and a cost of over $30,000,000), NO COLLUSION!
28,298 Retweets **119,532** Likes
5:01 AM - 8 Dec 2018

Donald J. Trump ✓
@realDonaldTrump

I am pleased to announce my nomination of four-star General Mark Milley, Chief of Staff of the United States Army – as the Chairman of the Joint Chiefs of Staff, replacing General Joe Dunford, who will be retiring....
14,875 Retweets **72,376** Likes
6:19 AM - 8 Dec 2018

 Donald J. Trump ✓
@realDonaldTrump

....I am thankful to both of these incredible men for their service to our Country! Date of transition to be determined.
10,561 Retweets **56,309** Likes
6:19 AM - 8 Dec 2018

 Donald J. Trump ✓
@realDonaldTrump

"This is collusion illusion, there is no smoking gun here. At this late date, after all that we have gone through, after millions have been spent, we have no Russian Collusion. There is nothing impeachable here." @GeraldoRivera Time for the Witch Hunt to END!
22,222 Retweets **90,237** Likes
8:01 AM - 8 Dec 2018

 Donald J. Trump ✓
@realDonaldTrump

Very sad day & night in Paris. Maybe it's time to end the ridiculous and extremely expensive Paris Agreement and return money back to the people in the form of lower taxes? The U.S. was way ahead of the curve on that and the only major country where emissions went down last year!
39,181 Retweets **151,275** Likes
9:22 AM - 8 Dec 2018

 Donald J. Trump ✓
@realDonaldTrump

Watched Da Nang Dick Blumenthal on television spewing facts almost as accurate as his bravery in Vietnam (which he never saw). As the bullets whizzed by Da Nang Dicks head, as he was saving soldiers....
19,662 Retweets **81,537** Likes
10:58 AM - 8 Dec 2018

 Donald J. Trump ✓
@realDonaldTrump

....left and right, he then woke up from his dream screaming that HE LIED. Next time I go to Vietnam I will ask "the Dick" to travel with me!
17,176 Retweets **75,049** Likes
10:58 AM - 8 Dec 2018

 Donald J. Trump ✓
@realDonaldTrump

Great honor to be headed to the Army-Navy game today. Will be there shortly, landing now!
11,709 Retweets **79,576** Likes
11:07 AM - 8 Dec 2018

 **Donald J. Trump** ✓
@realDonaldTrump

#ArmyNavyGame
18,294 Retweets **94,495** Likes
3:22 PM - 8 Dec 2018

President Trumps Tweets 2018: A Historical Archive of President Trump's Tweets

Donald J. Trump ✓
@realDonaldTrump

It was my honor to attend today's #ArmyNavyGame in Philadelphia. A GREAT game played all around by our HEROES. Congratulations @ArmyWP_Football on the win!

21,318 Retweets **105,868** Likes
3:31 PM - 8 Dec 2018

Donald J. Trump ✓
@realDonaldTrump

On 245 occasions, former FBI Director James Comey told House investigators he didn't know, didn't recall, or couldn't remember things when asked. Opened investigations on 4 Americans (not 2) - didn't know who signed off and didn't know Christopher Steele. All lies!

35,672 Retweets **129,097** Likes
5:38 AM - 9 Dec 2018

Donald J. Trump ✓
@realDonaldTrump

Leakin' James Comey must have set a record for who lied the most to Congress in one day. His Friday testimony was so untruthful! This whole deal is a Rigged Fraud headed up by dishonest people who would do anything so that I could not become President. They are now exposed!

32,471 Retweets **124,250** Likes
5:53 AM - 9 Dec 2018

Donald J. Trump ✓
@realDonaldTrump

The Trump Administration has accomplished more than any other U.S. Administration in its first two (not even) years of existence, & we are having a great time doing it! All of this despite the Fake News Media, which has gone totally out of its mind-truly the Enemy of the People!

33,301 Retweets **141,916** Likes
2:43 PM - 9 Dec 2018

Donald J. Trump ✓
@realDonaldTrump

I am in the process of interviewing some really great people for the position of White House Chief of Staff. Fake News has been saying with certainty it was Nick Ayers, a spectacular person who will always be with our #MAGA agenda. I will be making a decision soon!

17,329 Retweets **87,406** Likes
5:27 PM - 9 Dec 2018

Donald J. Trump ✓
@realDonaldTrump

"Democrats can't find a Smoking Gun tying the Trump campaign to Russia after James Comey's testimony. No Smoking Gun...No Collusion." @FoxNews That's because there was NO COLLUSION. So now the Dems go to a simple private transaction, wrongly call it a campaign contribution,...

25,245 Retweets **104,794** Likes
3:46 AM - 10 Dec 2018

Donald J. Trump ✓
@realDonaldTrump

....which it was not (but even if it was, it is only a CIVIL CASE, like Obama's - but it was done correctly by a lawyer and there would not even be a fine. Lawyer's liability if he made a mistake, not me). Cohen just trying to get his sentence reduced. WITCH HUNT!

22,947 Retweets **101,074** Likes
4:00 AM - 10 Dec 2018

Donald J. Trump ✓
@realDonaldTrump

James Comey's behind closed doors testimony reveals that "there was not evidence of Campaign Collusion" with Russia when he left the FBI. In other words, the Witch Hunt is illegal and should never have been started!
27,065 Retweets **107,141** Likes
6:11 PM - 10 Dec 2018

Donald J. Trump ✓
@realDonaldTrump

"Former FBI Director James Comey under fire for his testimony acknowledging he knew that the Democrats paid for that phony Trump Dossier." @LouDobbs Details on Tuesday night.
20,945 Retweets **81,171** Likes
6:28 PM - 10 Dec 2018

Donald J. Trump ✓
@realDonaldTrump

Despite the large Caravans that WERE forming and heading to our Country, people have not been able to get through our newly built Walls, makeshift Walls & Fences, or Border Patrol Officers & Military. They are now staying in Mexico or going back to their original countries.......
20,287 Retweets **93,608** Likes
3:52 AM - 11 Dec 2018

Donald J. Trump ✓
@realDonaldTrump

.....Ice, Border Patrol and our Military have done a FANTASTIC job of securing our Southern Border. A Great Wall would be, however, a far easier & less expensive solution. We have already built large new sections & fully renovated others, making them like new. The Democrats,.....
16,117 Retweets **74,862** Likes
4:04 AM - 11 Dec 2018

Donald J. Trump ✓
@realDonaldTrump

....however, for strictly political reasons and because they have been pulled so far left, do NOT want Border Security. They want Open Borders for anyone to come in. This brings large scale crime and disease. Our Southern Border is now Secure and will remain that way.......
20,706 Retweets **92,172** Likes
4:12 AM - 11 Dec 2018

Donald J. Trump ✓
@realDonaldTrump

.....I look forward to my meeting with Chuck Schumer & Nancy Pelosi. In 2006, Democrats voted for a Wall, and they were right to do so. Today, they no longer want Border Security. They will fight it at all cost, and Nancy must get votes for Speaker. But the Wall will get built...
15,347 Retweets **68,749** Likes
4:30 AM - 11 Dec 2018

Donald J. Trump ✓
@realDonaldTrump

....People do not yet realize how much of the Wall, including really effective renovation, has already been built. If the Democrats do not give us the votes to secure our Country, the Military will build the remaining sections of the Wall. They know how important it is!
28,478 Retweets **119,626** Likes
4:42 AM - 11 Dec 2018

President Trumps Tweets 2018: A Historical Archive of President Trump's Tweets

Donald J. Trump ✓
@realDonaldTrump

Great job by Michael Anton on @foxandfriends. A true National Security expert!
8,881 Retweets **47,723** Likes
5:11 AM - 11 Dec 2018

Donald J. Trump ✓
@realDonaldTrump

Very productive conversations going on with China! Watch for some important announcements!
16,605 Retweets **81,650** Likes
5:19 AM - 11 Dec 2018

Donald J. Trump ✓
@realDonaldTrump

Fake News has it purposely wrong. Many, over ten, are vying for and wanting the White House Chief of Staff position. Why wouldn't someone want one of the truly great and meaningful jobs in Washington. Please report news correctly. Thank you!
20,699 Retweets **91,578** Likes
5:30 AM - 11 Dec 2018

Donald J. Trump ✓
@realDonaldTrump

James Comey just totally exposed his partisan stance by urging his fellow Democrats to take back the White House in 2020. In other words, he is and has been a Democrat. Comey had no right heading the FBI at any time, but especially after his mind exploded!
26,474 Retweets **104,894** Likes
10:50 AM - 11 Dec 2018

Donald J. Trump ✓
@realDonaldTrump

"I don't care what you think of the President...it cannot bleed over to the FBI...Comey is confirming there is bias in the FBI..." -Chris Swecker
23,325 Retweets **97,884** Likes
10:55 AM - 11 Dec 2018

Donald J. Trump ✓
@realDonaldTrump

Thanks to Leader McConnell for agreeing to bring a Senate vote on Criminal Justice this week! These historic changes will make communities SAFER and SAVE tremendous taxpayers dollars. It brings much needed hope to many families during the Holiday Season.
21,960 Retweets **104,310** Likes
2:09 PM - 11 Dec 2018

Donald J. Trump ✓
@realDonaldTrump

Another very bad terror attack in France. We are going to strengthen our borders even more. Chuck and Nancy must give us the votes to get additional Border Security!
36,786 Retweets **164,069** Likes
4:34 AM - 12 Dec 2018

Donald J. Trump ✓
@realDonaldTrump

The Democrats and President Obama gave Iran 150 Billion Dollars and got nothing, but they can't give 5 Billion Dollars for National Security and a Wall?
61,295 Retweets **194,346** Likes
4:50 AM - 12 Dec 2018

Anthony T. Michalisko

Donald J. Trump ✓
@realDonaldTrump

.@FLOTUS Melania will be interviewed by @SeanHannity tonight on @FoxNews at 9:00pmE!
13,021 Retweets **76,159** Likes
3:50 PM - 12 Dec 2018

Donald J. Trump ✓
@realDonaldTrump

I often stated, "One way or the other, Mexico is going to pay for the Wall." This has never changed. Our new deal with Mexico (and Canada), the USMCA, is so much better than the old, very costly & anti-USA NAFTA deal, that just by the money we save, MEXICO IS PAYING FOR THE WALL!
27,554 Retweets **117,678** Likes
4:38 AM - 13 Dec 2018

Donald J. Trump ✓
@realDonaldTrump

I never directed Michael Cohen to break the law. He was a lawyer and he is supposed to know the law. It is called "advice of counsel," and a lawyer has great liability if a mistake is made. That is why they get paid. Despite that many campaign finance lawyers have strongly......
18,105 Retweets **78,687** Likes
5:17 AM - 13 Dec 2018

Donald J. Trump ✓
@realDonaldTrump

....stated that I did nothing wrong with respect to campaign finance laws, if they even apply, because this was not campaign finance. Cohen was guilty on many charges unrelated to me, but he plead to two campaign charges which were not criminal and of which he probably was not...
16,150 Retweets **71,477** Likes
5:25 AM - 13 Dec 2018

Donald J. Trump ✓
@realDonaldTrump

....guilty even on a civil basis. Those charges were just agreed to by him in order to embarrass the president and get a much reduced prison sentence, which he did-including the fact that his family was temporarily let off the hook. As a lawyer, Michael has great liability to me!
15,633 Retweets **73,187** Likes
5:39 AM - 13 Dec 2018

Donald J. Trump ✓
@realDonaldTrump

They gave General Flynn a great deal because they were embarrassed by the way he was treated - the FBI said he didn't lie and they overrode the FBI. They want to scare everybody into making up stories that are not true by catching them in the smallest of misstatements. Sad!.....
23,898 Retweets **96,718** Likes
8:07 AM - 13 Dec 2018

Donald J. Trump ✓
@realDonaldTrump

WITCH HUNT!
23,743 Retweets **103,418** Likes
8:08 AM - 13 Dec 2018

Donald J. Trump ✓
@realDonaldTrump

If it was a Conservative that said what "crazed" Mika Brzezinski stated on her show yesterday, using a certain horrible term, that person would be banned permanently from television....
20,000 Retweets **79,385** Likes
9:34 AM - 13 Dec 2018

Donald J. Trump ✓
@realDonaldTrump

....She will probably be given a pass, despite their terrible ratings. Congratulations to @RichardGrenell, our great Ambassador to Germany, for having the courage to take this horrible issue on!
12,691 Retweets **56,021** Likes
9:34 AM - 13 Dec 2018

Donald J. Trump ✓
@realDonaldTrump

Just did an interview with @HARRISFAULKNER on @FoxNews, airing now (1pmE.) Enjoy!
7,749 Retweets **45,955** Likes
10:00 AM - 13 Dec 2018

Donald J. Trump ✓
@realDonaldTrump

Happy 382nd Birthday @USNationalGuard. Our entire Nation is forever grateful for all you do 24/7/365. We love you! #Guard382
13,301 Retweets **60,185** Likes
10:13 AM - 13 Dec 2018

Donald J. Trump ✓
@realDonaldTrump

Today, it was my honor to welcome our Nation's newly elected Governors to the @WhiteHouse!
10,894 Retweets **57,220** Likes
12:24 PM - 13 Dec 2018

Donald J. Trump ✓
@realDonaldTrump

Let's not do a shutdown, Democrats - do what's right for the American People!
38,771 Retweets **128,786** Likes
1:21 PM - 13 Dec 2018

Donald J. Trump ✓
@realDonaldTrump

China just announced that their economy is growing much slower than anticipated because of our Trade War with them. They have just suspended U.S. Tariff Hikes. U.S. is doing very well. China wants to make a big and very comprehensive deal. It could happen, and rather soon!
27,243 Retweets **128,368** Likes
8:35 AM - 14 Dec 2018

Donald J. Trump ✓
@realDonaldTrump

Many people have asked how we are doing in our negotiations with North Korea - I always reply by saying we are in no hurry, there is wonderful potential for great economic success for that country....
13,960 Retweets **70,466** Likes
10:17 AM - 14 Dec 2018

Donald J. Trump ✓
@realDonaldTrump

....Kim Jong Un sees it better than anyone and will fully take advantage of it for his people. We are doing just fine!
11,573 Retweets **58,952** Likes
10:17 AM - 14 Dec 2018

Donald J. Trump ✓
@realDonaldTrump

Thank you to @tim_cook for agreeing to expand operations in the U.S. and thereby creating thousands of jobs!
13,212 Retweets **60,963** Likes
10:19 AM - 14 Dec 2018

Donald J. Trump ✓
@realDonaldTrump

I am pleased to announce that Mick Mulvaney, Director of the Office of Management & Budget, will be named Acting White House Chief of Staff, replacing General John Kelly, who has served our Country with distinction. Mick has done an outstanding job while in the Administration....
17,437 Retweets **79,595** Likes
2:18 PM - 14 Dec 2018

Donald J. Trump ✓
@realDonaldTrump

....I look forward to working with him in this new capacity as we continue to MAKE AMERICA GREAT AGAIN! John will be staying until the end of the year. He is a GREAT PATRIOT and I want to personally thank him for his service!
12,676 Retweets **62,243** Likes
2:18 PM - 14 Dec 2018

Donald J. Trump ✓
@realDonaldTrump

For the record, there were MANY people who wanted to be the White House Chief of Staff. Mick M will do a GREAT job!
13,320 Retweets **71,805** Likes
4:31 PM - 14 Dec 2018

Donald J. Trump ✓
@realDonaldTrump

As I predicted all along, Obamacare has been struck down as an UNCONSTITUTIONAL disaster! Now Congress must pass a STRONG law that provides GREAT healthcare and protects pre-existing conditions. Mitch and Nancy, get it done!
32,534 Retweets **132,831** Likes
6:07 PM - 14 Dec 2018

Donald J. Trump ✓
@realDonaldTrump

Wow, but not surprisingly, ObamaCare was just ruled UNCONSTITUTIONAL by a highly respected judge in Texas. Great news for America!
31,162 Retweets **133,302** Likes
6:16 PM - 14 Dec 2018

Donald J. Trump ✓
@realDonaldTrump

Secretary of the Interior @RyanZinke will be leaving the Administration at the end of the year after having served for a period of almost two years. Ryan has accomplished much during his tenure and I want to thank him for his service to our Nation.......
11,980 Retweets **64,637** Likes
6:14 AM - 15 Dec 2018

Donald J. Trump ✓
@realDonaldTrump

.......The Trump Administration will be announcing the new Secretary of the Interior next week.
11,203 Retweets **62,814** Likes
6:18 AM - 15 Dec 2018

President Trumps Tweets 2018: A Historical Archive of President Trump's Tweets

Donald J. Trump ✓
@realDonaldTrump

Never in the history of our Country has the "press" been more dishonest than it is today. Stories that should be good, are bad. Stories that should be bad, are horrible. Many stories, like with the REAL story on Russia, Clinton & the DNC, seldom get reported. Too bad!
37,948 Retweets **143,340** Likes
7:37 AM - 15 Dec 2018

Donald J. Trump ✓
@realDonaldTrump

The pathetic and dishonest Weekly Standard, run by failed prognosticator Bill Kristol (who, like many others, never had a clue), is flat broke and out of business. Too bad. May it rest in peace!
23,530 Retweets **104,385** Likes
8:15 AM - 15 Dec 2018

Donald J. Trump ✓
@realDonaldTrump

Wow, 19,000 Texts between Lisa Page and her lover, Peter S of the FBI, in charge of the Russia Hoax, were just reported as being wiped clean and gone. Such a big story that will never be covered by the Fake News. Witch Hunt!
36,242 Retweets **121,738** Likes
8:45 AM - 15 Dec 2018

Donald J. Trump ✓
@realDonaldTrump

A REAL scandal is the one sided coverage, hour by hour, of networks like NBC & Democrat spin machines like Saturday Night Live. It is all nothing less than unfair news coverage and Dem commercials. Should be tested in courts, can't be legal? Only defame & belittle! Collusion?
24,190 Retweets **96,861** Likes
5:58 AM - 16 Dec 2018

Donald J. Trump ✓
@realDonaldTrump

So where are all the missing Text messages between fired FBI agents Peter S and the lovely Lisa Page, his lover. Just reported that they have been erased and wiped clean. What an outrage as the totally compromised and conflicted Witch Hunt moves ever so slowly forward. Want them!
25,939 Retweets **101,296** Likes
6:11 AM - 16 Dec 2018

Donald J. Trump ✓
@realDonaldTrump

Remember, Michael Cohen only became a "Rat" after the FBI did something which was absolutely unthinkable & unheard of until the Witch Hunt was illegally started. They BROKE INTO AN ATTORNEY'S OFFICE! Why didn't they break into the DNC to get the Server, or Crooked's office?
32,115 Retweets **126,329** Likes
6:39 AM - 16 Dec 2018

Donald J. Trump ✓
@realDonaldTrump

At the request of many, I will be reviewing the case of a "U.S. Military hero," Major Matt Golsteyn, who is charged with murder. He could face the death penalty from our own government after he admitted to killing a Terrorist bomb maker while overseas. @PeteHegseth @FoxNews
26,065 Retweets **99,394** Likes
7:03 AM - 16 Dec 2018

Donald J. Trump ✓
@realDonaldTrump

Judge Ken Starr, former Solicitor Generel & Independent Counsel, just stated that, after two years, "there is no evidence or proof of collusion" & further that "there is no evidence that there was a campaign financing violation involving the President." Thank you Judge. @FoxNews
21,882 Retweets **82,996** Likes
7:20 AM - 16 Dec 2018

Donald J. Trump ✓
@realDonaldTrump

The Democrats policy of Child Seperation on the Border during the Obama Administration was far worse than the way we handle it now. Remember the 2014 picture of children in cages - the Obama years. However, if you don't separate, FAR more people will come. Smugglers use the kids!
24,535 Retweets **93,723** Likes
8:25 AM - 16 Dec 2018

Donald J. Trump ✓
@realDonaldTrump

Required television watching is last weeks @marthamaccallum interview with the wonderful wife of Rod Blagojevich and the @trish_regan interview with a Jerome Corsi. If that doesn't tell you something about what has been going on in our Country, nothing will. Very sad!
14,659 Retweets **56,633** Likes
12:29 PM - 16 Dec 2018

Donald J. Trump ✓
@realDonaldTrump

"It looks here as though General Flynn's defenses are incidental to something larger which is for the prosecution to figure out if it can find a path to Donald Trump without quite knowing what that crime might be. It stops looking like prosecution and more looking like.....
16,156 Retweets **64,205** Likes
12:29 PM - 16 Dec 2018

Donald J. Trump ✓
@realDonaldTrump

....a persecution of the President." Daniel Henninger, The Wall Street Journal. Thank you, people are starting to see and understand what this Witch Hunt is all about. Jeff Sessions should be ashamed of himself for allowing this total HOAX to get started in the first place!
21,700 Retweets **88,359** Likes
12:37 PM - 16 Dec 2018

Donald J. Trump ✓
@realDonaldTrump

...The Russian Witch Hunt Hoax, started as the "insurance policy" long before I even got elected, is very bad for our Country. They are Entrapping people for misstatements, lies or unrelated things that took place many years ago. Nothing to do with Collusion. A Democrat Scam!
29,162 Retweets **107,335** Likes
12:56 PM - 16 Dec 2018

Donald J. Trump ✓
@realDonaldTrump

The DEDUCTIBLE which comes with ObamaCare is so high that it is practically not even useable! Hurts families badly. We have a chance, working with the Democrats, to deliver great HealthCare! A confirming Supreme Court Decision will lead to GREAT HealthCare results for Americans!
20,910 Retweets **89,800** Likes
5:02 AM - 17 Dec 2018

President Trumps Tweets 2018: A Historical Archive of President Trump's Tweets

Donald J. Trump ✓
@realDonaldTrump

It is incredible that with a very strong dollar and virtually no inflation, the outside world blowing up around us, Paris is burning and China way down, the Fed is even considering yet another interest rate hike. Take the Victory!
25,130 Retweets **106,546** Likes
5:27 AM - 17 Dec 2018

Donald J. Trump ✓
@realDonaldTrump

Anytime you hear a Democrat saying that you can have good Border Security without a Wall, write them off as just another politician following the party line. Time for us to save billions of dollars a year and have, at the same time, far greater safety and control!
32,443 Retweets **133,258** Likes
8:05 AM - 17 Dec 2018

Donald J. Trump ✓
@realDonaldTrump

Today I am making good on my promise to defend our Farmers & Ranchers from unjustified trade retaliation by foreign nations. I have authorized Secretary Perdue to implement the 2nd round of Market Facilitation Payments. Our economy is stronger than ever—we stand with our Farmers!
25,031 Retweets **112,625** Likes
1:14 PM - 17 Dec 2018

Donald J. Trump ✓
@realDonaldTrump

Biggest outrage yet in the long, winding and highly conflicted Mueller Witch Hunt is the fact that 19,000 demanded Text messages between Peter Strzok and his FBI lover, Lisa Page, were purposely & illegally deleted. Would have explained whole Hoax, which is now under protest!
20,258 Retweets **76,049** Likes
3:28 AM - 18 Dec 2018

Donald J. Trump ✓
@realDonaldTrump

Good luck today in court to General Michael Flynn. Will be interesting to see what he has to say, despite tremendous pressure being put on him, about Russian Collusion in our great and, obviously, highly successful political campaign. There was no Collusion!
18,557 Retweets **77,887** Likes
3:41 AM - 18 Dec 2018

Donald J. Trump ✓
@realDonaldTrump

I hope the people over at the Fed will read today's Wall Street Journal Editorial before they make yet another mistake. Also, don't let the market become any more illiquid than it already is. Stop with the 50 B's. Feel the market, don't just go by meaningless numbers. Good luck!
16,500 Retweets **70,330** Likes
4:13 AM - 18 Dec 2018

Donald J. Trump ✓
@realDonaldTrump

Facebook, Twitter and Google are so biased toward the Dems it is ridiculous! Twitter, in fact, has made it much more difficult for people to join @realDonaldTrump. They have removed many names & greatly slowed the level and speed of increase. They have acknowledged-done NOTHING!
26,345 Retweets **96,334** Likes
4:26 AM - 18 Dec 2018

Donald J. Trump ✓
@realDonaldTrump

Illegal immigration costs the United States more than 200 Billion Dollars a year. How was this allowed to happen?
24,894 Retweets **92,263** Likes
4:55 AM - 18 Dec 2018

Donald J. Trump ✓
@realDonaldTrump

Russia Dossier reporter now doubts dopey Christopher Steele's claims! "When you get into the details of the Steele Dossier, the specific allegations, we have not seen the evidence to support them. There's good grounds to think that some of the more sensational allegations.....
14,488 Retweets **57,018** Likes
5:14 AM - 18 Dec 2018

Donald J. Trump ✓
@realDonaldTrump

....WILL NEVER BE PROVEN AND ARE LIKELY FALSE." Thank you to Michael Isikoff, Yahoo, for honesty. What this means is that the FISA WARRANTS and the whole Russian Witch Hunt is a Fraud and a Hoax which should be ended immediately. Also, it was paid for by Crooked Hillary & DNC!
19,460 Retweets **75,842** Likes
5:22 AM - 18 Dec 2018

Donald J. Trump ✓
@realDonaldTrump

Michael Isikoff was the first to report Dossier allegations and now seriously doubts the Dossier claims. The whole Russian Collusion thing was a HOAX, but who is going to restore the good name of so many people whose reputations have been destroyed?
21,238 Retweets **82,019** Likes
5:32 AM - 18 Dec 2018

Donald J. Trump ✓
@realDonaldTrump

"President Donald J. Trump's Commission on School Safety examined ways to make our schools safe for all students and teachers."
10,816 Retweets **45,671** Likes
2:42 PM - 18 Dec 2018

Donald J. Trump ✓
@realDonaldTrump

Congratulations to @MarthaMcSally on her appointment by Governor @DougDucey as the Great new Senator from Arizona - I have no doubt she will do a fantastic job!
11,617 Retweets **57,885** Likes
4:59 PM - 18 Dec 2018

Donald J. Trump ✓
@realDonaldTrump

The Democrats, are saying loud and clear that they do not want to build a Concrete Wall - but we are not building a Concrete Wall, we are building artistically designed steel slats, so that you can easily see through it....
22,852 Retweets **98,873** Likes
5:13 PM - 18 Dec 2018

President Trumps Tweets 2018: A Historical Archive of President Trump's Tweets

Donald J. Trump ✓
@realDonaldTrump

....It will be beautiful and, at the same time, give our Country the security that our citizens deserve. It will go up fast and save us BILLIONS of dollars a month once completed!
18,512 Retweets **81,752** Likes
5:13 PM - 18 Dec 2018

Donald J. Trump ✓
@realDonaldTrump

America is the greatest Country in the world and my job is to fight for ALL citizens, even those who have made mistakes. Congratulations to the Senate on the bi-partisan passing of a historic Criminal Justice Reform Bill....
20,647 Retweets **97,417** Likes
6:07 PM - 18 Dec 2018

Donald J. Trump ✓
@realDonaldTrump

....This will keep our communities safer, and provide hope and a second chance, to those who earn it. In addition to everything else, billions of dollars will be saved. I look forward to signing this into law!
13,725 Retweets **67,055** Likes
6:07 PM - 18 Dec 2018

Donald J. Trump ✓
@realDonaldTrump

In our Country, so much money has been poured down the drain, for so many years, but when it comes to Border Security and the Military, the Democrats fight to the death. We won on the Military, which is being completely rebuilt. One way or the other, we will win on the Wall!
25,288 Retweets **109,676** Likes
4:35 AM - 19 Dec 2018

Donald J. Trump ✓
@realDonaldTrump

Mexico is paying (indirectly) for the Wall through the new USMCA, the replacement for NAFTA! Far more money coming to the U.S. Because of the tremendous dangers at the Border, including large scale criminal and drug inflow, the United States Military will build the Wall!
23,954 Retweets **98,828** Likes
5:43 AM - 19 Dec 2018

Donald J. Trump ✓
@realDonaldTrump

We have defeated ISIS in Syria, my only reason for being there during the Trump Presidency.
25,524 Retweets **116,733** Likes
6:29 AM - 19 Dec 2018

Donald J. Trump ✓
@realDonaldTrump

The Trump Foundation has done great work and given away lots of money, both mine and others, to great charities over the years - with me taking NO fees, rent, salaries etc. Now, as usual, I am getting slammed by Cuomo and the Dems in a long running civil lawsuit started by.....
16,282 Retweets **65,794** Likes
6:44 AM - 19 Dec 2018

Donald J. Trump ✓
@realDonaldTrump

...sleazebag AG Eric Schneiderman, who has since resigned over horrific women abuse, when I wanted to close the Foundation so as not to be in conflict with politics. Shady Eric was head of New Yorkers for Clinton, and refused to even look at the corrupt Clinton Foundation......
20,672 Retweets **80,635** Likes
6:56 AM - 19 Dec 2018

Donald J. Trump ✓
@realDonaldTrump

....In any event, it goes on and on & the new AG, who is now being replaced by yet another AG (who openly campaigned on a GET TRUMP agenda), does little else but rant, rave & politic against me. Will never be treated fairly by these people - a total double standard of "justice."
17,280 Retweets **72,633** Likes
7:05 AM - 19 Dec 2018

Donald J. Trump ✓
@realDonaldTrump

After historic victories against ISIS, it's time to bring our great young people home!
29,396 Retweets **118,571** Likes
3:10 PM - 19 Dec 2018

Donald J. Trump ✓
@realDonaldTrump

Col. Jim Carafano on @IngrahamAngle "Trump has made the Middle East a better place. When Trump came into office, ISIS was running amuck in the Middle East. Over a million refugees poured into Western Europe - none of that is happening today. That's all due to Trump."
15,627 Retweets **63,010** Likes
9:04 PM - 19 Dec 2018

Donald J. Trump ✓
@realDonaldTrump

"Trump gets no credit for what he's done in the Middle East." @IngrahamAngle So true, thank you Laura!
15,142 Retweets **74,315** Likes
9:17 PM - 19 Dec 2018

Donald J. Trump ✓
@realDonaldTrump

"I'm proud of the President today to hear that he is declaring victory in Syria." Senator Rand Paul. "I couldn't agree more with the presidents decision. By definition, this is the opposite of an Obama decision. Senator Mike Lee
13,158 Retweets **60,475** Likes
3:25 AM - 20 Dec 2018

Donald J. Trump ✓
@realDonaldTrump

Getting out of Syria was no surprise. I've been campaigning on it for years, and six months ago, when I very publicly wanted to do it, I agreed to stay longer. Russia, Iran, Syria & others are the local enemy of ISIS. We were doing there work. Time to come home & rebuild. #MAGA
16,808 Retweets **72,204** Likes
3:42 AM - 20 Dec 2018

President Trumps Tweets 2018: A Historical Archive of President Trump's Tweets

Donald J. Trump ✓
@realDonaldTrump

Does the USA want to be the Policeman of the Middle East, getting NOTHING but spending precious lives and trillions of dollars protecting others who, in almost all cases, do not appreciate what we are doing? Do we want to be there forever? Time for others to finally fight.....

26,017 Retweets **109,948** Likes
3:56 AM - 20 Dec 2018

Donald J. Trump ✓
@realDonaldTrump

....Russia, Iran, Syria & many others are not happy about the U.S. leaving, despite what the Fake News says, because now they will have to fight ISIS and others, who they hate, without us. I am building by far the most powerful military in the world. ISIS hits us they are doomed!

16,936 Retweets **74,564** Likes
4:16 AM - 20 Dec 2018

Donald J. Trump ✓
@realDonaldTrump

The Democrats, who know Steel Slats (Wall) are necessary for Border Security, are putting politics over Country. What they are just beginning to realize is that I will not sign any of their legislation, including infrastructure, unless it has perfect Border Security. U.S.A. WINS!

22,888 Retweets **94,469** Likes
4:28 AM - 20 Dec 2018

Donald J. Trump ✓
@realDonaldTrump

With so much talk about the Wall, people are losing sight of the great job being done on our Southern Border by Border Patrol, ICE and our great Military. Remember the Caravans? Well, they didn't get through and none are forming or on their way. Border is tight. Fake News silent!

24,050 Retweets **101,172** Likes
4:39 AM - 20 Dec 2018

Donald J. Trump ✓
@realDonaldTrump

When I begrudgingly signed the Omnibus Bill, I was promised the Wall and Border Security by leadership. Would be done by end of year (NOW). It didn't happen! We foolishly fight for Border Security for other countries - but not for our beloved U.S.A. Not good!

30,304 Retweets **119,968** Likes
7:28 AM - 20 Dec 2018

Donald J. Trump ✓
@realDonaldTrump

Congress just passed the Criminal Justice Reform Bill known as the #FirstStepAct. Congratulations! This is a great bi-partisan achievement for everybody. When both parties work together we can keep our Country safer. A wonderful thing for the U.S.A.!!

13,689 Retweets **64,910** Likes
11:16 AM - 20 Dec 2018

Donald J. Trump ✓
@realDonaldTrump

So hard to believe that Lindsey Graham would be against saving soldier lives & billions of $$$. Why are we fighting for our enemy, Syria, by staying & killing ISIS for them, Russia, Iran & other locals? Time to focus on our Country & bring our youth back home where they belong!

25,228 Retweets **118,087** Likes
11:22 AM - 20 Dec 2018

Donald J. Trump ✓
@realDonaldTrump

Farm Bill signing in 15 minutes! #Emmys #TBT
36,226 Retweets **132,284** Likes
12:14 PM - 20 Dec 2018

Donald J. Trump ✓
@realDonaldTrump

Democrats, it is time to come together and put the SAFETY of the AMERICAN PEOPLE before POLITICS. Border security must become a #1 priority!
24,228 Retweets **93,654** Likes
1:48 PM - 20 Dec 2018

Donald J. Trump ✓
@realDonaldTrump

General Jim Mattis will be retiring, with distinction, at the end of February, after having served my Administration as Secretary of Defense for the past two years. During Jim's tenure, tremendous progress has been made, especially with respect to the purchase of new fighting....
20,654 Retweets **90,865** Likes
2:21 PM - 20 Dec 2018

Donald J. Trump ✓
@realDonaldTrump

....equipment. General Mattis was a great help to me in getting allies and other countries to pay their share of military obligations. A new Secretary of Defense will be named shortly. I greatly thank Jim for his service!
15,917 Retweets **75,018** Likes
2:21 PM - 20 Dec 2018

Donald J. Trump ✓
@realDonaldTrump

Thank you to our GREAT Republican Members of Congress for your VOTE to fund Border Security and the Wall. The final numbers were 217-185 and many have said that the enthusiasm was greater than they have ever seen before. So proud of you all. Now on to the Senate!
28,351 Retweets **125,268** Likes
7:13 PM - 20 Dec 2018

Donald J. Trump ✓
@realDonaldTrump

Soon to be Speaker Nancy Pelosi said, last week live from the Oval Office, that the Republicans didn't have the votes for Border Security. Today the House Republicans voted and won, 217-185. Nancy does not have to apologize. All I want is GREAT BORDER SECURITY!
28,189 Retweets **113,127** Likes
7:20 PM - 20 Dec 2018

Donald J. Trump ✓
@realDonaldTrump

Senator Mitch McConnell should fight for the Wall and Border Security as hard as he fought for anything. He will need Democrat votes, but as shown in the House, good things happen. If enough Dems don't vote, it will be a Democrat Shutdown! House Republicans were great yesterday!
16,593 Retweets **73,249** Likes
3:50 AM - 21 Dec 2018

President Trumps Tweets 2018: A Historical Archive of President Trump's Tweets

Donald J. Trump ✓
@realDonaldTrump

The Democrats are trying to belittle the concept of a Wall, calling it old fashioned. The fact is there is nothing else's that will work, and that has been true for thousands of years. It's like the wheel, there is nothing better. I know tech better than anyone, & technology.....
22,063 Retweets **101,281** Likes
3:58 AM - 21 Dec 2018

Donald J. Trump ✓
@realDonaldTrump

.....on a Border is only effective in conjunction with a Wall. Properly designed and built Walls work, and the Democrats are lying when they say they don't. In Israel the Wall is 99.9% successful. Will not be any different on our Southern Border! Hundreds of $Billions saved!
15,582 Retweets **67,948** Likes
4:10 AM - 21 Dec 2018

Donald J. Trump ✓
@realDonaldTrump

No matter what happens today in the Senate, Republican House Members should be very proud of themselves. They flew back to Washington from all parts of the World in order to vote for Border Security and the Wall. Not one Democrat voted yes, and we won big. I am very proud of you!
17,819 Retweets **78,125** Likes
4:19 AM - 21 Dec 2018

Donald J. Trump ✓
@realDonaldTrump

The Democrats, whose votes we need in the Senate, will probably vote against Border Security and the Wall even though they know it is DESPERATELY NEEDED. If the Dems vote no, there will be a shutdown that will last for a very long time. People don't want Open Borders and Crime!
19,337 Retweets **81,582** Likes
4:24 AM - 21 Dec 2018

Donald J. Trump ✓
@realDonaldTrump

House Republican Vote, 217-185.
11,100 Retweets **62,603** Likes
4:27 AM - 21 Dec 2018

Donald J. Trump ✓
@realDonaldTrump

Shutdown today if Democrats do not vote for Border Security!
23,237 Retweets **104,725** Likes
4:31 AM - 21 Dec 2018

Donald J. Trump ✓
@realDonaldTrump

Even President Ronald Reagan tried for 8 years to build a Border Wall, or Fence, and was unable to do so. Others also have tried. We will get it done, one way or the other!
20,752 Retweets **93,214** Likes
4:38 AM - 21 Dec 2018

Donald J. Trump ✓
@realDonaldTrump

Mitch, use the Nuclear Option and get it done! Our Country is counting on you!
28,519 Retweets **118,884** Likes
5:02 AM - 21 Dec 2018

Donald J. Trump ✓
@realDonaldTrump

Thank you @SteveDaines for being willing to go with the so-called nuclear option in order to win on DESPERATELY NEEDED Border Security! Have my total support.
15,951 Retweets **69,823** Likes
5:08 AM - 21 Dec 2018

Donald J. Trump ✓
@realDonaldTrump

There has never been a president who has been tougher (but fair) on China or Russia - Never, just look at the facts. The Fake News tries so hard to paint the opposite picture.
17,272 Retweets **78,064** Likes
6:41 AM - 21 Dec 2018

Donald J. Trump ✓
@realDonaldTrump

General Anthony Tata, author, "Dark Winter." I think the President is making the exact right move in Syria. All the geniuses who are protesting the withdrawal of troops from Syria are the same geniuses who cooked the books on ISIS intelligence and gave rise to ISIS."
21,921 Retweets **80,666** Likes
6:50 AM - 21 Dec 2018

Donald J. Trump ✓
@realDonaldTrump

The Democrats now own the shutdown!
29,590 Retweets **13,0672** Likes
7:07 AM - 21 Dec 2018

I've done more damage to ISIS than all recent presidents....not even close!
21,551 Retweets **113,478** Likes
7:31 AM - 21 Dec 2018

Donald J. Trump ✓
@realDonaldTrump

Today, it was my great honor to sign the #FirstStepAct - a monumental bi-partisan win for the American people!
13,670 Retweets **58,726** Likes
11:28 AM - 21 Dec 2018

Donald J. Trump ✓
@realDonaldTrump

Today, it was my honor to sign into law H.R. 7213, the "Countering Weapons of Mass Destruction Act of 2018." The Act redesignates the @DHSgov Domestic Nuclear Detection Office as the Countering Weapons of Mass Destruction Office.
11,305 Retweets **50,880** Likes
11:56 AM - 21 Dec 2018

Donald J. Trump ✓
@realDonaldTrump

A design of our Steel Slat Barrier which is totally effective while at the same time beautiful!
33,445 Retweets **138,598** Likes
2:14 PM - 21 Dec 2018

President Trumps Tweets 2018: A Historical Archive of President Trump's Tweets

Donald J. Trump ✓
@realDonaldTrump

Some of the many Bills that I am signing in the Oval Office right now. Cancelled my trip on Air Force One to Florida while we wait to see if the Democrats will help us to protect America's Southern Border!
22,682 Retweets **103,894** Likes
3:23 PM - 21 Dec 2018

Donald J. Trump ✓
@realDonaldTrump

Wishing Supreme Court Justice Ruth Bader Ginsburg a full and speedy recovery!
16,052 Retweets **113,554** Likes
4:16 PM - 21 Dec 2018

Donald J. Trump ✓
@realDonaldTrump

OUR GREAT COUNTRY MUST HAVE BORDER SECURITY!
38,165 Retweets **150,175** Likes
6:49 PM - 21 Dec 2018

Donald J. Trump ✓
@realDonaldTrump

I am in the White House, working hard. News reports concerning the Shutdown and Syria are mostly FAKE. We are negotiating with the Democrats on desperately needed Border Security (Gangs, Drugs, Human Trafficking & more) but it could be a long stay. On Syria, we were originally...
20,944 Retweets **90,769** Likes
8:18 AM - 22 Dec 2018

Donald J. Trump ✓
@realDonaldTrump

....going to be there for three months, and that was seven years ago - we never left. When I became President, ISIS was going wild. Now ISIS is largely defeated and other local countries, including Turkey, should be able to easily take care of whatever remains. We're coming home!
25,454 Retweets **117,921** Likes
8:30 AM - 22 Dec 2018

Donald J. Trump ✓
@realDonaldTrump

Will be having lunch in White House residence with large group concerning Border Security.
17,276 Retweets **93,759** Likes
9:02 AM - 22 Dec 2018

Donald J. Trump ✓
@realDonaldTrump

The crisis of illegal activity at our Southern Border is real and will not stop until we build a great Steel Barrier or Wall. Let work begin!
24,788 Retweets **111,116** Likes
12:03 PM - 22 Dec 2018

Donald J. Trump ✓
@realDonaldTrump

I won an election, said to be one of the greatest of all time, based on getting out of endless & costly foreign wars & also based on Strong Borders which will keep our Country safe. We fight for the borders of other countries, but we won't fight for the borders of our own!
40,151 Retweets **175,564** Likes
12:28 PM - 22 Dec 2018

Donald J. Trump ✓
@realDonaldTrump

Senate adjourns until December 27th.
14,231 Retweets **64,919** Likes
1:12 PM - 22 Dec 2018

Donald J. Trump ✓
@realDonaldTrump

I will not be going to Florida because of the Shutdown - Staying in the White House! #MAGA
23,909 Retweets **121,158** Likes
3:58 PM - 22 Dec 2018

Donald J. Trump ✓
@realDonaldTrump

Brett McGurk, who I do not know, was appointed by President Obama in 2015. Was supposed to leave in February but he just resigned prior to leaving. Grandstander? The Fake News is making such a big deal about this nothing event!
19,475 Retweets **86,601** Likes
5:48 PM - 22 Dec 2018

Donald J. Trump ✓
@realDonaldTrump

If anybody but your favorite President, Donald J. Trump, announced that, after decimating ISIS in Syria, we were going to bring our troops back home (happy & healthy), that person would be the most popular hero in America. With me, hit hard instead by the Fake News Media. Crazy!
33,844 Retweets **153,602** Likes
5:59 PM - 22 Dec 2018

Donald J. Trump ✓
@realDonaldTrump

When President Obama ingloriously fired Jim Mattis, I gave him a second chance. Some thought I shouldn't, I thought I should. Interesting relationship-but I also gave all of the resources that he never really had. Allies are very important-but not when they take advantage of U.S.
25,500 Retweets **115,813** Likes
6:20 PM - 22 Dec 2018

Donald J. Trump ✓
@realDonaldTrump

The only way to stop drugs, gangs, human trafficking, criminal elements and much else from coming into our Country is with a Wall or Barrier. Drones and all of the rest are wonderful and lots of fun, but it is only a good old fashioned Wall that works!
32,372 Retweets **143,510** Likes
6:17 AM - 23 Dec 2018

Donald J. Trump ✓
@realDonaldTrump

I am pleased to announce that our very talented Deputy Secretary of Defense, Patrick Shanahan, will assume the title of Acting Secretary of Defense starting January 1, 2019. Patrick has a long list of accomplishments while serving as Deputy, & previously Boeing. He will be great!
18,488 Retweets **87,083** Likes
8:46 AM - 23 Dec 2018

Donald J. Trump ✓
@realDonaldTrump

I just had a long and productive call with President @RT_Erdogan of Turkey. We discussed ISIS, our mutual involvement in Syria, & the slow & highly coordinated pullout of U.S. troops from the area. After many years they are coming home. We also discussed heavily expanded Trade.
17,811 Retweets **80,977** Likes
8:59 AM - 23 Dec 2018

President Trumps Tweets 2018: A Historical Archive of President Trump's Tweets

Donald J. Trump ✓
@realDonaldTrump

Unthinkable devastation from the tsunami disaster in Indonesia. More than two hundred dead and nearly a thousand injured or unaccounted for. We are praying for recovery and healing. America is with you!
15,979 Retweets **79,668** Likes
9:13 AM - 23 Dec 2018

Donald J. Trump ✓
@realDonaldTrump

We signed two pieces of major legislation this week, Criminal Justice Reform and the Farm Bill. These are two Big Deals, but all the Fake News Media wants to talk about is "the mistake" of bringing our young people back home from the Never Ending Wars. It all began 19 years ago!
22,964 Retweets **94,518** Likes
11:45 AM - 23 Dec 2018

Donald J. Trump ✓
@realDonaldTrump

Senator Bob Corker just stated that, "I'm so priveledged to serve in the Senate for twelve years, and that's what I told the people of our state that's what I'd do, serve for two terms." But that is Not True - wanted to run but poll numbers TANKED when I wouldn't endorse him.....
16,542 Retweets **78,517** Likes
11:56 AM - 23 Dec 2018

Donald J. Trump ✓
@realDonaldTrump

.....Bob Corker was responsible for giving us the horrible Iran Nuclear Deal, which I ended, yet he badmouths me for wanting to bring our young people safely back home. Bob wanted to run and asked for my endorsement. I said NO and the game was over. #MAGA I LOVE TENNESSEE!
21,647 Retweets **97,685** Likes
12:20 PM - 23 Dec 2018

Donald J. Trump ✓
@realDonaldTrump

Thanks @RandPaul "I am very proud of the President. This is exactly what he promised, and I think the people agree with him. We've been at war too long and in too many places...spent several trillion dollars on these wars everywhere. He's different...that's why he got elected."
25,268 Retweets **109,480** Likes
1:18 PM - 23 Dec 2018

Donald J. Trump ✓
@realDonaldTrump

"It should not be the job of America to replace regimes around the world. This is what President Trump recognized in Iraq, that it was the biggest foreign policy disaster of the last several decades, and he's right...The generals still don't get the mistake." @RandPaul
22,084 Retweets **89,820** Likes
7:32 PM - 23 Dec 2018

Donald J. Trump ✓
@realDonaldTrump

Mitch McConnell just told a group of people, and me, that he has been in the U.S. Senate for 32 years and the last two have been by far the best & most productive of his career. Tax & Regulation Cuts, VA Choice, Farm Bill, Criminal Justice Reform, Judgeships & much more. Great!
26,483 Retweets **130,325** Likes
7:47 PM - 23 Dec 2018

Donald J. Trump ✓
@realDonaldTrump

The most important way to stop gangs, drugs, human trafficking and massive crime is at our Southern Border. We need Border Security, and as EVERYONE knows, you can't have Border Security without a Wall. The Drones & Technology are just bells and whistles. Safety for America!
24,085 Retweets **100,773** Likes
8:05 PM - 23 Dec 2018

Donald J. Trump ✓
@realDonaldTrump

"The President has been remarkable. I do not doubt that he will thrive in this new environment, and he will be a constant reminder of what populism is." Thank you to Tammy Bruce and Steve Hilton. Presidential Harassment has been with me from the beginning!
16,101 Retweets **78,715** Likes
8:26 PM - 23 Dec 2018

President @RT_Erdogan of Turkey has very strongly informed me that he will eradicate whatever is left of ISIS in Syria....and he is a man who can do it plus, Turkey is right "next door." Our troops are coming home!
21,687 Retweets **97,080** Likes
8:54 PM - 23 Dec 2018

Donald J. Trump ✓
@realDonaldTrump

Virtually every Democrat we are dealing with today strongly supported a Border Wall or Fence. It was only when I made it an important part of my campaign, because people and drugs were pouring into our Country unchecked, that they turned against it. Desperately needed!
25,312 Retweets **108,934** Likes
6:31 AM - 24 Dec 2018

Donald J. Trump ✓
@realDonaldTrump

To those few Senators who think I don't like or appreciate being allied with other countries, they are wrong, I DO. What I don't like, however, is when many of these same countries take advantage of their friendship with the United States, both in Military Protection and Trade...
22,190 Retweets **98,796** Likes
6:41 AM - 24 Dec 2018

Donald J. Trump ✓
@realDonaldTrump

....We are substantially subsidizing the Militaries of many VERY rich countries all over the world, while at the same time these countries take total advantage of the U.S., and our TAXPAYERS, on Trade. General Mattis did not see this as a problem. I DO, and it is being fixed!
25,119 Retweets **107,521** Likes
6:59 AM - 24 Dec 2018

Donald J. Trump ✓
@realDonaldTrump

For all of the sympathizers out there of Brett McGurk remember, he was the Obama appointee who was responsible for loading up airplanes with 1.8 Billion Dollars in CASH & sending it to Iran as part of the horrific Iran Nuclear Deal (now terminated) approved by Little Bob Corker.
28,640 Retweets **99,077** Likes
7:23 AM - 24 Dec 2018

President Trumps Tweets 2018: A Historical Archive of President Trump's Tweets

Donald J. Trump ✓
@realDonaldTrump

AMERICA IS RESPECTED AGAIN!
28,409 Retweets **156,718** Likes
7:33 AM - 24 Dec 2018

Donald J. Trump ✓
@realDonaldTrump

The only problem our economy has is the Fed. They don't have a feel for the Market, they don't understand necessary Trade Wars or Strong Dollars or even Democrat Shutdowns over Borders. The Fed is like a powerful golfer who can't score because he has no touch - he can't putt!
30,508 Retweets **125,022** Likes
7:55 AM - 24 Dec 2018

Donald J. Trump ✓
@realDonaldTrump

I never "lashed out" at the Acting Attorney General of the U.S., a man for whom I have great respect. This is a made up story, one of many, by the Fake News Media!
19,239 Retweets **88,333** Likes
8:55 AM - 24 Dec 2018

Donald J. Trump ✓
@realDonaldTrump

The Wall is different than the 25 Billion Dollars in Border Security. The complete Wall will be built with the Shutdown money plus funds already in hand. The reporting has been inaccurate on the point. The problem is, without the Wall, much of the rest of Dollars are wasted!
25,415 Retweets **101,326** Likes
9:10 AM - 24 Dec 2018

Donald J. Trump ✓

Saudi Arabia has now agreed to spend the necessary money needed to help rebuild Syria, instead of the United States. See? Isn't it nice when immensely wealthy countries help rebuild their neighbors rather than a Great Country, the U.S., that is 5000 miles away. Thanks to Saudi A!
38,832 Retweets **156,892** Likes
9:23 AM - 24 Dec 2018

Donald J. Trump ✓
@realDonaldTrump

I am all alone (poor me) in the White House waiting for the Democrats to come back and make a deal on desperately needed Border Security. At some point the Democrats not wanting to make a deal will cost our Country more money than the Border Wall we are all talking about. Crazy!
37,860 Retweets **181,954** Likes
9:32 AM - 24 Dec 2018

Donald J. Trump ✓
@realDonaldTrump

Christmas Eve briefing with my team working on North Korea – Progress being made. Looking forward to my next summit with Chairman Kim!
17,566 Retweets **88,627** Likes
1:14 PM - 24 Dec 2018

Donald J. Trump ✓
@realDonaldTrump

I am in the Oval Office & just gave out a 115 mile long contract for another large section of the Wall in Texas. We are already building and renovating many miles of Wall, some complete. Democrats must end Shutdown and finish funding. Billions of Dollars, & lives, will be saved!
41,153 Retweets **182,040** Likes
2:24 PM - 24 Dec 2018

Donald J. Trump ✓
@realDonaldTrump

Merry Christmas!
89,254 Retweets **508,327** Likes
4:59 AM - 25 Dec 2018

Donald J. Trump ✓
@realDonaldTrump

I hope everyone, even the Fake News Media, is having a great Christmas! Our Country is doing very well. We are securing our Borders, making great new Trade Deals, and bringing our Troops Back Home. We are finally putting America First. MERRY CHRISTMAS! #MAGA
46,596 Retweets **249,842** Likes
3:18 PM - 25 Dec 2018

Donald J. Trump ✓
@realDonaldTrump

.@FLOTUS Melania and I were honored to visit our incredible troops at Al Asad Air Base in Iraq. GOD BLESS THE U.S.A.!
50,441 Retweets **222,873** Likes
12:35 PM - 26 Dec 2018

Donald J. Trump ✓
@realDonaldTrump

Just returned from visiting our troops in Iraq and Germany. One thing is certain, we have incredible people representing our Country - people that know how to win!
29,623 Retweets **168,756** Likes
3:59 AM - 27 Dec 2018

Donald J. Trump ✓
@realDonaldTrump

Have the Democrats finally realized that we desperately need Border Security and a Wall on the Southern Border. Need to stop Drugs, Human Trafficking,Gang Members & Criminals from coming into our Country. Do the Dems realize that most of the people not getting paid are Democrats?
30,542 Retweets **131,861** Likes
4:06 AM - 27 Dec 2018

Donald J. Trump ✓
@realDonaldTrump

The Democrats OBSTRUCTION of the desperately needed Wall, where they almost all recently agreed it should be built, is exceeded only by their OBSTRUCTION of 350 great people wanting & expecting to come into Government after being delayed for more than two years, a U.S. record!
20,172 Retweets **84,780** Likes
11:41 AM - 27 Dec 2018

President Trumps Tweets 2018: A Historical Archive of President Trump's Tweets

Donald J. Trump ✓
@realDonaldTrump

The reason the DACA for Wall deal didn't get done was that a ridiculous court decision from the 9th Circuit allowed DACA to remain, thereby setting up a Supreme Court case. After ruling, Dems dropped deal - and that's where we are today, Democrat obstruction of the needed Wall.
21,140 Retweets **81,965** Likes
11:44 AM - 27 Dec 2018

Donald J. Trump ✓
@realDonaldTrump

"Border Patrol Agents want the Wall." Democrat's say they don't want the Wall (even though they know it is really needed), and they don't want ICE. They don't have much to campaign on, do they? An Open Southern Border and the large scale crime that comes with such stupidity!
24,281 Retweets **105,281** Likes
12:39 PM - 27 Dec 2018

Donald J. Trump ✓
@realDonaldTrump

There is right now a full scale manhunt going on in California for an illegal immigrant accused of shooting and killing a police officer during a traffic stop. Time to get tough on Border Security. Build the Wall!
36,523 Retweets **146,277** Likes
1:04 PM - 27 Dec 2018

Donald J. Trump ✓
@realDonaldTrump

I totally agree!
45,963 Retweets **179,981** Likes
1:04 PM - 27 Dec 2018

Donald J. Trump ✓
@realDonaldTrump

Brad Blakeman: "The American people understand that we have been played by foreign actors who would rather have us fight their battles for them. The President says look, this is your neighborhood, you've got to stand up to protect yourselves. Don't always look to America."
19,646 Retweets **85,166** Likes
1:26 PM - 27 Dec 2018

Donald J. Trump ✓
@realDonaldTrump

This isn't about the Wall, everybody knows that a Wall will work perfectly (In Israel the Wall works 99.9%). This is only about the Dems not letting Donald Trump & the Republicans have a win. They may have the 10 Senate votes, but we have the issue, Border Security. 2020!
31,406 Retweets **127,902** Likes
2:10 PM - 27 Dec 2018

Donald J. Trump ✓
@realDonaldTrump

CNN & others within the Fake News Universe were going wild about my signing MAGA hats for our military in Iraq and Germany. If these brave young people ask me to sign their hat, I will sign. Can you imagine my saying NO? We brought or gave NO hats as the Fake News first reported!
43,772 Retweets **181,435** Likes
3:23 PM - 27 Dec 2018

Donald J. Trump ✓
@realDonaldTrump

We will be forced to close the Southern Border entirely if the Obstructionist Democrats do not give us the money to finish the Wall & also change the ridiculous immigration laws that our Country is saddled with. Hard to believe there was a Congress & President who would approve!
36,280 Retweets **156,425** Likes
4:16 AM - 28 Dec 2018

Donald J. Trump ✓
@realDonaldTrump

....The United States looses soooo much money on Trade with Mexico under NAFTA, over 75 Billion Dollars a year (not including Drug Money which would be many times that amount), that I would consider closing the Southern Border a "profit making operation." We build a Wall or.....
23,736 Retweets **101,103** Likes
4:42 AM - 28 Dec 2018

Donald J. Trump ✓
@realDonaldTrump

......close the Southern Border. Bring our car industry back into the United States where it belongs. Go back to pre-NAFTA, before so many of our companies and jobs were so foolishly sent to Mexico. Either we build (finish) the Wall or we close the Border......
25,309 Retweets **108,158** Likes
4:49 AM - 28 Dec 2018

Donald J. Trump ✓
@realDonaldTrump

.....Honduras, Guatemala and El Salvador are doing nothing for the United States but taking our money. Word is that a new Caravan is forming in Honduras and they are doing nothing about it. We will be cutting off all aid to these 3 countries - taking advantage of U.S. for years!
39,548 Retweets **167,132** Likes
5:06 AM - 28 Dec 2018

Donald J. Trump ✓
@realDonaldTrump

Thank you to Sean Parnell for the nice comments on @foxandfriends about the troops wonderful reaction to Melania and I in Iraq and Germany. Great things are happening!
21,407 Retweets **113,861** Likes
6:51 AM - 28 Dec 2018

Donald J. Trump ✓
@realDonaldTrump

The Mueller Angry Democrats recently deleted approximately 19,000 Text messages between FBI Agent Lisa Page and her lover, Agent Peter S. These Texts were asked for and INVALUABLE to the truth of the Witch Hunt Hoax. This is a total Obstruction of Justice. All Texts Demanded!
32,048 Retweets **112,010** Likes
7:42 AM - 29 Dec 2018

Donald J. Trump ✓
@realDonaldTrump

I am in the White House waiting for the Democrats to come on over and make a deal on Border Security. From what I hear, they are spending so much time on Presidential Harassment that they have little time left for things like stopping crime and our military!
30,009 Retweets **127,523** Likes
7:52 AM - 29 Dec 2018

President Trumps Tweets 2018: A Historical Archive of President Trump's Tweets

Donald J. Trump ✓
@realDonaldTrump

Just had a long and very good call with President Xi of China. Deal is moving along very well. If made, it will be very comprehensive, covering all subjects, areas and points of dispute. Big progress being made!
27,724 Retweets **142,064** Likes
8:03 AM - 29 Dec 2018

Donald J. Trump ✓
@realDonaldTrump

Any deaths of children or others at the Border are strictly the fault of the Democrats and their pathetic immigration policies that allow people to make the long trek thinking they can enter our country illegally. They can't. If we had a Wall, they wouldn't even try! The two.....
29,363 Retweets **120,614** Likes
10:30 AM - 29 Dec 2018

Donald J. Trump ✓
@realDonaldTrump

...children in question were very sick before they were given over to Border Patrol. The father of the young girl said it was not their fault, he hadn't given her water in days. Border Patrol needs the Wall and it will all end. They are working so hard & getting so little credit!
30,202 Retweets **129,715** Likes
10:36 AM - 29 Dec 2018

Donald J. Trump ✓
@realDonaldTrump

For those that naively ask why didn't the Republicans get approval to build the Wall over the last year, it is because IN THE SENATE WE NEED 10 DEMOCRAT VOTES, and they will gives us "NONE" for Border Security! Now we have to do it the hard way, with a Shutdown. Too bad! @FoxNews
34,525 Retweets **144,271** Likes
11:25 AM - 29 Dec 2018

Donald J. Trump ✓
@realDonaldTrump

2018 is being called "THE YEAR OF THE WORKER" by Steve Moore, co-author of "Trumponomics." It was indeed a great year for the American Worker with the "best job market in 50 years, and the lowest unemployment rate ever for blacks and Hispanics and all workers. Big wage gains."
25,797 Retweets **109,238** Likes
1:06 PM - 29 Dec 2018

Donald J. Trump ✓
@realDonaldTrump

"Absolutely nothing" (on Russian Collusion). Kimberley Strassel, The Wall Street Journal. The Russian Collusion fabrication is the greatest Hoax in the history of American politics. The only Russian Collusion was with Hillary and the Democrats!
30,777 Retweets **118,155** Likes
7:01 PM - 29 Dec 2018

Donald J. Trump ✓
@realDonaldTrump

"It turns out to be true now, that the Department of Justice and the FBI, under President Obama, rigged the investigation for Hillary and really turned the screws on Trump, and now it looks like in a corrupt & illegal way. The facts are out now. Whole Hoax exposed. @JesseBWatters
44,877 Retweets **150,051** Likes
7:15 PM - 29 Dec 2018

Donald J. Trump ✓
@realDonaldTrump

Veterans on President Trump's handling of Border Security - 62% Approval Rating. On being a strong leader - 59%. AP Poll. Thank you!
25,749 Retweets **123,564** Likes
7:28 AM - 30 Dec 2018

Donald J. Trump ✓
@realDonaldTrump

Great work by my Administration over the holidays to save Coast Guard pay during this #SchumerShutdown. No thanks to the Democrats who left town and are not concerned about the safety and security of Americans!
32,041 Retweets **130,761** Likes
8:56 AM - 30 Dec 2018

Donald J. Trump ✓
@realDonaldTrump

President and Mrs. Obama built/has a ten foot Wall around their D.C. mansion/compound. I agree, totally necessary for their safety and security. The U.S. needs the same thing, slightly larger version!
61,730 Retweets **233,299** Likes
1:59 PM - 30 Dec 2018

Donald J. Trump ✓
@realDonaldTrump

An all concrete Wall was NEVER ABANDONED, as has been reported by the media. Some areas will be all concrete but the experts at Border Patrol prefer a Wall that is see through (thereby making it possible to see what is happening on both sides). Makes sense to me!
20,779 Retweets **96,655** Likes
4:51 AM - 31 Dec 2018

Donald J. Trump ✓
@realDonaldTrump

If anybody but Donald Trump did what I did in Syria, which was an ISIS loaded mess when I became President, they would be a national hero. ISIS is mostly gone, we're slowly sending our troops back home to be with their families, while at the same time fighting ISIS remnants......
17,379 Retweets **79,095** Likes
5:03 AM - 31 Dec 2018

Donald J. Trump ✓
@realDonaldTrump

...I campaigned on getting out of Syria and other places. Now when I start getting out the Fake News Media, or some failed Generals who were unable to do the job before I arrived, like to complain about me & my tactics, which are working. Just doing what I said I was going to do!
22,000 Retweets **100,819** Likes
5:12 AM - 31 Dec 2018

Donald J. Trump ✓
@realDonaldTrump

.....Except the results are FAR BETTER than I ever said they were going to be! I campaigned against the NEVER ENDING WARS, remember!
15,081 Retweets **72,353** Likes
5:19 AM - 31 Dec 2018

President Trumps Tweets 2018: A Historical Archive of President Trump's Tweets

Donald J. Trump
@realDonaldTrump

I campaigned on Border Security, which you cannot have without a strong and powerful Wall. Our Southern Border has long been an "Open Wound," where drugs, criminals (including human traffickers) and illegals would pour into our Country. Dems should get back here an fix now!
21,960 Retweets **90,883** Likes
5:29 AM - 31 Dec 2018

Donald J. Trump
@realDonaldTrump

I am the only person in America who could say that, "I'm bringing our great troops back home, with victory," and get BAD press. It is Fake News and Pundits who have FAILED for years that are doing the complaining. If I stayed in Endless Wars forever, they would still be unhappy!
25,252 Retweets **111,582** Likes
6:38 AM - 31 Dec 2018

Donald J. Trump
@realDonaldTrump

I'm in the Oval Office. Democrats, come back from vacation now and give us the votes necessary for Border Security, including the Wall. You voted yes in 2006 and 2013. One more yes, but with me in office, I'll get it built, and Fast!
30,742 Retweets **131,151** Likes
7:37 AM - 31 Dec 2018

Donald J. Trump
@realDonaldTrump

It's incredible how Democrats can all use their ridiculous sound bite and say that a Wall doesn't work. It does, and properly built, almost 100%! They say it's old technology - but so is the wheel. They now say it is immoral- but it is far more immoral for people to be dying!
29,355 Retweets **125,931** Likes
7:39 AM - 31 Dec 2018

Donald J. Trump
@realDonaldTrump

Heads of countries are calling wanting to know why Senator Schumer is not approving their otherwise approved Ambassadors!? Likewise in Government lawyers and others are being delayed at a record pace! 360 great and hardworking people are waiting for approval from....
20,519 Retweets **74,566** Likes
12:02 PM - 31 Dec 2018

Donald J. Trump
@realDonaldTrump

....Senator Schumer, more than a year longer than any other Administration in history. These are people who have been approved by committees and all others, yet Schumer continues to hold them back from serving their Country! Very Unfair!
17,027 Retweets **63,013** Likes
12:02 PM - 31 Dec 2018

Donald J. Trump
@realDonaldTrump

HAPPY NEW YEAR!
32,999 Retweets **132,907** Likes
3:53 PM - 31 Dec 2018

Donald J. Trump
@realDonaldTrump

MEXICO IS PAYING FOR THE WALL through the many billions of dollars a year that the U.S.A. is saving through the new Trade Deal, the USMCA, that will replace the horrendous NAFTA Trade Deal, which has so badly hurt our Country. Mexico & Canada will also thrive - good for all!

24,125 Retweets **104,900** Likes

4:40 PM - 31 Dec 2018

Thank you for purchasing this book.

Buy other books in this series online,

www.anthonymichalisko.com

or

Available on AMAZON

KEYWORD

"Anthony Michalisko"

"Trump Tweets Book"

Follow Anthony on Twitter

@realMichalisko

MERCHANDISE

www.anthonymichalisko.com